BANGKOK
HANDBOOK

THE PROPERTY OF
RONALD LESLIE BELL
PHONE? 1 (780) 444-5192

EDMONTON, ALBERTA,
CANADA

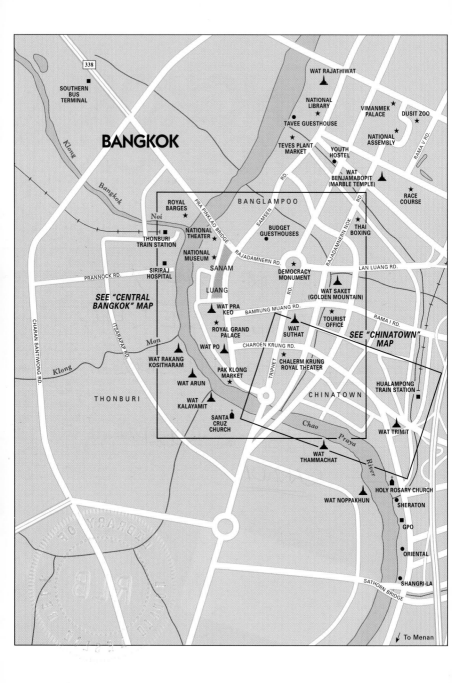

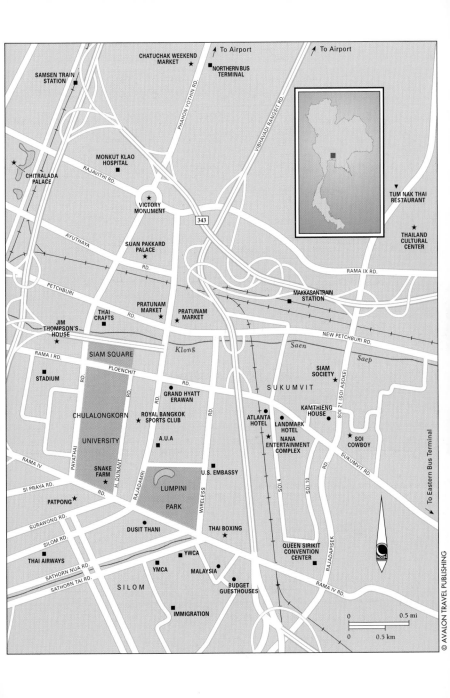

BANGKOK
HANDBOOK
THIRD EDITION

CARL PARKES

MOON
TRAVEL
HANDBOOKS

BANGKOK HANDBOOK
THIRD EDITION

Published by
Avalon Travel Publishing
5855 Beaudry St.
Emeryville, CA 94608, USA

Please send all comments,
corrections, additions,
amendments, and critiques to:

**BANGKOK HANDBOOK
MOON TRAVEL HANDBOOKS
5855 BEAUDRY ST.
EMERYVILLE, CA 94608, USA
e-mail: travel@moon.com
www.moon.com**

Some photos and illustrations are used by permission
and are the property of the original copyright owners.

ISBN: 1-56691-159-1
ISSN: 1078-5272

Printing History
1st edition—1992
3rd edition—January 2000

Editors: Gina Wilson Birtcil, Elizabeth Larson, Jeannie Trizzino
Production & Design: Selena Littrell, David Hurst
Cartography: Brian Bardwell, Allen Leech, Mike Morgenfeld
Index: Valerie Sellers Blanton

5 4 3 2 1 0

Front cover photo: Bangkok, courtesy of SuperStock, Inc.

All photos by Carl Parkes unless otherwise noted.
All illustrations by Bob Race unless otherwise noted.

Distributed in the United States and Canada by Publishers Group West

Printed in the United States of America

Dedicated to Joe Biz,
the people of Thailand,
and all my friends in San Francisco

CONTENTS

INTRODUCTION . . . . **1~35**

The Land 5
  Geographical Regions; Climate

History 8
  Kingdoms Before Bangkok; The Foundation of Bangkok; The Early
  Kings; Siam Meets the West; The End of Absolute Monarchy; Rise
  of the Military; The Present King

The People 21
  The Thais; Thai Society; The Chinese; Conduct and Customs for the
  Traveler; Language

Temple Architecture 28

The Performing Arts 31
  Dance and Drama

SPECIAL TOPICS

Sightseeing Highlights . . . .*3*   *A Question of Succession* *20*
Name Game . . . .*4*   *Responsible Tourism* *22*
Thai or Tai? . . . .*9*   *Meditation in Thailand* *29*
The King and I—Reality or Racism? . . .*14*   *Movies Filmed in Thailand* *33-35*
Farewell Siam *18*

BANGKOK BASICS . . . . **36~96**

Planning Your Trip 36
  Allocating Your Time; Figuring the Cost; What to Bring

Festivals 40

Accommodations 44

Food and Drink 46
  Common Dishes; Drinks; Dining Tips and Etiquette

Shopping 52
  Best Buys

Health 54
  Before You Go; Common Health Problems; AIDS Alert; Health
  Facilities

Safety 58
  Theft and Fraud; Illegal Drugs; Women Travelers; Resources

Visas and Officialdom 61
  Passports; Visas and Entry Permits; Customs and Currency
  Controls; Other Useful Documents

Money 65
  Thai Currency; Traveler's Checks; Money Transfers; Credit Cards;
  ATM Withdrawals

Measurements and Communications.........................70
   Mail; Telephone; Time; Measurements
Sources of Travel Information 74
   Government Agencies; Maps; The Internet; Bookstores and
   Libraries
Getting There 78
   By Air; By Air from North America; Airport Arrival
Getting Around..85
   By Air; By Train; Government Bus; Private Bus; Getting around
   Town; Tours

SPECIAL TOPICS

Bring the Kids!...........................*39*   *Sidewalk Snacks and Desserts* *49*
The Dreaded Chili......................*48*   *Thai Time*.................................*75*

BANGKOK SIGHTS ....97~141
Introduction 97
   Getting Your Bearings; Addresses; Suggested Walking Tours
Central Bangkok Attractions...............................104
   The Old Royal City; More of the Old Royal City; The New Royal City
Chinatown Attractions.....................................122
Thonburi Attractions 128
Attractions near Siam Square...............................130
River and Canal Tours.....................................133
   Up the Chao Praya River; Oriental Hotel to Banglampoo; Exploring
   the Canals
Outskirts of Bangkok.......................................137
   North of Bangkok; South of Bangkok; West of Bangkok

SPECIAL TOPICS

Requiem for a City ....*98*   *Floating Sleeves and*
Cheap Fun in Bangkok................*100*   *Painted Faces*........................*123*
Admission Fees and Cautions ....*103*   *Roman-Robot Fantasies* *131*
Sports at Sanam Luang ....*105*   *A Riverside Walk and*
Magical Medallions ....*119*   *the Oriental Hotel* *132*
                                         Organized River Tours *136*

ACCOMMODATIONS ....142~160
   General Information; Banglampoo and Khao San Road; Malaysia
   Hotel Area; Chinatown; Train Station Area; Little India; Silom Road;
   Siam Square; Sukumvit Road; Airport Area

FOOD ....161~172
   Banglampoo; Malaysia Hotel Area; Silom Road; Siam Square;
   Sukumvit Road

ENTERTAINMENT AND SHOPPING .... 173~188

Entertainment 173
Cultural Performances; Nightlife; Discos, Nightclubs, and Bars

Shopping 185
Where to Shop

SPECIAL TOPICS

Thai Kickboxing .... *178*   *Live Thai Rock 'N' Roll* *181*

EAST COAST .... 189~217

Bangkok to Pattaya 192
Bang Saen; Si Racha; Ko Si Chang

Pattaya 197
Attractions around Town; Attractions outside Pattaya; Islands near
Pattaya; Water Activities; Sports; Accommodations; Food; Nightlife;
Information and Services; Transportation

SPECIAL TOPIC

Weird Wheels *195*

VICINITY OF BANGKOK .... 218~261

West of Bangkok 218
Nakhon Pathom; Kanchanaburi; South of Kanchanaburi; North of
Kanchanaburi—Route 3199; Route 323 to the Burmese Border

North of Bangkok 238
Bang Pa In; Ayuthaya; Lopburi; Saraburi and Pra Buddhabat

SPECIAL TOPICS

A Life for Every Sleeper .... *227*   *Just Say No at Opium*
The Arts of Ayuthaya .... *244-245*   *Pipe Monastery* *260*
Cosmic Symbology and
  the Architecture of Ayuthaya *249*

APPENDIX .... 262~284

Suggested Resources 262
The Thai Language 273
Glossary 282

INDEXES .... 285~294

Accommodations Index 285
Restaurant Index 287
General Index 289

MAPS

COLOR SUPPLEMENT
Bangkok .... ii-iii

INTRODUCTION
Thailand...................................2
Western Colonial Expansion
(1785-1909) 15

BANGKOK BASICS
Skytrain Routes.....................106-107

BANGKOK SIGHTS
Central Bangkok.....................106-107
Wat Pra Keo and the Royal Palace 108
National Museum........................110
Wat Po.....................................115
Chinatown 124-125
Wat Arun..................................129
Chao Praya River........................134
Damnern Saduak Floating Market.......140

ACCOMMODATIONS
Banglampoo 145

Malaysia Hotel Area......................148
Silom, Surawong, and New Roads. 152-153
Siam Square and Pratunam 155
Sukumvit Road 158-159

EAST COAST
East Coast of Thailand...................190
Bang Saen...............................192
Si Racha 193
Pattaya....................................196
North Pattaya 198
South Pattaya........................200-201

VICINITY OF BANGKOK
Vicinity of Bangkok 219
Nakhon Pathom 221
Nakhon Pathom Chedi 222
Kanchanaburi.............................225
Kanchanaburi Region 233
Ayuthaya..................................241
Wat Pra Sri Samphet....................247
Central Lopburi 255
New Lopburi 258-259

MAP SYMBOLS

- — — INTERNATIONAL BORDER
- ·· — ·· PROVINCE BORDER
- ——— MAIN ROAD
- ——— OTHER ROAD
- — — — CART PATH, ROUGH ROAD (MAY BE PAVED IN PART)
- · — · — · PATH, TRAIL
- —⊐ ⊏— BORDER CROSSING
- BOAT ROUTE, FERRY ROUTE
- +++++ RAILROAD
- ═══ BRIDGE

- ★ RUINS. ATTRACTIONS
- ● ACCOMMODATIONS
- ■ SIGHT, POINT OF NOTE
- ○ CITY
- ○ TOWN, VILLAGE
- ▲ MOUNTAIN
- ② NUMBERED ROAD
- ✈ INTERNATIONAL AIRPORT
- ✈ SMALL AIRPORT, AIRSTRIP

GH = GUESTHOUSE

- ▲ WAT
- ✝ CHURCH, CATHEDRAL
- ⌂ TEMPLE, PAGODA
- ▲ STUPA
- ▮ MOSQUE
- WATER
- 𝗔 WATERFALL

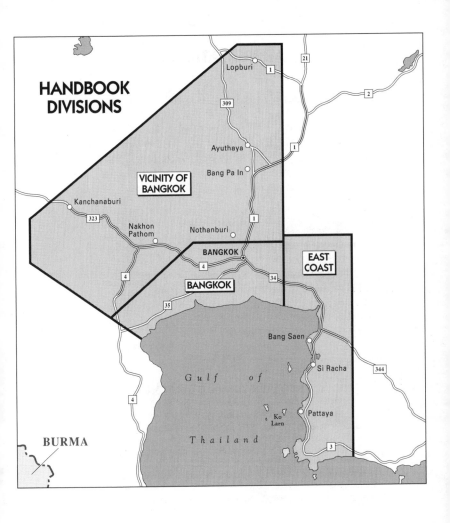

ABBREVIATIONS

a/c—air-conditioned
ASEAN—Association of Southeast Asian Nations
B—*baht*
B.E.—Buddhist Era
BCP—Myanmar Communist Party
BKS—Borisat Khon Song or Bor Kor Sor (bus company in Thailand)
d—double occupancy
GPO—General Post Office
Hwy.—Highway
km—kilometer
KMT—Kuomintang National Army
KNU—Karen National Union
kph—kilometers per hour
NAUI—National Association of Underwater Instructors
PADI—Professional Association of Dive Instructors
pp—per person
s—single occupancy
TAT—Tourist Authority of Thailand

NOTE ON TRANSLITERATION

Transliterating Thai words into Roman script is a vexing proposition,
since several divergent systems are used throughout the country. The
Thais themselves are as inconsistent as travel writers, often spelling a single destination a half-dozen ways. For example, a small town south of
Bangkok can be spelled Phetchburi, Petchaburi, or Petchburi, while the old
capital north of Bangkok can be spelled Ayudaya, Ayutthaya, or Ayuthaya.
Place names in this book follow the most common and shortened usage,
though alternative spellings are often included for reference.

ACKNOWLEDGEMENTS

Writers write alone, but survive only with generous doses of help and encouragement from friends, family, and associates. Top marks at Moon Publications go to editors Jeannie Trizzino, Gina Birtcil, and Elizabeth Larson, art director Dave Hurst, and map makers Mike Morgenfeld and Brian Bardwell, all of whom labored well beyond the call of duty. Gratitude is also given to founder Bill Dalton, publisher Bill Newlin, and other Moonbeams who helped realize the book.

I am also indebted to the people of Thailand, who took me into their homes and left me with memories to last a lifetime.

Contributions from Readers

I would also like to thank the many readers who wrote to me about their travel adventures:

United States: Chris Baker (Oakland), Susan Brown (NY), Burt Blackburn (Alexandria), Thom Burns (Ocean Park), W. S. Butterfield (Savannah), Alan Cartledge (AZ), Robert Chiang (San Antonio), Frank Cotter (Mounds View), Pat Crowley (San Diego), Stephen Downes (Marion), Mike Ellis (Niles), Rhys Evans (Grover City), Kathleen Flynn (Los Angeles), Jean Fournier (San Leandro), Leigh Fox (Guam), Leslie Freeman (Boise), Steve Gilman (Norcross), Lester Hamersly (Index), Stefan Hammond (San Francisco), Dr. Martin Hane (Chicago), Celeste Holmes (Oakland), Harry Hunter (Olympia), Terry Nakazono (Gardena), Martin Offenberger (La Habra), Irene Malone (San Pablo), Angelo Mercure (San Diego), Dan Moody (Studio City), Ms. Jan Morris (Louisville), James Patterson (Santa Cruz), Mark Peters (Muscatine), John Pierkarski (Huntington Beach), Michael Newman (LA), Roger Post (San Diego), Anna Redding (Atlanta), Rachel Rinaldo (Wilton), William Ring (San Diego), Yancey Rousek (Los Angeles), Claudia Siegel (Hackensack), Steve Stawarz (San Jose), Jefferson Swycaffer (San Diego), Michael Triff (Atlanta), Ray VarnBuhler (Wilseyville), Murray Westgate (Las Vegas), Chantal Yang (Cambridge), George Young (League City).

Australia: Gary Deering, Greg Duffy (Burleigh Waters), Martin Ellison (Darlinghurst), Cas Liber (Elizabeth Bay), Kevin Mulrain (Sydney), Morgana Oliver (Wodonga), Catherine Spence (Mona Vale), Keith Stephans (Noose), Amy Thomas (Bellevue Heights).

Austria: Herber Walland (Graz).

Belgium: Guy Crouna (Tieuen).

Canada: Michael Buckley (Vancouver), Bob Cadloff (Montreal), Melvin Green (Toronto), Pat and Tom Jorgrinson (Webb), Bruce Moore (Ganges), Lenny Morgan (Richmond), Bob Olajos (Peterborough), Scott Pegg (Vancouver), Laura White (Toronto), Tanya Whiteside (Ottawa).

China: Philip Drury.

England: Alan Cummings, Amanda Dixon (Cheam), Tim Eyre (Nottingham), H. L. Freeman (London), Linda Grace (Oxford), Mark Gregory (Leeds), David Host (Bulkington), John Maidment (Southbourne), Anthony Maude (Canterbury), C. Miller (London), Peter Moorhouse (Seathwaite), Anna Oldman (High Wycombe), Tina Ottman (Cambridge), Tim Prentice (Kent), Nick Slade (Flackwell Health), Lois Tadd (Chesham), David Veale (Fishbourne).

Germany: Christiane Moll (Berlin), Marcus Muller (Tubingen), Ralf Neugebauer (Lubeck), Wolfgang and Mosgit (Brey), Hans Zagorski (Gunterleben).

Japan: Bruce Swenson.

Netherlands: Vander Bel-Kampschuur (Eindhoven), Maarten Camps (Ryswyh), Claantie van der Grinten (Ryswyh), E. Cornelissen (Castricum), Rick Dubbeldam (Sas Van Gert), Jan Valkenbury (Heerlen), Michel van Dam (Den Haag), Erik van Velzen (Zoetermeer), Herbert Walland.

New Zealand: Gordon Boshell (Aro Valley), Barry Wells (Wellington).

Spain: Sevvy (Madrid).

Sweden: Stefan Samuelsson (Lomma).

Switzerland: Rolf Huber (Uitikon-Waldegg), Katharina Hug (Enalinpes).

continues on next page

Thailand: Jamie Donahoe who helped with my Bangkok restaurant reviews and Gary Hacker for setting me straight about Pattaya.

A Personal Note

Finally, I would like to extend my deepest gratitude and sincerest love to all my friends in San Francisco and throughout the world:

Terra and radio king Nickola, Norton (ready for another courier flight?), Dean (Wolfman) Bowden, Eric Dibbern and Sue, Roy T. Maloney, John Kaeuper, Jimbo & Kelly, Linda & Geek (now in Geneva), sexy El & handsome Dave, Vince "Dude," never-forgotten Lee & Pam, Ab Fab-Seinfeld Brucie, beam-me-up Scotty (Scotch!) & Juiceteen, lovely Rita & Eric, Dara & Roger (cool kids), amazing Amos, Zenbullet Stefan, Joel, Cuba Chris, Russian Vera, Peachy, sweet Cathy, Deke (Vegas?), Rich & Rens, Dave "Art Seen" Howard, Hai "Baby," tattoo Jerome (sans Harley), Ed Samarin, Chris & Ben, Juggler Ray (Key West), Joe C. and wife (Baja), Nancy Chandler, Kim Kacere, Michael, Rita & Eric (Santa Barbara), Susan T., Karen C. (thanks for the visit), Larsen (you still owe me $40), Zimme da Giant, Guru Das, Joe & Divine Dyan, Terri "The Terror," Stephanie (love all three), Hugh Linton (you started it all), Donna, Hazel & Rick, Richard (North Beach '75), Dianne (Aspen '76), Nam Chu (R.I.P.), Doctor Bob & German Ralph, Homeless Jim, June, Sheila, party Marty, Bill Bodewes (Amsterdam), Gary Flynn (Down Under), Michael Buckley (Vancouver), Joe & Nancy (Japan), David Stanley (Canada), Marael (Boots fan!), Joe Biz (R.I.P.) & Bob Nilsen (Chico), Rachel (Singapore), Nicole (Paris), Escola Nova de Samba, Lulu and the Atomics, sister Claud, fab Stan, cool Kev & (cooler) Heath, Mom & Dad.

REQUEST FOR COMMENTS

Travel books are collaborations between authors and readers. While every effort has been made to keep this book accurate and timely, travel conditions change quickly in a region as dynamic as Thailand. Please let us know about price hikes, new guesthouses, closed restaurants, transportation tips, and anything else that may prove useful to the next traveler. Your information will be checked in the field and then carefully interwoven into the next edition of this book. Moon Publications and the author deeply appreciate all suggestions sent in by our readers.

A Reader Profile questionnaire in the back of this book will help us find out who you are and your impressions about this guide. All correspondents will be acknowledged and the best letters will receive a new copy of any requested guide to Southeast Asia.

You may e-mail the author directly at:

cparkes@moon.com

or send your Reader Profile and travel suggestions via snailmail to:

Carl Parkes
Thailand Handbook
Moon Publications
5855 Beaudry Street
Emeryville, CA 94608
USA

DAVID HURST

INTRODUCTION

Bangkok and the Golden Triangle, Kanchanaburi and the River Kwai, Sukothai and Siam—these are destinations to fire the imagination. In a world gone increasingly dull, Thailand and its capital city of Bangkok remain worlds of magic and mystery, adventure and romance, far-flung destinations still strange and exciting in a Westernized world.

Thailand's romantic image began with the writers and adventurers who recorded their early journeys of discovery and voyages of inner exploration. Tales of intrigue by Marco Polo were followed by the stories of Conrad, Verne, Hesse, Maugham, Gurdjieff, Malraux, Fleming, Ginsberg, and Watts. Today, a new generation of writers—Theroux, Iyer, and Krich—continue to explore and interpret the brave new world of Thailand and Southeast Asia.

Thailand's image as an Eastern paradise has also been fueled by Hollywood films such as *The King and I* and *The Beach,* and by sobriquets bestowed by creative copywriters and the national tourist office—Land of Smiles, Treasures of a Kingdom, Amazing Thailand. While the hyperbole may be excessive, Thailand unquestionably deserves its accolade as one of the world's premier destinations, a region that richly rewards the discriminating visitor.

A World of Choices
Travelers heading off to Southeast Asia often ask this writer for a specific recommendation on "the best country" in the area. After 15 years of wandering the region, I've learned that each country offers unique strengths appealing to different types of travelers.

Singapore may no longer be the exotic land of Conrad and Kipling, but the island state features the best food and most comfortable travel conditions in all of Southeast Asia. The Philippines may lack remarkable cuisine, and travel conditions are often rugged, but the archipelago offers outstanding beaches, superb diving, and the friendliest people in Asia. Myanmar remains controlled by one of the world's most repressive regimes, and internal transport is nothing short of an ordeal, but the isolated nation is a miraculous place for adventurous travelers. And then there is Indonesia, a bewildering expanse of islands far too expansive to explore properly in any time frame—but where else can you find such an amazing diversity of cultures, religions, peoples, and histories?

MYANMAR

Mae Sai   Chiang Saen
Thaton   Chiang Rai
Mae Hong Song
Chiang Mai

Salween River   Mekong River   LAOS   Gulf of Tonkin

Mae Sariang   Lampang
Nan River
Yom River
Ping River

RANGOON (YANGON)

Mae Sot   Sukothai   Phitsanulok

Loei   Nong Khai   Nakhon Phanom
Udon Thani   Mukdahan

Khon Kaen   Chi River

THAILAND   Mekong River

Mun River   Ubon Ratchathani

Chao Praya River   Lopburi   Nakhon Ratchasima (Khorat)

Kanchanaburi   Ayuthaya

BANGKOK   Aranyaprathet   **CAMBODIA**

Andaman   Petchburi   Pattaya
Chanthaburi
Sea   Trat

PHNOM PENH   Mekong River   **SAIGON**

Gulf   of   Thailand

Chumphon

Ko Samui
Surat Thani

Nakhon Si Thammarat

Phuket   Phattalung
Trang

Hat Yai

Sungai Golok

MALAYSIA

VIETNAM

0   200 mi
0   200 km

© AVALON TRAVEL PUBLISHING

SIGHTSEEING HIGHLIGHTS

The following sketches will provide a quick glimpse of the national highlights in and around Bangkok.

Bangkok

Thailand's rich and kaleidoscopic tapestry of tourist attractions is enough to keep most travelers busy for years, though a single region can be explored well in several weeks. Visitors generally fly into Bangkok, a chaotic and unnerving metropolis of immense traffic jams and modern high-rises. Appalled by the overcrowding, overdevelopment and pollution, many travelers make the mistake of pausing only long enough to buy a plane ticket before moving on.

While Bangkok is certainly an urban planner's nightmare, it is also home to dozens of dazzling Buddhist temples, outstanding restaurants, superb shopping, and one of the liveliest nightlife scenes in the world. You'll be surprised at the vitality and friendliness of many of its eight million residents . . . if you survive the heat and congestion.

East Coast

This area features historical monuments, beaches, and natural wonders—all within a 200-km radius of Bangkok.

Pattaya: Thailand's eastern seaboard boasts several highly developed beach resorts; Pattaya is the most famous. One of the largest resorts in Asia, this low-powered Riviera of the East annually attracts over a million pleasure-seekers to its breathtaking range of water sports, restaurants, and legendary nightlife. Lively, chaotic, exciting, polluted, highly commercialized, and tacky, Pattaya in the past catered almost exclusively to military personnel or single businessmen who filled the bars and nightclubs. Today the resort appeals primarily to families, with attractions such as zoos, botanical gardens, and water parks. Although the beaches are inferior to those of Phuket or Ko Samui, the proximity to Bangkok makes Pattaya convenient for visitors with limited time.

Ko Chang: On the border of Cambodia lies the newest island resort in Thailand, with excellent beaches, magnificent topography, and dozens of untouched islands nearby. Ko Chang is rapidly developing into another Ko Samui; go now before the hotels arrive.

West of Bangkok

A quick and relaxing journey into Thai countryside can be made just west of Bangkok.

Nakhon Pathom: Often visited on a day-trip from Bangkok or as a stop en route to Kanchanaburi, this small town one hour west of Bangkok is home to the world's tallest Buddhist monument.

Damnern Saduak: Thailand's most authentic floating market, two hours south of Bangkok, Damnern Saduak is much less commercialized than the capital's artificial floating bazaar. You can join a tour or explore it yourself with an early start.

Kanchanaburi: This beautiful and relaxing region, three hours west of Bangkok, offers inexpensive floating guesthouses, refreshing waterfalls, hiking, national parks, and cool caves filled with Buddhas. Highly recommended for history buffs, nature lovers, and anyone annoyed with Bangkok's traffic jams. The bridge over the River Kwai is located here.

North of Bangkok

Historical sites north of Bangkok can be visited on day-trips, but the vast number of monuments and lengthy travel times demand a tour of several days.

Ayuthaya: For over 400 years the riverine-island town of Ayuthaya, two hours north of Bangkok, served as the second royal capital of Thailand. Though largely destroyed by the Burmese in 1767, many of the restored architectural ruins provide eloquent testimony to the splendor of Thailand's most powerful empire. Ayuthaya and Sukothai are Thailand's largest and most impressive archaeological sites.

Lopburi: Although nothing special, Lopburi features some modest Khmer ruins and an old summer capital for Ayuthayan kings. It also makes a convenient stopover en route to the northeast.

All these factors make the selection of Southeast Asia's top destination a difficult call.

And yet, this travel writer always recommends first-time visitors head directly to Thailand. No other country offers such an outstanding array of attractions in such a compact package. Do you dream of crystalline beaches and brilliant islands? Thailand offers world-class resorts with five-star amenities as well as remote islands untouched by the forces of modern tourism. Culture fans can seek out authentic festivals, tour archaeological parks, or visit 20 superb museums scattered around the country.

Thailand is exotic. Thai religious architecture is almost unbelievable—a riotous fantasy of color, shapes, and mythological creatures that often appear inspired by Disney. Outdoor enthusiasts can enjoy hilltribe trekking in the north, river rafting in the Golden Triangle, and scuba diving over pristine coral in the remote south. Thailand guarantees superb shopping—the best in Asia—world-renowned cuisine, notorious nightlife, and all types of environments, from national parks to remote jungles.

Most important, Thailand is home to the Thais, wonderful people who have graciously preserved their traditions while accepting the conveniences of modern life.

Thailand remains one of the few nations in Asia where modernization has failed to triumph over local traditions. Many feel this strength is due to the fact that Thailand was never colonized by Western powers, but this author believes credit should be given to Buddhism, the world religion that teaches compassion and forgiveness rather than judgmental approaches to life. Buddhism, independence, and perhaps the tropical heat have given the Thais an extraordinary sense of serenity and a lack of the psychological tension so common to Western life.

The happy result is a wacky, wild, and wonderful society that can be neatly summarized by three common Thai phrases: *"chai yen"* ("cool heart"), *"mai pen rai"* ("what will be, will be"), and *"sanuk"* ("life is a pleasure"). This approach to life means the Thais maintain a cool heart, refuse to worry about the future, and always live for pleasure. No wonder Thailand is my top choice in Asia.

Brave New World

The visitor should arrive in Thailand with open eyes, leaving false expectations back home. Thailand today hardly resembles world described by writers of earlier generations; this is no place for sentimental colonialism or quaint longing for unspoiled paradise forever lost. Modern Thailand is a highly developed nation, where the average citizen prefers Hollywood and holograms over meditation and mantras.

Western influences pervade even the remotest corners of the country. Ko Samui, once an unknown and untouched destination privy to a select group of world travelers, now ranks as a favorite stop for package tourists from Europe and Australia. Other destinations are overwhelmed with tourists and marred by schlock shops, sacrificing their souls for economic reward.

Still, travelers who venture off the beaten track will find destinations where nobody speaks a word of English and young schoolgirls run from the sight of a gangly Westerner. Even as you read this paragraph, somewhere in Thailand an adventurous backpacker sits on a deserted beach on an untouched island, smiling at the villagers and believing himself or herself the luckiest person in the world.

NAME GAME

*T*he official name of the country formally known in English as Burma has been changed to the Union of Myanmar (MEE-an-ma). The current government (SLORC) says the change is intended to better reflect the country's ethnic diversity and provide Romanized spellings more phonetically in tune with local pronunciations. However, pro-democracy opposition groups claim it's yet another historical distortion by the military junta.

The name change has been adopted by most members of the international press, and the country's official UN designation is Myanmar. Yet some publications still use the older terminology as a sign of nonrecognition of the Burmese government. However, there is historical and linguistic support for the use of the "new" terms, which are gaining acceptance worldwide. Therefore, in this book we use the name Myanmar, as well as Yangon (Rangoon), Bagan (Pagan), etc.

To see the real Thailand—the Thailand that lies beneath the Western veneer—you must travel with wide eyes and an open mind. Avoid spending money simply to isolate yourself against what appears to be an alien culture. Treat residents and other travelers as you would have them treat you, and resist measuring people by your standards or cultural values. Keep a cool heart, an optimistic attitude, and an openness to chance encounters. Believe in *chai yen, mai pen rai,* and *sanuk.*

Your first stops in Thailand will most likely be Bangkok and perhaps a few of the nearby destinations described in this book. Have a great adventure.

THE LAND

GEOGRAPHICAL REGIONS

Thailand, a melange of subtropical and temperate zones situated between five and 21 degrees north of the equator, offers the visitor a diverse and varied topography encompassing fertile alluvial plains, rugged mountains, rough savannah, tropical rainforests, and a sandy, irregular coastline facing the Andaman Sea to the west and Gulf of Thailand to the east.

The country is set in the center of mainland Southeast Asia, bordered by Myanmar to the west, Laos in the north, Cambodia to the east, and Malaysia down south. The insular kingdom stretches over 1,800 km from north to south, and contains a total land mass of 513,115 square km—roughly equivalent to the size of France or slightly smaller than Texas.

Thailand's shape somewhat resembles an elephant's head, with the trunk forming the southern peninsula and Bangkok sited in the elephant's mouth. The capital lies approximately 14° north of the equator, roughly in line with Manila, Madras, and Khartoum.

Some national boundaries are defined by natural features, such as the long and winding Mekong River that demarcates much of the border with Laos. Other borders are ill-defined lines established in modern times by treaties with the British and French. Subsequent reinterpretations of these arrangements caused many 20th century territorial disputes, most notably the controversy over the exact location of Preah Vihar. In 1962 the famed Khmer temple was awarded by an International Court of Justice to Cambodia, though the temple steps were judged to be in Thailand.

Landforms and drainage divide the country into six natural regions. Each differs from the others in population, resources, natural features, historical background, ethnic and linguistic groups, and the level of social and economic development.

traditional boats (with untraditional motors) on the beach

Thailand has its own system of land measurement. The basic units are the *wa* (four square km) and the *rai* (400 square *wa*, 1,600 square meters, or 0.16 hectares). One square km equals 625 *rai*.

Bangkok and Vicinity

Much of Thailand's political and economic development occurred in the flat patchwork of emerald-green paddies around the capital city of Bangkok. Now the contemporary core of modern Thailand, the alluvial plains and highly developed irrigation systems that surround the city have long served as the rice bowl of Asia; this was the homeland of the region's earliest settlers.

Although many rice fields have been lost to urban encroachment and industrial estates, annual floods and rich soils still allow the region to support the most densely populated area of Thailand. Bangkok and vicinity encompass only 1.5% of the nation's total land mass but over 15% of the total population.

The most important geographical characteristic of lower and central Thailand is the Menam or Chao Praya River, the Nile of Siam. This Mississippi-like stretch of water, together with its tributaries, drains an estimated one-third of the nation. The dual moniker itself demonstrates its importance. Menam means "mother of waters" or "river," while Chao Praya is an aristocratic title signifying female nobility. Thus the full term translates to "Noble lady, mother of waters." Most Thais simply say "Menam."

The annual flooding of the lower Menam delta is both a blessing and a curse. Each year during the June-Nov. monsoon season, heavy rains inundate the alluvial lowlands that stretch from the mouth of the Menam to the historic town of Lopburi, 130 km north. Farmers are thankful for the soaking but Bangkok residents must once again suffer through another season of flooded streets. The floods are due to the low-lying nature of Bangkok and nearby towns; the capital is only two meters above sea level. The river is still tidal at Ayuthaya, 95 km inland yet just four meters above sea level.

East Coast

The southeastern coastal regions of Trat, Chantaburi, Rayong, and Chonburi are often placed in the same geographical group as the northeast, despite their completely unique charms. Somewhat isolated from mainstream travel, this stretch of superb beaches and remote islands also includes the land wedged between the Gulf of Thailand and the Phnom Damrek mountain range to the north.

To the west stretch the flattened summits of the Banthat range, outliers of the Cardomoms, which form the untamed frontier with Cambodia. Smugglers, Khmer army commanders, and independent miners live here, working the pits that supply Thailand with most of its rubies and sapphires.

The region nearest Bangkok has been transformed into new cities and industrial parks designed to take advantage of cheaper land and better roads to the shipping centers near Bangkok. Beyond these bedroom communities and huge shipping facilities lie the beach resort towns of Pattaya and Rayong. The coastline continues southeast to Trat, which serves as the launching point for boats to Ko Chang, a peaceful island graced with fine beaches and towering mountains.

CLIMATE

Thailand lies in a tropical zone and shares the same weather patterns as most Southeast Asian countries situated north of the equator. Although there's little you can do about the weather after arrival, an understanding of the elements can help you choose beforehand the season best suited to your personality.

Monsoons, not latitude, determine the seasons in Thailand. Monsoons are seasonal winds that change direction during the year as a result of differences in temperature and pressure between land and sea. Derived from the Arabic word *mansim*, monsoons are the life source for farms across the country.

Regional Variations

The climate of Thailand varies widely from region to region. Rainfall patterns and temperature levels described apply to Bangkok, as well as the central plains, the north, and the northeast. These insular regions are subjected only to the summer monsoon, which brings three distinct seasons: dry (Dec.-Feb.), hot (March-June), and rainy (June-Dec.). Variations within seasons and be-

AVERAGE HUMIDITY–BANGKOK

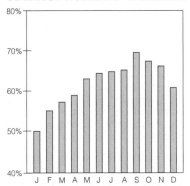

MAXIMUM TEMPERATURE–BANGKOK

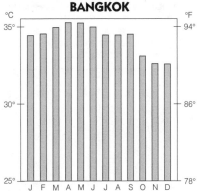

RAINFALL–BANGKOK

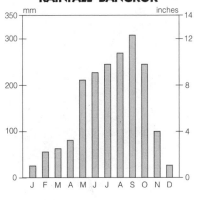

tween years can alter these monthly guidelines.

There can be significant differences in rainfall levels between the west and east coasts depending on the strength of the storm. Travelers on Ko Samui surprised by sudden showers might find drier conditions across the peninsula on Phuket.

The Dry Season (December-February)

The dry and cooler season begins in the early winter as temperatures start to drop and the land begins to cool faster than the sea. The high-pressure zone which gradually builds over mainland Southeast Asia forces winds to blow from the land to the sea, from the northeast to the southwest. This northeastern monsoon brings pleasant, dry, and somewhat cooler weather.

Temperatures drop to tolerable levels in Bangkok and the central plains, but can approach freezing in the far northern provinces. Sweaters and jackets sold by sidewalk vendors are often necessary for mountain trekking or motorcycle touring north of Chiang Rai.

Thailand's dry season is a popular time to tour the kingdom, especially for those intolerant of heat and humidity. The chief disadvantages are the sheer number of tourists who arrive during the winter months, the scarcity of rooms, and the high-season prices demanded by some proprietors.

The Hot Season (March-June)

The hot season begins to build in March, blazes through April and May, and keeps sizzling brains until the arrival of the summer monsoons. Temperatures during the peak months of April and May often reach 35-40°C and barely drop during the evening. Conditions are worsened by the debilitating humidity, which hovers over 80% night and day.

Few visitors can tolerate this hellish season—especially in Bangkok—without air-conditioned rooms and plenty of cold showers.

The Wet Season (June-November)

The wet season begins when warm, humid air masses flow northeastward from the Indian Ocean and move toward the large low pressure zone over mainland Asia. As the winds blow over the cooler sea and on to the warmer land surfaces, humidity levels soar. This southwestern monsoon brings the rainy season, which continues until the winds reverse direction in the early winter.

The amount of rainfall varies with topography and the region's alignment with the approaching storm. Towns in the extreme northeast receive minimal rainfall, while the southwest coastal resorts of Phuket and Krabi are deluged Aug.-November.

Some travelers feel the rainy season is the best time to visit Thailand. Although the monsoons last five or six months, rainfall is sporadic and intermittent, not continuous. Most days are crisp and perfectly clear. The downpours that arrive in the late afternoon or early evening are heavy but relatively brief. Monsoons mean the kingdom is green, vibrant, and alive: nature at its most beautiful. Rather than view brown landscapes and harvested fields, you'll gaze across brilliant green paddies to glistening mountains covered with exuberant vegetation.

The rainy season also insures there will be fewer tourists, lower prices, and plentiful rooms. And what's wrong with rain? Seasoned travelers agree the violent but brief rains of summer provide the real drama of Asia, an opportunity to witness nature in all her uncontrolled fury.

HISTORY

KINGDOMS BEFORE BANGKOK

Bangkok is one of the youngest kingdoms in Southeast Asia, though its historical and cultural references reach far back in time to earlier Thai empires that once thrived in the central plains of the country.

Sukothai, 1238-1360
The brief but brilliant kingdom of Sukothai marks the true beginning of the Thai nation and to this day remains a source of great pride to the Thai people. While Sukothai's preeminence lasted less than 150 years, it gave rise to uniquely personified forms of architecture, sculpture, and governance.

Under the leadership of King Ramkamheng (1278-1318), revered today as the father of modern Thailand, Sukothai fused Khmer and Mon political traditions into a dynamic kingdom that stretched from Laos to Malaysia. Military power and economic prosperity fueled the development of such highly refined artistic achievements as the world-renowned Sawankalok celadon and supremely sensitive Buddhist images. Even today Sukothai is considered one of the most remarkable empires in the long history of Southeast Asia.

Thailand's first national empire, Sukothai arose from the collapse of Khmer hegemony and the threat posed by the Mongol armies of Kublai Khan.

By the mid-13th century, Khan had successfully mounted campaigns against the Chinese and conquered the quasi-independent Tai kingdom of Nanchao in Yunnan Province. Heady with success, he then set out to conquer the emergent powers of present-day Thailand. Threatened with serious military challenge, Thai principalities consolidated their power and prepared for what appeared to be a final conflagration.

soaring wats *in Ayuthaya, once a medieval metropolis*

THAI OR TAI?

Thai is a political term referring to any citizen of Thailand, whether that person is of Tai, Chinese, Indian, or Western descent. If you've got a Thai passport, you are legally a "Thai."

On the other hand, Tai is a cultural and linguistic term which denotes a broad spectrum of peoples who migrated into Thailand over the last several millennia. Contemporary Tais spread over much of Southeast Asia but are known by regional names such as Tai, Lao, Shan, Lu, and Chuang. Tais speak a monosyllabic and tonal language with some degree of mutual intelligibility among the regional groups. In most cases, Tais have adapted to local conditions and assumed many of the conventions of the indigenous population. For example, the Tais who settled in the lower Chao Praya valley converted to the Theravada Buddhism favored by the Mons, while the Tais in Cambodia adopted Hinduism, the prominent religion of the Chams. An estimated 80 million Tais live throughout Southeast Asia, a cultural group comparable in number to the French or Germans.

Some Thais are not Tai—Hindus in Bangkok, Malay Muslims in the south—while many Tais are not Thai—Cambodians, Shans, and Chuangs in southern China.

Another factor in the creation of Sukothai was the decline of the Khmer Empire after the death of King Jayavarman VII in 1220. As the Cambodian empire weakened, regional Thai rulers, long under the thumb of Khmer domination, revolted and established their own power bases. The most significant event occurred around 1240 when a pair of disgruntled princes from two small Thai principalities gathered an army and marched on the main Khmer outpost at Sukothai. The Khmers resisted but were quickly defeated by Thai forces led by Prince Indraditya—the first sovereign of an independent Thai nation.

Although loosely functioning as a kingdom, Sukothai remained a rather insignificant outpost until 1278, when it was attacked by the ruler of Mae Sot. Threatened with certain defeat, Sukothai was saved through the efforts of Rama, the 19-year-old son of Indraditya. Rama rallied his troops and then, according to legend, killed the king of

Mae Sot during a hand-to-hand battle on elephantback. For his bravery, Rama was accorded the title of Ramkamheng—Rama the Bold.

King Ramkamheng (r. 1278-1318) established the first independent Thai nation through a combination of diplomatic skills and statesmanship, rather than military prowess. At the time of his ascension in 1278, Sukothai consisted of little more than the city itself and a few neighboring communities. By the end of his 40-year reign, Ramkamheng had increased his territorial holdings tenfold to include Luang Prabang in the north, the Mon homelands near Bangkok, and the peninsula south to Nakhon Si Thammarat. These gains were all accomplished through diplomatic relations and family intermarriages, rather than military conquest.

Ramkamheng today is honored as a capable administrator who brought peace to a divided land, an astute legislator who encouraged free trade and open borders, and a talented statesman who willingly absorbed many of the best elements from the Khmers, Mons, Indians, and Chinese. Ramkamheng also invented the Thai script, fusing the Mon and Khmer alphabets with Thai tonal inflections—an achievement denoted in a stele dated 1292 describing the idyllic conditions of his kingdom. Finally, Ramkamheng codified traditional laws into written canon, abolished slavery, and unified his nation under the umbrella of Buddhism. Small wonder the Thais have such great respect for Rama the Bold.

Sukothai declined after the death of Ramkamheng in 1318; his successors appeared more involved with religious matters than with the maintenance of the empire. Three kings followed Ramkamheng but all failed to repulse Burmese attacks and retard the rise of Ayuthaya to the south.

Ayuthaya, 1350-1767

By the end of the 14th century, several small but well-organized principalities ruled over much of what is now Thailand—most notably the Lanna and Sukothai Kingdoms. Other Southeast Asian powers—the Burmese at Bagan, the Khmers at Angkor, and the Mongol Chinese—were in steep decline. Conditions were ideal for the rise of Ayuthaya as the leading power in Southeast Asia.

The Kingdom of Ayuthaya was established in 1350 by King U Thong of Suphanburi, a principality which dominated the western side of the Chao Praya River basin. Suphanburi was predominantly a Siamese and Theravada Buddhist state which competed with Lopburi, the old Angkorian cultural and administrative center, for control of central Thailand after the decline of Sukothai. According to legend, U Thong moved his capital from Suphanburi to Ayuthaya to escape an outbreak of smallpox and occupy a more strategic location at the confluence of the Chao Praya, Lopburi, and Pasak Rivers. Military defense against the Burmese was a major factor in the choice of Ayuthaya.

The strategy proved successful. Within a few years, U Thong (renamed King Ramathibodi I) had united the whole of central Siam, from Sukothai in the north to the Malay Peninsula in the south. For the next 417 years, Ayuthaya served as the heart and soul of the Thai state—the religious, cultural, and commercial capital of modern Siam.

In the final years of his reign, Ramathibodi seized Angkor and most of present-day Cambodia. Efforts to control his domestic territories were frustrated by persistent rebellions in Sukothai and the need for repeated military campaigns against the Lanna Kingdom of Chiang Mai. Ramathibodi died in 1369.

Western contact with Siam began in 1511 when Ayuthaya received a diplomatic mission from the Portuguese. Encouraged by their annexation of the Muslim trading entrepot of Malacca, the Portuguese were anxious to expand their commercial contacts within Southeast Asia. Five years later, the two nations concluded a treaty granting the Portuguese permission to conduct trade in exchange for Portuguese arms, ammunition, and warfare training. Portuguese mercenaries later fought in battles against Chiang Mai and helped Ayuthaya defeat other regional powers.

Western contact with Siam dramatically increased during the reign of King Ekatosarot until, by the early 17th century, Ayuthaya was regarded by Western powers as a useful trading site and stopover point on the long voyages to China and Japan. Each Western nation competed vigorously to establish trading connections with the Thai crown. The initial Dutch contract signed in 1605 was followed by agreements with the Eng-

lish in 1612, the Danes in 1621, and the French in 1662. Commercial links were also maintained by Japanese traders who comprised a sizable community until their retreat to Cambodia in 1628.

European influence reached its zenith during the reign of King Narai (1656-1688). During his tenure, Ayuthaya was regarded as the strongest military power and grandest city in all of Southeast Asia. Western visitors described the realm as a splendid metropolis with a population larger than those of contemporary London or Paris. Within the city walls stood glorious palaces, hundreds of resplendent temples, and entire communities for military leaders, scholars, and artisans.

Europeans described an awe-inspiring walled city some 10 km in circumference interlaced with more than 50 km of interconnecting canals. Many of these waterways were flanked by monumental Buddha images and exquisitely executed and richly embellished *objets d'art*. Outside the walled enclosure existed vast foreign settlements, factories, and warehouses designed to serve the Western trade community. Visitors were amazed by the grandeur and opulence of this most splendid and cosmopolitan of all Asian cities.

Ayuthaya was also the major military and economic powerhouse within Southeast Asia. After the submission of Sukothai and containment of Lanna, Ayuthaya ruled over an empire that stretched from Laos and Malaysia to Angkor and Burma. Economic success was insured by the large contingent of foreign traders who positioned the city as the hub of international trade between China and the West. Ayuthaya shone as the brightest star in the East.

After the death of Narai and execution of Phaulkon, Ayuthaya entered a period of self-imposed isolation for almost 150 years. The French were forced from Siam, though British and Dutch traders continued to maintain small posts. Missionaries imprisoned during the palace coup were released and given permission to proselytize, despite their noted lack of earlier success in converting the population.

The political nemesis of Siam, Burma was by the mid-18th century poised for yet another attack on the Siamese capital. Initial forays were led by King Alaungpaya, a powerful leader and magnetic personality who single-handedly restored the Kingdom of Ava and recaptured the

Mon Kingdom of Bago. Alaungpaya next set his sights on Ayuthaya. His attack of April 1760 might have leveled the city had not a Burmese cannon burst outside the city walls. The explosion killed Alaungpaya and sparked a hasty Burmese retreat.

The final siege began in 1763. Burmese forces initially besieged Chiang Mai and Lamphun; both cities fell within six months. Burmese troops then quickly conquered Chiang Rai, Nan, and Luang Prabang. Massing for the final assault on Ayuthaya, the main Burmese force departed Chiang Mai and headed south through easily captured Thai outposts at Sawankhalok, Sukothai, Phitsanulok, and Nakhon Sawan. Another Burmese expedition concurrently left Bago, marching across Three Pagodas Pass into Siamese territory. The southern flank took Kanchanaburi, Ratchburi, and Petchburi. Siam was now largely in Burmese hands. In February 1766 the two Burmese expeditions joined forces just outside the walls of Ayuthaya.

A terrible war ensued. Thai citizens over the next year valiantly resisted superior Burmese forces despite the famines, epidemics, and horrible fires that consumed most of the city. Conditions grew so grim that the king of Ayuthaya offered to surrender his empire in exchange for his life. The Burmese, however, demanded unconditional surrender.

Finally, on 7 April 1767, Ayuthaya fell to the Burmese. Retaliation was swift and completely horrific. In an unprecedented orgy of vandalism, murder, and destruction, most of the population was killed and the entire city was burned to the ground. The royal family and over 100,000 Siamese captives were marched back to Burma and sold as slaves. Mass slaughter and wholesale slavery reduced the population to under 10,000 people in a city which once held over one million.

The Burmese did more than simply kill the population. With complete disregard for their common religion, Burmese forces destroyed the artistic and literary heritage of Ayuthaya by pulling down many of the magnificent Buddhist temples and melting down most of the golden Buddha images—a savage act which still profoundly shocks the Thais. Ayuthaya was almost completely obliterated in the holocaust.

THE FOUNDATION OF BANGKOK

Early History of Bangkok

Prior to the arrival of King Taksin, Thonburi and Bangkok on the opposite side of the river were little more than small villages with a customs port, an old fort constructed by the French in the previous century, and a rudimentary collection of simple huts inhabited by Chinese merchants and traders. The customs port had long served the shipping trade intended for Ayuthaya, as this was the furthest point up the Chao Praya navigable by most seagoing vessels. Cargo was often checked through the customs port in Thonburi, transferred to smaller boats, and shipped upstream some 80 km to the capital at Ayuthaya.

Bangkok itself, the poor cousin to Thonburi, passed its time as a simple village *(bang)* amid an orchard of trees whose fruit to Western visitors appeared to be either olives or plums. Splitting the difference, Western mapmakers settled on the Thai compromise word of *kok* (plum-olive) and gave the small village the moniker of Bangkok, the village of plum-olive trees.

Today, unless a Thai is condescending to foreign ignorance, he or she will never call the capital city Bangkok but rather Krung Thep, "City of Angels." Krung Thep actually begins the string of honorariums that comprise the official name, a mammoth tongue twister which, according to Guinness, forms the longest place-name in the world.

Thonburi (Money Town) with its important customs port was the more active of the two riverine villages, though today little remains of its early architecture aside from Wat Arun, the famous Temple of the Dawn, largely reconstructed in 1842. Bangkok lacked the commercial vitality of "Money Town," but compensated with its larger collection of temples which survive to the day such as Wat Po, Wat Saket, Wat Samplum, and Wat Sampeng.

General Taksin, 1767-1782

The destruction of Ayuthaya was devastating but, as is typical in Thai history, not a permanent setback. Shortly before the fall of Ayuthaya, an ambitious half-Chinese provincial governor from Tak in western Thailand quietly fled southeast to Chantaburi with an expedition of some

500 soldiers. Taksin soon rallied his soldiers and returned to fight the Burmese.

Taksin marched into a fortuitous situation. Most of the Burmese troops stationed at Ayuthaya had been called away to resist Chinese aggression along the northern Burmese border. Remarkably, within seven months Taksin had defeated a dispirited Burmese garrison, recaptured the ruined Ayuthaya, and reestablished the Thai kingdom.

Taksin soon realized that Ayuthaya was finished as a viable capital, as it lay dangerously exposed to Burmese military threats and distant from international trade routes. It had also been completely destroyed after several generations of warfare with the Burmese. After a propitious dream, Taksin transferred his capital to Thonburi, a small town on the banks of the Chao Praya River just opposite present-day Bangkok.

Although blessed with a brilliant tactical mind and financial support from the Chinese mercantile community, Taksin proved himself a rather inept ruler. Consumed with administrative matters in Thonburi, Taksin turned command of his army over to two brothers—Chao Phraya Chakri and Chao Phraya Sarasih—who in turn liberated Chiang Mai from Burmese domination and brought most of Cambodia and Laos under Thai suzerainty. During the Laotian campaign, Chao Phraya Chakri captured the famed Emerald Buddha, returning it to Thonburi in 1779. Now installed in Wat Pra Keo, the jadeite image remains the single most venerated statue in modern Thailand.

Taksin, in the meantime, was going mad. French missionaries reported he imagined himself a living reincarnation of the Buddha, spending his days in silent meditation attempting to fly. Monks who refused to acknowledge his divinity were flogged and sentenced to menial labor. Plagued with paranoia and delusions of grandeur, Taksin imprisoned and tortured his wife, his sons, his heir apparent, and many high officials. The situation deteriorated until his ministers and generals staged a revolt, forcing Taksin to abdicate the throne. This solution to unpopular rule—the military coup—remains a cornerstone of contemporary Thai politics.

Taksin was executed in the manner prescribed for royalty: placed in a velvet sack and gently beaten to death with a sandalwood club.

THE EARLY KINGS

King Ramathibodi—Rama I, 1782-1809

The popular Chao Phraya Chakri, on expedition in Cambodia, was recalled to Thonburi and crowned King Rama, first ruler of the Chakri dynasty which continues to the present day. Fearful of attack by Burmese forces, Rama I transferred his capital from Thonburi across the river to present-day Bangkok.

He then began to recreate the former magnificence of Ayuthaya with the construction of the royal palaces, temples, and even canals which characterized the former capital. Rama I, formally known during his reign as Ramathibodi, also enshrined in his royal temple the Emerald Buddha captured from the Laotians and removed to Siam.

The city continues to be called Bangkok by Western mapmakers, though Rama I renamed it a multisyllabled Sanskrit moniker abbreviated as Krung Thep, or "City of Angels." This island created by the construction of a semicircular canal was named *Ratankosin,* a term that means the "Resting Place of the Emerald Buddha."

To consecrate his new capital for the purposes of statecraft and religion, Rama I forced the Chinese merchants living within the canal perimeter to move south to a district now known as Sampeng, the first active commercial district in the new kingdom and the site of today's Chinatown.

On 6 April, 1782, Rama I proclaimed the establishment of a new city to be called Krung Thep, a new and sacred administrative center known as Ratanakosin, and a new dynasty called Chakri. Two weeks later, at an exact time decreed by court astrologers and geomancers, he consecrated the city's Lak Muang, a sacred pillar honoring the Hindu god Shiva that ensured divine protection over the new empire.

Along with the original semicircular canal—Klong Lawd—that runs from Pak Klong Talat market in the south to Phra Pinklao Bridge in the north, Rama I ordered the construction of two additional semicircular canals, each bisected by a labyrinth of canals that formed the early "roads" of the capital. Early Bangkok had only three formal roads: a dirt path inside the walls of the new palace grounds, a second just outside the walls, and Bamrung Muang, an elephant track running east from the exterior road.

Rama I spent much of his reign consolidating his empire, devising a new code of civil law which served the state for the next century, and issuing a series of ecclesiastical verdicts intended to restore discipline to the monkhood. He also oversaw the brilliant defeat of the Burmese during their 1785 invasion, in which some 70,000 Thai soldiers defended Bangkok against 100,000 Burmese. This encounter marked the final attempt by the Burmese to conquer their Siamese neighbors.

By the end of his reign, Rama I had created a new empire significantly more powerful and complex than had previously existed in Ayuthaya.

Phra Phutthalaetia—Rama II, 1809-1824

After the death of Rama I, his 41-year-old son, Prince Phutthalaetia, ascended to the throne, becoming the second king in the Chakri dynasty. Peace and prosperity within Siam allowed him to concentrate on the arts and literature. His chief accomplishment was penning the famous Thai verse play the *Inao,* adapted from a Javanese legend, and a version of the Ramakien frequently staged in the Royal Palace. Rama II also funded the reconstruction of Wat Arun (the Temple of Dawn) in Thonburi; he is said to have personally carved the massive doors at Wat Suthat.

Rama II reestablished formal relations with the West, allowing the Portuguese to open an embassy and trading post a few blocks south of his royal palace.

King Phra Nangklao—Rama III, 1824-1851

The chief shortcoming of Rama II and the Thai crown in general was the failure to clearly define royal succession. In the event of an undesignated *uparaja* (heir), royal selection was left to a council of senior officials, princes, and Buddhist prelates. At the time of Rama II's death, Prince Mongkut—the king's eldest son by the queen—had just entered the priesthood at the age of 20 and was not considered ready to assume the crown. After a series of debates, palace nobles asked Prince Chesda, the son of a consort, to claim the throne under the assumed title of Phra Nangklao. He ruled under the assumed title of Phra Nangklao.

Rama III was a devout Buddhist who renovated Wat Po and supported the monastic studies of Prince Mongkut, who wisely remained out of royal politics. Phra Nangklao was also a political and social conservative who distrusted the West and resisted trade and diplomatic advances from both Joseph Balestier on behalf of the United States and Sir James Brooke from Britain. The king correctly understood that the primary threat to Siamese independence came not from Burma or Cambodia but from the rising forces of the West. He finally signed trade agreements with the United Kingdom in 1826 and the United States in 1833.

On another enlightened note, Rama III invited Baptists to establish a mission in Bangkok. This religious group went on to introduce the smallpox vaccine and printing presses to Siam.

SIAM MEETS THE WEST

King Mongkut—Rama IV, 1851-1868

Thailand's modern phase began with the reign of King Mongkut (Rama IV) who maintained the independence of his country while the rest of Southeast Asia was methodically carved up and annexed by France (Indochina), Britain (Burma and Malaya), and Holland (Indonesia).

Prior to his accession to the throne on the death of his half-brother, Mongkut lived for 27 years as a monk in Buddhist temples around Bangkok. His religious tenure proved excellent preparation for the crown. During his monastic life, Mongkut studied English, Latin, Pali, Sanskrit, and Khmer; pursued Western history, geography, and mathematics; founded the Thammayut (Dhammakaiya) sect of Buddhism which stressed strict adherence to Theravada Buddhist ideals; and elevated Wat Bowonivet in Bangkok (where he served as chief abbot) to a major center of Buddhist thought and Western studies. He also came to understand that Siam could only survive as an independent nation by rapid modernization and close cooperation with Western powers.

Mongkut initiated diplomatic relations with most European powers and the United States. Trade treaties were signed with Britain in 1855, France in 1856, and Denmark and Holland in 1862. By negotiating these diplomatic and trade agreements, Mongkut cleverly played one colonial power against another, making Siam a neutral buffer zone between the competing nations.

THE KING AND I ~ REALITY OR RACISM?

*K*ing Mongkut, unfortunately, is largely known to the Western world as theautocratic despot who sang and danced his way through the film *The King and I*.

Starring Yul Brynner as the monarch and Deborah Kerr as his governess, the Rodgers and Hammerstein film is based on Margaret Landon's 1943 best-seller *Anna and the King of Siam* which was, in turn, based on the writings of one Anna Leonowens. Her two fanciful novels—*The English Governess at the Court of Siam* (1870) and *Romance of the Harem* (1873)—described her experiences as an English teacher in the court of King Mongkut.

Born in India in 1831, Anna married a clerk who took her to Penang, where he died in 1859. Unsure of her future, Anna moved to Singapore and then to Bangkok in 1862, where she broke with most of her family, including a grandnephew, Boris Karloff of *Frankenstein* fame. In Bangkok, she hooked up with American Protestant missionaries such as Dr. Dan Bradley, who reinforced her Christian prejudices during her employment as the English instructor to the king's children.

Her five years of service in the court made little impact on the king—his only written reference to Leonowens was an appendix to a shopping list. After completing her contract, Leonowens moved to the U.S., where she wrote her memoirs and made a living giving lectures about life in the Siamese court.

The Western world largely believed the story of Anna Leonowens until an English scholar wrote a biography of her family in the early 1970s. Dr. Bristowe discovered Anna had lied about her age, her birthplace, and the background of her husband, who was a clerk rather than a military officer. Worse yet, her memoirs were filled with glaring errors regarding Thai history, Buddhism, and activities within the royal court. Leonowens essentially plagiarized old books on Myanmar and invented all sorts of wild tales to help boost book sales. She neither spoke Thai nor had access to workings of the inner court. In the end, she portrayed King Mongkut as some sort of primitive despot and herself as the Victorian Christian who single-handedly modernized the backward nation.

Nothing could be farther from the truth. King Mongkut is universally regarded as an enlightened ruler whose imaginative diplomacy secured Thailand's sovereignty against Western colonialists. He also modernized his nation by reforming the legal system and encouraging contact with the West, leading the way by employing English teachers for his sons.

Leonowens, on the other hand, was a puritanical widow of low social standing whose colorful fabrications caused a great deal of embarrassment to the Thai government. After all, no group of people enjoy having others laugh at one of its most respected leaders.

Today, both the book and the film are banned in Thailand.

Mongkut brought his country into the modern era by introducing political and social reforms. One of his early edicts allowed his subjects to gaze upon his face. He also used royal commands to attempt to improve the conditions of slaves and women. Mongkut continued to Westernize his nation by supporting the work of Christian missionaries and hiring European tutors—most notably Anna Leonowens—for his sons.

On a more prosaic note, Mongkut ordered the construction in 1863 of Bangkok's first paved road, called Charoen Krung ("Prosperous City") by the Thais and "New Road" by the Western residents. This 6.5 km road running southeast from the palace and along the river past the Oriental Hotel quickly become the commercial center of the growing city, favored by both local Chinese and Thai merchants and the foreign community, which constructed their homes and diplomatic offices within blocks of the Oriental Hotel. He later constructed Silom and Sathorn roads to aid in the rapid expansion of his city.

Mongkut also helped to popularize modern science, though his quest for knowledge tragically led to his death. In 1868 he correctly predicted a solar eclipse from his royal palace in Petchburi, then went south to observe it near Prachuap Khiri Khan. There he contracted malaria during the observation and died three weeks later in Bangkok. Chulalongkorn, his senior son, claimed the throne.

WESTERN COLONIAL EXPANSION (1785 - 1909)

(map)

Labels on map: MANDALAY, UPPER BURMA, MYANMAR, LOWER BURMA, YANGON, RAKHINE, CHIANG MAI, LUANG PRABANG, VIENTIANE, TONKIN, HANOI, CHINA, LAOS, HUE, FRENCH, VIETNAM, ANNAM, BRITISH, SIAM, BANGKOK, TENASSERIM, ANDAMAN SEA, CAMBODIA, PHNOM PENH, GULF OF SIAM, SAIGON, COCHIN CHINA, PHUKET, KEDAH, PENANG, MALAYA, BRITISH

0   300 km

THAI TERRITORIAL LOSSES (1785 - 1909):
1. Penang ceded to Britain;
   ceded by Sultan of Kedah (1785 - 1800)
2. Cambodia ceded to France; Franco-Siamese Treaty (1867)
3. Northeast Laos to France; seized (1888)
4. Laos ceded to France; Franco-Siamese Treaty (1893)
5. Mekong Region ceded to France; Franco-Siamese Treaty (1904)
6. West Cambodia ceded to France; Franco-Siamese Treaty (1907)
7. Malay States ceded to Britain; Anglo-Siamese Treaty (1909)

BRITISH EXPANSION:
Arakan; First Anglo-Burmese War (1826)
Tenasserim; First Anglo-Burmese War (1826)
Lower Burma; Second Anglo-Burmese War (1852)
Upper Burma; Third Anglo-Burmese War (1885)
Malay States; annexed (1874-1909)

FRENCH EXPANSION:
Cochin China; ceded by Tu Duc (1862-1867)
Annam; seized (1887)
Tonkin; seized (1887)

King Chulalongkorn—Rama V, 1868-1910

Mongkut's son, Chulalongkorn, ascended the throne at the age of 15 and reigned over Siam for 42 years, continuing his father's policies of transforming Thailand from a medieval kingdom into a modern and progressive nation. Chulalongkorn abolished slavery in 1905, as well as ceremonial prostration before the king, and constructed the first railways, strengthened the national infrastructure through public projects, and adopted European concepts of government, education, and justice.

In 1886 he opened the first hospital in Siam, Siriraj (Thonburi), and in 1892 established the first post and telegraph office. He also constructed a national library, museum, and important religious sites, such as the Marble Temple in Bangkok, the last major Buddhist temple erected in the city. His two visits to Europe helped introduce Siam to the outside world.

Chulalongkorn nevertheless clung to some autocratic customs, including polygamy on a grand scale, keeping a grand total of 92 wives who bore him some 77 children. Opium was strictly regulated but remained a lucrative government monopoly. He also continued to appoint men of royal descent to high administrative posts, a practice that offended some of the European-educated elite. At the same time he hired a grand total of 549 foreign advisers, the largest number British.

His greatest political success was to successfully balance the territorial ambitions of the British and French. By the latter half of the 19th century, France controlled Indochina and England laid claim to Burma and Malaya. The final question appeared to be whether France or Great Britain would seize Siam.

The French approached from the east. In 1863 the French signed an agreement with the Cambodian king which effectively made his country a colonial protectorate. Alarmed, Chulalongkorn modernized his army and prepared to meet the French challenge. Siam resisted until 1893, when a French blockade of Bangkok forced Chulalongkorn to cede Laos and western Cambodia to the French.

The British approached from the south. In 1909 the four Thai-controlled Malayan states of Kelantan, Trengganu, Kedah, and Perlis were given to the British in exchange for diplomatic recognition of Siamese territorial rights. Chulalongkorn's skillful diplomacy and large but strategic land concessions allowed Thailand to remain the only nation in Southeast Asia never colonized by the West.

Chulalongkorn, the most honored of all past kings, is the only ruler recognized each year by a national holiday, on 23 October.

King Vajiravudh—Rama VI, 1910-1925

The death of Chulalongkorn in 1910 left Thailand with neatly defined borders on all sides and a centralized government dominated by royalty and a Western-educated bureaucracy. It also saw the rise of a new bourgeois intelligentsia unhappy with its lack of power within the royalist government.

Vajiravudh was a flamboyant, Oxford-educated prince who continued his father's process of modernization. Among his notable edicts was the 1913 law commanding all Thais to adopt surnames (Thais previously used only first names) and his 1921 introduction of compulsory universal education. He also reformed the calendar along Western lines and established the first national university, which he named after his father. Vajiravudh wisely sent an expeditionary force to France in June 1918 to participate in the final battles of WW II. Goodwill generated by this gesture allowed the Thais to renegotiate many of the unequal treaties previously signed with Western powers.

Vajiravudh made a few blunders. His extravagance almost bankrupted the government and he left behind only one heir, a daughter born one day before his death in 1925. More ominously, Vajiravudh antagonized the military by creating a nationwide paramilitary corps recruited exclusively from the civil service. In 1912 a group of young army lieutenants—angered with their downgrading—plotted a military coup to overthrow his government. The revolt was quickly crushed but military leaders remained disenchanted with absolute monarchy.

THE END OF ABSOLUTE MONARCHY

King Prajadhipok—Rama VII, 1925-1935

Prajadhipok, Chulalongkorn's 76th child and final son, reigned as Siam's last absolute monarch. His was also the shortest and most controversial rule in the history of the Chakri dynasty.

Prajadhipok claimed the throne under difficult circumstances. As a military officer educated at Eton, he never expected to be crowned king and was never properly trained in civil and administrative matters. Early reforms improved the economic situation created by his predecessor, but the worldwide depression of the early 1930s forced Prajadhipok to cut salaries, raise taxes, and alienate many of his bureaucrats and military leaders. Prajadhipok understood political reform was inevitable but received little support from his government. Despite his efforts, his proposals for a democratic constitution were rejected by advisors who feared loss of status and position.

The pressure cooker finally blew in 1932 when a bloodless coup d'etat instigated by French-educated Thai intellectuals and supported by the military toppled the absolute monarchy. The coup leaders included a number of nationalists who remained major figures for the next three decades. Pridi Panomyong, one of the country's leading intellectuals, was a young leftist lawyer trained in France who served as the leader of the government's civilian faction. Phibul Songkram was an ambitious junior army officer who used his ministerial powers to assert the superior efficiency of the military over the civilian bureaucracy headed by Pridi. The third player was an old-line military officer named Phraya Phanon, who, as the first prime minister, maintained a precarious balance between the Pridi and Phibul factions in the new government.

After the coup, King Prajadhipok served in a minor role until deteriorating relationships with the new rulers forced him to flee to England. Prajadhipok formally abdicated on 2 March 1935. The National Assembly in Bangkok then invited Ananda Mahidol, the 10-year-old son of Prince Mahidol of Songkla and nephew to Prajadhipok, to ascend to the throne. A regency council was appointed to serve while Mahidol continued his studies in Switzerland.

RISE OF THE MILITARY

Phibul and the Nationalist Regime, 1938-1944
Relations in the 1930s between the civilian cabinet led by Pridi and the military forces headed by Field Marshal Phibul continued to deteriorate to the point of insurrection. Faced with a military threat he could no longer contain, Prime Minister Phanon retired in late 1938 to be replaced by Phibul.

The Phibul regime sold nationalism to the public by changing the name of the country, initiating a series of anti-Chinese measures to reassert Thai hegemony, and stirring up old animosities against the French, who still occupied former Thai territories. Thailand had never forgiven the French for their blockade of 1893 and the subsequent loss of Siamese control over portions of Laos and Cambodia. Sensing an opportunity to avenge the French seizure and reclaim lost lands, Phibul cultivated closer relations with Japan, praising that country as the only Asian nation to successfully challenge the West.

On 8 December 1941 Japanese forces invaded Thailand at nine points, chiefly along the southern peninsula to support the invasion of Malaya and Singapore. Facing certain defeat, Prime Minister Phibul quickly signed an agreement which guaranteed continued Thai independence in exchange for unimpeded Japanese passage through Thailand toward British-held Burma.

Thailand then formed a military alliance with Japan and issued a declaration of war against the United States and Great Britain. Pridi resigned in protest but accepted a position as chief regent for the absent Prince Mahidol. Whether a cynical move or sensible acceptance of a de facto situation, Thailand's alliance with Japan allowed the Thais to remain sovereign and relatively unscathed throughout the war.

Fortunately, the Thai ambassador in Washington, Seni Pramoj, refused to deliver the declaration of war to the American government. Seni simply filed the document away in his desk and never brought up the event in political discussion. It proved a wise move, since America never formally declared war on Thailand and continued to regard the Thai people as supporters of Allied efforts. Seni later worked with the American Office of Strategic Services, a precursor to the Central Intelligence Agency, and helped establish the Free Thai movement coordinated by Pridi back in Bangkok.

As the war dragged on, relations between Japan and Thailand deteriorated. By mid-1944 political winds and the tides of warfare were shifting against the Japanese and Prime Minister Phibul. The prime minister had become closely associated with General Tojo, who was disgraced in Tokyo. Authoritarian rule and military dictatorships were losing favor around the world. Sensing the imminent defeat of Japan, the National Assembly demanded the resignation of Phibul and the reintroduction of civilian rule.

Following the fall of Japan, Thailand lost its territories reclaimed under Japanese occupation but, thanks to American pressure against the wishes of Britain and France, was never punished for its alliance with the island nation. Phibul went into internal exile in June 1944, replaced by the first predominantly civilian government since the 1932 coup.

King Ananda Mahidol—Rama VIII, 1935-1946
After the bloodless coup of 1932 and the abdication of Vajiravudh in 1935, the Thai crown passed to Ananda Mahidol, a 10-year-old prince born in Germany. The son of Prince Mahidol of Songkhla and grandson of Chulalongkorn, Mahidol occasionally visited Thailand but largely remained in Europe away from the ongoing power struggles between military and civilian factions.

Ananda returned from his studies in Switzerland to occupy the throne as Rama VIII in December 1945. The following month saw the first openly democratic elections in almost a decade. Pridi was elected prime minister, the head of a civilian government.

The jubilant mood that followed was shattered on 9 June 1946 when King Ananda was found dead in his bedroom at the royal palace—

FAREWELL SIAM

The name change of a nation is always a curious affair. Visitors to Thailand often wonder what happened to that wonderfully romantic name Siam. As with Myanmar, Sri Lanka (Ceylon), and Irian Jaya (New Guinea), the truth lies in political intrigue.

After Prime Minister Phanon retired in 1938 and Field Marshall Phibul took over in 1939, Phibul renamed Siam Thailand, or, more properly, Muang Thai—"Land of the Thai." The official line was that Siam was not a Thai word but a creation of foreign powers and therefore unacceptable to a free and independent nation. It was also argued that 23 million Thai-speaking citizens needed to be reflected in the nation's name.

Some criticized the new English name as being a bastardized conjunction—Thai being a local word and "land" being English—but the nomenclature served to unite the nation in the face of approaching war. A greater loss, perhaps, was the disappearance of the word Siam, which carried such vivid and exotic overtones.

There were other reasons for the change. Phibul was a right-wing, ultranationalist military leader who supported many of the xenophobic politics and nationalistic policies being advocated at the time in Germany and Italy. Among his chief concerns was the domination of the Thai economy by the Chinese, who had long comprised a sizable portion of the population. The Chinese had migrated to Siam in large numbers since the early 18th century and, with a flair for business, soon dominated many of the major industries, including the opium trade and tax collection, both despised occupations. Unlike earlier immigrants, Chinese arrivals in the 20th century resisted assimilation into Thai society by supporting a separate structure of social halls and Chinese-language schools. Legislation enacted after the turn of the century was often intended to force the integration of the Chinese into Thai society. To a large degree these laws were successful, as many Chinese changed their names to Thai derivatives and started to speak only Thai in public. But their domination of the economy remained an obvious source of resentment among less fortunate Thais.

In 1939, Phibul introduced his "Thailand for the Thai" economic plan, which levied heavy taxes on Chinese-owned businesses while offering state subsidies to Thai-owned enterprises. Chinese opium addicts were deported from the country, Chinese immigration was restricted, and numerous occupations previously held by Chinese were reserved for Thais. Phibul used another weapon to show the world that the country was controlled by the Thais and not the Chinese: Muang Thai or Thailand—Land of the Thais.

---

shot in the head under mysterious circumstances. Murder, conspiracy, or suicide? An official announcement that afternoon said the king had accidentally shot himself while examining his Colt .45 automatic, but a subsequent government commission that included American and British doctors concluded the king had probably been murdered or committed suicide.

The government bungled the investigation. Two years after his death, three of the king's bodyguards were arrested and charged with complicity in his murder. The three attendants responsible for the king's safety spent the next six years in a long, messy trial that resulted in their acquittal, retrial, guilty verdict, and 1954 execution.

Public opinion, however, held Prime Minister Pridi morally responsible for the murder, due to his long promotion of antiroyalist sentiments. Pridi resigned as prime minister in August 1946 and left the country on an extended vacation. The civilian government remained haunted by the unexplained death of Ananda and plagued with economic problems and persistent levels of bureaucratic corruption.

THE PRESENT KING

King Bhumibol Adulyadej—Rama IX (1946-present)

The present king, Bhumibol Adulyadej, was born on 5 December 1927 in Cambridge, Massachusetts, where his father was studying medicine at Harvard University. Bhumibol's birth was an inauspicious event, hardly noted by the Siamese press; the American-born Thai was considered a highly unlikely candidate to ever reach the throne.

According to Siamese laws of royal succession, Bhumibol on the day of his birth was outranked by the reigning King Prajadhipok (his uncle), Bhumibol's father (Prince Mahidol of Songkhla), and his elder brother, Prince Ananda. But fate intervened in a remarkable way. Prince Mahidol died abruptly in 1929 and Prajadhipok abdicated without a designated heir (he only had one daughter) in 1935. Prince Ananda briefly served as King Rama VIII until his mysterious death in 1946. Prince Bhumibol then became king of Thailand at the age of 19.

The young king finished his education at Lausanne University in Switzerland before returning to Thailand to claim the throne as Rama IX. Prior to this homecoming, Bhumibol lost an eye in a car accident, but also was introduced to Mom Rajawongse Sirikit, the beautiful daughter of the Thai ambassador to France. Bhumibol married Sirikit in April 1950, one week prior to his coronation. He then took his full, royal name: Phrabaat Somdet Boramintara Maha Phumipol Phonadunyadet.

The young king vowed to prove himself a worthy successor to his predecessors and "rule with dharma for the benefit and happiness of the Siamese people." His early years were more noted for his love of the arts, music, and the social whirl of Bangkok society. Perhaps his deepest love was the world of jazz, where he proved himself a talented jazz saxophonist at formal university graduations, state functions, and even impromptu jam sessions held in the inner sanctums of the Royal Palace.

During his jazz period, the king led all-star late-night sessions with such luminaries as bandleader Les Brown and singer Patti Page. In 1960, the king played with the Benny Goodman band in New York; Goodman offered the king a job in his orchestra. Lionel Hampton, jazz's greatest vibest, called him the "coolest king in the land." Bhumibol's jazz compositions include "Hungry Man's Blues," "Blue Night," "Falling Rain," and the alma mater theme song for Chulalongkorn University. His compositional career peaked with the release of his three-movement "Manohra Ballet," a complex piece based on a classical Thai story accompanied by a variety of blues moods, Thai musical themes, and improvised melodies inspired by Coltrane and Monk. The work itself, previewed in Vienna during a state visit, earned Bhumibol the first admission of any Asian citizen to the Viennese Institute of Music and Art.

Bhumibol also has proved himself a talented artist, often using members of the royal family in his small- to medium-sized oils. A rare retrospective of his paintings in 1987 to honor his 60th birthday revealed his evolutionary style from portrait realism to semi-abstracts filled with bold colors and original design.

The king also has a great fondness for yachting. Despite the automobile accident that blinded him in one eye, Bhumibol's deft handling and intriguing boat designs won him the Gold Medal at the Southeast Asian Games in 1967. Bhumibol in this respect is similar to other national leaders who love the sea: King Constantine of Greece, King Olav of Norway, the duke of Edinburgh.

Bhumibol's interests changed with time, from jazz and sailing to more serious matters of social and political justice. In what is now the longest reign of any Thai king, Bhumibol has earned immense popularity as the working monarch who guides and unifies the nation as head of state and protector of national traditions. He also works ceaselessly to promote rural development, oversee construction of new roads to help the poor farmers of the northeast, and encourage the opium growers of the north to experiment with alternative cash crops. The king is aided in his humanitarian efforts by his wife, Queen Sirikit, who oversees a foundation to preserve traditional arts and crafts.

Bhumibol is a wealthy man, with major financial interests in the Siam Cement Corporation and the many large banks managed by the Crown Property Bureau. This organization is the second-largest asset holder and fourth-largest investor in the country, with widely varied financial interests that include the Dusit Thani and Siam Intercontinental Hotels, offshore mining, and Honda car assembly.

In July 1988 Bhumibol became Thailand's longest reigning monarch after 42 eventful years on the throne. In 1996, His Majesty's 50 years of leadership were honored with nationwide festivals and celebrations, while in 1999 the King presided over the final year of the Amazing Thailand tourism campaign.

A QUESTION OF SUCCESSION

King Bhumibol and Queen Sirikit have four children, Princess Ubol Ratana (born 1951), Crown Prince Vajiralongkorn (1952), Princess Mahachakri Sirindhorn (1955), and Princess Chulabhorn (1957).

The nation now faces one of the more controversial quagmires of modern Thai politics—the question of royal succession. Thailand's rules of succession are taken from a royal decree issued by King Tilok (1448-88), who sought to standardize succession when most kings were in polygamous relationships and produced hundreds of potential heirs. Tilok established the tradition still observed today that the king's senior son was first in line for the throne, followed by his brother, known as the *uparaja,* and then by other male offspring of the king.

According to these traditions, Crown Prince Vajiralongkorn, the sole son of Bhumibol, should claim the throne upon the death or abdication of his father. However, the situation changed dramatically in 1981, after new laws approved by the Thai Parliament made it theoretically possible for any member of the royal family to take the throne. Although Vajiralongkorn was officially designated crown prince and heir to the throne when he turned 20 years of age in 1972, in the event of illness, death, or voluntary declination, the throne might pass to one of his sisters.

The next ruler probably won't be the eldest daughter, Princess Ubol Ratana (Ubolrat), who attended M.I.T. in Massachusetts where she fell in love with and married an American student, Peter Jensen. The newlyweds moved to Los Angeles, where the princess studied statistics and public health at U.C.L.A. Because she married a foreigner, Ubolrat lost her title and royal allowance and later found work as a marketing assistant with a computer company in Los Angeles—quite a change from royal life in Bangkok.

Today Ubolrat and Peter reside in Los Angeles, where Peter works in the mining industry and Ubolrat raises their three children. Ubolrat appears satisfied to be uninvolved with the political and social intrigues of the royal family. She is also on good terms with her family, who had her reinstated as princess a few years ago.

The next ruler probably won't be Princess Chulabhorn, third eldest daughter of the king and queen. Even though she's four steps down from the throne, Chulabhorn lacks the command of government affairs and social issues so vital for national leadership. Chulabhorn married a Thai commoner in 1982.

Could the next king be a queen? If public popularity held sway, the next monarch would probably be Bhumibol's second daughter, Princess Sirindhorn, a woman of many accomplishments, including academic distinction—she's a lecturer at two of Thailand's most prestigious universities and recipient of a string of degrees in sociology, the humanities, history, and education. Sirindhorn also presides over the Red Cross and, much like her beloved father, works incessantly to help the poor of Thailand.

Sirindhorn was elevated in 1981 to the rank of *Maha Chakri,* a title virtually equivalent to crown princess. Despite Princess Sirindhorn's popularity, the next monarch will most likely be Crown Prince Vajiralongkorn. He attended school at London's prestigious Royal College of Defense Studies and currently holds the rank of major general in the Royal Guards Regiment, military credentials being important in the political structure of Thailand. Vajiralongkorn has one daughter by his first wife, Princess Somsawali, and five younger children by his unofficial consort (or second wife), Yuwatida Surasawadee. The 1993 divorce of Vajiralongkorn and Somsawali ended an unhappy relationship similar to that of Britain's Prince Charles and Princess Diana, although Vajiralongkorn certainly received better treatment from the press than his British counterpart. Vajiralongkorn then married Surasawadee.

The crown prince is heir apparent, but Sirindhorn continues to be a popular candidate among the Thai people, who consider her a righteous choice for the throne. The question of royal succession is one of the favorite topics among the Thais, who constantly whisper the latest rumors circulating about the royal family. Negative publicity about the king, queen, or children is forbidden in Thai publications, but speculation comes up almost daily in most conversations.

Visitors may want to discuss the issue with a Thai, but remember most Thais are reluctant to discuss royal matters with a foreigner and deeply resent criticisms given by outsiders.

THE PEOPLE

THE THAIS

Thailand is one of the most racially homogeneous countries in Southeast Asia—almost 80% of the country's 60 million inhabitants are Thai, speak a dialect of the Thai language, read a unified Thai script, and follow the Buddhist faith. The remainder of the population is comprised of ethnic Chinese (8-12%), Malay (4-6%), and minority groups (3-5%) such as Vietnamese, Cambodians, Burmese, and various hill peoples.

Thais are similar in physique and complexion to peoples of most neighboring countries, including Indonesia and the Philippines, and are roughly categorized as Deutero-Malay. As a racially tolerant people, they have assimilated large numbers of Chinese, Burmese, Mons, and Khmers to a degree that precludes any typical Thai physiognomy or physique. The degree of Chinese blood distinguishes Thais the most; genetic traces from other Southeast Asian peoples is significant.

Thais speak a dialect of the Tai (Thai) language, the lingua franca of those living in a remarkably diverse region that ranges from southern China to northern Borneo and from central Myanmar to the east coast of Vietnam. Their particular version, Siamese Tai, is an isolative and tonal language related to Lao and Shan, and is derived primarily from Sinitic sources or the Kadai language, related to Indonesian.

The so-called "Core Thai" majority can be divided into four regional groups: central Thai (36%), northeastern Thai (32%), northern Thai (8%), and southern Thai (8%).

Central Thais

This political, social, and culturally dominant group lives in the Chao Praya River basin and makes up the largest segment of the population.

Although their numbers barely exceed those of the Thai-Lao in the northeast, central Thais control the government, the military, the taxation system, and most forms of national development, a concentration of power resented by distant residents. These residents feel neglected in terms of economic development and controlled in matters of regional sovereignty—most notably the insistence of the central government that the central Thai dialect ("standard Thai") be taught in all public schools. Other unpopular programs include news programs broadcast in standard Thai over public radio systems and political appointees from Bangkok assigned to positions removed from their area of origin.

*little girl at
Floating Market*

RESPONSIBLE TOURISM

*T*ourism, some say, broadens the mind, enriches our lives, spreads prosperity dissolves political barriers, and promotes international peace. While concurring with most of these sentiments, others feel mass tourism often destroys what it seeks to discover; it disrupts the economy by funneling dollars into international travel consortiums rather than local enterprise, exploits the people who find themselves ever more dependent on the tourist dollar, and reinforces cultural stereotypes rather than encouraging authentic dialogue between peoples. Responsible tourism is a movement that attempts to address both the virtues and vices of mass tourism by making each traveler more sensitive to these issues. The fundamental tenet is travel should benefit *both* the traveler and the host country, and travelers should travel softly and thoughtfully, with great awareness of their impact on the people and the environment.

Spearheading this movement is the Center for Responsible Tourism (2 Kensington Rd., San Anselmo, CA 94960), a Christian group that holds annual conferences on the impact of mass tourism, publishes a thought-provoking newsletter, and offers workshops on how to lead a responsible tour. Visitors are encouraged to seek out low-impact and locally based travel experiences by patronizing cafes, guesthouses, and pensions owned by indigenous people. Their guidelines:

1. Travel in a spirit of humility, with a genuine desire to meet and talk with the local people.
2. Sensitize yourself to the feelings of your hosts.
3. Cultivate the habit of listening and observing, rather than merely hearing and seeing.
4. Realize that other people's concepts of time and thought patterns may be dramatically different—not inferior—to your own.
5. Seek out the richness of foreign cultures, not just the escapist lures of tourist posters.
6. Respect and understand local customs.
7. Ask questions and keep a sense of humor.
8. Understand your role as a guest in the country; do not expect special privileges.
9. Spend wisely and bargain with compassion.
10. Fulfill any obligations or promises you make to local people.
11. Reflect on your daily experiences; seek to deepen your understanding of the people, the culture, and the environment.

Regional stereotypes are fading, but central Thais have long characterized northern and northeastern Thais as semi-barbaric country bumpkins, while the latter consider speakers of the central dialect to be untrustworthy, exploitative carpetbaggers. At the same time, northern groups often feel inferior to the central Thais, who represent (and control) national progress, prestige, wealth, and power.

THAI SOCIETY

Thai society is often described as a world of polite behavior, tolerance, and eternal pacifism—characteristics that complement their good-natured approach to life. To a large degree, this assessment rings true. Thais certainly smile more than most other peoples, and there are few outward signs of the anxieties and neurotic behavior that plague many Western societies. This lack of psychological tension insures that Westerners remember Thailand chiefly for the genuinely warm and friendly people rather than the glittering temples or lovely beaches.

Thailand's happy state of affairs often is credited to the major religion, Buddhism, and the traditional value system, which places great importance on the sanctity of family, friends, and social harmony. Credit also must be given to their belief that life is to be enjoyed without restraint, provided the individual's activities do not impinge on the rights of another person. Thais generally refuse to be fanatical about productivity, deadlines, and goals.

Thais also detest conflict and will go to great pains to avoid confrontation and preserve harmony between individuals. The attitude of *jai yen* (cool heart) is strongly favored over *jai rohn* (hot heart). Criticism—a definite sign of a hot heart—may be valued as an honest characteristic in the West, but Thais consider direct criticism a personal attack that ruins face and may demand serious retribution in the future.

The above attitudes can be summarized by the popular, and perhaps most important, phrase *mai pen rai,* which means "never mind."

Names

Thais have personal first names such as Porn ("Blessings"), Boon ("Good Deeds"), Sri or Siri ("Glory"), Som ("Fulfillment"), or Arun ("Dawn"). Since Thais normally address each other by their first name rather than their family name, don't be surprised if they call you "Mr. John" or "Miss Judy." The prefix Khun is the ubiquitous title which substitutes for Mr. or Mrs. Affectionate nicknames such as Frog, Rat, Pig, Fat, or Shrimp are more popular than first names.

Buddhist Values

Buddhism—the most important element in Thai society—teaches a system of beliefs quite different from those of the West. Buddhist theology is based on doctrines of causality unlike those of Christianity.

Buddhism sees life as endless suffering (illness, disappointment, decrepitude, decay, and death) caused by desire, attachment, and the craving for ego satisfaction. Salvation occurs when the individual achieves nirvana and frees the self from the endless cycles of reincarnation.

Buddhism considers life a series of predetermined events dictated by the karma accumulated over a previous lifetime. It assigns no sense of moral shame to the actions of an individual but rather regulates life through nonjudgmental precepts such as karma and reincarnation. Buddhists are concerned about the cycles of reincarnation rather than an impending day of judgment or an eternity in heaven or hell.

Furthermore, the very basis of Buddhism leaves many questions about the nature of existence unanswered and refuses to synthesize the contradictory, opposed, and complementary experiences of life. The big picture is left as it is: contradictory, opposed, and complementary. In this sense, Buddhism parallels existentialist philosophy, which sees life as a series of random and impermanent events without easily defined meanings, and placing responsibility with the individual in determining morality and values.

These fundamental aspects of Buddhism—free choice, predetermination, sin, punishment, heaven, hell, reincarnation—give the Thais their unique outlook on life. One fundamental is that Thais subjugate their egos to a remarkable degree, since ego gratification is considered mankind's chief source of pain and suffering. Yet equally important are their beliefs in predetermination and reluctance to judge individuals on the basis of sin or guilt.

The results are obvious as you travel around the country. Thais disregard with ease many of the commonplace aggravations that infuriate Western visitors such as delayed buses, vague answers, and incompetent waiters. They also disregard—or at least tolerate—evildoers such as pickpockets and prostitutes; individuals assume sole responsibility for the consequences of their karma.

Agrarian Values

The Thai agrarian system of values starts with the family, then moves upward through households, neighborhoods, villages, and extended communities until the pyramid forms the extended family of Thailand. This explains their respect for parents and other people in positions of authority, their need for social harmony, and their dedication to community and nation. Perhaps the most important result of this devotion to family, community, and nation—rather than to the individual—is the sense of emotional security it provides, a feeling of belonging beyond the comprehension of most Westerners.

Codes of behavior for relating to community members are instilled from earliest childhood. Respect for elders is taught through a complex system of titles, which are imbued with overtones of rank to indicate the amount of deference due each position. Social relationships are not egalitarian, as in the West, but rather hierarchically ordered. Children are taught the importance of moral goodness *(bunkhun),* gratefulness *(katanju),* reciprocity *(kaan tob thaen),* respect *(nap thay),* and inhibition *(krengjai)*—the ability to never impose upon the peace of other individuals.

Once learned, these systems of interaction remain viable as the child matures and moves into the hierarchies of school, office, and government. Many later move to Bangkok and assume the lifestyles of jaded youth *(way ruan)* but most continue to follow the values of an earlier era.

Emotional security allows most Thais to interact with fellow citizens and foreign visitors on a surprisingly warm basis. For example, Thais often address complete strangers with surprisingly familiar terms, such as "aunt" for female mango sellers and "younger brother" for waiters in a cafe. Westerners also will be greeted on intimate levels provided they appear friendly and *taam sabai*—comfortable with their environment.

Social Hierarchy

Thai society differs from Western societies in many ways, including social hierarchy, attitudes toward authority, emotional expression, and concepts of time and work.

Perhaps the fundamental difference is the stratification of Thai society into carefully defined levels, a social hierarchy alien to Western societies that place great value on the ideals of equality and egalitarianism.

Thai society has traditionally given top status to the king, who enjoys the titles The Lord of the Land *(phra kha paedin)* and The Lord of Life *(phra kha chiwit)*. Just below the king are the royal princes and members of the royal court, followed by government officials deemed important enough to receive honorific titles. The middle classes are judged according to their wealth and access to political power, while the remainder of the population is ranked by other factors such as age, social connections, lineal descent, earnings, and education.

This traditional system, in place since the Sukothai era, changed after the fall of the absolute monarchy when military leaders, the bureaucratic elite, and Chinese entrepreneurs gained power and weakened the strength of hereditary royalty.

On a more common level, Thais consider the search for social ranking an important element of all social interaction. Social conduct can only occur after status has been determined, often through direct questions such as "How much do you earn?" and "How old are you?" Westerners unaccustomed to such inquiries should consider them a form of flattery or simple curiosity rather than an invasion of privacy.

Even the Thai language includes dozens of forms of personal and impersonal pronouns depending on the social status of the speaker and listener.

Authority

In contrast to most Westerners' natural distrust of authority—especially absolute authority—Thais respect their rulers, whether royalty, military captains, or community leaders. This respect is derived from the client-patron relationship that requires superiors to provide protection and leadership in exchange for the services and respect of subordinates.

Beneath the Smile

As noted above, Thailand is often described as a nation of easygoing, carefree, and gracious people who lack visible signs of anger and aggression. Another viewpoint was offered in the mid-19th century by Anna Leonowens (of *The King and I* fame), who wrote that "in common with most of the Asiatic races, the Siamese are apt to be indolent, improvident, greedy, intemperate, servile, cruel, vain, inquisitive, superstitious, and cowardly."

The truth is that Thai society is more complicated, enigmatic, and ambiguous than either of these viewpoints.

Thai citizens do value smooth interaction and the avoidance of overt conflict. Polite smiles and polite speech accompanied by genuine kindness and interest in others help maintain the social harmony so highly valued by Thais. Yet this image of pleasantness hides certain psychological pressures held within by the individual and society—pressures created by the elevation of importance and high status over self-expression and communication.

Thailand is, in fact, a very violent country, as shown by the lurid crime stories in Thai newspapers such as the *Bangkok Post.* Goons, gangsters, and godfathers pack guns to prove their machismo and protect themselves against drive-by assassins. Thailand's per capita prison population is high, and petty crime and violence appear highly endemic.

Government statistics list the leading causes of death as homicide, suicide, accidents, poisoning, heart disease, and hypertension. Suicide rates have risen from 5.4 to 6.8 per 100,000 citizens over the last decade, and a disproportionate percentage of the population appears to suffer from neurotic behavior. American Express cites Thailand as having one of the highest ratios of fraudulent to legitimate cards of all its worldwide markets, second only to that in the United States. The number of prostitutes is estimated at one percent of the population, yet AIDS cases per capita rank among the highest in the world. Statistics released from the Office of Narcotics Control Board suggest amphetamine and other substance abuse (glue and paint sniffing, marijuana, opium, heroin) are serious problems in 40% of Thailand's 70,000 communities.

Murder is commonplace in the land of smiles. According to figures provided by the Police Research and Planning Division, Thailand's murder rate hovers around 8.5 victims per 100,000—about the same as the rate in the United States, the so-called murder capital of the world. Although remarkably high, present figures seem insignificant compared to those of the previous decade, when murder rates were double or even triple that level. And death comes cheap according to the *Far Eastern Economic Review,* which states gunmen can be hired for as little as US$1,000 per murder.

Perhaps the most ominous aspect of societal decline is the disappearance of traditional and religious values, as typified by the incidents following the Air Lauda crash in the early 1990s. This event was described by the *Bangkok Post* as a "shocking occurrence that mirrored the uglier aspects of the society which we are part of—from naked greed to social breakdown and our own hypocrisy." While relatives mourned the victims of the crash, local villagers looted the dead without any sense of shame, remorse, or fear of the law. Fingers of the dead were chopped off for rings; corpses were stripped for gold necklaces and Rolex watches.

International coverage of the looting raised many questions about the famous kindness and generosity of Thai villagers and about the very nature of Thai society. Observers agreed the incident went deeper than simple greed: the looting of Air Lauda mirrored the breakdown of social order, the pervasiveness of theft and corruption, and the loss of traditional values without the development of a new code of civil ethics and responsibilities.

Blame for the shocking incident was placed on a variety of factors. Many political scientists emphasized that the public views law enforcement officials as "thieves in uniforms," and that this attitude breeds a sense of lawlessness that in turn justifies abuse, corruption, and exploitation on all levels. Thai society can no longer rely on morality for personal restraint, and respect or fear of the law is dissipating.

The public has called for greater emphasis on education and religion to solve the problems of moral erosion. Many social scientists disagree that these institutions can reform Thai society, pointing out that the educational system continues to promote submissiveness and ethnocentricity, and the moral influence of Buddhism has declined due to widespread malpractice among the clergy.

THE CHINESE

Thailand's largest and most important minority group is the Chinese. Early immigrants included the Hokkiens, who arrived during the late 18th century to serve as compradores and tax collectors for the Thai royalty, and the near-destitute Teochews, who became the leading merchants in early Bangkok. Later arrivals included thousands of economic refugees fleeing massive crop failures and widespread starvation in 20th-century China.

As elsewhere in Southeast Asia, Chinese immigrants worked hard, educated their children, and today completely dominate the trade and finance sectors of the local economy. Estimates show that 60% of Thailand's largest companies is controlled by Sino-Thais (Thai nationals of Chinese descent), and almost 100% of Thai banks are controlled by a handful of extremely wealthy Sino-Thai families.

But unlike other countries in Southeast Asia, in Thailand the massive concentration of wealth in Chinese hands has not brought widespread racial conflicts or discriminatory legislation. Racial harmony could be attributed to widespread intermarriage. According to legend, King Mongkut (himself of Chinese lineage) encouraged Chinese immigration and intermarriage with Thai women—social intercourse he hoped would give future generations the traditional Chinese qualities of industry and thrift.

As a result, it is now difficult if not impossible to distinguish ethnic Thais from Sino-Thais; perhaps 50% of Bangkok's population is ethnically

Chinese calligrapher

Chinese. Sino-Thais have Thai surnames and speak Thai rather than Chinese. Consequently, the Thai government has rarely been motivated to pass discriminatory laws but has let the Chinese help build the economic miracle of modern Thailand.

CONDUCT AND CUSTOMS FOR THE TRAVELER

Asian Bureaucracy

Dealing with immigration officials, ticket clerks, and tourist officers is much smoother if you dress properly and keep your emotions under control. You must never lose your cool no matter how slow, mismanaged, or disorganized the situation. Yelling and table pounding will only screw up things for you—in fact, Thai paper pushers *enjoy* slowing up for the obnoxious foreigner.

Smile, be polite, try humor, then firmly ask for help and suggestions. Stubborn bureaucrats can suddenly become extraordinarily helpful to the tourist who keeps his or her cool and knows how to play the game.

Royalty

Thais hold the royal family in great reverence. All visitors are expected to show respect to all royal images, including national anthems preceding movies and royal portraits on Thai currency. While some Thais may tactfully criticize their

government or local politicians, Thai royalty is beyond reproach and never openly criticized.

Buddha Images

Thais are a deeply religious people who consider all Buddhist images extremely sacred—no matter what their age or condition. Sacrilegious acts are punishable by imprisonment—even when committed by foreign visitors. Many years ago, two Mormon missionaries posed for photographs on top of a Buddha image in Sukothai. The developing lab in Bangkok turned the negatives over to a Bangkok newspaper, which published the offending photographs on the front page. Public outrage was so strong the foreigners were arrested and jailed.

Sports Illustrated was refused permission in 1988 to use religious shrines as backdrops for its annual swimsuit issue. On the island of Phuket in 1989, Kara Young, an international model, was arrested with photographer Sante d'Razzion of the French *Vogue* magazine for posing beside a religious monument. Kara and Sante were charged with desecration of a religious monument, even though the two had been invited to Thailand by the TAT and assured fashion photography was allowed at the monument. Both were booked in Phuket and briefly confined to their hotels before being allowed to leave the country.

And in 1995, deputy minister Pramote Sukhum lodged a government complaint against the

French firm Le Clerc for its portrayal of Buddha on the label of a liquor bottle.

Monks

Monks must be treated with respect. Monks cannot touch or be touched by females, or accept anything from the hand of a woman. Rear seats in buses are reserved for monks; other passengers should vacate these seats when necessary. Never stand over seated monks since they should always remain at the highest elevation.

Temple Dress

All Buddhist temples in Thailand have very strict dress codes. Shorts are not acceptable attire in Buddhist temples; men should wear long pants and clean short-sleeved shirts. Women are best covered in either pants or long skirts, and shoulders should not be exposed. Leather sandals are better than shoes since footwear must be constantly removed. Rubber flip-flops are considered proper only in the bathroom, not in religious shrines. Buddhist temples are *extremely* sacred places; please dress appropriately.

Modest Dress

A clean and conservative appearance is absolutely necessary when dealing with border officials, customs clerks, local police, and bureaucrats. A great deal of ill feeling has been generated by travelers who dress immodestly. When in doubt, look at the locals and dress as they do.

Shorts are considered improper and low-class attire in Thailand, only acceptable for schoolchildren, street beggars, and common laborers—not wealthy tourists! Except at beach resorts, you should never wear skimpy shorts, halter tops, low-cut blouses, or anything else that will offend the locals. Long slacks and collared shirts are recommended for men in urban environments. Women should keep well covered. Swimwear is only acceptable on the beach.

Emotions

Face is very important in Thailand. Candor and emotional honesty—qualities highly prized in Western society—are considered embarrassing and counterproductive in the East. Never lose your temper or raise your voice no matter how frustrating or desperate the situation. Only patience, humor, and *chai yen* (cool heart) bring results in Thailand.

Personal Space

Thais believe the head—the most sacred part of the body—is inhabited by the *kwan,* the spiritual force of life. Never pat a Thai on the head even in the friendliest of circumstances. Standing over someone—especially someone older, wiser, or more enlightened than yourself—is also considered rude behavior since it implies social superiority. As a sign of courtesy, lower your head as you pass a group of people. When in doubt, watch other Thais.

Conversely, the feet are considered the lowest and dirtiest part of the body. The worst possible insult to a Thai is to point your unholy foot at his or her sacred head. Keep your feet under control; fold them underneath you when sitting down, don't point them toward another person, and never place them on a coffee table.

The left hand is also unclean and should not be used to eat, receive gifts, or shake hands. Aggressive stances such as crossed arms or waving your arms are also considered boorish.

A Graceful Welcome

Thailand's traditional form of greeting is the *wai,* a prayerlike gesture accompanied with a slight bow. Social status is indicated by the height of your *wai* and depth of your bow: inferiors initiate the *wai,* while superiors return the *wai* with just a smile. Under no circumstances should you *wai* waiters or waitresses, children, or clerks—this only makes you look ridiculous! Save your respect for royalty, monks, and immigration officials.

LANGUAGE

The Thai language is tonal (like Chinese) and quite difficult for most Westerners to learn. In most cases, this is not a major problem for Western visitors; many younger Thais speak some English and, with each passing year, the level of proficiency within the country improves. Communication may still present problems in the smaller towns and remote regions of the kingdom, though visitors traveling only to the major destinations will have few problems.

And yet, anyone who wishes to make true personal contact in Thailand should make an effort to learn a minimal amount of the language. By starting with a small core of basic words and phrases, almost anyone can make simple conversation and open up doors that would otherwise be closed.

Start with the basic greetings and then learn the numbering system to help with bargaining. Another important aspect is to learn directions when you can't find your hotel or the train station.

Determined visitors can be up and running within a few weeks. Spend two months working on the language and you'll be amazed at how well you communicate with most Thais.

Once you've mastered a simple vocabulary, you'll find that prices drop quickly and that ordinary Thais will treat you with greater respect. The rewards are worth the effort. To learn more about the Thai language see the **The Thai Language** in the appendix.

TEMPLE ARCHITECTURE

Thailand has over 30,000 Buddhist temples that share, to a large degree, common types of structures. The following descriptions will help you sort through the dazzling yet bewildering array of buildings found throughout the country.

Wat

An entire religious complex is known as a *wat*. This term does not properly translate to "temple," since temple implies a singular place dedicated to the worship of a god while *wats* are multiple buildings dedicated to the veneration, not worship, of the Buddha. *Wats* serve as religious institutions, schools, community meeting halls, hospitals, entertainment venues, and homes for the aged and abandoned. Some even serve as drug rehabilitation centers.

The title of a *wat* often explains much about its history and function. Some are named after the kings who constructed them, such as Ayuthaya's Wat Pra Ram, named for King Ramathibodi. Others use the word Rat, Raja, or Racha to indicate Thai royalty either constructed or restored the building. Others are named for their Buddha images, such as Wat Pra Keo in Bangkok, which holds the Keo or Emerald Buddha. *Pra,* the term which often precedes important Buddha images, means "honorable." Thailand's most important *wats* are called Wat Mahathat, a term that indicates they hold a great *(maha)* relic *(that)* of the Buddha. Wat Mahathats are found in Bangkok, Chiang Rai, Sukothai, Ayuthaya, Phitsanulok, Petchburi, Nakhon Si Thammarat, Yasothon, and Chai Nat.

Bot

Bots, the most important and sacred structure in the religious compound, are assembly halls where monks meet to perform ceremonies and ordinations, meditate, deliver sermons to laypeople, and recite the *patimokkha* (disciplinary rules).

On the exterior, ground plans vary from quadrilateral *cellas* with single doors to elaborate cruciform designs with multiple entrances. All are identified by *bai semas,* eight boundary stones defining the consecrated ground and helping to ward off evil spirits. *Bai semas* are often protected by small tabernacles richly decorated with spires and runic symbols. You'll find *bot* window shutters and doors carved and decorated with gold leaf and mirrored tiles, or engraved with mother-of-pearl designs. But the most arresting sights are the multitier roofs covered with brilliant glazed tiles. Roof extremities end with *chofas,* graceful curls which represent either *nagas* or mythological *garudas.* Wriggling down the edges of the bargeboards are more *nagas* that act as heavenly staircases between earthly existence and Buddhist nirvana. Some of the best artwork is found in the triangular pediments: images of Vishnu riding Garuda or Indra riding elephant-headed Erawan.

In the interior, stunning murals often follow identical arrangements. Paintings behind the primary Buddha image depict scenes from the *Traiphum,* the Buddhist cosmological order of heaven, earth, and hell. Take a close look at the punishments of the damned—they might remind you of the Hieronymus Bosch painting of Dante's Inferno. Less interesting side walls are decorated with incidents from the life or earlier incarnations of the Buddha. The most spectacular murals, always located on the front wall above the main entrance, depict either the Buddha's enlighten-

MEDITATION IN THAILAND

*I*ncreasing numbers of travelers are investigating Buddhism and *vipassana* (insight) or *samatha* (calmness) meditation during their visits to Thailand.

Students of Buddhism cite several reasons to study in Thailand. Many feel Thai centers offer a superior atmosphere and purer level of instruction than Western locales. Thailand welcomes visitors who arrive with a genuine desire to study and practice the teachings of Buddha. Western novices are highly respected within Thai society, as are all Thai monks, earning great merit for their devotions to the dharma.

Another reason to study meditation in Thailand is the affordability. Month-long meditation retreats in the U.S. and Europe can be prohibitively expensive, but Thais believe Buddhism is a priceless gift that must be offered in the proper spirit. As a result, meditation retreats are free, aside from small donations to cover basic expenses such as rooms and meals.

Students of meditation need not worry about language difficulties. Today, almost a dozen temples and monasteries are supervised by Western monks who teach meditation practices in English. Other temples use Thai language as the medium of instruction, but have Western monks who conduct additional classes in English. A listing of temples offering courses in English or maintaining a sizable community of Western monks follows.

Finally, Thai meditation centers provide the opportunity to break the bonds of Western conditioning and enter the spiritual realm of Southeast Asia.

Most visitors interested in learning about Buddhist meditation arrive with the standard two-month visa, extendable for another 30 days. Students intending to study more than three months might consider obtaining a three-month nonimmigrant visa from a Thai consulate. These visas can be extended up to 12 months, but only with great difficulty. Note most temples have limited residential space and prefer that prospective students write in advance regarding meditation retreats.

The best resource on locations of meditation *wats* is *A Guide to Buddhist Monasteries and Meditation Centres in Thailand* researched and written by Bill Weir, *vipassana* devotee and author extraordinaire of Moon handbooks to Arizona and Utah. Bill spent seven months of travel updating the original 1970s guide written by Jack Kornfield. An updated edition released in 1995 includes new information on visas, travel conditions, health, language, forms of instruction, accommodations and quality of meals in each monastery; daily meditation schedules; and ordination procedures.

Bill's handy 100-page guide (US$8) is available from the World Fellowship of Buddhists, 33 Sukumvit Rd., Bangkok 10110. In the U.S., contact Insight Meditation West (Spirit Rock) at P.O. Box 909, Woodacre, CA 94973, tel. (415) 488-0170.

Another useful source of printed information is the small Mahamakut Bookstore on Pra Sumen Road, just across from Wat Bowonivet. The English-language section includes books published by the Pali Text Society, the Buddhist Publication Society, and Mahmakut Rajavidyalaya Press.

Bangkok

Bangkok is a fine spot to conduct some initial research, though noise and pollution make this a difficult place for serious meditation.

World Fellowship of Buddhists: English-language meditation classes for Western visitors are held on the first Sunday of every month, 1400-1730 in their headquarters on Sukumvit Road. Their small bookstore sells English literature on Buddhism and Weir's guide to meditation temples in Thailand. Located at 33 Sukumvit Rd. (between Soi 1 and Soi 3), Bangkok 10110, Thailand, tel. (02) 251-1188.

Wat Mahathat: The International Buddhist Meditation Centre (I.B.M.C.) in the Dhamma Vicaya Hall to the rear of Wat Mahathat is an excellent information source on Buddhism and meditation retreats. Founded by a former Thai monk and his English wife, along with scholars from adjacent Mahachulalongkorn Buddhist University, the center sponsors weekly lectures on Thai Buddhism and weekend meditation retreats to nearby temples. Their weekend at Buddha Monton in Nakhon Pathom costs 500B for food, accommodations, and transportation from Wat Mahathat. Upcoming English-language lectures are listed in the *Bangkok Post*. The center also publishes a list of meditation *wats* that welcome guests. For further information contact Vorasak and Helen Jandamit, c/o The International Buddhist Meditation Centre, 26/9 Chompol Lane, Lardprao Lane 15, Bangkok 10900, Thailand, tel. (02) 511-0439.

ment or his temptation by Mara. Shoes must be removed before entering all *bots* in Thailand.

Viharn

Secondary assembly halls where laypeople pay homage to the principal Buddha image are *viharns,* architecturally identical to *bots* except for the lack of consecrated boundary stones. Larger *viharns* are surrounded by magnificently decorated cloisters filled with rows of gilded Buddha images.

Chedi

Chedi is the Thai term for the Indian stupa. In ancient times, these dome-shaped monuments held such relics of the Buddha as pieces of bone or hair. Later prototypes were erected over the remains of kings or saints, and today anybody with sufficient *baht* can order a *chedi* constructed for his or her ashes. A *chedi* consists of a three-tiered base representing heaven, hell, and earth, with a bulbous stupa on top. The small pavilion *(harmika)* near the summit symbolizes the Buddha's seat of meditation. Above is a multitiered

and highly stylized umbrella ringed with moldings representing the 33 Buddhist heavens. The pinnacle is often capped with crystals and precious jewels. The world's largest *chedi* stands in Nakhon Pathom, one hour west of Bangkok.

Prang

These towering spires, among Thailand's most distinctive and exciting monumental structures, trace their architectural heritage to the corner towers of Cambodian temples. Although the phallic-shaped structures rest on square bases like *chedis,* many have achieved a more elegant and slender outline than Kampuchean prototypes. Lower tiers are often ringed by a frieze of demons who appear to be, depending on your perspective, either dancing or supporting the tower. Summits are typically crowned by the Hindu thunderbolt, symbol of Shiva and a religious holdover from ancient traditions. Thailand's most famous *prang* is Wat Arun, just across the river from the Grand Palace in Bangkok.

Mondop

These square, pyramidal-roofed structures enshrine highly venerated objects such as palm-leaf Tripitakas (Buddhist bibles) or footprints of the Buddha. Thailand's most famous example is the *mondop* of the Temple of the Buddha's Footprint at Saraburi.

Prasat

Elegant buildings with ground plans in the form of a Greek cross, *prasats* may either serve reli-

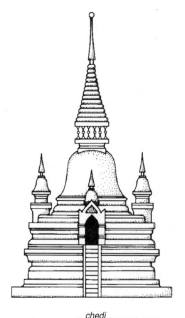

chedi

religious prasat

TERRA MUZICK

gious or royal functions. Those designed for secular or royal purposes are capped with familiar multiple rooflines; religious *prasats* are crowned with *prangs*. Thailand's most famous *prasat* is at Bang Pa In, one hour north of Bangkok.

Other Structures

A **sala** is an open-walled structure used by pilgrims to escape the heat and by monks as a casual dining room. *Salas* also serve as overnight shelters for pilgrims during temple festivals.

A bell or drum tower that summons monks to services and meals is called **ho rakang.** The **ho trai,** an elevated, graceful library, houses Buddhist canonical texts. The *ho trai* is built on stilts to prevent rats and white ants from devouring the precious manuscripts.

The **kutis** are the monks' quarters, often the simplest yet most attractive buildings in the *wat* complex. Older *kutis* frequently dangle on the verge of collapse; those in Petchburi are most evocative.

The **Kanbarien** Hall hosts religious instruction.

prang

TERRA MUZICK

THE PERFORMING ARTS

DANCE AND DRAMA

Khon

The glory of Thai classic theater is the *khon,* a stunning spectacle of warriors, demons, and monkeys in brilliant costumes who perform acrobatics and highly stylized movements. *Khon* has its roots in court-sponsored ballets which thrived under royal patronage until the military revolution of 1932 ended Thailand's absolute monarchy.

Accompanied by the surrealistic sounds of the Thai *pipat* orchestra, the *khon* typically takes its storyline from either the Javanese *Inao* legend or the Indian Ramayana, called the Ramakien ("Glory of Rama") in Thailand. Actors and actresses never speak, but rather mime narration provided by professional troubadours and choruses. Originally a masked drama, modern *khon* features unmasked heroes and celestial beings, though demons and monkeys continue to wear bizarre head coverings. *Khon* is an endangered art form; the only remaining venue in Thailand is Bangkok's National Theater. Performances are

sponsored several times yearly—superb theatrical experiences not to be missed.

Lakhon

While *khon* is male-oriented and relies on virtuosity in strength and muscular exertion, the courtly *lakhon* impresses its audience with feminine grace and elegant fluidity. *Lakhon* presents episodes from the Ramakien, *Manora* folktales of southern Thailand, and *Lakhon Jatri* itinerant folk dances used to exorcise evil spirits. *Lakhon* is traditionally accompanied by a chorus and lead singers instead of *khon*-style recitation, though these distinctions are no longer strictly followed.

The costumes of elaborately embroidered cloth and glittering ornaments surpass the brilliance of the *khon*. Actresses are unencumbered by masks, allowing them to combine singing and dialogue with dance. Highly refined body gestures display a complex encyclopedia of movements while emotion is conveyed by demure dartings of the eyes and highly stylized, very specific movements of the hands. The dance itself lacks the dramatic leaps and whirling pirouettes of Western ballet but a great deal of dramatic tension and sensuality are achieved by the movement of the upper torso. *Khon* and *lakhon* are often combined into grand shows for the benefit of both visitors and Thais.

Likay

If *khon* and *lakhon* are classical art, then *likay* is slapstick comedy performed for the masses. The obvious lack of deep artistic talent is made up for with unabashed exuberance and a strong sense of earthiness. A form of people's theater performed at most provincial fairs, *likay* relies heavily on predictable plots, outrageous double entendres, and lowball comedy. Performers interact directly with the audience, which responds with raucous laughter at the political sarcasm and sexual innuendo. Costumes worn by the untalented but enthusiastic actors run from gaudy jewelry to heavy makeup. It is ironic that television, the universal destroyer of traditional theater, has helped keep *likay* alive by broadcasting daily performances of soap-opera sophistication.

MOVIES FILMED IN THAILAND

*M*ore than 100 films and documentaries were shot in Thailand over the last few decades, primarily Vietnam War pictures which substituted Thailand topography for Vietnam's.

Over the years, Thailand has seen the likes of Sylvester Stallone in *Rambo III,* Jean Claude Van Damme in *Kick Boxer,* erotic classics such as *Emmanuelle in Bangkok* and Private Video's *Private Goes to Bali* (actually filmed in Thailand), as well as lighter fare, such as *Air America,* and Disney's *Operation Dumbo Drop.* Recent efforts include the James Bond flick, *Tomorrow Never Dies,* and Leonardo DiCaprio in *The Beach.*

Films highlighting Thailand's landscape include:

Chang (1927): Although filmmakers Ernest Schoedsack and Merian Cooper will be forever associated with their 1933 classic *King Kong,* the inventive pair accomplished some of their greatest work with their depiction of Siamese peasant life near Nan. Filmed on location, *Chang* ("Elephant") established a cinematic blueprint for *King Kong,* complete with roaming jungle cats and marauding herds of elephants.

Anna and the King of Siam (1946): The original film account of King Mongkut (Rex Harrison) and his nanny (Irene Dunne) wasn't filmed in Thailand but the staging is reasonably authentic, except for the Balinese *gong kebayar* gamelan style of music which didn't exist until the 20th century.

The King and I (1956): Though Yul Brynner and Deborah Kerr never left the Hollywood soundstage, the costumes and set designs look quite accurate, except for the Japanese lantern in the garden. Based on the fictional life of a former governess, *The King and I* was immediately banned in Thailand due to Brynner's unfavorable portrayal of King Mongkut, one of the nation's most honored and accomplished rulers.

Around the World in 80 Days (1956): The classic story of Phileas Fogg and company includes a shot of David Niven as he watches the royal barges on the Chao Praya in Bangkok.

The Ugly American (1963): After a visit to Southeast Asia in 1958, Marlon Brando agreed to star in this film based on the controversial William Lederer novel about diplomatic intrigue and anti-American sentiments in the mythical country of Sarkhan. Brando, ever the political idealist, portrayed a quaintly simplistic American ambassador who struggles against the rising tide of communism. The well-intended film included extensive footage of Bangkok, the Thai countryside, and historic temples, but the complex political issues and obscurity of the region doomed it to commercial failure.

The Man with the Golden Gun (1973): Many of the brilliant chase scenes in this James Bond flick were filmed in Phangnga Bay, near Phuket in southern Thailand. Soon afterward, one of the towering limestone pinnacles was dubbed "James Bond Rock" by local tour promoters, a clever marketing ploy still used some 25 years after the film's release. The film also includes a wild car chase down an almost rural Sukumvit Road in Bangkok, an impossible feat today given the bone-crushing traffic.

Emmanuelle in Bangkok (1976): A French softcore romp largely staged in Bangkok with endless, mindless, jerky, poorly focused shots of Thai kids playing in the Bangkok *klongs.*

The Deer Hunter (1978): Most of the hair-raising river scenes in this Vietnam War classic were filmed on the River Kwai near the town of Kanchanaburi. The bar scenes might also look familiar since most were shot inside the Mississippi Queen on Patpong Road in Bangkok. *Deer Hunter* won a slew of Academy Awards and started the mania for Vietnam-era films.

Uncommon Valor (1983): Gene Hackman, Robert Stack, and Patrick Swayze (in one of his early roles) tell about Vietnam Vets who return to rescue imprisoned comrades held captive on some dusty hill in Thailand.

The Killing Fields (1984): This production, based on Sydney Schanberg's *The Life and Death of Dith Pran,* won several Academy Awards for its powerful depiction of the Cambodian holocaust. Most of the exterior scenes were shot in Thailand, including footage of Hua Hin's Railway Hotel, which doubled as the correspondent's hotel in war-torn Phnom Penh. Bangkok, Patpong Road, and Bang Tao Beach on Phuket were also used as backdrops. Finally, the elegant old Government House in Phuket town served as a replica of the French Embassy in Phnom Penh.

Volunteers (1985): This comedy-adventure flick about the American Peace Corps was filmed in Bangkok and around Mae Hong Son. Despite the leading roles of Tom Hanks and John Candy, *Volunteers* was quickly relegated to video rentals.

continues on next page

MOVIES FILMED IN THAILAND
(continued)

Platoon (1987): This film garnered Oliver Stone an Academy Award for Best Director of the Year, and Willem Dafoe a nomination for Best Supporting Actor. Street scenes of old Saigon were re-created by constructing fiberglass replicas of old blue-and-yellow Renault taxis. Chinese-Thai extras were hired to ensure a Vietnamese look.

Swimming to Cambodia (1987): Spalding Gray, San Francisco's famed but now hated monologist (he prefers New York), used his experiences as an actor in the filming of *The Killing Fields* to explore the social and political undercurrents of contemporary Southeast Asia. Jonathan Demme directed.

Good Morning Vietnam (1987): Hollywood's first Vietnam War comedy starred Robin Williams as a zany disc jockey who entertains troops via the American Forces Radio Service. The atmosphere of old Saigon was successfully re-created by production designers who arrived months in advance to scout locations and work on elaborate transformations, such as turning a small food store into the Minh Ngoc GI Bar, complete with American flags and flashing jukebox. Most of the Saigon street scenes were filmed along Rajadamnern Avenue. Director Barry Levinson sensibly used Bangkok's notorious Patpong Road as the substitute for Saigon's equally notorious brothel district along Tu Do Street.

Rambo III (1988): This film begins with our hero, played by Sylvester Stallone, meditating about the truths of life in a Thai monastery; he quickly decides to chuck the robes and do battle with the Soviets in Central Asia. The opening scenes were filmed in Bangkok and the meditation sessions at Wat Buddhaphat, a hillside temple about one hour southeast of Chiang Mai, near the weaving village of Pasang.

Air America (1990): This *M*A*S*H* rehash centers around a pair of wild and crazy U.S. pilots—played by Mel Gibson and Robert Downey, Jr.—working for Air America, the secret airline operated by the CIA out of Laos during the Vietnam War. *Air America* was largely filmed around Mae Hong Son in northern Thailand, including a dramatic scene of an elephant being airlifted over the Burmese-style temples around Chang Khom Lake.

Casualties of War (1991): The war drama, directed by Brian De Palma and starring Michael J. Fox and Sean Penn, was filmed in Kanchanaburi and on the island of Phuket.

The Good Woman of Bangkok (1991): Loosely based on Bertolt Brecht's *The Good Woman of Szechuan,* this documentary features a 25-year-old prostitute named Aoi, who made the confession in exchange for enough cash to quit her job and buy a farm in her old village. Any traveler foolish enough to fall for a Thai prostitute should see this film.

Heaven and Earth (1993): Oliver Stone's final Vietnam War film approaches the conflict from the viewpoint of a Vietnamese woman who sympathizes with the communist cause but loves an American GI. The film was shot in Vietnam and around Phangnga Bay near Phuket in southern Thailand.

Street Fighter (1994): Jean Claude Van Damme makes his first appearance in Thailand in this hokey film, based on a video game, which is plagued with cheesy effects and costumes cloned from Nazi and sci-fi films.

Men of War (1994): Starring Swedish-born Dolph Lundgren, this film about hardened mercenaries and innocent natives was mostly filmed on Ao Nang Beach and in Khao Phanom Bencha National Park near Krabi. The "Cavern of the Dead" was created inside the caves of Suan Si Nakawan National Park near Phangnga; the boxing scenes were staged in Bangkok.

Day of Reckoning (1994): A flash-in-the-pan dirge with rogue travel guide Fred Dyer touring around Bangkok with a brief visit to the phallic shrine in the back yard of the Hilton International.

Operation Dumbo Drop (1995): This Walt Disney film about elephants and their mahouts was filmed over a two-month period in Mae Hong Son, Kanchanaburi, Chiang Mai, and Lopburi. Although the film starred Ray Liotta and Danny Glover, the real star was Pathet Thai, an elephant born in Thailand, raised in the United States, and returned to Thailand to assume the lead role as Dumbo.

The Quest (1995): Roger Moore, star of the 1973 James Bond film, returns to Thailand to play a villain opposite Jean Claude Van Damme. The Belgian kickboxer apparently was an old Thailand fan, as he married Darry Lapier at the Bangkok Regent Hotel in 1994.

Mortal Kombat (1995): This flick and its 1997 follow-up were largely filmed in Bangkok and on the beaches near Krabi.

Cutthroat Island (1995): A big budget Hollywood blockbuster which did even worse in box office receipts than *The Quest* and *Mortal Kombat,* despite the drawing power of Hollywood stars Matthew Modine and Geena Davis. Geena pouts while the area around Krabi substitutes for the Caribbean, including some great shots of the ship inside Maya Bay on Ko Phi Phi—the same wonderful location where Leonardo DiCaprio wandered aimlessly in *The Beach*.

The Phantom (1996): Billy Zane (the evil husband in *Titanic*) as the Man in Purple Tights and Treat Williams as Xander Drax can't rescue the early half of this film shot in Thailand, though the latter half in New York features some nifty costumes from the 1930s.

***Mortal Kombat II* (1997):** The Japanese robot action craze returned to Thailand with several scenes filmed in Ayuthaya, the ancient capital. After its release, some Thais protested the apparent sacrilegious desecration of the 600-year-old temples of Ayuthaya. Actually, the problem was that the plywood and styrofoam sets back in Hollywood were so realistic that it appeared on screen that Ayuthaya was going up in smoke.

Tomorrow Never Dies (1997): James Bond (Pierce Brosnan) and Michelle Yeoh tear up the streets of Bangkok, including some clips of the soaring Baiyoke Tower (tallest building in town) and a motorcycle chase which almost ended the career of Ms. Yeoh. Although these scenes supposedly took place in Vietnam, sharp-eyed viewers will find a significant amount of Thai script and a Thai flag waving from a mast in the harbor. Other goofs include the impossibility of helicopters hovering in place with their rotors tilted forward (a cool effect, but

beyond the laws of physics) and the fact that Bond's car is actually a BMW 740i V8 and not a 750i V12.

Return to Paradise (1998): This highly acclaimed but largely ignored film revolves around two friends who must choose whether to help a third friend who was arrested in Malaysia for drug possession, starring Joaquin Phoenix and Anne Heche. The drug connection banned filming in Malaysia but areas around Krabi in southern Thailand substituted for the Malaysian prison.

Brokedown Palace (1999): Claire Danes and Kate Beckinsale are arrested for drug smuggling while vacationing in Thailand.

The Beach (1999): The biggest film to be lensed in Thailand since the 1973 James Bond flick *The Man with the Golden Gun,* starred Leonardo DiCaprio and was directed by Danny Boyle *(Trainspotting). The Beach* caused a national uproar after the Fox production company asked to use Maya Bay on Ko Phi Phi as a central film set, planting over 100 coconut trees to enhance the atmosphere of the film, apparently an environmental assault on the pristine atmosphere of southern Thailand (cough, cough). Despite the protests, the film was completed in mid-1999 with additional scenes filmed at the On On Hotel in Phuket Town and at a waterfall in Khao Yai National Park. The film was based on an award-winning novel by British author Alex Garland and tells the story of a young backpacker who discovers an Edenic beach and takes up residence, only to ruin the island paradise. Beautiful Maya Bay was featured on the cover of the second edition of *Thailand Handbook*.

BANGKOK BASICS
PLANNING YOUR TRIP

Before you leave for Thailand, you'll need to do a few things:

- Learn something about Thailand's history, people, and culture
- Figure out your personal interests and motivations for travel
- Pick your preferred destinations and activities
- Estimate your time and total expenditures
- Plan an itinerary and travel route
- Obtain necessary documents
- Check your health and safety needs
- Purchase an airline ticket
- Pack your bag
- Grab a taxi
- Head for the airport!

ALLOCATING YOUR TIME

Bangkok takes about a week to casually explore, though Thailand is a large country which requires a minimum of a month for proper exploration. Visitors on shorter schedules should consider an organized tour or limit themselves to a few destinations such as Bangkok, Chiang Mai, and an island in the south. Visitors with more time can add other places, such as Ayuthaya and Sukothai for historical ruins, the northeast for Khmer monuments and traditional culture, and the remote beaches and islands in the deep south.

Be prepared for serendipity—Thailand is a place where the firmest of plans quickly go astray.

FIGURING THE COST

Everybody needs to estimate expenditures, whether traveling for two weeks or two years.

The basic rule is that time and money are inversely related. Short-term travelers must spend substantially more for guaranteed hotel reservations and air connections. Long-term travelers willing to use local transportation, stay in budget hotels, and eat at streetstalls can travel as cheaply in Thailand as anywhere in the world.

Expenses vary widely, but there are a few guidelines. Budget travelers should figure on about US$500-800 per month for land costs such as accommodations, meals, local transportation, and shopping. Shoestring types who laze on beaches and survive on fried rice can escape for US$250-400 per month.

Midlevel travelers who need better hotels with private bath and clean sheets will probably spend US$800-1,200 per month. This level of travel includes a mix of fan-cooled rooms and a/c hotels, budget cafes and better restaurants, buses and trains supplemented with taxis and rental cars, and occasional splurges such as first-class restaurants and extravagant shopping sprees.

Travelers who demand a/c rooms every night and shudder at the thought of eating from streetstalls should allow US$1,500-2,000 per month. Anyone spending over US$2,000 per month is probably missing the best parts of travel—meeting the people and gaining true insight into this wonderful country.

Total costs can be figured by considering costs in four basic categories: airfare, accommodations, local transportation, and food.

Airfare

Airfare depletes a big chunk of everybody's budget, but you'll be surprised at how many kilometers can be covered per dollar with some planning and careful shopping. Roundtrip airfare from the United States or Europe should average US$800-1,100. Except for a few short connections, there is little need for internal air flights.

Independent travelers should buy a one-way ticket to Bangkok and onward tickets from travel agencies along the way. Discount agencies in Thailand offer some of the world's lowest prices, due to fierce competition and the unwillingness of local agents to follow fares suggested by international airline consortiums.

Accommodations

While transportation costs are rather fixed, sleeping expenses can be carefully controlled. Accommodations are incredibly cheap all over Thailand: simple rooms under 100B can be found in almost every town in every province. Spend a few dollars more, and you can stay in simple but spotlessly clean rooms including clean sheets and a private bathroom with fresh towels. Visitors on shorter vacations will find the nation's upscale hotels and resorts among the finest in the

SAMPLE PRICES IN THAILAND

The following list will help you gauge local prices. The current exchange rate is 25B *(baht)* = US$1.

ACCOMMODATIONS

Camping (National Park): 5-10B
Budget Guesthouse: 50-150B
Budget Hotel: 150-300B
Moderate Hotel: US$25-60
Luxury Hotel: US$100-150
Super-luxury Hotel: US$150-500

FOOD

Fried Rice: 8-15B
Rice Dish With Meat: 15-30B
Budget Cafe: 40-60B
Moderate Restaurant: 100-250B
Luxury Restaurant: US$10+
Thai Beer (pint): 30-40B
Thai Beer (liter): 60-80B
Mekong Whiskey (pint): 40-60B
Thai Cigarettes: 15-20B
Coke: 5-8B
Fruit: 20-25B

TRANSPORTATION

Taxi from Bangkok Airport to City Center: 300B
Local Taxi: 100-200B
Bangkok to Chiang Mai by air: US$70
Bangkok to Phuket by air: US$85
Bus from Bangkok-Chiang Mai: 250-350B
Bus from Bangkok-Phuket: 300-400B

SUPPLIES AND SERVICES

Soap: 5-7B
Band-Aid: 1B
Rubber Sandals: 20-40B
Music Cassette: 20-40B
Batteries: 25-30B
Haircut: 20-30B
Shirt: 80-150B
Shorts: 35-60B
Movie Ticket: 10-25B
Film (36 exposures): 100-125B
Film Processing (36 slides): 50-80B

world. All this makes Thailand a real jewel for travelers of all budgets.

The best news is the *baht* devaluation of 1997-98 has made Thailand about 30-40% cheaper than before the economic crisis. This applies to local train fares, buses, and all guesthouses and hotels which quote their rates in local currency.

On the other hand, luxury hotels have recently started quoting their room prices in U.S. dollars rather than *baht*, which means that a large gap now exists between the midlevel and luxury accommodation levels. Anyone who wishes to do Thailand in style, but not break the bank, should seek out quality hotels that still quote room prices in local *baht!*

Local Transportation

Trains, buses, taxis, and other forms of internal transportation are ridiculously cheap by Western standards. For example, a 36-hour train ride from Hat Yai to Bangkok costs under US$20 in second class, an overnight bus from Bangkok to Chiang Mai is US$12-15, a taxi from the Bangkok airport to most hotels runs US$8-10.

Food

In Thailand finding excellent meals at bargain prices involves the same process as anywhere else in the world. Avoid those places signposted "We Speak English" or displaying credit card stickers. Search out cafes filled with local customers, not groups of tourists. Don't be shy about streetstalls and simple cafes; these often provide the tastiest food at rock-bottom prices. By carefully patronizing a selection of local cafes and quality streetstalls, it's surprisingly easy to enjoy three outstanding meals for under US$10 a day.

WHAT TO BRING

Overpacking is perhaps the most serious mistake made by first-time travelers. Experienced vagabonders know that heavy, bulky luggage absolutely guarantees a hellish vacation. Travel light and you'll be free to choose your style of travel. With a single carry-on pack weighing less than 10 kg you can board the plane assured your bags won't be pilfered, damaged, or lost by baggage handlers. You're first off the plane and cheerfully skip the long wait at the baggage

carousel. You grab the first bus and get the best room at the hotel.

Choosing Your Bag

First consideration should be given to your bag. The best modern invention for world travel is the convertible backpack/shoulder bag with zip-away shoulder straps. Huge suitcases that withstand gorilla attacks and truck collisions are more appropriate for group tours and those moving permanently to a new country.

Serious trekking packs with external frames work best for backpackers mainly interested in hiking and camping. Your bag should have an internal-frame, single-cell, lockable compartment without outside pockets to tempt thieves. A light, soft, and functional bag should fit under an airplane seat and measure no more than 18 by 21 by 13 inches.

Impossible, you say? It's done every day by thousands of experienced travelers who know they are the most liberated people on the road.

Baggage Allowances

Regulations on baggage vary with the airline, the route, and the class of your ticket; ask in advance. In general, international flights from the United States permit two bags of legal size weighing no more than 70 pounds to be checked. A third piece may be brought onto the plane if it fits into the overhead compartment or under the seat.

Baggage limits between international destinations outside the United States are often determined not by piece but by weight—40 kg for first class, 30 kg second class, and 20 kg economy. Flights between foreign cities that connect with transpacific flights to the United States are determined by piece, not by weight.

Special Needs for Female Travelers

Women travelers should bring along yeast infection medicine and an ample supply of tampons as these items can be difficult to find in Thailand.

Packing Tips

An important consideration is what to pack. Rule of thumb: total weight should never exceed 10 kg (22 pounds). Avoid bag bondage by laying out everything you think you need, then cut the pile

BRING THE KIDS!

*T*raveling with children in Thailand may be slower, more expensive, riskier, and harder work than going childless, but it can also be the most rewarding travel experience of your life. Cultural barriers such as race and language seem to disappear in the presence of children, who help us remember the essential goodness and unity of humankind. Children speak a universal language that reduces personal barriers and helps us see the world through fresh, new eyes.

Best of all, children are treated like divine creatures throughout Southeast Asia. Adored and honored for their sheer rareness, Western children often become the center of all social events. Finding a baby-sitter is no problem; though keeping track of your children as they are passed around the crowd can sometimes be alarming.

On the road, accept the fact that children need more time to recover from jet lag, and tired children are grumpy children. Itineraries are subject to change no matter how ambitious your plans, and children are often more impressed with flying kites than with some solid-gold Buddha.

Detailed preparation and packing lists are essential, as are reading topical bedtime stories to prepare your children for their upcoming adventure. More useful ideas are given in *Travel with Children* from Lonely Planet (tel. 800-275-8555) and *Traveling with Children and Enjoying It* from Globe Pequot Press (tel. 800-243-0495). *Family Travel Times* (tel. 212-206-0688) is a monthly newsletter with travel tips. *Family Travel Guides* (tel. 510-527-5849) has a catalog with over 200 books and articles on family travel. How about a tour? **Rascals in Paradise** (tel. 800-872-7225) specializes in adventurous vacations for families.

---

in half. To truly appreciate the importance of traveling light, pack up and take a practice stroll around your neighborhood carrying your bag(s) on the hottest day of the year.

Take the absolute minimum and do some shopping on the road. The reasons are obvious: Asia is a giant shopping bazaar filled with everything from toothpaste to light cotton clothing, prices are much lower than back home, and local products are perfectly suited for the weather.

Minimize by bringing only two sets of garments: wash one, wear one. A spartan wardrobe means freedom and flexibility, plus it's great fun to purchase a new wardrobe when the old clothing no longer comes clean. Give some serious thought to what you *don't* need. Sleeping bags, parkas, bedding, and foul-weather gear are completely unnecessary in Thailand. Many travelers buy an umbrella when it rains and a sweater when it gets chilly.

It's a good idea to pack everything into individual plastic bags. Put underwear and socks in one bag, shirts in another, medical and sewing supplies into a third. Place the larger bags with pants and shirts at the bottom of your pack and smaller packages with books and socks at the top. Plastic compartmentalization keeps your bag neat and organized, and possibly even dry

when the longtail boat capsizes in northern Thailand!

Here's a list of suggested items to include in your gear:

• two pairs of long pants—one casual, one formal
• one stylish pair of shorts
• two short-sleeved shirts with pockets
• five pairs of underwear and socks
• modest bathing suit
• one pair of comfortable walking shoes
• sandals or rubber thongs
• mini towel
• mini umbrella
• medical kit
• insect repellent
• International Drivers License
• photocopies of essential documents
• spare passport photos
• sunglasses
• plastic Ziploc freezer bags
• sewing kit
• two small padlocks
• alarm clock or alarm wristwatch
• Swiss Army knife
• good Thai dictionary
• *Thailand Handbook* or *Bangkok Handbook*

FESTIVALS

The Thais are fun-loving people whose love of *sanuk* brings celebrations and festivals almost every week of the year. Whether a colorful parade filled with costumed participants, or a solemn procession to honor Buddha, all provide great entertainment for both participants and spectators alike.

The following festivals, described in greater detail under each chapter, are worth planning into your itinerary—despite the time or additional expense required.

The Lunar Calendar

Festival dating is an inexact science in Thailand since nature has provided the world with two obvious time markers—the sun and the moon. Festivals can be based on the familiar solar-based Gregorian calendar of 12 months and 365 days, or on the lunar-based calendar of 13 moons with 28 days each.

The disparity between the two systems makes dating difficult. Thai national holidays are set by Western calendars and fall on fixed dates, but festivals connected with Buddhism or agricultural cycles are generally dated by the lunar calendar and change from year to year.

To complicate matters further, Thais use a different lunar calendar than the Chinese; the Thai lunar new year (Songkram) takes place in November while the Chinese lunar new year generally occurs in February. And both systems use a solar calendar for solstice-oriented festivals but make adjustments by adding a lunar month once every three solar years.

Approximate dates are given below, but details should be checked with the tourist office and their *Major Events & Festivals* calendar, or in the entertainment section of the *Bangkok Post*.

National Holidays

Thailand has 13 official holidays celebrated nationwide, including the birthdays of Queen Sirikit and King Bhumibol, the founding of the Chakri dynasty (1782), Bhumibol's coronation (1950), and the reign of King Chulalongkorn.

National holidays also include the three major Buddhist events, plus New Year's Day, Labor Day, Constitution Day, and Songkram (the Thai New Year).

National holidays are as follows:

1 January—New Years Day

February—Makha Puja

6 April—Chakri Day

13 April—Songkram

1 May—Labor Day

Buddhist monks

5 May—Coronation Day
May—Visakha Puja
July—Asanha Puja
12 August—Queen's Birthday
23 October—Chulalongkorn Day
5 December—King's Birthday
10 December—Constitution Day

Buddhist Festivals

Most Thai celebrations are religious, designed to honor the teachings of the Buddha. Most are lunar-based holidays held on the day or evening of the full moon.

The three most important Buddhist events are public holidays celebrated nationwide in all temples. Makha Puja, third lunar month, February, marks the major sermon of the Buddha; Visakha Puja, sixth lunar month, May, commemorates the birth, death, and enlightenment of the Buddha; and Asanha Puja, eighth lunar month, August or September, honors the Buddha's first sermon.

Two other important Buddhist events (not national holidays) are Khao Phansa, the time for young boys to enter the monkhood at the beginning of the rainy season; and That Kathin, the end of the rainy season when laypeople present new robes to senior members of the *sangha.*

Many smaller regional festivals are only celebrated in a single town or province.

Brahmanic Festivals

Brahmanic ceremonies honor the elemental spirits of Hinduism still deeply ingrained within Thai society. These are often centered around ancient rites performed by white-robed priests, such as the Royal Ploughing Ceremony held at Sanam Luang in Bangkok.

Brahmanic festivals also include Loy Krathong (Festival of Lights), a thanksgiving ceremony associated with animist Hindu traditions, and rocket festivals that feature elements of pre-Buddhist tradition.

Nature Festivals

Rural festivals are often determined by the vagaries of nature and the annual cycles of rainfall and drought.

Brahma

Pre-monsoon festivals designed to ensure bountiful rainfall and plentiful crops, such as the ploughing ceremony in Bangkok and rocket festivals in the north, are held in May and June before the onset of the monsoons. Post-monsoon harvest festivals take place during the cool season from November to February. Temple fairs neatly coincide with a period of low farm activity.

Agricultural festivals are often based on fruit and vegetable harvests, depending on the region and maturity cycle of the fruit. Many of these fairs are highlighted by the selection of a beauty queen, who then serves as Miss Rambutan, Miss Banana, or Lychee Queen. Curiously, Thailand lacks a durian festival, though Ko Samui would be the perfect location.

Popular fruit fairs include:

March	Chachonengsao	Mango Festival
April	Damnern Saduak	Grape Fair
May	Chiang Rai	Lychee Fair
May	Rayong	Fruit Festival
June	Chanthaburi	Fruit Festival
August	Surat Thani	Rambutan Fair
August	Lamphun	Longan Fair
September	Kamphang Phet	Banana Fair
September	Uttaradit	Langsat Fair

Regional Festivals

Almost every large town in Thailand has a festival unique to the region. Some are based on an historical event such as a military victory (the Don Chedi Fair in Suphanburi) or the foundation date of the city. Others honor an important product or craft (Borsang Umbrella Fair), a regional hobby (Chana Dove Festival), a famous resident (Rayong Suthorn Phu Day), or a sporting event (Phuket King's Cup Regatta). Chinese events include the traditional (Chinese New Year in Nakhon Sawan) and the modern (Phuket Vegetarian Festival).

The newest wrinkle seems to be festivals created solely to draw Thai and *farang* tourists, and localized events elevated to national status through the promotional efforts of the

TAT. Examples include River Kwai Week and the Surin Elephant Roundup, respectively.

January

The year begins with the three-day hangover of New Year's Day; nobody on earth celebrates the new year like the Thais.

Only festivals held in Bangkok or other destinations in this book are described below.

Don Chedi Memorial Fair: In 1592, Prince (later king) Naresuan defeated the prince of Myanmar on an elephantback duel that saved Ayuthaya from Burmese occupation. The actual battle site was lost until 1913 when Prince Damrong rediscovered the ancient *chedi* marking the site of the battle, now reenacted during the week-long festivities held just outside Suphanburi, two hours west of Bangkok. Late January.

February

February is highlighted by Buddhist ceremonies, historical light-and-sound presentations, giant straw birds, orchids, beauty queens, and Chinese New Year.

Makha Puja: The Buddhist "All Saints Day" celebrates the spontaneous gathering of 1,250 disciples at Bodhgaya, India, when Buddha outlined his principal doctrines. The event is now honored with the release of fish and caged birds, sermons, and the burning of incense. After sunset, monks lead a lovely candle-lit procession of pilgrims on a triple circumambulation of Buddhist temples throughout the kingdom. Full moon of the third lunar month.

Chinese New Year: The most important social, moral, and personal festival of the Thai-Chinese is also a time for spiritual renewal, family reunions, and social harmony. The old are honored with mandarin oranges while the young receive red envelopes filled with lucky money. All debts are settled and salaried workers receive year-end bonuses. Miniature peach trees symbolizing good luck are exchanged as everyone calls out, *"Gung hay fah choi,"* or "Good luck making money." Clothes are purchased, houses are cleaned, and calligraphers paint messages of good luck on red banners. A special salad of raw fish and 20 vegetables is prepared, while the image of the Kitchen God (a deity who reports everyone's activities to the Jade Emperor) is courted with special candies, sweet wine, hell

money, and perhaps a dab of sticky opium to seal his lips against speaking evil. After the bribe, he's taken outside and burned.

Chinese New Year is a fairly restrained event in most of Thailand except for towns with large Chinese populations, most notably Nakhon Sawan. Late February-early March.

March

Wat Pra Buddhapat Fair: Buddhist devotees make an annual pilgrimage to the Temple of the Holy Footprint in Saraburi. The temple houses the most famous footprint in the kingdom and is one of only six royal temples in the country honored with the rank *Raja Vorama Viharn*. The massive footprint, identified by its 108 auspicious marks, is enshrined under a *mondop* constructed during the reign of King Rama I. Early March.

April

The hottest month of the year is the time for beach escapes and water festivals.

Pattaya Festival: Thailand's original beach resort hosts a week-long run of beauty queens, floral floats, fireworks, cultural and not-so-cultural dance, kite competitions, car races, and revelry from the prostitutes in this Baghdad-by-the-Bay. Early April.

Chonburi Fair: The booming business town one hour south of Bangkok sponsors a 10-day fair which includes an opening-day parade, exhibitions of handicrafts, pop concerts, *likay* (folk dance) shows, beauty contests, and open-air movies. Early April.

Chakri Day: A national holiday to commemorate the reign of Rama I, the founder of the Chakri dynasty, and the only day of the year it's possible to visit the sealed chapel within Wat Pra Keo. 6 April.

Songkran: Thailand's New Year is celebrated nationwide as the sun moves into Aries; Buddha images are purified with holy water, and young people honor their parents by pouring perfumed water over their hands.

Songkran ("move" or "change") is actually a time when *sanuk*-crazed Thais convert a religious ritual into a wild-and-crazy water-throwing festival involving white powder, water pistols, and buckets of freezing liquids. The more creative folks hire fire department trucks and cruise the streets searching for innocent tourists—the prime targets and hopeless victims who should leave their cameras, dignity, and inhibitions in their hotel rooms. 13-15 April.

Pra Pradang Songkran Festival: The Mon community in Samut Prakan, south of Bangkok, sponsors a Mon Songkran festival with parades, beauty queens, and nonstop deluges of water. Tours can be booked through the Siam Society. 13-15 April.

May

Visaka Puja and pre-harvest festivals are May highlights.

Visaka Puja: This most sacred of all Buddhist holidays commemorates the birth, death, and enlightenment of Buddha with merit-making ceremonies identical to those of Maha Puja. During the day, temples are decorated with lanterns and lights, while at night the grounds come alive with the serene beauty of candlelight processions. Full moon of the sixth lunar month.

Coronation Day: King Bhumibol's ascension to the throne is commemorated with a private ceremony in the royal chapel. 5 May.

Royal Ploughing Ceremony: A colorful pageant of Hindu origins, which marks the beginning of the rice-planting season and seeks to ensure a bumper crop for the coming year. Staged on the Sanam Luang field in Bangkok and observed by the king and queen, the ceremony begins as a richly decorated plough is slowly pulled by buffaloes. Brahman priests and government ministers scatter rice seeds across the grounds. The Brahmans predict the upcoming season by interpreting the fall of the seeds, a highly prized commodity by farmers who eagerly gather the blowing kernels. Early May; the exact date is determined by Brahmanic priests.

June

The beginning of the rainy season slows down the festival cycle as farmers wait out the rains and young men serve as novice priests.

Suthorn Phu Day: The town of Rayong honors the literary works of Thailand's most famous poet, Suthorn Phu (1787-1855), with puppet shows and readings of his greatest works. 26 June.

July

Several major events occur at the beginning of the Buddhist Lent, the annual three-month rains retreat. It's an auspicious time for young Thai males to enter the Buddhist priesthood for a period of prayers, meditation, and religious studies.

Asalha Puja: Asalha Puja commemorates Buddha's first sermon to his five disciples and marks the beginning of the annual rains' retreat. Full moon of the eighth lunar month.

Khao Phansa: The day after Asalha Puja marks the first day of the novice retreat; a popular time for ordination ceremonies across the country. First day of the waning moon of the eighth lunar month.

August

Queen's Birthday: Municipal buildings are illuminated with colored lights during this national holiday that honors Her Majesty Queen Sirikit. 12 August.

October

The festival schedule picks up after the end of the rainy season.

Tod Kathin: The end of "Buddhist Lent" and the rainy season is marked by Wan Ok Phansa, celebrated with an increasing number of boat races around the country and the presentation of new robes to senior members of the *sangha*. Tod Kathin lasts until the next full moon, but each temple may only celebrate a single day of receiving gifts. The period also marks the return of Lord Buddha to the earth after teaching his doctrines in the heavens. Full moon of the 11th lunar month.

Chulalongkorn Day: Thailand's beloved King Rama V is honored with a national holiday during which wreaths are laid at his equestrian statue in the Royal Plaza near the old National Assembly. 23 October.

November

November marks the beginning of the cool season and a season of low farm activity, when rural Thais have extra time for village festivals and temple fairs.

Loy Kratong: Loy ("to float") Kratong ("a leaf cup")—the most charming festival in Thailand—honors both Buddhist traditions and the ancient water spirit of Mae Kong Ka, the Mother Waters of the Ganges River. Loy Kratong perhaps dates back to Hindu India, but the present form was developed by the Thais at Sukothai to honor the rains which had watered the earth and to wash away the sins of the previous year.

Loy Kratong begins with a full-day parade of beauty queens, floral floats, and hundreds of participants dressed in historical costumes. As the sun falls, pilgrims launch thousands of tiny banana-leaf boats, each carrying a single candle, onto the rivers and lakes throughout the kingdom—a wonderful, delicate illusion enhanced by the light of the full moon.

Loy Kratong is celebrated in both Sukothai and Chiang Mai, though Sukothai provides a superior venue due to smaller crowds and a more authentic setting among towering *chedis* and brightly illuminated temples. Full moon in the 12th lunar month.

Wat Saket Fair: Bangkok's most spectacular temple fair features folk drama, foodstalls, pop concerts, and candlelight processions around the Golden Mountain. Mid-November.

Pra Pathom Chedi Fair: Folk dramas, beauty pageants, and a parade take place at Pra Pathom Chedi, the world's tallest Buddhist monument. Nakhon Pathom. Late November.

Phimai Historical Fair: A relatively new festival designed to honor Khmer culture and attract both Thai and *farang* visitors to the premier Cambodian monument near Nakhon Ratchasima. The TAT and Fine Arts Department-sponsored event includes a procession of the *nak prok* Buddha image, *chak nak duk dam ban* folk dances, and a *son et lumière* shown across the backdrop of the Phimai sanctuary. Late November.

River Kwai Historical Week: Another newly created festival that relates the grim history of this world-famous bridge. Festivities include a light-and-sound show complete with booming cannons and voice-over narration. The week-long event includes historical exhibitions, cultural performances, and rides across the bridge on vintage WW II steam engines. Late November.

Ayuthaya Swan Boat Races: An international event which attracts local and foreign crews to the championships of the fall racing season. Late November.

December

King's Birthday: The birthday of King Adulyadej Bhumibol is celebrated with a grand parade and citywide decorations of flags, royal portraits, and brilliantly colored lights along Rajadamnern Klang Avenue. 5 December.

Thais may not be Christians, but the habit of exchanging gifts and putting up decorated trees around the end of December is almost as popular in the Buddhist kingdom as in the Land of the Rising Sun. A curious twist is the tree decorations produced by dozens of companies around the country: velvet house lizards, red-hot chili peppers, and sequinned *nagas* known for their devotion to Lord Buddha rather than Lord Jesus. 25 December.

ACCOMMODATIONS

Reservations?

Most travelers worry about finding proper accommodations their first night in Bangkok, especially those with late-night arrivals at the somewhat remote airport. Relating the current situation is difficult; although Bangkok is presently overstocked with hotel rooms, gluts often turn into droughts within a few years.

Reservations are highly recommended during the high tourist season from early December to late February, but are generally unnecessary during other times of the year. A hotel reservation desk at the Bangkok airport will check on hotel vacancies and make your reservations at good quality hotels.

The best way to make reservations is to contact your travel agent or a student travel agent. You can make reservations directly by sending a fax to the hotel in Bangkok, stating the date and time of your arrival (they may provide complimentary transportation from the airport) and length of stay, and inquiring about confirmation details such as credit card numbers and deposits. International phone calls are not recommended due to the language barrier.

Another excellent way to make a reservation is to use the hotel website on the Internet. Most mid-range and luxury hotels now have websites where you can check photos of the rooms and make an instant reservation—often at an "Internet discount rate."

For toll-free numbers of popular hotel companies, check the chart, "International Hotel Chains."

Guesthouses

Budget travelers who can accept simple rooms and common baths can sleep for under 100B everywhere, except possibly Bangkok and upscale tourist resorts such as Phuket and Pattaya.

The guesthouse phenomenon began about two decades ago as young backpackers crossed Thailand on the Kathmandu-to-Bali trail. Intrigued by these curiously dressed foreigners, and recognizing the potential for a small profit, enterprising Thai families opened up extra rooms and put up hand-painted signs marked "homestay" or "guesthouse." Coconut farmers on undiscovered islands such as Phuket and Ko Samui erected simple wooden A-frames and called them "bungalows."

Today, guesthouses specifically geared toward Western travelers and charging 50-100B for a basic room with shared bath can be found in all major tourist centers, on most beaches, and in some of the strangest nooks and crannies of the nation. The few towns that lack guesthouses need only wait until some bright soul opens up his or her home or English-language school to a Western backpacker.

Guesthouses range from simple beach shacks to three-story concrete warehouses with small swimming pools. The only unifying elements are low prices and the Western clientele. Guesthouses in larger towns and cities may be packed together in a curious variation on those much-maligned "tourist ghettos"—the "backpackers' ghetto." Although some travelers resent the pseudo-hip mentality that permeates these scenes, many regard them as convenient spots to relax for a few days and hang out with other budget travelers.

Though towns without great appeal or significant sights may lack authentic guesthouses, budget Thai hotels with acceptable rooms will invariably be found around the train and bus stations. Note that many travelers feel the most memorable guesthouses are those situated in small and remote villages, well off the tourist trail and rarely visited by curious *farangs*.

Hotels

Budget: An excellent compromise between low-end guesthouses and expensive resorts are budget hotels specifically geared to Thai tourists and Thai businesspeople. These hotels are found in most towns and are perfectly adequate for travelers uncomfortable with shoestring accommodations but unwilling to spend copious amounts of cash. Hotels with fan-cooled rooms cost US$5-15, while a/c rooms are US$10-25, depending

INTERNATIONAL HOTEL CHAIN TOLL-FREE NUMBERS

Accor Group	(800) 221-4542
Ammanresorts	(800) 447-7462
ANA Hotels	(800) ANA-HOTELS
Best Western	(800) 528-1234
Choice Hotels	(800) 4-CHOICE
Club Med	(800) CLUB-MED
Conrad Hotels/Hilton	(800) HILTONS
Dusit Hotels	(800) 44-UTELL
Four Seasons	(800) 332-3442
Golden Tulips	(800) 344-1212
Holiday Inn	(800) HOLIDAY
Hyatt International	(800) 327-0200
Insignia Resorts	(800) 467-4464
Intercontinental	(800) 327-0200
ITT Sheraton	(800) 334-8484
Mandarin Oriental	(800) 526-6566
Marriott Hotels	(800) 228-9290
Meridien Hotels	(800) 543-4300
New Otani	(800) 421-8797
Nikko Hotels	(800) NIKKO-US
Omni Hotels	(800) THE-OMNI
Pan Pacific	(800) 538-4040
Peninsula	(800) 462-7899
Radisson Hotels	(800) 777-7800
Regent Hotels	(800) 545-4000
Renaissance Hotels	(800) 228-9898
Shangri-La	(800) 942-5050
Sterling Hotels	(800) 637-7200
Westin Hotels	(800) 228-3000

on the location and time of year. Each room will generally be furnished with a double bed fitted with clean sheets, decent furniture including a chair and writing table, and a private bathroom stocked with fresh towels and a small bar of soap.

Moderate: Hotel rooms in the US$25-50 range usually include a queen- or king-sized bed, individually controlled a/c, color TV, telephone, around-the-clock room service, small pool, restaurant, cocktail lounge, and other services such as a travel agency and car rental outlet. These hotels are located in all larger towns and most smaller places frequented by tourists or upscale Thai businesspeople.

Hotels priced US$50-100 could be ranked as either moderate or luxury depending on the location. For example, Bangkok hotels priced US$50-100 are ranked as moderately priced hotels when their rates are compared to average hotel rack rates in the capital. Similarly priced hotels in smaller towns would probably be of better quality and so placed in the luxury category. Your money goes farther, of course, outside of Bangkok.

Luxury: Thailand's premier hotels and beach resorts are ranked among the finest in the world for their superb architecture, wonderful ambience, and unrivaled level of service. The "Best Hotels of the World" listed in *Travel & Leisure* and recommended by readers of *Condé Nast Traveler* consistently include the Oriental and Shangri-La in Bangkok, the Amandari on Phuket, and the Baan Na Taling and Tongsai Bay Resort on Ko Samui. Room rates in luxury hotels can range US$100-500.

As noted above, many luxury hotels and a handful of mid-range properties are now quoting their room rates in U.S. dollars rather than local Thai *baht*. This has effectively killed off any savings you might find after the *baht* devaluation of 1997-98, so you'll save serious money by moving down a few notches and staying at an upper middle level hotel rather than at the absolutely top level.

Single and Double Rooms

Single rooms mean just one bed, while double rooms have two beds. Very few hotels in Thailand make this distinction or charge a different rate for either room. Even luxury hotels, which once charged slightly higher rates for double rooms, have dropped the practice. They now charge an identical rate whether you want a single or double room—whether you have two people per room or your entire family.

Just ask at the front desk for a room with two beds and, in most cases, they will take care of you at no extra charge.

FOOD AND DRINK

The cuisine of Thailand is unquestionably one of the highlights of a visit to the East. Twenty years ago, Thai food was largely unknown outside the country except to a handful of Westerners returning from the land of *sanuk* and *tom kha kai.*

Today, Thai cooking has emerged from relative obscurity to become one of the most popular and highly regarded culinary forms in the world. The dramatic proliferation of Siamese restaurants in every corner of the planet has made Thai food such an international favorite it now threatens to replace Chinese as the world's leading Asian cuisine.

COMMON DISHES

Soups

Soup is an essential component in almost every meal in Thailand. Breakfast will start with a bland and thickened rice soup accompanied by a few simple side dishes. Lunch will often be a hearty bowl of *kuay teow* from a sidewalk vendor or open-fronted kitchen. Dinner will generally include a lighter soup, either delicate or hot and spicy, to complement the principal dishes of curries and rice plates.

The hot-and-sour broth *tom yam kung* is prepared with fragrant lemongrass, kaffir lime leaves to make it sour, chilies for the heat, fresh and lightly blanched straw mushrooms, fish sauce as a substitute for salt, fresh coriander for the garnish, and large tiger shrimp. The broth is Thailand's classic dish. There are many variations on this dish. When prepared with chicken, it's called *tom yam kai.* Vegetarian versions can be made with whole mushrooms and fresh tomatoes.

Another delicious soup is *tom kha kai*—a rich chicken and coconut-milk soup flavored with lemongrass, lime leaves, galangal, and shallots. This essential element of Thai cuisine is served throughout the country.

Khao tom (thick rice soup) can be served with fish *(khao tom pla),* pork *(khao tom mu),* or prawns *(khao tom kung).* Other noteworthy soups include *kaeng chut,* a mild flavored soup with vegetables and pork; and *kaeng liang,* a spicy soup with shrimp, vegetables, basil, and pepper.

Rice Dishes

The central ingredient in most Thai meals is a plate of steamed or boiled rice. The most common variety is the translucent long-grained type grown in several grades. Sticky or glutinous rice is an opaque, short-grained variety favored in the north and northeast. Brown, unpolished rice and varieties of red rice are occasionally used in special dishes. Popular rice dishes include:

khao daeng	red rice
khao hawn mali	jasmine rice
khao kaeng	rice with curry
khao man kai	steamed rice with marinated Hainan-style chicken
khao mu daeng	rice with Chinese-style red pork
khao na kai	steamed rice with sliced chicken
khao na pet	steamed rice with roast duck
khao pat	fried rice
khao pat kai	fried rice with chicken
khao pat kung	fried rice with shrimp
khao pat mu	fried rice with pork

Noodle Dishes

In Thailand, consuming noodles is a near-religious experience that defines the soul of the nation and the Thai way of life. For more information on the types of noodles, refer to "The Noodle Vendor" below. Some good noodle dishes to try are *bah mee haeng:* wheat noodles with meat and vegetable served dry without broth or meat gravy; *bah mee nam:* wheat noodles in broth with vegetables and meat; *bah mee ratna:* wheat noodles in meat gravy; and *kuay teow:* Chinese-style noodle soup—a lunchtime favorite from street vendors and open-air kitchens.

Kuay teow haeng is rice noodles served dry without any type of liquid soup or meat gravy. The classic *kuay teow pat thai* consists of rice vermicelli fried with small shrimp, bean sprouts, and fish sauce.

More noodle possibilities include: *kuay teow ratna,* rice noodles in a meat gravy of pork, broccoli, and oyster sauce; *mee krob,* rice vermicelli noodles fried and flavored with meats and vegetables in a tangy sweet-and-sour sauce; *pat si yii,* fried thin noodles with soy sauce; *pat thai,* thin rice noodles fried with tofu, vegetables, egg, and peanuts.

Curry Dishes

Curries are considered native to India, Pakistan, Sri Lanka, and other neighboring countries. Curries are created by cooking meats, fish, and vegetables in a combination of herbs and spices known as curry pastes to create stewlike dishes.

In Thailand, the word *kaeng* (liquid) is used to define curries. Coconut milk is often incorporated into a curry paste; this mixture is called *krung kaeng* (city of liquids). The most common are *krung kaeng ped* (red curry) which takes its color from fiery peppers, and *krung kaeng keo wan* (green curry) made from green chilies and often incorporated into poultry dishes. *Krung kaeng som* is an orange curry generally used in soups, while *krung kaeng kari* is yellow and often used for chicken and beef curries.

Among the most popular dishes in the country is *kaeng pet.* This spicy curry is made from sweet coconut milk and flavored with lemongrass, chilies, and shrimp paste. It is served with either pork, chicken, beef, fish, or prawns.

A milder version of a Muslim curry from India, *kaeng mussaman* is laced with beef, potato, onion, coconut milk, and peanut. The Thai name is a corruption of the word "Muslim." True to its foreign origins, this curry uses many spices absent from the Thai culinary repertoire, such as cinnamon, nutmeg, and other sweet spices.

Kaeng wan is a green curry thickened with coconut milk, eggplant, sweet basil, and lime leaves. Green curries have an innocent appearssance but can often be extremely hot; be careful.

Kaeng kari, a yellow curry laced with turmeric, is a milder version of Indian curry. *Kaeng baa,* however, is Thailand's hottest curry—for veteran fire-eaters only.

Salads

Thai salads *(yam)* often consist of edible leaves and succulent flowers native to the country, in combination with distinctive mints and fish sauces. Toppings include crushed peanuts, dried chilies, garlic flakes, chopped coriander leaves, dried shrimp, and flakes of unsweetened coconut. Salads are often garnished with lime wedges and pickled garlic cloves carved into flowers.

Som tam, a shredded salad from northeastern Thailand, contains shredded raw papaya, diced long beans, dried shrimp, and toasted peanuts,

THE DREADED CHILI

The Thai love affair with the fiery chili *(prik)* has given rise to the apparently indestructible myth that all Thai food is unbearably hot and spicy. While some dishes will instantly wreak havoc on the taste buds of *farangs,* the truth is many Thai recipes are not spicy and many Thais themselves cannot tolerate and tend to avoid the more aggressive dishes.

The origins of the chili pepper are almost as surprising as their effect on the uninitiated. In the year that every American schoolchild knows so well, a Portuguese captain on one of Christopher's ships discovered in the Caribbean some elongated little fruits in attractive hues of red and green. The pint-sized pepper traveled back to Europe and on to Thailand in the early 16th century with Portuguese merchants visiting the Siamese trading kingdom of Ayuthaya. For the spice-loving Siamese, the discovery of something more pungent than their beloved black pepper was taken with great enthusiasm.

Today, Thai cooking employs over 40 varieties of chilies, which are green when immature but change to yellow, orange, and red as they ripen. The hottest parts are the seeds and internal membranes, which can be removed, though this defeats the purpose of cooking with *Capsicum annum.* Bite unexpectedly into some varieties and you're launched on a breathtaking roller-coaster ride unrivaled by any other spice known to the human race.

As a general rule, chilies vary in pungency in inverse proportion to their size. Practical jokers sometimes urge newcomers to start with the smaller varieties and work their way up to the larger peppers. Novices should note the intensity of fire increases as the chili becomes smaller. For example, the large green-and-yellow *prik yuak* are as mild as green bell peppers in the West, while *prik num* and *prik chi fa,* middle-sized varieties from the north, are also relatively harmless. The thermometer rises sharply when the chilies start to resemble finger-sized torpedoes.

It is the tiny *prik kee noo* that packs a wallop so terrifying even experienced Thais treat the deceptive missile with deference and respect. Descriptively translated as "rat shit peppers" on account of their shape, these innocent-looking projectiles are guaranteed to clear your sinuses and have been know to make grown men cry.

Travelers who wish to avoid these experiences can push the suckers aside or order food as *mai phet* ("not hot") or *phet nit noy* ("a little hot"). Another tip—remember even the hottest of chilies loses much of its fierce flavor when safely cocooned in a mouthful of rice. In other words, the antidote for an overdose of chili is to eat more rice to remove the slippery oil, not panic and dive for a glass of water or beer. Finally, when sweat breaks out on your forehead and drips into your eyes, resist the sudden urge to wipe your eyes with the back of your hand. There are few experiences in life more painful than an eyeful of chili oil.

all pounded in a mortar together with palm sugar, lemon juice, fish sauce, and hot chilies. Many, many travelers survive solely on *som tam, tom kha kai, kuay teow* and *pat thai,* washed down with icy bottles of Singha beer.

Larb ped, a salad of ground duck, is served on a bed of lettuce with spice and acidic lemon to balance the richer flavors of the meat. Other meat salads include *yam kung,* prawn salad made with fish sauce, lime juice, finely chopped garlic, chili powder, minced lemongrass, red onion, coriander leaves, lettuce, and mint leaves; *yam nang mu,* pork skin salad; *yam neua,* a combination of grilled strips of beef with fresh coriander, mint, basil, spring onion, garlic, shallots, lime juice, fish sauce, chilies, and sugar; and *yam pla muk,* squid salad sautéed with onions, chilies, lemongrass, and mint leaves. *Yam pla muk* has great acid balance and is generally served with lettuce to help cut the biting heat.

More good salads to try are *yam tang kwa,* cucumber salad; *yam het,* mushroom salad; *yam mamuang,* green mango salad; and *yam wun sen,* cellophane noodle salad.

DRINKS

Water

Thais don't drink water directly from the tap; most purchase purified water *(nam deum khuat)* bottled in plastic containers.

Many cafes and restaurants serve free glasses along with unsealed bottles of boiled water *(nam tom)*, drinking water *(nam deum)*, or plain water *(nam plao)*. All are safe to drink even if served at room temperature or having a pale straw color. Most are tinted with a weak infusion of tea leaves to signify the water has been boiled. Drinking water provided in cafes and restaurants will not make you sick, and it's more economical than bottled water, which generally costs 5-15B.

Larger cafes and restaurants keep their containers of boiled water, soft drinks, and fruit juices refrigerated, but smaller cafes add ice *(nam khaeng)* to glasses and takeaway containers, i.e., plastic bags. All ice in Thailand is produced in government-licensed factories inspected to guarantee hygienic and potable ice. However, problems sometimes arise in transportation, so ice served in remote locations is best avoided.

Fruit Juices
Fresh-squeezed fruit juices such as *nam som* (orange juice) and *nam manao* (lemon juice)

SIDEWALK SNACKS AND DESSERTS

*M*any of the most popular foods in Thailand fall into a category called *kap klaem* (drinking foods), intended for consumption when people gather for a glass of Mekong whiskey or a few rounds of Singha beer. Similar to *tapas* in Spain or *pupus* in Hawaii, these snacks are actually miniature meals in themselves that often provide some of the most convenient and tasty dining in the country.

These snacks and other sweets can be purchased from *mae khar harb rey*, a traveling woman who sells her goods from baskets levered on strong sticks *(mai khan)* balanced between her shoulders. She typically wears the *ngorb*, a broad-brimmed hat made from palm leaves, and a sarong of colorful cotton. Inside her two swinging baskets rest a wondrous collection of tiny pots, crockery, and cutlery used to serve her assortment of condiments and snacks. The following treats are offered by *mae khar harb rey*, as well as sidewalk vendors and small cafes:

kai sam yang: a plate of fried chicken with peanuts, chopped ginger, and fiery peppers; often consumed with beer and various forms of *yam*

satay: barbecued skewers of meat served with peanut sauce and cucumbers in vinegar and sugar

sang kaya: custard made from coconut milk, sugar, and eggs

chow kway: black-grass pudding shredded and mixed with a sugar syrup over ice

boh bok: green-grass drink made from crushed vines and sugar water. Bitter.

roti sai mai: small flat pancakes with strands of green or pink spun sugar wrapped inside

kanom buang: batter poured on a hot griddle, then folded over and filled with shredded coconut, egg yolk, and green onions

tong krob: golden yellow balls made from egg yolks and rice flour, then dusted with sugar

kao glab pat maw: thin crepe filled with fried shrimp, pork, peanuts, sugar, coconut, and even fish sauce. Delicious.

thua thawt: fried peanuts

What would you like to try today?

are often served with a little salt or sugar. If you prefer straight juice, no salt, add the words *mai sai kleua* (without salt).

Fruit juices blended or squeezed may be called either *nam khan* (squeezed juice) or *nam pon* (mixed juice) as in *nam malakan pon* (papaya shake or smoothie).

The most widespread fruit juice is sugarcane juice *(nam awy)*. It's served year-round no matter what particular fruit may be in season.

Coffee

Thais consider Nescafé and other instant coffees superior to freshly ground coffee, perhaps because of the foreign association or the convenience factor. But decent coffee beans are grown in the north and south and brewed by filtration in many local cafes.

Thais use condensed milk in coffee rather than the plain milk used in the West. Although overly sweet to some Western palates, this authentic coffee can be ordered in morning markets by asking for *kafae thung* (big coffee). To enjoy a steaming cup of black coffee, ask for *kafae dam* (black coffee) followed by *mai sai nam tan* (without sugar).

Another caffeinated treat is iced coffee *(kafae yen)* made from freshly brewed black coffee laced with condensed milk.

Beer

The perfect complement to a Thai dinner is an ice-cold bottle of locally produced beer. Thai beer is strong and tasty, brewed according to German recipes. Beer is the fastest growing beverage in Thailand according to government statistics, which show consumption soaring from 98 million liters in 1987 to almost 400 million liters in recent years.

Thai beer is excellent, though not exactly an inexpensive drink. High excise taxes imposed by the government make beer one of the few consumer products almost as costly as it is in the West. Excise taxes run 30B per large bottle of beer, or 50% of the total price for most alcoholic beverages in the country. A large beer (630 ml) costs 50-60B in Bangkok—about half the minimum wage of a local worker.

Singha Beer: The oldest and most popular beer in Thailand is the Singha brand produced by Boon Rawd Brewery. Boon Rawd was founded in August 1933 by nobleman Phya Bhirom Bhakdi after he realized that the arrival of bridges would quickly ruin his ferryboat transportation business. Bhakdi went to Germany, learned the skills necessary to brew European-style beer, and returned to uncork his first bottle of Singha in 1934. Today, Boon Rawd Brewery is one of the kingdom's most successful companies boasting extensive holdings in farms, bottled water, manufacturing plants, brewpubs, restaurants, and a golf course.

The current success is credited to Bhakdi's son, Prachuab, who served his brewmaster apprenticeship in Munich and took over the helm of Boon Rawd upon the death of his father in the 1950s. The present-day brewery, near the Chao Praya River in Bangkok, uses barley grown on farms near Chiang Mai and imported German hops which cannot survive in the heat of Thailand. Singha beer has an alcohol content of 6.0 percent, a heady punch much appreciated by the average Thai beer drinker, while the lighter Singha Gold weighs in at a reasonable 4.6 percent.

Carlsberg: Singha holds almost 65% of the domestic beer market. Second place goes to Carlsberg, jointly owned by Thai and Danish interests and heavily backed by the makers of Mekong whiskey and an energy drink called Krating Daeng. Since its launch in 1993, Carlsberg has seized almost 20% of the domestic beer market by using the distribution system established by the makers of Mekong, and by raising the alcohol content to match that of Singha. Carlsberg, a sweeter beer than the more bitter Singha and Kloster brews, is priced midway between Singha and Kloster.

Kloster and Amarit: Thai Amarit Brewery, in third place with only seven percent of the market share, produces Kloster (the name is leased from a German company) and Amarit NB. Kloster is an upscale beer generally enjoyed by expatriates and wealthy Thais who like the bitter kick and exclusive image.

Heineken: Thai beer drinkers were given another choice in 1995 with the second arrival of Heineken into the Thai market. Heineken's first attempt to penetrate the market in 1990-91 was abandoned due to poor distribution, but the current partnership includes the national distributor of Coca-Cola. For the first time since Boon Rawd opened in 1933, Singha has some real competition in the national beer market.

Whiskey

Approach with extreme caution the whiskeys of Thailand; the 70-proof molasses-based spirits pack an abnormal, almost psychotropic wallop—the tequila of Thailand.

Whiskey has long been one of the country's leading moneymakers, contributing more than five percent of the national budget through excise taxes and license fees. The leading brand is **Mekong,** manufactured by the Suramaharas group, which has thrived under a 15-year production contract tied to generous concessions to the government. Suramaharas also produces the less-expensive **Kwangthong** brand. Whiskeys made by the Suramaharas group are sold in liters *(klom)* for about 120B, half-liters *(baen),* and quarter liters *(kok).*

Spirited competition is provided by the Surathip Group and their line of 12 **Hong** (swan) brands. Labels carry variations on the word Hong—Hong Thong, Hong Ngoen, Hong Yok, Hong Tho. Hong whiskeys are somewhat cheaper than Suramaharas brands and generally found in rural rather than urban areas.

The two liquor consortiums waged a bloody war of price cuts and foolish discounting until they were forced into an uneasy merger in the late 1980s. The merger helped recharge government revenues by allowing the quasi-independent companies to raise prices, equalize distribution, and escape many of the onerous production quotas imposed by the government.

Premium whiskeys designed to compete with prestigious imports such as Johnnie Walker, Seagrams, and Chivas Regal are being introduced into Thailand. New arrivals packaged in fancy boxes complete with labels in English include VO Royal Thai whiskey and Golden Cat VO from United Winery Company. The chief problems are government taxes that have been jacked up to unrealistic and perhaps unsustainable levels.

The result of sharply rising taxes has been increased popularity of budget liquors. One beneficiary has been Pramuanphon Distillery (United Winery Company) in Nakhon Pathom and its line of budget whiskeys called Maew Thong (Gold Cat), Sing Chao Praya (Chao Praya Lion), and Singharat (The Lion King).

Other Liquors

Imbibers who can't handle the powerful kick of Mekong or the overwhelming aromas of moonshine might try Sang Thip, a distilled rum made from sugarcane. It's slightly more expensive but much more palatable than moonshine or regional whiskeys.

Perhaps the biggest effect of skyrocketing liquor taxes has been the illegal distillation of moonshine whiskey and various types of white liquors. White liquor, or *lao khao,* is generally made from sticky rice and carries an odor that rises above even the heaviest of dilutions.

Lao khao and other homemade brews can easily undercut the price of legal whiskeys, giving rise to the following joke. What are the only two households in each village that don't produce moonshine? Answer: the government excise office and the Buddhist *wat.* Some even have doubts about the *wat.*

DINING TIPS
AND ETIQUETTE

Ordering a Meal

Ordering a meal outside a tourist area can often be challenging since few restaurants offer English menus or employ waiters who speak English. One solution is to point to a dish being served to other patrons; another is to memorize the names of a few Thai dishes served throughout the country. In many smaller cafes and restaurants, customers often wander into the kitchen and point to the pots of food that look promising.

You could also surrender yourself to the waiter and say, *"Mee arai phe set?"* "What's special?" Many upcountry restaurants feature regional specialties—only found by trusting the proprietor.

The typical Thai meal includes dishes that complement each other and provide a range of flavors. Such a selection may include a spicy curry entree with meat or chicken, a stir-fried rice dish, a salad of vegetables flavored with lime and chili, a hot-and-sour soup of the *yam* type, noodles, and a variety of pepper sauces and pastes that show the genius of Thai cooking in its purest form.

The assemblage of dishes is placed on the table and each customer is presented with a plate of rice as the centerpiece. Dishes are eaten in no particular order.

Dining Etiquette

Thais still respect the visitor who uses proper etiquette and understands the correct use of utensils and dining procedures.

Do not allow food to spill on the table, and avoid loud and flamboyant behavior when dining with well-bred Thais. Customs dictate that a spoonful of plain rice be consumed first to acknowledge the importance of rice as the central ingredient of Thai cuisine. Also, to indicate restraint, only one or two spoonfuls of food should be taken from the common platter when dining with guests.

At formal meals, it is considered polite to allow the host to first serve himself or offer the opportunity to a guest. Do not dive into a meal without first acknowledging the generosity and rights of the host.

Utensils

Westerners befuddled by chopsticks will happily note that Thais eat all meals with forks and spoons except for a limited number of Chinese noodle dishes which are handled by chopsticks. The main instrument is a large spoon *(chawn)* held by the right hand, which is filled by a fork *(sawm)* held in the left hand. Food should be pushed in a direction away from the body onto the spoon, then lifted into the mouth.

Thais consider it bizarre to eat any type of food with a fork and believe, like the Chinese, that knives *(mid)* belong in the kitchen, not in the dining room.

When finished with the meal, place utensils face down together on the plate or in a 4:20 clockface position to signal that you're finished. Any other configuration indicates additional food will be consumed and that the waiter should not clear the plates.

Condiments

Tables are generally set with a variety of condiments.

A fermented fish sauce made from anchovies or shrimp paste, **nam pla** is rich in B vitamins and protein and is a substitute for salt and pepper in most Thai recipes. Made from salted and fermented fish or shrimp, the translucent brown liquid comes in small bottles or in Chinese sauce dishes filled with chopped chilies *(nam pla prik)* and a squeeze of lime. When combined with additional ingredients, *nam pla* becomes *nam prik.* Fish sauce is to Thai cuisine what soy sauce is to Japanese and Chinese dishes.

Nam som is a vinegar-green chili extract mixed with orange juice to make "sour water." A hot and pungent pepper sauce, **nam prik,** is made from fresh chilies, salt, sugar, vinegar, and any number of optional ingredients. **Thua** can consist of dried beans, peas, or peanuts.

Tipping

Traditional Thai customs do not include tipping, but a smile signals appreciation of the restaurant staff. Good service *(borikan dee)* is considered a given ingredient, though a small tip of 10-20B is appreciated by the underpaid staff. Larger hotels and restaurants that cater to tourists often include a 10-15% tip on the final bill.

SHOPPING

The Tourist Authority of Thailand strongly suggests that all visitors to Thailand shop with great care. Far too many tourists are overcharged and sold fraudulent merchandise with worthless guarantees.

Bargaining

Bargaining is absolutely necessary except in the large department stores. It's challenging and fun—*if* you keep your sense of humor. Haggle with a smile; let the shopkeeper laugh at your ridiculous offer while smiling back at his absurd asking price. Bargaining is a game, not a life-

or-death struggle. Expect a discount of 20-30%. As elsewhere in Asia, knowing a few numbers and key phrases will send prices plunging.

Refunds, Receipts, and Guarantees

As a general rule, goods once purchased cannot be exchanged or returned. Deposits are also nonrefundable. Carefully examine all merchandise since receipts and guarantees issued by local retailers are of dubious value after you have returned home.

Touts and Fakes

Touts are paid commissions for rounding up customers. All expenses, including taxi rides and lunches, are added to your bill. Avoid them.

Thailand enjoys a reputation as the Counterfeit Capital of Asia. Most fakes, such as ersatz Lacoste shirts and Cartier watches, are advertised and sold as fakes. More dangerous to your pocketbook is colored glass being peddled as rubies, and newly manufactured Buddhas sold as genuine antiques. Experts at Bangkok's National Museum estimate that 90% of the items sold at the city's antique stores are counterfeit! Unless you are an expert or are prepared to gamble large sums of money, a sound policy is to shun expensive jewelry and pricey antiques.

BEST BUYS

Silk

Thai silk is world famous for both its high quality and beautiful designs. Be cautious, however, of silk fabric being sold at extraordinarily good prices. Cheap silk is often just rayon or rough silk cleverly interwoven with synthetics. A yard of high-quality silk, hand-woven and dyed with modern, colorfast German dyes, should sell for about 500-800B per meter. Check for variations in the size of the silk thread, which gives Thai silk its distinctive uneven texture. Or burn a small piece: synthetics turn to ash but real silk forms little sweatlike beads and does not disintegrate.

Precious Stones

Thailand, once one of the world's primary sources of precious stones, has now almost completely exhausted its domestic supply. Last year Thailand was forced to import over 80% of the gemstones cut in the country, including a worthless milk-white rock called a geuda (corundum) which is found in great quantities in Sri Lanka. When heated to temperatures between 2,912 and 3,272°, this nondescript stone becomes a "sapphire." This scientific process helps explain the flood of inexpensive sapphires in Bangkok! Several years ago it was revealed that Miss Thailand wore a tiara of artificial stones, and letters in the *Bangkok Post* regularly complain about stones being sold at five times their fair value from *government-backed* lapidaries. Little help is offered by the TAT.

The jewelry racket is pushed by friendly, clean-cut students and *tuk tuk* drivers who take you anywhere for just 10B. All are crooks and should be avoided.

The bottom line: if you intend to make a sizable purchase of precious stones in Thailand, ask the jeweler to accompany you to a facility for an independent appraisal. The Tourist Police are completely helpless. The Asian Institute of Gemological Sciences on Silom Road can determine the nature of the stone, but will not offer a monetary valuation. Gem receipts should always be marked "Subject to identification and appraisal by a registered gemologist." Some shops will offer 50% refunds to unhappy customers, but require you to sign a declaration that removes them from all further legal prosecution. You could also pay with a credit card and cancel payments if you have been defrauded.

Antiques

As mentioned before, most Thai wooden antiques are actually clever fakes produced by "instant antique" factories where hundreds of wooden images are carved, treated with special chemicals, and aged under the sun. All antiques, regardless of type or age, can only be exported with written permission from the Antique Art Business Division (tel. 02-224-1370) of the Fine Arts Department in Bangkok. Obtain registration and permission by taking the piece to the Fine Arts Department on Na Prathat Road across from Sanam Luang, together with two six- by nine-cm photographs of the object. An export fee of 50-300B may be charged depending on the piece. This permit must be obtained at least five days in advance of departure. Store owners can often obtain this permit for a nominal fee. Confirm that the shop can handle this process; once the sale has been completed, some shops find little motivation to follow through with the procedure.

Fake antiques do not require export permits. However, since airport customs officials are not antique experts, they often confuse fakes with authentic antiques and block export as you try to get on the plane.

Buddha Images

Thai laws prohibit the export of *all* Buddha images and images of other deities dating from before the 18th century. The only exceptions to this rule are Buddhist amulets. The problem has apparently been misguided tourists who have converted their Buddha images into lamps and doorstops, a sacrilegious act that infuriates Thais. Buddha images can be exported for reasons of religious homage, educational purposes, and cultural exchange programs. Letters of certification issued by your organization must be submitted to the Fine Arts Department in Bangkok.

As a result of government pressure, most Buddhas sold in Bangkok (whether real or fake) are exclusively Burmese images, which are exempt from the law. Rather than worrying about exporting a Buddha, many shoppers opt for images of kneeling monks and female deities.

Hilltribe Handicrafts

Thai hilltribes are well known for their elaborate jewelry, colorful textiles, and esoteric items such as opium pipes and bamboo flutes. All are best purchased in Chiang Mai. Consider your purchases carefully; hilltribe souvenirs which seem exotic in Thailand quickly lose their charm back home. Practical items such as wearable clothing and high-quality handicrafts generally make more sense than a trunkload of cheap and junky oddities.

Other Goods

Bronzeware cutlery sets siliconized to prevent tarnishing are excellent buys in Thailand. Another popular gift is nielloware, a special type of silver inlaid with black enamel designs and crafted into lighters, ashtrays, and bracelets. Celadon pottery, a cottage industry centered in Chiang Mai, attempts to reproduce the sublime glazes of Sawankalok prototypes. Thai lacquerware, similar to Burmese models, is also produced in Chiang Mai.

HEALTH

Thailand is a healthy place and it's unlikely you will lose even a single day to sickness. The secret to healthy travel is adequate preparation, watching your health during your travels, and understanding how to find adequate medical attention in an emergency.

BEFORE YOU GO

U.S. Government Health Advice

Current health recommendations from the United States government can be checked by calling the **Centers for Disease Control** (CDC) in Atlanta, Georgia, at (404) 332-4559 for general information and a printout of fax services, and (404) 639-1610 for malaria tips. The annual CDC publication, *Health Information for International Travel,* is available from the U.S. Government Printing Office at (202) 783-3238.

A handy new service is the **CDC Fax Information Service,** which sends country-specific information to your fax machine in a few minutes. Call (404) 332-4565 and follow the voice prompts for instant advice on disease risk and prevention by region, diarrhea, disease outbreak bulletins, prescription drugs recommended for malaria, the biweekly *Blue Sheets,* and updates on AIDS.

Armed with this information, you'll feel reassured about the situation in Thailand and less willing to purchase unnecessary pills and shots from doctors burdened with yacht payments.

Vaccinations

Contact a doctor who specializes in travel medicine for a general health checkup, necessary shots, and perhaps the International Certificate of Vaccination, a small yellow booklet which records your immunizations. Occasionally immigration officials demand this card from visitors arriving from an area infected with yellow fever. The CDC does not recommended a yellow fever vaccination, unless you intend to travel to or from a country in Africa or South America.

Cholera and smallpox vaccination requirements for Thailand have been dropped, though the normal "childhood" vaccinations should be up to date: tetanus, diphtheria, typhoid, measles, mumps, rubella (MMR vaccine), pertussis (DTP vaccine), and polio. Obtain booster shots, if necessary, from your doctor.

A vaccination clinic operated by the Thai Red Cross Society (tel. 02-252-0161) is located in Bangkok at the corner of Rama IV and Henri Dunant Roads.

International Health Certificate

Under the International Health Regulations adopted by the World Health Organization (WHO), a country, under certain conditions, may require from travelers an International Certificate of Vaccination against yellow fever. However, the WHO has recently eliminated the special page for cholera vaccinations, and visitors no longer need an international certificate for entry into Thailand.

COMMON HEALTH PROBLEMS

Diarrhea

The United States Centers for Disease Control reports that the most frequent problem is common traveler's diarrhea, transmitted by bacteria and parasites found in contaminated food or water. Common sense will minimize the risks: eat only thoroughly cooked food, drink bottled water, wear shoes, resist swimming in fresh waters possibly contaminated with schistomiasis flatworms, and avoid contact with insects, particularly mosquitoes.

Two drugs recommended by the National Institutes of Health for mild diarrhea can be purchased over the counter: Pepto-Bismol Diarrhea Control and Imodium A-D. Both contain loperamide, an antidiarrheal not found in regular Pepto-Bismol.

An alternative to loperamide is three days of a single 500ml dosage of the antibiotic ciprofloxacin, approved by the Food and Drug Administration for traveler's diarrhea.

Hepatitis A

The two main varieties of hepatitis, hepatitis A and B, are highly contagious liver diseases marked by debilitating, long-term symptoms such as jaundice and a feeling of malaise.

Hepatitis A ("infectious hepatitis") is spread by contaminated water and food—conditions common in countries with poor standards of hygiene and sanitation. The disease is transmitted through fecal-oral contact and is often spread by infected food handlers who don't wash their hands. Hepatitis A is a widespread problem in Myanmar, India, Nepal, and Indochina, but is rarely contracted in Thailand by travelers who exercise caution with their drink and food. On the other hand, hepatitis A is serious. Statistics show

each infected adult in the United States spends US$2,600 in lost wages, US$700 in medical costs, and an additional US$2,800 for hospitalization. About 20% of those infected experience a relapse and an estimated three percent of adults over 49 years will die from hepatitis A.

Until a few years ago, hepatitis A was regarded as an incurable condition without any effective form of prevention or treatment. A dose of gamma globulin (immune serum globulin) is still the only known antibody which reduces the likelihood of contracting the disease. Gamma globulin's effect wears off after one month, declining to near zero after three months, while also possibly reducing the natural immune systems of the body. Antibiotics administered after infection were useless and other drugs only increased liver damage. The only treatment remained rest and liquids; travelers were told to "go home and rest."

Fortunately, in early 1995, the U.S. Food and Drug Administration approved a new vaccine called Havrix, the first vaccine proven effective in the prevention of hepatitis A. Developed by SmithKline Beecham, Havrix requires two injections one month apart with a booster after six months; it should be taken at least three weeks prior to departure. The newly approved drug is somewhat expensive—US$50-60 for each of the two injections—but recommended for its long-term immunity, estimated to be up to 10 or 15 years. Obtain more information from SmithKline Beecham, tel. (800) 437-2829.

Hepatitis B

Hepatitis B, formerly called serum hepatitis, also affects the liver but is passed through sexual conduct and the exchange of body fluids such as blood or semen.

Hepatitis B is a more serious disease and is of particular risk to homosexuals, intravenous drug users, and health workers who handle body fluids. The disease can cause irreparable liver damage or even liver cancer.

Hepatitis B can be prevented by a course of three shots of vaccine (Hepvac B) over a five-month period, with a booster shot every four or five years.

Malaria

After a general checkup, discuss malaria with your doctor.

The nine-page CDC regional profile on Southeast Asia recently stated that the risk of malaria in Thailand throughout the year is low in all parts of the country, except for limited border areas with Cambodia, Myanmar, and Laos. Another danger spot is the newly developed island resort of Ko Chang near the Cambodian border. Visitors who stick to the standard routes have little risk of exposure and should perhaps avoid powerful anti-malarial drugs.

Travelers who plan to get well off the beaten track—explore remote jungles during the rainy season, camp around equatorial lakes—should take malaria pills, remain well covered, wear dark clothing, use mosquito nets, purchase insect repellents which contain DEET (diethylmetatoluamide), and faithfully follow the recommended regimen of anti-malarial pills.

Malaria Pills

Prescription drugs recommended by the CDC to treat malaria include chloroquine, mefloquine, doxcycline, proguanil, and primaquine. These drugs resist various strains of malaria with different side effects. About 50% of malaria cases in Thailand are due to *plasmodium falciparum,* a parasite which gives flulike malaise and high fever with shakes, and which if not treated can lead to organ disease, anemia, and even death.

As a general rule, visitors who've been in risk areas should consider any fever as a sign of malaria and seek early diagnosis and treatment for an uncomplicated and complete cure. Malaria clinics are located throughout Thailand; free anti-malarials are provided to those found bloodsmear positive. Medical care in Thailand is excellent.

The CDC currently recommends the use of **doxcycline** for travelers intending to spend significant time around the borders of Cambodia and Myanmar. Doxycycline is a more effective drug than mefloquine described below, due to mefloquine-resistant malarial mosquitoes found in the border districts.

Common trade names for doxycycline include Vibramycine, Banndoclin, Doxin, Dumoxin, Interdoxin, and Siclidon. The chief disadvantage to doxycycline is that it must be taken every day at an adult dose of 100 milligrams, beginning the day before entering the malarious area and four weeks after departure. One possible side effect is skin photosensitivity that may result in a sunburn.

Travelers should also ask their doctor about the suitability of **mefloquine,** marketed in the U.S. under the trade name Lariam. The adult dosage is 250 milligrams once a week. Mefloquine has been proven effective against the chloroquine- and Fansidar-resistant strain *P. falciparum,* but is no longer recommended as a malaria prophylaxis due to mefloquine-resistant parasites found in the border areas. Mefloquine in low doses also carries side effects such as gastrointestinal disturbances and dizziness.

Chloroquine is a possible choice for travelers who cannot take mefloquine or doxycycline. The adult dosage is 500 milligrams once a week, starting one week before entering a malarious area, then weekly for four weeks after leaving the area. Chloroquine is marketed in the U.S. under the brand name Aralen and elsewhere as Resochin, Avoclor, Nivaguine, and Kalguin.

Because many mosquitoes in the area have developed an immunity, chloroquine is no longer recommended for visitors to Southeast Asia. It is still effective in the Caribbean, South America, and parts of the Middle East.

The CDC recommends that travelers taking chloroquine should simultaneously take **proguanil.** It's not available in the United States but can be purchased overseas under the brand name Paludrine. The dosage is 200 milligrams daily in combination with a weekly dose of chloroquine.

Fansidar, the trade name for sulfadoxine and pyrimethamine, is a powerful and potentially dangerous drug taken only as temporary self treatment. Fansidar is also sold as Maloprim, the trade name on dapsone and pyrimethamin. The CDC advises that Fansidar should be taken to treat a fever only if professional medical assistance is not available within 24 hours.

Health Concerns for Women Travelers

Female visitors to Thailand should be aware that the extreme heat often brings on yeast infections. Yeast infection medicine can be difficult to locate, so bring along an ample supply for your trip.

Tampons are available in most larger towns but scarce if you intend to get off the beaten track for any amount of time. Feminine products are easily found in larger urban centers such as

Bangkok, but your preferred brand may be hard to find. If this is a concern for you, bring an adequate supply of your own.

AIDS ALERT

Thailand's sex industry has taken an ominous turn since authorities first detected AIDS in 1984. According to a report issued in 1998 by the head of the European Union's AIDS program in Bangkok, more than one million Thais are HIV-positive, a figure slightly higher than the Health Ministry estimate of 800,000. The same study also showed that more than 222,000 Thais had died of the disease since 1985, compared to the 24,667 deaths reported by the Public Health Ministry. An additional 270,000 Thais have full-blown AIDS but have not yet died of the disease—three times more than the official estimate. The World Health Organization estimates that, by the year 2005, over two million Thais could contract the AIDS virus and up to 500,000 may die from it.

In 1999 the *Far Eastern Economic Review* published an article estimating that AIDs now infects 2.6% of the Thai population, or three to five times the per capita infection rate in the Philippines, India, and Indonesia. Recent international conferences have pointed out the epicenters of the epidemic in Asia are still Thailand and India, which has the highest HIV-infection rate of any country in the world.

In Thailand, AIDS is most commonly spread through heterosexual intercourse rather than anal sex or shared needles. Mechai Viravaidya, former head of the government's anti-AIDS program, estimates that up to 50% of the prostitutes in Thailand carry the virus and up to 10% of the male population is infected. The epidemic is most advanced in the provinces of northwestern Thailand, where government surveys estimate over 75% of the prostitutes carry the AIDS virus and up to 20% of young men aged 20-24 are HIV-positive.

The eeriest quality of the raging epidemic is its invisibility. Most people infected with AIDS or who are HIV-positive do not develop symptoms until years after infection and continue to engage in unprotected sex, unwittingly infecting their partners. A disturbing twist has been the discovery of a new and unusual strain of the AIDS virus that occurs almost exclusively in heterosexuals in northern Thailand and resembles the strains believed to have originated in central Africa. Some theorize this mutation may explain the rapid spread of AIDS within the Thai heterosexual community.

Initially, the Thai government played down the problem, fearing negative publicity would kill the tourist industry and cut into the nation's largest source of foreign capital. The government claim that the AIDS virus was solely a Western disease soon gave way to a scheme to officially certify prostitutes as clean and ready for work. Another measure restricted HIV-positive people to prescribed activities and movements and threatened detention for those who refused to comply with the orders.

The reality of AIDS finally began to enter the national consciousness in the early 1990s. The man responsible for the new thinking was Mechai Viravaidya, who initiated mandatory radio and TV broadcasts of commercials warning against the dangers of AIDS and popularized the use of condoms so much he was dubbed "The Condom King." Mechai even opened a restaurant—Cabbages and Condoms—near his headquarters in Bangkok. Here he stocks condom key chains and other unique souvenirs. Infection rates fell so dramatically that in 1994 Mechai was awarded the prestigious Magsaysay Award for his remarkable campaign.

Mechai forced the government to accept that the human and economic costs of AIDS far outweighed whatever negative publicity could be incurred by a public campaign against the disease. Mechai's education program—free condoms, school seminars, prostitute outreach programs—so sharply reduced the infection rate that cases now double every two years rather than twice a year as in the late 1980s. The so-called projected vulnerability for AIDS is now estimated to be higher in India, Pakistan, and the Philippines than in Thailand.

The problem with success is that statistics can be used to downplay the situation and provide comforting reassurances to potential visitors. Some tourism officials or others with vested interests dislike public discussion of the problem and somehow wish to turn the clock back to the carefree early 1980s. And statistics can be twisted to prove almost any position on the epidemic.

The fact is Thailand still has a serious problem with AIDS, and the epidemic must remain a cause for concern and ongoing action. AIDS is a worldwide phenomenon; discussions about the problem should not be interpreted as a negative reflection on the country or the character of the people. Sexually active Westerners and Thais alike would do well to practice the only form of safe sex: complete abstinence.

HEALTH FACILITIES

Medical Care

All of the following hospitals have English-speaking doctors; many are foreign trained and familiar with Western medicine. All provide 24-hour emergency service, ambulances, and a full range of medical and surgical work.

Treatment prices vary depending on the hospital and the patient's needs, but standard private rooms with meals average 1,500-3,500B per day, extra for VIP rooms. Rooms are modern, clean, and luxuriously furnished with color TV, stocked fridge, bathroom with amenities, sofa, coffee table, and balcony.

A deposit of 20,000B is generally required on arrival and all major credit cards are accepted. For longer stays, health insurance can be obtained from Blue Cross (tel. 02-235-5832) and South East Insurance (tel. 02-233-7080).

Recommended hospitals include:

Bangkok Christian Hospital, 124 Silom Rd., tel. (02) 233-6981

Bangkok General Hospital, Soi Soonvijai (Soi 47), New Petchburi Rd., tel. (02) 318-0066, fax (02) 318-1546

Bangkok Adventist Mission Hospital, 430 Phitsanulok Rd., tel. (02) 281-1422

Bumrungrad Hospital, 33 Soi 3, Sukumvit Rd., tel. (02) 253-0250

Phayathai Hospital, 364/1 Sri Ayudhaya Rd., tel. (02) 245-2620

Samitivej Hospital, 133 Soi 49, Sukumvit Rd., tel. (02) 392-0011.

Dental Care

Hospitals with dental facilities include Bangkok Adventist Mission, Bangkok General, Bumrungrad, and Samitivej. The following clinics have English-speaking dentists. Call for an appointment.

Dental Polyclinic, 211/3 New Petchburi Rd., tel. (02) 314-5070

Dental Hospital, 88 Soi 49, Sukumvit Rd., tel. (02) 260-5000

Orthodontic Centre, 542/1 Ploenchit Rd., tel. (02) 251-7613

Ploenchit Clinic, Maneeya Bldg., Ploenchit Rd., tel. (02) 251-1567

Siam Dental Clinic, 412/11 Soi 6, Siam Square, tel. (02) 251-6315.

SAFETY

THEFT AND FRAUD

Losing your passport, air ticket, traveler's checks, or cash to a thief can be a devastating experience, but with a certain amount of caution you shouldn't have any problem. Theft in Thailand happens usually by stealth rather than force; armed robbery is rare except in isolated situations. I've traveled for almost 20 years around Southeast Asia and have yet to lose anything of great value.

First, minimize your risk by bringing as few valuables as possible. Leave the expensive jewelry, gold necklaces, flashy camera bags, and other ostentatious signs of wealth at home.

Keep your gear in full sight whenever possible while riding trains or buses and be cautious about pickpockets in crowds, on buses, during festivals, and at boat harbors. A common problem in Bangkok is razor-blade artists on public buses; carry your bag directly in front of you and be extra alert whenever somebody presses against you.

To speed up the replacement of valuable documents, keep duplicate copies of all valuable papers separate from the papers themselves. Immediately report any theft to the local police and obtain a written report including traveler's check serial numbers. This helps you collect on insurance claims after you return home.

Finally, try to maintain a balance between

paranoia and trust. Most Thais are extraordinarily honest, so don't worry about everybody who wants to show you around or practice English.

Hotel Security

Check the security of your hotel room and ask for a room with a private lock and lockable windows. Valuables should generally be checked in the hotel safe and an accurate receipt obtained from the front desk. This may not always be necessary in better hotels with good security, but be cautious about fellow travelers in dormitories and other shared living situations.

Tourist Assistance Center

Complaints about theft, fraud, and unfair business practices can be directed to the tourist police subdivision of the Tourism Authority of Thailand. They are powerless to help if you have only been overcharged, but sometimes are effective when you have purchased fragments of colored glass that you thought were precious gems. You can also contact the Tourist Police for additional help on more serious crimes. Tourist Assistance Center, 372 Bamrung Muang Rd., tel. (02) 282-8129.

Tourist Police

Serious crimes beyond the scope of the TAC are handled by this division of the National Police Department. First take your problems to the TAC office on Bamrung Muang Road and if you are unsatisfied with their results, move up the ladder to National Police Department. You can contact them at their head office or seek out any of the 500 police officers who station themselves at police kiosks in popular tourist venues. 29/1 Soi Lang Suan, Poenchit Rd., tel. (02) 255-2964.

ILLEGAL DRUGS

Knockout Drugs

Many Western visitors are robbed each year by professional con artists who often spend hours, even days, gaining your confidence before administering a powerful sleeping drug. *Never* accept food or drink from a stranger, and be wary of strangers who offer tours of the city or private boat cruises in Bangkok.

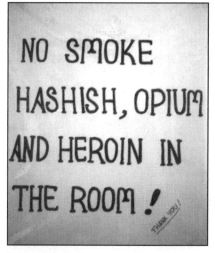

Drug Penalties

Thailand is a country with all sorts of illegal drugs, from marijuana and downers to opium and heroin. The current favorite is speed, which has overtaken the old standbys of opium and heroin.

However, unless you care to spend the next 20 years of your life in prison, don't mess with drugs in Thailand. Local law enforcement officials make little distinction between marijuana and heroin, and penalties are harsh. Several hundred foreigners have been incarcerated in Bangkok and Chiang Mai prisons on drug charges—not pleasant places to spend a large portion of your life. Even the smallest quantities bring mandatory sentences; life imprisonment is common for sizable seizures.

Cautious travelers completely free of drugs sometimes find themselves in serious trouble with the authorities. Raids conducted by uniformed police at popular travelers' hotels in Bangkok and Chiang Mai often involve drugs planted by overzealous officers. Taxi and *tuk tuk* drivers sell drugs to travelers and turn them in for the reward and return of the drug. Arrested, booked, and fingerprinted, the frightened Westerner spends a night in jail before posting a sizable bail and passport as collateral. A few embassies will bail their nationals out of jail and get them on the first plane back home; others leave them to the mercy of the Thai legal system.

The obvious message with illegal narcotics in Thailand is *don't*.

WOMEN TRAVELERS

Should women travel alone in Thailand? During my 15 years of traveling around the country, I've talked to countless solo women travelers and most tell me Thailand is one of the safer and more comfortable places for women traveling alone. One reason for this is that Buddhism places great emphasis on respect for females and encourages harmonious relationships between the sexes. Thais are generally shy people who have a deep fear of shame; this discourages much of the sexual harassment common in more religiously fundamentalist countries. Finally, Thailand's crime rate is much lower than that of any Western nation.

However, Thai society has long considered females inferior to men. Thai women are controlled by legal, cultural, and social restrictions. For this reason, many Thai females of the younger generation may be deeply interested in your views on equality and women's rights. It also means that some Thai males will view you as a docile member of a disenfranchised sex. Another viewpoint held by many Thai males is that Western women are morally loose individuals who seek constant sexual satisfaction, an idea created by many pornographic American movies and influential pop idols.

Though Thai males seldom hassle Western females or grope women in public, solo females may experience intimidation and improper behavior by Thai males. The best approach to minimize sexual harassment is to use common sense and follow cultural norms. Attending to your manner of dress is perhaps the first step in preventing unwanted male attention. Dress as conservatively as the location demands; don't show skin except on tourist beaches and Westernized resorts, and remember that modest dress is extremely important in the deep south, where scantily dressed females will find themselves in serious trouble with Muslim authorities.

Women can further minimize sexual harassment by traveling with a Western male; avoiding direct eye contact with Thai men, which is considered an invitation for sex; keeping off lonely streets in the evenings; remaining cool, not flirtatious, with hotel employees and others in the tourism industry; and using humor as a tool to diffuse potentially dangerous situations. Finally, when harassed, groped in public, or verbally abused, yell loudly at the offender. This alerts bystanders and publicly embarrasses the male, who will most likely flee the scene. Don't feel apologetic or worry about being rude—it's your vacation and offensive males should not be allowed to ruin it.

RESOURCES

U.S. Government Travel Warnings

Hear recorded travel warnings 24 hours a day by calling the Citizens Emergency Center of the U.S. State Department at (202) 647-5225. To speak with a human operator, call the Bureau of Consular Affairs at (202) 647-1488 during business hours, 0900-1700 EST. Desk officers (tel. 202-647-2000) may offer additional tips.

However, the most reliable and comprehensive advice is obtained by calling the American embassy in the specific country and asking for the consular section. To obtain these telephone numbers, call the Bureau of Public Affairs at (202) 647-6575 or check the State Department's *Key Officers of Foreign Service Posts* updated three times a year. The booklet costs US$1.75 and is available from Government Printing Office bookstores or by calling the order department at (202) 783-3238.

VISAS AND OFFICIALDOM

PASSPORTS

American Passports

Essential travel documents include a valid passport and the necessary visa. Passports should be valid for at least six months from the day of entry, though visitors intending to stay longer should ensure their passports are valid for at least one year.

American passports are issued by U.S. Passport Agency offices in 13 cities:

• Boston	(617) 565-6990
• Chicago	(312) 353-7155
• Dallas	(214) 653-7691
• Honolulu	(808) 522-8283
• Los Angeles	(310) 235-7070
• Miami	(305) 536-4681
• New Orleans	(504) 589-6161
• New York	(212) 399-5290
• Philadelphia	(215) 597-7480
• San Francisco	(415) 744-4010
• Seattle	(206) 220-7777
• Washington	(202) 647-0518

Passports are also available from some post offices and court houses. Passports are valid for 10 years and cost US$65, renewals US$50. Allow at least five weeks for processing, especially during the busy spring and summer months.

Call the U.S. Passport Information office at (202) 647-0518 for their 24-hour recording about fees, documentation, and other requirements. You can request the brochures, *Passports: Applying For Them the Easy Way* and *Foreign Entry Requirements,* from the Consumer Information Center in Pueblo, CO 81009.

Canadian Passports

Canadians can apply for passports at 28 regional offices as well as post offices and travel agencies. Passports are valid for five years; processing usually takes about three weeks. For information on fees, documentation, and other requirements in English and French, call their 24-hour recording at (819) 994-3500 or (800) 567-6868.

Safeguard Your Documents

Losing your passport and other important documents can be a nightmare. Passports can be replaced at overseas embassies and consulates with proof of citizenship, but replacement takes from two days to two weeks depending on circumstances and your nationality. In an emergency, request an immediate temporary traveling permit that allows quick return to your country.

The following precautions will reduce hassles and speed up replacement of important documents. Before you depart, photocopy your passport, airline tickets, identification cards, insurance policies, and credit cards. Leave this information with someone you trust and can contact quickly in an emergency.

While on the road, carry another set of photocopies separate from the original documents to speed replacement after loss. Remember to stash some money in a secret compartment to avoid poverty in the event of a robbery.

VISAS AND ENTRY PERMITS

Visas are stamps placed in your passport by foreign governments that permit you to visit that country for a limited time and for a specified purpose, such as tourism or business.

The visa situation in Thailand changed dramatically in July 1996 after the Ministry of the Interior approved new immigration regulations that created a free-entry permit good for 30 days. The package also included other visa regulations that offer new benefits for long-term visitors.

Most nations maintain diplomatic relations with Thailand and have embassies in Bangkok. Embassies are generally open Mon.-Fri., but accept visa applications only 0900-1200. Some issue visas within two hours, while others require your passport be left overnight. Embassies are spread out all over town and can be *extremely* time-consuming to reach with public transportation. If you need a visa, it's often easier to let a travel agency obtain it for a nominal fee. Addresses, phone numbers, and operating hours of diplomatic missions are listed in most tourist magazines and booklets.

Several different types of visas are available, such as tourist, transit, and nonimmigrant. With these visas, you're note allowed to work in Thailand.

30-Day Entry Permit

Nationals from 56 favored nations, who intend to stay 30 days or less and have sufficient funds and proof of onward passage, may now enter the country without a visa. Immigration officers at the airport in Bangkok will automatically give the permit on arrival. Permits are also given to those who arrive by bus or train from Malaysia and visitors who arrive by cruise ship. This system is essentially an extension of the former 15-day free-entry permit system, which brought complaints from tour operators and hotel chains selling longer excursions.

Citizens from several lucky countries, such as South Korea and Sweden, can stay up to 90 days without a visa in accordance with bilateral agreements between governments. Nationals of another 76 countries, most of which have no existing Thai consulate or embassy, are given 15-day tourist visas on arrival.

Extensions: The 30-day entry permit can be extended for up to 10 additional days, at the discretion of immigration, for 500B. While this may prove useful, travelers who intend to stay longer than 30 days should obtain a 60-day tourist visa, in advance, from a Thai diplomatic mission.

Overstay Fines: Visitors on a 30-day entry permit are generally fined 100B for each day they overstay the limit, up to a maximum of 20,000B. The fines are collected by immigration officers, who conducted a roaring trade from their small glass office at the airport.

Re-Entry Permits

Visitors intending to exit, then re-enter Thailand—and who want to avoid time-consuming delays at overseas Thai immigration offices—can obtain a re-entry permit from any Thai embassy or consulate. This is a sensible option for travelers heading to Myanmar and who wish to return without trekking over to the Thai embassy in Yangon.

Re-entry permits cost 500B at the Thai Immigration Department on Soi Suan Plu (tel. 02-286-4231) in Bangkok, just off Sathorn Thai Road. It's open weekdays from 0830-1630 and Saturdays 0830-1200 with a skeleton staff during lunch hours.

CUSTOMS AND CURRENCY CONTROLS

Customs upon Arrival

Thailand prohibits the import of drugs, guns, pornography, and harpoons for underwater fishing.

Otherwise, customs officials allow you to bring in a reasonable amount of clothes, toiletries, photographic equipment and five rolls of film, business equipment such as laptops and power drills, a carton of cigarettes, and a liter of your favorite booze. These are duty free, but valuable merchandise should be declared to avoid problems on departure.

Customs officials sometimes question visitors carrying expensive gadgets which could be profitably resold in the country. Those bringing in a single stereo or digital assistant are usually allowed to pass, though a refundable deposit may be required from suspicious types. Expensive merchandise imported in large quantities (a dozen Rolexes, six Nikons) will be confiscated and held until your departure.

Exchange Controls

All visitors to Thailand are legally required to bring a minimum amount of currency as determined by their visa category. Visitors who arrive without a visa and receive the 30-day entry permit are required to bring at least US$250 in cash, traveler's checks, bank draft, or letter of credit. The same sum is required for visitors with a 60-day tourist visa. This formality is rarely enforced and immigration officers only check backpackers who arrive with one-way tickets and appear to be potential basketcases. As with all officialdom in Thailand, clean dress and a pleasant demeanor make the wheels of travel turn smoothly.

Thailand specifies no legal limit on the amount of Thai or foreign currency brought into or exported from the country, but amounts over US$10,000 or 50,000B must be declared with customs officials.

THAI DIPLOMATIC OFFICES

Australia: 111 Empire Circuit, Canberra, ACT 2600, tel. 273-1149
Exchange Bldg., 56 Pitt St., Sydney
464 Saint Kilda Rd., Melbourne

Canada: 85 Range Rd., #704, Ottawa, Ontario, K1N8J6, tel. (613) 237-0476
250 University Ave., 7th Fl. Toronto 110
1155 Dorchester Blvd., #1005, Montreal 102
700 W. George St., 26th Fl. Vancouver

China: 40 Guang Hua Lu, Beijing, tel. 521903 or 522282

Denmark: Norgesmindevej 1B, 2900 Hellerup, Copenhagen, tel. 01-62-50-10

France: 8 Rue Greuze, Paris 75116, tel. 4704-3222

Germany: Ubierstrasse 65, 53173 Bonn 2, tel. (0228) 355065

Hong Kong: 8 Cotton Tree Dr., 8th Fl. Central, tel. 521-6481

India: 56 Nyaya Marg, Chankyapuri, Delhi 110021, tel. 605679
18-B Mandeville Gardens, Calcutta 7000019, tel. 460836

Italy: Nomentana 132, 00162 Rome, tel. 832-0729

Japan: 14-6 Kami Osaki 3-Chome, Shinagawa-ku, Tokyo, tel. 441-1386

Laos: Thanon Phonkheng, Vientiane Poste 128,
tel. 2508, 2543

Malaysia: 206 Jalan Ampang, 504505 Kuala Lumpur, tel. 488222
1 Jalan Tunkoabdul Rahman, Penang, tel. 23352 4426
Jalan Pengkalan Chepa, Kota Baru, tel. 782545

Myanmar: 91 Pyi Rd., Yangon, tel. 82471, 76555

Netherlands: Buitenrustweg 1, 2517 KD, Den Hague, tel. (070) 345-2088

New Zealand: 2 Cook St., Karori, Wellington 5, tel. 735385

Philippines: 107 Rada St., Makati, Manila, tel. 815-4219

Singapore: 370 Orchard Rd., Singapore 0923, tel. 737-2158

Switzerland: Eigerstrasse 60, 3007 Bern, tel. (031) 462281

United Kingdom: 30 Queens Gate, London SW7 5JB, tel. (01) 589-2834

U.S.A.: 2300 Kalorma Rd. NW, Washington, D.C. 20008, tel. (202) 482-7200
801 N. Labrae Ave., Los Angeles, CA 90038, tel. (213) 937-1894
53 Park Place #505, New York, NY 10007, tel. (212) 732-8166

Vietnam: So Nha El, Kho Ngoai Giao Doan, Hanoi, tel. 56043

Customs upon Departure

Thailand has few restrictions on exported items except for images of Buddha and other religious deities. The purpose is to prevent Buddhas from ending up as lamp fixtures or garden decorations in some *farang's* home. The only exception is small Buddha images worn around the neck as amulets.

Buddha images may also be exported by worshipping Buddhists and those involved with cultural exchanges and academic pursuits. To legally export a Buddha or fragment of a religious deity, a license must be obtained from the Fine Arts Department of the Bangkok National Museum, the Chiang Mai National Museum, or the Songkhla National Museum. The application requires sending two postcard-sized photos of the frontal view of the Buddha image, and a photocopy of your passport to the Fine Arts Department. Allow five days to complete the application process.

Judging from the number of Thai Buddhas in art shops around the world, regulations against their exportation appear less than effective. Some claim Thai art dealers, in tandem with government officials, falsify documents for quick and easy export to foreign collectors around the world.

The same regulations regarding Buddhas also apply to anything considered an "antique" in Thailand. All antiques—whether of Ban Chiang vintage or produced last week in somebody's backyard—must be duly registered with the Fine Arts Department of the National Museum to obtain an export license. The problem is that customs officials at the Bangkok Airport are less than fully trained in recognizing antiques and often confiscate anything that appears of great value or great antiquity.

U.S. Government Customs

Residents of the United States, including each member of the family regardless of age, may bring home US$400 worth of foreign goods duty-free. Goods may be pooled among family members to maximize the legal exemption. A flat 10% duty applies to the next US$1,000 worth of goods; above US$1,400 the rate varies according to the merchandise. In addition, travelers may bring back duty-free one liter of alcohol, 100 non-Cuban cigars, 200 cigarettes, and antiques and works of art more than 100 years old.

Canadian Customs

Canadians may bring back C$300 worth of goods duty-free provided you have been out of the country more than seven days. Canadians should check on other rules regarding time limits and exemptions by contacting the Revenue Canada Customs, Excise and Taxation Department, 2265 St. Laurent Blvd. S, Ottawa, Ontario, K1G 4K3, tel. (613) 957-0275. Ask for the free brochure, *I Declare.*

OTHER USEFUL DOCUMENTS

International Student Identity Card (ISIC)

The green-and-white ISIC card brings very few airline or hotel discounts in Southeast Asia, but is very useful in Europe and the United States. The card, however, can be recommended for the insurance policies which cover up to US$3,000 in total medical expenses as well as US$100 per day in a hospital. The annual fee for the card is US$16.

Students 12-25 years of age can apply at any of the 43 offices of Council Travel Services (tel. 212-661-1450), STA Travel (tel. 800-777-0112), Let's Go Travel (tel. 800-553-8746), and the Canadian student travel agency, Travel CUTS (tel. 416-798-CUTS). The ISIC Association Head Office (tel. 45-33-93-9393) is P.O. Box 9045, 1000 Copenhagen, Denmark.

International Drivers License

An international drivers license is required to rent cars and motorcycles in Thailand. International car rental agencies such as Avis and Hertz follow the rules, but motorcycles can generally be rented without the license. International permits are available from any office of the Canadian or American Automobile Association (AAA).

International Youth Hostel Card

Though invaluable in Europe and expensive in Asian countries such as Japan, the IYHF card is of very limited use in Thailand, which only has a handful of hostels. Youth hostel offices throughout the world sell membership cards and their *International Youth Hostel Handbook* to Africa, America, Asia, and Australasia.

MONEY

Smart travelers bring a combination of cash, traveler's checks, credit cards, and a bank ATM (Automatic Teller Machine) card. Each has its own advantages and drawbacks depending on the circumstances.

Cash is useful in emergencies, so stash a few U.S. twenties in your pack, well removed from your main money supply. Traveler's checks remain the favorite form of money despite the growing popularity of bank cards. Credit and debit cards used for withdrawals from bank ATMs are slowly becoming a feasible alternative to traveler's checks, though a few kinks need to be worked out before traveler's checks can be completely discarded.

The secret to successful money management is to keep your money working in interest-bearing accounts, minimize fees for transfers of funds, demand commission-free traveler's checks, and bring along a credit or debit card.

THAI CURRENCY

Thailand's basic unit of currency is the *baht* (B) divided into 100 *stang*. Coins are issued in one, two, five, and ten *baht* denominations. The 25 and 50 *stang* coins are rarely seen due to their low value and general scarcity. Shopkeepers compensate by routinely rounding prices off to the nearest *baht* or giving sweets in lieu of *stang*.

Thai coinage is quite confusing. Coins of all values have been issued over the years in various shapes and sizes. For example, the five-*baht* coin, once a monstrous nickel-and-copper heavyweight, is down to the size of an American quarter. The one-*baht* coin has gone from the size of an American quarter to the size of an American dime. And 10-*baht* coins are smaller but more valuable than one-*baht* coins.

To further confuse matters, old coins stamped with Thai script continue to circulate

amid new coins stamped with both Thai and English script.

The results can be bizarre. A fistful of change might include two sizes of copper 25 and 50 *stang* coins, three sizes of silver one-*baht* coins (only the middle size works in public phones), three completely different five-*baht* coins (one has nine edges, one a copper rim, and the other is all silver), and a copper-and-silver 10-*baht* coin designed with a small brass center encircled by a silver ring.

Fortunately, paper currency bears Arabic numerals and is printed in different colors and different sizes. Denominations include 10B (brown), 20B (green), 50B (blue), 100B (red), 500B (purple), and 1,000B (beige). Currency should not be defaced, crumpled up, or otherwise mistreated in public since all notes feature images of the king and denigration of the royal family is among the greatest of all cultural taboos.

Exchange Rates

The Thai *baht* once was pegged to a basket of currencies heavily weighted toward the dollar. It remained extremely stable, vis-à-vis the dollar, until the currency crisis of 1997-98. The economic meltdown of Thailand and the remainder of Southeast Asia forced the Bank of Thailand to finally abandon its monetary defense of the *baht* and accept new exchange levels as set by international forces.

The *baht* fell from its long-standing exchange rate of 25 per dollar to as low as 57 per dollar in early 1998. By late 1998, an improving economy and stabilizing measures introduced by the government of Chuan Leekpai had improved the exchange rate, at least from the standpoint of Thai citizens.

The rate stood at around 38 Thai *baht* per U.S. dollar in early 1999, though daily and ongoing fluctuations mean you will find a different rate on your arrival.

There is no black market for *baht* and therefore no reason to bring in large amounts of Thai currency.

Maximizing your Rate

The subject of exchange rates is popular for almost all visitors, whether student backpackers or wealthy clients attached to an escorted tour.

Traveler's checks bring slightly higher rates than cash, and larger-denomination checks bring higher rates than lower denominations. Note that all currency exchanges are subject to the same 20B commission fee. Exchange rates are higher in Bangkok than in smaller towns, and higher in Thailand than outside the country.

Banks and legal moneychangers post higher rates than hotels, guesthouses, rail and bus stations, shopping centers, and the corner liquor store. Bank rates vary slightly depending on the bank. Exactly which banking system offers the highest rate is subject to debate, though some financial sleuths claim higher rates are consistently given at Thai Farmers Bank and Bangkok Bank. Actually, it varies from town to town and probably depends more on local economies than on a unified banking policy.

You'll get a slightly higher rate inside a bank building than from mobile exchange offices located outside on the front lawn or sidewalk. Other currency booths, however, are conveniently located in the most unlikely spots—remote piers, next to the beach, at festivals and parades—and often stay open until 2100 or 2200, perfect hours for that late-night bowl of *tom yam gai.*

A popular misconception is that exchange rates at the Bangkok airport must be grossly unreasonable. Actually, rates at the airport are excellent and, aside from convenience, there's little reason to bring bushels of *baht* from home. On arrival, exchange enough at the airport to cover your ride into town and your first few days of basic expenses.

Value-Added Tax

Several years ago, Thailand introduced a seven percent value-added tax (VAT) to the *retailer's* cost of certain goods and services. The measure was designed to replace the nine percent graduated business tax and to reduce net prices for consumers.

Few merchants understood the tax and many shops immediately tacked a seven percent tax onto the *consumer's* price of goods, creating confusion and anger among shoppers who resented the price gouging. Most merchants now understand the law but some continue to illegally add VAT surcharges to the bills of unwary customers. Shoppers should point out that VAT surcharges are illegal and report uncooperative shop owners to the TAT police.

The government also has a VAT refund plan for tourists, so if you intend to spend a great deal of money in the country, inquire with your hotel or the tourist office for details.

TRAVELER'S CHECKS

Most of your currency will probably be in traveler's checks, the familiar standby that provides a degree of safety and fairly quick refunds when lost or stolen. The most widely recognized brands are American Express, Bank of America, Citicorp, Thomas Cook, Visa, and MasterCard. Most of your checks should be in larger denominations, such as US$50s and US$100s, to minimize paperwork and garner the slightly higher exchange rates given over smaller denominations. Bring a few smaller checks to cash when exchange rates are dismal and to minimize the aggravation of excess currency at the end of your trip.

Keep a list of serial numbers and an accurate record of each exchange. This provides a running balance of your finances and helps speed up the refund process in the event of loss.

Fees

Traveler's checks are safe and convenient but they certainly aren't free. Most banks and commercial issuers charge one to three percent for purchase, then keep all accrued interest until the checks are cashed. Banks make far more profit using your float than whatever sales fees they might collect. These fees can be minimized by purchasing only commission-free checks and keeping your funds in interest-bearing accounts until the moment of transfer.

MONEY TRANSFERS

Money can be transferred from banks, private companies, and stock brokerage firms at home to financial institutions in Thailand. Be sure to open an account prior to departure and request a list of their international affiliates. Ask about all transfer fees and for suggestions on more economical methods of receiving money abroad.

Bank Transfers
Bank transfers by telex are safe and fast but quite expensive due to mandatory service charges, US$20 per transaction; telex fees, US$20 each way; commissions on traveler's checks, one to three percent; and currency spreads between the buy and sell rates. Bank fees for wire transfers average 6-10% or US$60-100 per US$1,000.

Transfers by mail take two or three weeks but eliminate the need for expensive telexes.

American Express
American Express MoneyGrams can be sent and received from any participating AMEX Travel Office. You don't need to be a cardholder. The first US$1,000 may be paid by credit card but additional amounts must be paid in cash. MoneyGrams take about 30 minutes, and funds can be picked up in either local currency or U.S. dollar traveler's checks.

MoneyGram service fees of 4-10% are based on the amount of funds transferred, the final destination, and method of payment. This means you'll pay US$40-100 per US$1,000, or about the same rate as bank transfers by telex.

AMEX cardholders can withdraw funds directly from their home account up to a limit of US$1,000 per week. This can be an economical alternative to MoneyGrams or wire transfers through banks. For more information and overseas AMEX locations, call (800) 926-9400 in the U.S. and (800) 933-3278 in Canada.

Western Union
Money can also be wired from Western Union to representative offices in Thailand. To wire money, take cash or a cashier's check to the nearest office of Western Union. Transfers take about 30 minutes. You can also use your Visa or Master-Card by calling (800) 325-6000 in the U.S. or (800) 321-2923 in Canada. Service fees range 4-10% depending on the amount transferred and method of payment.

Brokerage Firms
Another option is to open a managed account at a large investment firm such as Merrill Lynch and use their international transfer services. Many travelers claim this is the fastest and most economical way to transfer funds.

International Money Orders
The Thai postal service has reciprocal agreements with 27 countries abroad, including the U.S., Canada, Great Britain, and Australia. Transfers take one day from your post office back home to a major destination such as Bangkok or Chiang Mai. Allow three or four days to post offices in smaller towns.

U.S. Embassies
Emergency funds *only* can be sent abroad through U.S. embassies or consulates. Fees are US$15-40 per US$1,000. More details are provided in the U.S. government brochure, *Sending Money to Overseas Citizens Abroad.* Call (202) 647-5225 or fax (202) 647-3000.

CREDIT CARDS

Smart travelers carry credit cards for several reasons. First, they're invaluable for major purchases such as airline tickets and electronic equipment since you don't need to haul around buckets of cash or a suitcase packed with traveler's checks. Credit cards provide interest-free loans until the bill arrives back home. Just be sure to make arrangements to have a friend or family member pay the bill if you're staying an extended amount of time.

Credit cards are also useful for instant cash advances from banks in Thailand. For example, you can walk into any branch of Thai Farmers

Bank, present your credit card to the clerk, fill out a short form, and quickly pocket up to US$500 in *baht*. Another advantage is that funds are normally converted into *baht* at the favorable interbank foreign exchange rate, the wholesale benchmark used by international banks.

Cash advances have some drawbacks. Advances are considered loans—not lines of credit—and interest charges accrue from the moment of transaction.

This biggest possible danger is that cash advances completed overseas often carry much higher transactions fees than similar services in the West. *Always inquire about the transaction fee!* If the fee is more than two or three percent of the total transaction, move to another bank.

Credit Card Guarantees

Warning: purchase protection is less than most travelers would assume.

Perhaps the blame lies with the aggressive marketing campaigns of the card companies or the general naivete of the public, but anyone contemplating large overseas purchases by credit card should read the fine print, very carefully. United States law states that credit card companies must provide a degree of protection against defective, switched, unauthentic, and inferior goods, but only on items purchased in your home state or within 100 miles of your home address. Did you notice this caveat on your credit card application?

On overseas purchases, credit cards only help with items that never arrive. There are no legal protections against defective, switched, and unauthentic merchandise purchased overseas with a credit card.

In most cases, the customer pays by credit card and agrees to let the merchant ship the items back home. Upon arrival (if it arrives at all), the customer discovers the item to be either defective, broken, or switched with an inferior replacement. The cardholder then turns to the credit card company for help. The card company attempts to resolve the issue by contacting the merchant by mail or phone, but companies are helpless if the merchant quibbles or fails to respond to their inquiries. The cardholder is not only stuck with the merchandise, but also legally obligated to pay the bill.

The most straightforward solution is to hand-carry all purchases back home. Otherwise, ask for an itemized invoice that details exactly what you bought, the date of purchase, and all shipping and insurance costs. Take several photographs of the store owner and yourself standing next the item. Write down the merchant's name, address, and phone number, and all other verbal guarantees. Detailed paperwork often helps settle problems with recalcitrant merchants.

Credit Card Fraud

American Express reports that Thailand has the highest ratio of fraudulent-to-legitimate cards of all its markets, second only in total monetary value to the United States.

Hotel Scams: Far too many visitors return home to discover that large bills have been run up by dishonest hotel employees who remove cards from stored luggage or hotel safes, then go on shopping sprees with the cooperation of unscrupulous merchants. You return home to find that you somehow purchased 20 color TVs and 16 stereo systems during your brief visit to Thailand.

Credit cards should be carefully guarded and carried on your person at all times. Whenever cards are checked with baggage handlers or in hotel safes, be sure to tightly seal all financial documents in theft-proof compartments and obtain a complete receipt of valuables, including credit cards and the serial numbers of all traveler's checks. Carefully inspect the contents of your package when you reclaim your valuables from the front desk or baggage storage room.

Duplicate Receipts: Fraud is also practiced by dishonest merchants who surreptitiously run cards through machines several times to produce multiple copies. The merchant then fills out the extra copies, forges your signature, and submits the receipts to a bank for collection.

The best prevention is to keep an eye on your credit card during purchases. Don't let the merchant disappear into a back room, and do remember to destroy all carbons after the transaction.

Illegal Surcharges: Merchants sometimes add illegal surcharges to credit card purchases, such as value-added taxes (VAT) and merchant fees from three to five percent collected by the credit card company. Both practices are against

Thai law and violate the legal agreements signed between the merchant and credit card company.

Customers charged such fees should immediately object and demand that all surcharges be eliminated from the bill. If the merchant refuses but you still want the item, ask for an itemized receipt that clearly states the cost of the product and the amount of surcharge. After your return home, submit photocopies of these receipts to your credit card company for a refund.

Lost Cards: Travelers who lose credit cards issued by Western or Thai banks should immediately contact the appropriate representative in Bangkok. Some major companies include: American Express, tel. (02) 273-0022 or 273-3660; Diners Club, tel. (02) 238-3660 or 236-7455; Visa and MasterCard, tel. (02) 246-0300; Thai Farmers Bank, tel. (02) 271-0234 or 273-1199; Siam Commercial Bank, tel. (02) 256-1361.

ATM WITHDRAWALS

A sensible alternative to carrying around wads of cash is to withdraw funds from ATM machines with a credit or debit card issued by a domestic or foreign bank. ATMs dispense cash 24 hours a day, seven days a week, then charge your credit card or debit your bank account. Debit cards are more widely honored than credit cards at Thai ATMs.

Debit cards are issued by banks in conjunction with either the Cirrus system owned by Visa or the PLUS system owned by MasterCard. Your MasterCard/Cirrus card will work at over 160 ATM machines located in airports, major hotels, and branches of Bangkok Bank and Siam Commercial Bank. The Visa/PLUS debit card works at regional ATMs and branches of Thai Farmers Bank. To obtain an international ATM directory, call MasterCard/Cirrus at (800) 424-7787 or Visa/PLUS at (800) 843-7587.

The most versatile and widely honored cards are those issued by either Thai Farmers Bank or Bangkok Bank. Both banks' ATM cards work at the ATMs of 15 other banks connected to a national system of interlocking networks. The two major ATM systems in Thailand—Siam Net and Bank Net—link over 1,500 ATMs across the country. Visitors spending a month or so in Thailand should seriously consider opening a local bank account and obtaining a debit card.

Daily withdrawal limits are predetermined by your bank, but usually range US$100-200 per day. Many machines have instructions in English on the screen or posted nearby. Thai *baht* is given but your account is debited in your national currency at favorable exchange rates.

Ghosts in the Machine

A few problems exist with automatic teller machines. Many ATMs in Asia do not have the ability to ask whether you want the money withdrawn from your checking or savings account, but will automatically try the primary (usually checking) account. Contact your institution prior to departure to ensure that sufficient funds are in your primary account and that your card withdraws from the correct account. It can be an unpleasant surprise to discover that your card is programmed to withdraw funds from your checking account when all your money is in your savings account.

Another consideration: overseas ATMs often do not accept PIN numbers longer than four digits. Travelers with six-digit PINs should ask their bank to reprogram their card with a four-digit number.

Finally, consider the fees. ATM withdrawals carry transaction fees, either flat fees demanded by the institution that issued the card, or transaction fees based on the amount of withdrawal. Visa and MasterCard fees are determined by the issuing bank, American Express charges a minimum of two percent or US$2 per transaction, Diners Club charges three to four percent.

MEASUREMENTS AND COMMUNICATIONS

MAIL

The Bangkok General Post Office (GPO) on Charoen Krung Road is open weekdays 0800-1800 and weekends and holidays 0900-1300. The GPO is a five-minute walk from the Tha Muang stop of the Chao Praya River Express.

Postal branch offices with overseas telephone services are located in several neighborhoods: Banglampoo, Trok Mayom Rd.; Silom, 113/6 Suriwong Center Rd.; Sukumvit, Sukumvit Soi 4; Sukumvit, Sukumvit Soi 23.

Postal Hours
The Bangkok GPO is open weekdays 0800-1800, weekends and holidays 0900-1300. The address for the Bangkok General Post Office is GPO, Charoen Krung Rd., Bangkok, Thailand. Provincial post offices elsewhere in Thailand are open weekdays 0830-1630 and Saturday 0900-1200.

Postal Rates
Airmail from Thailand takes 10-14 days; mail by sea requires three or four months. Airmail from the U.S. takes 7-10 days to reach Bangkok. All mail should be registered and receipts retained to trace missing parcels. All valuable parcels should also be insured at the rate of 10B per 2,000B value of goods.

Rates for parcels over one kg are determined by weight in one-kg increments, by country of destination, and by method of delivery (airmail or surface). Maximum weight is 20 kg. Postal rates to the United States and Europe are almost identical.

Mail Pickup
When retrieving mail, bring your passport or other legal identification to the poste restante counter. The service fee is 1B for each piece of mail, 2B per parcel. Letters held over three months are returned to sender.

Letters sent to you should be marked "hold" and directed to poste restante, the French term for general delivery. Since Thais write their last name first and their first names last, postal clerks sometimes misfile letters under the first name

("given" name) rather than the surname ("family" name). To ensure proper delivery, family names should be both capitalized and underlined on the outside of the envelope. If missing anticipated mail, ask the postal clerk to check under your first name.

Mail intended for the Bangkok GPO should be addressed: NAME, Poste Restante, General Post Office, Charoen Krung Rd., Bangkok, Thailand 10500.

All mail should be registered and receipts retained to trace missing parcels. It's a good idea to insure valuable parcels at the rate of 10B per 2,000B value of goods.

Travelers with an American Express credit card or using American Express traveler's checks can receive mail at the AMEX office at Sea Tours, tel. (02) 251-4862, in Siam Center, Suite 414, 965 Rama I Rd., Bangkok. A complete list of AMEX offices is available from AMEX (tel. 800-528-4800) in their booklet, *Travelers Companion*.

Parcel Post
All packages must be officially boxed and sealed at special counters inside the main post office or at nearby private agencies. Don't pack a box and expect to just drop it at the post office.

Bring all goods to the post office for inspection. Assuming you aren't smuggling drugs or rare antiques, you may then purchase a cardboard box and string, pack your goods, weigh the contents, purchase stamps, and deliver your assembled masterpiece to the appropriate window.

Packing services inside the Bangkok GPO do all the work for a reasonable fee. Private packing agencies located nearby can help with the packing and shipping of parcels that weigh over 20 kg.

Packages that require overseas delivery within four days can go via the Express Mail Service (EMS) offered at major post offices. The cost is 320B per 250 grams, or US$22 per pound.

Fast delivery services are also offered by commercial shippers such as DHL, Federal Express, UPS, and TNT Express.

TELEPHONE

The Telephone Organization of Thailand (TOT) under the authority of a government agency appropriately called the Communications Authority of Thailand (CAT) operates the phone system. Telephones are fairly reliable except during floods and thunderstorms when connections can be cut for periods of a few hours to several days.

A few idiosyncrasies surround the telephone system in Thailand. Thai telephone area codes always begin with a zero. For example, the area code for Bangkok is 02 and the code for Chiang Mai is 053. This zero is used for calls inside the country but *dropped for international calls or faxes to the country*. For example, to reach Bangkok from the United States you first dial 011 (the international access code), 66 (Thailand's country code), and 2 (city code). Don't dial 02. This is why hotels in Bangkok always list their phone number with a 662 prefix rather than 6602.

Another confusing fact: telephone numbers often have several different final digits to handle multiple incoming calls. Therefore you'll often see strange phone numbers such as 233-4501-09 or 233-4401/09. Advanced multiline systems are still considered an exotic technology in Thailand.

Another vexing problem is that telephone numbers seem to change with the seasons, a horrible curse cast upon society by the TOT.

Not only do numbers change quickly, telephone directories list people by their first names rather than their family names.

Finally, travelers attempting to make hotel reservations or contact a business in Thailand will have better luck sending a fax or e-mail rather than attempting a phone call. Faxes eliminate language barrier difficulties and produce a hard copy that hotel receptionists can decipher in their free time. E-mail is even better since it's free and a guaranteed way to find out if your message was received.

International Calls to Thailand

International calls to Thailand from the United States are placed by dialing the international

INTERNATIONAL DIRECT DIAL CODES

From Thailand, dial 001 followed by the country code:

WESTERN NATIONS

Australia	61
Canada	1
France	33
Germany	49
Ireland	353
Netherlands	31
New Zealand	64
United Kingdom	44
U.S.A.	1

SOUTHEAST ASIA

Brunei	673
Myanmar	95
Cambodia	855
Hong Kong	852
Indonesia	62
Laos	856
Macau	853
Malaysia	60
Philippines	63
Singapore	65
Thailand	66
Vietnam	84

access code for calls from America (011), the country code for Thailand (66), the area code for the particular city (drop the zero), and finally, the local number. To make an operator-assisted call including person-to-person, collect, or calling card, dial the international access code for operator-assisted calls (01) and give the country code for Thailand (66), the area code, and local telephone number.

Before calling Thailand and waking your friends or business partners at some hellish hour, you might consider the time differential. For more information, refer to the section on "Time" in this chapter.

International Calls from Thailand

International calls from Thailand are made by dialing the international access code for Thailand (001), followed by country code, area code, and finally the local number.

Phone calls made from hotels are generally the most expensive option due to heavy surcharges and stiff connection fees. To avoid surcharges on multiple calls, press the pound key (#) after your first call and you usually won't have to rekey your card number or pay another surcharge.

International telephone calls at the lowest possible prices are available from discount calling plans offered by AT&T USA Direct, MCI Call USA, and Sprint Global Fone. These programs allow travelers to dial a toll-free access number (listed below) and speak directly with an operator in their home country.

Discount calls through AT&T, MCI, and Sprint also can be made on special "Home Direct" phones at CAT Telecom Centers. To make an international call, fill out the bilingual form with your name and telephone details, pay a deposit to cover the estimated cost, and find an empty phone booth to make your call. Larger CAT Telecoms permit you to dial the number, but smaller offices require the assistance of an operator.

Operators are required for collect calls, for person-to-person calls, for station-to-station calls, and to use your international calling card. Operator assistance is 100.

CAT Telecom Centers with Home Direct Phones are located at the GPO on Charoen Krung Road (open 24 hours), the airport post office, the Wall Street Building on Suriwong Road, the Queen Sirikit National Convention Centre, the World Trade Center, Sogo Department Store,

---

USEFUL BANGKOK PHONE NUMBERS
(Bangkok area code is 02)

Airport (Arrivals) 535-1301
Airport (Departures) 535-1385
Airport (Domestic) 535-1253
Airport (International) 535-1111
Eastern Bus Terminal (a/c) 391-9829
Eastern Bus Terminal (Ordinary) . 391-2504
Fire 199
General Post Office 233-1050
Hualampong Train Station (Info.) . 223-7010
Hualampong Train Station 223-3762
  (Advance Booking)
Immigration 286-9176
International Calls 100
Northern Bus Terminal (a/c) . . . 279-4484
Northern Bus Terminal (Ordinary) . 271-0101
Phone Information 13
Southern Bus Terminal (a/c) . . . 391-9829
Southern Bus Terminal (Ordinary) 434-5558
Tourist Police 1699
  Crime Suppression Div. 225-0085
Train Station 223-7010

---

the Thaniya Building on Silom Road, and the Banglampoo and Hualampong post offices.

To use the Home Direct service, call 0001-999 followed by the access number. Access numbers for several countries include:

Australia: 61-1000
Canada: 15-1000
Germany: 49-1000
Netherlands: 31-1035
New Zealand: 64-1066
UK: 44-1066
USA: AT&T, 11111; MCI, 12001;
  Sprint, 13871

ISD International Calls

The Communications Authority of Thailand (CAT) provides international telephone service through their International Subscriber Dialing (ISD) and International Operator Direct Connection, often called "Home Direct."

ISD calls can be made from all CAT Telecom Centers and from most private phones. Home Direct calls can be made *only* from CAT Telecom Centers and from a limited number of private phones.

CAT Telecom Centers are located near central post offices and are open daily 0800-2200. To make an international call, fill out the bilingual form with your name and telephone details, pay a deposit to cover the estimated cost, and find an empty phone booth to make your call. Larger CAT Telecoms permit you to dial the number but smaller offices require the assistance of an operator. Operators are also required for all collect calls, person-to-person calls, and station-to-station calls, and to use your international calling card. Operator assistance is 100.

Fax Services

CAT Telecom Offices at GPOs throughout the country also offer fax, telegraph, and telex services. International faxes cost 100-150B for the first page and 65-100B for each additional page depending on the destination and amount of transmission time.

Local Telephone Calls

Pay phones in Bangkok are painted distinct colors and often marked with a blue triangle. Phone booths painted with red roofs and red horizontal stripes are for local calls only, which cost 1B for three minutes. Note that only the medium-sized 1B coin fits the slot. Warning beeps signal the end of the three-minute period, but additional coins will keep the line open. The remaining time is noted by a small display inside the booth.

Local calls can also be made from small pay phones inside restaurants, hotels, and shops. Most are painted a bright red or pale blue and cost 5B for three minutes.

Domestic Long-Distance Calls

The phone booths painted with blue roofs and metallic stripes are for long-distance calls within Thailand. These phones accept 1B, 5B, and 10B coins but are rarely seen outside Bangkok and busy tourist zones.

Local and domestic long-distance calls can also be made from "card phones" located in supermarkets, financial districts, and hotel districts. Card phones are painted with green stripes and only accept payment by telephone cards. Markets and shops such as 7-Eleven sell phone cards in 100B denominations.

Domestic long-distance phone calls are made by dialing the area code followed by the local phone number.

TIME

Thailand is seven hours ahead of Greenwich mean time (GMT+7).

During winter months, Thailand is 15 hours ahead of San Francisco and Los Angeles, 13 hours ahead of Chicago, 12 hours ahead of New York, seven hours ahead of London, and three hours behind Sydney. Daylight saving time will add one hour to these figures.

From another perspective, Bangkok at noon is San Francisco at 2100 (the previous day), Chicago and New Orleans at 2300, New York at midnight, Auckland at 1700, Sydney at 1500, Perth at 1300, London at 0500, and Paris at 0600.

Business Hours

Government offices and private businesses keep similar hours to businesses in foreign countries. National museums and major GPOs have special opening hours and days. Most **government offices** are open Mon.-Fri. 0830-1200 and 1300-1630. **National museums** are open Wed.-Sun. 0830-1200 and 1300-1630; closed on Monday, Tuesday, and national holidays. **Post offices** operate Mon.-Fri. 0830-1630, Saturday 0900-1200, closed Sunday and holidays. GPOs in Bangkok and Chiang Mai stay open until 2200.

INTERNATIONAL CLOCK FOR THAILAND	
San Francisco	-14
New York	-12
Honolulu	-17
London	-7
Paris	-6
Sydney	+3
Bonn	-6
Tokyo	+2

You can frequent **tourist offices** daily except holidays 0830-1630. **Banks** are open Mon.-Fri. 0830-1530. Foreign exchange offices adjacent to banks in Bangkok and other tourist destinations are open daily 0830-2200. Most **shopping centers** are open daily 0830-1700; smaller shops stay open until around 2200.

MEASUREMENTS

Electricity
Electric current is 220 V, 50 cycles. The standard wall outlets accept electrical appliances with two round poles. Some outlets accept flat two-bladed plugs while others accept both round and flat. Electrical adapters and voltage convertors are available from travel supply shops in your

home country, from better hotels in Thailand, and at all electrical stores in Thailand.

Weights and Measures
Temperature is expressed in degrees Celsius.

The metric system serves as the national standard of measurement except for a few items still measured according to the traditional Thai system.

Land, for example, is parceled into *waa, ngaan,* and *rai.* Gold is measured in a unit of weight confusingly called the *baht,* which is approximately 15.2 grams. *Baht*—rather than

---

TRADITIONAL THAI MEASUREMENTS

LAND MEASUREMENTS

waa: 4 sq. meters (100 sq. *waa*)
ngaan: 400 sq. meters
rai: 1600 sq. meters (4 *ngaan*)

WEIGHT

baht: 15.2 grams
taleung: 60 grams (4 *baht*)
chang: 1.2 kg (20 *taleung*)
haap: 60 kg (50 *chang*)

DISTANCE

niu: 2.2 cm
kheup: 25 cm (12 *niu*)
sawk: 50 cm (2 *kheup*)
waa: 2 meters (4 *sawk*)
sen: 40 meters (20 *waa*)
yoht: 16 km (400 *sen*)

---

ounces or grams—will be quoted when you buy gold jewelry anywhere in the country.

Most of the older measurement terms listed in the chart "Traditional Thai Measurements" have been abandoned except by a few carpenters, traditional boat builders, and hilltribe merchants when speaking about their crops (i.e., opium).

SOURCES OF TRAVEL INFORMATION

The following section will help you obtain background details and travel information before you leave for Thailand.

First visit your public library for titles on Thai history, culture, people, traditions, political developments, and artistic heritage. Unless you live in a major city, libraries rarely carry much on Thailand aside from musty copies of *The King and I* and dated guidebooks such as *Nagel's Encyclopedic Guide to Thailand.* Ask your librarian to order a copy of *Thailand Handbook* or *Bangkok Handbook* from Moon Publications.

A list of recommended readings is located in the back of this guidebook. I've indicated my

personal favorites and best choices for travelers with limited reading time. The more you learn about Thailand beforehand, the more you will appreciate your travel experience.

Travel agents experienced with Thailand are a godsend, but rare as whale's teeth. Student travel agencies listed in this chapter can sometimes offer reliable travel advice.

The Internet is also an amazing source of information about Thailand.

Best of all, seek out and talk with travelers who have been to Thailand or other areas in Southeast Asia. Throughout the world, an amazing number of people have traveled the region and love to relate their travel experiences.

GOVERNMENT AGENCIES

U.S. Government Information

Current travel conditions and safety advisories on worldwide destinations can be obtained from the new Consular Information Program, which replaced an outmoded and highly criticized system of travel advisories.

Two categories of information exist: travel warnings to avoid certain destinations, and consular information sheets to every country in the world. Both can be heard on tape 24 hours a day by calling the Citizens Emergency Center of the U.S. State Department at (202) 647-5225. Follow the taped recording of menu options. To avoid voice mail and speak with a human operator, call the Bureau of Consular Affairs at (202) 647-1488 dur-

THAI TIME

The Buddhist Calendar

The Western Gregorian calendar, introduced to Thailand in 1899, is used for all national and social events, but Thais also consult the Buddhist calendar for some religious events and life cycle ceremonies. Buddhist calendars and the Buddhist Era (B.E.) date from 543 B.C., the year Buddha attained enlightenment and entered nirvana. Thus, A.D. 1998 equals 2541 B.E. in the Buddhist Era.

To add to the chronological confusion, the Buddhist Era in Thailand is one year behind that of Myanmar, Sri Lanka, and India. The situation is similar to that experienced by the Christian world, which took many moons to decide on the exact year of the birth of Christ. It was, of course, Pope Gregory XIII, who finally settled the issue in 1592 by imposing his system and namesake on our Western calendar.

The Lunar Calendar

The Thais also use the lunar calendar to set the dates of many religious ceremonies. The lunar calendar comes from Chinese astrologers who calculated that a complete cycle of the moon takes about 29.5 days. Lunar calendars probably worked well until somebody decided that the lunar year should somehow correspond to the Western calendar.

The problem is that the Western year is divided into 12 months with a total of 365 days (except for leap years), while the lunar year is 12 months with only 354 days. Over a period of years, the difference of 11 days causes the lunar year to gradually creep ahead of the Western calendar. In an attempt to realign the two systems, an extra eighth lunar month is shoved into the lunar year every two or three years.

The Thais also celebrate some lunar-based holidays on days unconnected with the lunar calendar. For example, the Thai New Year (Songkram) takes place each year on 13 April, though the lunar new year generally falls in either February or March.

The Thai Day

Another curious twist on time concerns the division of the day.

While urban Thai citizens observe a 24-hour day divided into two 12-hour segments (midnight to noon and noon to midnight), they also divide the day into four periods of six hours, each given a different term.

This system is the legacy of earlier days when village watchmen used wooden drums and clackers to signal the hour and assure everyone that all was well within the neighborhood. Villagers slept peacefully unless signaled by unexpected drumming or disturbed by the eerie absence of the hourly clack.

Today, the six-hour shifts of the night watchman are reflected in the terminology of time. *Chao* refers to the period between 0600 and 1100, *klung wun* is midday, *bai mong* is 1300, and *bai song* means 1400. Evening hours after 1800 are *yen* with another number to indicate the exact hour, while *keun* replaces *yen* after 2200.

To further complicate the issue, Thais also divide the day into four base hours plus the familiar periods of noon and midnight. *Dee neung* is 0100 in Western time, *neung muang chao* is "one in the morning" (0700 in Western time), *bai muang* is "one in the afternoon" (1300 to Westerners), *thum neung* is "one in the evening" (1900 for foreigners).

Thais also name the days after the planets, in much the same way that Westerners name the days after planetary names of Greek origin. Each day is associated with a particular color. For example, Sunday is associated with red while the lucky color for Wednesday is pink or lilac.

Whew. As you might expect, this refusal to compartmentalize the day according to Western thought should be considered when someone invites you to breakfast at "three in the morning." That's breakfast at 0900.

ing normal business hours. Desk officers at (202) 647-2000 may offer additional tips.

The same information can be obtained by fax, (202) 647-3000.

The Consular Affairs Bulletin Board (CABB) can accessed using your computer modem via their website. This convenient service allows you to review warnings, information sheets, tips for travelers, medical information, and daily updates of the *Overseas Security Advisory Council Reports.*

Tourist Authority of Thailand

The Tourist Authority of Thailand (TAT) can help you with general travel information such as glossy brochures and lists of upcoming festivals. Tourism employees are friendly, and the department is well funded compared to other government tourist offices in Southeast Asia. You'll need to request specific topics as most handouts are kept well hidden.

The TAT head office is at 372 Bamrung Muang Rd., Bangkok 10100, Thailand, tel. (662) 226-0060, fax (662) 224-6221. A bulletin board lists upcoming festivals, dance performances, and warnings about safety and rip-offs.

Airport TAT: Not as much information but useful for free tourist magazines and last-second tips on transportation into town. Their kiosk is in the arrival area. Open daily 0800-midnight.

Wat Pra Keo TAT: A small tourist outlet is just opposite the royal temple on Na Pra Lan Road. Open daily 0830-1930.

Chatuchak TAT: A final and often deserted TAT kiosk operates weekends at the famous flea market on the outskirts of town near the Northern Bus Terminal. Open daily 0830-1930.

MAPS

Sprawling and confusing Bangkok requires a good map. Two essential ones are Nancy Chandler's map and a bus route map if you intend to spend much time in Bangkok. Buy both to quickly understand the layout of Bangkok. Maps can be purchased at most bookstores and from many guesthouses and hotels.

Nancy Chandler's Map of Bangkok: Nancy's map has been the best tourist map of the city

for over a decade, sensibly drawn with color codes and sectional details, plus inside tips on restaurants and popular shopping districts. Somewhat expensive, but highly recommended for all visitors to Bangkok.

Bangkok Bus Map: Most of the bus routes in Bangkok are shown on this map published by the Bangkok Guide Company. This useful if somewhat outdated resource also includes tidbits on markets, guesthouses, bookshops, river and canal tours, embassies, and airline offices. The same company also produces a small booklet with greater detail on the myriad bus routes, although most visitors will not need to dig this deep into the transportation permutations of this bewildering city.

Groovy Map & Guide of Bangkok: A relatively new map researched by a local expat with sightseeing and shopping tips, plus a full-page map of the core city with a limited number of bus routes. Although somewhat basic, the clean and colorful layout makes this the most understandable map of the city and is probably quite adequate for most first-time visitors.

Association of Siamese Architects: The Fine Arts Department publishes four colorful hand-drawn cultural maps with details on Bangkok and the canals of Thonburi. The map of Thonburi is somewhat useful, but the other maps are too vague and sketchy.

THE INTERNET

Internet Cafes in Thailand

Several dozen Internet cafes now provide Web access in all the major destinations including Bangkok (mostly in Banglampoo), Chiang Mai, Phuket, and Ko Samui. Internet connections cost about 2B per minute in tourist-oriented venues but only 1B per minute in cafes serving primarily a Thai clientele.

The best way to check your e-mail is to set up an account with a free e-mail service (Hotmail, Yahoo, etc.) and then check your Hotmail account from an Internet cafe in Thailand. Most services allow you to pull e-mail messages directly off your chief Internet Service Provider by checking your POP account.

BOOKSTORES AND LIBRARIES

Bookstores

Bangkok's bookstores are probably the best in all of Southeast Asia, although the largest and most complete bookstore is now Tower Books in Singapore. Thailand has two major publishers and book distributors.

Asia Books: The largest selection of English-language books in Bangkok is found in Asia Books, a large chain especially strong on bestsellers, modern literature, business, art, travel, Thailand, and reference works. All the following Asia Books outlets are open daily 1000-2100. The Landmark Z branch specializes in art and architecture.

Stores around Bangkok include: Main Store, 221 Sukumvit Soi 15, tel. (02) 252-7277; Central City, 309 Bangna Rd., tel. (02) 361-0743; Landmark Plaza, Sukumvit Soi 3, tel. (02) 253-5839; Peninsula Plaza, Rajadamri Rd., tel. (02) 253-9786; Thaniya Plaza, Silom Rd., tel. (02) 231-2106; Times Square, Sukumvit Soi 12, tel. (02) 250-0162; World Trade Center, Rajadamri Rd., tel. (02) 255-6209.

D.K. (Duang Kamol) Books: Khun Suk Soongsang, founder and chair of Duang Kamol, opened his first bookstore at Siam Square in 1970, which he named after a book written by a close friend. Today, D.K. is Thailand's largest book distributor with over 60 stores nationwide, including 23 in Bangkok alone.

They also run the biggest bookshop in Thailand at Seacon Square in the suburb of Bangkapi. This superstore, the size of a football field, displays almost one million books, plus puts on publishing seminars, writing workshops, book signings, and special exhibitions. The store also includes a restaurant and "vinotech" offering quality wines personally selected by Khun Suk, a well-known wine connoisseur.

A few D.K. outlets include: Mahboonkrong Centre, Rama 1 Rd., tel. (02) 217-9301; Pratunam, 90/21 Ratchaprarob Rd., tel. (02) 245-5586; Seacon Square, Srinakarin Rd., tel. (02) 393-8040; Siam Square, Rama 1 Rd. Soi 2, tel. (02) 251-1467; Sukumvit Centre, Sukumvit Soi 8, tel. (02) 252-6261.

Independent Bookstores

A handful of both small and large bookstores are scattered around town.

Kinokuniya: Just about the largest selection of English-language books in town with everything from glossy, coffee table tomes to classics and regional guides. Emporium Shopping Center, Sukumvit Soi 24, tel. (02) 664-8554.

The Bookseller: Excellent selection of English-language books and foreign magazines, plus discount tables for bargains. 81 Patpong Rd., tel. (02) 233-1717.

Book Gallery: Limited number of books but Bangkok's best selection of international magazines. 12/1 Sukumvit Soi 33, tel. (02) 260-6215.

Fine Arts Gift Shop: Specializes in art, music, and Asian culture in a logical location just opposite the Royal Palace near Silpakorn University. Naprathat Rd.

White Lotus: For new and rare books on Asia, plus old maps and prints, order their catalog at GPO Box 1141, Bangkok 10501. White Lotus has was relocating at the time of publication.

Used Books

Used English-language books are carried at the following bookstores and markets.

Chatuchak Weekend Market: Visit sections 22 and 25 to plow through enormous stacks of used antiquarian books and magazines, including back issues of *Sawasdee* magazine. Paholyothin Rd. Weekends 0900-1800.

Elite Used Books: An old favorite that stocks titles on subjects from fiction and travel to politics and history. This is where most of the expats in Bangkok trade their books for newer titles. 593/5 Sukumvit Soi 33, tel. (02) 258-0221.

Khao San Road: All sorts of backpacker books, including ragged copies of Moon Publications' *Southeast Asia Handbook*. Shops here sell everything used from modern and classic literature to popular fiction, new age novels, used travel guides, and foreign-language novels.

Libraries

Libraries in Bangkok are good places to escape the heat and conduct some background research on the country.

National Library: One of the few libraries in the country, the National Library north of Banglampoo has a small number of English-language books but an extensive selection of Thai manuscripts. The air-conditioned periodicals room has a good stock of English-language magazines. Samsen Rd., tel. (02) 281-5212. Open daily 0930-1930.

Chulalongkorn University: Thailand's premier institution of higher education has an extensive range of books which can be read in an air-conditioned environment. Visitors can purchase a one-day membership pass which allows use of computers equipped with CD-ROM and Internet access. Phayathai Rd., tel. (02) 215-4100. Open daily except Sunday 0900-2100.

American University Alumni (AUA): Features a decent library sponsored by the U.S. Information Service, plus a good selection of American magazines and background reading on Thai history and culture. Visitors can borrow books and use the photocopy machine. 179 Rajadamri Rd., tel. (02) 252-8953. Open weekdays 0800-1700.

Neilson Hays Library: Constructed in 1922 by Dr. Hays to commemorate his wife (Jennie Neilson Hays) and her devotion to the Bangkok Ladies Library Association, this historic structure offers over 20,000 hardbacks, a magazine section, used paperbacks for sale, and a Rotunda Gallery that sponsors monthly art exhibitions and sales. Visitors can browse but membership is required to check out books. 195 Suriwong Rd. near the British Club, tel. (02) 233-1731. Open daily 0930-1600.

Siam Society: The scholarly collection of books at the Siam Society attracts a continual stream of visitors conducting research on the arts, culture, customs, and history of Thailand. Now holding over 10,000 volumes, the library preserves many rare and valuable works, some photocopied and rebound or microfilmed for permanent storage. Informative brochures and booklets are sold at the front desk, but only members are allowed to enter the research facilities. Sukumvit Soi 21, tel. (02) 258-3491. Open Tues.-Sat. 0900-1600.

GETTING THERE

BY AIR

Thailand is centrally located in the heart of Southeast Asia and is served by over 50 international airlines from all major world capitals. Most international airlines fly to Bangkok's Don Muang International Airport, though direct flights are also available to international airports in Penang, Hat Yai, and Chiang Mai. Travel times to Bangkok are 16-20 hours from San Francisco, Los Angeles, and Seattle; 20-24 hours from Chicago; and 22-26 hours from New York via the West Coast.

Some airlines provide complimentary overnight accommodations in Tokyo, Seoul, Taipei, or Hong Kong—a good way to break up the long and tiring journey. The following tips may save you time and money while you search for the perfect airline ticket.

Fares

All major airlines in North America conform to the price guidelines issued by the International Air Transport Association (IATA). Roundtrip advance-purchase weekday fares from the U.S.

West Coast are currently US$1,124 (low season) and US$1,231 (high season). Roundtrip is US$1,440 from New York.

Tickets purchased directly from the airlines cost more than tickets purchased from budget agencies and consolidators, but often carry fewer restrictions and cancellation penalties. Special promotional fares offered by the airlines may even match the discounters, such as roundtrips during the winter months priced US$880-940.

Thailand can be reached on dozens of airlines with a variety of tickets sold at all possible prices. Read the travel section of your Sunday newspaper for advertised bargains, then call airlines, student travel agencies, and discount wholesalers for their prices and ticket restrictions. Determined travelers can plan itineraries and discover obscure air routes by studying the *Official Airline Guide* at the library.

Ticket prices vary enormously depending on dozens of factors, including type of ticket, season, choice of airline, your flexibility, and experience of the travel agent. It's confusing, but since airfare comprises a major portion of total travel expenses, no amount of time getting it right is wasted. The rule of thumb is that price and restrictions are inversely related; the cheaper the ticket the more hassles such as penalties, odd departure hours, layovers, and risk of last-minute cancellations.

First Class and Business Tickets: First class (coded F) and business class (coded J) are designed for travelers who need maximum flexibility and comfort, and are willing to pay the price.

Economy Tickets: Economy class tickets (coded Y) are cheaper than first and business classes, plus they often lack the advance-purchase requirements and cancellation charges.

Advance-purchase excursion (APEX) Tickets: APEX tickets—the airlines' main method for deep discounts—are about 25% less than economy class tickets but often come loaded with restrictions which require advance payment, dictate your length of stay, and carry heavy penalties for cancellations or amendments.

Super-APEX: Super-APEX tickets, somewhat cheaper than regular APEX, are limited in quantity and often sell out quickly. APEX and Super-APEX tickets are recommended for visitors with limited time who need guaranteed air reservations.

Low and High Seasons

All airlines and discount agencies price their tickets according to the season.

Airlines in North America and Europe consider the low season the winter months Oct.-April and the high season the summer months May-September. The holiday period Dec.-Jan. is also considered a high season. An intermediate or "shoulder season" is often wedged between the high and low seasons.

The high season for airlines in Australia and New Zealand runs December to 15 January, school holiday periods are shoulder seasons, and the low season is the rest of the year.

Sold-Out Flights

The holiday season Dec.-Jan. can be a difficult time to obtain tickets. Not only are prices about 20% higher, the shortage of seats makes confirmed reservations on specific days a real chore.

This exasperating situation was created by the reluctance of Thai Airways International (THAI) to allow additional flights into the capital by other international carriers. As with other Asian-based airlines, THAI feels they're at an unfair disadvantage against U.S. airlines that have huge domestic networks to feed their transpacific routes. Airlines in the U.S. also benefit from fifth-freedom rights, which allow them to pick up passengers and fly on to a third country in Asia. THAI further argues that U.S. carriers can now fly direct to more Asian destinations with new long-haul aircraft, but won't because of higher yields on intra-Asian routes.

Travelers are advised to make reservations several months in advance to ensure reserved seats on the most convenient dates. After arrival in Bangkok, be sure to reconfirm departure dates to avoid losing your reservation.

Passengers are required to reconfirm all flights at least 72 hours prior to departure. **Reconfirmation** is not necessary on the first flight of your itinerary or on flights with a layover of less than 72 hours. Passengers who fail to reconfirm their flights may have their seats automatically canceled and given to other passengers. Some passengers even reconfirm their reconfirmations!

Nonstop, Direct, Connecting?

Airline terminology is almost as confusing as its ticketing policies. Flights are either nonstop, direct, or connecting. A nonstop flight requires no change of planes and makes no stops. A direct flight stops at least once and may involve a change of planes. The flight number remains the same and the second plane must wait for any delayed arrivals. A connecting flight involves different planes and different flight numbers. Connecting planes are not required to wait for delayed flights on the first leg.

No airline flies nonstop from North America to Thailand. All direct flights require a stop for refueling and possible change of planes in either Tokyo, Seoul, Taipei, Manila, or Hong Kong. A stop in Honolulu is often included.

Getting Bumped

Bumping is another problem encountered by an increasing number of passengers heading off to Southeast Asia. The situation has been created by airline executives who routinely overbook flights to maximize their profits and meet yield management goals. Who gets bumped is often based on check-in time: those who checked in last are the first to be bumped. Passengers denied boarding against their will are entitled to compensation, provided they have fulfilled certain requirements, such as confirming their reservation and checking in before the deadline.

Airline managers know that compensation for bumped passengers is a small price to pay to maximize aircraft capacity. The compensation depends on the price of the ticket and the length of delay until the next available flight. Compensation can be free domestic tickets, cash up to US$400, discount coupons for other destinations, or complimentary hotels and meals. Believe it or not, some passengers actually attempt to get bumped to pick up these benefits.

Proof of Onward Passage

Some countries in Asia require incoming travelers to show proof of onward passage. Proof of onward passage can be a plane ticket to some foreign destination or a miscellaneous charge order (MCO). Fortunately, Thai immigration rarely checks for onward tickets unless they dislike your appearance.

If you're concerned about not having proof of onward passage, you could purchase the cheapest outbound ticket (Hat Yai to Phuket for example) and request a refund after you've passed through immigration in Bangkok. Be sure to buy this ticket with cash or traveler's checks from a major airline carrier. Requesting a refund for an unused ticket with an obscure airline can be a Kafkaesque experience.

Ticket Tips

Bargain tickets sold by major airlines and discount travel agencies often carry heavy restrictions to prevent passengers from changing their minds and thereby saddling the airline with empty seats. Travelers should read the fine print and understand the restrictions, which aren't always spelled out in airline advertisements. Most airlines only give cash refunds in the event of death—not for a sudden change of plans, marriage, birth of a child, traffic delays, or nervous breakdown at the check-in counter. Passengers who need to cancel their flights may, depending on the type of ticket, be able to have the value applied toward the purchase of another nonrefund-

able ticket for up to one year after the first was issued. Other tickets are partially refundable but penalties can be 25-75% of the ticket value.

Tickets issued by travel agents will be marked either "OK," "RQ," or "on request." The OK stamp next to the destination indicates the travel agent has checked with the airline and the seat has been reserved in your name. An RQ or "on request" stamp means your seat has not been confirmed by your agent and you are going to be on standby. This is a big problem with many travel agencies in Bangkok. Be sure your ticket is marked "OK" before payment.

Airline tickets cannot be legally transferred from one passenger to another, despite the advertisements placed in newspapers and on bulletin boards in youth hostels and guesthouses. International departures are usually checked by matching the name on the ticket with the name on the passport.

Tickets purchased from mileage brokers are prohibited by airlines and subject to seizure at the airport. In other words, mileage certificates obtained from frequent flyer programs and sold to the public at steep discounts are nontransferable.

Tour conductor tickets given to travel agents as a reward for selling seats on group tours cannot be legally sold or transferred but may be given away as presents. Always check your bargain ticket to see if it's marked "no fare" or "no miles," two terms given by discount operators to denote budget tickets without fare guarantees or mileage benefits.

For passengers, air travel is getting worse. The number of passengers angry enough to complain to the Department of Transportation has risen to record levels in recent years. A few tips may help reduce the aggravation.

Try to avoid flying on weekends or holidays when airport congestion is bad and flight cancellations and delays are most common. Avoid rush hours in the early mornings and evenings. Request your boarding pass when you make your reservation or take advantage of the new "ticketless" travel options offered by many airlines.

Don't check additional baggage; carry everything possible onto the plane. Ask your travel agent about legal limits and pack accordingly. Remove old airport destination tags and write your permanent business address and phone number at your destination on your luggage tag.

File claims for lost baggage before you leave the airport.

Know your legal rights. Contact the U.S. Department of Transportation's Office of Consumer Affairs (tel. 202-366-2220) for a copy of *Fly Rights: A Guide to Air Travel in the U.S.*

Resources for Budget Tickets

The cheapest tickets to Asia are sold by wholesalers who take advantage of special rates for group tours by purchasing large blocks of unsold seats. Once an airline concludes it can't sell all of its seats, **consolidators** are offered a whopping 20-40% commission to do the job. They then use most of the commission to offer clients reduced ticket prices.

The drawbacks are these companies rarely provide travel counseling, they keep you guessing about which airline they'll fly, tickets often carry penalties, and routings can be slow and byzantine. Try to get the cheapest ticket, on the best airline, with the fewest unnecessary stops. Consolidators sell tickets through student bureaus, independent travel agents, and travel clubs. In fact, you can buy consolidator tickets from almost everyone except the consolidators themselves and the airlines.

Roundtrip prices currently average US$500-600 from the U.S. West Coast cities to Tokyo, US$550/650 low season/high season to Hong Kong, and US$750-950 to Bangkok, Singapore, and Manila. East Coast departures add US$150-200. Current fares are advertised in the Sunday travel sections of major newspapers such as the *New York Times, Los Angeles Times,* and *San Francisco Chronicle-Examiner.* Advance planning is essential since the best deals often sell out months in advance.

The following penalties and restrictions may apply to consolidator tickets: Peak fares in effect June-Aug. mean an extra US$50-100; tickets purchased less than 90 days in advance are subject to an additional US$50-150; flight cancellations or changes before the ticket issue usually cost US$50; and cancellations within 30 days of departure or any time after the ticket has been issued cost you up to 25% of the fare.

Travel Clubs: These clearinghouses sell leftover space on airlines, cruises, and tours at a 15-50% discount. Many specialize in cruise discounts and all charge an annual membership fee of US$20-50. **Warning:** Most are honest, but some travel clubs are fraudulent scams. Proceed with caution.

Contact the following companies for more details: Cruise Line, tel. (800) 327-3021; Cruises Inc., tel. (800) 854-0500; Entertainment Travel, tel. (800) 445-4137; Great American Traveler, tel. (800) 548-2812; Privilege Card, tel. (800) 236-9732; Traveler's Advantage, tel. (800) 548-1116; Vacations To Go, tel. (800) 338-4962.

Couriers: Aside from working as a travel agent or hijacking a plane, the cheapest way to reach Southeast Asia is to carry urgent mail for a courier company. Anyone can do this, and it's perfectly legal—no drugs or guns are carried, just stock certificates and registered mail. However, you're generally limited to carry-on luggage, and length of stay averages two to four weeks.

The best source of accurate information on courier flights is an extremely helpful monthly newsletter from **Travel Unlimited,** P.O. Box 1058, Allston, MA 02134. Editor Tom Lantos charges US$25 for 12 monthly issues; a great deal since you'll save hundreds on your first flight, whether heading to Asia, Europe, or South America.

Standby Couriers: Absolutely the cheapest way to reach Thailand is as a standby courier. Call any of the courier companies listed in the chart "Courier Phone Numbers" and tell them you can replace passengers who cancel their reservations at the last moment. Courier companies welcome standby volunteers. Companies are legally allowed to confiscate the nonrefundable deposit paid by the client, in many cases the full value of the ticket.

Standby prices decline as the departure approaches. For example, a flight leaving in five days may be discounted only US$100-150, since the courier company has plenty of time to find a replacement. Flights departing in under two days force the company to offer ridiculous fares, such as US$100 roundtrip to Bangkok.

BY AIR FROM NORTH AMERICA

Planning Your Route

By now you've studied the historical, geographical, and cultural background of the country, decided where to go and your motivations for travel, decided what activities carry the strongest appeal, determined your allotted time and monetary limits, and formed a general itinerary for your adventure. You've taken care of legal documents, checked your health, surfed the Internet, and packed your bag. You've also learned about types of tickets, pitfalls, and cheaper travel options from couriers and consolidators.

One last task before purchasing a ticket and hopping on a plane is to plan your route. Of course, if time is limited, you can just fly directly to Bangkok. However, if you have extra time and are flexible about deadlines, you might visit a few other countries, whether starting from the United States, Australia, or Europe.

Americans can reach Thailand direct from the U.S. West Coast via the northern loop through Japan and Hong Kong, or across the South Pacific.

Northern Loop: The north Pacific loop includes optional stops in Japan, Korea, Taiwan, and Hong Kong before continuing into China or down to Bangkok. This one-way ticket—often on an airline such as Korean Air or China Air—costs under US$900 from budget travel agencies in San Francisco and Los Angeles.

South Pacific Loop: The southern loop includes stops in the South Pacific, New Zealand, and Australia before arriving in Bali and continuing up to Thailand. This ticket—often standby on various carriers—costs around US$1,200-1,400 to Bali from student agencies.

Roundtrip: Another popular and relatively inexpensive itinerary begins with the northern Pacific loop, travels through Thailand and Southeast Asia, routes across the South Pacific, then returns to the United States. This journey covers most of Asia for about US$2,000 in total airfare—a once-in-a-lifetime experience.

Major Airlines in North America

U.S. East Coast travelers can use the North American airlines listed below or a European airline such as Swissair (17 hours, change in Zurich) or Finnair (18 hours, change in Helsinki).

Northwest Airlines (NWA): Northwest Airlines has the most gateways to Bangkok, with flights from Los Angeles, San Francisco, Seattle, Chicago, Dallas, Detroit, Washington, D.C., and New York. The airline also offers the fastest flights with a stop and change of planes in Tokyo. Fares are identical to those of other major airlines.

AIRLINE TOLL-FREE NUMBERS

Cathay Pacific	(800) 233-2742
China Airlines	(800) 227-5118
Delta	(800) 241-4141
Finnair	(800) 950-5000
Garuda	(800) 342-7832
Japan	(800) 525-3663
KLM	(800) 347-7747
Malaysian	(800) 421-8641
Northwest	(800) 447-4747
Philippines	(800) 435-9725
Silk Air	(800) 745-5247
Singapore	(800) 742-3333
Swiss Air	(800) 221-4750
Thai	(800) 426-5204
United	(800) 538-2929

lines. Daily service from Toronto via Detroit or Los Angeles costs US$1,566.

United Airlines (UA): United Airlines flies daily to Bangkok from Canada (Toronto and Vancouver) and from major U.S. cities via Tokyo, Taipei, or Seoul. United offers low-priced promotional fares during the winter. Contact their travel division (tel. 800-328-6877) for information on organized tours.

Canadian Airlines International (CP): Canadian Airlines flies daily from Toronto and Montreal via Vancouver to Bangkok. Promotional fares are available during the winter months, but rates on U.S. carriers departing from the United States are generally much lower.

Asian Airlines

Asian carriers are considered some of the finest in the world in terms of safety records, service, and food.

Thai Airways International (THAI): THAI flies daily from Los Angeles, three times weekly from Seattle, and twice weekly from Toronto. All flights stop in either Tokyo or Taipei; the fastest route is Los Angeles to Bangkok via Seoul.

THAI's frequent flyer program shares benefits with the Mileage Plus Program from United Airlines. Members of either program can now accrue miles and redeem awards on a reciprocal basis. THAI also sells package tours that include transportation, accommodations, and sightseeing.

On the downside, THAI has problems with overbooked flights during the busy holiday season Dec.-Feb. when the airline may bump passengers, delay flights, and change schedules without prior notification.

Other Airlines: Singapore Airlines, Malaysian Airlines, Philippine Airlines, Korean Air, China Air, Japan Airlines, Cathay Pacific, and other Asian-based airlines offer super-APEX flights from U.S. West Coast cities to Bangkok for US$900-1100.

Budget Travel Agencies in North America

Some of the best advice on airline ticketing can be found at agencies which specialize in the youth and student markets.

Student Travel Australia: STA serves not only students and youths, but also nonstudents and tour groups. In the United States call (800) 777-0112 for the nearest office.

Hostelling International (HI): The former International Youth Hostel Federation (IYH) and their associated American Youth Hostels (AYH) provide budget travel information and confirmed reservations at any of almost 200 hostels in the U.S. and abroad. HI-AYH, 733 15th St. NW, Suite 840, Washington, D.C. 20005, tel. (202) 783-6161.

Air Brokers International: A dependable discount agency with many years of experience in the Asian market. Air Brokers sells discount tickets and can help with circle-Pacific and round-the-world airfares. Air Brokers International, 323 Geary St., Suite 411, San Francisco, CA 94102, tel. (800) 883-3273, fax (415) 397-4767.

Council Travel: This excellent travel organization, a division of the Council on International Educational Exchange, has 37 offices in the U.S. and representatives in Europe and Australia. Prices are low and service reliable since they deal only with reputable airlines to minimize travel problems. Best of all, Council Travel sales agents are experienced travelers who often have firsthand knowledge of Southeast Asia.

Council Travel also sells the Youth Hostel Association Card, International Student Identity Card (ISIC), Youth International Educational Exchange Card (for nonstudents under 26), plus travel and health insurance. Larger offices in some major cities include: San Francisco, tel. (415) 421-3473;

Los Angeles, tel. (213) 208-3551; Seattle, tel. (206) 632-2448; Chicago, tel. (312) 951-0585; Boston, tel. (617) 266-1926; New York, tel. (212) 661-1450.

AIRPORT ARRIVAL

Bangkok International Airport

Bangkok's Don Muang International Airport, 25 km north of the city, is a busy, modern place with all the standard facilities.

After arrival, you first pass through immigration control to have your visa stamped or to obtain a 30-day Permit to Stay, which is stamped on your immigration card, not in your passport. Custom formalities is fastest through the green lanes marked "Nothing to Declare."

Passengers connecting directly to domestic flights to Chiang Mai, Phuket, Ko Samui, and Hat Yai can take the free shuttle bus to the domestic terminal.

After immigration and customs, you enter the arrival lounge filled with irritating taxi touts who direct you toward expensive private coaches and limousines; give these guys a miss unless you want to pay double the ordinary rate.

The arrival lounge has a post office, left-luggage facilities that charge 20B per day per item, an emergency medical clinic staffed 24 hours a day, and international and local phones. Two restaurants, including an inexpensive self-service cafe and a deluxe joint, are located on the fourth floor. Baggage trolleys are free.

Tourist Office: First stop should be the Tourism Authority of Thailand counter for maps, weekly magazines, and other free information. Current prices for transportation into town are posted here.

Thai Hotel Association: Hotel reservations at member hotels can be made at the adjacent THA counter. They also will call and check on room vacancies, but the cheapest listing (the Miami Hotel) starts at 800B per night.

Airport Bank: While some airports in Asia offer poor exchange rates, rates are very good at the Thai Military Bank inside the arrival lounge.

Taxi into Bangkok

Bangkok's hotels are 30-90 minutes from the airport, depending on traffic. A variety of transportation is available, but ordinary taxis and minibuses are the most popular choices.

Metered taxis are the best option for groups of travelers and solo travelers who want to quickly reach their hotel. A few private taxi companies have offices inside the arrival terminal, but these services are more expensive than the ordinary metered taxis outside.

Finding the taxi booth outside is somewhat tricky since there are few signs pointing the way. Go out the front door then walk left about 100 meters until you see the taxi booth on the sidewalk. You pick up a ticket from one of the girls working the counter and then give this ticket to the next available taxi driver. This coupon system is intended to discourage cheating by the taxi drivers.

When you get in your taxi, be sure the driver turns on his meter. Your fare will be the meter total, plus another 50B airport surcharge, plus whatever tolls are collected on the way. It's best to pay your toll directly rather than let the driver pay for you.

Some hotels only require that you drive on a single tollway, while more distant hotels, such as those near Silom Road, require travel on two tollways. As of this writing, each tollway costs 30B and the average taxi fare is 200-300B. To reach a Silom Road hotel such as the Oriental would therefore cost 250B taxi fare, plus 50B airport surcharge, plus 60B for two tollways, giving a total of 360B to this particular hotel.

Taxi from Bangkok to the Airport

Metered taxis to the airport cost 250-350B including tollway surcharges and take 30-90 minutes depending on traffic. Excess *baht* can be re-exchanged into foreign currency at the Thai Military Bank, and last-minute international phone calls can be made from the phone booth in the arrival lounge. The fourth floor features an inexpensive food mall and a semiluxurious restaurant operated by Thai International.

Airport departure tax is 500B for international flights and 100B for domestic flights.

Airport Bus

Several years ago, the Bangkok Mass Transit Authority (BMTA) started running three buses from the airport to various neighborhoods in Bangkok. The fare is 70B per passenger.

The airport bus counter is about 200 meters to the left of the arrival lounge. Walk out the door then turn left and walk past the taxi counter to the bus area. Ignore all touts.

Airport Bus A1: This bus heads down the tollway and exits near Victory Monument and then continues down Rajadamri Road to Lumpini Park and Silom Road. This bus reaches the hotels near Pratunam (Indra Regent, Baiyoke Tower, Amari Watergate), Siam Square (Le Meridien President, Grand Hyatt Erawan, Siam Intercontinental, Novotel Siam Square, The Regent), and finally the hotels near Silom Road (Dusit Thani, Pan Pacific, Tawana Ramada, Holiday Inn Crowne Plaza, Oriental, Shangri-La). It can also drop you fairly close to the Malaysia Hotel and guesthouses near Soi Ngam Duphli.

Airport Bus A2: This is the bus for guesthouses and hotels in Banglampoo and along Khao San Road. The bus takes the Don Muang Expressway to Victory Monument to Payathai and Petchaburi roads before heading past Democracy Monument to Banglampoo, where it stops at Tanao Road and drops off all the backpackers heading for Khao San Road. The bus then continues around Banglampoo and terminates at Sanam Luang near the Grand Palace.

Airport Bus A3: This is the bus for hotels on Sukumvit Road. After taking the first expressway to the Din Daeng exit, the bus gets on a second expressway until it makes another exit right at Sukumvit Road. The bus continues down Sukumvit past Soi Asoke (Sukumvit Soi 23) to Ekamai (Soi 53) until it reaches the Eastern Bus Terminal and finally terminates at the Tonglor Police Station.

GETTING AROUND

BY AIR

Thai Airways International

Domestic flights are chiefly provided by Thai Airways International (THAI) which merged with the domestic carrier, Thai Airways Company, several years ago. The consolidation benefits international travelers, who can now purchase all necessary tickets in one package to ensure a worry-free trip with guaranteed connections and seats.

Thailand's Civil Aviation Board has approved the start of two new airlines—Bangkok Airways and Orient Express Air—a decision that effectively breaks the monopoly enjoyed by flag carrier Thai International, 92% of which is owned by the Finance Ministry (no wonder it took so long). The new airlines are permitted to operate on the same routes as Thai, including international and domestic routes. Bangkok Airways has been up and running for several years, but Orient Express is still seeking funding and may never come into existence.

THAI serves 23 domestic airports and several nearby countries with a variety of aircraft, including Airbus 300s and Boeing 737s to larger destinations, and Avro 748s and Shorts 330s to smaller airports. Fares on routes served by both large and small craft will be higher with the larger planes.

Internal flights are fairly expensive when compared to rail or bus travel, but are recommended for those routes not served by train or only reached by long and grinding bus journeys. For example, the flight from Chiang Mai to Mae Hong Song takes only 30 minutes and costs 380B; the bone-crushing bus ride takes at least 12 hours and costs 140B. Another recommended flight is from Ubon Ratchathani to Phuket, a three-hour flight instead of two days of hard travel by bus and train. The 90-minute flight from Chiang Mai to Phuket is also a godsend.

THAI Air Passes: Thai Airways sells a Discover Thailand Air Pass for US$240 that includes four coupons good for four flights anywhere in the country. Additional coupons up to a total of eight can be purchased for an additional US$50 each. The first leg must start in Bangkok and sectors cannot be repeated. Full payment and reservation for the first sector must be made outside Thailand prior to arrival in the country. The air pass is sold at all Thai Airways offices outside the country.

The ticket is only worthwhile for carefully planned journeys that involve travel from the far north to the deep south. The limitation on sector repeats also makes it difficult to maximize any possible savings.

Bangkok Airways

Bangkok Airways, Thailand's only domestic airline, launched service in 1991 after the Ministry of Transportation decreed that private carriers could operate on routes not served from Bangkok by Thai Airways. Bangkok Airways was formed to take advantage of lower overhead, which allows the airline to turn a profit even on less profitable routes to smaller destinations within Thailand.

Thai Airways seems to tolerate the competition but also may be attempting to steal away any profitable routes with their subsidiary airlines. In 1995, THAI announced plans to pull their Cambodia International Airlines out of Cambodia and rename the airline Orient Express Air. The first planned route was from Chiang Mai to cities in northeastern Thailand, though as of this writing the airline has never flown a single route. Coincidentally, Bangkok Airways' most profitable route has reportedly been their service from Bangkok to Phnom Penh in Cambodia.

The primary route of Bangkok Airways is from Bangkok to Ko Samui. Additional destinations from Bangkok include Phuket via Ko Samui and Chiang Mai via Sukothai. Flights also run between Ko Samui and Phuket—a useful connection for serious island hoppers.

Sukothai is intended to be a primary airport stop for many Bangkok Airways flights. Destinations planned include Sukothai to Chiang Rai, Udon Thani, Kunming in southern China, and Mandalay in Myanmar. From Ko Samui, they plan to offer flights to Hua Hin, U-Tapao near

Pattaya, Hat Yai in the south, and Medan in Sumatra. Anticipated flights from Bangkok include Loei, Krabi, and Ranong.

Bangkok Airways also provides international service from Bangkok to Phnom Penh and Siem Reap.

Bangkok Airways' head office (tel. 02-229-3434, fax 02-229-3450) is located in Queen Sirikit National Convention Centre, New Ratchadaphisek Rd., Klong Toey, Bangkok 10110. Bangkok Airways branch offices are located in Hua Hin, Pattaya, Phuket, and Ko Samui near the boat landing.

BY TRAIN

Trains are the best form of transportation when leaving Bangkok. Operated by the State Railway of Thailand (SRT), trains are clean and comfortable, fares are inexpensive, and there is no more pleasant or scenic way to enjoy the countryside. Much safer than buses, trains provide an excellent way to meet other travelers and the Thai people.

Train service is normally quite punctual, and many of the coaches have attached restaurant cars where you order a meal and enjoy a drink before slipping back into your a/c sleeping berth.

Perhaps the chief advantage is that train rides get you off the crowded highways and carry you through countryside unblemished by factories, housing tracts, and other signs of progress. Unlike a bus where you are pinned to your seat, you can wander around the coach or throw open the window to enjoy the passing views.

Hualampong Train Station: Bangkok has two train stations. Hualampong, tel. (02) 223-7010, on Rama IV Rd. is the main station from where most trains arrive and depart.

Bangkok Noi Train Station: This station, tel. (02) 411-3102, on Arun Amarin Rd. in Thonburi, is used by local trains to Hua Hin and Kanchanaburi.

Schedules: Train schedules are available free of charge from the Rail Travel Aids counter in Bangkok's Hualampong station—handy resources for anyone riding the trains in Thailand.

Several types of schedules are available. The condensed English-language timetables include fares and schedules for selected trains on the four primary trunk lines. Condensed Thai-language schedules also are available, as are unabridged Thai-language timetables that include fares and schedules for all trains on all lines.

To obtain further information, contact the Hualampong Information Counter at (02) 223-7010 or (02) 223-7020.

Advance Bookings: Train reservations can be made 90 days in advance at Bangkok's Hualampong train station. Be sure to reserve a seat at least one week in advance during holidays, during weekends, and on popular routes such as Bangkok to Chiang Mai or Hat Yai.

Reservations can be made Mon.-Fri. 0830-1600 and weekends and holidays 0830-noon at the Advance Booking Office (tel. 02-223-3762 or 02-223-7788) in the back-right corner of Hualampong station. Ticket windows on the left side of the station are for same-day purchases. To make a reservation, take a queue number and wait for your number to appear on one of the electronic boards, then report to the proper desk for your particular line—southern or north and northeastern.

Travel Agencies: Reservations can also be made through travel agencies in Bangkok. Authorized agents who can make reservations and deliver tickets without a service charge are listed in the preceding section on Tours. All other agencies will generally charge around 200-400B to collect the ticket.

Rail Routes

There are four main train routes in Thailand, along with a few minor side extensions kept open to serve local villagers. Bangkok is the hub for the rail system, which radiates off to the major regions within the country.

Northern Line: This line starts at the Hualampong train station in Bangkok and passes through Ayuthaya, Lopburi, Nakhon Sawan, Phitsanulok, Uttaradit, and Lampang before terminating in Chiang Mai. A spur from Den Chai, a town between Uttaradit and Lampang, up to Chiang Rai is under construction and planned for completion in 1997.

Northeastern Line: This service also begins at Hualampong train station in Bangkok, then heads up to Ayuthaya and Saraburi before reaching the junction at Kaeng Khoi, where it splits into two separate lines. One spur continues to Nakhon Ratchasima (Korat), then goes due east to Buriram, Surin, Sisaket, and Ubon Ratchathani near the Laotian border. The other spur detours north to Khon Kaen and Udon Thani until it ends at Nong Khai on the banks of the Mekong and just opposite Laos.

Eastern Line: The rarely used line leaves Bangkok for Chachoengsao and Prachinburi before terminating at Aranyaprathet on the Cambodian border. Discussions have taken place about reopening the line from Aranyaprathet to Poipet, Battambang, and Phnom Penh in Cambodia, but no one expects much action for the next few years. However, buses now go from Aranyaprathet to Siem Reap, so this train route may gain some popularity in the near future as tourism increases to Cambodia.

Southern Line: This immensely popular line also leaves from Hualampong train station and first heads west to Nakhon Pathom before changing directions and heading south to Petchburi, Hau Hin, Prachuap Khiri Khan, Chumphon, Surat Thani, Phattalung, and Hat Yai. The southern line splits at Hat Yai, one spur going through Yala to Sungai Golok on the border with the east coast of Malaysia, the other continuing due south to Padang Besar on the western border of peninsular Malaysia. This is the train route which continues south to Kuala Lumpur and Singapore.

Probably the most useful spur is the route from Nakhon Pathom through Kanchanaburi to Nam Tok in the direction of Three Pagodas Pass and the Burmese border. Tourists often board the train in Kanchanaburi and ride the rolling coaches along the former "Death Railway," immortalized in the film *The Bridge on the River Kwai*. The State Railways of Thailand has discussed renovating the rail line from Nam Tok to the Burmese border to encourage tourism and, more importantly, complete the rail link from Bangkok to Yangon.

A second spur with great potential is the line from Phumpin near Surat Thani, to Khiri Rattanikhom near Chieo Lan reservoir. The SRT has discussed extending this line down to Phuket, thereby providing direct rail connections between Bangkok and Thailand's most popular resort island.

An extension from Bangkok to Pattaya opened several years ago to provide an alternative to the congested highway that connects the capital with the beach community. The line has been underutilized and service may be discontinued in the near future. Another side route connects Thung Song, near Nakhon Si Thammarat in southern Thailand, with Trang and Kantang on the west coast of peninsular Thailand.

Train Types

Three different types of train are operated by the State Railways of Thailand. Note that the comfort zone of each type of train varies widely depending on whether you are traveling in first, second, or third class compartments.

Ordinary Trains: Diesel railcars and ordinary trains offer the cheapest fares and most basic services but also stop at every single station and town along the way. Languishing ordinary trains are rolling bargains but very, very slow—best avoided except on short journeys during the day.

Rapid Trains: Rapid trains *(rot raew)* haul only second- and third-class cars. Rapids provide better cabins and are slightly faster than ordinary trains since they aren't required to stop at every possible town. Rapid trains, however, are hardly "rapid" since they do stop at approximately every second or third town, a tiring ritual on longer journeys. The chief advantage to rapid trains is experienced on long overnight journeys—having a sleeper makes the trip relatively inexpensive, comfortable, and tolerable since you sleep through most of it.

Express Trains: Express trains *(rot duan)* haul only second- and first-class cars. Express service is faster than rapid; trains only stop at major destinations and can therefore pick up some serious speed between stations. The fastest express services are dubbed special express trains *(rot duan phiset)*.

Train Classes

Trains are divided into three classes that vary in terms of comfort and amenities depending on the type of train. Not all classes are available on all types of trains. For example, ordinary trains often haul only third-class coaches, while first-class coaches exclusively are generally hooked to express and special express trains. Train fares and schedules are listed in the back of this book.

Third Class: Third-class seats are quite cheap but can only be recommended on shorter journeys of under three or four hours. Most coaches have two rows of facing wooden benches designed for three passengers. The padded third-class seats on rapid trains are almost tolerable on longer trips. All seats are nonreserved and coaches are often packed to the gunwales. Sleeping space is on the floor with discarded peanut shells and abandoned bottles of Mekong. Third class costs about the same as an ordinary bus.

Second Class: Depending on the type of train, second class offers a choice of padded seats that often recline enough for sleeping, a/c carriages fitted with individualized reclining seats, and fan-cooled sleepers recommended for overnight travel.

Regular coach cars become sleeping compartments when ordinary seats are folded down into bunk beds by the train attendants. The clever transformation takes place shortly after dinner has been cleared and the bills settled by the porters. Sleeping berths are quite comfortable, with clean sheets; sliding curtains provide a degree of privacy. Choose lower berths if possible since they have more legroom and are removed from the bright ceiling lights that shine throughout the night.

Second class costs about twice third class, or the equivalent of a private bus with air-conditioning. Second-class trains with sleepers are more expensive than night buses, but are far safer and infinitely more comfortable—the best way to cover long distances at a reasonable cost with minimal discomfort.

First Class: Traveling first class guarantees a private compartment with individually controlled air-conditioning, an electric fan, fold-down washbasins with mirror and towels, and either one or two berths that convert into sleepers. First-class coaches are only available on express and special express trains. First-class rail travel is a delightful experience that costs double the second-class fare or about the same as airfare.

Supplemental Charges

Supplementary charges are placed on all trains except diesels and ordinary services. To compute the total cost, you must add the supplemental charges for superior types of train (rapid,

express, special express), charges for a/c, and various charges for sleeping berths. For example, a lower sleeping berth in second class with a/c on an express train costs the basic fare, plus extra charges for express service (60B), sleeper (220B), and a/c (70-120B).

Other supplemental charges include:

• rapid trains	40B
• express trains	60B
• special express trains	80B
• a/c (with catering)	120B
• a/c (no catering)	70B
• sleeper (2nd fan upper)	100-130B
• sleeper (2nd fan lower)	150-200B
• sleeper (2nd a/c upper)	220B
• sleeper (2nd a/c lower)	270B
• sleeper (1st a/c cabin)	520B
• Malaysia crossing (express)	200B
• Malaysia crossing (all a/c trains)	250B

Timetables

Train schedules are available free of charge from the Rail Travel Aids counter in Bangkok's Hualampong station—handy resources for anyone riding the trains in Thailand.

Several types of schedules are available. The condensed English-language timetables include fares and schedules for selected trains on the four primary trunk lines. You can also obtain condensed Thai-language schedules, as well as unabridged Thai-language timetables that include fares and schedules for all trains on all lines.

English-language schedules come in two colors: red brochures with condensed timetables for the southern line, and green brochures that detail the northern, northeastern, and eastern lines. Rules on refunds, breaks in journeys, ticket alterations, and validity of return tickets are included with each brochure.

To obtain further information, contact the Hualampong Information Counter, tel. (02) 223-7010 or 223-7020.

Train Tips

Ticket Validity: Tickets are valid only for the date and train as specified on the ticket.

Ticket Expiration: Roundtrip tickets expire 30-60 days after the initial departure date depending on the length of journey.

Change of Departure Date: Passengers may change their journey to a later or earlier date for a fee of 10B. Departures can be postponed twice up to a total of seven days. Postponement must be made within three hours after departure.

Break of Journey: Passengers who break their journey are not entitled to refunds or further use of the ticket.

Refunds: Passengers may apply for refunds on unused tickets at the point of purchase not more than three hours after departure of the train. Cancellation fees vary 10-40% according to the time of notification and face value of the ticket.

Children's Fares: Children under three years of age can travel free provided they do not require separate seats. Children 3-12 years of age are accepted at half the adult fare.

Luggage Allowance: Passengers are allowed to carry personal luggage free of charge up to 30 kg in third class, 40 kg in second class, and 50 kg in first class.

Seat Selection: To avoid sunstroke, reserve or grab a seat on north-south lines on the side of the carriage away from the sun.

Cautions: Train travel is quite safe but you should not accept offers of free food or drink from strangers, since there is a chance of drugging and robbery. Beware of pickpockets and thieves; sleep with a money belt and padlock your gear to an immobile object such as a luggage rack.

Meals

Meal service is provided in dining cars attached to express trains and to passengers in their seats in second- and first-class coaches. Prices are reasonable and the quality of the Thai fare is fairly high, but some Western dishes, such as breakfast items, are less than inspiring. Vendors also walk the aisles hawking soft drinks, beer, Thai whiskey, and comic books loaned for a small rental fee. Passengers can bring along their own meals and drinks.

Be wary of train staff and independent entrepreneurs handing out what appear to be complimentary face wipes or bags of peanuts. In most cases, the attendant will return later to collect fees from anyone who used the product. You should also confirm the price of meals before ordering and carefully check your bill for overcharges and lousy math.

Station Facilities

All train stations have baggage storage rooms that cost 10-20B per day depending on the size of the luggage. Most cloakrooms are open daily 0700-1800, longer hours in major stations.

All stations have a small cafe or kiosk selling basic food supplies and bottled water. The Bangkok station has a small post office, information booth in the center of the main floor, travel agency, advance-booking service in the rear, showers, and money-exchange facilities operated by the Bangkok Bank. The station in Hat Yai even has a hotel on the premises.

Thailand Rail Pass

Two types of *Visit Thailand Rail Passes* are available to holders of international passports at the Advance Booking Office in the Hualampong train station. Both passes can be used to make advance reservations or to take trains on the day of departure.

Blue Pass: The Blue Pass permits 20 days of unlimited second- and third-class travel for 1,100B adult, 550B children ages 4-12. Supplemental charges for superior trains and sleepers are *not* included.

Red Pass: The Red Pass allows 20 days of unlimited second- and third-class travel for 2,000B adult, 1,100B children ages 4-12. This pass includes all supplemental charges.

Both passes offer some degree of convenience but only provide significant savings for visitors doing a great deal of rail travel in the kingdom. The chief advantage will be realized by someone traveling from Bangkok to Chiang Mai, back to Bangkok and up to Nong Khai, then south to Ko Samui or Hat Yai in less than 20 days.

Advance Bookings

Train reservations can be made 90 days in advance at the Hualampong train station in Bangkok and at terminus train stations elsewhere in the country.

Reservations are essential during holidays, on weekends, and on popular routes such as Bangkok to Chiang Mai or Bangkok to Hat Yai. These busy seasons and routes should be booked at least one or two weeks prior to departure, especially if you intend to reserve a sleeping berth. Most trains to the northeast still have room even a few days in advance.

Roundtrip reservations do not guarantee a seat on the return journey. You should reserve your seat at the station upon arrival at your destination—an important consideration at the train stations in Chiang Mai and Surat Thani.

Reservations are impossible from most stations located midway on a trunk line, an inconvenience which limits you to third-class coaches from places such as Nakhon Ratchasima and Sukothai.

Booking Procedure: Reservations can be made Mon.-Fri. 0830-1600 and weekends and holidays 0830-1200 at the Advance Booking Office (tel. 02-223-3762 or 223-7788) in the back-right corner of Hualampong station. Ticket windows on the left side of the station are for same-day purchases. To make a reservation, take a queue number and wait for it to appear on one of the electronic boards, then report to the proper desk for your particular line—southern or north and northeastern.

Travel Agencies: Reservations can also be made through authorized travel agencies in Bangkok for an additional service charge of 50-100B. Be wary of unauthorized agencies that sometimes take the money but fail to deliver the tickets.

Special Excursions

The State Railways of Thailand offers a variety of organized excursions on weekends and holidays to popular tourist destinations such as national parks and historical monuments. A selection of the more popular programs would include Erawan National Park near Kanchanaburi (one day; 350B), the floating market at Damnern Saduak (one day; 380B), and Phimai Historical Park near Nakhon Ratchasima (two days; 1,600B).

The SRT also sells convenient transportation packages to Kanchanaburi and Ko Samui. The Ko Samui package includes your train from Bangkok to the Phumpin station, bus transportation to Surat Thani, and the boat ride across to Ko Samui—the easiest way to reach the island at minimal cost. These one-day excursions, weekend getaways, and special transportation packages can be booked through the Advance Booking Office at Hualampong train station in Bangkok.

GOVERNMENT BUS

Bus transport in Thailand is fast, clean, and reasonably comfortable on shorter journeys, and serves every settlement from big cities to small villages. In many cases, unless you have the luxury of private transportation, buses are the only way to reach a given locale.

Bus services are provided by the government and by a host of private companies; both offer regular and air-conditioned coaches. Superior types of buses provide reclining airline-style seats and video movies plus smiling hostesses who crank up the air-conditioning and serve icy drinks to their frozen customers.

Perhaps the best choice are buses operated by the government transport company called **Baw Kaw Saw** (BKS) or **Bor Kor Sor,** an abbreviation of Borisat Khon Song—"The Transportation Company."

The cheapest and slowest BKS buses are the orange ordinary buses *(rot mai thamada);* these cover every short route and reach every possible hamlet in the country. Each bus is staffed by a driver, fare collector, and optional attendant who yells "stop" and "go" to make sure all hand-wavers are picked up on the road.

Ordinary buses are fine for shorter journeys but are often packed beyond comprehension since drivers and attendants work on salary plus commission. This incentive program also inspires drivers to hang around the bus terminal for interminable periods in the hopes of finding a few more passengers.

Your best bet for bus transportation in Thailand are the air-conditioned government buses called either *rot air* (air bus), *rot prap akata* (special service bus), *rot mai duann* (express bus), or *rot tour* (tour bus). Whatever *rot* you ride, all will be fast and reasonably comfortable, and will often cost substantially less than private buses with similar amenities. Departures are less frequent than ordinary buses and not all towns are served, but whenever possible, a/c buses operated by the BKS generally offer the best combination of value and comfort.

On longer routes, Baw Kaw Saw also operates two or three superior versions of a/c buses. Regular a/c models *(chan song)* have about 44 seats that may be too tightly arranged for long-legged Westerners. First-class buses *(chan nung)* have the same number of seats but include toilets in the rear. VIP buses, a relatively new creation, have been altered to hold 34 seats instead of the standard 44 seats. This seating arrangement provides additional legroom for leggy *farangs*.

The latest word in spaciousness is the so-called "Super-VIP" bus or "sleeper" *(rot nawn),* which cuts the seat count down to just 24 passengers. Although more expensive, super-VIP coaches allow the seats to recline to near-horizontal positions.

Bus Terminals

Baw Kaw Saw terminals are located in every town in Thailand, often on the outskirts to minimize bus traffic zooming through the city center. BKS terminals in smaller towns are often located within walking distance of guesthouses and hotels; in larger cities you may require public transportation to reach the BKS terminal.

Air-conditioned and ordinary buses may depart from different terminals in the same city. In some cities, these terminals are adjacent to each other but elsewhere may be on opposite sides of town.

Departures and Tickets

Ordinary buses leave throughout the day without any apparent departure schedule. For short or medium-length journeys, simply show up at any hour and simply board the next available bus heading to your destination. Long-distance buses often depart in clusters in the early morning hours 0500-0900 and in the evenings 1700-2100.

Purchase tickets on the more popular routes a day in advance or, for evening departures, arrive by 1700 to locate the next available seat. Ordinary bus tickets are sold on the bus.

Few buses display their destination in Roman script, but Western travelers are invariably offered assistance from a concerned Thai. If not, check with the ticket office or repeat your intended destination to the bus driver or attendant.

Meals

Most overnight buses operated by the government and by privately owned companies stop for a complimentary meal in the middle of the night, often in the middle of nowhere at what appears to be a cafe owned by the second cousin of the bus driver.

Budget companies often stop at horrifically illuminated restaurants that serve little more than a bowl of vegetable soup or fried rice, while more expensive lines stop for buffet meals and seafood specialties cooked to surprisingly high standards.

In any event, hang onto your BKS bus ticket to provide proof of purchase to the restaurant crew.

PRIVATE BUS

Several dozen private bus companies provide services between most major tourist destinations such as Bangkok, Chiang Mai, Ko Samui, and Phuket. Smaller destinations, including Ko Samet, Ko Chang, and Krabi, are often served by minibuses rather than full-sized coaches.

As with superior BKS buses operated by the Thai government, privately owned bus companies allot reserved seats to their customers and provide a/c, blankets, pillows, snacks, drinks, and, more ominously, videos during the longer journeys. All buses are fitted with window curtains that allow you to ignore the outside world racing by at the speed of light.

Private companies operate several different types of bus priced according to the seat arrangement and levels of service. The most popular services are the VIP buses designed to hold 34 passengers instead of the standard 44 sardines, and "Super VIP" buses (sleepers) which reduce the count to just 24 seats.

Although more expensive, VIP and Super-VIP coaches provide essential legroom for tall *farangs* and, on the Super VIPs, permit seats to recline to near-horizontal positions.

Also note that private companies often misleadingly call their coaches "tour buses" and themselves "tour companies," although no tours are offered and real "tour buses" are identical to buses operated by the government.

Bookings

Tickets can be purchased through most hotels, guesthouses, and travel agencies, and from the head office of the bus company. Note that some budget agencies collect money, then fail to deliver the proper ticket; it's best to purchase tickets from a reputable company or directly from the bus office to avoid complications.

Selecting the Company

Recommending a particular bus company is difficult since companies rise and fall with the seasons, and the quality of service is unpredictable. All bus companies in Thailand are theoretically licensed by the government and required to depart from private bus terminals located adjacent to the Baw Kaw Saw terminal. Some do and some don't, but the private companies that do leave from government terminals are generally more dependable and honest than companies that hustle customers from guesthouses and hotels.

Although getting out to the Baw Kaw Saw terminal can be a hassle in larger cities—especially Bangkok—the reward is that you can choose from an economical government bus or a private bus that will probably be safer and less dishonest than freelance operators.

Safety

Safety, ah, safety. An entire book could be written on the wonders of bus travel in Thailand. Thais pay for speedy service and expect their bus drivers to reach the destination in record-breaking time, often fueled by prodigious amounts of amphetamines and a hell-bent-for-leather attitude.

Traffic accidents kill over 15,000 Thais per year, a chilling statistic recently put forth by the Land Transport Department, which also pointed out that traffic accidents are now the biggest killer of young people in the country. The Ministry of Public Health claims that half the deaths are the result of drunken driving.

Read the *Bangkok Post* for any length of time and you'll come across the classic story about the bus stewardess who serves all the passengers complimentary Cokes heavily laced with sleep-inducing drugs. After the riders have miraculously nodded off, the stewardess and bus driver calmly relieve the entire entourage of their wallets, jewelry, and cameras before hightailing it back to their provincial hideaway. Of course, one rider wisely declined the beverage, but then had to play dead while his pockets were rifled and his Rolex cut from his wrist.

What can you do to avoid making the obituary column of the *Bangkok Post?* First, never accept food or drink from strangers. Buses operated by Baw Kaw Saw tend to have less accidents than buses from private companies, and private buses

that depart from Baw Kaw Saw terminals tend to be safer than independent operators who depart from cafes and street corners.

Select a safe seat. Although seats at the front of the bus have additional legroom and guarantee great views out the front window, front-row passengers are also the first to die in head-on crashes.

Government or Private Bus?

Private buses on popular routes such as Bangkok-Chiang Mai will cost about the same as government buses, but services and meals will be probably be less comprehensive than those on government buses.

Most other routes served by private companies tend to be more expensive than government buses. For example, Bangkok-Surat Thani fares are 30-70% more expensive on private lines. Services are identical. One advantage could be that private companies often provide pickup from your hotel or guesthouse.

But pickup services are sporadic and undependable. You might wait an extra 30 minutes at your hotel, then be shuttled to some strange neighborhood where you're dumped in a cafe and told to wait for the main bus. Two hours later, another minibus shuttles you to another location where you're once again told to wait for the bus. When the bus finally arrives and accepts passengers, it leaves for another cafe to pick up three more travelers shuttled over from another part of town. At this point, the pickup service seems a twisted joke invented for torture rather than convenience.

The complimentary pickup service offered by private bus companies is often more stressful and a sheer waste of time; you're better off taking local transportation over to the government bus terminal.

GETTING AROUND TOWN

Bangkok is a hot, bewildering metropolis without any recognizable city center—a place where only the certified insane attempt to walk any great distance. Aside from roaming the neighborhood near your hotel, a taxi, *tuk tuk,* or bus will be necessary. The good news is that public transportation is very cheap; the bad news is that traffic and air pollution are among the world's worst. Avoid rush hours, 0800-1000 and 1500-1800, when the entire city comes to a complete standstill.

Taxis

In 1993, the Thai government passed a law requiring all taxis in Bangkok to install and use meters. In one bold move, the government finally ended one of Thailand's longest nightmares. No more haggling with drivers over the proper fare. No more bailing out of cabs after the driver suddenly doubles the fare en route to your destination. No more bizarre, late-night, completely baffling routes on a short journey that winds up taking over an hour.

Meter Rates: Metered taxis charge 35B at the outset for the first two km, and 2B for each extra kilometer. Freeway tolls must also be paid by the passenger. Bangkok—the Gridlock Capital of the World—protects the cabdriver by including a surcharge of 1B per minute when the traffic slows to under 5 kph. When you're stuck at a traffic light for 20 minutes or crawling down Sukumvit Road at a speed slower than the average pedestrian (most people *walk* at 5 kph), expect surcharges, then try to relax.

Metered taxis can be ordered by calling (02) 319-9911 24 hours a day.

Taxi Types: Any taxi with the sign "Taxi Meter" will have an installed meter, but the level of service varies between companies. The green-and-yellow taxis are driven by the owners and generally tend to be cleaner and driven with more care. Pink, blue, or red taxis are rented from various cooperatives and drivers seem to have less regard for the value of human life or the general appearance of their vehicle. Taxis with signs proclaiming "Taxi Taxi" are hoping that confused tourists will mistake them for a metered taxi. Taxis with black and white license plates are illegal; these often overcharge passengers and intimidate tourists with thinly veiled threats.

Problems: A few problems exist with the new system. Some drivers refuse to use meters and will only take passengers at set fares. Other drivers shut down their meters during long traffic jams, then attempt to negotiate a fixed fare. Meters are sometimes altered to run at higher speeds, or the driver forgets to reset the meter for the new passenger. You should always check the meter before setting off and refuse to pay any additional surcharges during the journey.

Tuk Tuks

Affectionately named after their obnoxious sounds that resemble chainsaws on acid, these motorized *samlors* are noisy three-wheelers that race around at terrifying speeds, take corners on two wheels, and scream through seemingly impossible gaps. *Tuk tuks* are the cheapest form of private transportation in Bangkok and generally cost 10-20% less than taxis. However, you must bargain hard and settle all fares in advance. Few drivers speak English or understand maps, so be sure to have your destination written down in Thai or know how to pronounce it properly.

Negotiation is usually done by raising a few fingers to indicate your offer: two for 20B, three for 30. Smile and grin during price negotiation. If the driver won't come down to a reasonable price then do the taxi ballet—walk away shaking your head until he pulls up and waves you inside. Then hold onto your seat.

Buses

The public bus system in Bangkok is operated by the Bangkok Metropolitan Transit Authority (BMTA). Several private bus companies also operate in the city.

Two maps with reasonably complete bus routes include the *Bangkok Bus Map* published by Bangkok Guide, and *Bangkok Thailand Tour 'n' Guide Map* by Thaveephol Charoen. The *Bangkok & Central Thailand Travel Map* from Periplus Editions also includes a fairly good summary of the bus routes.

Before setting off, study your bus map and write down all possible bus numbers that go to your destination. Service is haphazard and some buses only pass once per hour.

Hours: Ordinary buses run daily 0500-midnight. Visitors unfamiliar with the bus system will find taxis more useful at night. Buses are quite sensible during rush hours when they speed along specially marked lanes.

Types: BMTA buses come in three colors. Light blue-and-white buses have no fan or air conditioning; these are being phased out. Red-and-cream buses have rotating fans to cool off passengers. Dark blue-and-white buses are air-conditioned coaches that can prove surprisingly comfortable.

Fares: Light blue-and-white buses charge 3B for journeys under 10 km and 4B for journeys over 10 km. Red-and-cream buses cost 3.5B for the first 10 km and 5B for longer journeys. The a/c dark blue-and-white buses charge 6B for the first 8 km and up to 16B for the longest distances, such as from the airport to Banglampoo.

The dark-blue a/c buses are relatively plentiful and worth every single extra *baht* over the crowded and hot non-a/c buses.

Minibuses

The BMTA also operates orange and green minibuses that race around town on unpublished routes. Unless you are positive about the destination, avoid these minibuses. Many have the same numbers as the larger buses but go to completely different sections of town.

The latest addition are red-and-gray air-conditioned "microbuses" that guarantee seats for every passenger and provide amenities such as newspapers, video programs, and mobile phones. Microbuses cost 15B and payment must be with exact change, a coupon, or a "smart card." There are 35 routes. All buses display the beginning point and terminus (Bang Khun Thien-Samrong, Siam Park-Silom, for example), but few visitors will be able to use these buses effectively until a route map is published.

BUS SERVICE FROM BANGKOK

DESTINATION	KM	HOURS	ORDINARY	A/C	VIP
EAST COAST					
Pattaya	136	2	35B	65B	80B
Chantaburi	240	6	50	100	140
Trat	320	8	80	150	200
NORTH					
Ayuthaya	75	1.5	25B	36B	50B
Phitsanulok	365	5.5	95	165	240
Lampang	610	9.5	150	270	330
Nan	680	11	170	290	340
Chiang Mai	715	10	160	300	480
Chiang Rai	850	12	190	360	530
NORTHEAST					
Korat	250	5	65B	120B	200B
Khon Kaen	445	7	110	200	300
Nong Khai	615	9	150	280	420
Ubon Ratchathani	679	10	160	300	440
SOUTH					
Kanchanaburi	100	2	25B	50B	60B
Hua Hin	205	4	70	100	130
Surat Thani	670	11	160	285	360
Trang	865	14	195	370	400
Krabi	870	14	195	380	420
Phuket	890	14	200	380	450
Hat Yai	990	16	240	430	500

Skytrain

After almost a decade of construction, Bangkok's newest form of public transportation finally opened to the public in December 1999, to honor the 72nd birthday of the present king.

Bangkok officials began serious talks about mass transit for the badly congested Thai capital in the 1980s, and early plans called for four privately built, elevated systems that were to crisscross the city but not connect to each other. One of the four systems was to be a "skytrain" built by Canada's SNC-Lavalin, but it fell into political quicksand in the early part of this decade as did two other projects. The existing Skytrain is a US$1.2 billion elevated mass transit train system constructed by Tanayong Co. Ltd. and the Bangkok Mass Transit System Corp.

The 23.5 km elevated train system consists of 35 three-carriage trains which ply the tracks daily from 0600 until midnight on two lines. The Sukumvit Line is 16.5 km long, running from Mor Chit Bus Terminal on Phahon Yothin Road to the end of Sukumvit at Sukumvit 77. It has 17 stations.

The other, the Silom Line with seven stations, starts from Sathorn Bridge and heads up Silom, Rajadamri, and Rama I Roads to the National Stadium. The two lines intersect at the Central Station at Siam Square on Rama I.

A few routes seem quite logical for the average visitor, such as starting on Silom Road and then transferring to Sukumvit Line to head out to the shopping and entertainment venues along Sukumvit. You could also continue along the Sukumvit Line to the Eastern Bus Terminal for bus connections to Pattaya and other destinations along the East Coast. The Skytrain will also prove useful for reaching the Weekend Market and the major shopping centers near Siam Square.

Riverboats

The **Chao Phaya Express Boat** is hands-down the best way to move between any locations on the river—especially useful between Banglampoo and the General Post Office. These open-air boats are fast, cheap, exciting, and a refreshing escape from the horrors of land transportation. Boats operate daily 0600-1800 and charge 3-15B depending on the distance.

Two other types of boats work the Chao Praya River. Short and stubby ferries called *reua kham fak* shuttle across the river. These cross-river barges charge 1B per crossing.

The other boats are noisy longtails called *hang yaos,* which roar along several canals in central Bangkok and charge 5-15B depending on their final destination. The longtail service on Pratunam Canal from Pratunam Market to Democracy Monument is quite useful.

TOURS

Budget Travel Agents

Bangkok has hundreds of budget and full-service travel agencies offering everything from nightclub tours to excursions to

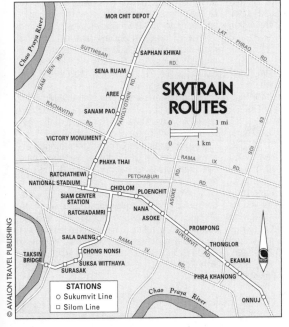

Angkor Wat. Most hotels have attached agencies, but check prices carefully before handing over your money. Rates vary widely around town. For example, a one-day tour of the Damnern Saduak floating market costs 700B from travel agents on Silom Road, but only 300B from discount shops in Banglampoo.

Travelers also should be aware that agencies often fail to deliver the proper ticket or make extravagant promises simply to make the sale. Double check all restrictions and limitations before making any sizable purchase. A few of the larger and more trustworthy travel agencies are listed below.

Student Travel Australia (STA), the world's largest student travel organization, is somewhat more expensive than bucket shops, but you won't need to worry about fraudulent activities. The Head Office is in the Wall Street Tower, 33 Surawong Rd., tel. (02) 233-2633; STA also has an office in Banglampoo: Thai Hotel, 78 Prachatipatai Rd., tel. (02) 281-5314.

ETC Travel is an agency recommended by readers. They staff the following offices: Head Office, Royal Hotel, 2 Rajadamnern Ave., tel. (02) 224-0023; Banglampoo, 180 Khao San Rd., tel. (02) 249-4414; Malaysia Hotel, 5/3 Soi Ngam Duphli, tel. (02) 356-7781.

Other Travel Agencies

Fully escorted tour packages to Vietnam, Cambodia, and Laos can be booked through the following agencies: Diethelm Travels, 140 Wireless Rd., tel. (02) 255-9150, fax (02) 256-0248; Exotissimo Travel, 21/17 Soi 4 Sukumvit, tel. (02) 253-5250, fax (02) 254-7683; SEA Tours, Siam Centre, Rama 1 Rd., Suite 414, tel. (02) 251-4862, fax (02) 253-2960; World Travel, 1053 Charoen Krung Rd., tel. (02) 233-5900, fax (02) 236-7169.

Most travel agencies will also make train reservations and pick up the tickets for you for an additional 100B surcharge. The following four agencies are licensed to make bookings and issue tickets without the surcharge: Airland Travels, 866 Ploenchit Rd., tel. (02) 251-9495; SEA Tours, Siam Centre, Rama 1 Rd., Suite 414, tel. (02) 251-4862; Songserm Travel, 172 Khao San Rd., tel. (02) 282-8080; Songserm Travel, 121 Soi Chalerm, Phayathai Rd., tel. (02) 255-8790; Viang Travels, Viengtai Hotel, 42 Rambutri Rd., tel. (02) 280-1385.

Educational Tours

Travel agents sell the standard assortment of Thailand tours, but many visitors prefer the educational tours sponsored by public and private organizations in Bangkok. Led by archaeologists, art historians, and other experts in their fields, these well-priced tours are highly recommended for all visitors.

Siam Society: Bangkok's leading private cultural organization sponsors monthly group tours to important historical and archaeological sites in Thailand. They also take groups to major festivals and conduct environmental surveys in national parks through their natural history section. Upcoming tours in Thailand and to Myanmar, Angkor, and China are listed in the *Bangkok Post.* For further information, call the Siam Society office in Bangkok or write and request a copy of their monthly newsletter, which lists upcoming lectures and group tours. Yearly membership at 1,500B includes access to their 20,000-volume library, subscriptions to the *Siam Society Newsletter* and *Journal of the Siam Society,* free admission to most lectures, and discounts on Society books and study trips. Siam Society, 131 Sukumvit 21, Soi Asoke (Soi 21), Bangkok 10110, tel. (02) 258-3491 or (02) 258-3494.

National Museum: The National Museum occasionally sponsors tours similar to the Siam Society's. Check the bulletin board in the museum ticket office for upcoming tours.

Volunteer Guide Group: Unique and personalized tours of Bangkok temples, plus overnight visits to nearby villagers, can be arranged through a small student-run group in Bangkok. Each visitor is accompanied by a student guide who will explain local customs and traditions. Public transportation is used and the tour is free except for a membership fee of 100B and travel expenses for your guide. Volunteer Guide Group, Box 24-1013, Ramkamheng Rd., Bangkok 10241.

BANGKOK SIGHTS
INTRODUCTION

Thailand's sprawling, dynamic, and frustrating capital offers more variety, sights, and wonders than any other destination in Asia. Far too many visitors, hearing of the horrendous traffic jams and searing pollution, stop only long enough to glimpse a few temples and pick up a cheap air ticket before departing for more idyllic environs. To some degree this is understandable. Packed into these sweltering plains of the lower Chao Praya River are some 10 million residents, 80% of the country's automobiles, and most of the nation's commercial headquarters—a city strangled by uncontrolled development. Without any semblance of a city center or urban planning, traffic grinds to a standstill during rush hours and dissolves into a swamp after summer monsoons. Worse yet is the monotonous sprawl of Chinese shophouses and faceless concrete towers that more closely resemble a Western labyrinth than anything remotely Eastern. It's an unnerving place.

To appreciate the charms and fascinations of Bangkok, focus instead on the positive: dozens of magnificent temples that form one of

Asia's great spectacles, countless restaurants with superb yet inexpensive food, legendary nightlife to satisfy all possible tastes, excellent shopping, and some of the friendliest people in the world. Few enjoy the heat, humidity, or traffic jams, but with patience and a sense of *mai pen rai,* Bangkok will cast an irresistible spell.

History
Unless a Thai is condescending to foreign ignorance, he or she will never call the capital city Bangkok ("City of Wild Plums"), but Krung Thep, "City of Angels." Krung Thep actually begins the string of honorariums which comprise the official name, a mammoth tongue twister which, according to Guinness, forms the longest place-name in the world.

Bangkok sprang from a small village or *bang* filled with wild olive and plum trees called *kok.* At first little more than a trading suburb to Thonburi ("Money Town"), Bangkok rose to prominence after Burmese forces destroyed Ayuthaya in 1767 and General Taksin moved his armies south. Taksin soon went insane (claiming to be

REQUIEM FOR A CITY

Once known as the Venice of the East, modern Bangkok is a City in Crisis. Economic boom times have transformed the once-charming town into an environmental horror show where street-level pollution has long since passed international danger levels, waterways not filled with concrete are clogged with garbage, and rush-hour traffic grinds to a complete standstill. One out of five residents lives in illegal slums with no piped water or electricity. Residential pollution, the unregulated dumping of dangerous chemicals and fertilizers, and a complete lack of oxygen have killed the Chao Praya River. Each day, Bangkok produces 5,400 tons of garbage but only 4,200 tons are collected; the remainder is dumped on street corners or in the waterways. Construction of artesian wells and high-rise buildings on soft soil is sinking the low-lying city under sea level, a horrifying prospect that may become reality.

But it is the horrendous traffic that typifies what is most frightening in the City of Angels. Bangkok's traffic crisis—almost certainly the worst in the world—is the result of government inaction and unwillingness to make tough decisions. The problem is that most cities throughout the world use 20-25% of their surface area for streets, but in Bangkok it's only six percent. Additionally, the number of cars doubles about every seven years, but the area of road surface increases much more slowly. The gridwork of roads found in all other major international cities has never been constructed in Bangkok. Instead, city authorities have let Bangkok grow without any form of urban planning, allowing the self-interest of private investors to undermine the controlling force of government policy.

The result is world-class traffic jams. According to the Traffic Committee, the average speed during rush hours has dropped to under four km per hour; people *walk* at five km per hour. The remainder of the day, traffic moves at just seven km per hour. When Dr. Sumet Jumsai, the nation's foremost authority on architecture and urban planning, was asked about Bangkok, he said, "It's irreversible destruction. The city is dying."

the final Buddha) and was dispatched to Buddhist nirvana in time-honored fashion—a sharp blow to the back of the neck.

With General Taksin out of the way, Rama I, Taksin's chief military commander, was recalled from Cambodia to found the dynasty which rules to the present day. Fearing further Burmese attacks, Rama I moved the city across the river and relocated the Chinese merchants south to Sampeng, today's Chinatown. Bangkok was formally established on 21 April 1782, with the consecration of the city's foundation pillar at Lak Muang. Rama I constructed his capital to rival once-glorious Ayuthaya: palaces were erected with brick salvaged from Ayuthaya, temples were filled with Ayuthayan Buddhas, and concentric canals were dug to emulate the watery kingdom. The city was then renamed Krung Thep, a title rather ignominiously ignored by Western cartographers, who continued to call it Bangkok.

Bangkok was first centered at the Royal Palace and Wat Pra Keo, a royal chapel constructed in 1785 to enshrine the statue of the Emerald Buddha. Modernization was slow until the coronation of King Mongkut (Rama IV) in 1851. Mongkut expanded the city limits, entered into treaties with the U.S. and several European powers, and, in 1862, ordered the construction of the first road over an old elephant trail which connected the Royal Palace with Chinatown. In the same year, Anna Leonowens arrived in Bangkok to become the governess of Mongkut's children and would later misrepresent them in her published reminiscences, *The English Governess at the Siamese Court*. This misleading yarn eventually inspired the stage and film musical, *The King and I.*

Chulalongkorn (King Rama V) ascended the throne in 1868 and introduced far-reaching reforms and Westernization. By 1908 Bangkok had a grand total of just 300 automobiles. After the death of Chulalongkorn in 1910, Bangkok was ruled by several more kings until a bloodless coup in 1932 changed the system of government from an absolute to a constitutional monarchy. A series of 18 military coups occurred from 1932 to the final takeover in 1991, while Bangkok's population soared from 1.5 million in 1960 to a present settlement of over 10 million.

GETTING YOUR BEARINGS

Bangkok isn't a compact or easily understandable city such as San Francisco, but a vast and octo- puslike metropolis spread haphazardly across 1,500 square km. Similar in many respects to Los Angeles (heat, smog, and traffic), Bangkok should be visualized as a multiplicity of neigh- borhoods with distinctive attractions, ethnic pop- ulations, variations of nightlife, and styles of hotels and restaurants that appeal to different types of travelers. The quickest way to orient yourself is to study Nancy Chandler's outstanding map of Bangkok and divide the city into the following neighborhoods. (For information on how to obtain this map, see **Maps** in the Introduction.)

Old Royal City
The old royal city around the Grand Palace has the largest concentration of sightseeing attrac- tions such as the Grand Palace, Wat Pra Keo, Wat Po, and the National Museum. Hotels and

the Grand Palace

DAVID HURST

noteworthy restaurants are relatively rare in this neighborhood, though this is one of Bangkok's few precincts that can be recommended for a walking tour (see below).

Banglampoo
Adjacent to the Old Royal City and the central pa- rade grounds of Sanam Luang is Banglampoo, a traditional Thai neighborhood which has become Bangkok's leading stopover for budget travel- ers. Banglampoo lacks great nightlife or shopping but compensates with a superb location near great temples and the Chao Praya River. Anyone looking for guesthouses under US$10 should head directly for its principal thoroughfare, Khao San Road.

New Royal City
Most of the important government offices and royal residences were moved here prior to WW II. Top draws are Chitralada Palace (the home of the present king), Vimanmek Palace, the out- standing Marble Temple, Parliament, and Dusit Zoo. No hotels.

Chinatown
Wedged between the Old Royal City and Silom Road is one of Southeast Asia's great Chinese neighborhoods and the single finest place to ex- perience a sensory overload of Asia. A map and suggested walking tour are provided in the fol- lowing pages. Chinatown hotels cater primarily to wealthy Chinese businesspeople, but a hand- ful of inexpensive guesthouses are located in adjacent Little India. Travelers searching for a strong and completely authentic encounter might consider staying here rather than in Banglampoo.

Silom
Bangkok's financial center and original tourist enclave is located along a major boulevard known as Silom Road. Sightseeing attractions are minimal and the congestion is unnerving, but Silom offers dozens of moderate to super-lux- ury hotels, exclusive restaurants, high-end shop- ping boutiques, great sidewalk shopping, and the infamous nightlife area of Patpong Road. Riverside hotels such as the Oriental and Shangri La are world famous for their extremely high levels of service.

Malaysia Hotel Area

This was once the budget travelers' center for Bangkok. However, hotels and guesthouses along Soi Ngam Duphli have sadly declined in recent years.

Siam Square

Bangkok's alternative to Silom Road is a relatively low-density neighborhood with ultra-elegant hotels and modern shopping centers. The lack of sightseeing attractions is balanced by the vast gardens which surround many of the hotels and the enormous shopping complexes which guarantee some of the best shopping in all of Asia. Hotels are generally expensive, although a few clean guesthouses are located near the house of Jim Thompson.

Sukumvit Road

Once considered on the outer fringes of Bangkok,

CHEAP FUN IN BANGKOK

Bangkok no longer ranks as the bargain center of the East, but visitors with limited funds can still enjoy themselves for a handful of *baht*. The secret is to find activities popular with Thais rather than with wealthy *farangs* on a two-week holiday. Here are a few suggestions:

Chao Praya Express River Cruise—For less than one U.S. dollar, you can enjoy one of the finest river trips in Asia. A 75-minute journey from the Oriental Hotel up to Nonthaburi in the north costs just 10B. Such a deal.

Wat Po Massage—Bangkok is filled with expensive emporiums offering both therapeutic and sexual massages for over 300B per hour. For an authentic rub in a safe environment, try the Wat Po Massage School where an hour's rub costs 150B.

Free Thai Dance—Colorful if somewhat amateurish Thai dance can be enjoyed at both the Lak Muang Shrine near the Grand Palace and the Erawan Shrine at the Erawan Grand Hyatt Hotel. Better performances, at the same reasonable price, can be seen on Sunday afternoons on the grassy courtyard at the National Theater.

Weekend Market—Bangkok's largest and most colorful market is held on weekends in Chatuchak Park. Operated largely by the Issan from the northeast, Chatuchak has everything imaginable at rock-bottom prices.

Meditation Classes—Free meditation instruction is given weekly at the International Buddhist Center at Sukumvit Soi 3, and inside the international hall at Wat Mahathat. Upcoming lectures are listed in the *Bangkok Post*.

Motorcycle Mania—Enjoy death-defying motorcycle stunts? Thanks to the ingenuity of Thai teenagers, you can now hire motorcycle taxis that weave through traffic with wild abandon. Hold onto your seat.

Tai Chi in the Park—Get up early and watch the old men go through their slow-motion paces in Lumpini Park. Then jog along the par course, feed the ducks, and paddle a boat around the small pond.

National Museum Tour—Best bets for an inexpensive culture fix are the free 0930 tours given at the National Museum. Admission is but 20B.

Golden Sunsets—Sunsets are best enjoyed on top of the Golden Mountain near Wat Saket, and from the luxurious Tiara Restaurant of the Dusit Thani Hotel. Somewhat different crowds, but the same great sunset.

Bus It—A cheap way to explore Bangkok is by public bus from city center to the end of the line. Stay on the bus and you'll return without fuss. Avoid all buses during rush-hour traffic.

Go Fly a Kite—From February to April, kite aficionados gather for aerial warfare at Sanam Luang. Watch the action; buy a kite and try your luck.

Street Dining—Foodstalls provide a wonderful opportunity to rest your aching feet while burning the roof of your mouth. Watch for Issan specialties: fried crickets and roasted grasshoppers.

Thai Movies—Whether kung fu from Hong Kong, sappy love stories with supernatural overtones, or slapstick comedy, Thai cinema is worth the experience. Tickets are cheap and most theaters are air-conditioned.

Say it with Flowers—Thai orchids are among the cheapest in the world. So surprise your partner with bouquets for under 30B.

Get High—Legal highs can be enjoyed at the top of rainbow-colored Baiyoke Towers, Bangkok's tallest building. Ride the elevator to the fourth floor and transfer to the express lift up to the Sky Lounge on the 43rd floor. If the smog god has smiled on you, enjoy the panoramic views and a soft drink.

Sukumvit has developed into the leading area for moderate-budget tourists. The biggest disadvantage is the enormous distance from Sukumvit to important temples and government services such as the General Post Office and the tourist office. However, Sukumvit has a great selection of hotels in the US$25-50 price range, many of the finest Thai restaurants in the country, wonderful sidewalk shopping including countless boutiques, and the mind-boggling nightlife of Nana Entertainment Plaza (NEP) and Soi Cowboy. Despite the relatively remote location and problems with noise and pollution, Sukumvit is recommended for midlevel-income travelers and anyone intrigued by the nightlife possibilities.

ADDRESSES

Sprawling Bangkok can be a difficult place to find an address, though a few tips might help in your search.

Street Names

The transliteration problem with turning Thai into English led to a series of different names for the same street, such as Ratchadamri Road also spelled as Rajadamri, Rajdamri, and Rat'dami roads. Another example is Petchburi Road, which can also be spelled Phetburi, Petburi, or Phetchaburi. Si Ayutthaya is the same as Sri Ayudhya.

Another problem is that some streets have two names—a Thai version and an English version—such as Charoen Krung Road, which is also know by its old English title of New Road, and Withaya Road, which is commonly known in English terminology as Wireless Road.

A final challenge is that pronunciation varies and a Thai person may not recognize your feeble attempts at proper intonation. The "th" sound is pronounced like a "t," so that Thanon, Thonburi, Sathron, and Nonthaburi are actually pronounced Tanon, Tonburi, Satom, and Nontaburi.

Street Types

The Thai word *thanon* translates to road, street, or avenue, and always means a major thoroughfare.

Moving down a few notches is a *soi,* a small street or lane, which generally leads off from a larger *thanon. Sois* are sometimes enlarged and widened until they more closely resemble a major road, such as Soi Asoke, which now ranks as a major highway through the Sukumvit district.

The smallest of all roads is a *trok,* which refers to a very small alley generally running off a slightly larger *soi.*

Finding an Address

Principal arteries help determine the location of an address, such as Silom, Khao San, or Sukumvit roads. Cross streets—generally called *sois*—are very useful, since they help pinpoint the exact location in a more precise fashion than the formal street address. For example, finding an address on Sukumvit Road is most easily accomplished by locating the corresponding *soi;* an address such as Sukumvit Soi 18 is much easier to find rather than 268 Sukumvit.

An address can be either simple or complex, depending on how it has been treated over the years by government agencies and local developers. Many locations are denoted by a series of numbers divided by slashes and hyphens, which indicate increasing degrees of exactness.

88/4-8 Soi 9, Sukumvit Road, involves a series of geographical symbols. The easiest way to find this address is to go to Sukumvit Road, proceed on to Soi 9, and then search out a sign or ask a local shopkeeper.

The 88/4-8 Soi 9 Sukumvit can also be written as 88/4-8 Sukumvit Soi 9 or simply just as 88-4-8 Sukumvit 9. Many times you'll just find the address listed as Sukumvit Soi 9.

What do all those numbers mean? The 88 refers to the original lot number which was assigned to the plot of land several decades ago; it may or may not refer to anything sensible since Bangkok (and most of Thailand) has been developed in an extremely haphazard fashion. The 4 after the slash refers to a building number or perhaps a block of buildings. Generally, you can find a small number 4 tacked onto the lower corner of the building, or you might have to ask around. The 8 is a more precise building number, which generally points out a specific structure within a block of buildings.

Mismatched Sois

Finally, city planning being what it is in Thailand, you'll find that sois on opposite sides of the road often don't match. Note that sois are usually even-numbered on one side of the road, odd-numbered on the other. You would expect Soi 8 to be opposite Soi 9 on Sukumvit Road, but don't hold your breath. As you move down Sukumvit, the disparity between opposite sois increases until you finally find that Soi 41 is opposite Soi 26, and Soi 55 is opposite Soi 38.

SUGGESTED WALKING TOURS

Finding your way around Bangkok can be difficult since street names are rarely marked and the numbering system for addresses is often baffling. Bear in mind that the larger thoroughfares *(thanon)* are intersected by smaller streets *(sois)* that often end in cul-de-sacs. Public transportation—whether in an ordinary bus or an a/c taxi—can be extremely time-consuming, especially during morning and evening rush hours when traffic grinds to a dead stop.

Faced with such obstacles, visitors often think that Bangkok is best experienced on an organized tour rather than a self-guided walking tour. Not true! While organized tours are convenient and relatively inexpensive, reasons to avoid them are plentiful: tour buses get stuck in traffic, visits to major monuments are frustratingly brief, shopping traps designed to extract kickbacks are commonplace, and only the most common (and hence touristy) sights are included in your tour. Worse yet, tours rarely allow an opportunity to freely wander around an ordinary Thai neighborhood and experience the charm and friendliness of the local residents.

Bangkok actually has several compact neighborhoods that can be easily enjoyed on self-guided walking tours by almost anybody with a good map and sense of adventure. A few tips: always get an early start to avoid the midday heat, bring along Nancy Chandler's map of Bangkok, and whenever possible use riverboats to reach your starting point.

First Day—Old Royal City
Temples within the Old Royal City and near the Royal Palace can be toured on foot in a single day. Only a slightly crazed tourist would attempt a single-day walking tour of *all* the temples within the Old Royal City; a leisurely two-day walking

tour is needed for the remaining sights such as Wat Suthat and the Golden Mountain.

Visitors staying in Banglampoo can easily walk over to the Grand Palace or National Museum to begin the tour. Visitors staying near Silom Road should take a public riverboat to the Tha Chang boat stop. From Sukumvit Road or Siam Square, take a taxi or public bus to the Grand Palace.

Begin your tour promptly at 0830 with the Grand Palace or enjoy a guided tour of the National Museum Tues.-Thurs. at 0930. Afterward, wander around the Sanam Luang, visit the amulet market near Wat Mahathat, enjoy some dancing at Lak Muang, and then tour Wat Po to see the Reclining Buddha. Finally, take a river shuttle across the Chao Praya River to Wat Arun. This concentration of temples will probably suffice for most visitors with only a casual interest in Thai religious architecture.

Second Day—Old Royal City
Your walking tour on the second day begins at the Royal Palace and heads away from the river toward Democracy Monument. A short visit can be made to Wat Rajapradit and the more impressive Wat Rajabopit before arriving at Wat Suthat, one of the most majestic temples in the old city. Adjacent to Wat Suthat stands the Giant Swing and a small but intriguing Brahman temple.

Nearby sights include a wonderful Chinese temple on Tanao Road and shops selling religious supplies and immense bronze Buddhas on Bamrung Muang Road. The tour ends with a visit to the amulet market at Wat Rajananda and the curious Lohaprasat before climbing to the summit of the Golden Mountain. Fast walkers can accomplish this tour in about four hours.

Third Day—Chinatown
Rather than tour the limited attractions in the New Royal City, spend your third day walking around Chinatown, Little India, and the adjoining riverside markets. The famous Golden Buddha is also located in this neighborhood. Best of all, strolling through Chinatown provides a welcome relief from the endless procession of temples, and gives you an opportunity to discover Chinese culture. An early start is essential to avoid the midday heat.

ADMISSION FEES AND CAUTIONS

The Grand Palace/Wat Pra Keo complex will probably be your first experience with the notorious two-tier fee system for selected temples, museums, and historical sites in Thailand. In late 1985 the Fine Arts Department began charging foreigners significantly higher admission fees than Thais. For example, entrance to the Grand Palace is 125B for foreigners but free for Thais. Major monuments in Ayuthaya and Sukothai now charge Westerners 20B admission to each temple but Thais only 5B. Although rarely noticed by tourists (lower entrance fees for locals are posted only in Thai script), this double standard has proven contentious for some travelers, who resent the gouge-the-rich-tourist mentality.

Tragically, this attitude—as propagated and approved by the Fine Arts Department and Thai government—has spread throughout Thailand. Many Thais consider tourists fair game for overcharging on everything from ice cream cones to antique Buddhas. There is no reason to play along with this game. Although there is little you can do about temple admissions, travelers who wish to avoid being ripped off on other purchases should learn the correct prices and refuse to pay any type of surcharge. Complaints about the double-pricing standard should be directed to museum directors, tour operators, editors of local newspapers, and upstairs at the Bangkok TAT office.

Cautions

Touts and con artists are plentiful around the Grand Palace; be extra cautious about free boat rides, invitations to lunch, or suspicious money-making schemes.

By far the most common scam is the free boat ride offered by a well-dressed young man who spends several hours gaining your confidence before inviting you on a boat tour of the Chao Praya and adjoining canals. At some point you will be forced to contribute an enormous amount of money for fuel, or risk being stranded in a remote location. Never get into a boat alone, no matter how honest or sincere your host may appear.

Almost as common and just as costly are the college students who offer unbelievable deals on Thai gems. These smooth-talking fellows will promise fabulous profits on gems purchased from reputable government-supervised stores. This is an absolute fraud: *never buy gems from a street tout.*

Dress Regulations

Please remember that foreign visitors to Buddhist temples must be properly dressed. *Shorts are never appropriate in temples.* Long pants or long dresses should be worn instead. Women should be well covered. Visitors wearing dirty jeans, T-shirts, or halter tops will be refused admittance. All visitors must wear shoes with closed heels and toes; those wearing sandals or rubber slippers will be refused entrance to all major temples, including Wat Pra Keo and the Royal Palace. Photographers should ask permission before taking flash photos inside temples.

Fourth Day—New Royal City

Begin your day with a river trip on the Chao Praya from Tha Orienten (Oriental Hotel boat stop) in the south to Tha Pra Arthit (Banglampoo) pier in the north. First, walk through the backpackers' enclave along Khao San Road and briefly visit Wat Bowonivet before heading up Rajadamnern Avenue to the tourist office and the magnificent Marble Temple. Farther on are the Vimanmek Palace and the Dusit Zoo—a long hike best aided with public transportation.

Fifth Day—Sukumvit to Siam Square

The best remaining walking tour is from Sukumvit Road to Siam Square, an easy-to-follow excursion which includes conventional tourist attractions such as Kamthieng and Jim Thompson's House, great sidewalk shopping along Sukumvit Road, comfortable air-conditioned shopping inside the Central and Zen centers, and plenty of great little restaurants and pubs for cold drinks. And not a temple in sight!

Begin your tour from Sukumvit Soi 21 (Siam Society and Soi Cowboy), and walk west past bookstores, local markets, sidewalk shops, tailors, and cafes to the expressway overpass where Sukumvit changes name to Ploenchit Road. Continue west to Central Department Store, the fascinating Erawan Shrine, newish World Trade Center (actually just a shopping complex), and Siam Square Shopping Center where Ploenchit—logically enough—becomes Rama I Road. Farther on is the immense Tokyu Shopping Center and finally, Jim Thompson's House, tucked away on a quiet side street.

Sixth Day—River Journeys

A full day can be enjoyed on the Chao Praya River and canals which circumscribe the city. For suggested itineraries see "River and Canal Tours" later in this chapter.

CENTRAL BANGKOK ATTRACTIONS

THE OLD ROYAL CITY

Wat Pra Keo

First stop for most visitors is the Grand Palace and its adjoining temple complex, Wat Pra Keo (Temple of the Emerald Buddha). Taken together, these brilliant and almost unbelievable monuments form one of the greatest spectacles in all of Southeast Asia. The following description follows a clockwise route corresponding to the map and legend.

Entrance (1): Entrance to both the temple complex and the Grand Palace is on Na Pralan Road opposite the Sanam Luang parade grounds. Walk past the government buildings and turn left down the narrow corridor.

Coin Museum (2): Your entry ticket includes admission to both the Coin Museum on the right and the Vimanmek Palace in northern Bangkok. Through the narrow gateway is a scene of almost unbelievable brilliance: golden spires and wonderfully ornate pavilions guarded by strange mythological creatures.

Ramakien Murals (3): The interior cloister murals depict tales from the Ramakien, the Thai version of the Ramayana. Originally painted during the reign of King Mongkut (1825-50), they have since been restored seven times including such occasions as the Rattanakosin bicentennial in 1982 and the king's 60th birthday celebration in 1987. The story begins by the north gate with the discovery of Sita, and advances through various adventures of her consort Rama and his assistant, the white monkey-god Hanuman. Much of the original artistic merit has been lost to the repeated restorations, though each mural still offers delightful depictions of ordinary Thai life: laughing children, demure concubines, grinning gamblers, and emaciated opium smokers. Marble tablets opposite each fresco provide explanatory texts composed by King Chulalongkorn.

Golden Chedi (4): This dazzling wonder was erected by King Mongkut and modeled after Ayuthaya's Pra Sri Ratana Chedi.

Mondop (5): Just beyond is a richly carved library with a solid-silver floor and interior set with a mother-of-pearl chest filled with sacred texts. Gracing the four interior corners are exquisite Buddha statues carved in a 14th-century Javanese style and miniature sacred white elephants, symbols of royal power. Normally closed to the public.

Angkor Wat Model (6): This miniature model of the famous Khmer temple was constructed by Rama IV when Cambodia was a vassal state of the Thai empire. If you're unable to visit Angkor, this fine model provides a convenient overview. Photographers can get an intriguing aerial view by standing on the railing.

Gabled *Viharn* (7): The Pra Viharn Yot, decorated with ceramics and porcelain, once held the historic Manangasila stone, which served as the throne for King Ramkamheng of Sukothai. Discovered by King Mongkut in the ruins of Sukothai during his monkhood, the stone has since been brought here.

Royal Mausoleum (8): The Pra Naga in the northwest corner of the complex holds urns containing the ashes of royal family members. Closed to the public.

Library (9): The west facade of the Montien Dharma, second library of the temple complex, is considered the finest of its kind in Thailand. As with other temple libraries, this building was constructed to protect sacred texts and copies of the Tripitaka, the holy Buddhist scripture.

Royal Pantheon (10): Ground plan of Prasat Pra Thepbidon is a Greek cross capped by a yellow *prang*. Standing inside are life-sized statues of the first seven kings of the Chakri dynasty. Open annually on 6 April.

Mythological Animals: Surrounding the magnificent Royal Pantheon are bizarre mythological animals such as the *kinaree*, a half-human, half-

SPORTS AT SANAM LUANG

*A*lthough the huge public ground in front of the Grand Palace is used for royal cremations and the annual ploughing ceremony, you'll more likely come across traditional Thai sports such as kite flying and *takraw* here.

Kite Fighting: Thailand is one of the few countries in the world where a children's sport has developed into a form of combat. Kite fighting began after an Ayuthayan governor quelled a local rebellion by flying massive kites over the besieged city and using jars of explosives to bomb it into submission. Less violent competitions, such as the coveted King's Cup in April, are held today between two different types of kites with gender-inspired characteristics. Male kites *(chulas)* are sturdy three-meter star-shaped fighting vessels fixed with bamboo barbs on reinforced strings. Female kites *(pakpao),* on the other hand, are one-meter kites set with long tails and loops of string. The male kite attempts to snag the female and drag her into his territory, while the female uses her superior speed and maneuverability to avoid the male and force him to the ground.

Takraw: One of Thailand's most popular sports, *takraw* comes in several versions. Circle *takraw* involves bouncing a light ball about the size of a grapefruit made of braided rattan, the object being to keep the ball in motion as long as possible without using the hands. Points are awarded for employing the least-accessible body parts such as knees, hips, and shoulders. Basket *takraw* players attempt to kick the rattan ball through a ring elevated 6-10 meters above the ground. Net *takraw*—unquestionably the most exciting version—is played almost exactly like volleyball without hands. Overhead serves and foot spikes in this variation require an amazing degree of dexterity and acrobatic skill.

Fish Fighting: Though formally banned by the Thai government, pairs of male Siamese fighting fish *(Betta splendens regan)* still do combat in the side streets for the benefit of gamblers. Captured in swamps and raised in freshwater tanks, when placed in common tanks these pugnacious fish transform themselves into vividly colored fighting creatures complete with quivering gills and flashing tails. Also popular is insect fighting, which pitches enormous horned male beetles against each other for the charms of a female attendant. The battle ends when the weaker beetle dies on its back.

---

bird creature of Himalayan origins; and glaring guardian lions known as *norasinghs.* Flanking the main entrance are slender *chedis* supported by a frieze of mythical *garuda* birds—important since the *garuda* is Vishnu's animal and Rama is the reincarnation of Vishnu.

Prangs (11): Covered with glazed ceramic tiles, eight Khmer *prangs* (spires) erected by Rama I symbolize the eight planets. Each color corresponds to a different celestial body. Two are located inside the palace walls; another six stand outside the grounds along the east gallery.

Chapel of the Emerald Buddha (12): Bangkok's Royal Temple is Thailand's most important and sacred *wat.* Constructed at the end of the 18th century by King Rama I, this splendid example of Thai aesthetics and religious architecture houses the Emerald Buddha, Thailand's most venerated image. So small and distant that it can hardly be seen, the green jasper (*not* jade or emerald) image symbolizes the independence, strength, and good fortune of the country.

Thais believe this religious talisman holds the magical power of the king, who thrice annually changes the holy garments from a golden tunic studded with diamonds during the hot season to a gilded monk's robe for the rainy season. A solid gold robe is placed over the image during the cool season. Shoes must be removed and photography is prohibited. Extreme respect should be shown in this chapel.

Interior walls are painted with superb frescoes. A few moments studying these murals will prove rewarding, since most Thai temples follow similar conventions as to mural placement. For example, murals between the window frames generally depict Jataka scenes from the life of Buddha. The universe is portrayed in Buddhist astrological representation on the back wall behind the altar. The wall fronting the altar (above the entrance) relates the temptation and victory of Buddha over Mara.

Two points of interest are located outside the chapel. Guarding the entrance are two mythical bronze lions, considered by art historians as

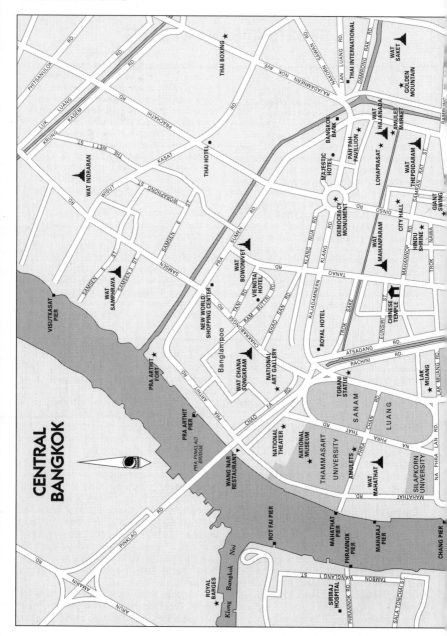

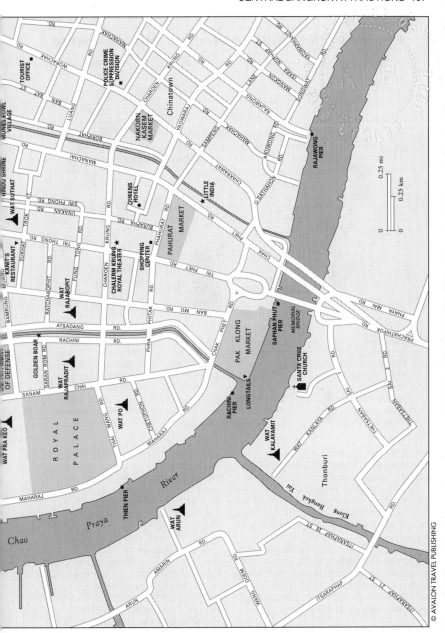

0.25 mi

0.25 km

0

0

© AVALON TRAVEL PUBLISHING

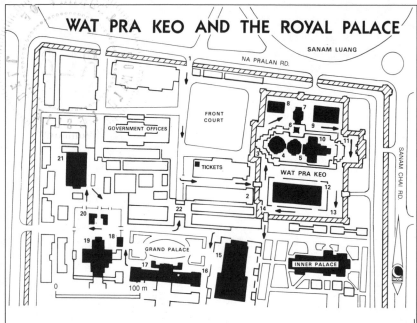

WAT PRA KEO AND THE ROYAL PALACE

SANAM LUANG

NA PRALAN RD.

FRONT COURT

GOVERNMENT OFFICES

TICKETS

WAT PRA KEO

GRAND PALACE

INNER PALACE

SANAM CHAI RD.

0   100 m

1. entrance
2. Coin Museum
3. Ramakien murals
4. Golden Chedi
5. Mondop
6. Angkor Wat model
7. Gabled Viharn
8. Royal Mausoleum
9. library
10. Royal Pantheon
11. prangs
12. Chapel of the Emerald Buddha
13. bell tower
14. yaks
15. Amarinda Audience Hall
16. Royal Collection of Weapons
17. Chakri Maha Prasat
18. Amporn Pimok Pavilion
19. Dusit Audience Hall
20. courtyard doorways
21. Wat Pra Keo Museum
22. Double Gates

masterpieces of Khmer art. Also note the un-usually ornate *bai sema* or boundary stones.

Bell Tower (13): An elaborate bell tower stands in the opposite corner. Bell towers typically summon monks for sermons and meals, though Wat Pra Keo no longer has resident monks.

Yaks **(14):** To exit the Wat Pra Keo compound you must pass towering manlike creatures called *yaks,* sharp-fanged mythological creatures dressed in Thai costumes and wielding huge clubs. *Kinarees* and *garudas* brandishing *nagas* complete the amazing scene.

Royal Palace
Bangkok's former royal palace, an intriguing blend of Italian Renaissance architecture and classical Thai roofing, was begun in 1783 by King Rama I and improved upon by subsequent rulers. As Wat Pra Keo evokes the East, the Grand Palace will remind you of Europe.

Amarinda Audience Hall (15): Originally the private residence of Rama I and the Hall of Justice, Vinchai Hall today serves as a royal venue for coronations and ceremonial state events. An antique boat-shaped throne on which early kings received homage stands behind the Western throne used by the present king.

Royal Collection of Weapons (16): A brief look at the history of Thai weaponry. Left of the weapon museum is a gateway leading to the Inner Palace, once the residence of the king's children and concubines. The king now celebrates his birthday here with friends and the local diplomatic corps. Closed to the public.

Grand Palace Audience Hall (17): Eccentric, half Western and half Asian, the **Chakri Maha Prasat** was constructed in 1882 by King Chulalongkorn to commemorate the centenary of the Chakri dynasty. Designed by a British architect, this Italian Renaissance palace was incongruously superimposed with a Thai *prasat* roof at the king's request—a strangely successful fusion of disparate styles. The Grand Palace served as the royal residence until King Ananda was shot in bed under mysterious circumstances in 1946. His brother, the current King Rama IX, subsequently moved out to the more spacious Chitralada Palace. Visitors are allowed inside the state reception room decorated with European furnishings.

Amporn Pimok Pavilion (18): At one time, Rama IV would alight from his elevated palanquin, present himself to the crowd below, enter this delicate little pavilion, remove his ceremonial hat and gown, and then proceed into the throne hall. So quintessentially Thai is the architecture that Rama V reproduced it at his Bang Pa In summer retreat, and a replica was exhibited at the 1892 World's Fair in Brussels.

Dusit Audience Hall (19): Mounted on a marble platform in the shape of a Latin cross, this magnificent building is widely considered Thailand's finest example of royal architecture. Once used for outdoor receptions, today the building serves for the ceremonial lying-in-state of deceased kings. Note the interior paintings, the throne built by King Mongkut, and the four guardian figures donated by wealthy Chinese businesspeople.

Courtyard Doorways (20): Exit the Grand Palace through these wooden doors delightfully carved and painted with colorful sentries.

Wat Pra Keo Museum (21): Features inside this fine little museum include a scale model of the Royal Palace and Wat Pra Keo complex— useful to sort out the confusing labyrinths. Javanese Buddhas and the famous Manangasila Throne are displayed upstairs. Best of all, it's air-conditioned!

Double Gates (22): Exit to the front courtyard and Na Pralan Road through the double gates.

Lak Muang

Across the road from the Royal Palace stands a newly renovated marble pavilion housing a lingam-shaped monument covered with gold leaf and adorned with flowers. This foundation stone, from which all distances in Thailand are measured, was placed here by King Rama I to provide a home for the unseen landlord-spirits of the city. Thais believe these magical spirits possess the power to grant wishes, win lotteries, guarantee healthy children, and protect the fate of the city.

Thai classical dance performances sponsored in the rear pavilion by satisfied supplicants include Ramakien routines, the most popular version being an Eastern *Swan Lake* called the Manora. Sponsors pay the dancers 100B for a short *ram tawai* (thanksgiving dance) while wealthy patrons ante up 1,000B for a longer drama. Early morning and late afternoon are the busiest and best times to watch the dancing— extra busy two or three days before a lottery.

National Museum

This museum—the largest and most comprehensive in Southeast Asia—serves as an excellent introduction to the arts of Thailand and the religious iconography of Buddhism.

Collections are open Wed.-Sun. 0900-1600. Admission is 20B. Tickets can be purchased and bags checked at the front entrance. Photography is prohibited. The bulletin board adjacent to the ticket counter often has notices on upcoming cultural and festival tours sponsored by the National Museum and the Siam Society —excellent tours at extremely good prices. Detailed information on the extensive holdings is provided in the *Guide to the National Museum Bangkok* sold at the front desk.

Orientation: The National Museum is comprised of a half dozen buildings. The Sivamokhapiman Hall holds the ticket office and Thai History rooms. Scattered on the outside grounds are the Royal Chariot Pavilion, Wat Buddhaisawan, and Red Pavilion, three excellent examples of traditional 18th-century architecture. To the rear is the Central Wing. Once used by the king's brother, these old royal structures have been subdivided into almost 20 rooms filled with everything from stuffed elephants to golden amulets. The two-storied South Wing, constructed in 1967, features early Thai statuary and artifacts from the Srivijaya, Dvaravati, and Lopburi Periods. The North Wing includes later artwork from the Sukothai, Ayuthaya, and Bangkok Periods.

The following highlights take three or four hours to cover. Visitors with limited time will probably best enjoy Wat Buddhaisawan, funeral chariots in the hall to the right, the Lopburi sculpture in the South Wing to the left, and the Sukothai Buddhas on the second floor of the North Wing.

Free Tours: To quickly sort through the artifacts, which range from Neolithic discoveries of Ban Chiang to contemporary Bangkok pieces, museum volunteers conduct free guided tours starting at 0930 from the ticket desk. These tours are highly recommended. Without a tour, the bewildering collections often confuse and frustrate Western visitors who lack any formal background in the basics of Asian art. English-language tours are given Tues.-Thurs. morning at 0930. French tours are given on Wednesday, German on Thursday, and Japanese on Tuesday. Special tours in Chinese and Spanish can also be arranged. Tours change frequently; call (02) 215-8173 for further information.

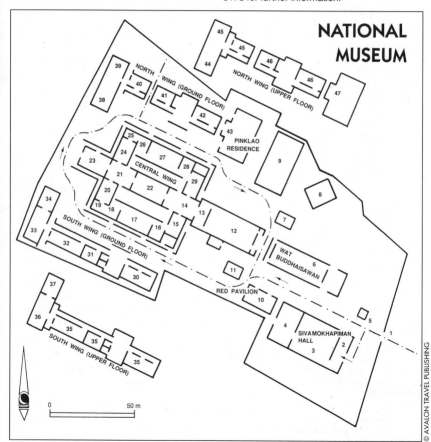

NATIONAL MUSEUM

NORTH WING (GROUND FLOOR)
NORTH WING (UPPER FLOOR)
PINKLAO RESIDENCE
CENTRAL WING
SOUTH WING (GROUND FLOOR)
SOUTH WING (UPPER FLOOR)
WAT BUDDHAISAWAN
RED PAVILION
SIVAMOKHAPIMAN HALL

0   50 m

© AVALON TRAVEL PUBLISHING

Sivamokhapiman Hall (2-4): The ticket office and bookstore are in the front, public restrooms to the rear.

Gallery of Thai History (3): Galleries to the rear of the admission counter are somewhat gloomy and confusing, but nevertheless help you sort through Thai epochs from Sukothai to the modern era. The prize exhibit is the famous Sukothai stele of King Ramkamheng, a stone slab which has generated a great deal of controversy regarding its authenticity. Also of interest are exhibits on possible origins of the Thai peoples, and dioramas of important events in Thai history.

Gallery of Pre-Thai History (4): Highlights include Paleolithic artifacts from Ban Kao near Kanchanaburi, and world-famous pottery and bronze ornaments from Ban Chiang in Udon Thani Province.

Wat Buddhaisawan (6): Finest among the assorted historic buildings on the museum grounds is this superb chapel, widely considered one of the best surviving examples of early Bangkok monastic architecture. Wat Buddhaisawan was constructed in 1787 to house a greatly revered Buddha image (Pra Buddha Sing) which, according to legend, was fashioned in Sri Lanka. However, two identical images are also found in Chiang Mai and Nakhon Si Thammarat, and, as you might expect, residents in

those communities are convinced that they possess the original Buddha. For the average visitor, it is the soaring interior roofline, shiny wooden floors, light streaming in through the open windows, and magnificent murals that remain the great attraction.

Chariot Hall (9): Stored inside this large shed are immense ceremonial carriages still used for royal open-air cremations in nearby Sanam Luang. The largest prototype weighs over 20 tons and requires the physical manpower of several hundred men outfitted in traditional palace uniforms. Also displayed is a replica of the royal cremation pavilion used by the late King Rama VI.

Red Pavilion (10): Once the home of Rama I's sister, the Tamnak Daeng (Red House) provides a quick look at the atmosphere and furnishings of a royal residence, circa 1782-1809. The Tamnak Daeng is constructed of prefabricated walls which allowed it to be moved several times before being placed on the museum grounds.

Audience Hall (12): Formerly the hall of the surrogate monarch (a deputy ruler appointed to succeed the ruling king), the Issaravinitchai Hall now houses special exhibits such as recent archaeological discoveries and shows that have returned from international tours.

Treasure Room (13): Includes golden jewelry and precious gems from U Thong and Nakhon

---

1. entrance
2. ticket office and bookstore
3. Gallery of Thai History
4. Gallery of Pre-Thai History
5. King Vijiravudh Pavilion
6. Wat Buddhaisawan
7. Heir to the Throne Pavilion
8. Sala
9. Chariot Hall
10. Red Pavilion
11. King Rama IV Pavilion
12. Audience Hall
13. treasure room
14. palanquins
15. shadow puppets
16. royal gifts
17. ceramics
18. models
19. stamps and coins
20. ivory

21. antique weaponry
22. royal regalia
23. woodcarvings
24. steles
25. model boats
26. curiosities
27. costumes and textiles
28. flags
29. musical instruments

SOUTH WING~GROUND FLOOR
30. Asian art
31. museum office
32. Khmer and Lopburi
33. Hindu sculpture
34. Lopburi

SOUTH WING~UPPER FLOOR
35. Dvaravati
36. Javanese images
37. Srivijaya

NORTH WING~GROUND FLOOR
38. coin gallery
39. Buddha images
40. textiles
41. decorative arts
42. Bangkok
43. photographs

NORTH WING~UPPER FLOOR
44. Lanna and Chiang Saen
45. Sukothai
46. Ayuthaya
47. Bangkok

Pathom, and a stunning collection of objects discovered at Wat Rajaburana in Ayuthaya.

Palanquins (14): Funeral palanquins and elephant howdahs used in royal processions are displayed in the Phimuk Monthain gallery. Finest piece is the exquisite ivory howdah presented to King Chulalongkorn by a Chiang Mai prince.

Shadow Puppets (15): Stage properties, *khon* masks worn by dignitaries of the court of Rama VI, Chinese marionettes, Siamese polo sticks, and a rare collection of giant shadow puppets make this one of the more intriguing rooms in the central museum.

Ceramics (17): Highlights of this room include 19th-century Bencharong ware, Sawankalok pottery, and Japanese and Chinese porcelains. Beautifully crafted mother-of-pearl screens are exhibited in the upstairs room.

Ivory (20): The sacred role of white elephants is noted here with carved ivory tusks and sculpted elephant armor incised with religious talismans.

Antique Weaponry (21): A life-sized elephant mounted by a Thai warrior and covered with battle regalia dominates a room filled with antique firearms and 18th-century swords.

Royal Regalia (22): The central room features thrones, a small royal pavilion, coronation regalia, and examples of the five traditional emblems of Thai royalty: *chatras* (tiered umbrellas), crowns, golden swords, fly whisks, and small golden shoes.

Woodcarvings (23): Extravagant teakwood carvings include circular monastery pulpits, Khmer *prangs,* mythological creatures such as *kinarees,* and a pair of doors salvaged from the Wat Suthat fire of 1959.

Steles (24): Resembling an ancient graveyard, this room displays teetering stones inscribed in Sanskrit, Pali, Khmer, and Thai.

Costumes and Textiles (27): A rare collection of Cambodian *ikats,* Indian brocades, Chinese silks, painted *phanung* garments, and Thai weavings executed with great skill. The upstairs room is devoted to religious artifacts and a monk's sole possessions: a begging bowl, three orange robes, a razor, a water sieve to filter out living creatures, a sash, and a small sewing pouch.

Musical Instruments (29): Thai and other Southeast Asian instruments (Javanese *game-*

lans, etc.) are displayed on an elevated veranda. Note the Thai *phipat* orchestra, comprised of xylophones, metallophones, gongs, cymbals, and flutes.

South Wing—Ground Floor (30-34)

Asian Art (30): This room demonstrates the overwhelming power and influence of Indian culture on early Thai art. Indian merchants, philosophers, and holy men reached Thailand shortly after the beginning of the Christian era, bringing with them Indian languages (Pali and Sanskrit), art, and religions which still influence modern Thai society. Among the highlights are 5th-century Sarnath Buddhas, 7th-century Gupta Buddhas, and 10th-century Pali-style steles. Also displayed are images from Sri Lanka, Myanmar, Tibet, China, and Japan.

Khmer and Lopburi (32 and 34): Khmer culture and political power extended across Thailand from the 8th to 13th centuries, reaching an apex in the northeast and at the small administrative outpost of Lopburi. This room, and the room beyond the director's office, illustrate both pure Khmer styles (Kompong Prae, Baphuon, and Bayon) and Khmer/Thai fusions called Lopburi, named after the town where the two styles were successfully blended.

Hindu Sculpture (33): Brahmanical devotional objects dating from the 3rd to 5th centuries have been discovered at two major sites in Thailand: Si Thep in Petchabun and the southern peninsula near Chaiya and Surat Thani. This room features a 7th-century stone Vishnu image found in southern Thailand near Takua Pa, considered the most impressive Hindu sculpture uncovered in Thailand.

South Wing—Upper Floor (35-37)

Dvaravati (35): The pre-Thai artistic period was dominated by Mon culture (6th-11th centuries). The Mon were a racial group who created empires at Nakhon Pathom near Bangkok and Haripunchai (modern-day Lamphun) in the north. Influenced by Indian post-Gupta styles and Amaravati traditions from South India and Sri Lanka, Mon art chiefly excelled in magnificent Buddhist sculpture with distinctive facial modelings. Displayed in these rooms are terra-cotta images in bas relief, stone Wheels of the Law which retell Buddha's first sermon at Sarnath, and extremely delicate busts which convey the inner calm of the enlightened Buddha.

Java (36): This small but worthwhile collection of images from central Java (Borobudur and Prambanan) and east Java (Singosari and Malang) was donated by the Dutch colonialists to King Chulalongkorn during a state visit in 1896. The more important pieces were returned in the 1920s.

Srivijaya (37): The kingdom of Srivijaya, with its center either in Sumatra or at Chaiya in peninsular Thailand, dominated much of Southeast Asia during its heyday from the 7th to 9th centuries. As an entrepot for trade between India, Indonesia, and China, the resulting art style blends various schools such as Mon, Indian, Indo-Javanese, Khmer, and Chinese. Bodhisattvas and eight-armed goddesses surround a marvelously sinuous Bodhisattva Avalokitesvara from Chaiya.

North Wing—Ground Floor (38-43)

Coin Gallery (38): Numismatists will enjoy the coin gallery collection of Chinese porcelain counters, 17th-century Cambodian coinage, bullet coins from the Sukothai era, and blocks of beaten metal which served as currency until the 19th century.

Buddha Images (39): Rather than a unified collection, this collection includes statues from various epochs. Dominating the enclosure is a colossal quartzite Buddha carved in Dvaravati style and seated in the so-called European fashion.

Textiles (40): Brocades, embroideries, cotton prints, and silks from the Bangkok Period.

Decorative Arts (41): Minor arts of the 19th and 20th centuries, such as lacquerware, ceramics, nielloware, silverwork, mother-of-pearl inlay, and illustrated manuscripts made of palm leaves and paper.

Bangkok (42): The Bangkok Period, also known as Rattanakosin, includes Thai art created since the founding of Bangkok in 1782. Early images imitated the styles of Ayuthaya with richly ornamented headdresses and impassive faces.

North Wing—Upper Floor (44-47)

Lanna (44): Lanna and Chiang Saen were art styles which flourished in Northern Thailand from the 13th to 16th centuries. Buddha images tend to be small but carefully cast with great attention.

Sukothai—(45): The following two rooms contain the supreme art of Thailand, and one of the great movements of Southeast Asian art. Sukothai was an enlightened empire which ruled much of Thailand from the 13th to 15th centuries. Highlights of the first room include a pair of magnificent bronze statues: a four-armed Vishnu with a strangely flaired robe, and an eight-armed Harihara with hands formed in various mudras. The following room features more Buddhas, including a black bronze walking Buddha cast in an androgynous style. Although the long hike through the museum has exhausted you, this room deserves a close and careful inspection.

Ayuthaya (46): Ayuthaya served as the Thai capital between the fall of Sukothai and the establishment of Bangkok. Buddhas created during this period continued the traditions of Sukothai with a gradual embellishment of the headpieces and robes. Bejewelled Buddhas in a pose of subduing Mara are particularly fine.

Bangkok (47): Final stop covers modern Thai Buddhas and the minor arts from the Bangkok (Rattanakosin) Period. The collection seems rather lifeless and formalized after the exquisite pieces in the Sukothai and Ayuthaya rooms.

Wat Mahathat

The "Temple of the Great Relic" was constructed during the reign of King Rama I and houses Mahachulalongkorn University, one of the two highest seats of Buddhist learning in the country. It also serves as national headquarters for the Mahanikaya sect practiced by over 90% of the Buddhist population.

Wat Mahathat has little of great architectural value, but it functions as an important center for the study of *vipassana* (insight) meditation. Westerners can obtain information on introductory seminars (given weekly in English, usually on Friday afternoon) and monthly meditation retreats from the International Buddhist Meditation Center, Dhamma Vicaya Hall, tel. (02) 511-0439, in the rear center of the temple complex. Weekly lecture times and subjects are often listed in the *Bangkok Post*.

Weekends and *wan pra* (Buddhist holy days) are excellent times to visit the lively outdoor market which runs right through the temple grounds.

With such great religious importance, it is hardly surprising that the temple serves as a major market for Buddhist amulets. Sales booths are found on Prachan Road near the Sanam Luang, and in a small *soi* (alley) which crosses Maharat Road and opens onto the riverside plaza. Located here are numerous shops filled with amulets, freshly cast Buddha images, and monk accessories such as begging bowls and orange robes.

National Art Gallery

The modern art museum opposite the National Theater exhibits traditional and contemporary works by both Thai and Western artists. Current shows are listed in the *Bangkok Post*. The gallery is open daily except Monday and Friday 0900-1600. Admission is 10B.

Earth Goddess Statue

Just opposite the Royal Hotel stands a small white pavilion and female statue erected by King Chulalongkorn as a public water fountain. This small monument merits a careful study since it illustrates one of the most beloved tales of Buddhist folklore, a story retold endlessly in murals and statues throughout Thailand.

According to legend, Buddha, in the throes of meditation, was repeatedly tempted by the evil goddess Mara and her sensual dancing ladies. Rather than submitting to temptation, the Buddha continued his meditation under the watchful gaze of the Earth Goddess Torani. So impressed was Torani with his courage, compassion, and moral willpower that she wrung her long hair, setting loose a tidal wave which swept away Mara and her evil armies.

Wat Po

Bangkok's oldest and largest temple complex, Wat Po was founded in the 16th century, when Ayuthaya was the capital, and radically remodeled between 1781 and 1801 by Rama I, who renamed the complex Wat Pra Chetupon. The area was extended in the 1830s by Rama III in his quest to establish an open-air university. This educational wonderland included inscriptions on traditional sciences, extracts from the Jatakas, marble tablets that taught the rules of traditional Thai massage, litanies of the reincarnations of Vishnu, treatises on astrology and palmistry, illustrations on world geography, and *rishi* figures contorted to demonstrate control over the physical body. In 1832 Rama III constructed an immense chapel on these grounds to house the statue of the Reclining Buddha; Wat Po is often called the Temple of the Reclining Buddha.

Wat Po today is one of the more fascinating temple complexes in Bangkok because of both its mystique and artistic achievement. Crammed into the courtyards is a bewildering number of chapels, rock gardens, bizarre statuary, educational tablets, bell towers, and small *chedis*. The complex has two major highlights: the superb *bot* to the right of the entrance, and the gigantic reclining Buddha in the rear courtyard. Guides are available at the front entrance on Soi Chetupon, though their services are hardly necessary. Guides charge 150B for one visitor, 200B for two, and 300B for three. Air-conditioned buses 6,8, and 12 all stop near Wat Po, or you can take a river boat to Tha Tien Pier.

Wat Po is open daily 0800-1700. Admission is 10B. Visitors can wander around the yards past closing hour but the Reclining Buddha is locked up firmly at 1700. Several travelers have recommended a visit on Sunday, when the temple school teaches young students Thai classical dance and how to play traditional Thai musical instruments.

The following walking tour follows a clockwise route.

Entrance (1): The principal entrance (in the back alley) is flanked by a pair of menacing Chinese guards wearing heavy armor and sporting sculpted beards. Other guardians scattered throughout the complex smoke cigars and wear European top hats! All of these humorous figures were cut from stone blocks taken from ship ballast on the Thailand-to-China trade route.

Yogi Figures (2): After purchasing your ticket and declining the services of a guide, you'll see several miniature mountains covered with figurines of holy men in contorted positions of meditation and massage. The fragile plaster-cast figures are periodically replaced.

Main *Bot* (8): The main temple at Wat Po is widely considered among the most elegant in all of Thailand and a masterpiece of Thai religious architecture. Note the remarkable proportions, elegant rooflines, and exquisite ornamental design on the doors and interiors. Entrance (5) to the *bot* central courtyard passes through an unusual double gallery (6 and 7) which features almost 400 gilded Ayuthaya-style Buddhas throughout and around the outer and inner chambers. All have recently been encased behind glass, a disturbing development. Each corner of the inner courtyard has a white-marble Khmer *prang* (3), and each of the four directional *viharns* (9) features an image of the Buddha. The most remarkable stands in the east *viharn* where the Buddha Lakanard dispenses blessings to the faithful.

Before entering the main *bot,* note the 16 fine bronze lions which guard the eight stairways, and the famous bas-reliefs which surround each base. These tablets relate the story of the Ramakien, the Thai version of the Hindu Ramayana.

Rubbings of woodcut copies (not the original stones) can be purchased at the souvenir shop. Also see the Chinese landscapes, *farangs* on horseback, and black-faced Moorish traders on the exquisite mother-of-pearl doorways.

The main doorway to the *bot* is to the east, away from the river. The interior features a high nave flanked by twin rows of thick square columns painted with floral patterns and hung with drawings of old Bangkok. Beware the loud-speaker system! Directly ahead is a well-illuminated Buddha magnificently elevated on a gilded wooden pedestal, an inspiring and extremely powerful image removed from Wat Sala Sina in Thonburi. Interior side wall murals have been

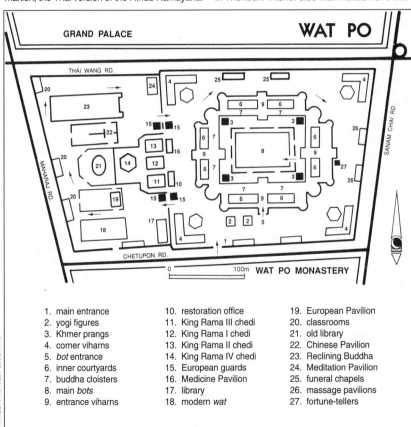

1. main entrance
2. yogi figures
3. Khmer prangs
4. corner viharns
5. *bot* entrance
6. inner courtyards
7. buddha cloisters
8. main *bots*
9. entrance viharns
10. restoration office
11. King Rama III chedi
12. King Rama I chedi
13. King Rama II chedi
14. King Rama IV chedi
15. European guards
16. Medicine Pavilion
17. library
18. modern *wat*
19. European Pavilion
20. classrooms
21. old library
22. Chinese Pavilion
23. Reclining Buddha
24. Meditation Pavilion
25. funeral chapels
26. massage pavilions
27. fortune-tellers

badly damaged from water seepage, but murals above the entrance remain in excellent condition; look for depictions of ordinary Thai life such as children in swings, bathing women, beggars, *klong* life, and wandering hermits.

Chedi Quartet (11-14): After touring the main *bot*, exit through the front entrance and walk past the main entrance and restoration committee headquarters to the quartet of Disneyesque-colored *chedis*. All have been recently redone with brilliant porcelains and rededicated to the first four kings of Thailand. The orange-and-brown *chedi* (11) on the left honors King Rama III, the central green *chedi* (12) is for Rama I, and the yellow-and-brown *chedi* (13) on the right honors Rama II. To the rear is a blue *chedi* (14) with red and white roses and green foliage, a monument constructed by Rama IV and dedicated to his wife, Queen Suriyothai, who was killed in battle defending the life of her husband. Great views can be enjoyed from the summit. Surrounding the *chedi* cloister are hundreds of standing Buddhas in the double-blessing pose.

West Courtyard Buildings (17-22): This courtyard features a half dozen halls of marginal interest. To the immediate left of the entrance is a new **Buddhist library** (17) and a modern *wat* (18) constructed with little style or imagination. The so-called **European Pavilion** (19)—more Chinese than Western—fronts a small pond flanked with monkey statues and a model of the *chedi* at Nakhon Pathom—a good place to relax and mix with the resident monks. Other buildings include **classrooms** (20); a display of traditional Thai musical instruments; an **old library** (21) restored with decorative flowers, green tiles, and small *nagas* at each corner; and the **Chinese Pavilion** (22) with its centerpiece bodhi tree.

Reclining Buddha (23): Certainly the most famous sight at Wat Po is the gigantic Reclining Buddha housed under a claustrophobic shed in the western courtyard. The 46- by 15-meter image, constructed of plaster over a brick core, represents the Buddha passing into nirvana. Thailand's largest reclining Buddha is difficult to appreciate in such tight settings, but special attention should be paid to the intricate mother-of-pearl designs on the footsoles which depict the 108 signs of the true Lord Buddha.

Massage Pavilions (26): As intriguing as the giant Buddha image is the College of Traditional Medicine in the eastern courtyard. This royal-sponsored mini-university of massage, herbal medicine, and Chinese acupuncture offers inexpensive, traditional Thai rubs: 80B for 30 minutes, 150B for one hour. Thirty hours of professional instruction spread over 10 days (three hours daily) or 15 days (two hours daily) costs 3,000B. **Fortune-tellers** (27) ply their trade in the adjacent courtyard.

MORE OF THE OLD ROYAL CITY

More temples and monuments lie east of the river. Time permitting after visiting the sights listed below, continue down Rajadamnern Avenue to Banglampoo and the Pra Arthit pier, or take a taxi to the Marble Temple in the New Royal City.

Wat Rajapradit

Constructed in 1864 by King Mongkut to complete the holy triumvirate of Ayuthayan temples, this picturesque but minor *wat* is noted for its widely diverse collection of architectural styles. This Thai-style *bot* is raised on a stone platform and surrounded by gray marble columns incised in an unusual checkerboard design. Interior murals offer clear views of Bangkok during the 1860s and royal ceremonies held 12 months a year. Resident monks can unlock the door. To the left is an Ayuthayan-style *prang* superbly carved with images of four-faced Brahma, while a Bayon-style *prang* stands to the right. To the rear of the *bot* is a Sinhalese-style *stupa* wedged between construction clutter and sleeping attendants.

Wat Rajapradit is open daily 0800-1900 and can be easily visited on the walk from the Grand Palace to Wat Suthat. No admission charge.

Before crossing the canal to Wat Rajabopit, you'll see a strange bronze pig near the banks. This funny little porcine monument commemorates the birth year of Queen Saowapha, a consort of King Chulalongkorn.

Wat Rajabopit

One of the more unusual temples in Bangkok, Wat Rajabopit was constructed in 1863 by King Chulalongkorn on the plan of the famous *stupa* at Nakhon Pathom. Entrance is made through doorways carved and painted with whimsical figures of European guards. Surrounding the *chedi* is a circular cloister decorated with ceramic tiles and interrupted at cardinal points by three *viharns* and the principal *bot* on the north. The *bot* displays familiar Thai rooflines on the exterior, but surprises you with its interior: a miniature Italian Gothic chapel inspired by Western models. Special note should be made of the Chinese Bencharong tiles which cover the exterior walls and blend beautifully with the darker golds and blues of the glazed roof tiles. Another glory of Wat Rajabopit is the symmetrical mother-of-pearl inlays in the 10 doors and 28 windows, some of the finest inlay work in all of Thailand.

To the west of the *chedi* courtyard is a royal cemetery constructed by Rama V to honor his parents and relatives. Tombs have been styled after Indian *chedis,* Cambodian *prangs,* and miniature Gothic cathedrals. The garden even includes a walkway reconstructed in Cambodian fashion with dancing *asparas* and roofline *nagas.*

Wat Rajabopit is open daily 0800-1700. No admission charge.

Wat Suthat

The massive *viharn* and *bot* of Wat Suthat form one of the most powerful and elegant monuments in Bangkok. The complex was initiated by Rama I in the early 19th century and completed by his two successors over the next three decades.

Wat Suthat is open daily 0800-1700. No admission charge. For the best effect, enter from Bamruang Road (opposite the Giant Swing) rather than from the side doors on Triphet Road.

Courtyard: The spacious and well-proportioned courtyard serves as an open museum filled with stone figurines, outstanding bronzework, and Buddha images in various poses. Surrounding the *viharn* balustrade are 28 hexagonal Chinese pagodas and eight genuine masterpieces: absolutely superb bronze horses that flank the four corners of the *viharn*. All have assumed a sheen of fine green patina; several retain their original red eyes. Chinese statuary of American sailors and Chinese warlords strategically stand near connecting doorways.

Viharn: The magnificent *viharn* of Wat Suthat—noted for its exceptional height and powerful proportions—exudes a monumental effect rarely witnessed in Thai religious archi-

tecture. The entire sanctuary is elevated on two ascending platforms and bordered by four Chinese stone pagodas which house Buddhas in various poses. Entrance to the central chapel is made through a grandiose portico which frames three massive wooden doors, carved under the direction of Rama III to depict the mythical forest of Himavada. Shoes must be checked outside.

The immense gathering hall houses an eight-meter 14th-century bronze Sakyamuni Buddha previously resident in Sukothai's Wat Mahathat. Widely considered one of the great masterpieces of Thai sculpture, the Pra Sakyamuni Buddha richly deserves the veneration accorded by pilgrims and the sumptuous setting created for it by Rama I and II. Other interior elements include partially restored frescoes that illustrate the lives of various bodhisattvas, eight square marble pillars which support the soaring roof, and an enormous carved wooden pedestal which buttresses the central image. A room with great power.

Bot: Looming beyond the wall which separates the anterior and posterior courtyards is an enormous whitewashed *bot,* constructed between 1839 and 1843 by King Rama III. The surrounding courtyard features elaborate *bai sema* boundary stones protected inside stone chambers, and various oddities such as stone European soldiers and sculpted trees. Entrance into the *bot* can be extremely tricky to find; try all possible gateways, including the small gate at the southwest corner.

Dominating the interior is a life-sized black Buddha figure donated by Rama III and a school of 80 kneeling disciples who listen to the master with backs turned to the entrance. But it is the interior murals—regarded as among the finest in Thailand—that are the chief draw in the *bot.* Dating from the reign of King Rama II (1809-1824) and painted in flat tints, these murals employ primitive perspectives which predate Western techniques. The 24 window panels retell the Jataka tales of previous incarnations of the Buddha, shutters illustrate the celestial city of Indra, and the front wall depicts Buddha overcoming the evil temptations of Mara.

A restoration committee headed by the Fine Arts Department has been charged with returning the badly damaged murals to original condition. After the remaining stucco has been resealed against the wall, the missing sections are sketched in and painted anew with special watercolors. Distinctive brush techniques are used to differentiate restorations from the original artwork.

Giant Swing

Opposite Wat Suthat tower a pair of red teak pillars once used for the Brahmanic Ceremony of the Swing, an annual festival which honored the earthly return of the Hindu god Shiva. Until being halted in 1935, teams of young Hindu priests would swing a full arch of 180 degrees and attempt to snatch a bag of gold coins between their teeth. Some bit the gold, others bit the dust.

Hindu Shrine

Though Brahmanism has been an integral part of Thai royal life since the 14th century, few temples in Bangkok exclusively honor the Hindu triumvirate of Brahma, Shiva, and Vishnu. These three small chapels, situated near the Giant Swing, pay homage with displays of an Ayuthayan-style Vishnu, dancing Nataraja Shivas, and four-headed Brahmas. A replica of the giant swing complete with golden chariot and mythical *kinaree* bird stands in front. Side chapels used for Brahmanic wedding ceremonies display other exquisite Hindu images. The rear alley serves as a production center for enormous bronze Buddhas.

A small Brahmanic Vishnu shrine is located on Mahachai Road adjacent to Wat Suthat.

Religious Supplies

Streets adjoining Wat Suthat specialize in religious paraphernalia such as bright orange robes, image stands, alms bowls, fans, and attractive umbrellas. Dozens of shops sell monstrous bronze images that eventually grace many of the temples in Thailand.

Baan Baht—the so-called "Monks' Bowl Village"—is a tiny corner of Bangkok where the forging of alms bowls clings tenuously to the old traditions. Much of this traditional craft has been lost to modern manufacturing methods.

Chinese Temple

Two blocks west of City Hall is a lively Chinese temple called San Chao Pah Sua. Unlike the sedate Buddhist *wat,* Chinese temples are a continual beehive of activity as worshippers arrive to burn incense and have their fortunes told with sticks and kidney-shaped blocks of wood. Caged birds at the front can be purchased and set free to improve your karma.

Wat Rajanada and the Amulet Market

Erected in 1846 by Rama III, the main sanctuary of Wat Rajanada features remarkable wall paintings of paradise and hell above the entrance, and side walls decorated with angels and celestial symbols. Entrance is made from a gate on the right side. The small *viharn* on the left is noted for its unusual design and the Rattanakosin-style Buddhas displayed on the central altar.

Wat Rajanada is chiefly noted for its popular amulet market at the far left end of the courtyard. Much of the informal street trade in amulets once conducted at Wat Mahathat has been moved into more permanent stalls on these grounds. Buddhist amulets may be legally taken out of the country without an official permit.

Lohaprasat

To the rear of Wat Rajanada stands a curious pink building which resembles, more than anything else, an ornate wedding cake festooned with 37 candle-spires. Lohaprasat was designed to resemble ancient temples in Sri Lanka and India which, according to legend, served as mansions for the Buddha and his disciples. The first thousand-room structure was erected in India by a rich disciple named Visakha, the second in Anaradapura by a Sri Lankan king who decorated the roof with precious stones and ivory. Both prototypes have long since disappeared, leaving Bangkok's structure the world's only surviving example of this unique style. Lohaprasat is now closed and no longer an active *wat,* but local groundskeepers can provide a key.

Pah Fah Pavilion

In a rare case of civic improvement, the recent destruction of an old eyesore on Rajadamnern Avenue and the subsequent erection of the Pah Fah Pavilion have created an attractive tableau of royal *salas,* Wat Rajanada, and the Lohaprasat.

MAGICAL MEDALLIONS

*T*hais believe that protection against malevolent spirits, reckless *phis,* and black magic can be guaranteed with amulets—small talismanic icons worn around the neck or waist. Extraordinarily powerful amulets derive their magic from having been blessed by Buddhist monks or issued by powerful organizations such as the military or monarchy. For example, those recognized by the king and distributed to policemen have acquired considerable renown for their protective powers. Small votive tablets found buried inside the relic chambers of ancient *stupas* are also deemed extra powerful. Amulet collection is big business in Thailand; over a dozen publications are devoted exclusively to their histories and personal accounts of their powers.

Each profession favors a certain style: taxi drivers wear amulets to protect against accidents, thieves to protect against the police. Even American soldiers during the Vietnam War became fascinated with their miraculous powers. Color is also important: white amulets arouse feelings of love, green protects against ghosts and wild animals, yellow promotes successful business deals, red offers protection against criminals. But black is the most powerful color— it provides *complete* invincibility.

Among the more bizarre amulets are those fashioned after the phallus *(palad khik)* and realistically carved from rare woods, ivory, or horn. Related to the Hindu lingam, *palad khik* are attached to cords and worn around the waist. A great way for travelers to make friends and influence people is to proudly wear an amulet of the king or queen.

Golden Mountain

One of the few places from which to peer (smog permitting) over sprawling Bangkok is high atop the 78-meter artificial mountain just outside the ancient capital walls. Modeled after a similar hill in Ayuthaya, the hilltop is surmounted by a modest *chedi* which enshrines Buddha relics donated to King Chulalongkorn by Lord Curzon, Viceroy of India. Visitors climbing the 320 steps are often approached by young monks anxious to practice their English and older, cynical monks more interested in rock music than nirvana. The walkway winds past graves fixed with photos of the deceased, Buddhist shrines, and miniature mountains. Summit views sweep across the Royal Palace, Wat Arun in Thonburi, and modern edifices such as the multihued Baiyoke Towers.

Wat Saket, at the foot of the mount, sponsors Bangkok's liveliest temple festival each November. Once used as a dumping ground for victims of plague, the *wat* is undistinguished aside from its late-Ayuthayan lacquered windows and the International Central Library of Buddhist Literature to the right of the main walkway. Admission is 5B to reach the top.

THE NEW ROYAL CITY

This area in northern Bangkok consists of a modern administrative center blessed with traditional temples, an old royal palace, and pleasant neighborhoods almost completely untouched by mass tourism. Also known as the Dusit or New Royal City, the region was established around the turn of the century by King Chulalongkorn to escape the cramped conditions in his riverside Royal Palace.

Various walking tours are possible depending on your time and interest. One option is a boat ride to the Pra Arthit pier in Banglampoo, followed by a quick look at Pra Arthit Fort and a stroll through the backpackers' center of Khao San Road. Wat Bowonivet and shopping in the New World Center are also recommended. The famous Wat Benjamabopit (Marble Temple) can be reached by taxi or by long hike along Rajadamnern Nok Avenue or through the neighborhoods which flank the Chao Praya River. Vimanmek Palace and the Dusit Zoo would complete the tour. Visitors short on time: don't miss the Marble Palace.

Pra Arthit Fort

Also known as Pra Sumane, this octagonal fort was constructed by King Rama I to defend the northern extremity of his young capital against Burmese and Cambodian invasion. The present reconstruction dates from 1982 and is based on old drawings and photographs.

Khao San Road

A walk through the neighborhood of Banglampoo is highly recommended for both travelers searching for inexpensive accomodations and tourists exploring the back streets of Bangkok. Khao San Road is not only one of the liveliest travelers' scenes between Kuta and Kathmandu, but also an excellent place for cheap plane tickets, inexpensive clothing, and delicious fruit smoothies. Shopping opportunities include several used bookstores with hard-to-find travel guides, sidewalk cassette emporiums, and a great selection of Thai handicrafts. Travel agents on Khao San Road sell the cheapest airline tickets in town, plus the most economical tours of Bangkok and outlying districts. The local notice boards hold information on upcoming Buddhist retreats, employment opportunities teaching English, and local merchants who pay cash for used Levis, Walkmans, and wives.

A few blocks north is a popular shopping district dominated by the New World Shopping Center; daily bargains are on the main floor and better-quality merchandise on the upper seven floors. Adjacent streets are filled with inexpensive clothing and foodstalls.

Wat Bowonivet

Wat Bowonivet is an architecturally modest but spiritually important temple where many of Thailand's kings and princes have traditionally served their monkhood. The temple was constructed in the early 19th century by King Rama III, but gained great fame when Prince Mongkut (of *The King and I* fame) founded the Thammayut sect of Thai Buddhism and served as chief abbot during a portion of his 27-year monkhood. Today, the complex serves as home to the Supreme Patriarch and as the national headquarters of the Thammayut monastic sect, an order which follows a stricter discipline than that of the traditional Mahanikaya. Because of its royal origin and highly disciplined form of Buddhism, Wat Bowonivet enjoys an elevated reputation among the Thai people.

Courtyard: Several small but noteworthy images are displayed in the courtyard off Pra Sumen Road. The overall plan revolves around a central gilded *chedi* with two symmetrical chapels to the north and south. To the right of the central

bot is a Buddha's footprint, a walking Buddha in the Sukothai style, two small Buddhas in the Lopburi style, and, on a raised niche, a Javanese Buddha perhaps imported from Borobudur. To the left is a Dvaravati Buddha. A beautiful reclining Buddha is located at the rear wall.

Bot: Though the *wat* lacks many of the graceful attributes so characteristic of other leading monasteries, a few special features make this temple worth a brief visit. The building is constructed in an unusual T-shape with its head facing north. Of special merit inside the *bot* is a bronze Sukothai Buddha, cast in 1257 to commemorate the country's liberation from Khmer rule and considered one of the finest of the period. Another Buddha image, finely bathed in diffused half-light, sits to the rear. Flanking these two Buddhas are standing images which represent Buddha's chief disciples, Mokkanlana and Saribut. The top tier of the gorgeously decorated gilt altar features a small image known as Pra Nirantaraj, one of 18 statues distributed among the monasteries of the Thammayut sect by King Mongkut.

The walls are blanketed with extraordinary murals. Far removed from the traditional concept of Thai art, these dark and mysterious frescoes are the highly personalized work of a Thai artist named Kru Ing Khong. Khong revolutionized classic Thai artwork with his original use of three-dimensional perspective, moody shading, and fascinating use of Western subjects: Englishmen at the horse races, American ships arriving with missionaries, colonial buildings, and Dutch windmills.

Murals between the windows depict various religious ceremonies, while high above the windows are 16 tableaux symbolic of the Buddhist Trinity: the Buddha, his Dharma, and the Sangha. Column murals relate the spiritual transformation of humanity, progressing from the dark and gloomy colors on the bottom to the lighter and more exalted hues near the ceiling. As a unified ensemble, the murals are unique in the history of Thai painting.

Chedi: Centerpiece of Wat Bowonivet is the great golden *chedi* which enshrines sacred relics and ashes of Thai royalty.

Viharns: Behind the *bot* and *chedi* are two *viharns,* normally closed to the public. The larger structure contains two famous statues brought from Sukothai and Phitsanulok; the smaller hall offers wall paintings depicting episodes from the famous Chinese story of Sam Kok.

Along with Wat Mahathat near the Grand Palace, Wat Bowonivet is a popular temple for meditation instruction. English-speaking visitors can inquire at the international section.

Wat Indraram

On the way to the Marble Temple, a brief diversion can be made to the 33-meter Buddha image at Wat Indraram. Constructed in 1830 of brick and plaster, this absolutely hideous Buddha redeems itself with great views from the tower to the rear of his head. A short taxi ride or long hike through traditional neighborhoods is required from Banglampoo to the Marble Temple in the New Royal City. The most direct route is down Rajadamnern Avenue, past Democracy Monument, but a more relaxing option is to cross the canal from the New World Shopping Center and head north through the winding alleys that skirt the Chao Praya River.

Wat Benjamabopit (Marble Temple)

The most famous attraction in the Dusit area, and one of the finest examples of modern Thai architecture, the Marble Temple is on Sri Ayuthaya Road near the Chitralada Palace.

Wat Benjamabopit was erected by Rama V at the turn of the century to replace an older temple torn down to expand the Dusit Palace. Designed by the half-brother of the king, the elegant complex is largely constructed of white Carrara marble imported from Italy, hence the popular nickname Marble Temple.

Wat Benjamabopit is open daily from sunrise until 1700. Admission is 10B. The *wat* is best visited in the early morning hours when resident monks gather to collect alms and chant in the chapel. Services are also held in the late afternoon.

Bot: Beyond the unusual ornamental railing which encircles the complex is a central hall with overlapping multiple roofs, and two small pavilions containing a bronze Buddha seated under a *naga* and a white alabaster image imported from Myanmar. The four directional gables are elaborately carved with Vishnu riding a *garuda* (east), the three-headed elephant Er-

awan (north), an *unalom* which represents the curl of the Buddha's forehair (west), and a Wheel of the Law (south). Guarding the *bot* are two mythical marble lions seated in the Burmese position. Considered as a unified ensemble, Wat Benjamabopit is a masterpiece of superb harmony and pleasing symmetry.

Dominating the interior is a large gold statue of Pra Buddha Chinarat, an excellent copy of the highly venerated image in Phitsanulok. An urn under the altar holds the ashes of King Chulalongkorn, while wall niches around the central image, transept, and nave contain murals of famous *prangs* and *chedis* from Sawankalok, Ayuthaya, Nakhon Pathom, Nakhon Si Thammarat, Lamphun, Nakhon Phanom, and Lopburi. Also note the vibrant and distinctive stained-glass windows designed by Siamese artists but crafted in Florence, Italy.

Gallery Statues: Perhaps the most famous sight at the Marble Temple is the outstanding collection of 53 Buddha statues displayed in the rear cloisters. To present a complete iconography to his subjects, King Chulalongkorn gathered together in one spot the finest examples—both originals and copies—of bronze Buddhas in the world. Taken together, they provide an amazing opportunity to study the artistic development and range of styles from Thailand, India, Sri Lanka, China, and Japan. Each has been carefully labeled with the country of origin and period—better than art school! Notable masterpieces include a Starving Buddha cast from an original in Lahore, two standing Buddhas of the Sukothai Period, Burmese images from Bagan, copies of Japanese and Chinese Buddhas, plus rare stone Dvaravati images protected against theft by iron grilles.

Vimanmek Palace

Vimanmek is a beautiful and gracious L-shaped palace believed to be one of the world's largest golden teakwood structures. The palace was designed by a German architect named Sandreczki and constructed in 1893 by King Rama V on Si Chang Island in the Gulf of Siam. Chulalongkorn's fascination with Western architecture was reflected in the Victorian style and gingerbread fretwork which allowed the sun to make lacy patterns on the walls. In 1901 the king ordered the unfinished palace disassembled and moved to his new royal enclave of Suan Dusit in Bangkok. Vimanmek ("Castle in the Clouds") served as a royal residence for Rama V and his family (92 wives and 77 children) until abandoned for larger quarters in 1908. The palace fell into disrepair until being completely renovated by Queen Sirikit and Princess Sirindorn in 1982, the year of the Bangkok Bicentennial.

Vimanmek today is a three-story, 81-room museum displaying a rich collection of royal regalia and the eclectic assemblage of King Chulalongkorn: period furniture, the country's first shower with a hidden water tank manually filled by royal pages, and a photograph of Thomas Edison inscribed "to the King and Queen of Siam."

The palace is open daily 0930-1630. Admission is 50B at the door, but free with your ticket stub from the Grand Palace. Complimentary guided tours are given hourly until 1500.

Dusit Zoo

Opposite Chitralada Palace, Thailand's largest zoo offers a modest collection of Asian animals such as elephants, rhinos, and monkeys. Also on the grounds is an artificial lake where pedalboats and rowboats can be rented. Though hardly spectacular, the zoo provides a welcome escape from the heat and congestion of Bangkok. Dusit Zoo is open daily 0800-1800. Admission is 20B.

CHINATOWN ATTRACTIONS

Chinatown is one of the most exotic and stimulating ethnic enclaves in Southeast Asia, and the extraordinary showcase of Old Bangkok. Bounded by the Chao Praya River on the west and Charoen Krung Road on the east, this seething, frenetic, jam-packed neighborhood offers visitors a chance to escape the temple rut and experience the old East of Maugham and Conrad. Although the main boulevards have now assumed the monotonous veneer of modernity, behind the facade lies the *real* Chinatown: smoky temples filled with robed Taoist monks, pharmacies selling antelope horn and cobra venom, rattan vendors, innumerable shops where Chinese merchants demonstrate their legendary commercial talents, jewelry emporiums piled high with gold chains and necklaces, and countless street peddlers who add to the perpetual spectacle.

Chinatown came about in the late 18th century after King Rama I asked Chinese merchants to vacate the land intended for his Grand Palace. Early Teochew (Chiu Chow) entrepreneurs built their thriving businesses along Sampeng Lane, a narrow and claustrophobic alley which served as a commercial center by day, but became an untamed district of brothels, gambling dens, and opium parlors at night. By the early 20th century, Soi Sampeng had been dubbed the Green Light District, since local brothels hung green rather than red lanterns over their doorways. Today,

Chinatown has traded its notorious reputation for the complacency of commerce, but enough exotic culture remains to make this one of the best places to explore in Bangkok.

Walking Tour: The scattered attractions and kaleidoscopic sense of disorder make an organized walking tour of Chinatown rather difficult. The following tour is simply meant to steer you in the right direction and help you find the more fascinating side streets and shopping districts. Visitors short on time should concentrate on Sampeng Lane, Wat Leng Nee Yee, the shopping alley of Soi 16, and the Pahurat Cloth Market.

Rajawong Pier

Begin with a boat ride from Silom Road or Banglampoo to Tha Rajawong (Rajawongse Pier) and walk up Rajawong (Ratchawong) Road past several banks and a lovely green trading firm constructed in a Moorish-German style. Turn left on Anuwong Road and then right on Krai Alley to the first sight.

Boonsamakan Vegetarian Hall

Bangkok's finest Chinese woodcarvings are displayed in this lovely yellow century-old vegetarian hall nestled away in a quiet back alley. Exterior details along the front porch include Chinese dragons and mythical phoenixes, miniature wooden tableaux of Chinese opera scenes protected

FLOATING SLEEVES AND PAINTED FACES

*C*hinese opera, a sometimes bewildering combination of high-pitched singing, clashing music, and stunning costumes, is an artistic expression with no real counterpart in the West. That alone makes it worth watching at least once. To compensate for the stark simplicity of the staging, costumes are brilliant and unbelievably elaborate—heavily embroidered gowns, superb makeup, and amazing sleeves that float expressively without support.

Although the dissonant music irritates some listeners, it can at times be ravishingly melodic and completely haunting. Stories taken from ancient Chinese folklore are told with symbolic gestures but few props. Role identification is linked to makeup, which ranges from the heavy paint worn in Peking-style opera (derived from older masked drama) to the lighter shades favored by the Cantonese. The more complicated a character the more complex the makeup: a red face indicates a courageous character, black a warrior's face, blue cruelty, white an evil personality, purple a barbarian warlords, yellow an emperor.

Costumes and movements are also highly stylized. The more important characters wear larger headdresses and express themselves with over 50 different hand and face movements. Cantonese opera is the most common genre, followed by highly refined Peking opera, considered the classic version. Soochow opera, with its lovely and soft melodies, is rarely performed.

Chinese opera is a dying art in Thailand, performed only in the lone theater in Bangkok's Chinatown.

Chinese opera star

behind glass cases, plus three-dimensional painted tilework of Chinese legends. All have been carved with great care by master craftspeople. Inside are three elaborately carved altars adorned with gilded masterpieces and eight-sided doors which lead into anterior chambers.

Chinese vegetarian halls are only crowded during the annual Vegetarian Festival, which honors the nine deities enshrined here on the main altar. Otherwise, this beautiful hall remains quiet and peaceful, unlike most Chinese shrines and temples which typically teem with worshippers. Just opposite is a stage used for Chinese opera troupes who perform during the Vegetarian Festival, held in the ninth month of the Chinese calendar.

Sampeng Lane

Soi Sampeng, or Soi Wainit 1, epitomizes what is most alluring and memorable about Chinatown. Much too narrow for cars, this canvas-roofed lane is crammed with shopkeepers, porters hauling heavy loads, wholesale and retail clothing merchants, and rare examples of prewar architecture. Walk slowly to enjoy the extraordinary scene. Sensory overload at its finest! A few shops are worth special attention.

Gold Shop: At the intersection of Soi Mangkorn is **Tang Toh Gang,** a remarkable seven-storied yellow building with an imposing tier of balconies designed by a Dutch architect. Tang Toh Gang once served as the central gold exchange for Chinatown.

Guan U Shrine: Left on Soi Issaranuparp is a small temple with a large wooden horse; feed him some oats and then ring the bell around his neck.

Talaad Kao (Old Market): Chinese visit this medieval market in the early morning hours to purchase fresh seafood as well as poultry and vegetables. Talaad Kao winds down around 1000, but an amazing amount of commercial activity continues through the day on Soi Issaranuparp.

Make a U-turn and walk past the Guan U Shrine and across Soi Sampeng.

Chinese Lanterns: Turn right on an alley off Soi Issaranuparp and look for the tiny shops where the ancient art of lantern making still survives.

Pei Ying School

Down the alley, hidden behind Lao Peng Tao Chinese Shrine on Songwat Road, is an imposing old European-style building once considered the most prestigious private primary school in Bangkok. Pei Ying was founded in 1916 by Teochew merchants to encourage the study of the Chinese language and customs. King Rama VII visited the school in 1927 and lectured the audience about his Chinese bloodline. However, since WW II the Thai government has limited the role of Chinese schools; today only five hours per week can be used for the study of Chinese at Pei Ying School.

Return to Soi Sampeng, walk south past the wholesale clothing outlets, and turn right on Yaowapanich Road. This street leads to Songwad Road, where you can view historic old mercantile buildings with fine doorway plasterwork of durians, mangosteens, and mangos.

Luang Kocha Mosque

Few people realize that Chinatown encompasses a sizable Indian and Muslim community. Luang Kocha Mosque (also Masjid Luang Kocha or Masjid Wat Koh) is a European-style building that more closely resembles a private English mansion than the center of worship for Chinatown Muslims. Deserted during the week, the mosque is packed on Friday afternoons; men worship upstairs while women discreetly pray behind curtains on the ground floor. The derelict graveyard to the rear has ancient tombstones of Yunnanese Muslim soldiers of the 93rd Division of the Chinese Nationalist Army.

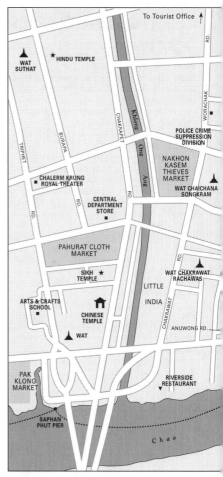

Wat Sampha Tawong

Wat Sampha Tawong, also known as Wat Koh, is chiefly noted for its grand and imposing three-story *bot,* a highly unusual if not altogether beautiful structure. Around the perimeter stand wooden monks' quarters and other auxiliary buildings.

The imposing *wat* has an unpleasant history. To pave the way for the construction of this lavish building some three decades ago, an ancient 18th-century *bot* decorated with murals dating from the reign of King Rama VI (1881-1925) was ordered demolished. Art lovers and historians vehemently protested, but their efforts failed to prevent the destruction of one of Thailand's great art treasures.

Wat Pathom Kongka

This unassuming temple, once known as Wat Sampeng, was constructed during the Ayuthaya Period and so predates the founding of Bangkok by nearly a century. One of the oldest *wats* in Bangkok, Wat Pathom Kongka served as an execution ground for nobles convicted of state crimes. Today, you're more likely to find traditional Chinese funerals in the open pavilions outside the cloistered courtyard.

The temple compound is split by Songwat Road. The main chapel with its *bai sema* stones enclosed in Cambodian-style huts and *viharn* surrounded by cement *stupas* lie close to the Chao Praya River. The monks' quarters and religious schools are on the other side of the road.

Golden Buddha

Wat Traimit, better known as the "Temple of the Golden Buddha," is one of Bangkok's most popular attractions and home of the world's largest golden Buddha. The gleaming Buddha deserves a brief look, but be forewarned: the image itself has little (if any) artistic value, and the entire complex has sadly disintegrated into a tawdry tourist trap, filled with pleading touts and barking escorts who herd around busloads of camera-toting tourists.

However, the history of the Buddha is worth recounting. According to local accounts, the three-meter statue once sat neglected and unloved in Wat Chotinaram, a disused temple in the business quarter of Bangkok. No one realized its true value since the Sukothai-era image had long been sealed in stucco to protect it from Burmese invaders. In 1953 the East Asiatic Company purchased the land and took over the premises. The Buddha was first moved to a temporary building, and later transferred in 1955 to Wat Traimit. During the process, workers dropped it from a crane and cracked its plaster skin. A heavy rainstorm that night further weakened the covering. The following morning, a resident abbot noticed a metallic glow emanating from the crack and ordered the protective shell peeled back. Underneath the stucco facade lay a 5.5-ton golden image.

Local abbots claim the Buddha is 75% pure gold, though scientific measurements have never been made. To the left of the statue is a piece of original stucco covering.

Wat Traimit is open daily 0830-1700. Admission is 10B.

Yaowaraj Road

This is the main boulevard which cuts through Chinatown. Stroll down this street to appreciate the spectacle: dazzling gold stores with mirrored interiors and richly carved wooden chairs, traditional calligraphers working on the sidewalk, herbal stores filled with antler horn and strange roots, cacophonous restaurants, and deafening noise from the people and traffic—sensory overload to rival anything in Asia.

Mr. Chew's Shark Fin Restaurant: Completely exhausted, you need to relax and enjoy a cold drink in this Yaowaraj Road establishment, which is famous for—what else—shark's fin soup and other expensive delicacies made from birds' nests and rhino horn. More luxurious settings are found in the air-conditioned Waikiki Cafe, on the ground level of the Chinatown Hotel.

Gold Shops: Chinese love gold, and nowhere else in Bangkok will you find so many gold shops packed together. Filled with every possible form of gold, the shops are themselves artistic creations with their glass facades, upswept ceilings, vermilion lacquer counters, gaudy red walls, glowing neon lights, carved wooden chairs, and legions of anxious salespeople.

Foreigners should note, however, that the unit weight used nationwide is the *baht* system, not the international metric system. One *baht* (no relation to the monetary unit) of ornamental gold equals 15.16 grams, while one *baht* of bullion gold is equal to 15.244 grams. Ornamental gold is only 96.7% pure, no matter what the salesperson claims.

Chinese Opera: Chalermrat Theater and its resident Tai Dong Chinese Opera Troupe are the last of five opera houses which existed before the onslaught of Chinese cinemas and home videos. Today, the opera company must alternate seasons with movies, but lucky visitors might stop in to experience the last of a dying breed. Performances are given Sunday afternoon and daily except Monday at 1900; admission is 100-400B.

Wedding Shops

From Yaowaraj Road, walk east along Plaeng Nam Road and then left on Charoen Krung Road, formerly New Road—King Rama V's name for the first formal road in Bangkok. To the left along Charoen Krung are small shops specializing in items for Chinese weddings, such as elaborately embroidered pink pillows, wedding invitations, delicate tea sets, and pink mattresses. Calligraphers on the street paint gold letters over a red background, auspicious colors for any occasion.

Soi 16 Market

This narrow covered alley, also known as Soi Issaranuparp, is a shorter version of Soi Sampeng with emphasis on food products rather than clothing and plastics. Ignore the filthy floor and enjoy the displays of Chinese snacks, fresh chickens, and exotic fruits. On the left is Lang Boya, a small Chinese temple marked with a sign proclaiming that "Tourists Are Welcome To Visit And Take Photographs Inside The Temple." Unlike many other groups in Asia, Chinese welcome discreet photographers inside their temples; a small donation is appropriate.

Wat Leng Nee Yee

Also called Wat Leng Noi Yi and Wat Mangkon Malawat, this "Dragon Flower Temple" is the most spectacular temple in Chinatown. It was founded in 1871 and has since become one of the most venerated sites for the Chinese of Thailand.

Above the imposing gateway is a nine-story tower which serves as a Museum of Religious Artifacts, not yet open to the public. Inside the spacious courtyard stands an old vegetarian hall and a traditional medicine shop where cures are prescribed by the Chinese god of medicine.

The central complex is divided into several *viharns.* The dominating hall features three gilded Buddhas draped with saffron robes and flanked by gilded statues of the 18 *arahats.* Also located in the central chamber is a fat Maitreya Buddha (the final Buddha before the destruction of the world), six Dharmapala figures found in every large Chinese temple, and the Four Heavenly Kings, Hindu deities converted to Buddhism. To the right is another hall with images of Taoist Star Deities who heal all illnesses; to the left are statues of Taoist patriarchs and the founder-abbot of the temple. The extreme left has a small but beautiful garden and vegetarian hall filled with elaborately carved furniture.

Services are held daily at 1600.

Alley of Religious Goods

Immediately to the south of Wat Leng Nee Yee is a narrow alley crammed with red and gold religious items: incense sticks, paper offerings shaped like gold bars, elaborate shrines for gods of the earth, and brilliantly colored attire for Chinese deities.

Wat Kanikaphon

Soi 16 continues up to a bright orange *wat* constructed by a former brothel madam to atone for her sins. Kanikaphon translates to "Women who sold women"! Attached to the temple is a Chinese *sanjao* (shrine) where devotees perform the *kong tek,* a ceremony in which paper goods fashioned after automobiles and yachts are burned to send to departed relatives. Never has it been so easy to please dead ancestors and ensure that they don't haunt the living.

Wat Kanmatuyaram

Tucked away in a small alley opposite Cathay Department Store is this small Buddhist temple built in 1864. Duck through the small iron doorway to see a striking, whitewashed, Sri Lankan-style *chedi* and a small *bot* graced with some of Thailand's most important murals. Executed in the reign of King Rama IV, these unretouched murals illustrate the lives of Bangkokians in the mid-18th century, and the various incarnations of the Buddha. Admittance is by official authorization only.

Wat Kusan Samakorn

This quaint Vietnamese temple features a seven-tiered Chinese pagoda on the left, and a small central chapel with a large robed Buddha. The original temple was built in 1854 by two Vietnamese monks, but reconstructed after a fire in 1913. Chinese paintings on the wall recount popular stories of 24 children who demonstrated gratitude toward their parents, an important trait in Chinese culture.

Wat Chaichana Songkram

Wat Chaichana Songkram ("Having Won the War") was constructed in the mid-18th century on land donated by a victorious army leader who served under King Rama III. Much of the complex is modern, but to the rear stand a pair of old bell-shaped *chedis,* a Khmer *prang,* and a two-story library filled with religious artifacts.

Nakhon Kasem Market

Once Bangkok's antique center, most of the dealers in the so-called "Thieves Market" have since moved to shopping centers near the tourist centers. A few dusty stores hold on, surrounded by hardware shops and copper merchants. Merchandise runs the gamut from imitation antiques to vintage clocks and Chinese porcelains.

Wat Chakrawat Rachawas

Though not a temple of great architectural merit, this sprawling complex satisfies curious travelers and allows visitors to witness the Chinese funerals held on a near-daily basis. The principal oddities are the crocodiles that sleep in the small pond off the central courtyard. The original croc was a one-eyed monster named Ai Bord; he now sits stuffed after losing a fight with a younger pondmate.

The *mondop* on the artificial hill which overlooks the pond houses a replica of a Buddha's footprint. To the rear is a grotto with statues of a supernatural Buddha shadow and a fat disciple who stuffed himself into obesity to end his sexual passions. Inside the nearby *bot* and *viharn,* both now under reconstruction, are excellent murals that feature life-sized angels and Jataka murals from the reign of King Rama V. All have been totally retouched.

Pahurat Cloth Market

Sampeng Lane terminates at the old cloth market where Sikh and Chinese merchants peddle Indian saris, Malaysian batiks, and Thai silks from enormous open-air tables. Also of interest are the Hindu wedding stores and shops selling accessories for Thai classical dancers.

Little India

Sikh Temple: Up a narrow alley off Chakrapet Road towers a seven-story white temple dedicated to the Sikh community of Thailand. A health clinic and maternity ward are located on the upper floors.

Indian Restaurants: Adjoining alleys all along Chakrapet are filled with travel agencies, which serve the Indian trade, and inexpensive *masala dosa* restaurants. A comfortable if somewhat expensive choice is the **Royal India Restaurant,** where you can dine in air-conditioned surroundings. Less expensive cafes include the **Moon Restaurant** in the rear alley adjacent to the canal, and the popular **Cha Cha Restaurant** on Chakrapet Road. All offer good food in earthy surroundings.

Pak Klong Market

Pak Klong Talaad, at the foot of the Memorial Bridge, is the city's largest wholesale fruit and vegetable market. The action begins at dawn as boats laden with foods arrive to unload their wares. By early afternoon the merchants have packed up and swept out the aisles, though this fascinating market at any hour offers an overpowering sense of medieval commerce.

River taxis back to Silom Road and Banglampoo leave from Saphan Phut dock at the terminus of Triphet Road, and from Rachini Pier just across the canal from Pak Klong.

THONBURI ATTRACTIONS

Thonburi, on the west bank of the Chao Praya River, briefly served as the capital of Thailand after the fall of Ayuthaya until Rama I moved his court to the opposite shore. Temples located near the river can be toured on foot by wandering through the narrow lanes; interior *wats* can be reached by public boat.

Wat Arun

This monumental 86-meter Khmer-style *prang,* one of Thailand's largest religious monuments, towers above the Chao Praya to form Bangkok's most impressive and famous landmark. Wat Arun was constructed by Rama II on the site of a former royal temple which once held the precious Emerald Buddha. Despite problems of erecting such a massive structure on the city's swampy soil, Rama III finally completed the complex in 1842. Rama IV added the final touch: thousands of multiglazed Chinese porcelains

donated by Buddhist devotees. The present king donates new robes to the resident monks on the occasion of the Tod Kathin Festival, a merit-making ceremony formerly done downriver from the Grand Palace in royal barges.

Better known as the Temple of the Dawn, Wat Arun symbolically represents the Buddhist universe, with its trident-capped central tower indicating Mt. Meru and the four smaller towers depicting the four worldly oceans. The central *prang* is intersected by four door niches with the god Indra riding his three-headed white elephant. Other figures include the moon god on his white horse and illustrations of the four most important episodes from the life of Buddha: birth, meditation under a protective *naga,* sermon to the five ascetics, and entry into nirvana. Visitors can make the steep climb up to the midway point for views over the Chao Praya and Thonburi.

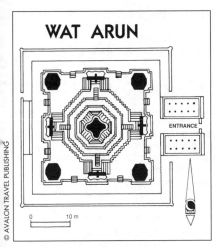

WAT ARUN

ENTRANCE

0   10 m

© AVALON TRAVEL PUBLISHING

Located on the grounds are several other worthwhile buildings. The *bot* in the northwest corner features four unusual *chedis* and interior murals which depict the life of Buddha. A restored *mondop* between the *bot* and *viharn* contains a Buddha footprint and twin towers used as belfries. The *viharn* behind the primary *chedi* contains a silver and gold Sukothai image brought back from Vientiane by Rama II.

Wat Arun is accessible by shuttle boat from the Tha Tien Pier behind Wat Po. Open daily 0800-1700. Admission is 10B.

Wat Kalayamit

Located near the entrance to Klong Bangkok Yai, this immense temple has dimensions dictated by the huge Buddha image it enshrines. Interior walls of the main *bot* and adjacent chapel are decorated with mural paintings dating from the reign of Rama III. The spacious courtyard is decorated with Chinese gateways and statues, and a bronze bell reputed to be the largest in Thailand. Thais of Chinese origin favor this temple and giant image, which they call Sam Po Gong.

Wat Prayoon

Also constructed during the reign of Rama III, Wat Prayoon consists of two chapels with mother-of-pearl decorations, an artificial hill decorated with *chedis,* frangipani trees, and a pool filled with turtles. According to legend, the hill was modeled after a mound of melted wax formed by a candle of Rama III.

Wat Suwannaram

This extremely well-proportioned and finely decorated *bot* near the Thonburi train station illustrates the transitional architecture of the Ayuthaya and Bangkok Periods. Interior frescoes are attributed to two famous painters from the court of Rama II. Lower murals display scenes from the last 10 Jataka tales of the previous lives of the Buddha, while the entrance wall features the victory of the Buddha over Mara. These 19th-century murals, remarkable for their sensitivity and originality of composition, are considered among the finest in Bangkok.

Wat Dusitaram

Though the primary *bot* is of little architectural interest, Wat Dusitaram, located near the Royal Barges Museum, also features interior murals of great interest. A traditional arrangement is followed. Side walls between the windows show episodes from the life of Buddha, the front fresco masterly renders the Buddhist victory over Mara, while the Buddhist cosmology is depicted on the back wall.

Royal Barges Museum

More than 50 longboats, all carefully restored for Bangkok's 1982 Rattanakosin bicentennial, are dry-docked inside the shed near Klong Bangkok Noi. Crafted in the early part of this century, and only waterborne for very special royal events, these barges are designed after mythical creatures featured in the Ramayana. The principal barge, *Sri Suphannahongse,* is named after the mythical swan which graces the prow. Perhaps the largest dugout in the world, this gilded 45-meter glider weighs over 15 tons and requires the efforts of 54 oarsmen and a rhythm keeper who bangs the beat in time with the chanting of ancient boat poems. Equally impressive is the 44-meter *Anantanagaraj,* with its carved figurehead of a seven-headed *naga.*

The museum is open daily 0800-1700. Admission is 30B.

Bangkok Floating Market

Thonburi's floating market epitomizes what is most crass and callous in the tourist trade. Once an authentic and colorful scene, the market completely died out in the 1960s as modernization forced boat vendors to move into shopping centers. Threatened with the loss of revenue, tour operators came up with a rather awful solution: hire a few Thai women to paddle around and *pretend* to be shopping. Disneyland feels genuine when compared to this outrage, perhaps the most contrived rip-off in the East.

ATTRACTIONS NEAR SIAM SQUARE

Jim Thompson's House

Jim Thompson was the legendary American architect-entrepreneur who settled in Thailand after WW II and almost single-handedly revived the moribund silk industry. No trace was found of Thompson after he disappeared in 1967 while hiking near Cameron Highlands. Jim's maze of seven Thai-style teak houses has since been converted into a small private museum filled with his priceless collection of Asian antiques, pottery, and curiosities. A small gift shop sells fine reproductions of Vessantara Jataka and Brahma Jati horoscopes.

Thompson's house, located off Rama I Road on Soi Kasemsan 2, is open Mon.-Sat. 0900-1600. Admission is 100B; the profits go to Bangkok's School for the Blind. A more comprehensive collection of Thai art is found in the National Museum; the modest layout here disappoints many visitors.

Phallic Shrine

Dedicated to Chao Tuptim, the pomegranate goddess and female animist spirit, this tangled mini-jungle shrine is noted for its hundreds of stylized and realistic phalluses contributed by childbearing devotees. Rather than simply a fertility symbol, the curious memorial also ensures prosperity since the lingam traditionally symbolizes both regeneration and good fortune in Thailand. Devotees of both sexes arrive daily to burn incense and donate brightly painted phalluses in all possible shapes and sizes.

The shrine is on the grounds of the Hilton Hotel at the end of Wireless Road next to Klong Saen Saep. Walk straight through the hotel lobby into the rear gardens, then walk right to the small shrine adjacent to the klong. No admission charge.

Siam Society

Publishers of the scholarly *Journal of the Siam Society,* this group also restores deteriorating murals and maintains a 10,000-volume library of rare and valuable editions. Research facilities are open to members only; write to the Executive Secretary, 131 Soi Asoke (21), Bangkok 10110, Thailand.

Of special interest to foreign visitors is the Society Travel Club (tel. 02-258-3491), which sponsors professionally led excursions to im-

Suan Pakkard Palace

portant temples, archaeological digs, and noteworthy festivals. These tours, unquestionably some of the best available in Thailand, are reasonably priced and open to the public. Upcoming tours are listed in the *Bangkok Post*.

Kamthieng House: To the left of the Siam Society headquarters is a restored century-old residence, formerly the home of a prominent family in Chiang Mai until being dismantled and reconstructed on the present site. Kamthieng is chiefly noted for its ethnological artifacts and collection of hilltribe costumes, plus exterior details such as teak lintels serving as magical talismans that hold ancestral spirits and guarantee the virility of the inhabitants.

Kamthieng House is on Soi 21 just off Sukumvit Road. Open Tues.-Sat. 0900-1700 and 1300-1700. Admission is 30B.

Suan Pakkard Palace

Bangkok can be a city of anachronisms. Hidden between the high-rises and construction sites are several charming homes surrounded by large, peaceful gardens. Suan Pakkard is an old Thai residence complex which was disassembled and brought down from Chiang Mai by Princess Chumbhot, one of Thailand's leading art collectors. The royal quarters were converted into a public museum after the death of Prince Chumbhot and his wife.

Five traditional houses cluster around small lotus ponds and meticulously trimmed lawns. All are filled with an eclectic range of Thai artifacts, from Ban Chiang pottery to Khmer sculpture. House I contains a Gandhara Buddha from Pakistan, an 8th-century Khmer goddess, and valuable celadon from Sawankalok. House II once served as the royal bedroom. House III, the reception area, features a gilded throne and a Chinese cabinet graced with five-colored Bencharong ceramics. The dining room, House IV, was constructed with leg wells for long-legged Western guests.

Suan Pakkard's most impressive structure is the 450-year-old Lacquer Palace to the rear of the gardens. Transferred from Ayuthaya in the face of Burmese invasion, the gold and black lacquer interior panels show the early influences of Westernization on traditional Thai art and chronicle everyday life in 16th-century Ayuthaya.

ROMAN-ROBOT FANTASIES

*F*rom Hong Kong to Singapore, economic success has dramatically transformed Asian skylines from low-rise colonial to high-tech Houston. But Bangkok's building boom has unleashed a wave of innovative architecture unrivaled anywhere else in the region. Refusing to clone Western prototypes, the architects of Bangkok have invented some amazing fantasies: corporate headquarters that resemble Roman palaces, condo complexes that fuse art deco facades with Thai rooflines, fast-food emporiums buried inside rocket ships, Mediterranean stucco homes, Bavarian half-timbered cottages—Hollywood holograms in the City of Angels.

This exciting movement is led by an iconoclastic architect named Sumet Jumsai and an innovative design firm called Plan Architect. Sumet's Bank of Asia Robot building near Silom Road—a humorous mixture of an external skeleton fitted with giant nuts and bolts—illustrates the marriage of high-tech themes with cartoon consciousness. The postmodern McDonald's on Ploenchit Road combines gleaming glass walls with Roman columns. Suburban developments include English castles complete with moats, and the new headquarters for *The Nation* newspaper, an 11-story sculpture inspired by the whimsical designs of cubist painter Georges Braque. Bangkok is now more than just Thai temples and nocturnal delights, it's home to some of the most creative modern architecture in the world.

The semiprivate gardens surrounding the home provide a welcome relief from the dirt and noise of Bangkok. Suan Pakkard is east of Banglampoo on Ayathaya Road and is open Mon.-Sat. 0900-1600. Admission is 150B.

Snake Farm

Also known as the Pasteur or Saowapha Institute, this snake farm is the world's second-oldest snake research facility—established in 1923 to develop antivenins and vaccines for poisonous snakebites. The serpentarium now houses over 1,000 snakes for both educational and medical purposes. Cholera, smallpox, typhoid inoculations, and rabies treatments are available.

A RIVERSIDE WALK AND THE ORIENTAL HOTEL

Bangkok's *farang* community once made their commercial and diplomatic headquarters on the banks of the Chao Praya, near New Road (now called Charoen Krung) and the venerable Oriental Hotel. Start this tour at the historic hotel, which consistently ranks as one of the world's finest. Wander into the nostalgic Authors Lounge and perhaps enjoy a cocktail on the riverside veranda. Fine antiques and designer silks are sold in the adjacent Oriental Plaza Shopping Center.

Just opposite the Oriental Hotel is a handsome white building constructed in 1901 to house one of Bangkok's original trading firms. **The East Asiatic Company** was founded by Dutch investors in 1897, and today ranks as one of the world's principal trading conglomerates. A Dutch flag still flies over the central cupola.

Slightly up Oriental Lane and on the right stands Bangkok's principal Catholic church, **Assumption Cathedral.** Constructed in 1910, the interior features a marble altar imported from France and a soaring roofline splashed with Technicolor hues.

Just north of the Oriental, you can stop and admire the **French Embassy.** Built in the mid-19th century, this lovely European-style residence still evokes the atmosphere of old Bangkok with its louvered shutters and spacious verandas.

The **Old Customs House** nearby once housed the head office of the Thai Customs Department. This sadly neglected 19th-century building is one of the finest remaining European structures in Bangkok. Fortunately, the future looks promising. The Treasury Department has registered the building with the Fine Arts Department as a historic site, and private investors intend to renovate and convert it into a Thai cultural hall.

Bangkok's community of Muslims worship in the small **Haroon Mosque** nestled in a narrow alley behind the Old Customs House.

Continue this tour by walking away from the river toward the GPO.

This neighborhood is home to a large community of Indians and Pakistanis who patronize the local cafes. Highly recommended is the **Sallim Restaurant** located in the alley beyond the GPO and past the Woodlands Hotel. Excellent food at rock-bottom prices.

Up from the GPO you'll find the **Portuguese Embassy.** The first Europeans to initiate trade with Siam were the Portuguese, from their maritime empire at Malacca. In 1820 they erected the first embassy in Thailand. Much has been reconstructed though original portions are still visible from the river and over the tall protective wall.

Final stop on your short walking tour is the four-story air-conditioned **River City Shopping Complex** adjoining the Sheraton Royal Orchid Hotel. Special art exhibits are often featured on the ground floor, while the third and fourth floors are devoted entirely to Asian antiques. An auction is held each month; exact dates are listed in the *Bangkok Post.*

The institute puts on a fascinating snake show. The demonstration begins with a 20-minute slide presentation on the work of the institute and dangers of Thailand's poisonous snakes. Afterward, the crowd gathers in the central pit to watch Siamese king cobras milked for their venom. Snake handlers gleefully squeeze the creatures only inches from your camera lens, close enough to watch the milky venom ooze from the fangs. The adjacent museum houses indigenous species such as green pit vipers, banded kraits, and other nonpoisonous snakes.

Near Lumpini Park on Rama IV Road, the Pasteur Institute is open daily 0830-1600. Snake shows are conducted weekdays 1030 and 1330, weekends 1030 only. Admission is 70B.

Erawan Shrine

Thailand's devotion to animist spirits and Hindu deities is best appreciated in the famous shrine on the grounds of the Erawan Grand Hyatt. The memorial was erected after hotel construction was halted by a series of seemingly random disasters: marble destined for the lobby disappeared at sea, workers died under mysterious circumstances, and cost overruns threatened to crush the hotel project. Spirit doctors, desperately summoned for advice, commanded the hotel owners to erect a shrine to Brahma. The mishaps ended and word of the miracle spread throughout Thailand.

Today, the Erawan Shrine hosts a continual circus of devotees bearing incense, flowers, and images of the elephant god Erawan, the three-headed mount of Brahma. Supplicants whose prayers have been fulfilled often sponsor performances of Thai dance. Western visitors are encouraged to make their own offerings; prices for goods are posted at the front entrance. This crazy and magical place amazes even more because of its bizarre location at a major Bangkok intersection, the corner of Ploenchit and Rajadamri Roads.

Lumpini Park

Bangkok's oldest park, Lumpini serves as one of the few green lungs for the congested city. Daytime heat empties the park, but early morning hours are an excellent time to watch the two categories of Lumpini fitness fanatics: traditionalists and modernists. The former, mostly older Thai folk, arrive at sunrise to practice the Chinese art of

tai chi. Designed to work the muscles in a slow-motion *kung fu*, the ancient dance is now accompanied by portable stereos playing Chinese dirges or modern disco. Competing with the traditionalists are joggers who pound the pavement on a 2.5-km circuit. Kite flyers, soccer players, and bodybuilders fill the park during the afternoon.

This oasis is nestled off Rama IV Road near Chulalongkorn University.

Wat Thamma Mongkol

Completed in 1985 as Bangkok's most modern temple, this 14-story, 95-meter-high blockhouse is capped with a traditional *chedi* which enshrines relics of the Buddha. It combines traditional religion with high-tech conveniences; an elevator whisks visitors to the top for spectacular views. Bangkok's tallest *chedi* is on Sukumvit Road at Soi 101.

RIVER AND CANAL TOURS

UP THE CHAO PRAYA RIVER

A boat cruise along the Chao Praya River is one of the highlights of any visit to Bangkok. River travel offers a rare opportunity to enjoy Bangkok without the hassles of congestion and pollution, plus it opens up fresh vistas impossible to experience from a public bus or taxi. Passengers of other boats seem ready to smile, plus you get an exhilarating sense of speed and a wonderful breeze on your face.

The following sights are included only in the central part of the route from Tha Orienten in the south to Pra Arthit Pier in Banglampoo. Public boats leave from the pier down the alley from the Oriental Hotel. Private tours cost 200-300B per hour, so unless you're looking for an expensive tour, ignore the touts who haunt the pier.

Boat Types

First, you'll need to recognize the three principal types of boats that operate on the Chao Praya.

Longtail Boats: Longtails *(hang yao)* are narrow, high-powered racers that serve the outlying canals.

Shuttle Boats: Shuttles are the squarish, slow boats that make short hauls across the river, useful for quickly crossing to Thonburi and visiting important temples such as Wat Arun.

Express Boats: Express boats *(rua duan)* are long, white boats with red stripes. Operated by the Chao Phya Express Boat Company, these run daily 0600-1800 every 20 minutes from the Krung Thep Bridge in south Bangkok to Nonthaburi, a suburb 18 km north. Note that *express boat service ends at 1800.* The one-way journey includes a total of 36 stops (26 on the Bangkok side and 10 on the Thonburi side) and takes approximately 75 minutes. Government-controlled fares range 5-10B depending on the distance. Rather than linger on the crowded rear landing, walk to the front of the boat where seats are more plentiful.

ORIENTAL HOTEL TO BANGLAMPOO

Holy Rosary Church

Just past the Sheraton Hotel complex, look for the recently restored church, constructed in 1787 by Portuguese Catholics who moved from Thonburi after the destruction of Ayuthaya by Burmese invaders.

Wat Thong Noppakhun and Wat Thammachat

Opposite, on the Thonburi side, are two little-

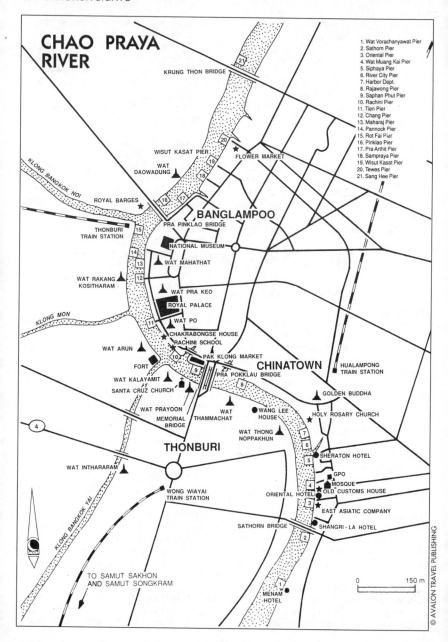

CHAO PRAYA RIVER

1. Wat Vorachanyawat Pier
2. Sathorn Pier
3. Oriental Pier
4. Wat Muang Kai Pier
5. Siphaya Pier
6. River City Pier
7. Harbor Dept.
8. Rajawong Pier
9. Saphan Phut Pier
10. Rachini Pier
11. Tien Pier
12. Chang Pier
13. Maharaj Pier
14. Pannock Pier
15. Rot Fai Pier
16. Pinklao Pier
17. Pra Arthit Pier
18. Sampraya Pier
19. Wisut Kasat Pier
20. Tewes Pier
21. Sang Hee Pier

KRUNG THON BRIDGE

KLONG BANGKOK NOI

WISUT KASAT PIER

FLOWER MARKET

WAT DAOWADUNG

ROYAL BARGES

THONBURI TRAIN STATION

PRA PINKLAO BRIDGE

BANGLAMPOO

NATIONAL MUSEUM

WAT MAHATHAT

WAT RAKANG KOSITHARAM

KLONG MON

WAT PRA KEO

ROYAL PALACE

WAT PO

CHAKRABONGSE HOUSE
RACHINI SCHOOL

WAT ARUN

PAK KLONG MARKET

CHINATOWN

FORT

HUALAMPONG TRAIN STATION

WAT KALAYAMIT
SANTA CRUZ CHURCH

PRA POKKLAU BRIDGE

GOLDEN BUDDHA

WAT PRAYOON

WAT THAMMACHAT

WANG LEE HOUSE

HOLY ROSARY CHURCH

MEMORIAL BRIDGE

WAT THONG NOPPAKHUN

THONBURI

WAT INTHARARAM

WONG WIAYAI TRAIN STATION

SHERATON HOTEL

GPO
MOSQUE
OLD CUSTOMS HOUSE

ORIENTAL HOTEL

EAST ASIATIC COMPANY

SATHORN BRIDGE

SHANGRI - LA HOTEL

KLONG BANGKOK YAI

TO SAMUT SAKHON
AND SAMUT SONGKRAM

0   150 m

MENAM HOTEL

© AVALON TRAVEL PUBLISHING

known temples featuring fine proportions in Ayuthaya style, and murals dating from the reigns of Rama III and IV.

Memorial Bridge and Tha Saphan Phut
Boats then glide under the iron-green Memorial Bridge to Tha Saphan Phut. Opened by King Rama VII in 1932, this pier leads to the colorful Pak Klong Market and the Little India neighborhood. Public longtails from this landing stage make inexpensive runs up Thonburi canals.

Wat Prayoon
Across from the Saphan Phut pier stands this temple, constructed during the reign of King Rama III and noted for its mother-of-pearl door decorations and artificial hill decorated with miniature *chedis* and frangipani trees.

Santa Cruz Church
Near Wat Prayoon, you'll see this unmistakable old church, constructed by Portuguese Catholics after the fall of Ayuthaya, but almost completely reconstructed in 1913. Note its distinctive narrow profile and towering cupola.

Wat Kalayamit
Adjacent to the Santa Cruz Church, this immense temple shelters an equally gigantic Buddha. Check out the interior mural dating from the reign of King Rama III.

Rachini School
A bit upriver on the Bangkok side, behind a low, white wall, stands a beautiful European-style building bearing the insignia of "Royal Seminary." Rachini School was the first school devoted to the education of Thai women and it is still regarded as the finest in Thailand.

Tha Rachini
Adjacent to Pak Klong Market is a busy little pier where shuttle boats cross to the Thonburi attractions of Wat Kalayamit and Santa Cruz Church. Adventurous visitors can enjoy a short walk from the pier through the winding alleys of the old Portuguese quarter.

Chakrabongse House
Past Tha Rachini, hidden behind the thick foliage, is one of the few remaining royal residences which once graced the riverbanks. Chakrabongse House was constructed in 1909 by an Italian architect for the son of King Rama V.

Tha Tien
From the next pier on the river (Tha Tien), travelers can access Wat Po, take a public ferry across to Wat Arun, and explore the canals of Thonburi on any of the waiting public longtails.

Wat Rakang Kositharam
One of the most original temples left from the Rattanakosin Period, this rarely visited structure is noted for its decorated roof supports of unusual size and elegance, retouched interior frescoes, and beautiful three-sectioned library restored several years ago by the Association of Siamese Architects. The opposite shore is dominated by Wat Po, the Grand Palace, and Wat Pra Keo.

Maharaj Pier
Further up the river on the Bangkok side, this distinctive red pier leads to Wat Mahathat, the National Museum, and Thammasart University. Long the hotbed of liberal politics, Thammasart earned worldwide attention in 1973 when a student-led revolution succeeded in overthrowing the military government. In 1976, the university was attacked and hundreds of students murdered after right-wing forces reseized power from the democratically elected government.

After a quick stop at Tha Rot Fai, terminus for the Thonburi Railway Station, express boats pull into Pra Arthit Pier and the backpackers' enclave of Banglampoo.

EXPLORING THE CANALS

Bangkok's waterways offer exceptional sightseeing opportunities and reveal what is most attractive about the city. Three major canals lead off the river: Klong Bangkok Yai in the south, Klong Mon in the center, and Klong Bangkok Noi in the north. All three arteries are intersected by dozens of smaller canals that wind through dense jungle and vine-choked foliage, all flanked with stilted houses and small temples rarely visited by Westerners. Best of all are the children who smile and wave as they cannonball into the murky waters.

Miraculously, the pollution and congestion of modern Bangkok seem light years away.

Private chartered longtail boats are somewhat expensive at 200-300B per hour, but hurried visitors who don't mind the rich tourist image may find it worth the cost.

Less pricey and more authentic are ordinary public longtails which race up and down the canals, picking up and dropping off Thai passengers until they finally turn around and return to their starting point. These longtails depart frequently from five piers in central Bangkok: Mahathat, Chang, Tien, Rachini, and Saphan Phut. Which pier to choose hardly matters since the scenery is similar throughout the canal network. Ignore the private operators and instead wait patiently for the next public longtail; fare is 10B in each direction or 20B roundtrip.

You have two options: stay on the boat for the roundtrip or disembark at one end and walk through the plantations to another canal to catch a longtail back to the starting point. Boat operators rarely speak English, but it's almost impossible to get lost. Just sit down, smile, and enjoy the ride.

Canal enthusiasts can purchase *50 Trips Through Siam's Canals* by George Veran or the re-cently published but rather sketchy *Bangkok's Waterways* by William Warren. The *Thonburi Canal* map by the Association of Architects is also useful.

Warning: Beware of slick professionals who offer free guided tours and then blackmail you for a 1,000B gasoline fare in the middle of the river. Never get into a longtail boat alone.

Klong Bangkok Noi

Ordinary longtails that travel up the northern canal of Klong Bangkok Noi depart from three different piers: Tha Tien dock near Wat Po, Tha Chang near Wat Pra Keo, and Tha Maharaj behind Wat Mahathat. Four different *hang yao* routes are possible, but most roar up Klong Bangkok Noi before exploring the smaller and more fascinating canals of Bang Sai, Bang Ramat, Bang Phrom, and Bang Yai. Attractions along these canals include the Royal Barge Museum, Wat Suwannaram, and Wat Suwankhiri. Make a roundtrip journey, or hop off to explore these Thonburi temples.

Klong Mon

Longtails up the central canal of Klong Mon leave from both Tha Chang (left side only) and Tha

---

ORGANIZED RIVER TOURS

*S*everal tour companies offer formal cruises along the Chao Praya and intersecting canals. Tickets can be purchased at the point of departure and from most travel agencies.

Moderate: Each Saturday and Sunday at 0800 a sleek boat leaves Maharaj Pier behind Thammasart University, stops briefly at the Thai Folk Arts and Crafts Center in Bang Sai, and reaches the Royal Summer Palace at Bang Pa In at noon. The return journey visits the fascinating Wat Pailom Stork Sanctuary before arriving back in Bangkok around sunset. This all-day river cruise costs 180-240B. A relaxing day except for the obnoxious loudspeaker. Contact Chao Praya Express Boat Company at (02) 222-5330 or (02) 225-3002.

Mit Chayo Phraya Express Boat Company offers all-day Bangkok Noi canal tours which leave Maharaj Pier daily at 0830 and cost 150B. Call (02) 225-6179 for further information.

Crystal Tour: Three-hour rice-barge tours to Klong Mon, Taling Chan, and Bangkok Noi leave from the Sheraton Royal Orchid Hotel daily at 1500. The 250B fee includes refreshments and soft drinks. Call (02) 251-3758.

World Travel Service: Four-hour longtail and rice-barge tours run up the Chao Praya River to Rama VI Bridge. Tours cost 320B, leave daily at 1400, and include a short visit to the Boonrawd Brewery. Call (02) 233-5900.

Asia Voyages: A teakwood rice barge makes an overnight cruise from Bangkok to Ayuthaya via Bang Pa In. The 3,000B fare includes onboard accommodation, tour guides, and all meals. Asia Voyages (tel. 02-235-4110) is the largest operator of private yachts in Thailand.

Oriental Queen: This air-conditioned cruiser leaves the Oriental Hotel daily at 0800 and returns around 1800. The 1,200B cruise includes a buffet lunch, a visit to Bang Pa In, a guided tour around the historic ruins of Ayuthaya, and splendid sunsets on the return voyage. Call World Travel Service at (02) 233-5900 for more information.

Tien. If you choose the more convenient pier at Tha Tien, you want the smaller landing to the right. Some longtails race up Klong Mon and then continue up the smaller canal of Bang Chuak Nang. For a longer and more colorful journey, ask for a boat heading for Bang Noi (not Bangkok Noi). The journey passes temples, orchid farms, and leaning coconut trees. Get off at the end when the driver makes his U-turn, wander 45 minutes south through traditional neighborhoods to Wat Chim on Klong Bang Waek, then flag down a longtail back to the Memorial Bridge.

Klong Bangkok Yai

Longtails up this southern canal depart from Tha Rachini, a few blocks south of Wat Po. After fol-lowing the river for some distance, the longtail veers off and follows the narrow *klongs* of Bang Dan, Phasi Charoen, or Sanam Chai. During perhaps the most colorful route in Thonburi, stops can be made at Wat Sang Krachai, Wat Werurachin, Wat Intararam, Wat Pak Nam, and a snake farm on Klong Sanam Chai.

Klong Tan

This unusual journey originates under the New Petchburi Road Bridge near Pratunam Market, and passes through beautiful residential neigh-borhoods to Klong Tan. Some boats go left to Bangkapi, while others turn right down Klong Tan to Sukothai Road Bridge at Soi 73. Buses return back to the center of town.

OUTSKIRTS OF BANGKOK

NORTH OF BANGKOK

Wat Thamakai

Located 28 km northeast of the city center near Bangkok Airport in Pathum Thani Province, this rural center was founded 20 years ago to offer instruction in Thamathayard meditation. The central *bot* is a marvel of modern Thai architecture which, unlike that of most Siamese temples, is characterized by pure, simple lines rather than highly ornate decoration. The theme of simplicity continues in the interior, where a black marble floor and plain white walls accent the presiding Buddha image illuminated with a single spotlight.

Wat Thamakai honors the legendary meditation techniques of a Bangkok monk named Pra Mongkol Thepmooni. As taught by the monk from Wat Paknam, meditation involves initial concentration on an imaginary crystal ball, then transferring that focal point to the center of the student's mind. There, the sphere expands to incorporate the universe and ultimately induces Thamakai, the visible Buddha.

Young Thai males come here to enter the monkhood during two-month retreats, held during the summer vacation months March-May. After a month of preparation, the students are ordained at a mass ceremony at the Marble Temple and then return to further their knowledge of Buddhism. Visitors will often find the initiates silently medi-tating under umbrellas arranged around the pond.

Public Thai-language lectures on meditation and the life of Buddha are given every Sunday 0930-1530. Visitors are requested to dress in white.

Prasart Museum

Notable private collections of Thai art can be viewed at Jim Thompson's House and Suan Pakkard Palace in Bangkok, in the Ancient City, and in the museum of Khun Prasart Vongsakul. Once a successful real estate developer, Prasart has spent the last decade constructing reduced-scale reproductions of historic Thai buildings and filling them with his priceless collection of Sukothai Buddhas, Bencharong porcelains, and paintings in the Thai classical style.

Prasart Museum is past the airport in the Bangkok suburb of Hua Mak. For further infor-mation, contact the Prasart Collection, Penin-sula Plaza, 153 Rajadamri Rd., Bangkok 10500, tel. (02) 253-9772.

Safari World

Southeast Asia's largest wildlife park includes a wildlife section toured by coaches, a bird park with walk-in aviary, Macaw Island, restaurants, and an amusement park. A friendly American from the San Francisco Bay Area oversees an-imal care and acquisitions.

Safari World is in Minburi District at Km 9 on Ramintra Road, 10 km northeast of downtown Bangkok. Take bus 26 from Victory Monument to Minburi, then a direct minibus. Open daily 1000-1800; tel. (02) 518-1000. Admission is 400B.

Siam Water Park
Also in the Bangkok suburb of Minburi, the park is popular with families and children who plunge down the longest water slides in Thailand. A small open zoo and botanical gardens are located on the grounds. Take bus 26 or 27 from Victory Monument. Open daily 1000-1800; tel. (02) 517-0075. Admission is 300B.

Nonthaburi
A pleasant day-trip can be made by express riverboat to Nonthaburi, a small town 20 km north of Bangkok. Disembark at the pier near the clock tower and walk left up to the Nonthaburi Prison. The Correctional Staff Training compound on the left has a small museum with displays of torture used to execute prisoners during the Ayuthaya and modern periods. Foreign prisoners convicted of drug crimes can occasionally be visited.

Central Nonthaburi has a floating restaurant and an old wooden provincial hall restored by the Fine Arts Department and converted into a museum of anthropology. Also worth visiting is the modern mosque, several Ayuthaya Period *wats,* and the Singha Brewery, where Thailand's most popular beer is brewed.

A ferry from the Nonthaburi dock leads across the Chao Praya to Wat Salak Dtai and Wat Chalerm Pra Kiet, a beautiful temple renowned for its architecture and idyllic location amid breadfruit trees and abandoned buildings.

Organized tours of nearby gardens are organized each weekend by the Suan Tan Noi Tour Company, tel. (02) 583-9279 or (02) 583-7853.

Wat Pailom Bird Sanctuary
Wat Pailom, near Pathum Thani on the Chao Praya River 32 km north of Bangkok, is one of the world's last sanctuaries for rare Indian open-billed storks *(Anastomus oscitans),* which migrate from Bangladesh each Dec.-June. Once a burial ground for execution victims, the bizarre landscape lies covered with denuded trees piled with over 10,000 enormous nests.

Tragically, Wat Pailom, one of the more remarkable nature reserves in Thailand, now seems doomed. Recently constructed upriver dams have choked off the water supply for the dipterocarpus trees, and modern fertilizers have poisoned the apple snail, the storks' primary source of food. The Wildlife Fund of Thailand is attempting to relocate the storks to more suitable colonies at Suphanburi and Ayuthaya.

Wat Pailom is best visited on the weekend river cruises leaving in the mornings from the Maharaj Pier. Contact the Chao Praya Express Boat Company at tel. (02) 222-5330 or (02) 225-3002.

SOUTH OF BANGKOK

Damnern Saduak Floating Market
The floating markets of Thailand are unique wonders. Amid the lowland canals and winding rivers, women in straw hats continue to paddle sampans piled high with vegetables, fruits, and flowers. Despite the popularity of fast-food restaurants and concrete shopping centers, authentic floating markets still serve several communities near Bangkok.

Don't bother visiting the completely artificial Wat Sai Floating Market in Bangkok, one of the worst examples of mercenary tourism in the world. Instead, make the journey to the small town of Damnern Saduak, 109 km southwest of Bangkok, midway between Nakhon Pathom and Samut Sakhon. Though firmly on the tourist route, it remains an authentic experience, but only before the busloads of tourists begin arriving at 0930. Visitors who arrive before 0900 will have the spectacle to themselves, but arrivals after 0930 will be deluged with thousands of tourists. Either be here early, or skip it.

Damnern Saduak has three floating markets. The principal market at Ton Kem is formed by a narrow canal flanked with foodstalls and souvenir shops. Handicraft bazaars in the rear should be avoided since the merchandise is overpriced and the vendors can be very aggressive. Farther south are the rarely visited markets at Her Kui and Khun Pitak. Photographers at Ton Kem will get their best shots from the bridge which crosses over the canal, and from the produce shed on the right. Chartered sampans cost 50-80B for a short 20-minute look and 250-300B for a one-hour tour, though everything of interest can be seen from the bridge and adjacent walkways.

The best way to experience the floating market at Damnern Saduak is to spend a night in

floating market

one of the nearby hotels.

Noknoi Hotel: The "Little Bird" hotel in the center of town is conveniently located near the bus stop, but is decrepit and only survivable for a single night. Highway 325, tel. (032) 251392, 120-180B fan, 200-250B a/c.

Ban Sukchoke Resort: Your best bet for comfort and atmosphere is this relatively new series of bungalows overlooking the canal. Facilities include a seafood restaurant, meeting rooms, and boat service to the floating market. Take a *tuk tuk* from the bus stop, or make arrangements with a travel agent in Bangkok. 103 M.5 Damnern Saduak, tel. (032) 253044, fax (032) 254301, 250B double bungalow, 400-600B rooms, 700-800B boathouse, 1,200-1,500B suites.

Guesthouse: A cheap but often deserted guesthouse may or may not be open. It's near the coconut factory on the right of the canal. Bare-bones bamboo huts cost 50-80B.

Damnern Saduak has plenty of **restaurants,** but most visitors will opt for the cafes which over-

hang the market. The coffee shop near the bridge is run by a friendly woman who can't understand why anyone would want Thai noodles for breakfast.

Getting There: Because of the distances involved, most visitors take an organized tour which includes a brief stop at the Nakhon Pathom *chedi* and an afternoon visit to the Rose Garden. Independent travelers can reach Damnern Saduak by public bus 78, leaving every 20 minutes from the Southern Bus Terminal in Thonburi.

To beat the tour buses, catch an early morning bus 0500-0700. The ride takes two hours and terminates in downtown Damnern Saduak. The floating market, located two km up the adjacent canal, can be reached by walking on the path to the right of the canal or by taking a public sampan for 10B at the bridge. You can also take a minibus from downtown or hike along the road south of the bridge just past the information booth.

From the western town of Kanchanaburi, take yellow bus 461 to Bang Pae and then bus 78 to Damnern Saduak. Allow two hours for the journey. Further details are available from Kanchanaburi guesthouses.

Motorcyclists will enjoy the cool, dark ride from Kanchanaburi to the Ratchaburi turnoff, then can follow the large English-language signs which point the way to Damnern Saduak. South of Bang Pae are a snake farm and several beautiful *wats,* including a new complex which resembles a Japanese Zen temple.

Ancient City

Ancient City, also called Muang Boran, is a 200-acre outdoor park and architectural museum filled with full-sized and reduced-scale replicas of Thailand's 65 most important monuments and temples. Constructed by an art-loving philanthropist and Bangkok's largest Mercedes-Benz dealer, Muang Boran provides an excellent introduction to the country's architecture, including reproductions of buildings which no longer exist, such as the Grand Palace of Ayuthaya. The complex is laid out in the shape of Thailand with monument locations mirroring the actual geography of the country.

Best suited for the visitor with a serious interest in architecture, the vast park is enormous, somewhat neglected, rarely visited, and murderously hot in the summer. Muang Boran pub-

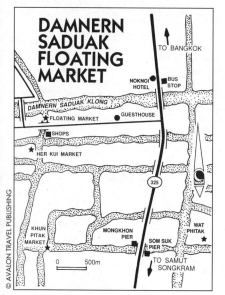

DAMNERN SADUAK FLOATING MARKET

TO BANGKOK

NOKNOI HOTEL BUS STOP

DAMNERN SADUAK KLONG

FLOATING MARKET GUESTHOUSE

SHOPS

HER KUI MARKET

325

KHUN PITAK MARKET MONGKHON PIER WAT PHITAK

SOM SUK PIER

0 500m

TO SAMUT SONGKRAM

© AVALON TRAVEL PUBLISHING

lishes a detailed guidebook to their park and a lavish bilingual periodical devoted to Thai art and architecture; old editions are heavily discounted.

Muang Boran is 33 km southeast of Bangkok along the old Sukumvit Highway. Muang Boran group tours (tel. 02-226-1963, 224-1057, or 222-8143) can be booked from travel agents or directly from their office at 78 Rajadamnern Ave. near Democracy Monument.

Independent travelers can take a/c bus 8 or 11 from Sukumvit Road to the clock tower in Samut Prakan, then minibus 38 to the front gate. Muang Boran is open daily 0830-1700. Admission is 150B.

Crocodile Farm

The world's largest reptile farm was founded in 1950 by a former hotel pageboy to save crocodiles from extinction and, parenthetically, turn their hides into wallets, briefcases, and shoes. Today, over 30,000 crocodiles patiently lounge around murky swimming pools waiting for their hourly wrestling matches and frenzied feedings at 1700. After their moment of glory, the beasts

are skinned into trendy suitcases and exotic dishes for Chinese restaurants. Also included is a small zoo blessed with oddities such as smoking chimpanzees and dancing elephants. Touristy and strange.

The Crocodile Farm (tel. 02-387-0020) is 33 km southeast of Bangkok in Samut Prakan, six km before Ancient City. Air-conditioned buses 8 and 11 from Sukumvit Road go directly to the entrance. Open daily 0800-1800. Admission is 400B.

WEST OF BANGKOK

Rose Garden

Located on the banks of the Nakorn Chaisri River and set amid beautiful landscaped gardens, this country resort features an eight-acre lake, aviaries with over 300 exotic birds, orchid and rose nurseries, championship 18-hole golf course, and replica of a Thai village where cottage industries such as silk weaving and umbrella painting are demonstrated. Overnight facilities include a resort hotel with 80 first-class rooms overlooking the river. Reservations can be made through travel agencies or by contacting the resort at (02) 259-3261.

The one-hour cultural show, given daily at 1500, is widely considered the finest in Thailand. No matter how contrived or touristy, this show consistently thrills with its nonstop performances of Thai dance, martial arts, a traditional wedding, Buddhist monkhood ordinations, *takraw,* and a demonstration of working elephants.

Rose Garden is 32 km west of Bangkok, on the road to Nakhon Pathom. Most travelers visit the park on a package tour which includes the floating market at Damnern Saduak and the *chedi* at Nakhon Pathom. Luxury hotels in Bangkok provide daily connections, as does Bangkok Sightseeing Travel Agency which charges 280B for a daily roundtrip bus ride at 1300 from the Indra Hotel. The resort can also be reached by public bus from the Southern Bus Terminal in Thonburi.

The Rose Garden is open daily 0800-1800. The 400B admission fee includes the gardens and cultural show.

Thai Human Imagery Museum

Prominent personalities and events in Thai history are examined in a small museum opened near the Rose Garden in 1987. Exhibits include figures of former kings of the Chakri dynasty, 15 great Buddhist monks with descriptions of their achievements, an upstairs hall dedicated to Confucius, and a demonstration room where the fiberglass figures were created. Artists fashioned the 40 figures from fiberglass rather than wax after considering the possible effects of Thailand's intense heat.

The museum is 31 km west of Bangkok. Open daily 0900-1800. Admission is 250B.

Samphran Elephant Park

This 22-acre farm sponsors daily demonstrations of crocodile wrestling, magic shows, an elephant tug-of-war, an elephant roundup, and re-creation of the famous elephant battle between King Naresuan the Great and a Burmese prince.

The park is 31 km west of Bangkok, on the left side of the road just one km before the Rose Garden. Open daily 0900-1800. Admission is 300B. For further information, you can telephone the park at (02) 284-1873.

ACCOMMODATIONS

Bangkok offers a wide range of hotels and guest-houses in all categories and possible price ranges. Budget homestays are plentiful in the Banglampoo District, while some of the finest hotels in the world are found near Siam Square and hugging the banks of the Chao Praya River.

Where to stay depends on your finances, and whether you want to be near the river, sightseeing attractions, nightlife centers, or shopping districts. The following summary will help you decide.

GENERAL INFORMATION

Districts

For quick orientation in Bangkok, think of the city as individual neighborhoods with distinct personalities, hotel price ranges, and styles of restaurants and nightclubs. The city has four major hotel districts (Banglampoo, Silom Road, Siam Square, and Sukumvit Road) and several less-frequented areas such as Chinatown and around the Malaysia Hotel.

Old Royal City: The old royal city around the Grand Palace has the largest concentration of sightseeing attractions but very few hotels or restaurants. Banglampoo is the best choice if you want to stay near the temples in the old royal city.

Banglampoo: Banglampoo has become the backpackers' headquarters, with dozens of budget guesthouses and inexpensive cafes. The area lacks great nightlife or shopping, but compensates with a superb location near great temples and the immensely convenient Chao Praya River. Anyone looking for guesthouses under US$10 should head directly for its principal thoroughfare, Khao San Road.

Chinatown and Little India: Chinatown hotels cater primarily to Chinese businesspeople, but a handful of inexpensive guesthouses are located in adjacent Little India. Travelers searching for a strong and completely authentic encounter with Indian culture might consider staying here rather than in Banglampoo.

Silom Road: Bangkok's original tourist enclave is located near the Chao Praya River and along a major boulevard known as Silom Road. Sightseeing attractions are minimal and the congestion is unnerving, but Silom offers dozens of moderate to super-luxury hotels, exclusive restaurants, high-end shopping boutiques, great sidewalk shopping, and the infamous nightlife area of Patpong Road.

Riverside hotels such as the Oriental and Shangri La are world famous for their extremely high levels of service, though budget accommodations are limited to some older properties and a few grungy Indian hotels near the GPO.

Malaysia Hotel Area: Once the budget travelers' center for Bangkok, hotels and guesthouses along Soi Ngam Duphli have sadly declined in recent years. Although the neighborhood can no longer be recommended, the nearby YMCA represents good value in the lower price range.

Siam Square: Bangkok's most luxurious hotel district is a relatively low-density neighborhood with ultra-elegant hotels and modern shopping centers. The lack of sightseeing attractions is balanced by the vast gardens that surround many of the hotels, and by the enormous shopping complexes that guarantee some of the best shopping in all of Asia. Hotels are expensive, but several low-priced and very clean guesthouses are located near Jim Thompson's House.

Sukumvit Road: Once considered on the outer fringes of Bangkok, Sukumvit has developed into the leading area for tourists seeking moderate-budget accommodations. The only drawback is the enormous distance to important temples and government services, but Sukumvit has the best selection of hotels in the US$25-50 price range.

Other positive notes to this neighborhood include countless excellent restaurants, sidewalk shopping, upscale boutiques, and racy nightlife in the Nana Entertainment Plaza (NEP) and along Soi Cowboy. Despite the remote location and problems with noise and pollution, Sukumvit is highly recommended for anyone motivated by nightlife and shopping.

Prices

Hotel prices and occupancy levels in Bangkok have followed a wild roller-coaster ride of boom-and-bust cycles since the early 1990s.

The economic collapse of 1997-98 effectively halted all hotel construction and stopped the hotel glut that had plagued Bangkok for almost a decade. At the same time, political problems in Indonesia (mostly affecting Bali) and Malaysia (after the freeze of the Malaysian currency) forced many major tour operators to redirect their groups to Thailand where peace and calm prevailed.

The result was that many destinations in Thailand—including Bangkok—are now running at near-capacity levels and a critical shortage of hotel rooms now exists. Visitors can always find a room, though advance reservations may be necessary during the busy winter months, especially December and January. More information below.

Prices cited in the hotel charts are published rack rates, subject to negotiation during periods of low occupancy and the slow season March-November. Most rooms, except for budget guesthouses, carry an additional 10% service charge and 11% government tax. Discounts are often given at the front desk for longer stays (three or more days) and for corporate accounts.

Luxury hotels have recently started to quote their prices in U.S. dollars rather than Thai *baht,* in an effort to stabilize prices and avoid the pitfalls of a wildly fluctuating currency. Those that quote prices in American currency are now substantially more expensive than those properties that continue to quote rates in local currency. Travelers seeking the best values are advised to move down a few notches and stay in smaller, midpriced hotels rather than the top-end properties.

Reservations

Advance reservations for moderate to luxury hotels are essential during the peak season from December to February. Reservations can be made by mail and by phone, though phone reservations are problematic since reservation clerks often have difficulty with English. Fax or Internet reservations are *highly* recommended since the hard-copy printout guarantees fewer mistakes than written or phone requests. Most of the better hotels in Bangkok now have websites where you can quickly and dependably make room reservations.

Fax numbers are listed with most hotel descriptions. The country code for Thailand is 66, and the area code for Bangkok is 02. Since the 0 at the beginning of the area code is dropped when dialing or faxing from overseas, Bangkok can be reached by dialing 662 (not 6602) followed by the seven-digit phone number.

Travelers arriving at the Bangkok airport without reservations can check on vacancies and make reservations at the Thai Hotel Association Reservation Counter in the arrival lounge. Hotels are listed according to price, with the cheapest rooms starting at around 800B. None of the guesthouses in Banglampoo or near the Malaysia Hotel belong to the Thai Hotel Association. Phone calls from the airport to the following guesthouses *might* turn up a vacancy and reservation.

BANGLAMPOO AND KHAO SAN ROAD

Bangkok's headquarters for backpackers and budget travelers is centered around this friendly little neighborhood just a few blocks from the temples and Chao Praya River. Named after the village *(bang)* where *lampoo* trees once thrived, Banglampoo now serves as a freak street for world travelers who hang out in the guesthouses, cafes, and travel agencies on Khao San Road.

There's a great deal of interest here. Early-morning risers can enjoy an espresso from one of the sidewalk cafes, while late-night strollers will love the sidewalk shopping and general sense of mayhem. People-watching in Banglampoo is excellent and prices on plane tickets, local tours, clothing, and other souvenirs are some of the best in town.

Best of all, Banglampoo is a friendly place with excellent vibes from both travelers and Thais who work the guesthouses and restaurants. Though it's undeniably a travelers' ghetto with all the standard trappings, much of the adjacent neighborhood exudes an authentic Thai atmosphere rarely found in the other tourist areas in Bangkok.

Guesthouse Overview

At last count, Banglampoo had over 70 guesthouses, which charge 60-100B for dorms, 80-300B for single rooms (rooms with one bed), and 120-400B for doubles (two beds). Rooms with private baths cost slightly more those with common baths. Many of the guesthouses also

have small air-conditioned rooms in the 400-800B price range. Guesthouses constructed in the last few years often have larger rooms with private baths for 300-900B. The trend appears to be toward better facilities at a slightly higher fee, though low-end rooms still vastly outnumber the more expensive ones.

Most Banglampoo guesthouses are identical in cleanliness and size. There isn't much sense in recommending specific guesthouses, since all will be fully booked simply from word-of-mouth reputation. A small selection of slightly better choices is shown on the map and briefly described here. Most guesthouses are located near Khao San Road.

Travelers who would like to distance themselves from the scene should check ones near the river or across the bridge to the north.

Banglampoo does have some drawbacks. Rooms are often small and claustrophobic, furnished with only a single bed. Theft can be a problem because of plywood walls and inadequate locks. Motorcycles which race around late at night can ruin your sleep; find a clean and comfortable room tucked away on a side street rather than directly on Khao San Road. Finally, Banglampoo is a trendy scene (banana pancakes, hippie clothes, etc.), which some travelers find unappealing.

Perhaps the worst problem in Banglampoo is that most guesthouses are perpetually filled from morning until night. Finding a room is time-consuming since reservation lists are rarely honored and rooms fill *immediately* after checkout. Room searches are best conducted in the early morning 0700-1100 when travelers depart for the airport and bus stations. Take the first available room, and transfer to another the following day if noise is a problem. Travelers arriving from the airport in the late afternoon or evening should expect a long—but ultimately successful —search. Take a taxi from the airport to Khao San Road, then leave your bags in a sidewalk cafe while you search for an available room. And keep smiling ... Bangkok is a great place once you find a room!

Transportation from the Airport

From the airport, the easiest way to reach Banglampoo is either by Airport Bus for 70B per person or a metered taxi for 350-450B.

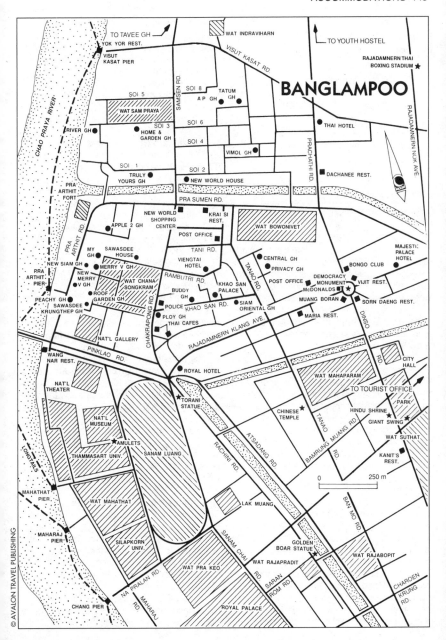

RAJADAMNERN AVENUE BUSES

39, 59	Airport
AC3, AC39	Airport
70	Boxing Stadium
12AC	New Petchburi
39AC	Northern Bus Terminal
45	Rama IV
15, 121	Silom
2, 11AC	Sukumvit, Eastern Bus Terminal

CHAKRABONGSE ROAD BUSES

| 3 | Weekend Market, Airport |

PRA SUMEN ROAD BUSES

| 53 | Chinatown, Train Station |

Taxi: Metered taxis leave from the stand outside to the far left of the exit. You must pay the metered fare, plus a 50B airport surcharge, plus any applicable tolls (30-60B). Ignore the more expensive private taxi services and limousine kiosks inside the terminal—walk outside the terminal door and then left about 100 meters. A taxi desk will give you a coupon, which you then turn over to the driver.

Airport Bus: There are three special Airport Buses to go to different sections of Bangkok. The "Route A2" bus goes from the airport down the tollway to Victory Monument, then Democracy Monument, and finally stops directly at Khao San Road. It then continues to Sanam Luang before looping back to the airport.

The bus leaves the airport every 30 minutes from 0500-midnight. Apart from the low fares and friendly service, passengers can watch videos prepared by the Tourism Authority of Thailand.

Khao San Road Guesthouses

Several dozen guesthouses are on Khao San Road or tucked away in the small alleys off the main street, though you might find places further afield far more pleasant.

Buddy Guesthouse: Located in the middle of Khao San Road, Buddy Guesthouse is a good place to begin your room search. Though it's perpetually filled, you can drop your bags here and enjoy a quick meal in the comfortable cafe

located in the rear. A less-packed restaurant is located upstairs. Buddy Guesthouse, like most other guesthouses in Banglampoo, has a variety of rooms from basic cubicles to small a/c rooms with private bath. 137 Khao San Rd., tel. (02) 282-4351, 80-350B.

Chart Guesthouse: An easy-to-find 20-room guesthouse with a great cafe. All rooms have fans; no a/c. 61 Khao San Rd., tel. (02) 280-3785, 100-300B.

Central and Privacy Guesthouses: Both Central and Privacy Guesthouses to the east of Tanao Road are quiet and somewhat run-down but exude a homey Thai feeling. Alleys branching off Khao San have several more peaceful guesthouses. 69 Tanao Rd., tel. (02) 282-0667, 60-180B.

C.H. Guesthouse: Big and popular place with 27 rooms and a packed video cafe on the ground floor. 216 Khao San Rd., tel. (02) 282-2023, 60-150B fan, 200-420B a/c.

Hello Guesthouse: A 30-room guesthouse with a popular streetside cafe. 63 Khao San Rd., tel. (02) 281-8579, 60-150B fan, 250-450B a/c.

Lek Guesthouse: One of the original guesthouses in Banglampoo. Always filled, but worth checking with Mr. Lek Saranukul. 125 Khao San Rd., tel. (02) 281-2775, 80-240B.

Ploy Guesthouse: A big place with very large rooms with private bath. Entrance is around the corner from Khao San Road. The lobby on the second floor includes a small cafe and the coldest soft drinks in Bangkok. 2 Khao San Rd., tel. (02) 282-1025, 80-300B.

Siam Oriental Guesthouse: Newish spot at the end of the road with large cafe, harried employees at the front desk, and decent rooms in all possible price ranges. 190 Khao San Rd., tel. (02) 629-0312, 350B fan, 400-650B a/c.

Guesthouses behind the Temple

For a slightly Felliniesque experience, walk through the passageways of Wat Chana Songkram (Chanasongkram) to the alleys and guesthouses that surround the temple in all directions. These very popular guesthouses are in a great location and well removed from the hubris of Khao San.

Apple 2 Guesthouse: Apple 2 is a long-running favorite located in a quiet back alley. The big rambling teak house with songbirds and upstairs rooms is also called Mama's. 11 Trok Kai Chae, tel. (02) 281-1219, 70-120B.

Merry V Guesthouse: One of the best guesthouses behind Wat Chana Songkram has clean rooms and a very comfortable restaurant. 33 Soi Chana Songkram, tel. (02) 282-9267, 100-450B.

New Siam Guesthouse: Popular five-story guesthouse with storage lockers and cozy cafe in the alley that connects the temple grounds with Pra Arthit Road. The lobby sign says "Enjoy your Life & Have a Nice Day." 21 Soi Chana Songkram, tel. (02) 282-4554, 200-375B fan, 500-600B a/c.

Roof Garden Guesthouse: Cheap, quiet, and almost completely deserted guesthouse at the far corner of the road behind the temple. Features an outstanding array of junk scattered around the lobby. 62 Soi Chana Songkram, tel. (02)629-0625, 80-180B.

Sawasdee House: Decent rooms, travel agency, Internet connections, and one of the largest open-air cafes in this neck of the woods. Very quiet location back from the busy streets. 147 Soi Rambutree, tel. (02) 281-8138, sawasdeehouse@hotmail.com, 100-450B.

Sawasdee Krungthep Inn: Clean and relatively new spot with small cafe decorated with old Bangkok photos. Superior rooms have a/c, cable TV, and hot showers. 45 Soi Chana Songkram, tel. (02) 629-0072, 250B fan, 350-450B a/c.

Phra Arthit Road Guesthouses

The road that skirts the river just west of Khao San has a half-dozen guesthouses that provide easy walking access to the Pra Arthit Pier.

New Merry V Guesthouse: A popular branch of the nearby guesthouse with a large, open-air restaurant, travel agency, storage lockers, and Internet cafe to check your e-mail. 18-20 Phra Athit Rd., tel. (02) 280-3315, 100-150B fan, 380-400B a/c.

Peachy Guesthouse: Slightly more expensive than Khao San cubicles, but the rooms are clean, spacious, and furnished with writing tables and standing closets. Air-conditioning is available. Perpetually filled, but sign the waiting list. Avoid rooms facing Pra Arthit Road or adjacent to the TV room. 10 Pra Arthit Rd., tel. (02) 281-6471, 120-360B.

Guesthouses North of Khao San Road

Some of Banglampoo's quietest guesthouses are across the bridge north of Khao San Road. All provide an opportunity to experience Thai homestays in a traditional neighborhood.

Samsen 6 Guesthouses: Another idyllic spot far removed from the hype of Banglampoo, near the midpriced Vorapong Guesthouse (250B fan, 300B a/c) and the less inexpensive AP, Tatum, and Vimol Guesthouses. Not a tourist in sight.

Tavee Guest House: To really escape the travelers' scene in Banglampoo, walk north up Chakrabongse Road and turn left on Sri Ayuthaya Road at the National Library. Near the river are three quiet guesthouses including the Shanti, Sawatdee, and Tavee. The latter is at 83 Sri Ayuthaya, tel. (02) 280-1447, 60B dorm, 120-150B private room.

Truly Yours Guesthouse: Samsen 1 Road has Truly Yours and Villa Guesthouse, while Samsen 3 Road has the River, Clean and Calm, and Home and Garden Guesthouses. Worth the walk. All charge 80-150B.

Youth Hostel: Bangkok's only hostel has a fan-cooled building with dorm beds (60B) and private rooms (200B), plus an a/c building with sex-segregated dorms (80B) and private rooms (220-450B). Clean but somewhat isolated. 25/2 Phitsanulok Rd., tel. (02) 281-0361, fax (02) 281-6834. No reservations accepted. Nonmembers must buy a one-year membership for 300B.

Moderate

Banglampoo isn't exclusively for budget travelers. Bridging the gap between the inexpensive guesthouses and the upscale hotels are several midpriced hotels and guesthouses that offer both fan and a/c rooms. During the fiery summer months March-June, paying extra for air-conditioning is worth it.

Khao San Palace Hotel: The dark and small rooms, probably the cheapest a/c rooms in Bangkok, come equipped with private baths, warm water, and horizontal mirrors geared to short-time business. 139 Khao San Rd., tel. (02) 282-0578, 360-580B.

Nith Charoen Hotel: Another good midpriced hotel in the heart of Banglampoo. Comfortable lounge with a useful bulletin board. 183 Khao San Rd., tel. (02) 281-9872, 300-340B fan, 420-560B a/c.

New World House: A large, modern apartment complex with luxury features at a bargain price. All rooms are a/c, with private bath, telephone, laundry service, and views over Banglampoo. Recommended for anyone who intends to stay a week or longer. Located just across the canal. Soi 2 Samsen, tel. (02) 281-5596, fax (02) 281-5597, 500B daily, 2,500-3,000B weekly, 8,000-12,000B monthly.

Luxury

Luxury is a relative term in Banglampoo. None of the following hotels compare with the Oriental or Shangri La, but all provide adequate facilities for travelers who want the location, with a touch of luxury.

Royal Hotel: This well-priced hotel is within easy walking distance of Bangkok's attractions—an excellent place in a great location. Reservations at this historic hotel (several people's revolutions have taken place inside this art deco building) can be made from the hotel counter at the airport. Budget travelers and overheated travel writers often spend their mornings in the a/c coffee shop reading the *Bangkok Post.* 2 Rajadamnern, tel. (02) 222-9111, fax (02) 224-2083, 1,000-1,800B.

Viengtai Hotel: Banglampoo's longtime favorite has sharply raised prices and failed to make any improvements; not recommended. 42 Rambutri Rd., tel. (02) 281-5788, fax (02) 281-8153, 1,400-1,800B.

Majestic Hotel: The best hotel in Banglampoo may be somewhat overpriced but compensates with an excellent restaurant and great location near the temples and tourist office. 97 Rajadamnern, tel. (02) 281-5610, fax (02) 280-0965, 1,800-3,200B.

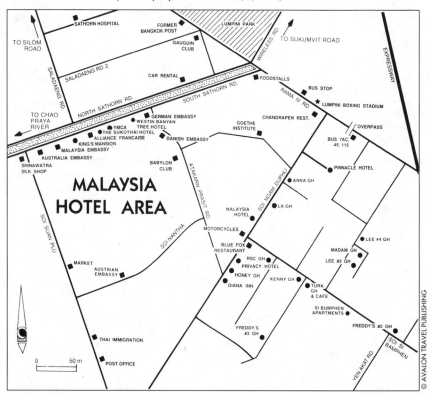

Thai: Another mid-range possibility but not in the best of locations. 78 Prachatipati, tel. (02) 282-2833, fax (02) 282-1299, 1,200-1,600B.

MALAYSIA HOTEL AREA

Surrounding the Malaysia Hotel are about a dozen budget guesthouses and several midpriced hotels which comprise Bangkok's original travelers' center. From the late 1960s to the early 1980s this neighborhood—also known as Soi Ngam Duphli after the main boulevard—was a hotbed of budget guesthouses, discount travel agencies, and banana-pancake cafes. Travelers on the Kathmandu-to-Bali trail made their home at the Malaysia, a near-legendary hotel that offered comfortable rooms at rock-bottom prices.

Unfortunately, the Malaysia Hotel raised its room rates and moved into the sex trade as travelers abandoned the neighborhood and moved over to Banglampoo to enjoy the far superior atmosphere and great location of Khao San Road. Today, the sex orientation has faded somewhat though the lobby of the Malaysia Hotel attracts legions of prostitutes after the bars close on Patong.

Soi Ngam Duphli today continues to offer some of the same kinds of services (guesthouses, budget travel agencies, etc.) or earlier days, but suffers from being noisier, more polluted, and far seedier than Banglampoo. Hard drugs and prostitutes (many gay) are now commonplace and yet the neighborhood survives with first-time visitors who haven't heard about Banglampoo, and those seeking inexpensive accommodations centrally located between the nightlife areas of Silom Road and Sukumvit.

From the airport take the Airport Bus in the direction of Silom Road or a direct taxi for about 350B including all tolls and airport surcharge.

Budget
Several of the budget guesthouses in this neighborhood are fairly comfortable and worth consideration despite the noise and pollution.

Anna Guesthouse: Dismal rooms though the downstairs travel agency may prove useful. 17 Soi Ngam Duphli, tel. (02) 679-6214, 100-180B.

L.A. Guesthouse: Another simple operation with fairly clean rooms but unfriendly manager. 27 Soi Ngam Duphli, tel. (02) 286-8556, 140-200B.

Kenny Guesthouse: Comfortable outdoor cafe with reasonable meals and tiny cubicles only fit for midgets. Soi Si Bamphen, 150-200B.

Turk Guesthouse and Cafe: A surprisingly decent Indian cafe on the ground floor and bare bones rooms upstairs. Avoid rooms facing the busy street. Soi Si Bamphen. 150-200B.

Freddy's #2 Guesthouse: A clean and friendly guesthouse recommended by many travelers. Freddy runs two other guesthouses in the neighborhood, though #2 is the best of the lot. Soi Si Bamphen, 100-150B.

Madam Guesthouse: The area's quietest guesthouses are located in a back alley and cul-de-sac off Soi Si Bamphen. All can be recommended for their solitude rather than cleanliness. Madam is a cozy if rustic homestay known for its friendly proprietor. Ramshackle rooms in the old house go from 100B.

Lee #3 Guesthouse: Adjacent to Madam Guesthouse, and far removed from the horrendous traffic that blasts along Soi Si Samphen, is another old house converted into a backpackers' crash pad. A popular place to nod out in the sunshine. Rooms cost 100-150B.

Honey Guesthouse: A somewhat clean and comfortable 35-room building just down from the Malaysia Hotel. Rooms are available with common or private bath, with fan or a/c. Hefty discounts are given for monthly residents. The adjacent **Diana Inn** (Greco-Roman style) is also recommended. 35 Soi Ngam Duphli, tel. (02) 286-3460, 180-200B inside rooms, 220-300B with balcony.

Moderate
Midpriced hotels in this neighborhood have sadly declined in recent years, but the nearby YMCA and King's Mansion are excellent value. These latter are located midway between the Malaysia

RAMA IV ROAD BUSES

5	Siam Square, Banglampoo
115	Silom, General Post Office
7AC	Train Station, Royal Palace

Hotel and Silom Road. For more information, see "Silom Road" below.

Malaysia Hotel: A decade ago, the legendary Malaysia was the favored gathering place for budget travelers who enjoyed the low rates, a/c rooms, swimming pool, and 24-hour room service. A large, very famous notice board offered tips on visas, crash pads, and how to see the world on a shoestring. Today, the notice board is gone, the coffee shop doubles as a pickup spot for prostitutes in the late evening, and the pub has been converted into a massage parlor. Rates have risen but are still reasonable by Bangkok standards. 54 Soi Ngam Duphli, tel. (02) 679-7127, fax (02) 287-1457, 620-900B.

Privacy Hotel: If the scene at the Malaysia turns you off, try this less-expensive but very run-down a/c alternative. 31 Soi Ngam Duphli, tel. (02) 286-2339, 320-364B.

Boston Inn: Once the best-value hotel in the neighborhood, the Boston Inn has finally collapsed and now seems beyond redemption.

CHINATOWN

Few travelers stay in Chinatown, but the chaotic neighborhood offers a chance to escape the standard tourist enclaves. Most hotels are on the main boulevards of Chakrapet, Yaowaraj, and Rajawong. Larger properties are signposted in English, while the smaller places, marked only with Chinese signs, are sometimes reluctant to take Westerners.

Chao Phaya Guesthouse: Beautifully situated on the banks of the Chao Praya River, this aging place is easily spotted from the river taxis that cruise between the Old Royal City and Silom Road. It's not in the best of condition, though Bangkok could use more waterfront guesthouses like this one. 1128 Songwad Rd., two blocks south of Rajawong Rd., tel. (02) 222-6344, 300-600B.

Riverview Guesthouse: Another riverside choice located north of the Royal Orchid Sheraton. The eight-floor hotel has both fan and a/c rooms and a restaurant with great views on the top floor. Somewhat funky but a great location. Reservations are recommended and call from the River City complex for free pick-up. 768 Soi Panurangsri, Songwad Rd., tel. (02) 234-5429, fax (02) 236-6199, 450-800B.

New Empire Hotel: Located near Wat Traimit, the New Empire is noisy and somewhat decrepit, but compensates with large rooms and a decent swimming pool in the handy location in the center of Chinatown. 572 Yaowaraj Rd., tel. (02) 234-6990, 450-900B a/c.

Chinatown Hotel: The largest and finest hotel in Chinatown is often filled with Chinese business travelers and tour groups. All rooms come with private bath, color TV, telephone, and minibars. 526 Yaowaraj Rd., tel. (02) 225-0203, fax (02) 226-1295, 1,200-1,500B.

TRAIN STATION AREA

The neighborhood around Hualampong train station is hectic and riddled with pickpockets, but it's a handy location near the restaurants and nightlife on Silom Road.

TT 2 Guesthouse: A popular place with decent rooms and spotless communal bathrooms, plus friendly management and a restaurant with good meals and homemade yogurt. It's somewhat tricky to find, hidden away in a quiet residential neighborhood about 10 minutes from Hualampong. From the station, walk left down Rama IV Road, right on Mahanakhon, left at the first alley (Soi Kaew Fa), then walk straight for five minutes to Soi Sawang. 516-518 Soi Sawang, Si Phraya Rd., tel. (02) 236-2946, fax (02) 236-3054. 180-280B.

TT 1 Guesthouse: Only 10 minutes from the train station. Turn left down Rama IV Road, and take a right on Mahanakhon. From here, follow the signs posted on every available telephone pole. Both TT 1 and TT 2 Guesthouses enforce a midnight curfew and have strict rules against drugs and prostitutes. 138 Soi Wat Mahaphuttharam, Mahanankhon Rd., tel. (02) 236-3053, 160-200B.

LITTLE INDIA

Over a dozen inexpensive Indian-owned hotels in the 150-300B price range are located in the alleys behind Pahurat Market. The clientele is almost exclusively Indian or Pakistani, and room conditions are extremely basic, but nobody cares how many people you pack into the cubicles.

On the other hand, this neighborhood has excellent authentic Indian cafes and enough atmosphere to transport you back to India itself. Best of all, not a tourist in sight.

Champ Guesthouse: Located in the heart of Little India and slightly better than most of the adjacent dives. Nearby guesthouses handle the overflow, plus several tasty and very inexpensive Indian cafes are within walking distance. Chakrapet Rd., 150-200B fan, 300-400B a/c.

Asia Guesthouse: Another option to consider is this small guesthouse tucked away in a quiet alley. Chakrapet Rd., 150-180 fan, 250-350B a/c.

Sunny Guesthouse: Just beyond the popular Cha Cha Restaurant is another fairly clean guesthouse that cheerfully accepts Westerners. Formerly called the Rani Guesthouse. Chakrapet Rd., 120-250B.

Golden Bangkok Guesthouse: Probably the best hotel in Little India, but only recommended for the seasoned traveler. Chakrapet Rd., 350-500B a/c.

SILOM ROAD

Silom Road, from the Chao Praya River to Rama IV Road, is both Bangkok's financial district and original tourist enclave. Once a luxurious residential neighborhood for wealthy merchants, today it has some of the city's finest luxury hotels and a large number of midpriced properties. The area also offers leading department stores, antique and jewelry shops, and the sleazy nightlife that thrives along notorious Patpong Road. Silom is exciting and vibrant, but also noisy and crowded with high-rises; an inner-city experience.

Budget
Silom accommodations are mostly in the midprice to upper price range, though a few inexpensive guesthouses and hotels priced under 1,000B are found in the side streets. Most of the low-end hotels are operated by Indians and Pakistanis.

Kabana Inn: Opposite the GPO and river taxis, the Kabana is another Indian-operated hotel with relatively clean rooms at bargain rates. All rooms are a/c with telephone and hot showers. 114 Charoen Krung Rd. (former New Rd.), tel. (02) 233-4652, 1,200-1,500B.

King's Mansion: Though constantly filled with long-term residents, this aging property is one of the better bargains in the Silom Road area. King's Mansion is located near many embassies, near Thai Immigration, and only 10 minutes from Silom and Patpong. Air-conditioned rooms with private bath cost under 8,000B per month. 31 South Sathorn (Sathorn Tai) Rd., tel. (02) 286-0940, 700-900B a/c with refrigerator and TV.

Madras Lodge: Better hotels that cater to the Indian community are on several alleys off Silom Road. Madras Lodge and Cafe is a newer three-story hotel about 200 meters down Vaithi Lane, two blocks east of the Hindu Temple. An exceptionally quiet location. Silom Soi 13, tel. (02) 235-6761, 280-350B fan, 450-600B a/c.

Naaz Guesthouse: Indians patronize several of the small and very inexpensive guesthouses on New Road near the GPO. Conditions are extremely rough, but if you want a cheap crash pad and don't mind the atmosphere, then the Naaz might be adequate. Similar spots are around the corner on Soi Puttaosod and to the rear on Nares Road. Several good Indian restaurants are nearby. 1159 Charoen Krung Rd., tel. (02) 235-9718, 350-500B a/c.

Swan Hotel: This inexpensive little hotel is ideally located within walking distance of the GPO, inexpensive Indian restaurants, and river taxis behind the Oriental. All rooms include private bath and telephone, plus there's a small pool and adequate coffee shop. The Swan needs some obvious improvement, but it remains an excellent value for budget travelers. Reservations are accepted for a/c rooms only, and flight number and arrival time are required. Credit cards and traveler's checks are not accepted. Charoen Krung Rd., Soi 31, tel. (02) 233-9060, 500-650B fan, 750-900B a/c.

Moderate
Bossotel Inn: Tucked away in the same alley as the Shangri-La is this small hotel that caters to businessmen on a budget and tourists who enjoy the neighborhood but don't want to break the bank. Rooms are basic but fairly clean and include a/c and private bath with hot showers. 55/8-9 Soi Charoendrung, tel. (02) 630-6120, fax (02) 237-3225, 1,000-1,600B.

New Rotel: A fairly new hotel with modern a/c rooms furnished with color TV, small refrig-

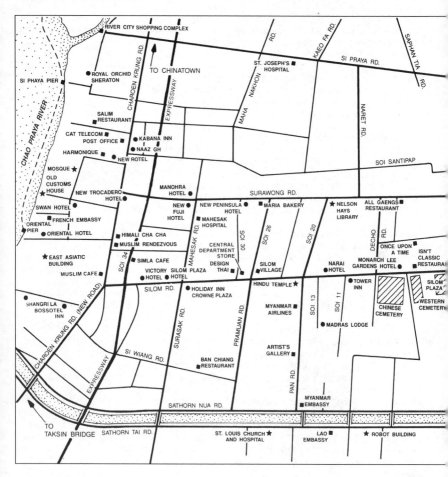

erator, and telephone. American breakfast is included. A fine place with friendly management. 1216 Charoen Krung Rd., tel. (02) 237-1094, fax (02) 237-1102, 1,100-1,400B.

Niagra Hotel: An old favorite in a quiet location off Silom Road with clean a/c rooms and hot showers. Soi Suksavitthaya, tel. (02) 233-5783, 600-900B.

Rose Hotel: Older property in need of renovation but in a convenient location for gay-oriented night owls prowling around Patpong. 118 Suriwongse Rd., tel. (02) 226-8268, 800-1,000B.

Suriwong Hotel: Another older hotel in decent condition that fills its rooms with solo males seeking action in nearby Patpong. Ask for a room on the upper floors. 31 Suriwongse Rd., tel. (02) 266-8257, fax (02) 266-8261, 700-1,000B.

Swissotel: Formerly the Swiss Guesthouse under the direction of Andy Ponnaz, this recently renovated and reconstructed Swiss-managed hotel has 57 a/c rooms with all the amenities. Good location, with swimming pool and restaurant. 3 Convent Rd., tel. (02) 233-5345, fax (02) 236-9425, 3,200-3,800B.

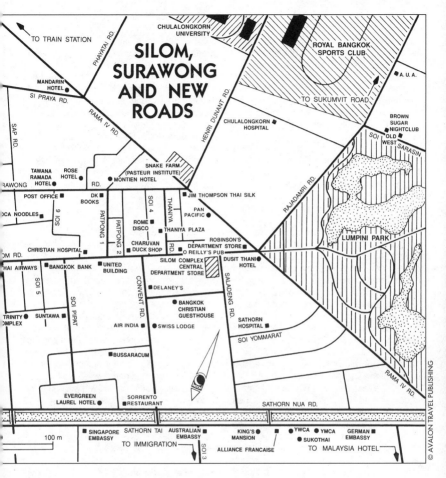

SILOM, SURAWONG AND NEW ROADS

YMCA Collins House: This modern, spotless, and comfortable hotel is one of the better hotel bargains in Bangkok. All rooms are a/c with private bath and mini refrigerator. There's also a pool and health club. Reservations require one night's deposit. 27 South Sathorn Rd., tel. (02) 287-1900, fax (02) 287-1996, 1,400-2,000B.

YWCA: The McFarland wing is less luxurious but also less expensive than the newer YMCA Collins House. Unfortunately, the swimming pool is perpetually filled with children. 13 South Sathorn Rd., tel. (02) 286-1936, 500-700B.

Luxury

Luxury hotels are the strong suit of this neighborhood. First choice are the fabulous hotels that face the Chao Praya River followed by newer properties both along the river and closer to Patpong.

Some hotels continue to quote prices in local currency and are now about 30% cheaper than several years ago (before the devaluation of 1997-98), while others have changed to a dollar basis and collect top fares no matter the current exchange rate.

© AVALON TRAVEL PUBLISHING

Dusit Thani Hotel: One of the most historic hotels in the country with a magnificent lobby, superb restaurants, and rooms in a variety of price categories. Rama IV Rd., tel. (02) 236-0450, fax (02) 236-6400, US$228-284.

Holiday Inn Crowne Plaza: Not the most inspiring exterior architecture but an excellent location between the river and Patong, plus spacious rooms decorated with Asian and European accents. 981 Silom Rd., tel. (02) 238-4300, fax (02) 283-5289, US$120-150.

Marriott Royal Garden Riverside Hotel: South of Silom Road and across the river in Thonburi is this welcome escape from the horrors of Bangkok with resorty amenities and an amazing array of activities. 257 Charoen Nakorn Rd., Thonburi, tel. (02) 476-0021, fax (02) 476-1120, US$177-222.

Monarch Lee Gardens: A decent midrange hotel in a coveted location near popular entertainment and business districts with European touches in the elegant lobby and equally impressive rooms. 188 Silom Rd., tel. (02) 238-1991, fax (02) 238-1999, US$100-125.

Montien Hotel: This locally owned and operated hotel has a strong French flair and is considerably less pretentious than most other luxury hotels in Bangkok. 54 Surawong Rd., tel. (02) 234-8060, fax (02) 236-5219, 2,500-3,800B.

Oriental Hotel: Since it first opened in 1876, this award-winning hotel on the banks of the Chao Praya has remained the undisputed grande dame of Bangkok. Much of the Oriental's fame comes from the authors who have stayed here: Somerset Maugham, Graham Greene, Noel Coward, and even (gasp) Barbara Cartland. Even if you can't afford to stay, take a look at the Writers' Bar, try the Siamese buffet lunch, or enjoy an evening cocktail on the terrace. The Oriental has a 100 million-*baht* health spa and Thai herbal-treatment center. Some of the old charm has given way to modernization, but the Oriental remains among the best hotels in the world. 48 Oriental Ave., tel. (02) 236-0400, fax (02) 236-1939, US$250-400.

Royal Orchid Sheraton Hotel: This hotel upriver from the Oriental has 700 rooms with uninterrupted views of the river. The adjacent River City Shopping Complex features two floors devoted to antiques. 2 Captain Bush Lane, tel. (02) 266-0123, fax (02) 237-2152, US$220-276.

Shangri La Hotel: This multimillion dollar hotel boasts 650 beautiful rooms facing the river and overlooking a stunning swimming pool. Facilities include a health club, business center, and spectacular glass-enclosed lobby with seven-meter-high windows. The central tower is supplemented by a newer 15-story wing. Many consider the Shangri La just as impressive than the Oriental. 89 Soi Wat Suan Plu, tel. (02) 236-7777, fax (02) 236-8579, US$180-280.

The Sukothai: Thailand's first capital serves as the inspiration for one of the newer luxury hotels in the Silom district. A good location away from the traffic and surrounded by greenery. 13 South Sathorn Rd., tel. (02) 287-0222, fax (02) 287-4980, US$210-275.

SIAM SQUARE

Named after the Siam Square Shopping Center on Rama I Road, but also known as Pratunam (after the Pratunam Canal and shopping center), this centrally located neighborhood is the city's premier shopping district and home to many of Bangkok's most exclusive hotels. Shopping opportunities include numerous air-conditioned complexes such as Central and Zen (both in the misnamed World Trade Centre), Tokyu, and Narayana Phand for Thai handicrafts, plus the colorful flea market known as Pratunam.

This area is also an entertainment center with dozens of cinemas and coffee shops patronized by trendy Thais. Finally, the Siam/Pratunam neighborhood lies conveniently between the nightlife centers of Sukumvit and the cultural attractions in the Old Royal City.

Budget to Moderate
Though mainly known as an upscale hotel district, several good-value guesthouses and hotels with rooms under 600B are found in an alley (Soi Kasemsan 1) opposite the National Stadium on Rama I Road. The following hotels are bunched together and can be quickly inspected.

Bed and Breakfast Guesthouse: A small and clean guesthouse with a/c rooms, hot showers, and telephone. Continental breakfast is included. 36/42 Soi Kasemsan 1, Rama 1 Rd., tel. (02) 215-3004, fax (02) 215-2493, 400-550B.

A-One Inn: Another relatively new and very

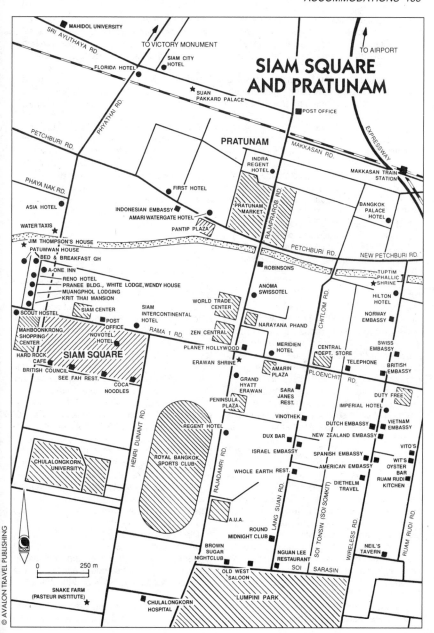

SIAM SQUARE AND PRATUNAM

clean guesthouse with friendly management and a/c room complete with private bath and telephone. Quiet, safe, and excellent value. 25/13 Soi Kasemsan 1, Rama 1 Rd., tel. (02) 216-3029, fax (02) 216-4771, 450-600B.

Muangphol Lodging Department: Somewhat ragged but recommended if other nearby spots are filled. All rooms are a/c with private bath. 931 Rama 1 Rd., tel. (02) 215-0033, fax (02) 216-8053, 450-550B.

Pranee Building: An older hotel operated by a motorcycle collector; don't miss his fine collection of Triumphs and antique cars in the front display room. Inexpensive monthly rentals. 931/12 Soi Kasemsan 1, tel. (02) 280-0033, fax (02) 216-8053, 350B small room with cold shower, 450-550B large room with hot shower.

Krit Thai Mansion: This clean and modern hotel is entered through the lobby restaurant and coffee shop. Easy to find since it faces Rama I Road. 931 Rama I Rd., tel. (02) 215-3042, fax (02) 216-2241, 900-1,200B.

Luxury

Like Silom Road, the Siam Square area excels in the expensive category. The following hotels are surrounded by immense grounds, a refreshing change from most properties hemmed in by concrete towers and noisy construction zones. Most hotels now quote their rooms prices in U.S. dollars rather than Thai *baht*.

Grand Hyatt Erawan: The venerable hotel with the famous religious shrine on its grounds was reconstructed several years ago in an amazing pseudo-Roman style; another first-class architectural monument for modern Bangkok. 494 Rajadamri Rd., tel. (02) 254-1234, fax (02) 253-5856, US$240-270.

Hilton International Hotel: Tucked away on the nine-acre Nai Lert Park and surrounded by gardens and bougainvilleas, Bangkok's Hilton is another tropical oasis in the middle of the noisy, polluted city. While somewhat distant from Silom Road and the temples in the old city, it's convenient for shopping, conducting business at the nearby embassies, and enjoying the nightlife along Sukumvit Road. Popular with business travelers. 2 Wireless (Withaya) Rd., tel. (02) 253-0123, fax (02) 253-6509, US$180-240.

Regent Hotel: Formerly known as the Bangkok Peninsula, this stately structure over-

looking the Royal Bangkok Sports Club is considered one of the city's finest hotels. Inside the enormous lobby is a grand staircase and hand-painted silk murals, which relate the colorful history of Bangkok. Actor and kickboxer Jean Claude Van Damme married Darry Lapier here in 1994. The afternoon high-tea ritual is worth experiencing. 155 Rajadamri Rd., tel. (02) 251-6127, fax (02) 253-9195, US$225-275.

Siam Intercontinental Hotel: Built on 26 acres of tropical gardens next to the Srapatum Palace, this oasis of tranquillity is far removed from the noise and grime of the city. Included in the tariff is a sensational array of sports facilities such as a mini-golf course and jogging trail. 967 Rama 1 Rd., tel. (02) 253-0355, fax (02) 253-2275, US$140-250.

SUKUMVIT ROAD

Thailand's longest road (it stretches all the way to Cambodia!) serves as the midpriced tourist center of Bangkok. Though very distant from the temples, Sukumvit offers dozens of good-value hotels in the moderate range, great sidewalk shopping, popular yet inexpensive restaurants, cozy English pubs, great bookstores, numerous tailor and shoe shops, and discount travel agencies. The racy nightlife scenes at Nana Entertainment Plaza (NEP) and Soi Cowboy are now far superior to the mess around Patpong.

Hotels on Sukumvit are available in all prices, but the neighborhood's claim to fame is the midpriced lodgings (600-1,200B) that flank Sukumvit from Soi 1 and Soi 63. Many of these are exceptional values with comfortable a/c rooms, swimming pools, travel services, taxis at the front door, and fine restaurants. Deluxe hotels above 3,000B are starting to appear, though it will be years before the neighborhood can compete with the five-star wonders on Silom Road and around Siam Square.

The best area to stay for shopping and entertainment is along Sukumvit between Soi 2 and Soi 13; hotels further afield are either a long walk or a very trick taxi ride. Best bet are the midpriced hotels near Soi 4 and the Nana Entertainment Plaza.

Visitors looking for long-term rentals and sublets should check the Villa Market bulletin board at Soi 33. Also listed are ads for used cars and motorcycles, plus furniture and miscellaneous goods being sold by departing expatriates.

Budget

Budget accommodations include over a dozen hotels with rooms for 600-900B. Many were constructed in the 1960s in Motel 6-style to serve the American military trade from Vietnam. Though extremely basic and in need of improvement, rooms are air-conditioned, and a small pool and restaurant are often included. Also described below are simple guesthouses constructed in the last few years; these won't have pools but the rooms will be cleaner. Budget travelers who spend more time sightseeing than lounging in their rooms will probably find all the following places suitable for a short stay.

Uncle Rey's Guesthouse: A clean but cramped high-rise with fully furnished, small a/c rooms, the guesthouse features private baths and hot showers. Tucked away in an alley near the Nana Hotel. No pool, no yard. Sukumvit Soi 4, tel. (02) 258-0318, fax (02) 258-4438, 600-900B.

Happy Inn: A small and very simple hotel with clean rooms and a good location near the nightlife and shopping centers. Sukumvit Soi 4, tel. (02) 252-6508, 500-600B.

Atlanta Hotel: An old travelers' favorite has clean rooms, a cheery little cafe, and a surprisingly good pool in the backyard. Proprietor Dr. Charles Henn, son of the German immigrant who founded the Atlanta in 1952, has recently renovated the property with attention to the increasingly rare 1950s decor. The cheapest hotel in the Sukumvit neighborhood. Highly recommended. Sukumvit Soi 2, tel. (02) 252-1650, fax (02) 255-2151, 300-400B fan, 450-700B a/c.

Miami Hotel: An old hotel offers dozens of decent rooms overlooking the courtyard swimming pool. Fan rooms are very basic, but all a/c rooms include TV, private bath, and maid service. One of the most popular cheapies on Sukumvit Road. Reservations can be made from the hotel counter at the Bangkok airport. Sukumvit Soi 13, tel. (02) 253-0369, fax (02) 253-1266, 550-650B a/c.

Crown Hotel: Another old hotel constructed for the American GI trade in the 1960s. Very funky, but the small pool provides a refreshing

---

SUKUMVIT ROAD BUSES

1AC	Chinatown, Wat Po
2	Banglampoo
8AC	Siam Square, Grand Palace
11AC	Banglampoo, National Museum
13AC	Northern Bus Terminal, Airport

---

dip in the hot afternoon. All rooms are air-conditioned; a longtime favorite with many visitors. Sukumvit Soi 29, tel. (02) 258-0318, 450-650B.

Moderate

Most of the better midpriced places are packed around the lower end of Sukumvit, within walking distance of Nana Entertainment Complex and dozens of small restaurants which characterize the neighborhood.

White Inn: This beautiful and unique lodge decorated in an old English-Tudor style features a/c rooms, swimming pool, and sun terrace. Although somewhat funky, it's in a quiet location and provides a welcome respite from the hell of Sukumvit. Sukumvit Soi 4, tel. (02) 252-7090, fax (02) 254-8865, 900-1,200B.

Nana City Inn: Great location just off Sukumvit with a popular café and decent if somewhat unimaginative rooms. 23/164 Sukumvit Soi 4, tel. (02) 253-4468, fax (02) 255-2449, 750-1,000B.

Dynasty Inn: Fine little place with a comfortable cocktail lounge, CNN on the cable TV, and very clean a/c rooms. Excellent location just opposite the Nana Hotel; often filled by noontime. Sukumvit Soi 4, tel. (02) 250-1397, fax (02) 255-4111, 900-1,200B.

Nana Hotel: A big hotel with all the standard facilities such as nightclubs and restaurants. Recently refurbished a/c rooms include private bath, TV, and refrigerator. The Nana is conveniently located within easy walking distance of nightlife and shopping districts; one of the better midpriced spreads on Sukumvit. Recommended for visitors who want a big hotel at a decent price. Sukumvit Soi 4, tel. (02) 252-0121, fax (02) 255-1769, 900-1,600B.

Grace Hotel: Big, sprawling hotel noted for its coffee shop full of low-end prostitutes but rooms are spacious and kept in good condition, plus you can walk to Sukumvit in just a few minutes.

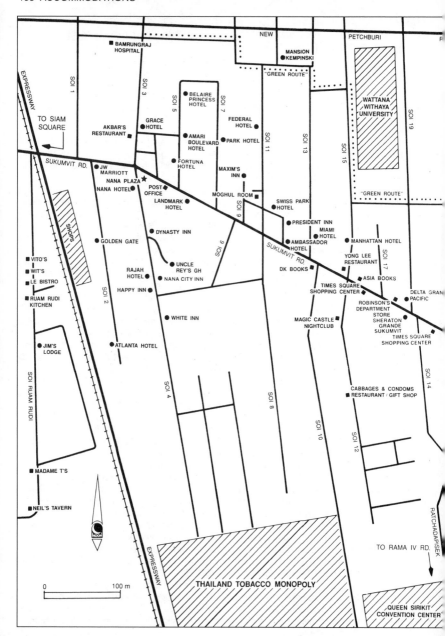

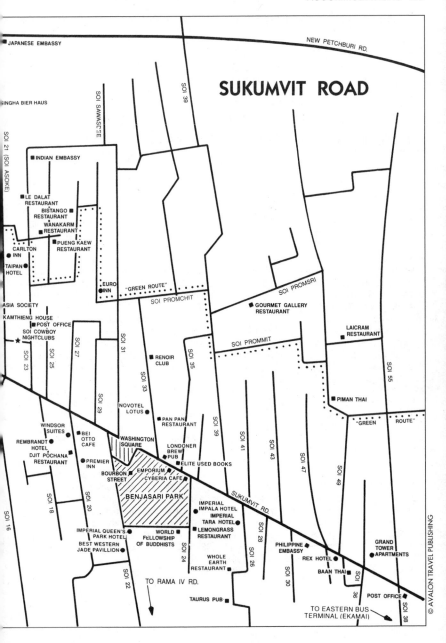

JAPANESE EMBASSY

NEW PETCHBURI RD.

SOI 39

SUKUMVIT ROAD

SINGHA BIER HAUS

SOI SAWASCEE

SOI 21 (SOI ASOKE)

INDIAN EMBASSY

LE DALAT RESTAURANT
BISTANGO RESTAURANT
WANAKARM RESTAURANT
PUENG KAEW RESTAURANT

CARLTON INN

TAIPAN HOTEL

EURO INN

"GREEN ROUTE"

SOI PROMSRI

SOI PROMCHIT

GOURMET GALLERY RESTAURANT

ASIA SOCIETY
KAMTHIENG HOUSE
POST OFFICE
SOI COWBOY NIGHTCLUBS

LAICRAM RESTAURANT

SOI PROMMIT

SOI 27

SOI 31

SOI 35

SOI 23

SOI 25

RENOIR CLUB

SOI 33

PIMAN THAI

SOI 29

SOI 55

NOVOTEL LOTUS

PAN PAN RESTAURANT

SOI 39

"GREEN ROUTE"

WINDSOR SUITES
BEI OTTO CAFE
REMBRANDT HOTEL
DJIT POCHANA RESTAURANT
PREMIER INN

WASHINGTON SQUARE

LONDONER BREW PUB

ELITE USED BOOKS

SOI 41

SOI 43

SOI 47

SOI 49

BOURBON STREET

EMPORIUM
CYBERIA CAFE

SOI 18

BENJASARI PARK

SUKUMVIT RD.

SOI 20

IMPERIAL IMPALA HOTEL
IMPERIAL TARA HOTEL
LEMONGRASS RESTAURANT

IMPERIAL QUEEN'S PARK HOTEL

WORLD FELLOWSHIP OF BUDDHISTS

BEST WESTERN JADE PAVILLION

PHILIPPINE EMBASSY

GRAND TOWER APARTMENTS

REX HOTEL

SOI 16

SOI 28

SOI 26

BAAN THAI

POST OFFICE

WHOLE EARTH RESTAURANT

SOI 24

SOI 30

SOI 36

SOI 38

SOI 22

TO RAMA IV RD.

TAURUS PUB

TO EASTERN BUS TERMINAL (EKAMAI)

© AVALON TRAVEL PUBLISHING

Sukumvit Soi 3, tel. (02) 253-0651, fax (02) 254-9020, 800-1,200B.

Maxim's Inn: Sukumvit in recent years has added a dozen small hotels in the *sois* near the Ambassador Hotel, especially between *sois* 9 and 13. All are clean and comfortable, but Maxim's is more luxurious and has a better location at the end of a short alley. If it's filled, check any of the adjacent hotels in the price range. Sukumvit Soi 9, tel. (02) 252-9911, fax (02) 253-5329, 900-1,200B.

President Inn: Several new, small inns are located in the short alleys near Soi 11. Most were constructed in the early 1990s, so the rooms and lobbies remain in good condition. Features clean a/c rooms with color TV, telephone, and mini-refrigerator. Sukumvit Soi 11, tel. (02) 255-4230, fax (02) 255-4235, 800-1,200B.

Luxury

A half-dozen luxury hotels have opened around Sukumvit in the last few years, though more refined properties are found near Siam Square and around Silom Road.

Ambassador Hotel: An enormous hotel that once served as the first and finest of its kind in the neighborhood, but has now fallen on hard times and chiefly attracts cheap group tours and a smattering of backpackers who want comfortable if funky rooms at bargain rates. Sukumvit Soi 11, tel. (02) 254-0444, fax (02) 253-4123, 2,200-2,800B.

Landmark Hotel: Sukumvit's largest luxury hotel enjoys a superb location near shops, restaurants, and nightclubs. Pluses include rooftop restaurants on the 31st floor, a swimming pool, health club, convention facilities, and a friendly staff. Sukumvit Soi 6, tel. (02) 254-0404, 3,800-5,000B.

Tara Hotel: Another fairly new hotel in the four-star range with a spacious lobby with teakwood carvings, garden swimming pool on the eighth floor, and a skyview cocktail lounge on the 22nd floor. Nice place but somewhat removed from the action. Sukumvit Soi 26, tel. (02) 259-0053, fax (02) 259-2896, 3,600-4,200B.

Swiss Park Hotel: A centrally located 108-room hotel with rooftop swimming pool, cafe on the seventh floor, and business center. Sukumvit Soi 11, tel. (02) 254-0228, fax (02) 254-0378, 3,000-3,600B.

AIRPORT AREA

Although there's no sights of interest out near the Bangkok Airport, a late arrival or early departure may necessitate an overnight stay in one of the nearby hotels. All hotels near the airport are overpriced and should only be used as a last resort.

Amari Airport Hotel: Expensive but very convenient—just walk from the airport on the 160-meter air-conditioned passageway which crosses the highway and leads directly to the hotel. Several travelers recommend the "three-hour special:" unlimited use of a room, the pool, the health club, and other facilities for just 600B. 333 Chert Vudtakas Rd., Don Muang, tel. (02) 566-1020, fax (02) 566-1941, 4,200-5,600B.

Rama Gardens Hotel: Five minutes by taxi from the airport. Another somewhat overpriced hotel that mainly caters to business travelers and conventioneers. 9/9 Vibhavadi Rangsit Rd., Bangkhen, tel. (02) 561-0022, fax (02) 561-1025. 4,600-5,400B.

Central Plaza Hotel: Another convention hotel about 20 minutes from the airport, 20 minutes from city center, and five minutes from the Chatuchak Weekend Market. 1695 Phaholyothin Rd., Chatuchak, tel. (02) 541-1234, fax (02) 541-1087, 4,800-6,400B.

Comfort Inn Airport: A well-priced hotel about five minutes south of the airport by taxi. Facilities include a restaurant, swimming pool, health club, and large air-conditioned rooms with color TV and mini-fridge. Call for free pick-up from the airport. Room prices are negotiable. 88/117 Vibhavadi Rangsit Rd., Don Muang, tel. (02) 552-8929, fax (02) 552-8920, 2,400-3,000B.

FOOD

Bangkok richly deserves its reputation as one of the world's great culinary destinations. Spread across the city are some 30,000 registered restaurants and countless streetstalls that produce some of the tastiest food in the East. Whether you try heart-pounding curries or aromatically smooth soups, it's almost impossible to go wrong in the City of Angels.

Gourmets with a serious interest in the restaurants of Thailand will find further information and a discount dining program in *The Restaurant Guide of Thailand* published annually by The Siam Dinner Club. *Bangkok Restaurant Guide* published in 1988 (the first and only edition) by Asia Books is dated, but is still recommended for the neighborhood maps and detailed descriptions of restaurant specialties. Gault Millau's *The Best of Thailand* attempts to "distinguish the truly superlative from the merely overrated" restaurants in Bangkok. Also check the restaurant listings in the *Bangkok Post* and local tourist magazines.

Most of the following summaries describe popular restaurants that have been in business for an extended period, or newer cafes that show great potential. The listings range from cheap sidewalk cafes, where you'll find some of the best food in Bangkok, to expensive Thai restaurants that specialize in regional and royal cuisines.

Specific restaurant recommendations are difficult for several reasons. Many establishments tend to change ownership and location with the seasons. Leading chefs often move to other restaurants, or open their own operations to exploit their culinary reputations. And, as elsewhere in the world, successful restaurants often rest on their laurels and eventually go into decline, raising prices and letting food quality suffer. For these reasons, take suggestions from fellow travelers and Bangkok residents.

BANGLAMPOO

Alfresco dining along Khao San Road is a pleasant way to meet other travelers and exchange information, though none of the cafes will win any awards for great cuisine or elaborate atmosphere. Banglampoo's other problem, besides the mediocre food, is the noisy video cafes that prohibit good conversation. Try to patronize video-free restaurants.

Inexpensive

Buddy Cafe: One of the more elegant cafes on Khao San Road is tucked away behind the Buddy Guesthouse. The food is bland but safe, a good introduction for first-time visitors fearful of chilies. The upstairs restaurant provides a pleasant escape from the mayhem of Khao San Road.

Streetstalls: If the cafes on Khao San seem overpriced and unimaginative, try the sidewalk stalls just north of Khao San on Rambutri and Tani roads. For half the price of Khao San cafes you can enjoy an authentic Thai meal and soak up an atmosphere a million times more authentic than back in the travelers ghetto. Tani Road has over a dozen sidewalk stalls completely accustomed to the antics of travelers and prepared to offer great meals at rock-bottom prices.

Thai Cafes: Several unpretentious cafes around the corner from Khao San on Chakrabongse (Chakraphong or Chakrapong) Road offer a good selection of unusual dishes. They are best in the morning when the food is freshest; very inexpensive. The no-name cafe at 8 Chakrabongse specializes in southern Thai dishes, #22 has good Chinese noodle dishes, and #28 spicy Thai curries.

Night Foodstalls: Authentic Thai food is found nightly in the foodstalls at the west end of Khao San Road and a few blocks north toward the New World Shopping Center.

New World Shopping Center: Nearly every shopping center in Thailand has a food complex on the top floor where the prices are rock bottom, the quality is good, and the service is near instantaneous. Try the numerous outlets on the eighth floor.

Chabad House: Simple cafe with Jewish kosher meals and a Hebrew message board near the front door. Meetings are held upstairs. 108/1 Rambutri Rd., tel. (02) 282-6388.

Chochana: Another Israeli cafe often packed out with Jewish backpackers and somewhat cheaper than the nearby Chabad House. 86 Chakrabongse Rd., tel. (02) 282-9948.

May Kaidee: Vegetarian cafe with streetside tables and small menu with tasty brown rice, tofu curry, fresh spring rolls, and *som tam jeh.* Open daily until 2100. 117 Tanao Rd., no phone.

Moderate

Krai Si: Small, clean, and very chilly restaurant with Japanese sushi, sashimi, tempura, and Western specialties. Look for the sidewalk sushi man. Pra Sumen Rd.

Royal Hotel Coffee Shop: An excellent place to relax in the morning, enjoy a good cup of coffee, and read the *Bangkok Post.* 2 Rajadamnern Ave.

Yok Yor: Also on the banks of the Chao Praya. Yok Yor serves Thai, Chinese, and Japanese dishes in a rather wild atmosphere: waitresses are dressed in sailor outfits and passengers disembarking from the river taxi saunter right through the restaurant! The restaurant offers dinner cruises for 60B plus meal; the boat leaves nightly at 2000. Try *hoh mok,* duck curry, and *noi na* ice cream for dessert. Yok Yor is on Wisut Kaset Rd., down from the National Bank, a very pleasant 30-minute walk through back alleys that skirt the river. 4 Visutkaset Rd., tel. (02) 280-1418.

Hemlock: One of the first trendy cafes in this neighborhood and still frequented for its well-prepared Thai dishes served without fuss. Nonsmoking section upstairs. 56 Pra Arthit Rd., tel. (02) 282-7507.

Apostrophe's Restaurant: The newest arty enclave serves up tasty Thai dishes in a very small but almost stylish setting. Pra Arthit Rd., tel. (02) 282-7040.

Maria Restaurant: Rajadamnern Avenue serves as an administrative center during the day and as restaurant row in the evening. Scattered along the broad avenue are a several moderately priced restaurants popular with Thai civil servants and businesspeople. Maria's is a large, air-conditioned place with both Chinese and Thai specialties.

Vijit's: Several old favorites are also located around Democracy Monument on Rajadamnern Avenue. All are patronized by Thais who seek a semi-luxurious yet casual restaurant. Vijit's resembles an old American diner from the 1950s, and serves both Asian and Western dishes. Both indoor and patio dining are offered. **Sorn Daeng Restaurant,** just across the circle, is another popular restaurant with a 1950s atmosphere. 77 Rajadamnern Ave., tel. (02) 282-0958.

Dachanee: A long-running Thai restaurant recommended by many tourist guides. The heavy decor is rather gloomy, but the traditionally prepared dishes and skillful presentation provide compensation. Prachathi Rd., tel. (02) 281-9332, open daily 1000-1900.

Kanit's: Both French specialties and Italian pizzas are served in very elegant surroundings. Considered the best European restaurant in this section of town. Owned by a friendly Thai woman and her German husband. 68 Ti Thong Rd., near the Giant Swing and Wat Suthat, tel. (02) 222-1020.

MALAYSIA HOTEL AREA

This neighborhood has few decent restaurants, but a string of inexpensive cafes with standard fare lines Soi Si Bamphen. The overpriced restaurant inside the Malaysia Hotel provides a welcome escape from the noxious fumes and noise that plague this area.

Inexpensive
Blue Fox: A quiet little spot of eccentric Thais and lonesome travelers escaping the searing heat, this restaurant has acceptable Western food, bland Thai dishes, and a pickup atmosphere in the evening. Soi Si Bamphen.

Foodstalls: Get tasty, authentic Thai food at the large collection of foodstalls just across Rama IV near the Lumpini Boxing Stadium. Point to a neighbor's dish or look inside the pots. More foodstalls are a few blocks south.

Moderate
Chandrapen: Large and fairly luxurious restaurant on Rama IV Road features Thai and Chinese specialties. The only upscale place within easy walking distance of the Malaysia Hotel.

Pinnacle Hotel: Comfortable a/c cafe with fairly good dishes in this moderately priced hotel just off the main drag. Soi Ngam Duphli.

Kiaow Tra Wang Chun: Popular Chinese cafe opposite the Chandrapen with decent Cantonese dishes but a surly staff. 5/4 Soi Ngam Duphli, tel. (02) 679-7019.

Ratsstube: German home cooking featuring stuffed sausages, sauerkraut, fried potatoes, and traditional desserts including *karamel koepfchen*. The large selection of imported German beers and kitchsy interior decor keeps this place busy with a largely Thai clientele. Goethe Institute, 101 Soi Ngam Duphli, tel. (02) 286-4258.

SILOM ROAD

Silom and Surawong Roads are gourmet ghettos, with dozens of great restaurants and hundreds of cheap cafes and streetstalls. The following suggestions include both classic joints in the high-price range and small spots rarely visited by Westerners.

Inexpensive
Charuvan Duck Shop: Around the corner from Patpong is an old travelers' favorite with, what else, duck specialties over rice and inexpensive curries. The food has unfortunately gone downhill and duck dishes are mostly rice with duck skin. An air-conditioned room is located behind the open-air cafe. Silom Soi 4, tel. (02) 234-2206.

Robinson's Department Store: For a quick bite at bargain prices, try the fast food outlets on the main floor or the well-stocked grocery store downstairs. Silom at Rama IV Rd.

Soi 20 Nightmarket: The few street vendors on this narrow alley during the day are joined by dozens of others after the sun sets. Try a *kuay teow* dish or the trusty point-and-order method.

Maria Bakery: A longtime favorite among local and foreign residents with an extensive selection of Vietnamese, Thai, and Western dishes, along with pizza, baked goods, and hearty breakfasts, served in a simple but air-conditioned dining room. 311/234 Surawong Rd., tel. (02) 234-6362.

Silom Village Trade Center: A very touristy shopping complex but with several decent restaurants at reasonable prices, including a seafood outlet in a patio environment, a popular coffee bar, a cozy Indian outlet for baked crab and spicy beef salad, and an upscale Thai restaurant for a pricey but first-rate dinner-dance show. 286 Silom Rd., tel. (02) 235-8760.

Central Department Store: Department stores often serve excellent food at rock-bottom prices in a clean but inevitably sterile environment. Once again, the coupon system; most dishes cost only 20-40B. Silom Plaza at Mahesak Rd., 5th floor.

Silom Plaza Hotel: Try the wonderful lunch buffet in the fifth-floor dining room with great views, air-conditioned comfort, and all-you-can-eat Thai, Korean, and Japanese dishes. Salad lovers will be in heaven. Open daily 1100-1400. 320 Silom Rd., tel. (02) 236-0333.

Coca Noodles: This palatial Chinese emporium specializes in Thai-style sukiyaki prepared at your table. It also features inexpensive noodle dishes and pricier seafood specialties. Eat noodles and avoid the more exotic offerings—such as shark's fin soup—and you'll walk away without draining the wallet. Surawong, 8 Soi Tantawan, tel. (02) 236-0107.

The Mango Tree: A place with great food, friendly service, and live Thai classical music, plus both indoor and outdoor seating. This popular spot is housed in an old residence with antique cameras displayed in the foyer. 37 Soi Tantawan, Suriwong Rd., tel. (02) 236-2820.

Tom's Quik Pizza: Vegetarians rejoice. When it's three in the morning and you're desperate for a veggie pizza, Tom's Quik Pizza comes to the rescue in under 15 minutes. However, beware of the transvestite heroin dealers upstairs. Patpong 1 Rd., tel. (02) 234-5460.

Anna's Cafe: New place but extremely popular and always packed out for its Thai dishes with a *farang* twist and vice versa. Named after the infamous Anna Leonowens, be sure to try the Anna's Salad and make reservations well in advance. 114 Soi Saladaeng, tel. (02) 632-0620.

Eat Me!: Not the most refined name for a restaurant, though this elegant L-shaped place serves up excellent Mediterranean dishes to local trendsetters and curious tourists alike. 1/6 Piphat Soi 2, off Convent Rd., tel. (02) 238-0931.

Indian Cafes

The Silom Road district has such a large range of Indian and Muslim cafes that it deserves its own category.

Budget Indian Cafes: Cheap open-air Muslim cafes on Charoen Krung Road serve delicious *murtabaks* and *parathas,* but noxious fumes blowing in from the road could kill you. A filling lunch or dinner costs under 50B per person. Indian street vendors sometimes gather opposite the Narai Hotel near the small Hindu temple.

The Indian restaurant next to the Manohra Hotel, has great food served under a video screen blasting out wild Hindu films, while the cafe in the Madras Lodge is recommended for its authentic atmosphere and South Indian special-

ties. Perhaps the best choices for excellent Indian and Malay food at rock-bottom prices are the simple, open-air cafes in the alleys near the GPO.

Woodlands Inn: Decent accommodations plus a small cafe with Indian, vegetarian, and nonvegetarian specialties and *halal* offerings. 1158 Charoen Krung Rd., tel. (02) 235-3894.

Bismi Restaurant: The alleys near the G.P.O are filled with numerous small cafes and a few somewhat upscale offerings including this relatively new spot that serves both north and south *halal* Indian dishes in a/c comfort. 1133 Charoen Krung Rd, tel. (02) 639-4469.

Tamil Nadu: Small and unpretentious cafe with outstanding samosas and dal plus a range of south Indian vegetarian dishes. Silom Soi 11, tel. (02) 235-6336.

Deen Muslim Restaurant: Another basic Indian cafe just opposite Silom Village known for its fried fish with chili, hot goat's milk, and rich, creamy lassi. 761 Silom Rd., tel. (02) 635-0441.

Simla Cafe: The less-expensive Simla Cafe, located off Silom Road in a small alley behind the Victory Hotel, is another popular choice for Indian and Pakistani dishes. 382 Soi Tat Mai, tel. (02) 234-6225.

Himali Cha Cha: The long-running Himali Cha Cha, up a small alley off New Road near the GPO, is known for its tasty curries, *kormas,* fruit-flavored *lassis,* tandoori-baked breads, and North Indian specialties served in an informal setting. Cha Cha, owner and head chef at Himali, was once Nehru's private chef. 1229 Charoen Krung Rd., tel. (02) 235-1569.

Indian Hut: Cozy cafe with north Indian dishes served in a/c comfort just opposite the Monohra Hotel. 311/2 Suriwong Rd., tel. (02) 237-8812.

Moderate

Most of the following restaurants are near Patpong Road or clustered around Charoen Krung Road near the river.

Bobby Arms: Almost a dozen excellent restaurants are located on Patpong Road such as this English pub where expatriates gather on Sunday evenings for drinks and Dixieland music. Patpong 2 Rd.

Trattoria d'Roberto: Known for its Italian specialties such as veal dishes and chocolate desserts. Patpong 2 Rd.

The Australian Club: A comfortable air-conditioned lounge with imported beers from Down Under, plus helpful literature on local nightlife spots. Patpong 1 Rd.

El Gordo's Cantina: Mexican tavern with south-of-the-border dishes plus live music nightly until midnight. Silom Soi 8, tel. (02) 237-1415.

Cairns Stonegrill Restaurant: An upmarket Aussie barbie where patrons grill their own selections on a heated slab of stone. 167 Surawong Rd., tel. (02) 634-3031.

Bua Garden: Rowdy and fun spot popular with large groups in celebration and the odd *farang* who wanders into this popular party enclave just off Silom Road near Patpong. 1 Soi Convent, tel. (02) 237-6640.

Via Convent: Mediterranean outlet run by Philippe Sdrigotti known for its pumpkin soup with blue cheese, pork scaloppine with balsamic vinegar, and grilled swordfish with capers. 1 Convent Rd., tel. (02) 266-7162.

Sun Far Myanmar Food Centre: One of Bangkok's few Burmese restaurants is predictably located near the Myanmar Embassy and serves regional dishes including the famous and highly recommended Burmese tea leaf salad. Closed daily at 2000. 107/1 Pan Rd., tel. (02) 266-8787.

Once Upon A Time: A wonderful romantic restaurant with outdoor dining under little twinkling lights. Nicely located in a quiet back alley, but within walking distance of most hotels. Decho Rd., Soi 1.

All Gaengs: Unlike most Thai restaurants, All Gaengs has been stylishly decorated with art deco touches and a shiny baby grand piano. Along with the jazz, enjoy shrimp curry, *yam* dishes, and *nuea daed dio,* a beef dish served with a spicy dipping sauce. 173/8-9 Surawong Rd., tel. (02) 233-3301.

Ban Chiang: Wonderful atmosphere in this old house (owned by a Thai movie star) converted into a restaurant; it's decorated with turn-of-the-century memorabilia such as vintage photos, grandfather clocks, and Thai antiques. Try the roast duck curry, minced chicken in coconut milk, or freshwater crab baked au natural. Quite popular with Thai gourmands and local expatriates. 14 Sriviang Rd., tel. (02) 236-7045.

Isn't Classic: An oddly named restaurant that serves fiery "Isn't" food from the Issan area

of Thailand. Try something on the English-language menu or Issan specialities such as spicy grilled chicken *(kai yang),* chopped meat salad *(laap, larb),* fiery papaya salad *(som tam),* or more exotic concoctions made from obscure animal parts—classic Issan from Isn't. 154/9 Silom Rd., tel. (02) 235-1087.

Thai Room: One of the stranger joints in town, this American-style, greasy spoon, highly honored time capsule has remained unchanged since it first opened during the Vietnam War. Glance around the room and you might see some wizened old veteran quietly reminiscing about whatever happened here in 1968, Peace Corp volunteers, or curious tourists perusing the English-language menu that lists over 400 items. Thai, Western, Mexican, Italian, and Thai/Mex/Italian dishes. Open until midnight or later. 30/37 Patpong 2 Rd., tel. (02) 233-7920.

Expensive

Sala Rim Nam: Alfresco dining on the banks of the Chao Praya is a memorable if expensive experience. This particular choice may be touristy but it's a beautiful restaurant with excellent Thai salads and traditional dance; use the free boat service from the Oriental Hotel. The set menu includes a classical Thai dance.

Salathip: The Shangri-La Hotel does an excellent Sunday brunch on the veranda overlooking the river.

River City Barbecue: On the rooftop of the River City Shopping Center, this self-service Mongolian barbecue cafe has excellent views from the tables at the edge of the roof. Adjacent to the Sheraton Royal Orchid Hotel.

Normandie Grill: A world-famous French restaurant located in pseudo-dining cars on the roof of the Oriental Hotel. One of the few restaurants in Bangkok that still strictly enforces the jacket and tie rule.

Bussaracum: Restaurants found in luxury hotels generally cater to the foreign palate and temper the degree of garlic and chilies used in their dishes. For something more authentic, try this elegant dining establishment featuring pungent dishes whose recipes stem from the royal palace. *Saengwa* (grilled prawns), *phat benjarong* (vegetables with meats), and *gang kari gai hang* (chicken curry) are recommended. Chef Boonchho has been selected one of the top 10 chefs in the world. 35 Soi Phipat 2, tel. (02) 235-5160. Bussaracum 2, a newer and more modern extension, is wedged inside the Trinity Complex. 425 Soi Phipat 2, tel. (02) 235-8915; very expensive.

Rueng Pueng: Traditional Thai dishes from all regions of the country plus outstanding salads are served in a converted Thai house—a common sight in Bangkok these days. 37 Soi 2, Saladeng Rd.

La Rotonde Grill: Wonderful views of Bangkok can be enjoyed from this revolving restaurant on top of Narai Hotel

Tiara Restaurant: Another restaurant with spectacular views on the 22nd floor of the Dusit Thani Hotel.

SIAM SQUARE

Many of the best restaurants in this neighborhood are located in luxury hotels, while inexpensive cafes and foodstalls are found in the air-conditioned shopping complexes.

Inexpensive
Shopping centers are your best bet for quick, inexpensive Thai and Western dishes. Many operate on the coupon system and are packed with teenagers high on the urban eating experience. For more information on the coupon system see "Other Dining Venues" under "Food and Drink" in the On The Road chapter of this book.

MBK Shopping Center: Mahboonkrong (MBK) is an enormous complex with a food center on the ground floor and a wonderland of stalls on the seventh floor that stretches for half a block. Menu boards are listed in Thai but you can practice the point-and-choose method favored by tourists from Kathmandu to Kuta. Other floors have midpriced restaurants serving steak, pizza, pasta, fried chicken, Filipino dishes, and all variations of Chinese cuisine. Rama 1 Rd.

Beer Garden: Afterwards, head up to the beer garden on the seventh floor for a brew and great views over the holocaust below. Open daily 0930-2200. Rama 1 Rd., tel. (02) 217-9491.

Siam Center: If you can't find anything to eat in MBK, don't despair. The Siam Center, just opposite Siam Square, has over a dozen cafes with Thai, Chinese, Japanese, and European dishes that average just 40-60B per dish. Many attempt to cash in on the nostalgic craze for pseudo-1950s American grub, but you'll do better by sticking to Thai or Chinese dishes. Ploenchit Rd.

Oldies Goldies: However, for an insight as to why America's leading export is modern culture—Elvis, Disney, Madonna—wander into Oldies Goldies on the fourth floor, where Thai teenagers embrace nostalgia, bobby socks, and other icons from *American Graffiti.* Rama 1 Rd.

See Fah Restaurant: In operation since 1936,

dried fish at the market

this cozy cafe/ice-cream parlor/patisserie is famed for its seafood specialties pictured on laminated English-language menus. See Fah is tucked away behind the fire house near the Novotel Hotel, tel. (02) 251-5517.

Inter Restaurant: Basic cafe with hearty Issan dishes popular with Chula students and office workers on break. Siam Square Soi 9, tel. (02) 255-4689.

New Light Coffee House: Another longtime favorite known for its Western and Asian dishes served in an unpretentious air-conditioned environment. 426/1-4 Siam Square, next to the Hard Rock Cafe, tel. (02) 251-9591.

World Trade Centre: The two food emporiums on the seventh floor of this massive shopping complex are comfortable places to dine and watch the crowds without busting your budget. Rama 1 at Rajadamri roads.

Vegeta: A large upmarket cafe with a wide selection of meat-free interpretations of Thai national dishes, plus Chinese cuisine using mock duck, bean curd, and gelatin dishes, plus vegetarian fish—almost indistinguishable from the real thing. Check out their all-you-can-eat weekend buffet lunch. World Trade Centre, tel. (02) 255-9569.

Sarah Jane's: A strange name for a small cafe that specializes in Issan dishes, not the home-style cooking you might expect from Ms. Sarah. 130 Wireless Rd., Sindhorn Tower, tel. (02) 650-9992.

Moderate

Coca Noodles: A colossal, noisy place packed with Chinese families and groups of hungry teenagers chowing down on a plethora of inexpensive noodle dishes, along with chicken, fish, and seafood specialties. Self-cook Mongolian barbecues and sukiyakis are the most popular dishes. 416/3-8 Siam Square, tel. (02) 251-6337.

Baan Khun Phor: An opportunity to dine among the owner's eccentric collection of Victorian and Thai artifacts, served by waitresses attired in traditional garb. Somewhat pricey but the food is decent, especially the spicy crab soup. 458/7-9 Siam Square Soi 8, tel. (02) 250-1733.

La Fontana: A sharp neo-Mediterranean cafe serving authentic pastas and Tuscan dishes, plus cakes, ice cream, and coffees. A Filipino

singer croons your favorites after 1800. Open daily 1000-2330. World Trade Center, 1st Floor, tel. (02) 255-9534.

Koreana: As the name suggests, a Korean restaurant with a variety of popular set menus plus Japanese dishes illustrated by photos on the menu. 446-450 Rama 1 Rd., Siam Square, tel. (02) 252-9398.

Siam Intercontinental: Some of Bangkok's least expensive splurges are the all-you-can-eat luncheon buffets served at the Siam Intercontinental and at other nearby hotels. diners must be well attired; no shorts or sandals. Rama 1 Rd.

Expensive

Thanying Princess: The original restaurant—located in a converted private house and owned by a Thai movie star—has been joined by a second branch in the World Trade Center, an upgraded version with a more elegant setting. Thanying is famed for Royal Thai cuisine, served with refined presentation and offering unusual selections such as fragrant chilled rice and marinated whole sea bass. World Trade Center, 6th floor, tel. (02) 255-9838.

Gianni's: An upscale Italian restaurant owned and operated by the president of the local Italian Chef's Organization, with reasonably priced set lunches and more expensive dinners in a fine location just off Ploenchit Road. Considered one of the best in town. 51/5 Soi Tonson, tel. (02) 252-1619.

Amarin Plaza: Upscale Japanese and Thai restaurants are located on the lower floor. Note the wild Greco-Roman-Thai architecture of the adjacent McDonald's for some insight into the Thai penchant for extravagant indulgence. Ploenchit Rd.

Soi Lang Suan

This road that runs from Lumpini Park to Central Department Store on Ploenchit Road has over a dozen very popular cafes and restaurants filled with both expats and locals plus a few curious tourists.

Pan Pan: One of Bangkok's favorite Italian trattorias provides a comfortable environment to try their wood-fired pizzas, linguine with salmon and vodka, the superbly decadent Chicken Godfather, and the thickest gelato in all of

Thailand. The newer branch at Sukumvit Soi 33 offers a buffet-style antipasti spread and a large selection of rich desserts. Some local residents abhor the food here, but tourists seem to come away satisfied with the experience. 45 Soi Lang Suan, tel. (02) 252-7104.

Airplane: A cheery Italian restaurant done with an airplane theme and set with simple tables and chairs. 65/9 Lang Suan Soi 3, tel. (02) 255-9940.

Nguan Lee Lang Suan: The south end of Soi Lang Suan at Lumpini Park features simple open-air dining patronized by expats, Thai families, and chefs from some of the best hotels in Bangkok. All arrive to try the huge selection of fresh seafood, plates of fresh vegetables, or chicken steamed in Chinese herbs *(kai tun yaa jiin)*. 101/25-26 Soi Lang Suan (at Soi Sarasin), tel. (02) 250-0936.

Dux Bar & Grill: You like ducks? This is your place. Duck motifs adorn everything from drinking glasses to menu selection, in an old house restored to great condition. 72/2 Soi Lang Suan, tel. (02) 252-5646.

Whole Earth Restaurant: Specializing in creative vegetarian dishes, the menu also features Thai and Indian selections that substitute tofu for meat and include garnishes such as fried mushrooms, cashew nuts, and pickled vegetables. Dine upstairs on traditional floor cushions rather than the conventional Western seating on the first floor. 93/3 Soi Lang Suan, tel. (02) 252-5574.

Le Moulin De Sommai: French restaurant with a homey brasserie atmosphere and decent continental food at reasonable prices. A fine place for an afternoon meal in the sunny front section. 93/3 Soi Lang Suan, tel. (02) 652-2513.

Soi Ruam Rudi (Rudee)

Another road just a few blocks from Soi Lang Suan with plenty of cafes and a selection of nightclubs.

Bali Restaurant: Situated in a relaxed old house with garden seating and known for its mildly spiced Indonesian dishes and variations on local Thai cuisine. 15/3 Soi Ruam Rudi, tel. (02) 250-0711.

Vito's Restaurant: Ruam Rudi Village, just a few steps down from Ploenchit Road, features several upscale restaurants popular with em-

bassy employees and local business people. Chef Gianni Favro serves up all forms of antipasti plus northern Italian dishes such as scallopini and frutta di mare. 20/2-3 Soi Ruam Rudi, tel. (02) 251-9455. Moderate.

Wit's Oyster Bar: The English food served here—baked oysters, Yorkshire puddings, seafood dishes—is favored by the fashionable set in Bangkok. 20/10 Soi Ruam Rudi, tel. (02) 251-9455.

Ruam Rudi Kitchen: One of the few Thai restaurants on the street and a comfortable spot that serves unusual Thai dishes such as *nam prik kai poo* (crab eggs in chili sauce). 48/10 Soi Ruam Rudi, tel. (02) 256-6253.

SUKUMVIT ROAD

Sukumvit Road and adjacent side roads offer the best selection of restaurants in Bangkok. Inexpensive streetstalls and midpriced restaurants are most plentiful along Sukumvit between the freeway and Soi Asoke. High-end restaurants are concentrated on the backstreets that run parallel to and north of Sukumvit. Three excellent neighborhoods to explore include Soi 23, the Green Route, and Soi 55. Specific restaurants in these popular enclaves are described below.

Inner Sukumvit Restaurants

Most visitors to this section of Bangkok stay at one of the numerous hotels (and flophouses) between the Expressway at Soi 1 and Soi 21 (Soi Asoke) that marks the outer limits of inner Sukumvit. Sois off Sukumvit are rather oddly numbered, but sois 1 to 21 are on the north side of the street, while sois 2 to 14 are on the south. And they don't exactly match up as you might expect: Soi 19 on the north side of Sukumvit is just opposite Soi 14 on the south side. Go figure.

In any event, if you are staying at an inner Sukumvit hotel, these will be your closest restaurants and all are within a reasonable walking distance—a big consideration in the hell that is Sukumvit.

Night Foodstalls: Some of the best food in Bangkok is found in the foodstalls along Sukumvit where most dishes are precooked and displayed in covered pots. Try *som tam,* a spicy salad made from shredded raw papaya and palm sugar; fried chicken with sticky rice; or *pad thai,* sautéed bean sprouts with chicken and peanuts. Delicious!

Foodstalls are near the Grace Hotel, near the infamously seedy Thermae Coffee Shop, at both ends of Soi Cowboy, at the Washington Square pub center, and on Sukumvit at Soi 38. Wonderful food and a great way to mix with the locals.

BH Vietnamese Restaurant: Wide selection of local dishes at very affordable prices. 70/1 Sukumvit Soi 1, tel. (02) 251-8933.

Atlanta Hotel: This historic old hotel has a fine little cafe with variations of Thai cuisine plus an expansive vegetarian menu that claims to offer the widest selection in Thailand. Most dishes drop the meat and substitute either tofu or "quorm," a vegetable protein mix that can be cooked in a bewildering variety of ways. Among the hits are *phaneng jay* (thick coconut curry with a pork substitute), *khaw muu yaang* (spicy pineapple curry), and *kaeng massaman* (mild Indian curry with quorm). The Atlanta Hotel, Sukumvit Soi 2, tel. (02) 252-6069.

Riley's Pub Cafe: Steaks, sandwiches, roasts, and oysters in this newer cafe just below Clouds Disco provides a welcome alternative to the Arabic cafes that dominate this neighborhood near the Grace Hotel. Sukumvit Soi 3, tel. (02) 626-4332.

Nasir Al-Masri: Perhaps the best Middle Eastern restaurant in a neighborhood chock-a-block with similar offerings. Also serves a range of Indian and Thai dishes under the direction of the Egyptian owner. Sukumvit Soi 3, tel. (02) 253-5582.

Akbar's: A top-quality Indian restaurant over 20 years in the same spot offering a wide choice of dishes from both north and south India. The Navrattan curry, chicken *korma,* mutton *marsala,* and *dahls* are recommended. Sukumvit Soi 3, tel. (02) 253-3479.

Restaurant Heidelberg: Chef Franco Vanoli provides three kinds of fondue—Swiss, French, and Chinese—in a pub-like setting near all the craziness of the Nana Entertainment Plaza. Open daily until midnight. Sukumvit Soi 4, tel. (02) 252-3584.

Dhaba Indian Cafe: Indian dishes plus live tabla music at dinnertime, then a very unique Hindi karaoke scene in the later hours. Hindi karaoke? Sukumvit Soi 10, tel. (02) 251-5404.

Cheap Charlie's: Where is the most popular expat gathering spot in Thailand? Believe it or not, this open-air and completely funky cafe may be the place. The place is cheap, packed, popular, and the flavor of the month since it lacks chairs, tables, and anything else that might be misconstrued as shop fixtures. Once again, go figure. Sukumvit Soi 11, tel. (02) 253-4648.

Ambassador Food Center: A few simple cafes hang on in this largely deserted corridor that once led to the entrance to this once-great hotel, now in steep decline. However, the remaining cafes and foodstalls are still worth checking out for their low prices and reasonably decent grub. The adjacent streetside cafe at Soi 11 is a good place to escape the midday heat and enjoy a very cheap luncheon buffet. Sukumvit Soi 11.

Moghul Room: Another popular Indian restaurant with all the standard items. Sukumvit Soi 11.

Bankeo Ruenkwan: This old and partially renovated house serves up top-quality seafood in a/c comfort. Sukumvit Soi 12, tel. (02) 251-8229.

Lum Gai Yia: Another inexpensive and simple cafe where the tables are just old oil drums topped by welded steel tables and just two dining options: a large wok full of soup of a self-serve barbecue where you do your own cooking on a small personal hotplate. Sukumvit Soi 12, tel. (02) 252-4279.

Cabbages and Condoms: Established over a decade ago by Mechai Viravaidhya, "Condom King" and former director of the national birth control center (next door), the restaurant features excellent food in air-conditioned comfort plus some truly strange items at the front desk—condom key chains and T-shirts you won't find back home. The place benefits the adjacent Population Development Association (PDA). Highly recommended. Sukumvit Soi 12, tel. (02) 252-7349.

Yong Lee Restaurant: A very funky cafe popular with budget travelers and local *farangs* who rave about the Thai and Chinese specialties. Sukumvit Soi 15.

Robinson's Department Store: Cheap eats in this pricey emporium include McDonald's on the main floor, and a downstairs Food Court with several self-service cafes that serve Thai and Japanese dishes. Sukumvit Soi 19.

Middle Sukumvit Road Restaurants

The middle of Sukumvit could possibly be defined as anything between Bangkok and Pattaya (the road runs all the way to Cambodia), but we'll call this section the area from Soi 21 (Soi Asoke on the north side and Ratchadapisek on the south) to just past Washington Square. These restaurants are too far to walk from hotels near Nana Entertainment Plaza, but taxis are plentiful and cheap and fairly quick after the evening traffic dies down.

Sally's Kitchenette: A Filipino place with regional dishes often served in small portions so you can experiment on a budget. The cheese ice cream is something unique. Sukumvit Soi 16, tel. (02) 261-3205.

The Cafe: This hotel coffee shop is superior to most others in town, and worth visiting for the lunch buffet when reservations are recommended. Dinners are served until 0200. Rembrandt Hotel, Sukumvit Soi 18, tel. (02) 261-7100.

Thong Lee Restaurant: A very popular and simple shophouse with good food at low prices. Try the *muu phad kapi* (spicy pork in shrimp paste), and the *yam hed sot* (fiery mushroom salad). Sukumvit Soi 20.

Djit Pochana: One of the most successful restaurant chains in Thailand with three outlets in Bangkok that serve authentic Thai dishes without compromise to Western palates, including an excellent-value luncheon buffet. Sukumvit Soi 20, tel. (02) 258-1605.

Singha Bier Haus: An imitation German chalet owned and operated by the Singha Beer Company where German and international dishes are served with musical entertainment ranging from polkas to Barbra Streisand imitators. Sukumvit Soi 21, tel. (02) 258-3951.

Alfredo: Pizzas, pastas, and other Italian dishes served in an old restored house under the watchful eye of a former champion pizza tosser. Sukumvit Soi 21, Asoke Tower, tel. (02) 258-3909.

Bourbon Street: Several very popular pubs and cafes are located in an old business complex know as Washington Square. This American-style bar and grill serves hearty breakfasts, spicy Cajun food, and local dishes plus a weekly Mexican buffet. Sukumvit Soi 22, tel. (02) 259-0328.

Larry's Dive Shop: Perhaps the only dive shop in the world that also provides a bar and grill

with Western and Asian dishes. Another Washington Square hangout. 8/3 Sukumvit Soi 22, tel. (02) 663-4563.

Khing Klao: A cozy little cafe just past Washington Square with Northern Thai specialties including various dishes made from Chiang Mai sausages and great *khao saoi* served amid a riot of clocks of every shape and size. Sukumvit Soi 22, tel. (02) 259-5623.

Lemongrass Restaurant: Embellished with antiques in both the interior dining room and exterior courtyard, Lemongrass offers atmosphere and regional dishes from all parts of Thailand such as the hot fish curry, barbecued chicken, *larb pla duk yang* (smoked catfish in northeastern style), and *nam takrai,* a cool sweetish drink brewed from lemongrass. Sukumvit Soi 24, tel. (02) 258-8637.

Tangerine's: Chinese emporium in the Capitol Club complex along with Paulaner Brauhaus serves Cantonese and Mandarin dishes along with decent ale and tangerine specialties. Even the air smells suspiciously like a lemon. Sukumvit Soi 24, tel. (02) 661-1210.

Seafood Market Restaurant: This expensive seafood restaurant (once located back on Soi Asoke) is worth a look even if the prices cause heart failure. Don't miss the enormous Phuket lobsters and giant prawns in a place that claims, "If it Swims, We Have It." Sukumvit Soi 24, tel. (02) 261-2071.

Whole Earth Restaurant: Somewhat upscale vegetarian dining venue serving fresh fruit smoothies, lassis, seafood dishes, and a range of brewed coffees along with new age music and floor cushions on the upper deck just off an alley near the Four Wing Hotel. Sukumvit Soi 26, tel. (02) 258-4900.

Joe's Place: One of the few Filipino cafes in town with all the standards including crispy *pata, adobo,* and *sinigang.* Packed on Sundays when Filipino families arrive after Church services. Sukumvit Soi 31, tel. (02) 259-8164.

Café Deco: Thai, Italian, and Mexican dishes but chiefly known for its "Thaitalian" creations that throw together two of the most famous cooking styles in the world. Sukumvit Soi 39, tel. (02) 258-8336.

Soi 23 Restaurants

Almost a dozen popular restaurants are scattered along Soi 23, a few blocks off Sukumvit Road.

Ruen Pak: An excellent-value cafe located in a renovated wooden house.

Thong U Rai: Traditional Thai dishes served in a pub atmosphere with live music.

Cue: A relatively expensive Swiss inn that serves French and European cuisine.

Le Dalat: A private, intimate house and very classy Vietnamese restaurant known for its *naem neuang,* a tasty version of Vietnamese egg rolls.

Wanakarm: For over two decades, this place has served Thais and *farangs* traditional dishes in air-conditioned dining rooms and in the romantic garden.

Pueng Kaew: Experimental Thai-Western dishes listed on both the Thai and English-language menus.

September: European cuisine in an Art Deco 1930s atmosphere.

Bistango: Western-style steakhouse with meat, chicken, and seafood specialties.

Black Scene: Trendy place with live jazz nightly at 2100.

Baan Kanitha: One of the most famous restaurants in Bangkok, known for its memorable decor, fine service, and classic Thai dishes created from both traditional and rare ingredients.

Club Tacoco: Mexican and Thai restaurant combo on the top floor of Prasarnmit Plaza with an outdoor terrace with fine views and live combo music in the evenings. Sukumvit Soi 23, tel. (02) 664-1217.

Thong U-Rai Chicken: Fairly grungy exterior but popular with locals for its unusual dishes such as deep-fried salted beef, Chiang Mai sausage, and Vietnamese oddities. Sukumvit Soi 23, tel. (02) 258-2777.

Soi 49 Restaurants (The Green Route)

Several of Bangkok's finest restaurants are located on the so-called "Green Route," a street that runs between Sois 39 and 63, midway between Sukumvit and New Petchburi Roads. All are tucked away off Sukumvit on or near Soi 49.

Gourmet Gallery: An elegant setting with creative cuisine and classical music.

The Library: An upscale restaurant owned by a Thai singer who invites in local celebrities and jazz-fusion musicians.

Laicram: Well-known Thai restaurant with royal dishes.

Piman: Features nightly performances of Thai classical dance.

Soi 55 Restaurants (Soi Thonglor)

Another concentration of fine restaurants is on Soi 55 (Soi Thonglor) between Sukumvit and the Green Route.

Art House: First-class Chinese restaurant set in a country house surrounded by formal gardens and a pleasant pond.

Barley House: A funky bohemian cafe, features nightly jazz and country bands.

L'Hexagone: Bangkok's finest French restaurant might be this place with its pastel interiors and wildly decorated bathrooms.

Sanuk Nuek: Much less formal is this simple cafe with live folk music.

Witch's Tavern: Victorian decor and English pub grub.

Singapore Chicken Rice: The name says it all as this cozy cafe serves up what is considered the best version of the classic Singaporean dish in the city. Also has the shortest menu in town with just two dishes: Hainanese chicken rice (of course) and a smaller dipper sampler. Sukumvit Soi 55, tel. (02) 392-4247.

Duke's: American steakhouse with an unusual decor centered around an interior waterfall and casino theme with imported steaks and venison dishes. Sukumvit Soi 55, tel. (02) 392-5096.

Outer Sukumvit Restaurants

Well, they aren't really as remote as they sound and these two offerings are among the most unique dining venues in Bangkok, but figure on a lengthy taxi ride.

Tum Nak Thai: For many years, Tum Nak held the world's record as the largest restaurant with 10 acres of land, a capacity of 3,000 seats, over 100 professional chefs, and 1,000 servers decked out in national costumes. Some waiters use roller skates to speed up service! A classical dance show is given nightly at 2000. 131 Ratchadapisek Rd., tel. (02) 277-8833.

Mang Gorn Luang: Several years ago, Tum Nak Thai recently lost its crown as the world's largest restaurant to the "Royal Dragon Seafood Restaurant" located at the base of the Bangna Trad Expressway in the southwest section of town. Leaving nothing to chance, this monstrous place boasts 5,000 seats, 1,200 roller-skating waiters, a 400-item menu, moored "happy boats" perfect for couples, soundproof karaoke pavilions for private parties, and a seven-story pagoda from which servers rocket down with heaping platters of steaming seafood. Has Hunter S. Thompson seen this place? Bangna Trad Expressway, tel. (02) 398-0037.

ENTERTAINMENT AND SHOPPING

ENTERTAINMENT

Mention entertainment in Bangkok and many visitors will immediately think of the brothels and massage parlors that have made Thai nightlife a world-famous phenomenon, but the city also offers a limited range of classical entertainment, from traditional dance to elaborate dramas. Culture vultures should take advantage of the opportunities in Bangkok, since Thai performing arts are almost exclusively found in the capital and, to a lesser degree, in Chiang Mai.

The three basic venues for cultural entertainment include free Thai dance at various locations, high-end spectacles at the National Theater and the Thailand Cultural Centre, and the familiar dinner-dance shows sponsored nightly by a dozen restaurants in Bangkok.

CULTURAL PERFORMANCES

Free Thai Dance
While professional performances of Thai dance-drama are both infrequent and pricey, travelers can easily enjoy the following free shows.

Lak Muang Shrine: Amateurish but authentic *likay* is sponsored around the clock by various donors in the pavilion to the rear of the City Pillar shrine, near the Grand Palace. Have a quick look, but don't expect a masterful performance from the young girls and tired grandmothers who slowly go through the paces.

Erawan Hotel Shrine: The famous shrine in the courtyard of the Grand Hyatt Erawan Hotel is among the more intriguing scenes in Bangkok. No matter what the hour, a steady stream of devotees arrives to offer flowers and wooden elephants, burn an unbelievable amount of incense, and hire the somewhat unenthusiastic dancers as gratitude for granted wishes.

Visitors are welcome to photograph the dancers and improve their karma by making offerings to four-faced Brahma, the Hindu deity associated with the shrine. Prices for incense and the small wooden elephants are posted at the entrance. Another sign gives prices to hire the dancers: four girls for 15 minutes costs 360B. Erawan Shrine, an amazing place, is most active in the early evening hours and just before the weekly lottery. Grand Hyatt Erawan Hotel, Ploenchit at Rajadamri roads.

Classical Dance and Drama

Considering the size and economic dominance of Bangkok, you would expect to find an overwhelming selection of dance, drama, music, art, and other cultural activities. Surprisingly, cultural events are limited to infrequent performances at the National Theater, smaller cultural centers, diplomatic centers, and local universities. A fairly complete listing of upcoming events is found in the *Bangkok Post* and in the Cultural Activities Programme published bimonthly by the Thailand Cultural Centre, available from the TAT office.

National Theater: Full-length *khon* performances are sponsored by the Fine Arts Department several times yearly in the National Theater. Though a somewhat expensive experience, these majestic pageants should not be missed if you are fortunate enough to be in Bangkok on the lucky weekend.

The National Theater also sponsors less elaborate cultural events on Saturday and Sunday at 1000 and 1400. Performances range from Thai variety shows to presentations of the *manora.* Special presentations are given on the last Friday of each month at 1730. Shows cost 40-100B and include a Thai-language commentary.

Perhaps the best option is the free student shows given Sunday afternoon on the front lawn. Schedules are sometimes listed in the *Bangkok Post,* but it's more dependable to simply wander by the National Theater on a Sunday morning and see if a crowd is gathering. Stageside spots can be reserved by leaving a blanket on the lawn. Local food vendors sell inexpensive snacks from the adjacent stalls.

Thailand Cultural Centre: Many of Bangkok's finest cultural performances take place in the newish cultural center on Ratchadphisek Rd., a few blocks north of New Petchburi Road en route to the airport. Opened by the king in 1987, the cultural center features a 200-seat main auditorium graced with outstanding Ramayana murals, a smaller 500-seat performance hall, and a library where fine-art exhibitions are held. Recent shows have included Thai classical music, folk puppet theater, demonstrations of *khon* drama, chamber orchestras, German vocal music, piano recitals, and opportunities to meet leading Thai artists. Pick up a complete schedule at the tourist office, or call (02) 245-7711 or (02) 247-0013 for more information.

BANGKOK RESTAURANTS
WITH THAI CLASSICAL DANCE

RESTAURANT	ADDRESS	AREA	PHONE
Baan Thai	Sukumvit Soi 32	Sukumvit	258-5403
Maneeya's Lotus Room	Ploenchit Rd.	Siam Square	252-6312
Chao Phraya	451 Arun Amrin Rd.	Thonburi	424-2389
Oriental Hotel	Charoen Krung Rd.	Silom	437-9417
Piman	Sukumvit Soi 49	Sukumvit	258-7866
Ruen Thep	Silom Village	Silom	233-9447
Indra Regent Hotel	Rajaprarop Rd.	Siam Square	251-1111
Sawasdee	66 Soi Phipat	Silom	237-6310
Siam Intercontinetal	Rama I Rd.	Siam Square	253-0355
Suwanahong	Sri Ayuthaya Rd.	Siam Square	245-4448
Tun Nak Thai	131 Rajadapisek	Sukumvit	277-3828

Chalerm Krung Royal Theater: The performing arts were given a major boost in 1994 with the opening of this high-tech *khon* center inside the historic Chalerm Krung theater in Pahurat, four blocks from the Royal Palace. Opened in 1993 as Thailand's largest and most sophisticated movie theater, Sala Chalerm Krung was also the first cinema to feature air-conditioning and was the scene of many important premiers such as *Ben Hur* and *Tea House of the August Moon.* After it fell on hard times and was closed for over a decade, financial support from private industry and a donation from King Rama VIII helped renovate and reopen the grand structure.

Today, the troupe of 170 dancers are complemented by a sophisticated light show, an 80,000-watt audio system, and other technological wonders that never distract from the sumptuous costumes and elaborate choreography. *Khon* and other Thai performances are held at 2000 several times weekly. 66 Charoen Krung Rd., tel. (02) 222-0437, 400-1,000B.

Dinner Dance Shows

First-time visitors who wish an overview of Thai dance can attend performances in almost a dozen air-conditioned Thai restaurants listed in the accompanying chart. While these highly abbreviated performances are somewhat artificial and resented by visitors who dislike the "instant culture" mentality, the performances are usually of a high standard, plus the glittering costumes and elegant dance styles are always impressive.

Dinner dance shows follow a standard arrangement. A northern Thai *khon toke*-style dinner is followed by brief demonstrations of *khon, lakhon,* and *likay* folk dancing, Thai martial arts, puppetry, and sword fighting. Dinner is usually served around 1900, and the show begins 60-90 minutes later. Photographers should arrive early and request a seat near the stage.

Prices for the dinner with show range 300-800B; some restaurants offer the show without a meal for 300-400B. Transportation from the hotel to the restaurant is often included with the ticket. Performance times and prices can be double-checked by calling the restaurant or inquiring with the TAT.

Dinner dance shows can be seen at several luxury hotels and at private restaurants in renovated homes. Purchase tickets from most travel agents or get the lowest prices from the bucket shops in Banglampoo and near the Malaysia Hotel.

Baan Thai: Like most Thai restaurants with dance performances, Baan Thai re-creates a traditional Thai house with polished teakwood floors, elegant furnishings, and tropical gardens. Nightly shows from 1900. 7 Sukumvit Soi 32, tel. (02) 258-5403.

Piman: One of Bangkok's more elegant and expensive shows takes place inside this beautiful reproduction of a Sukothai-era house. 46 Sukumvit Soi 49, tel. (02) 258-7866.

Chao Phraya Restaurant: Travelers staying in the guesthouses of Banglampoo often attend the cultural show across the Pinklau Bridge in Thonburi. Packages sold by travel agents include transportation, dinner, show, and possibly a cocktail in the adjacent Paradise Music Hall.

Hotel Shows: Dance performances are also given at the **Sala Rim Nam Restaurant** across the river from the Oriental Hotel (free boat service), and at the **Sala Thai Restaurant** on the rooftop of the Indra Regent.

NIGHTLIFE

Bangkok's nightlife is perhaps the most notorious in the world. Bars, brothels, live sex shows, massage parlors, gay nightclubs, roving transvestites, sex cabarets, all-night coffee shops thick with call girls, child prostitutes, and barbershops that provide more than just haircuts—the range of sexual services is simply amazing. Bangkok alone has an estimated 100,000 prostitutes, and it's said that almost one-fifth of all visitors to Thailand come for sex. Despite the devastating effect of AIDS, local opposition, and the conservative moral attitudes of the Thai people, Thailand's roaring sex industry seems destined to remain a major attraction.

It all begins at the Bangkok Airport, where male visitors are sometimes propositioned by transvestites who boldly drag their unsuspecting prey into terminal bathrooms. Airport taxi drivers often negotiate the fare, then offer up girls in all ages and prices. Many Bangkok hotels—from low-end to prestigious—also serve as "knock-

knock" emporiums, where spare girls are sold by the employees or sent uninvited up to rooms at night.

The scene continues throughout the city. Over on Patpong, street touts thrust out Polaroids of young women and well-worn scraps of cardboard that list their sexual talents. Teams of transvestites cruise the tourist enclaves. Local publications such as *This Week in Bangkok* advertise escort services, marriage agencies, gay nightclubs, barbershops, and go-go bars wedged between brief descriptions of temples and upcoming Rotary Club functions.

First-time visitors often assume that prostitution in Thailand is a hangover from the Vietnam War era when American servicemen took their R&R in Bangkok and Pattaya. Actually, Thai society has long been tolerant of prostitution; brothels were commonplace in Chinatown and in the Pratunam *klongs* before the arrival of mass tourism. Today, even the smallest of Thai towns have long-established houses frequented exclusively by local men; *farangs* are often refused admittance in the belief that AIDS is a foreign disease.

Visitors are also surprised to learn that prostitution is illegal in Thailand. For that matter, even topless dancing is prohibited, not to mention the other services available in the massage parlors and darkened nightclubs. Proposals have been made to legalize prostitution to control AIDS, but most Thais prefer to keep the business as private as possible. Police periodically raid brothels and go-go bars, but this formality is done more to ensure a steady stream of payoffs than to stop the flesh trade.

The Bangkok Scene

Nightclubs and girlie bars that cater to foreigners are concentrated in several neighborhoods. The most notorious area is Patpong Road between Silom and Surawong Roads. To briefly experience the mayhem you could spend a few hours wandering through the clubs, but the insistent hawkers and surprisingly aggressive nature of the shopkeepers is a complete turn off.

The second-largest number of clubs is located on Soi Cowboy, a short street near the intersection of Sukumvit Road and Soi 21.

But the best area for this type of entertainment is the roaring Nana Entertainment Plaza

(NEP), also called Nana Plaza, just off Sukumvit Road on Soi 4. Serious party animals generally find a hotel in this neighborhood and spend the rest of their vacation haunting the bars and nightclubs on both sides of Sukumvit, spending their early evenings in NEP and later hours at the disco inside the nearby Nana Hotel or down the street at the Thermae.

Washington Square on Sukumvit near Soi 22 is another nightlife center but very quiet and more geared to simple meals and cocktails than the girlie bar scene.

Tidbits and gossip about the bar scene in Bangkok can be culled from Bernard Trink's column in the Friday *Bangkok Post*. Trink does a good job describing what's happening and offers dependable tips. His column is posted on the *Bangkok Post* website.

Patpong

Bangkok's most notorious red-light district is on Patpong 1 and 2 between Silom and Surawong Roads. Once owned by the Patpong family and made popular by American soldiers on leave from Vietnam, this infamous collection of go-go bars, cocktail lounges, live shows, street vendors, pushy touts, and preteen hustlers forms a scene straight from Dante's *Inferno.*

During the day Patpong is almost deserted except for a pair of excellent bookstores and several cozy pubs that screen the latest videos in air-conditioned comfort. Between 1800 and 2000 the bars spring to life with smaller crowds and happy-hour prices. A lively but completely obnoxious night market now takes place along Patpong 1 and on the sidewalks of Silom and Surawong Roads. After 2000, some 30-50 go-go bars and live-show nightclubs operate at full tilt.

Single males, Western females, and even families are welcome to enter a club, watch a show, and perhaps attempt a conversation with the unexpectedly friendly ladies. Surprisingly, *farang* women are often the center of attention and soon become the conversation centerpiece for the entire bar.

Patpong 1: The best strategy for selecting a club is to walk the entire street and quickly peek inside the flashier establishments. Better clubs on Patpong 1 include those owned by the King's Group such as **King's Castle, Queen's Cas-**

tle, and the **Mississippi Club,** where scenes from *The Deer Hunter* were filmed. Patpong also served as Saigon's Tu Do Street for Robin Williams's *Good Morning Vietnam.* The **Kangaroo Club** on the north end is an Australian-run pub that provides an air-conditioned escape. **Napoleon Lounge** is an old favorite that serves as a daytime restaurant and nighttime jazz club.

Patpong 2: This narrow alley provides an easy alternative to the madness on Patpong 1. **Bobby's Arms** has a Sunday evening music fest of straight-ahead mainstream jazz performed by both Western and Thai artists. The open-air beer bars (also called bar beers!) on Patpong 2 are less intimidating options where you can relax and watch the passing crowd. Women in the north-end watering holes are friendly and under less pressure to push drinks than their counterparts on Patpong 1. Several of the bars allows patrons to go-go dance with the women.

Live Sex Shows: The most irritating activity on Patpong is the hordes of overly aggressive barkers who accost Westerners with offers of private shows featuring young girls whose special talents are explicitly listed on calling cards. After performing their bizarre biological feats, the girls are joined by a young Thai male who tests his endurance, perhaps knocking over your drink in the process.

Very few visitors enjoy these shows, but if you must, be sure to establish the total cover charge and price for drinks *before* going upstairs for the show—misunderstandings are common. Tourists who are presented with extortionate bills should pay up, then contact the tourist police on the Surawong Road end of Patpong 1, or the larger police station at the intersection of Silom and Rama IV Roads. The tourist police will collect your refund and correct the situation for the next visitor.

Patpong 3 (Silom Soi 4): This dead-end alley off Silom Road is home to several gay clubs that feature transvestites *(gatoeis)* in hilarious follies revues. Solo women and mixed couples are welcome to have a drink and enjoy the show. Also on this alley are several small restaurants such as the **Telephone Cafe** and the wildly popular **Rome Club** disco, where trendy gays and visiting *farangs* come to enjoy the superb sound and lighting system.

Soi Taniya: Japan comes to Bangkok. Taniya Road, three short blocks east of Patpong, more closely resembles a nightlife district in Tokyo than Bangkok. Just for an odd experience, walk past the private gate (the Japanese have apparently purchased the entire street) and pseudo-art-deco Thaniya Plaza building to glance at the Japanese nightclubs, laser karaoke bars, and sushi joints all marked with Japanese script. Most are private clubs that bar admittance to Westerners unless accompanied by a member.

Nana Entertainment Plaza (NEP)
Bangkok's greatest go-go bar scene features three floors of clubs, cafes, and rock 'n' roll cabarets with outstanding sound systems.

Ground floor of the U-shaped complex has a few open-air beer bars for drinks without hassles, especially during happy hours from 1800-2000. The better clubs are all on the second floor. **Asian Intrigue** sponsors rather campy music revues nightly at 2000 and 2300 that run the gamut from Thai classical dancers to simulated love scenes; popular with single males and mixed couples. **Woodstock** is a dark and smoky lounge that features disco tunes, girls, and some of the better rock bands in Bangkok. Other bars on the second floor include the **Farang Connection, Blackout, Hog's Breath Saloon** ("better than no breath at all"), **Sexy Night,** and **Three Roses.**

Nana Entertainment Complex is on Soi 4, directly across from the Nana Hotel.

Soi Cowboy
Bangkok's second-most-active bar area is off Sukumvit Road between Sois 21 and 23. The area gets its name from a black American nicknamed "Cowboy" who owned one of the first bars on the street. Crowds tend to be smaller and made up of Western expatriates rather than locals and tourists. Soi Cowboy is also a good place to meet Western residents and pick up inside tips and anecdotes about the nightlife scene in Bangkok. Set with terrific foodstalls and friendly pubs, Soi Cowboy is the slow and sleazy counterpoint to the flash and glitter of Patpong.

Bars tend to change name and ownership with the seasons, but the current favorites in-

THAI KICKBOXING

T hai boxing is the street fighter's dream of Western boxing mixed with karate and a bit of *tae kwon do*. Barefoot pugilists prior to WW II wrapped their hands in hemp mixed with ground glass; the fight went on for as long as anyone could stand, or had any blood left. Today the boxers wear lightly padded gloves and a few rules have been introduced to control the carnage.

An interesting ritual takes place before the match begins. Wailing music from a small orchestra of Javanese pipe, two drums, and cymbal sets the mood. Often fixed with colored cords and protective amulets, the two contestants enter the ring, kneel and pray to the spirits for victory, then begin a surrealistic slow-motion dance designed to show off their talents while emulating their teachers' movements. Spectators make their bets as the boxers pound and kick each other with ever-increasing frenzy. The drama is heightened by the cacophonous musical accompaniment. At the end of five three-minute rounds, or the merciful intervention of the referee, the fight ends and a winner is declared by the judges.

Thai kickboxing can be experienced at the Lumpini Stadium on Rama IV Road (near the Malaysia Hotel) every Tuesday and Friday at 1800, and Saturday at 1800 and 1330. Superior boxers meet at Rajadamnern Stadium (near the TAT office) every Monday, Wednesday, and Thursday at 1800, and on Sunday at 1700 and 2000. Admission is 50-200B. This spectacle is best watched from ringside rather than with the rabble up in the circular gallery.

clude **Midnight** featuring a dance show around midnight, a country-western pub with live bands sensibly called **Country Road,** brightly illuminated **Tilac,** and the very popular **Five Star,** also with live music. Smaller bars and pubs include the **Apache** with wooden Indians posted above the entrance, **New Klymaxx, New Crazy Cats, Rawhide, Shadow, Long Gun, Toy Bar, Black & White, New Loretta, Dandy Bar, Cowboy Two,** and *After Skool* with, what else, a schoolgirl theme.

The far end of the street is chock-a-block with small bars and cozy nightclubs worth checking out such as **Cowboy One, Big Blue, New Hare & Hound, Suzi Wong, D.L. Irish Pub, Pam's, Our Place, Bluebird** ("Three Floors of Fun"), **Tony's, Moonshine Joint,** and **Virgo.**

Several of these clubs have been enlarged by knocking down the walls between two smaller bars.

Adjacent Soi 23 offers several good British pubs that serve bangers and mash along with the latest videos. Top choices include **The Old Dutch Cafe** right on the corner, the **B.H. International Restaurant & Beer House** just across Soi 23, the **Ship Inn** (a British pub), and the **Old Siam** for Thai fare in a cozy setting.

Washington Square

Another low-key nightlife scene is located on the south side of Sukumvit Road between Sois 22 and 24. Behind the Washington Cinema, which dominates the square, you'll find a small cluster of cheap foodstalls and nightclubs that evoke an American atmosphere. Darts, snooker, videos, and Sunday afternoon barbecues are the main attractions rather than go-go girls and sex shows.

The liveliest spot is the popular **Bourbon Street,** which features Cajun creole cuisine and live Dixieland and other jazz on weekends by the Bourbon Street Ramblers. Other American West saloons include the **Texas Lone Star Saloon** with "Food, Wimmin & Likker," the well-named **No Probl'm Cocktail Lounge,** the **Prince of Wales Pub, Happy Pub, Square One Pub,** and the **Silver Dollar Bar** ("No Weapons Allowed").

Denny's Corner is another cowboy-style bar and restaurant with American grub and inexpensive brew.

Late Night Clubs and Coffee Shops

Moving sharply downscale several notches is a handful of coffee shops that allow freelance prostitutes to ply their trade. Most are rather deserted until about midnight when the bars on Patpong and Soi Cowboy close their doors. Bar girls who haven't found a date then grab a *tuk tuk* to the Grace or Thermae and hang out until sunrise.

Angels: By far the most popular and inviting late-night spot for music, dance, and girls is the almost chic nightclub on the ground floor of the Nana Hotel, just opposite Nana Plaza. Although the club is almost completely deserted until 2200, almost every table fills in the next 30 minutes, so arrive at exact the right moment to grab a table near the dance floor. Nana Hotel, Sukumvit Soi 2.

Grace Hotel Coffeeshop: Bangkok's formerly great late-night hangout has lost much of its sheen and now is favored by a heavily Arab clientele, but this longtime classic may be worth a quick visit to see what floats to the surface in the early morning hours. Sukumvit Soi 3.

Thermae Coffeeshop: The famous old rendezvous closed down at its former location several years ago but has reopened in a somewhat more upscale setting with all the familiar trappings—hordes of freelance ladies who pack the cozy club after the other nightclubs close around 0200. Sukumvit Soi 15, under the Ruam Chitt Plaza building.

Massage Parlors

Countless massage parlors, Turkish baths, and steam baths are found throughout Bangkok. Large numbers have cropped up on lower Sukumvit and along New Petchburi Road, north of Sukumvit. Massage parlors come in two varieties: legitimate places that offer traditional "ancient massage" for 200-400B per hour, and sex houses filled with numbered women waiting in viewing rooms. These giant pleasure palaces are equipped with one-way mirrors through which customers watch up to 250 masseuses file their nails and zone out on TV while waiting for a customer.

It's a flesh market of the most curious type. Customers make their selection by picking a woman and giving her number to the parlor manager. The chosen is called out, the style of massage is decided, and the bill is paid at the cashier's counter.

Transvestite Revues

"Boys Will Be Girls" is a familiar theme here in the Land of Smiles. For several decades, female-impersonator revues have been a popular form of entertainment in the seaside resort of Pattaya, but today these revues take place in Bangkok and Patong Beach on Phuket. The small gay clubs around Silom Soi 4 put on minor revues in intimate surroundings, but tourists generally favor the more elaborate and professional shows held at the following two clubs.

Calypso Cabaret: The one-hour performance includes dancing sailoresses, comedy skits with audience participation, leather queens, Thai and Chinese dancers in stunning costumes, and above all, a delightful sense of humor and good cheer. Photographers are welcome but arrive early to secure a good seat in this uncomfortably small auditorium. Shows nightly at 2015 and 2145, 600B includes one drink. Asia Hotel, 296 Phayathai Rd., tel. (02) 261-6355.

Mambo: Formed from Calypso's former touring company, this equally professional troupe is now the only choice on Sukumvit after Calypso left the Ambassador Hotel several years ago.

male Monroes

Reservations are recommended for either of the twice nightly shows. Shows nightly at 2000 and 2145, 600B includes one drink. Sukumvit Soi 31, tel. (02) 662-0441.

DISCOS, NIGHTCLUBS, AND BARS

The nightlife scene in Bangkok is unrivaled, even by the hedonist pleasures of Manila or Hong Kong. Within easy walking distance or a short cab ride from most hotels are pubs, nightclubs, discos, and cabarets offering everything from country-western tunes to all-night rave scenes packed with trendy Thais and the curious *farang*.

Nightclubs and bars in luxury hotels are okay, but don't compare with the local venues that offer live music and entertainment from about 2100 to the early morning hours. Cover charges at clubs with bands or DJ services run 50-150B during the week and 120-300B on weekends, but a complimentary drink or two is often included in the cover charge. The larger and newer venues feature DJs, private karaoke lounges, restaurants and bars, and "videotheques" where music is backed by laser rock videos.

The following section is arranged by neighborhood.

Banglampoo
The backpackers' enclave near Khao San Road remains an entertainment dry zone though a handful of small spots are worth checking out before heading off to the brighter lights elsewhere in the city.

Gulliver's Traveller's Tavern: After years of suffering through cheap cafes and dismal clubs, Khao San finally has a professionally designed and operated venue where upmarket backpackers can escape the heat and enjoy a decent meal along with pub games and live music. Khao San at Chakraphonse Rd., tel. (02) 629-1988.

Hemlock: Small but sophisticated cafe and pub with trendy decor and sophisticated music just opposite the express boat pier. 56 Pra Arthit Rd., tel. (02) 282-7507.

Joy Luck Club: A longtime favorite just around the corner from the Hemlock with reasonably priced meals and light music. Open daily

noon to 0200. 8 Pra Sumen, Pra Arthid Rd., tel. (02) 280-3307.

Song Muai: Popular and very crowded two-storey pub cafe with inexpensive food and drink and loud music to keep the place jumping. 169 Tanao Rd., tel. (02) 622-1205.

Silom Soi 4
While nearby Patpong Road is mostly go-go bars with dancing girls, the adjacent streets offer dozens of clubs and discos that cater to all sorts of musical tastes and sexual persuasions. Silom Soi 4 has the largest concentration of clubs.

Cactus Club: Owner Brian Sullivan operates a colorful, Spanish-style nightclub with dance floor, long bar, and uncharacteristically high ceiling for a small club on this alley. The place is easily spotted by its distinct green neon light that draws in the loyal mix of Thais and expats. 114/15 Silom Soi 4, tel. (02) 233-8821.

Molly's Jump: An American-style theme bar based on the career of a famed Australian music promoter decorated with photos of Ian "Molly"

Meldrun with his singer and musician friends. Downstairs is the dance floor while upstairs is a pool table, satellite TV, and cocktail lounge. 86-8 Silom Soi 4, tel. (02) 235-5891.

Milk Bar: A near-legendary hangout for the artistic Thai set (singers, actors, designers, wannabees) who lift the rafters of the small, 1950s-style interior. Popular spot for a drink before moving on to Deeper, Sphinx, or the D.J. Station. 114/10 Silom Soi 4, no phone, no credit.

Film Mix: A movie-themed cafe with dance music that attracts the spillover from nearby Kool Spot. 114/5 Silom Soi 4, tel. (02) 235-3877.

Kool Spot: Another addition to the crazy alley near Patpong. This music-and-dance bar is set with stone flagging and curvy mirrors facing a long enamel bartop fashioned in the shape of a snake; you'll see the dragon eyes flashing after a few pitchers of Kamikazes. 114/6 Silom Soi 4, tel. (02) 266-4820.

Speed: DJ dance music and themed Saturday hip-hop nights make this about the most crowded and interesting club in the neighborhood. 80 Silom Soi 4.

Hyper: A longtime favorite with a trendy people-watching crowd and laid-back music for the dance inclined. Open nightly 2100-0200. 114/14 Silom Soi 4, tel. (02) 238-5257.

Silom Road Area

Several other pubs and nightclubs are around Silom but not tucked away in lively Soi 4.

Delaney's: Clean and comfortable Irish pub with Guiness and Kilkeeny's plus Irish food and live bands most nights with an emphasis on folk music and jazz combos. Just across the street from Patpong. 1/5 Convent Rd., tel. (02) 266-7160.

O'Reillys Irish Pub: Another safe escape from the madness of Patpong with dependable grub and drinks without the hassle of hostesses or grubby merchants. 62/1 Silom at Thaniya Rd., tel. (02) 632-7515.

FM 228 An entertainment complex that combines live music, a karaoke lounge, an American restaurant, and a videotheque hall—perfect for the occasional rave party. 323 Silom Rd., United Centre Bldg., 5th floor, tel. (02) 231-1228.

Radio City: Formerly Mars and then Smile but still a dependable choice for DJs spinning

---

LIVE THAI ROCK 'N' ROLL

*U*nlike Manila in the Philippines, most of the clubs in Bangkok feature recorded music rather than live entertainment. The scene, however, has improved with the arrival of *dontree pher cheevit,* a fresh musical force that has traded the traditional love themes for issues of social injustice.

Early efforts at political consciousness by a group named Caravan proved too radical for public airing, but Carabao in the late 1980s caused a major sensation with their song "Made in Thailand." The hit both ridiculed Thai obsession with foreign-made goods and inadvertently promoted the government's Buy-Thai program! Other Carabao songs have described the plight of Bangkok's prostitutes and poor rural farmers. Instead of simply plagiarizing Western pop melodies to back up Thai lyrics, Carabao has successfully fused American country rock with traditional Thai music. Remember the 1986 disco hit "One Night in Bangkok"? Banned in Thailand.

---

oldies and live bands on weekends. 76/1-3 Patpong Soi 1, tel. (02) 234-6902.

Barbican: Not on Patpong or one of its nearby alleys but a trendy nightclub stuck directly in the heart of Japanese Patpong with an upstairs restaurant, international newspapers on the ground floor, and a small disco that welcomes all visitors and rocks until dawn. 9/4 Soi Taniya, Silom Rd., tel. (02) 234-3590.

Silom Gay Clubs

Almost a dozen gay clubs are scattered around Patpong, often in Soi 4.

Rome Club: A relatively large number of fashionably dressed gays, trendy art-club types, *farang* visitors, and *gatoeis* hang out in the upstairs annex despite the disco's ban against their gay clientele. The scene peaks around midnight and winds down around 3 a.m, but this once-famed club has lost much of its glamour as the trendsetters have move on to greener lawns. 90 Silom Soi 4, tel. (02) 233-8836.

Deeper: A slow but steady decline at the Rome Club has sent patrons—both gay and straight—to other, nearby clubs. Deeper is popular with trendsetters and creative *farangs* who party and dance until dawn. Be sure to visit the adjacent Deep Bar and try a jug of their lethal Kamikaze (250B) that glows in the ultraviolet lights in the bar's dark recesses. 82 Silom Soi 4, tel. (02) 233-2930.

Telephone: The eight-year-old bar/restaurant has survived the onslaught of newer clubs and continues to draw a regular clientele. However, few folks use the table phones in this era of cellular madness. Have you ever seen so many people packing "handphones?" 114/11-13 Silom Soi 4, tel. (02) 234-3279.

Sphinx: A predominantly gay bar with terraced seating on two spacious floors, creamy Egyptian decor, dance rooms on the upper floors, and a balcony for watching the lip-synching drag shows nightly at midnight or later. Excellent food, too. 98-104 Silom Soi 4, tel. (02) 234-7249.

The Balcony: An offshoot of the Telephone Club with fan-cooled open frontage and breezy balconies for people watching. 86-8 Silom Soi 4, tel. (02) 235-5891.

Bank Studio: Techno dance club with third floor karaoke plus amusing cabaret show around midnight. Mostly a Thai clientele but *farang* and women are welcome. Silom Soi 6, tel. (02) 236-6385.

Disco Disco (DD): Small but packed-out place with two bars and nonstop dance music provided by young Thai DJs. Open nightly 2100-0200. Silom Soi 2, tel. (02) 234-6151.

DJ Station: Gay disco with an unpretentious atmosphere and campy cabaret show nightly around midnight. 8/6-8 Silom Soi 2, tel. (02) 266-4029.

JJ Park: An old favorite known for its tasty Thai food, friendly clientele, and great sounds like live bands, plus attractive setting fixed up with snazzy copper panels. Also, a late-night cabaret show with performers drawn from nearby clubs. 8/3 Silom Soi 2, tel. (02) 233-3247.

Sarasin Road

For many years, Bangkok had few bars in the traditional sense since cafes could legally sell beer and spirits, and Thais generally preferred to socialize with friends at home rather than in public. But over the last few years Bangkok has exploded with dozens of new clubs that cater to both foreigners and locals with rock,

country-western, jazz, and other forms of popular music.

The scene started in the late 1980s with the launching of several clubs on Soi Sarasin, just off Rajadamnern Road near Lumpini Park, where clubs modeled themselves after European bistros and cater to an older and more professional crowd rather than the teenybopper set that frequents the Silom Road discos.

Brown Sugar: Arguably the city's best choice for adult contemporary and jazz music featuring three bands per night, ranging from Manop Varonitipas on sax to local pop master Tewan Sapsanyokorn, who plays saxophone, Thai flute, and electric violin with his group Tewan Novel-Jazz. The place has become expensive (drinks run 120-180B) but the good vibes and excellent music have attracted folks such as Willem Dafoe, Gregory Hines, and Spyro Gyra. Cover charge runs 150-300B. 231/19 Sarasin Rd., tel. (02) 250-0103.

Old West Saloon: A longtime favorite that recreates the American Wild West in a down-to-earth atmosphere. Two bands play country-western nightly, there's no cover, and the place is filled with all kinds of kitsch such as cattle skulls, American Indian photos, and other cowboy memorabilia. 231/17 Sarasin Rd., tel. (02) 250-0103.

Blue's Bar: A two-floor fashionable music club that features alternative and classic rock, plus decent food for the designer set. The place has dropped their former 1980s music in favor of more hip rap but still remains among the better clubs in this neck of the woods. 231/16 Sarasin Rd., tel. (02) 252-7335.

Hi Park: Lively hangout for young and trendy Thais who are well dressed and have money to burn. The downstairs area gets overly boisterous, though a quieter balcony is just upstairs. 231/18 Sarasin Rd., tel. (02) 250-0090.

Soi Lang Suan

Around the corner from Soi Sarasin is another street with a good selection of pubs favored by local expats and upscale Thais.

Round Midnight: The club caters to jazzophiles and lovers of salsa and samba but also features bands playing rock classics and easy listening during the week. Packed on weekends. No cover. 106/12 Soi Lang Suan, tel. (02) 251-0652.

Bee'z: Small and cozy spot with nightly entertainment, mostly folk but also flamenco guitarists and other low-key forms that allow conversation. 63/10 Soi Lang Suan, tel. (02) 252-4630.

Ad Makers: A Western bar with plenty of rough wood and live bands that play your requests, plus a full menu and food served until 0200. 51/51 Soi Lang Suan, tel. (02) 652-0168.

Siam Square

This rather conservative neighborhood will never win any awards for Bangkok party central, though a few places might be worth a quick look.

Hard Rock Cafe: Have you picked up your T-shirt yet? The standard array of rock memorabilia plus live bands most nights starting around 2200. Siam Square Soi 1, tel. (02) 251-0792.

Planet Hollywood: Another American-themed restaurant and nightclub with movie stuff and some of the worst food in the city. Business has been disappointing since this place opened several years ago and this outlet may close in the near future. Ploenchit Rd., Gaysorn Plaza, tel. (02) 656-1358.

Hartmannsdorfer Bauhaus: German microbrewery in an elegant setting with fresh brew and beer hall food at reasonable prices. Rama 1 Rd., Discovery Center, tel. (02) 658-0223.

Sukumvit

The wilder and raunchier spots are near the upper end of Sukumvit, while the classier spots with jazz and otherwise are farther down and tucked away in the side alleys. The following are described starting from inner Sukumvit all the way out to Ekamai at Soi 63.

Woodstock: Entertainment in this funky club alternates between live rock 'n' roll bands on weekends and recorded music during the week. It's oriented toward cruising males but a great place for live music to suit all persuasions. Check the overwhelming collection of *Far Side* cartoons in the men's room. Nana Entertainment Plaza, Sukumvit Soi 4, tel. (02) 258-2565.

Jool's: A longtime favorite for those in the know, Jool's is the Sukumvit counterpart to Bobby's Arms on Patpong. But here you don't have to hassle with the bar touts and other promoters of sleaze to enjoy the British pub food, imported beers, and good conversation from local denizens. Prices are low, but don't ring the bell unless you intend to buy drinks for the everyone. 21/3 Soi 4 Sukumvit Rd., tel. (02) 252-6413.

Grace Hotel Streetstalls: Not really a pub, disco, or nightclub in any sense of the word, but the streetstall vendors near the Grace Hotel provide tasty food at rock-bottom prices, plus their honest chatter is an authentic form of Thai entertainment. Soi 1 and Soi 3.

Huntsman Pub: Somewhat sedate but an excellent place to escape the nearby madness and enjoy a drink or meal along with the talented bands that play nightly until 0100. A comfortable venue for those not interested in the girlie bar scene that dominates this area. Landmark Plaza, Sukumvit Soi 6, tel. (02) 254-0404.

Victoria Bar & Pub: An old favorite in operation for over 15 years with imported brews and unique versions of Swiss fondue. 9/1 Sukumvit Soi 7, tel. (02) 484-9717.

Discovery: Large disco with massive dance floor, balconied pub, and open-air porch for escaping the crowds that frequent the retro nights and gay events held weekly. Sukumvit Soi 12, tel. (02) 653-0246.

Isaan 19: Unique Isaan Lao disco with *mor lam* music in a cramped setting just above the Country Road nightclub. Sukumvit Soi 19.

Imageries By The Glass: Strange name but an impressive place with decent food and a non-stop array of bands performing from early evening until closing at 0200. Sukumvit Soi 24, tel. (02) 258-7010.

Taurus Brew House: Upmarket and trendy disco, featuring Latin and funk sounds, both recorded and live. Few Westerners in sight, but a venue that has survived and thrived over the last few years for its attention to detail and outstanding selection of live bands. A very dressy place with a 500B minimum (two drinks included) but among the better places in town. Sukumvit Soi 26, tel. (02) 661-3535.

The Bull's Head: British pub with grub, brew, and a variety of theme nights such as a quiz program on Tuesday and an oldies music session on Fridays. Sukumvit Soi 33, tel. (02) 259-4444.

Londoner Brew House: Another popular English-style pub with homemade bitters and nightly music from retro disco to live bands playing golden oldies. Sukumvit Soi 33, UBC Bldg., tel. (02) 261-0238.

Sukumvit Soi 33: Several cozy clubs—curiously named after European painters—are tucked away in a quiet alley. All offer happy hour drink specials and are popular with Western expatriates who live nearby. Two standards are **Vincent Van Gogh** and the **Renoir Club.**

Axil Cafe: Fashionable boutique with heavy attitude favored by hip young Thais on an early evening bender before moving on to more raucous digs. Sukumvit Soi 39, tel. (02) 261-6232.

Blues Jazz: Classy pub with excellent entertainment and decent food at decent prices, though the remote location holds tourist visits down to a minimum. Sukumvit Soi 53, tel. (02) 258-7747.

Witch's Tavern: Enormous pub with a long bar and music lounge worked by Filipino and Hong Kong bands specializing in jazz, soul, and easy-listening classics. Reasonable prices for beer and spirits. Sukumvit Soi 55, tel. (02) 390-2646.

Barley Castle Pub: Impressive nightclub with pop and jazz band performing nightly until 0100 or 0200 depending on their mood. Sukumvit Soi 55, tel. (02) 390-2646.

Harmonics: Cozy little cafe with reasonably priced food and wafting guitar music, then livelier three-piece bands until the closing hours. Sukumvit Soi 55, tel. (02)390-4484.

Café 50: Trendy and very hip cafe with downstairs cafe and upstairs bar with folk music evenings, plus appearances by Thai movie and soap opera idols. Sukumvit Soi 61, tel. (02) 381-1773.

Major Bowl Pub & Restaurant: A flashy newer bowling rink with dance music and designer restaurant serving Thai and Western dishes to the late-night crowd. 122/39 Sukumvit Soi 63 (Ekamai), tel. (02) 714-2849.

Washington Square

This assortment of simple pubs and nightclubs has long been the favorite watering hole for many Western expats living in the nearby apartments and condominium complexes. The "Square" at Sukumvit Soi 22 is rather tame when compared to Patong or Soi Cowboy; the food is familiar and you won't have to hassle with teenyboppers or Thai trendsetters of questionable sexual persuasion. This is not a place for people who prefer videotheques and flashing lights.

Bourbon Street: A local hangout for a cheap breakfast, leisurely Sunday brunch, creole cuisine, a Mexican buffet on Tuesday evenings, and entertainment provided by local expats who enjoy meeting the tourist and traveler. 29/4-6 Washington Square, Sukumvit 22, tel. (02) 259-0328.

Denny's Corner: An alfresco bar and restaurant on the edge of the square that guarantees a good place to nurse a beer and watch the passing parade. No entertainment or music, but a pleasant spot to hang out for a few hours. 13 Washington Square, Sukumvit 22, tel. (02) 259-5684.

The Prince of Wales: Another old favorite known for its inexpensive food, cold beer, and shaggy carpets that have been nailed to the walls for unknown reasons. 37 Washington Square, Sukumvit 22, tel. (02) 258-4204.

Silver Dollar: Another expat watering hole with homey vibes and an excellent barbecue on Sunday from noon to late afternoon. Modeled after the American Old West, it now resembles something from the *Gunsmoke* era. 550 Washington Square, Sukumvit 22, tel. (02) 258-2033.

Bangkapi

Bangkapi is in eastern Bangkok near Ramkamheng University, about 15 km northeast of Silom Road or 10 km from the beginning of Sukumvit Road. A taxi from Sukumvit should cost about 150B.

NASA Spacedrome: Bangkok's flashiest disco is a multimillion-dollar dance emporium that packs in over 2,000 sweating bodies every weekend. At midnight, a spaceship descends to the floor amid smoke, flashing lights, and the theme song from *2001: A Space Odyssey.* For sheer spectacle, nothing else compares in Thailand. Afterwards, the house Gypsy Band plays until 0300. 999 Ramkamheng Rd., 100 meters north of New Petchburi Rd., tel. (02) 314-6530.

Thonburi

Travelers in Banglampoo will find the following disco easy to reach and a convenient spot to experience modern Thai culture.

Another gigantic dance emporium with the standard amenities of flashing lights, laser videos, and booming disco music, it's a very wild place on weekends. **The Paradise** is on

Arun Amarin Road in Thonburi, just across the bridge from Banglampoo; a good choice for trav-elers staying on Khao San Road. Taxis from Khao San Road cost 50-80B.

SHOPPING

Bangkok enjoys a well-deserved reputation as the shopping capital of Southeast Asia with its range of products from Thai silks, gemstones, tai-lor-made suits and dresses, to inexpensive shoes, bronzeware, and traditional handicrafts. Even the imported items such as electronics, watches, and cameras are much cheaper in the duty-free ports of Hong Kong or Singapore. It's impossible to beat the deals in Bangkok.

Prices are fairly uniform across town, but se-lection varies slightly between neighborhoods: Chinatown is best for gold chains and photog-raphy equipment, Silom Road for silks and an-tiques, Sukumvit for leather goods and tailors, shopping centers near Siam Square for high fashion, Pratunan for cheap clothing, Banglam-poo for handicrafts and tribal artifacts.

Serious shoppers should purchase Nancy Chandler's outstanding *Market Map of Bangkok* and *Shopping in Exotic Thailand,* published by Impact Publications.

WHERE TO SHOP

Merchants recommended by the Tourism Au-thority of Thailand are listed in the TAT publi-cation, the *Official Shopping Guide,* and de-noted on shop front windows by a decal of a female vendor seated with a pair of baskets. Unfortunately, this regulation means very little in Bangkok, so conduct your shopping with extreme caution.

Silk
Thai silk is heavy and coarse and not enjoyed by everyone, though you might want to investigate the product at any of the following shops.

Jim Thompson Silk: Thailand's most famed outlet for traditional Thai silk is expensive though the quality is considered the world's finest. Thompson has outlets all over Southeast Asia in-cluding four in Bangkok on Surawong Road near Rama 4 Road, in the Oriental Hotel (of course),

in Isetan at the World Trade Center, and at the Grand Hyatt Erawan Hotel.

Shinawatra Silk: Another respected silk out-let with shops on South Sathorn Road near Silom and at Sukumvit Soi 23.

Kanitha: This well-known boutique has been producing world-famous designer fashions made from silk and other fabrics for over 20 years. Silom Rd.

Design Thai: Small but worthwhile shop with decades of experience. 304 Silom Rd.

Antiques
Authentic antiques are extremely rare in Thai-land—and cost a fortune—but hundreds of shops sell "instant antiques" that are so convincing that only an expert could tell the difference. Most shopkeepers are very honest about this situa-tion, but shop around as prices vary enormously.

River City Shopping Complex: Bangkok's best selection of antiques and fake antiques is in-side this four-story complex right on the river adjacent to the Sheraton Royal Orchid Hotel. A major antique auction is held here on the first Saturday of each month.

Silom and Charoen Krung roads are other good sources of antiques, with antique and pseudoantique shops as far as the eye can see.

Elephant House: Burmese antiques, teak furniture, and decorative artwork in a famous old shop in an alley just off Sathorn Tai Road. This place has been around for several decades and has quite the reputation. 67/12 Soi Pra Phinit, tel. (02) 286-2780.

Krishna's Antiques: Four floors of exquisite crafts and rare collectibles. Sukumvit Soi 6.

L'Arcadia: A small shop that specializes in Burmese antiques and reproductions; ask to see their upstairs showcase. Sukumvit Soi 23.

Rasi Sayam: Another small but high-quality shop operated by Honathan Hayssen, a Stanford MBA graduate. Most of the items are instant an-tiques but of unusually high quality. Sukumvit Soi 23.

Buddha for sale

Handicrafts

Most handicrafts are best purchased in Chiang Mai, on the highway that runs between Chiang Mai and Sankamphang, though the following shops sell good quality merchandise at fair prices.

Narayana Phand: Supported by the Thai government but actually a private enterprise, this sprawling store (the largest of its kind in Thailand) has every possible handicraft at fixed prices—Thai silk, cotton, bronzeware, ceramics, lacquerware, Thai dolls, teakwood products, antique reproductions, and other indigenous handicrafts. This is a good place to get an initial idea of prices before setting off to other shops scattered around town. Rajadamri Rd., tel. (02) 252-4670.

Chitralada: Another handicraft emporium, under the support of the Royal Family, which aims to encourage and promote native handicrafts, and provide employment to the handicapped who create many of the items for sale. Chitralada now has 12 outlets in Thailand, including seven in Bangkok at the Oriental Hotel shopping complex, Grand Palace, Vimanmek Mansion, Amporn Palace, Thaniya Plaza on Silom Road, Amari Watergate Hotel, and the Marriott Royal Garden Riverside Hotel.

Once again, prices are fixed and very reasonable, making this a good place to learn something about the quality and price range of local handicrafts.

Central Bangkok Shopping Centers

Service and selection are unrivaled at the immense shopping complexes throughout Bangkok, many of which are located in the Siam Square-Ploenchit-Rama 1 Road area.

World Trade Center: Probably the largest and most interesting shopping complex in Bangkok provides eight floors of shops, anchored on one end by the midpriced Zen Central shopping center and the more upscale Isetan at the other flank. Almost everything imaginable is sold here, plus there's plenty of budget cafes and better restaurants on the upper floors. Some of the more familiar outlets are Asia Books, Tower Records, and a new Duty Free outlet. Bad name though—this place has absolutely nothing to do with "world trade." Rama 1 at Rajadamri Rd.

Mahboonkrong (MBK) Center: Bangkok's first large indoor shopping mall includes endless arcades full of trinkets, restaurants, six cinemas, a concert hall, and the upscale Japanese-owned Tokyu Department Store. The place is now somewhat outdated and sells more schlock than quality, but don't miss the wonderful food emporiums on the ground floor and an older food center on the seventh. Rama 1 at Phyathai Rd.

Siam Square: Bangkok's original shopping complex (an open-air affair), opened in the 1960s, looks fairly forlorn these days after a fire gutted many of the centrally located shops, though renovation is in progress and this old favorite may return to favor in a few years. Today, there's a handful of small and utilitarian shops and several popular restaurants in the rear section of the complex. Rama 1 at Phyathai Rd.

Gaysorn Plaza: A new and very stylish shopping center with trendy boutiques and several upscale Thai handicraft shops on the second floor. Planet Hollywood occupies much of the ground floor while Narayana Phand, another famous handicraft outlet, is right next door. Ploenchit at Rajadamri Rd.

Siam Center: Just opposite Siam Square is a small but reasonably priced shopping complex with clothing and shoe stores catering mostly to teenagers. Rama 1 Rd.

Siam Discovery Center: Adjacent to the Siam Center is a rather quiet shopping complex catering primarily to children and young adults. Rama 1 at Phyathai Rd.

Amarin Plaza: Prices are atmospheric but some of the highest-quality goods are sold in the Romanesque complex on Ploenchit Road. Sogo—the main department store anchor—has expanded into a building adjacent to the Erawan Grand Hyatt Hotel. Ploenchit at Rajadamri Rd.

Peninsula Plaza: Over 70 small boutiques and a comprehensive branch of Asia Books are located in the small but almost dazzling shopping center on Rajadamri Road near the Regent Hotel. Rajadamri Rd. just south of Ploenchit.

Central Chidlom: A very large and relatively new branch of the largest chain of department stores in Thailand, with reasonably priced goods and handicrafts, especially when compared to Japanese-based chains such as Isetan, Sogo, and Tokyu. Ploenchit at Chidlom Rd.

Duty Free Shop: Much to the dismay of local merchants, the Tourism Authority of Thailand operates a duty-free shop on Ploenchit Road where the liquor and tobacco sections offer great bargains, though better prices on other goods are available elsewhere. Another outlet is in the nearby World Trade Center.

Panthip Plaza: A few blocks from the World Trade Center is a small shopping complex chiefly visited for its dozen-plus computer stores. Pirated software has been illegal for several years now, though some shops still sell discs under the counter to familiar faces. Phetburi Road near the Amari Watergate Hotel.

Sukumvit Road Shopping Centers

Sukumvit isn't a shopper's paradise though a few shopping centers have opened in recent years.

Ploenchit Center: Small but useful shopping complex right at the beginning of Sukumvit near the Expressway and JW Marriott Hotel.

The Emporium: Bangkok's newest shopping center is almost exclusively comprised of pricey boutiques, far beyond the means of most Thais and many visiting *farangs* for that matter. The place is largely deserted but provides a welcome escape from the heat if you're actually walking down this messed-up road. Sukumvit Soi 24.

Silom Road Shopping Centers

Shopping around Silom Road and Charoen Krung Road (New Road) tends to be somewhat expensive, as most shops are geared to tourists staying in the nearby upscale hotels.

Central: Thailand's original department store chain has branches on Silom Road (the smallest and least useful outlet), a much better store on Ploenchit Road, a new addition in the Zen Complex, and an immense emporium in the Lard Prao neighborhood. All stores have an upstairs handicraft market and a mind-boggling selection of quality clothes at reasonable prices.

Oriental Place: Top-end shops offering mostly arts, antiques, expensive handicrafts, and fine clothing in the European Renaissance shopping complex near the Oriental Hotel.

River City Shopping Complex: Thailand's largest and most distinguished venue for fine arts and antiques, with four floors of amazing shops plus a handful of smaller spots for inexpensive trinkets. River City holds a monthly antique auction and often has fairly good art and handicraft shows on the main floor. There are several good, reasonably priced restaurants, plus a barbecue cafe on the top floor with outstanding views over the river and Thonburi.

Silom Village: Small shopping center with a handful of antique and handicraft shops where prices are lower than in the exclusive places mentioned above, but much higher than you will find in Chiang Mai or in the government-sponsored stores mentioned above under Handicrafts.

Chatuchak Weekend Market

The granddaddy of all Thai flea markets is Chatuchak's monstrous affair out near the airport on Paholyothin Road. Once located on the Sanam Luang near the Royal Palace, Chatuchak now sprawls over 35 acres with hundreds of booths selling everything imaginable at rock-bottom prices. An attempt has been made to sectionalize areas selling one kind of product, but most visitors are content to simply wander around and see what they discover.

Items for sale include used books and magazines (including back issues of *Sawasdee*), real and fake antiques, textiles and hilltribe artifacts, used Levi 501s, fruit, Siamese fighting fish, and endangered birds and other prohibited species. Afterwards, eat at the famous Djit Pochana Restaurant down Paholyothin Road toward the airport; their inexpensive luncheon buffet is highly recommended.

To reach the market, take a bus and watch for the large carnival tent on the left. Open weekends 0900-1800 and Friday evenings 1800-2300.

Street and Produce Markets

Shopping in Bangkok can be roughly divided into air-conditioned shopping malls and traditional markets where Thai housewives pick up their vegetables. The following local venues are great for photographs and a glimpse of old Bangkok, a slice of life that is rapidly disappearing from modern Thailand. Best choices are the aforementioned Chatuchak Market for general shopping, Pratunam for clothing, and Pak Klong for authentic atmosphere.

Pratunam Market: A sprawling rabbit warren of hygienic foodstalls, vegetable wholesalers, and shoe merchants is located at the intersection of Petchburi and Rajaprarop Roads, slightly north of Siam Square. Pratunam is famous as the best place in Bangkok to shop for inexpensive clothing. Open 24 hours; don't get lost!

Pak Klong Market: Thailand's most colorful and smelly vegetable/fruit market hangs over the riverbanks near the Memorial Bridge. Bangkok's answer to London's Covent Garden is a fascinating experience, a hive of ceaseless activity where porters wheel about stacks of crates while old ladies peddle enormous piles of fragrant orchids. Bring your camera and nose plugs.

Banglampoo Market: Conveniently located near the budget guesthouses on Khao San Road are several alleys packed with inexpensive clothing and backpackers' supplies. The adjacent New World Department Store has great bargains on the main floor and an inexpensive self-serve cafeteria on top.

Teves Flower Market: A permanent sidewalk market with plants and (occasionally) flowers flanks a canal one km north of Banglampoo, near the National Library.

Thieves' Market: Touted in many tourist books as an antique shopping district, the only antiques and thieves located here are the shopkeepers. Best buys include brassware, imitation antiques, old furniture, Chinese porcelains, and industrial supplies. Located near Chinatown and correctly called Nakhon Kasem. Most of the better merchants have abandoned the area and moved into posher digs along Silom and Sukumvit Roads. Bargaining is *de rigueur*.

EAST COAST

With over 2,600 km of coastline along the Gulf of Thailand and Andaman Sea, Thailand offers a wide selection of beaches and resorts with everything from first-class resorts to perfect tranquility on unspoiled islands. While most of the better beaches and island resorts are located down south, the east coast between Bangkok and Cambodia is blessed with good beaches and pristine islands that can be reached in less than a day from Bangkok with public transportation.

But the east coast is more than just beaches and offshore islands. It is an area rich in natural resources where Thailand's future has been laid. Government officials and economic planners have chosen the eastern seaboard as the new economic growth zone for the 21st century. Discoveries of immense deposits of natural gas and the urgent need for an alternative deepwater port to Bangkok have brought massive development on an unparalleled scale. City planners envision a megalopolis of cities stretching from Bangkok to Rayong, forming a gigantic economic engine which would rival the eastern seaboard of the United States and the Tokyo-Osaka region.

Pattaya—the original beach resort in Thailand—is now flanked by the deepwater port at Laem Chabang to the north and massive oil refineries to the south. Entire cities, soon to be home to over a million Thai citizens, are under construction at breakneck speed. More than any other region, the east coast represents the future of Thailand.

Sightseeing Highlights

The twin attributes of beach resorts and economic development have given the east coast a schizoid personality that combines pleasure with business. The end result of all this development is that the best tourist destinations are being pushed farther east toward Cambodia as travelers seek out the more idyllic beaches and islands. Visitors with sufficient time may enjoy a leisurely journey, stopping at each of the following destinations, but hurried travelers should head directly to the beach or island that has the strongest appeal. Distances from Bangkok appear after each destination.

Bang Saen (103 km): Although rarely visited by Western visitors, Bang Saen is a pleasant beach with an authentic Thai flavor where

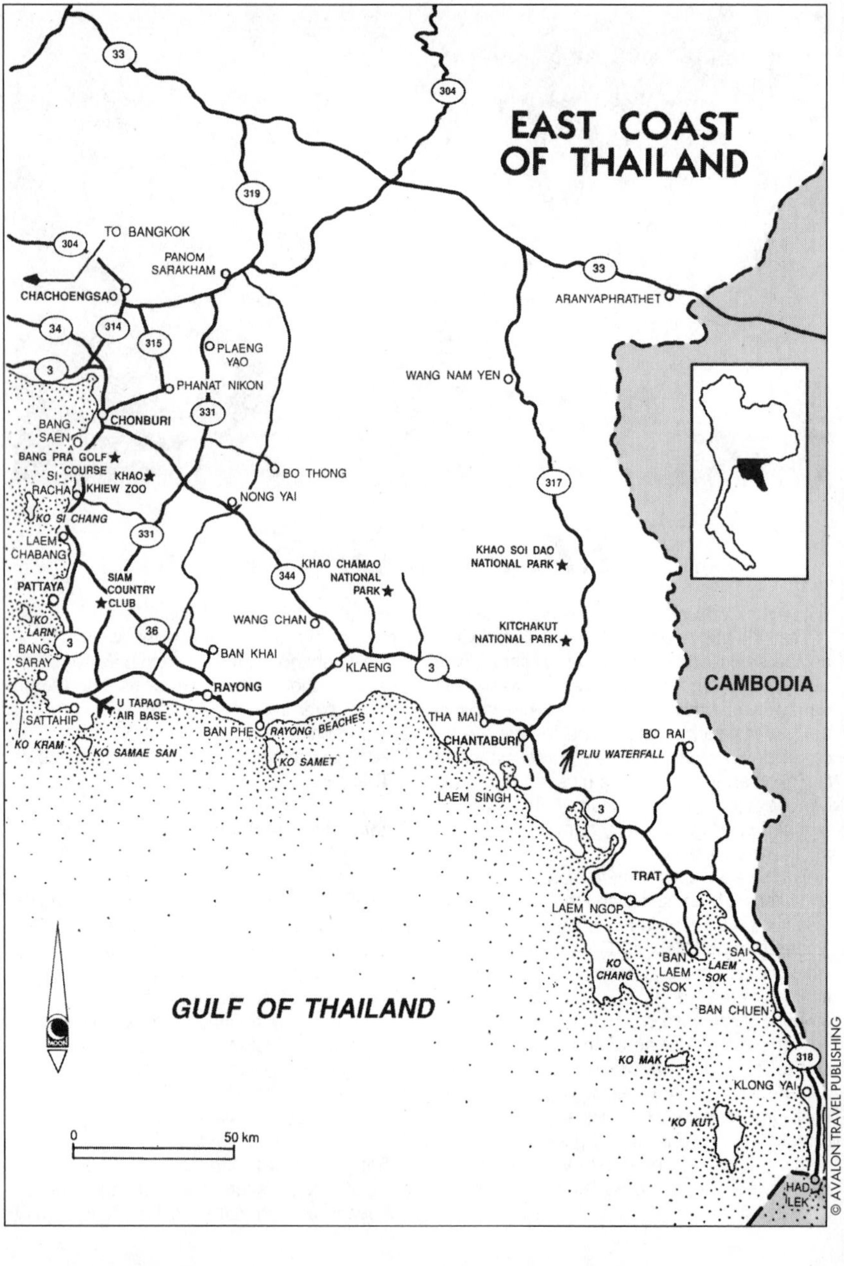

EAST COAST
OF THAILAND
TO BANGKOK
33
304
319
34
314
315
3
331
317
344
36
318
PANOM SARAKHAM
CHACHOENGSAO
PLAENG YAO
PHANAT NIKON
CHONBURI
BANG SAEN
BANG PRA GOLF COURSE
SI RACHA
KHAO KHIEW ZOO
KO SI CHANG
BO THONG
NONG YAI
LAEM CHABANG
SIAM COUNTRY CLUB
PATTAYA
KO LARN
BANG SARAY
SATTAHIP
KO KRAM
KO SAMAE SAN
U TAPAO AIR BASE
BAN KHAI
RAYONG
BAN PHE
RAYONG BEACHES
KO SAMET
WANG CHAN
KLAENG
KHAO CHAMAO NATIONAL PARK
THA MAI
CHANTABURI
LAEM SINGH
ARANYAPHRATHET
WANG NAM YEN
KHAO SOI DAO NATIONAL PARK
KITCHAKUT NATIONAL PARK
PLIU WATERFALL
BO RAI
CAMBODIA
TRAT
LAEM NGOP
KO CHANG
BAN LAEM SOK
LAEM SOK
SAI
BAN CHUEN
KO MAK
KLONG YAI
KO KUT
HAD LEK
GULF OF THAILAND
0
50 km
MOON
© AVALON TRAVEL PUBLISHING

locals come to picnic and relax on beach chairs. The beach is surprisingly clean and relatively deserted during the week. Day-trippers might consider a quick visit to Bang Saen rather than fight the traffic farther south to Pattaya.

Si Racha and Ko Si Chang (118 km): The busy little fishing town of Si Racha chiefly serves as departure point for the long, narrow island of Ko Si Chang. The southern tip of the island holds the remains of an old royal summer palace used by King Chulalongkorn in the late 19th century. Though a very modest historical monument, Ko Si Chang can easily be visited en route to Pattaya.

Pattaya (137 km): After two decades of uncontrolled growth, Thailand's original beach resort is trying to restore its image with an aggressive and highly publicized improvement campaign. The resort's personality is split between upscale hotels catering to families and group tours, and a raucous nightlife suited to bachelors and sailors. Pattaya's mediocre beach compensates with all types of recreation from parasailing to scuba diving.

Rayong (185 km): Rayong town is an uninspiring place but the southern coastline offers fairly good sand and accommodations from budget bungalows to mid-range hotels.

Ko Samet (210 km): Discovered by budget travelers a decade ago, Ko Samet is now favored by Thai families and group tourists rushing down from Pattaya. The island offers some of the cleanest and finest sand in Thailand, though its popularity and easy accessibility have brought problems of overdevelopment and pollution. Budget travelers have largely abandoned Ko Samet for the more remote island of Ko Chang.

Chanthaburi (320 km): The large town of Chanthaburi lies in an area famed for rubber, rubies, and tropical fruits such as rambutan and durian. Chanthaburi is a rather ordinary town aside from its gem industry and nearby natural attractions such as waterfalls and national parks.

Trat (315 km): Thailand's southeasternmost province and town is the jumping-off point for the islands scattered along the Thai-Cambodian border. Most travelers head directly to Laem Ngop, 15 km southeast, where boats leave throughout the day for Ko Chang and other tropical islands.

Ko Chang (360 km): Thailand's second-largest island after Phuket was officially opened to tourism in 1990 after a series of travel articles publicized its wonderful beaches and unspoiled topography. Following the development cycle of Phuket and Ko Samui, Ko Chang will unquestionably be Thailand's next major island resort as sun-lovers relentlessly march eastward in search of the perfect beach. Over a dozen islands are located farther south, perhaps the final island escapes in Thailand.

Getting There

All of the east coast beaches are located along the Sukumvit Highway (Route 3), which stretch-

Ko Chang huts

es almost 400 km from central Bangkok to the Cambodian border. Buses from Bangkok's Eastern Bus Terminal (Ekamai) on Sukumvit Road depart every 15-30 minutes throughout the day for all possible destinations on the eastern seaboard. Buses to distant destinations such as Chanthaburi and Trat leave mornings only, 0600-noon.

Private bus and tour operators offer similar services in small air-conditioned minivans to major destinations such as Pattaya, Ko Samet, and Ko Chang. Private minibuses are convenient since pickup is made from your hotel in Bangkok, though public buses from the Eastern Bus Terminal are cheaper, safer, just as fast, and much more comfortable for the long haul.

BANGKOK TO PATTAYA

BANG SAEN

Southeast of Bangkok, six km past the commercial city of Chonburi, lies the beach resort of Bang Saen. Once the premier weekend escape for Bangkokians, Bang Saen was replaced by Pattaya after the arrival of better highways and faster buses. Today it caters to economy-minded Thai families and groups of teenagers, who rest under umbrellas or stroll along the two-km-long beach lined with coconut palms and casuarina trees.

Buses from Bangkok stop just beyond the Bang Saen intersection. Minitrucks continue four km down the road to the beach.

Attractions

Bang Saen is only average as a beach resort, though the lack of high-powered development gives it a degree of charm and a refreshingly laid-back atmosphere. A small information office is located adjacent to Ocean World.

The Beach: The beach itself is clean and relatively uncrowded on weekdays, but solidly packed on weekends and holidays. The water varies from a nice marine blue to muddy shallows at low tide. Beachside vendors rent multicolored umbrellas, chairs, and inner tubes, and sell snacks and beverages. Being a novelty at the Bang Saen beach, Westerners often find themselves invited to join locals for food and endless rounds of Mekong.

Ocean World: Popular with Thai parents and their children, this water amusement park has several swimming pools, slides, and a small roller coaster. Open daily 0930-1800.

University Aquarium: The medium-sized aquarium, on the road between the highway and the beach, was presented in 1982 to Srinakharinwirot University by the Japanese government.

Tropical marine life from the Gulf of Thailand is featured.

Monkey Cliff: A community of wild monkeys inhabits the hill and Chinese shrine at the north end of Bang Saen beach. The small temple honors the goddess spirit of a wife whose fisherman husband never returned from a fishing expedition. Chinese ascribe magical powers to the site and come to fly kites to honor the faithful wife.

Khao Khiew Open Zoo: Tour groups often visit this open-air zoo located 18 km from Bang Saen up a side road off Sukumvit Highway. The zoo was opened in 1973 to provide overflow for the cramped Dusit Zoo in Bangkok.

Bang Pra Golf Course: Located midway up the road to the zoo, the 18-hole, 7,249-yard course has a 54-room motel, lodge, and swim-

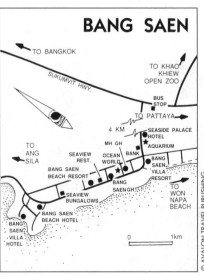

BANG SAEN

TO BANGKOK

SUKUMVIT HWY.

TO KHAO KHIEW OPEN ZOO

BUS STOP

TO PATTAYA

4 KM

SEASIDE PALACE HOTEL

MH GH

AQUARIUM

TO ANG SILA

SEAVIEW REST.

OCEAN WORLD

BANK

BANG SAEN

BANG SAEN BEACH RESORT

BANG SAEN VILLA RESORT

BANG SAEN GH

TO WON NAPA BEACH

SEAVIEW BUNGALOWS

BANG SAEN BEACH HOTEL

BANG SAEN VILLA HOTEL

0   1km

© AVALON TRAVEL PUBLISHING

ming pool. Tambon Bang Pra, Bangkok reservation tel. (02) 240-9170, 1,500-2,300B.

Accommodations

Bang Saen Villa Resort: The only hotel on the beach; it has a swimming pool, airy restaurant, and small banquet room. 140-16 Mu 14 Tambon Saensuk, Chonburi 20130, tel. (038) 381772, fax (038) 383221, 680-980B.

Bang Saen Beach Resort: A 40-acre landscaped resort with swimming pool, "gathering terrace," and accommodations in the 29-room hotel complex and 102 individual bungalows. The resort is operated by the TAT as a training site for their nearby College of Tourism. 55-150 Tambon Saensuk, Chonburi 20130, Bangkok tel. (02) 428-3262, local tel. (038) 381675, 550-750B fan bungalows, 800-1,200B a/c.

Guesthouses: Several inexpensive guesthouses in the 300-500B range are located on the beachfront road near Ocean World. Try the Seaside Palace, Seaview Bungalows, Picnic, and Sansabai Bungalows.

SI RACHA

The next place of interest on Sukumvit Highway is the busy fishing village of Si Racha, best known as the production center for a pungent sweet fish sauce called *nam prik si racha.* Si Racha has won awards as the cleanest town in the kingdom. Facilities include several banks, postal center, and immigration office.

Attractions

Temples: Surasak 2 Singha Road has the small Wat Sri Maha Racha on the north side, and a larger Chinese temple in a back alley to the south. The market is worth a wander, as are the stilted houses flanking the nearby pier.

Ko Loi: For a quick trip, ask the *samlor* driver to take you to a famous offshore island linked to the mainland by a 1.5-km bridge. Here you can visit the Ko Loi Temple featuring a *chedi, viharn,* and lifelike wax statue of a monk known for his miraculous healing powers. In 1959 the monk disappeared for good, allegedly with all the donations, but superstitious Thais continue to visit his shrine. The causeway is flanked with

colorful fishing boats laden with arrow-shaped fish traps constructed from nipa palm. Fare is 10B each direction.

Accommodations

Few visitors spend the night in Si Racha, though several inexpensive hotels are located along the waterfront and on the roads which connect the highway with the seashore. All have breezy open-air restaurants where you can enjoy the local seafood specialties.

Samchai Hotel: Located on the rickety pier across from Surasak 1 Road, the Samchai has both fan-cooled and a/c rooms. 3 Chomchonpon Rd., tel. (038) 311134, 140-200B fan, 350B a/c.

Siri Wattana Hotel: Another seaside hotel offering rooms with or without private bath, plus views over the ocean; probably the best budget choice in town. 35 Chomchonpon Rd., tel. (038) 311307, 140-160B.

Grand Bungalows: Better rooms are found in the hotel on the southern pier. 9 Chomchonpon Rd., tel. (038) 311079, 400-1,000B.

Restaurants

Seafood Restaurants: Lining the seafront are several seafood restaurants serving local specialties such as sautéed oysters and shellfish. One popular restaurant is located at the end of the pier past the houses on stilts. Few have English menus or list prices, so check carefully before ordering.

Central Market: The most economical spot for meals is the market near the clock tower and opposite city hall.

Home & Garden Restaurant: On Jermjonpol Road near the Sukumvit Highway is a more luxurious if less atmospheric restaurant.

Transportation

Buses from Bangkok's Eastern Bus Terminal take about 60 minutes to reach Si Racha, from where you can walk or hire a *samlor* down to the waterfront and departure pier for Ko Si Chang. Hail buses to Bangkok and Pattaya from the highway or depart from the station on Chomchonpon Road just past the Srivichai Hotel.

KO SI CHANG

Ko Si Chang, about 12 km off the coast from Si Racha, once served as Thailand's custom port and was listed among the country's most popular weekend destinations. Today it's a sleepy place chiefly visited for the decaying palace of King Chulalongkorn and its highly revered Chinese temple. The long and narrow island has a small fishing village with several guesthouses and an arid climate suitable for prickly pear cactus and other desert plants.

Attractions

Ko Si Chang's two principal sights can be seen as you approach on the boat ride from Si Racha: a Chinese temple standing prominently to the right, and the ruins of the old royal palace to the left. Si Chang is very compact and both sites are within walking distance from the arrival pier. Alternatively, hire a *samlor* for a three-hour, 80B tour that includes the Chinese temple, the old royal place, a tiny beach on the north coast, mango plantations, and a Buddhist cave in the center of the island.

Chinese Temple: It's a hot climb up to San Chao Por Khao Yai, but you're rewarded with outstanding marbled floors inside the shrine, a cool natural grotto with Buddha images, plus a

Buddha's footprint and excellent views from the 268-meter summit. This temple is much revered by the Chinese, who visit the shrine in great numbers at Chinese New Year.

Chulalongkorn's Summer Palace: The ruins of King Rama V's old summer retreat are one km left of town at the end of a roadway too narrow for cars. Construction began in 1889 after Rama's physician recommended Si Chang as a place of rest and recuperation for his royal consort and her son. Among the early buildings were the two-story Wattana Palace, the octagonal-shaped Phongsri on a nearby hill, and the Aphirom with front and rear porches. A well was dug to supply water, a lighthouse erected to provide safe passage for passing ships, and 26 roads constructed to link the scattered residences.

In 1892 the king erected a royal compound with four throne halls, 14 royal domiciles, and a royal hillside *chedi* to honor the birth of his new son. Constructed entirely of teakwood, one of the four throne halls was later disassembled and transferred to Bangkok, where it was restored and reopened as the Vimanmek Palace. The final visit to Ko Si Chang of King Chulalongkorn in 1893 was cut short when French gunships, in a territorial dispute, attacked the Thai Navy and occupied the island from 1893 until 1907.

The remaining buildings were deserted and largely disassembled for firewood over time until 1978, when Chulalongkorn University established a marine science research center on the island. In 1991 the Thai government in conjunction with the Fine Arts Department announced an ambitious restoration project.

The surviving foundations, crumbling staircases, beautiful flowering trees, and eerie reservoir blanketed with dead leaves form a pleasant if somewhat unspectacular sight. The Bell Rock near the top of the hill rings nicely when struck with a stick. It's hard to locate: look for Thai script in yellow paint. The Asdangnimitr Temple, farther up the hill, once served as the king's meditation chambers but is now locked to protect Rama's portrait and a Buddha image cursed with ungainly large ears.

Budget Accommodations

A few basic guesthouses are located near the dock, but it's more pleasant to stay outside town on a beach.

WEIRD WHEELS

*T*he most amazing sidelight to Si Racha is its bizarre but strangely elegant *samlors*, three-wheeled motorbike-rickshaws elongated to outrageous lengths and fitted with huge car or smaller motorcycle engines. Originally constructed from Harley Davidson bikes, these contraptions roamed the streets of Bangkok before being banished to Si Racha since they were not equipped with reverse gears. All have numbers painted on the side, which serve as license plates. Local drivers include Thongkam Sonri, who parks his tricycle near the Savings Bank; Somsak Parnsomboon, who hails from Lopburi; and Urai Chantawat, one of the few female drivers in Si Racha. All can provide sightseeing tours at about 60B per hour.

Unfortunately, their days are numbered since new licenses are no longer issued. The original 499 vehicles now number under 100, and the remaining permits command up to 10,000B each. Motorcycle enthusiasts will love these contraptions!

Camping: Camping is permitted anywhere on the island, including all the beaches and even the grounds of the old royal palace.

Tiew Pai Guesthouse: The most accessible and among the more popular choices is the simple guesthouse with clean rooms at the south end of town. The management offers halfday boat trips around the island that stop at Hin Klom (Round Stone Beach) and small Tawang Beach for swimming and snorkeling. Scuba divers can explore underwater wrecks during the dive season Nov.-February. Atsadang Rd., tel. (038) 216048, 60B dorm, 150-200B fan, 400-600B air-conditioned.

Benz Bungalow: A crazy and creative place unlike the cookie-cutter molds of most Thai hotels. The owner has formed eccentric bungalows from local stone rather than the standard cinder block, and added fans or air-conditioning for his clientele. Benz is located on the road to Tha Wong Beach, just before the entrance to the Aquatic Resources Research Institute, or about one km south of the ferry pier. Hire a *tuk tuk* if your pack is overloaded. Hat Tha Wong Rd., tel. (038) 216091, 400B fan, 600B a/c.

Green House: Travelers happy to stay near the rather rustic town might try the simple but clean guesthouse toward the Chinese temple on the edge of town. Atsadang Rd., tel. (038) 216024, 100-140B.

Sri Pitsanuk Bungalow: A more remote spot but a great location on the edge of a cliff overlooking Hat Tham Beach. It's a one-km walk past the Tiew Pai Guesthouse up the narrow road heading to the tiny beach. Hat Tham Beach, tel. (038) 216024, 300-880B.

Top Bungalows: Just before Sri Pitsanuk is another set of bungalows owned and operated by a local taxi driver, but the rooms lack a view and are generally deserted during the day. Hat Tham Beach, tel. (038) 216001, 200-650B.

Moderate Accommodations

Sichang View Resort: One of the rare upscale resorts with better facilities geared to wealthier clients from Bangkok. Also located toward the Chinese temple. Atsadang Rd., tel. (038) 216210, 800-1,200B.

Sichang Palace: A three-story 65-room hotel in the middle of town with swimming pool, restaurant, and all a/c rooms with private baths. Atsadang Rd., tel. (038) 216276, 1,000-1,600B.

Practical Information

All of the following facilities are located in the main town.

Thai Farmers Bank: Currency exchange at reasonable rates. 9 Atsadang Rd., tel. (038) 216132, open Mon.-Fri. 0830-1530.

Post Office: Atsadang Rd., tel. (038) 216227. Standard services but important parcels should be mailed from Bangkok or Pattaya.

Motorcycle Rentals: Motorcycles can be rented at 150B per day at the Tiew Pai Guesthouse from the owner, who also provides advice on hidden beaches and rather obscure destinations.

Transportation

Ko Si Chang can be reached with small fishing boats which depart hourly from the Si Racha pier on Soi 14, between the seafood restaurants. The shuttle sputters past Russian ocean liners, a large naval station, and cargo ships before docking at the island's nondescript Chinese fishing village.

The last boat back to Si Racha departs at 1700.

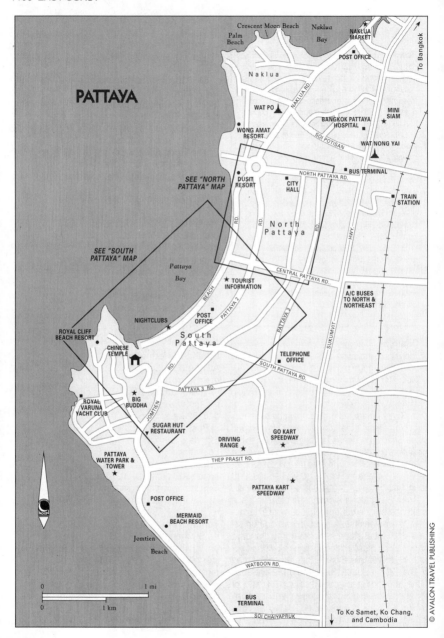

PATTAYA

Once a sleepy fishing village popular with harried Bangkokians and American GIs on R&R, Pattaya has since mushroomed into a major beach resort smothered with high-rise hotels, roaring discos, fine restaurants, throbbing go-go bars, and lively nightclubs. Those seeking peace and solitude on a deserted beach should forget Pattaya and head south or east to the less commercialized beaches. Visitors who seek out nonstop entertainment and a honky-tonk environment will love Pattaya, one of the most convoluted and schizophrenic destinations in the world.

Today, this low-powered Riviera of Southeast Asia is undergoing an image crisis as it transforms from a bachelor's paradise to a sophisticated retreat catering to middle-aged couples and families. Pattaya's image problem stems from inadequate sewage facilities, flooding, uncontrolled commercial sprawl, drugs, prostitution, a mysterious series of murders, and water pollution so severe that tourist officials strongly discourage swimming anywhere along South Pattaya Beach. The *Far Eastern Economic Review* once cited Pattaya's problems as a classic lesson for other Asian countries of the dangers of unplanned tourism development.

Criticism from travel agents, tour operators, and local hotel owners has finally pushed local authorities into action. Several new water-treatment plants are under construction, and south Pattaya will soon be renovated with a landfill project, a new beachfront road, a pedestrian promenade, piers for excursion boats, parks, and a concert hall. The main road was still torn up for a new sewer system as of this writing, though most of these projects should be completed by 2000.

Both despised and loved, Pattaya may yet prove itself the first Asian resort destroyed by tourism but saved by government intervention.

Although it's still fashionable to condemn Pattaya as superficial, overbuilt, unplanned, congested, polluted, tawdry, and having nothing to do with the *real* Thailand (all true), most of the three million annual visitors seem to come away satisfied with its wide range of hedonistic offerings.

Recent Transformations

Pattaya is also undergoing a transformation from holiday resort town to a major commercial city due to the economic growth of the entire eastern seaboard. The new deepwater port at Laem Chabang, 20 km north, has necessitated the construction of several new towns to house the estimated 100,000 Thais involved in the massive project. Another major construction project at Map Taphut, south of Pattaya near Rayong, is now attracting dozens of large international companies such as Michelin and Mitsubishi, which have established giant manufacturing complexes and brought in hundreds of expats to keep the gears of the machinery running smoothly.

All this growth has brought in new hotels, new housing estates, expanded highways, modern shopping centers, four international hospitals, five international schools, and a real estate boom that seems to accelerate with each passing year. And, in a sign of the times, Father Brennan at the local orphanage recently was ordered to quit farming pigs as the city limits are no longer considered fit for rural activities.

ATTRACTIONS AROUND TOWN

Big Buddha Hill (Khao Pra Yai)

Fine views over Pattaya can be enjoyed from two small hills in south Pattaya. The closer hill is capped with a microwave station operated by Naval Broadcasting, while Pattaya Hill to the south features a large seated Buddha image surrounded by seven mini-Buddhas representing the seven days of the week.

Mini Siam

Over 100 miniature reproductions of Siamese temples and palaces are located on Sukumvit Road, about three km northeast from central Pattaya. Recent additions include the Eiffel Tower, Big Ben, and a Thai cultural show given at 1600. 387 Moo 6 Sukumvit Rd., tel. (038) 421628, 300B. Open daily 0800-2200.

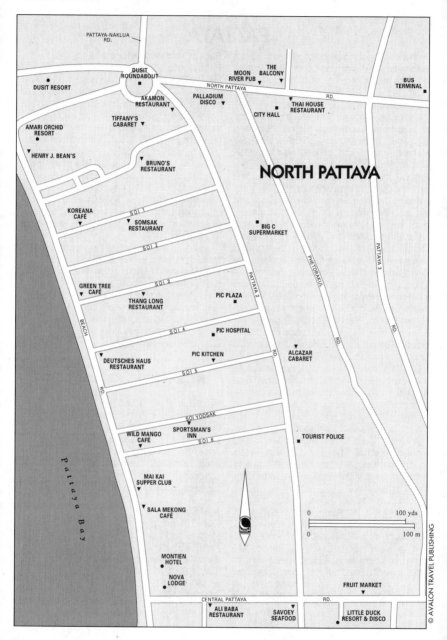

PATTAYA-NAKLUA RD.

DUSIT ROUNDABOUT

DUSIT RESORT

AKAMON RESTAURANT

TIFFANY'S CABARET

AMARI ORCHID RESORT

HENRY J. BEAN'S

BRUNO'S RESTAURANT

MOON RIVER PUB

THE BALCONY

NORTH PATTAYA

PALLADIUM DISCO

CITY HALL

THAI HOUSE RESTAURANT

BUS TERMINAL

RD.

NORTH PATTAYA

KOREANA CAFÉ

SOI 1

SOMSAK RESTAURANT

SOI 2

BIG C SUPERMARKET

GREEN TREE CAFÉ

SOI 3

THANG LONG RESTAURANT

PIC PLAZA

PATTAYA 2

PHETDRAKUL RD.

PATTAYA 3 RD.

SOI 4

PIC HOSPITAL

DEUTSCHES HAUS RESTAURANT

PIC KITCHEN

SOI 5

ALCAZAR CABARET

SOI YODSAK

WILD MANGO CAFÉ

SPORTSMAN'S INN

SOI 6

TOURIST POLICE

BEACH RD.

MAI KAI SUPPER CLUB

SALA MEKONG CAFÉ

Pattaya Bay

Moon

0   100 yds

0   100 m

MONTIEN HOTEL

NOVA LODGE

FRUIT MARKET

CENTRAL PATTAYA

ALI BABA RESTAURANT

SAVOEY SEAFOOD

RD.

LITTLE DUCK RESORT & DISCO

© AVALON TRAVEL PUBLISHING

ATTRACTIONS OUTSIDE PATTAYA

Many of the most popular attractions are located in the countryside outside Pattaya. All can be reached with rented car or motorcycle, though travel agents sell tickets that include free roundtrip transportation from your hotel.

Nong Nooch Tropical Gardens
A 600-acre tourist resort—by far the best attraction in the Pattaya region—features landscaped gardens, a mini zoo and aviary, an orchid garden, a man-made lake for rowing, and two restaurants—one Thai and one Western. The highlight to this park is the cultural show with its elephant performances and Thai classical dances, held daily at 1000, 1500, and 1545. This very impressive show features over 100 participants decked out in full Thai regalia.

Visitors can visit the village with their own rented vehicle or join one of the halfday tours that depart Pattaya daily at 0900 and 1300. Sukumvit Rd., Km 163, tel. (038) 429321, 350-400B.

Pattaya Elephant Village
Pachyderms haul logs and play soccer at the elephant *kraal* five km from town on the road to the Siam Country Club. Demonstrations are given by the mahouts and the featured elephant show involves dozens of participants. A two-hour elephant trek into nearby bush country can be arranged with advance notice. Elephants now lead the unemployed list after teak logging was banned in Thailand several years ago. Siam Country Club Rd., tel. (038) 249853, 300B admission, 700B for elephant treks.

Crocodile Farm and Million Year Stone Park
Yet another Thai crocodile farm but with a difference—the petrified trees at this park are over a million years old. Along with the crocodile show is a small zoo with elephants, camels, lions, bears, and tigers. Siam Country Club Rd., tel. (038) 249347, 300B.

Wat Yansangwararam
Seven architecturally unique pavilions and temples in Thai, Chinese, Japanese, Indian, and Western styles are located in a 360-*rai* park 15 km south of Pattaya. Also on the grounds is a primary temple constructed in modern Thai style and a magnificent Chinese museum noted for its fine examples of Chinese painting and scrolls, ancient bronzes, carved granite wall reliefs, and a small scale replica of the excavated tomb from Xian province. Sukumvit Rd., three km north of Nong Nooch Tropical Gardens. Open daily 0600-1800.

Bang Saray
A small, relatively undisturbed fishing village known for game fishing and seafood restaurants lies some 20 km south of Pattaya. Fisherman's Lodge, headquarters for the Thailand Game Fishing Association, sponsors fishing trips and has 16 standard a/c rooms from 800B. The lodge also features a swimming pool and marina.

ISLANDS NEAR PATTAYA

Ko Larn
Islands near Pattaya offer better sand and diving than the mainland beaches. The only island with schedule boat service is Ko Larn, about 45 minutes by boat from Pattaya.

Tours usually include Ko Rin or Ko Pai before stopping at Ko Larn ("Coral Island"), a highly developed resort fixed with several upscale hotels, pricey restaurants, golf course, and dive shops. Coral Island is a fanciful rendition of its rather prosaic name (true translation: Bald Island). Pack food and drinks if you're counting your *baht*.

Beaches: Ta Waen Beach on the northwest coast is the most impressive stretch of sand but also the most commercialized and best avoided on weekends when hordes of Thai tourists flood the island. Daeng Beach around the northern cape is smaller and less crowded but often bothered with jet boats that buzz just offshore. Thien Beach on the southwest side of the island provides a long expanse of white sand but lacks the scenic appeal of Ta Waen. Samae Beach and Nual Beach to the south of Thien Beach are fairly remote and provide more privacy but can be somewhat tricky to reach unless you hire a motorcycle from either Thien or Ta Waen beaches.

Transportation: Converted fishing trawlers leave from the south Pattaya pier daily at 0800

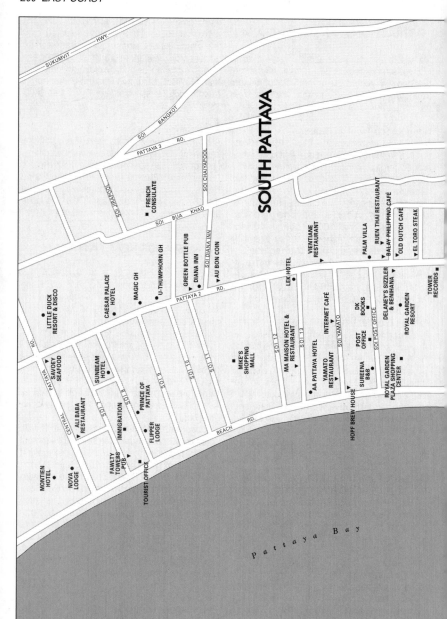

SUKUMVIT HWY.

SOI BANGKOT

PATTAYA 3 RD.

SOI JIRAPOOL

SOI CHAIYAPOOL

SOUTH PATTAYA

■ FRENCH CONSULATE

SOI BUA KHAO

GREEN BOTTLE PUB ▼
▼ DIANA INN
SOI DIANA INN
▼ AU BON COIN

VIENTIANE RESTAURANT

PALM VILLA ●
RUEN THAI RESTAURANT
▼ BALAY-PHILIPPINO CAFÉ
▼ OLD DUTCH CAFÉ
▼ EL TORO STEAK

U-THUMPHORN GH ●

MAGIC GH ●

CAESAR PALACE HOTEL ■

LITTLE DUCK RESORT & DISCO ■

PATTAYA 2 RD.

LEK HOTEL ●

INTERNET CAFÉ ■

DK BOOKS ■

DELANEY'S SIZZLER & BENIHANA ▼

ROYAL GARDEN RESORT ●

TOWER RECORDS ■

SAVOEY SEAFOOD ●

PATTAYA RD.

SUNBEAM HOTEL ■

SOI 9

SOI 10

SOI 11

MIKE'S SHOPPING MALL ■

SOI 12

MA MAISON HOTEL & RESTAURANT ▼

SOI 13

AA PATTAYA HOTEL ■

YAMATO RESTAURANT ▼

SOI YAMATO

POST OFFICE ■

SOI POST OFFICE

SUREENA B&B ■

ROYAL GARDEN PLAZA SHOPPING CENTER ■

PRINCE OF PATTAYA ●

SOI 8

ALI BABA RESTAURANT ▼

CENTRAL RD.

IMMIGRATION ■

FLIPPER LODGE ●

FAWLTY TOWERS PUB ▼

MONTIEN HOTEL ■

NOVA LODGE ●

TOURIST OFFICE ■

BEACH RD.

HOPF BREW HOUSE ▼

Pattaya Bay

ANZAC HOTEL

BLUE PARROT
TEX-MEX

PATTAYALAND SOI 1
PATTAYALAND SOI 2
PATTAYALAND SOI 3

MIKE'S
DEPARTMENT
STORE & HOTEL

SWISS FOOD

SOUTH

RD.

PATTAYA

SOI 15

SOI 17

SOI 14

BAMBOO BAR
& NIGHTCLUB

SOI DIAMOND (FOOT TRAFFIC ONLY)

BARS & NIGHTCLUBS

SOI P 72 (WALKWAY)

BARS & NIGHTCLUBS

SOI BJ (WALKWAY)

SOI SAENSUMRAN

MOTTA
MAHAL

SOI 16

PRATUMNOK RD.

JOMTIEN RD.

PATTAYA 3 RD.

RD.

NEW PIER

LOBSTER POT

MARINE DISCO

FOOD FAIR

SIMON CABARET

NANG NUAL RESTAURANT

MON AMI PIERROT CAFÉ

19TH CAFÉ

BEACH

RD.

ATHA-LINDA DR.

PRATUMNOK RD.

ROYAL CLIFF
BEACH RESORT

100 yds.
100 m
0
0

and 1000 and cost 50-100B roundtrip. These boats return at 1200, 1400, and 1700.

Several travel agencies also arrange more expensive excursions, while glass-bottom boat trips are also available. Prices vary depending on quality of meals, diving equipment, and number of islands visited.

Islands near Ko Larn

Ko Larn may be uncomfortably commercialized and probably not worth visiting on weekends, though several nearby islands provide a welcome escape from the crowds.

Ko Sak and Ko Krok: These two small and relatively unspoiled islands with good diving can be reached by chartered boat from Ko Larn.

Ko Pai: Ko Pai and its nearby islands—Ko Luam, Ko Klung Badan, and Ko Manvichai—are under the supervision of the Royal Thai Navy and kept in far more pristine condition than all other islands in the Pattaya region. Travel time is about two hours and these islands can only be reached by private boat charter or with any of the dive companies which make regular excursions to these remote outposts. No accommodations or restaurants so remember to bring along food and water.

WATER ACTIVITIES

Named after the southwestern monsoon wind that sweeps the east coast during the summer months, Pattaya is a beach resort dedicated to the pursuit of pleasure and love of *sanuk*. The range of activities is nothing short of amazing—sunbathing, parasailing, skin diving, golf, gamefishing, zoos, night markets, and the world-famous nightlife.

Traditional culture is not much in evidence within the city limits. But to remind visitors that Pattaya is located in exotic Thailand rather than Miami Beach or Waikiki, outlying attractions include an elephant camp, Buddhist temples, and an orchid farm with Thai dancers.

Beaches

Pattaya's biggest disappointments are the narrow and brownish four-km beach, vastly inferior to the crystalline shores of Phuket or Samui, and the polluted waters that are declared a haz-

ardous zone by a government-sponsored study on environmental pollution. Better sand and cleaner waters can be found at Jomtien Beach, south of Pattaya, and Wong Amat Beach, north of Pattaya in the suburb of Naklua. Wong Amat is recommended as the best option to central Pattaya.

Water Sports

Pattaya offers a wide range of water sports. Most are now found on Jomtien Beach since Pattaya Bay is crowded with powerboats and fishing trawlers. Prices are negotiable, subject to change, and higher on weekends and holidays. For a general guide to current prices, check local publications such as *Pattaya This Week* and *Explore Pattaya*. Check fuel supplies and condition of equipment, and never sign papers that promise liability. Fleecing ignorant tourists is big business here in Pattaya.

Scuba

Pattaya has almost a dozen scuba diving shops that sponsor PADI and NAUI certification courses, and multiday dive expeditions for licensed divers. A single-day two-dive excursion to nearby islands with all equipment, boat rental, and instruction starts at 2,500B per day. Two days of instruction and three dive days cost 5,500B, while full PADI certification runs 9,000B. Deep wreck, photography, and rescue courses are also offered.

Scuba diving is centered on the offshore Ko Lan archipelago, though farther islands such as Ko Pai, Ko Luam, and Ko Rim offer better opportunities since they are managed by the Royal Thai Navy. The best dive spots with underwater wrecks are located south of Pattaya near the naval base at Sattahip. These diveable wrecks include the *Hardeep* at Samaesan (20 meters) and the *Bremen* near Sattahip (30 meters).

Dave's Divers' Den: Among the oldest and more reliable dive operators in the region. 190/11 Central Pattaya Rd., tel. (038) 429387.

Dolphin Diving Centre: Another reputable company owned and operated by professional divers who provide instruction in English, German, and French. 183/29 Soi Post Office, tel. (01) 944-0992.

Seafari: Bill and Pat Burbridge also provide top-notch instruction and arrange daily dive trips

white sand and clear water: an antidote for urban stress

around the Pattaya waters. 359/2 Soi 5, tel. (038) 429060, fax (038) 424708.

Mermaid Dive School: Pattaya's only dive shop with compressor, tanks, and oxygen on board their private boat. 75/124 Moo 12, Soi Mermaid, Jomtien, tel. (038) 232219, fax (038) 232221.

Windsurfing

Visitors undeterred by the pollution can rent sailboards at Jomtien Beach. Pattaya Beach is simply too crowded and dangerous for windsurfing. October to June are considered the best months, though the summer monsoon months can kick up some intimidating surf for the inexperienced. International windsurfing tournaments take place in early December, while the Siam World Cup—a national competition—is held in either April or May.

Yacht and Boat Rentals

All types of boats can be rented by the hour at Jomtien Beach, including Lasers, 16-foot catamarans, and Hobie Cat sailboats. Yacht and sailboat charters by the day, weekend, or longer periods are available from several specialized agencies in Pattaya and south down in Sattahip.

Bamroong Sailing & Paramotor Centre Resort: Five km south of town is Chak Nok Lake where a sailing school offers windsurfing and sailing instruction on waters far more dependable than you would find in the open ocean. They also provide archery lessons, off-road jeep terrain, and training courses in microlight aviation. Facilities include a restaurant and limited bungalow accommodations. Chak Nok Lake, Sukumvit Rd., tel. (01) 946-7859.

Ocean Marina Yacht Club: Large international marina with spacious clubhouse, bar, several restaurants, and facilities for yachters and sailors including pontoon moorings, slip rentals, dry storage, and repairs through the nearby Concord Boatyard. This club also provides boat sales, rentals, and charters. Sukumvit Km 157, just past Ambassador Hotel, Jomtien, tel. (038) 237300.

Royal Varuna Yacht Club: A private club on a fine, unspoiled beach with rack storage, boat repairs, chandlery, large swimming pool, terrace restaurant, and short and long-term accommodations. Although there are no formal boat rentals, club members frequently seek crew for day trips and longer excursions around the islands off the east coast of Thailand. Races are organized most weekends. The resort is a few minutes south of Pattaya near the Cosy Beach Hotel and Island View Hotel. Royal Varuna Yacht Club, tel. (038) 250115.

Fishing Trips

Big-game fishing at 1,000-1,500B per day can be arranged at most travel agencies and directly at several bars in South Pattaya.

Deutsches Haus: Arranges fishing expeditions for a minimum party of four passengers and will, of course, cook your catch right on the boat. Beach Road at Soi 4, tel. (038) 428725.

Bang Saray Fishing Club: This place in Bang Saray, 20 km east of Pattaya, also arranges multiday fishing excursions for big game such as marlin, king mackerel, shark, and barracuda.

Panarak Park: Freshwater fishing plus restaurant and play area for the kids. Siam Country Club Rd., tel. (038) 249156.

Pattaya Tower and Water Park

An enormous beachfront park with water slides, swimming pools, and restaurants—a perfect place for families to swim in clean, clear waters. The park is located between Pattaya and Jomtien Beach.

Towering over the water park is an enormous seaside hotel block capped by a soaring concrete pinnacle with revolving restaurant. Great views from the top of the 240-meter high structure. After lunch, you can ride the elevator back down to the ground floor or leap out of the window and return to earth on an absurdly perilous "sky shuttle." This contraption hooks you into a small chair which is released from the tower and follows metal guidelines down to the ground.

Pattaya Park Beach Resort: This relatively new hotel complex has 730 rooms and suites with all the standard resort amenities. 345 Jomtien Beach, tel. (038) 251210, fax (038) 251209, 800-1,800B.

SPORTS

Golf

Pattaya is one of the golfing centers of Thailand with almost 20 golf courses in Pattaya or within a one hour drive.

Golf fees: Greens fees on weekends range from 450B to 1,000B, while weekday rates are heavily discounted. Special rates are given to holders of Pattaya Sports Club or Pattaya Golf Association cards. Pattaya Sport Club cards are sold at Kronborg Hotel on Soi Diana off Pattaya 2 Road, while Pattaya Golf Association cards are available at Siam Golf and Country Club and the Greenway Driving Range.

Tours and Tournaments: Golf tours and tournaments are organized through several

clubs on Pattaya Beach Road, easily found by looking for the bags of clubs piled behind the pool table.

Siam Golf and Country Club: One of Thailand's finest course is 20 minutes from downtown Pattaya through the archway on Sukumvit Road just opposite Central Pattaya Road. The 7,016-yard course is one of the oldest in the country with plenty of old trees and tight fairways. 50 Tambol Poeng, Siam Country Club Rd., tel. (038) 249381.

Royal Thai Navy Course: Phu Ta Luang Golf Course, 35 minutes south near the naval town of Sattahip, also ranks among the oldest courses in the country with 27 very challenging holes of golf, plus a fine clubhouse with all possible amenities. Sukumvit Rd., Ban Chang, tel. (038) 431189.

Bang Phra International Golf Club: A long 18-hole professional golf course with driving range and large clubhouse complete with hotel, restaurant, and even Japanese-style bath tubs in the luxurious locker rooms. 45 Moo 6 Tambon, Bang Phra, tel. (038) 341149.

Great Lake Golf Course: A Nick Faldo-designed course with a tricky layout and loads of bunkers. 77 Moo 5, Rayong, tel. (01) 321-1913.

Horseback Riding

Several horseback riding centers are outside town, generally up in the mountains.

Horse Sports Center Pattaya: Willi Netzer and his crew lead organized rides through the countryside and jungle in the Kao Camin hills just east of Pattaya. Rides cost about 700B per hour. Instruction also is provided for beginners and intermediates, and monthly discounted memberships are available. Rayong Highway, tel. (038) 251984.

Thai Boxing Instruction

The latest wrinkle to activities in Pattaya seems to be the various Thai boxing schools that have opened in recent years. The gyms are hardly luxurious but the instruction is professional and rates are reasonable.

Universe Gym: Fitness center with weekly Thai boxing instruction. Soi 2, tel. (038) 421027.

World Class Gym: One of the better operations in town with daily aerobic classes, dance instruction, weight training, and Thai boxing classes for beginners and intermediates. Visitors can use the day rates or sign up for a short-term membership. Pattaya 2nd Rd. Soi 12, tel. (038) 411116.

Sityodthong International School of Boxing: The only facility in Pattaya dedicated strictly to the sport of Thai boxing, located about three km north of town. 90 Moo 6, Nongprue, Sukumvit Rd., tel. (038) 429018.

Mountain Bikes

As with horseback riding centers, most of Pattaya's mountain bike centers are outside town at the edge of the mountains.

Mountain Bike Club Challenger: The largest facility on the east coast with hourly mountain bike rentals and escorted rides through the nearby jungles. Laem Chabang Country Club, tel. (01) 239-5615.

Go-carts

Several surprisingly elaborate go-cart venues have opened in recent years and appear to be doing quite well with the thrill-seeking crowd.

K.R. International Kart Circuit: The biggest and best operation of its kind in the Pattaya area with professional instruction and weekend races with specially modified carts. A pair of Englishmen run this outfit. 62/125 Moo 2 Thep Prasit Rd., tel. (038) 300349.

Pattaya Kart Speedway: The original go-cart place with two tracks (one for beginners and one for advanced drivers) and dual carts for parent-and-kid teams. Thep Prasit Rd., tel. (038) 422044.

Mini Siam: The amusement park at the north end of town has a single cart track only suitable for experienced drivers. 387 Sukumvit Rd., tel. (038) 421628.

Bira Circuit

Named after Prince Bira, one of Thailand's best-known racing enthusiasts, this 2.4-km racetrack has international events and a popular race school managed by Pacemakers AG, a European-based company involved in the racing-tire business. Rentals cost 600-900B per hour and include go-carts, Formula 3 models, and Ford 2000s. Highway 36, Km 14.

ACCOMMODATIONS

Hotel Districts

Pattaya is divided into several districts.

North Pattaya and Wong Amat Beach have swankier deluxe hotels, fine restaurants, and low-key nightlife suitable for families with children. Wong Amat Beach is recommended for its fairly luxurious hotels tucked away in a semi-rural setting on the best beach in the area. North Pattaya is a fairly classy and clean area but it's too far to walk to the nightclubs in south Pattaya and you'll need to flag down a baht bus to go just about anywhere.

Central Pattaya is the place for families or couples who wish to be within walking distance of the nightclubs in south Pattaya, but removed enough to escape the solo males who fill most of the guesthouses and hotels in that particular neighborhood. For many visitors, this is the best part of town.

South Pattaya has budget hotels and restaurants, plus notorious nightlife that ranges from go-go bars to transvestite cabarets that rage until dawn. This area is best left to the single male traveler.

Jomtien Beach to the south is a family resort region with luxurious hotels, soaring condo complexes, and the best selection of water sports in the region.

Hotel Prices

Some 280 guesthouses, hotels, and condominiums are estimated to be operating in and around Pattaya, with a total of over 35,000 rooms.

Tariffs vary according to day and season. Weekdays are cheaper than weekends, and rates are cut about 40% during the slow season May-Oct. Business has been booming in recent years with high occupancy levels provided by the political and economic problems of neighboring Malaysia and Indonesia. And yet rates remain at extremely reasonable levels and there appears to be little pressure to raise prices.

Contrary to popular belief, Pattaya has a good selection of fan-cooled hotels in the 150-300B price range and a/c rooms in the 400-600B range. The cheapest places are just basic cubicles but come equipped with adequate furniture and private bath, and are perfectly acceptable for short stays.

Pattaya's cheapest hotels are located in south Pattaya on Soi Post Office, Soi Yamato, and Soi 13. These places are recommended for single males rather than couples or families.

The following hotel descriptions start from the south end of Pattaya—near the nightclubs and restaurants—and move north to the quieter areas in central and northern Pattaya.

Budget—Soi Post Office

Soi Post Office (Post Office Alley)—a very utilitarian street—has several travel agencies, the well-stocked D.K. Books, real estate agencies with photos of available properties in the front windows, translation and general business services, a dive shop, overseas call outlets, Internet cafes, a used book exchange, a wine shop, and almost every other service you may need.

Several budget-priced guesthouse are also on this street, with decent fan rooms for 200-250B and a/c rooms for just 300-350B, such as **Sureena Bed and Breakfast** and, at the far end of the street, the French-owned **Riviera Beach Hotel** where a/c rooms start from 400B.

Malibu Bar, at the end of the road, puts on a rankly amateurish nightclub show with transvestites and Thai dancers.

Budget—Soi Yamato

Named after a well-known Japanese restaurant just off Beach Road, this rather claustrophobic alley has eight hotels in the 200-450B price range. **Siam Guesthouse** and the adjacent **Porn Hotel** at the eastern end of the road have a/c rooms from 350B and several fan rooms for just 200B. **Sailor Inn** a few steps down is a Norwegian Bar with a few inexpensive rooms upstairs. German-operated **Eiger Bar** has fan rooms from 220-300B.

Hotel Norge is, as you might imagine, a Norwegian haunt with a/c rooms from 350B. **Nipa Guesthouse** and **The Rising Sun Hotel** in the middle of the block also have both fan-cooled and a/c rooms at bargain rates. **Texxan Inn** is owned by a retired USAF officer who serves enormous breakfasts and has nightly CNN broadcasts 1900-2000. **Europa Inn, Joiles Momei Hotel,** and **PS Guesthouse** at the western end of the street are other low-priced choices.

Once again, this street is best suited to single males rather than couples or families.

Budget—Soi 13

This is the northernmost street in south Pattaya which isn't strictly aimed at solo males travelers, but still isn't quite mainstream enough to attract the average visitor. It's also a strangely deserted street with wide stretches of open land between the limited number of guesthouses and hotels.

Starting from Beach Road, you'll first find the large and relatively decent **AA Pattaya Hotel** with 82 rooms priced from 850-1,200B. Heading east along the alley you then reach **Ma Maison Hotel and Restaurant** followed by the **Chris Guesthouse,** where rooms start at 250B. The clean and comfortable **Inn of the Golden Crab,** with a small swimming pool, provides short-term rentals but not rooms by the night (weekly rentals only).

Sportsman Grill, just opposite the **Inn of the Golden Crab,** provides the best dining on the street. The final two accommodations on this very quiet street are **The White House,** almost to the end of the road, and **Lek Hotel** at the corner of Pattaya 2 Road. Both have rooms in the 350-500B price range.

Budget—Soi 8

This narrow street in Central Pattaya just south of Central Pattaya Road is an excellent choice for couples who wish to be near the nightlife action but don't want to descend into the hardcore bachelor enclaves to the south. Quite a number of small clubs and beer bars are scattered along this road, but the atmosphere is fairly friendly and couples and female travelers will find this neighborhood perfectly acceptable for a few nights. Places here tend to be in the midmarket level with a/c rooms and private baths.

Starting from Pattaya 2 Road to the west, you first come across the **Elephant & Castle Pub, Rovers Return Hotel, Top House,** and **Mongkol Guesthouse** at the southern corner of the intersection. These are the least expensive choices on the street with small rooms from 300B.

Just opposite this budget hive is the rather nondescript **Highfive Hotel** with motel-like rooms at bargain rates. Heading west toward the beach is the popular if somewhat sterile **Sunbeam Hotel** surrounded by dozens of beer bars and a few struggling go-go bars. The **Sunshine Hotel** across the street also has rooms in the 350-750B price range.

A few steps to the west is the very large and fairly new hotel complex modestly known as the **Prince of Pattaya Beach Hotel** with several levels of clean and comfortable rooms from 450-1,200B. The outdoor cafes directly in front of this hotel and just across the street are some of the most comfortable places to relax at night and watch the passing parade of Western drunks and local transvestites.

Eastiny Inn & Minimart across the street is small but has decent rooms from 450B while the older **Flipper Lodge Hotel,** adjacent to the **Prince of Pattaya,** provides acceptable rooms in the same price range.

Budget—Pattaya 2 Road
Along with the budget spots mentioned above, almost a dozen inexpensive guesthouses and hotels are located back on Pattaya 2 Road just opposite Soi 6, 10, 11, and 12. Many have posted signs which announce their special room deals, which range from 150-450B. The low-end places are just simple guesthouses with barely survivable cubicles, but you'll also find plenty of decent hotels with small pools and cozy cafes with a/c rooms priced from just 250B. You can walk to the beach in about two minutes.

Hotel names and special promotions seem to change with the seasons, so it's best to just wander down the street and inspect a few places before checking in.

Magic Guesthouse: A French-owned and operated guesthouse with small but clean rooms in a handy location. Pattaya 2 Rd., Soi 9, tel. (038) 720211, 150-400B.

U-Thumphorn: Basic but very inexpensive guesthouse with simple fan-cooled rooms. Pattaya 2 Rd., Soi 10, tel. (038) 421350, 150-250B.

Apex Hotel: A large and reasonably modern hotel with near-spacious rooms at bargain rates. Also has a small pool and good deals on breakfast buffets. You may need to bargain at the front desk, though this hotel seems to perpetually post prices for special discount rooms just outside the front door. 216/2 Pattaya 2 Rd., Soi 11, tel. (038) 429233, 250-500B.

Diana Inn: Simple rooms and a good pool make this a popular spot for budget travelers who want basic frills at low cost. Pattaya 2 Rd., Soi 11, tel. (038) 429675, fax (038) 424566, 450-600B.

Palm Villa: Pattaya's venerable budget hotel has all a/c rooms, an attractive swimming pool, and is within easy walking distance of the bars. Pattaya 2 Rd., Soi 13, tel. (038) 428153, 400-600B.

Moderate—South Pattaya
Most Pattaya hotels priced in the 600-1,500B price range include a/c rooms with private bath, a restaurant, and a small swimming pool. Some charge an additional 20% for tax and service.

Honey Lodge: A clean, quiet, and well-located hotel with a spacious swimming pool and discounts for long-term visitors. 529 Soi 10, Pattaya 2 Rd., tel. (038) 421543, fax (038) 421946, 350-700B.

Lek Hotel: A relatively new hotel with large swimming pool, billiards hall, and rooftop terrace. All rooms furnished with TV, refrigerator, and hot showers. Pattaya 2 Rd., Soi 13, tel. (038) 425550, fax (038) 426629, 800-1,000B.

Caesar Palace Hotel: Las Vegas comes to Pattaya in this pseudo-Romanesque 200-room hotel. The compound includes a large pool and tennis courts. Pattaya 2 Rd., Soi 10, tel. (038) 428607, fax (038) 422140, 900-1,400B.

Luxury
Four luxury hotels are located in Pattaya between Jomtien Beach to the south and Naklua to the north.

Royal Garden Resort: Superb location and wonderful views from rooms facing the beach make this the ideal location for upscale visitors to Pattaya who wish to be near the action and shopping venues in the adjacent complex. The resort lies in a garden setting with swimming pool, health club, and a variety of restaurants from Benihana's to their Saturday night seafood buffet artfully arranged around a series of ponds. South Pattaya Beach Rd., tel. (038) 428122, fax (038) 429926, US$100-180.

Amari Orchid Resort: Tucked away at the north end of town with some of the finest gardens in the region and a vaguely European feel to the property. Popular with tour groups and others drawn to the personality of this large Thai hotel chain. North Pattaya Beach Rd., tel. (038) 428161, fax (038) 428165, 1,800-3,600B.

Montien Pattaya: Considered one of the best in the region with beautiful rooms and all possible amenities in a handy location near the center of town. Central Pattaya Beach Rd., tel. (038) 428155, fax (038) 423155, 2,500-3,500B.

Dusit Resort Hotel: Situated on 15 acres of lovely gardens with great views, two swimming pools, three tennis courts, sauna, billiards, and a health club. Best hotel in north Pattaya, but far removed from the nightclubs and restaurants in the southern part of town—attracts mostly a Thai clientele. North Pattaya Beach Rd., North Pattaya, tel. (038) 425611, fax (038) 428239, 2,600-4,500B.

Naklua Hotels

Naklua is the residential neighborhood just north of Pattaya where many locals live and several intimate midpriced resorts are located near some of the finest beaches in the region.

Wong Amat: Far from the madding crowd, this low-rise bungalow, nicely set on the best beach in Pattaya, may not be the most spectacular place in town, but it remains popular with discriminating Europeans who wish to escape the southern crowds. Wong Amat Beach, tel. (038) 426990, fax (038) 428599, 1,800-3,000B.

Jomtien Beach

Jomtien Beach—a few kilometers south of Pattaya—is somewhat less expensive than staying directly in Pattaya but offers almost no nightlife, and restaurants tend to be unimaginative. On the other hand, Jomtien provides a great beach and the best selection of water sports activities on the entire east coast, and is the preferred destination for many families.

The Icon: Situated between Pattaya and Jomtien is the first so-called "boutique" hotel in the region with 24 finely furnished rooms plus trendy restaurant and swimming pool. 146/8 Thappraya Rd., tel. (038) 250300, fax (038) 250838, 1,200-1,800B.

Mermaid's Beach Resort: European escape with 100 well-designed rooms, private dive boats, and swimming pool just 100 meters from the sandy beach. Jomtien Beach Rd., tel. (038) 232210, fax (038) 231908, 850-1,400B.

Ambassador Jomtien: Thailand's largest hotel has international restaurants, an amoeba-shaped swimming pool, and 5,000 rooms with views over the Gulf of Thailand. Monstrous in conception. Jomtien Beach Rd., tel. (038) 255501, fax (038) 255731, 1,200-3,000B.

Royal Cliff Hotel: Midway between Pattaya and Jomtien Beach, Pattaya's most expensive and exclusive hotel offers four individual hotels with 86 executive suites in their Royal Wing, private butlers, several beautiful pools, and elevators down to the private beach. Cliff Rd., tel. (038) 250421, fax (038) 250511, 4,500-8,000B.

FOOD

Pattaya's dining choices include everything from Arabic and French to Scottish and Japanese—Thai food is an endangered species here. Seafood is the emphasis due to the town's location on the Gulf of Thailand. Many of the best Thai restaurants are not located on Beach Road, but on the side roads leading up to Sukumvit Highway.

Streetstalls

The most inexpensive dining in Pattaya is at the dozens of simple foodstalls which open nightly at dusk at several locations around town.

Soi Diamond: Good cheap alfresco dining, popular with hookers, transvestites, and sailors, can be enjoyed along Soi Diamond, Soi Post Office, Soi Yamato, and Soi Pattayaland 1 and 2. Look for the stalls that sell Thai herbal wines at 10B per shot.

Thai

As you might expect, Pattaya is a place where it can be difficult to find decent Thai food but you always pick up a Swiss fondue or German sausage at any hour of the day.

PIC Kitchen: Classical Thai cooking in a lovely setting accompanied by jazz musicians and traditional Thai dancers on Wednesday evening. Great atmosphere. Pattaya 2 Rd., Soi 5, tel. (038) 428374.

Ruen Thai: Open-air restaurant with traditional Thai dancing nightly at 1930. 485/3 Pattaya 2 Road opposite Royal Garden Hotel in south Pattaya, tel. (038) 425911.

Thai House: An upscale restaurant with traditional Thai dishes and nightly Thai dancing and music starting around 2000. Somewhat isolated near City Hall in the north of town. 171 Pattaya North Rd., tel. (038) 370579.

Sugar Hut: Certainly doesn't sound even vaguely Thai, but this extremely elegant spot decorated in Ayuthaya style specializes in authentic Thai dishes such as roast duck in curry and seafood with coconut sauces. A very beautiful place and well worth the splurge. Pattaya-Jomtien Rd., tel. (038) 251686.

Sala Maekong: Simple, beachfront, open-air cafe with good food at rock-bottom prices. Beach Rd., Soi 6, North Pattaya, tel. (038) 428645.

Somsak: Another traditional open-air Thai cafe with casual atmosphere and decent food. Beach Rd., 436/24 Soi 1, South Pattaya, tel. (038) 410485.

Wild Mango: Fine name for an inexpensive spot which serves delicious food at very reasonable prices. The managers are friendly and many of the staff speak decent English. Beach Rd., 437/93 Soi 6, Central Pattaya, tel. (038) 361363.

Japanese

Thai and Chinese predominate in the Asian cuisine department, though you can also find restaurants which serve many other Asian styles of cooking, including Japanese, Korean, Indian, Polynesian, and Indonesian.

Benihana: The classic Japanese restaurant with tasty food and amusing jokes from the chef. Beach Rd., Royal Garden Plaza, tel. (038) 425029.

Akamon: Another popular Japanese venue with sushi and tempura in an inconvenient location near the Tiffany Cabaret. Pattaya 2 Rd., North Pattaya, tel. (038) 423727.

Yamato: Such an old-time favorite that the adjacent alley is often just called "Soi Yamato." Japanese favorites, sushi, and sashimi served at dinner only. 219/51 Soi Yamato, South Pattaya, tel. (038) 429685.

Vietnamese and Lao

Thang Long: Vietnamese and Thai dishes in a small cafe at very reasonable prices. Beach Rd., Soi 3, South Pattaya, tel. (038) 425487.

Vientiane: Perhaps the only place in town with Lao dishes along with a large selection of Thai and Chinese specialties as noted on their extensive menu. Moderately priced but service is good and the atmosphere is somewhat unique. 185 Pattaya 2 Rd., near Palm Villa Hotel.

Indian

Indian restaurants tend to be somewhat overpriced but the food provides a welcome change from a steady diet of Thai rice dishes or American fast food.

Ali Baba: Indian restaurant known for its vegetarian dishes and Tandoori cuisine. Open for

streetstalls offer delicious and inexpensive dining options

both lunch and dinner. 14 Central Pattaya Rd., tel. (038) 429262.

Motta Mahal: Somewhat hectic atmosphere near the Marine Plaza Hotel but a wide selection of Indian, Arabic, Pakistani, Bengali, and even Thai dishes. 323/26 Soi Saen Samran, South Pattaya, tel. (038) 429630.

Korean

Krung Seoul: The best Korean food in town served in a spotless little cafe just opposite the Royal Garden Plaza shopping complex. 215/46 Pattaya 2 Rd., tel. (038) 426248.

Koreana: A surprisingly large restaurant (seats over 300) near many of the seedy hotels in South Pattaya. The place is clean, however, and serves all the classic Korean dishes from kim chi to beef bulgogi. 436 Beach Rd., Soi 1, tel. (038) 429635.

More Asian

Filipino, Indonesian, and even Polynesian food can be enjoyed in this multicultural beach resort.

Bahay Philipino: The only Filipino cafe in town is just across the road from the Royal Garden Hotel. Pattaya 2 Rd., tel. (038) 426191.

Mai Kai Supper Club: The only Polynesian restaurant in town is located near the Hotel Tropicana. Also serves a wide selection of seafood dishes plus offers live band entertainment in the evenings. Beach Rd., North Pattaya, tel. (038) 428645.

Dolf Riks: Indonesian dishes and Thai specialties prepared by an Indonesian-born food critic and artist. 116/8 Pattaya-Naklua Rd., tel. (038) 367585.

English and Irish

Most expatriates here are of European extraction so expect an inordinate number of Swiss, German, and Italian cafes. English and Irish places tend to be pubs rather than formal restaurants.

Delaney's Irish Pub: A very large and popular place with Guinness, Killkenny, and Carlsberg on draft, plus a variety of Irish and English pub food. Happy hours daily from 1100-1300 and 1700-1900. Beach Rd., tel. (038) 710641.

Anzac: Typical English pub food plus Thai dishes, pool table, and TV with weekly sporting events. A popular place with expat families and

Europeans on short vacations. Open daily from 0700-0300. 325/22 Soi Pattayaland 1, tel. (038) 427822.

Fawlty Towers: Traditional English pub and cafe with British food, snacks, and football games on the telly. Beach Rd., Soi 7, tel. (038) 420853.

Greg's Kitchen: The English chef does a mean job with roasts, traditional pies, and hearty breakfasts. 370/21 Pattaya 2 Rd., tel. (038) 361227.

Sportsman's Inn: Another English cafe/pub with respectable breakfasts and traditional roasts. 437/124 Soi Yodsak, North Pattaya, tel. (038) 429152.

Dutch

Old Dutch: Cozy spot with Dutch decorations and Thai plus Continental cuisine. Open around the clock and popular for breakfasts. 215/62 Pattaya 2 Rd., opposite Royal Garden Plaza, South Pattaya, tel. (038) 723177.

German

Zeppelin: German cafe with traditional fare and not a Led Zeppelin CD in sight. Beach Rd., just north of Central Rd., Nova Lodge Hotel, Central Pattaya, tel. (038) 420016.

Deutsches Haus: German, Thai, and international cuisine served in a comfortable a/c environment. This place also operates a deep-sea fishing yacht, which you can charter and then catch your own seafood. Beach Rd., Soi 4, tel. (038) 428725.

Swiss

Swiss Food: Not the most creative name but a popular and centrally located cafe with traditional Swiss fare, in the heart of the action. The three-course daily set menu is a good deal. 29 Soi Diamond, tel. (038) 423991.

Chalet Swiss: Swiss, International, and Thai cuisine served in the heart of South Pattaya. 220 Beach Rd., tel. (038) 429255.

French

Mon Ami Pierrot: French restaurant supervised by a French chef who prepares at least four set menus each day. Open for dinner only. 220/3 Beach Rd., South Pattaya, tel. (038) 429792.

Bruno's Restaurant and Wine Bar: An elegant French-Thai restaurant with second-floor wine bar with almost 200 different wines; also serves international dishes at reasonable prices. 463/77 Sri Nakorn Centre, North Pattaya, tel. (038) 361073.

Ma Maison: French and Continental dishes plus steaks and pastries in a casual open-air atmosphere adjacent to a small swimming pool. Beach Rd., Soi 13, South Pattaya, tel. (038) 429318.

Le Cafe Royale: A piano bar and sophisticated restaurant in a very seedy district surrounded by gay clubs and low-end strip joints—that must be the appeal. 325/102 Pattayaland Soi 3, South Pattaya, tel. (038) 423515.

Au Bon Coin: Small European cafe with steaks, continental entrees, and daily specials at reasonable cost. 216/59 Pattaya 2 Rd., tel. (038) 421978.

The Balcony: French, Thai, and Western dishes plus a great assortment of pastries. Soi Ananthakul, North Pattaya just beyond Thai Garden Resort, tel. (038) 411429.

19th Hole: Certainly doesn't sound French, but this large bar complex serves French cuisine along with juices from the juice bar, ice creams, and diversions from 10 snooker tables to backgammon and other pub games. Beach Rd., Sophon Plaza, 2nd floor, tel. (038) 429152.

Italian

La Gritta: An old favorite with Italian cuisine and nightly piano entertainment. Pasta with clams and other seafood dishes are recommended. Amari Orchid Hotel, Beach Rd., North Pattaya, tel. (038) 428161.

Borsolino: Another cozy cafe in the heart of the nightlife district with both Thai and Italian ala carte dishes plus bargain-priced set menus which change daily. Soi Diamond, tel. (038) 424450.

American

American-style pubs and steak houses have been gaining in popularity in recent years and now seem almost as common as Swiss fondue joints and German sausage cafes.

Hopf Brew House: Unquestionably the most successful new restaurant, brewpub, and entertainment venue in Pattaya with upscale atmosphere, excellent food, and the healthiest looking crowd in town. Great for families, Western couples, and even bachelors who wish to escape the seediness of South Pattaya for a few hours. The place is huge—takes up an entire city block—but can be absolutely packed on weekends. Live bands most nights (the best in town) plus beer brewed on the premises, not to mention excellent Western and European food. 219 Beach Rd., Soi Post Office, South Pattaya, tel. (038) 710650.

Henry J. Bean's Bar & Grill: Great spot in a finely restored old building with decent Western grub, beers on tap, and live bands nightly except Monday starting around 2030. Amari Orchid Resort, Beach Rd., North Pattaya, tel. (038) 334881.

Sizzler: Some of the best steaks in town, plus chicken, seafood platters, pasta dishes, and a remarkable salad bar—probably the best reason to visit this American chain. Prices are reasonable and the adjoining shopping complex is a delight to explore (it's a/c). Royal Garden Plaza, Beach Rd., tel. (038) 428128.

Captain's Corner Steak House: Just south of Pattaya on the road to Jomtien this attractive garden restaurant known for its nightly all-you-can-eat "Texas Style Bar-B-Q." Pattaya-Jomtien Rd., tel. (038) 364318.

Maxwell's American Diner: Nostalgia lives on with period music (1950s to '70s only) and basic American grub from shakes and burgers to steaks and cakes. 217/14 Pattaya 2 Rd., Soi 8, South Pattaya, tel. (038) 361247.

El Toro Steak House: As the name implies, a place for steaks in all shapes and fashions from flambe and pepper to Diane and tartare. 215/31 Pattaya 2 Rd., opposite Royal Garden Hotel, tel. (028) 426238.

Green Bottle: Combination entertainment venue (pool table, darts, nightly vocalist) and restaurant which serves steaks, duck, and plenty of fresh seafood dishes. 216/9 Pattaya 2 Rd., opposite Mike Shopping Mall, tel. (03) 429675.

Green Tree: Despite the Western name, this a/c spot serves up Thai, Chinese, and Western dishes along with live musical entertainment most evenings. Beach Rd., Soi 3, North Pattaya, tel. (038) 428586.

Moon River Pub: Cozy little spot near the Thai Garden Resort known for its Saturday evening buffets and live entertainment most evenings. The atmosphere is American Country & Western. North Pattaya Rd., tel. (038) 370614.

American Fast Food Chains: If it's American and fast, then Pattaya's got it: Burger King, Dunkin Donuts, Swensen's, Bud's Ice Cream, A&W, KFC, McDonald's, Pizza Hut, and whatever else you can imagine.

Tex-Mex

The latest food craze to sweep Pattaya is the Tex-Mex food of the American Southwest.

Blue Parrot: The best Tex-Mex food in Pattaya, including fajitas, enchiladas, and nachos. Margaritas are popular, plus there's more sleaze outside the door that you could swing a stick at. 325/151 Soi Pattayaland 2, tel. (038) 424885.

Moonshine: Another Tex-Mex outlet with pool tables, darts, and live music in a raunchy, sleazy part of town. Beach Rd., Soi Diamond, South Pattaya, tel. (038) 411820.

Rancho Tejas: An open-air, family sort of place popular with expats, packed for the Sunday brunches, Thursday buffets, and weekend barbecues. The house band plays Thursday to Sunday starting nightly at 1900. Pattaya-Naklua Rd., Soi Potisan, Naklua, tel. (038) 428787.

Wild Chicken: Tex-Mex plus a variety of chicken specialties in a lively bar setting and a pair of TV blasting away with sporting events. Soi Post Office at Pattaya 2 Rd., tel. (038) 424006.

Seafood

Seafood is a big item here in Pattaya where almost a dozen decidedly upscale restaurants provide absolutely fresh seafood at rather startling prices.

Food Fair: Seafood restaurants at the south end of Beach Road let you personally select your entree, cooking styles, and accompanying sauce, but it's advisable to avoid well-dressed touts and to double-check cooking charges before ordering. Beach Rd., South Pattaya.

Nang Nual: Another longtime favorite with expensive if completely fresh seafood. Beach Rd., South Pattaya, opposite Soi 14, tel. (038) 428708.

Lobster Pot: Another pricey but fun seafood emporium with interior dining spaces and an outdoor terrace restaurant, perfect for sunsets. The restaurant is open daily from 1000 until well after midnight. 228 Beach Rd., South Pattaya, tel. (038) 426083.

Savoey Seafood: One of the few seafood restaurants in town not located on Beach Road, but with an extensive menu at cheaper prices than down by the sea. Somewhat noisy due to its location at a major intersection but quite an authentic dining experience. 164 Central Pattaya Rd., at the corner of Pattaya 2 Rd., tel. (038) 428580.

Restaurants with a View

Several restaurants around town provide decent views of Pattaya and the beach, but one place deserves a special mention for its outrageous panoramic views.

The Pinnacle Revolving Restaurant: A few kilometers south of Pattaya and just slightly north of Jomtien Beach is an amazing tower with revolving restaurants situated on the 52nd and 53rd floors. The views are spectacular. Visitors can just pay for the elevator ride to the top and enjoy the vistas or try the reasonably priced international buffet lunch or more expensive dinner option. Dinners are recommended for the sunsets. Pattaya Water Park, 345 Jomtien Beach Rd., tel. (038) 251201.

NIGHTLIFE

South Pattaya between Soi 13 and Soi 16 is a nonstop barrage of heady go-go bars, seedy nightclubs, high-tech discos, and outrageous live shows that cater to every possible sexual persuasion. It's an amazing experience to wander down Pattaya Beach Road past mud wrestlers, Thai kickboxers, open-air cinemas, touts, transvestite clubs, and whatever new gimmick sweeps the night scene. Much of the action revolves around open-air beer bars in South Pattaya, where friendly women hail customers from the street.

Soi Diamond

A good place to start is Soi Diamond, a small and totally crazy lane a short walk beyond South Pattaya Road. Lively women working the narrow alley drag reluctant customers up to the bar stools and push them into the better bars such as **Caligula** (live shows), **Blackout** (better furnishings), **Baby A Go-Go** (best club on Soi Diamond), and **Limmatquai** (inexpensive drinks).

transvestite follies

Before you leave the lower section of this surrealistic alley, ride the circular **Chiquita Bar** that revolves like a carousel; Hunter S. Thompson on acid would love this place.

Other nightclubs near the main road worth a look (and then perhaps a drink) include Blue Hawaii, Vixens, Super Girl, and Paris Go-Go.

Heading deeper up Soi Diamond, you then pass the **Diamond Beach Hotel** on the right and then the road narrows and the mid-alley beer bars completely disappear. **Starlights** on the left is a transvestite bar (so beware), followed by the **Jungle Pub, Mama Restaurant,** the delightfully named **Lassi Beer Bar** (lassis and beer?), **Casa Italia Restaurant,** and finally the **Lucky Corner Bar** almost where Soi Diamond reaches Pattaya 2 Road.

Soi BJ and Golden Mile Plaza

Another large concentration of nightclubs and go-go bars is located about five minutes south of Soi Diamond, on another narrow lane that has been mysteriously nicknamed Soi BJ, though the large sign over the entertainment complex calls the place the Golden Mile Plaza.

In any event, this alley isn't as much fun as Soi Diamond, though it does provide the aimless visitor with another dozen beer bars to explore and the lively **Happy A Go-Go** at the end of the alley.

Pattayaland

Pattaya has several dozen gay clubs, mostly located on Pattayaland Sois 1, 2 and 3 in South Pattaya. The neighborhood isn't strictly gay and offers plenty for straight travelers such as British pubs, a French piano bar, inexpensive Thai cafes, guesthouses, several budget hotels, go-go bars with lovely girls, and mundane services such as travel agencies and dive shops.

Pattayaland Soi 1: Just one block south of Royal Garden Plaza shopping complex is this busy alley packed with all manners of pubs, bars, nightclubs, crash pads, and other assorted things. Starting from Beach Road, you'll first pass the Aquanauts Diving Center, Papillon Go-Go Bar, Why Not Cabaret? (a boys show), followed by the Whooters & Pool (I assume this place is straight), the Sugar Shack, and then Dave's G.B. Bar.

On the left in the middle of the block is Tai Boys Boys Club (this place calls itself "the Funny Bar"), then the Gentleman Boy's Club, Winner's Boys, Billion Beer Bar (nice name), and finally the Winner Guesthouse. Spots to explore on the right side of this road include City Boys Club, Dey Mosquetos Beer Bar, Tatoo by Big, and Charlie Boys.

Pattayaland Soi 2: More fun and games on this busy street that connects Beach Road with Pattaya 2 Road. The west end of the road near the ocean has the Bubbles Club, Cheers Pub, Viking Beachcomber Cafe, the very popular Palmers Cafe, the Blue Parrot Cafe mentioned above, and Bobby Joe's Guesthouse and Bar. Most of these places are aimed at the straight rather than gay crowd.

Pattayaland Soi 3: This half-block long lane features a mixture of straight go-go nightclubs and a scattering of gay spots for those so inclined. Among the more prominent pubs and nightclubs are the Shamrock Bar, the very lively Misty's Go-Go, Lipstick A Go-Go (also popular), Miss Din's Beer Bar, the cleverly named Classroom Fun A Go-Go Sports Bar, Cats Go-Go Fun Bar, and the A-Bomb Boys Club.

The road curves around this concentration of nightclubs and continues down to Pattaya 2 Road, flanked with another nonstop collection of clubs, restaurants, and places to crash such as Amor Restaurant, Cocobanana Pub, Hotel Serene, Ambiance Hotel, and a Thai porcelain shop (quite out of place).

At the end of this street is the Le Cafe Royale Hotel & Piano Bar, Toy Boys Nightclub, and La Bodega Restaurant. If you need more diversion, walk across Pattaya 2 Road to the Boat Bakery, Simpatico Italian Restaurant, and a towering Russian karaoke palace that opened just a few years ago. Whew!

Transvestite Shows

Pattaya's best entertainment options are the hilarious transvestite shows that take place nightly in two extravagant cabarets in the north end of Pattaya on Pattaya 2 Road. Cheaper and far less professional transvestite shows are given in the larger nightclubs in South Pattaya, an area known as "The Strip."

Alcazar Cabaret: Professional shows of world-class caliber are given here every night of the year, by a company of almost 100 *gatoeis* who perform three times nightly in their 800-seat theater. . . the largest transvestite show troupe on earth. 78/14 Pattaya 2 Rd., tel. (038) 428746. 300-500B includes your first drink. The price varies depending on where you buy your ticket—directly at the cabaret or from a street vendor (or travel agency) that may tack on a hefty commission.

Tiffany's: Tiffany's is an 850-seat theater with over 65 performers who pose for photo sessions after the three nightly shows. Pattaya 2 Rd., tel. (038) 429642. 300-500B includes your first drink.

Simon Cabaret: Inside this enormous nightclub, somewhat seedy and filled with freelancers, you'll find a rather amateurish yet humorous nightly transvestite show, plus other entertainment oddities such as Thai boxing between local professionals and drunken tourists. The place was very quiet at last inspection and may have finally closed after a very long run. Beach Rd., South Pattaya, "The Strip." If this enormous open-air brothel remains in business, expect a

modest cover charge of 50-100B depending on where you sit.

Marine Bar: Another monstrous open-air nightclub catering to "girls, guys, and in-betweens." This legendary nightclub also appears to be in financial trouble and may be closed on your arrival. If not, enjoy yourself.

If you haven't noticed by now, transvestites *(gatoeis)* are plentiful here in Pattaya. Since most Westerners have a difficult time distinguishing between women and *gatoeis,* proceed with caution unless you seek a wild war story.

Nightclubs and Discos

Pattaya has several large dance clubs filled with Thai teenagers, cruising call girls, and Western tourists.

Disco Duck: A long-time favorite with large video screens, live band, light shows and entertainment alternatives such as pool tables in the outside hall. Mostly for young Thais rather than Western tourists. Little Duck Pattaya Resort Hotel, Central Pattaya Rd., tel. (038) 428782.

Pattaya Palladium: An enormous place that bills itself as the largest disco in Thailand if not all of Southeast Asia; the claimed capacity is 5000 souls. This place has DJs on weekdays and live bands on weekends. Pattaya 2 Rd., tel. (038) 424933. The 200-300B entrance fee includes two drinks.

Moon River Pub: Popular country and western nightclub with live bands, line dancing, and an abundance of local expats rather than tourists. North Pattaya Rd., tel. (038) 370614.

Bamboo Bar: An excellent place to hear outstanding Thai rock bands and soak up the authentic atmosphere. No cover charge and there's plenty of seating among the tropical decor. Attracts an older and more sophisticated crowd for its quality rock bands and occasional visits by jazz groups down from Bangkok. South Pattaya Rd., between Beach Road and Pattaya 2 Rd., tel. 421361.

INFORMATION AND SERVICES

Tourist Office

The TAT office doles out maps and hotel lists, and can help with upcoming festivals and sporting events. They also have information on other east coast destinations such as Rayong, Chanthaburi, Trat, and Ko Chang. 382 Beach Rd., tel. (038) 428750.

Tourist Police
Contact this group for emergency help. Pattaya 2 Rd., tel. (038) 429371.

Maps
The TAT office distributes a decent free map. The *Pattaya/Eastern Part* map published by Prannok Witthaya has a larger-scale version of Pattaya plus an excellent map of the entire eastern seaboard, but this map is out of print and now very difficult to find.

The best map of Pattaya is the one that comes with *A Guide to Living in Pattaya & Rayong* compiled by the Pattaya International Ladies Club. You can also buy the map separate from the book, which you don't really need unless you intend to move to Pattaya.

Tourist Magazines
The latest word on hotels, restaurants, and nightlife can be culled from free magazines such as *Explore Pattaya* and *Pattaya This Week.* Trink's gossipy column in the *Bangkok Post* is also worth checking for bar and restaurant promotions. English-language local newspapers such as the *Pattaya Mail* cover real estate investments and advertise bankrupt nightclubs for sale.

Books
Duang Kamol Bookstore (D.K. Books) on Soi Post Office offers novels, literature, and magazines, and has a decent selection of travel guides. As of this writing, there are no current and/or comprehensive English-language guides to Pattaya and the east coast of Thailand.

The best collection of books and magazines is found in Bookazine in the Royal Garden Plaza shopping complex. The first floor has maps and books about Thailand and Asia, while the second floor is the place for international newspapers and magazines

Visas
Visas may be quickly extended at the Chonburi Immigration office on Soi 8 just off Beach Road. Visa photos and the necessary copies can be made at the small office just outside their front gate.

Telephone
International calls can be made 24 hours daily from all major hotels, from the exchange service in south Pattaya, and from dozens of public phones scattered around town. The telephone area code for Pattaya is (038).

Post Office
The Pattaya Post Office (tel. 038-429341) is located, sensibly enough, on Soi Post Office between Sois 13 and 14.

Travel Agencies
Budget travel agencies are most plentiful on Soi Post Office and Soi Yamato. Day tours offered include Ko Samet, Chonburi temples and museums, Chanthaburi gem mines, Bangkok, Damnern Saduak Floating Market, Ayuthaya, and River Kwai. The Chonburi and Chanthaburi tours are worthwhile, but the other excursions are far too time-consuming as one-day options. Prices for tours and international travel vary widely, so shop around before signing those traveler's checks.

Cautions
Pattaya police urge visitors not to carry too much money, never to accept drinks or food from strangers (knockout drugs are common), to keep off motorcycles unless you're an experienced driver, and to check prices before buying *anything.*

TRANSPORTATION

Getting There
Pattaya is 147 km southeast of Bangkok.

Train: The State Railways of Thailand has daily service at 0700 from Hualamphong station. The three-hour journey passes attractive scenery and is a wonderful alternative to the buses.

Bus: Ordinary and a/c buses depart every 30 minutes 0630-2100 from Bangkok's Eastern Bus Terminal on Sukumvit Road Soi 63 and from the Northern Bus Terminal. These government-franchised buses cost 85-100B a/c and take about three hours to reach the small, very poorly marked *bor kor sor* (government) bus station on North Pattaya Road near the Sukumvit Highway.

The beach and most hotels are about four km down the road. You can hire a private *song-tao* to your hotel for about 60B, or take a public *songtao* and pay 10-20B per person.

Private bus companies operate daily a/c buses from major Bangkok hotels direct to your hotel in Pattaya. These buses cost double the a/c government buses but avoid the hassle of getting to the government bus station on Sukumvit Road.

From Bangkok Airport: Buses depart from Bangkok Airport daily at 0600, 1400, and 1830. Tickets cost 200-240B and are sold at the transportation desk in the arrival lounge.

Getting Around

Pattaya is a relatively small town that can be easily explored on foot or with public transportation.

Songtaos: Compact Pattaya is served by *songtaos* that cruise the main roads and—within the city limits—should charge a flat fee of just 5B. In reality, this never happens, since all *songtao* drivers are thieves who will charge whatever they think they can get from unsuspecting tourists.

Fleecing Western visitors is a big business in this town. Just get on a vehicle, get off at your destination, hand the driver five *baht* and walk away. Don't look back. Ignore his pleas and threats. The man is a thief.

Motorcycles: An excellent way to avoid obnoxious minitruck drivers and reach outlying attractions is rented motorcycle. All bikes should be checked carefully for damage before depositing your passport with the rental agency and taking off. International Drivers Licenses are rarely checked.

Small bikes under 150cc cost 150-200B per day and are perfectly adequate for local rides. Larger bikes fitted with an amazing variety of illegal modifications are available from vendors on Pattaya Beach Road. All of these monster bikes are imported as disassembled parts from Japan and reconstructed by local motorcycle enthusiasts. Most are for sale at very low prices (50,000B for a late-model Ninja 750), but few are legally registered with the Thai government.

No matter what size you select, be very careful riding around town; a frightening number of

tourists end their vacations on the streets of Pattaya.

Cars and Jeeps: Both self- and chauffeur-driven cars can be hired from **Avis** at the Dusit Resort in north Pattaya, the Royal Garden Hotel in central Pattaya, and the Royal Cliff Hotel towards Jomtien Beach. **Hertz** has closed down. Jeeps can be rented from vendors on Beach Road but be advised that insurance is rarely available and visitors are held responsible for any damage or injury caused in an accident.

Leaving Pattaya

To Bangkok (Eastern Bus Terminal): Ordinary and a/c government buses depart every 30 minutes 0600-2100 from the government bus terminal on North Pattaya Road near the Sukumvit Highway. These buses terminate in Bangkok at the Eastern Bus Terminal (Ekamai) on Sukumvit Road Soi 63, from where city buses continue into town.

Private bus companies provide pickup at Pattaya hotels and drop-off at major hotels in Bangkok. A very popular service; tickets should be purchased several days in advance.

To Bangkok (Northern Bus Terminal): Visitors heading from Pattaya north to Chiang Mai should take a bus direct from Pattaya's bus terminal on North Pattaya Road to Bangkok's Northern Bus Terminal (Morchit). This connection saves precious hours and avoids the traffic snarls that plague Bangkok. This bus leaves every 30 minutes.

To Bangkok Airport: Buses from the terminal on North Pattaya Road to Bangkok Airport cost 200-240B and depart every two hours 0700-1700. Figure on around three hours to reach the airport.

To North and Northeast Thailand: Destinations in the north, such as Chiang Mai and Mae Sai, and northeastern towns such as Korat and Ubon, can be reached directly by buses departing from a private bus terminal located on Sukumvit Highway near Central Pattaya Road. Buses to Chiang Mai depart at 1330 and 1645, to Korat and Khon Kaen every 15 minutes 2100-2330.

These departures should be confirmed with the tourist office in Pattaya.

Train to Bangkok: One train leaves Pattaya daily at 1450 and takes almost three hours to reach Hualamphong train station.

To Rayong and Ko Samet: Orange public buses to Rayong can be hailed on the main highway. Minibuses continue from Rayong down to Ban Phe, the departure point for boats to Ko Samet. Private minibus service is available from Pattaya to Ban Phe, though you'll pay three times the ordinary rate for the convenience.

VICINITY OF BANGKOK

WEST OF BANGKOK

West of Bangkok lie the three provinces of Nakhon Pathom, Ratchaburi, and Kanchanaburi. Nakhon Pathom and Ratchaburi Provinces are alluvial lowlands once almost entirely covered with ricefields and coconut palms. Today, both are peppered with towns that have transformed themselves from tiny hamlets into thriving industrial estates in less than a generation. Kanchanaburi Province is chiefly known for its bridge over Kwai Yai River and for natural wonders such as lakes, waterfalls, and national parks.

Sightseeing Highlights

The region northwest of Bangkok to the Burmese border offers an outstanding range of attractions, from Buddhist *stupas* and war monuments to Khmer temples and stunning landscapes. Urban sprawl now connects Bangkok with Nakhon Pathom, and Kanchanaburi is firmly on the tourist trail, but the remainder of the region remains largely untouched by mass tourism.

Nakhon Pathom: The world's tallest Buddhist monument is located in this nondescript town about one hour (54 km) west of Bangkok.

Nakhon Pathom is generally visited on a day tour from Bangkok, or as an afternoon pause en route to Kanchanaburi.

Ratchaburi: Almost 50 km southwest of Nakhon Pathom, Ratchaburi is a busy commercial town known for several historic *wats* and the production of huge water jars used in households throughout Thailand. Bamboo reed pipes are still handcrafted in the nearby village of Ban Ko Bua.

Kanchanaburi: This town, 122 km west of Bangkok, is one of Thailand's upcoming centers for both domestic and international tourism. Westerners generally visit the famous bridge and cemeteries that commemorate the events of WW II, while domestic tourists use Kanchanaburi as a weekend escape from the horrors of Bangkok. The medium-sized town is beautifully situated on the River Kwai and within easy day-trips to nearby waterfalls and national parks, a combination that often inspires Western visitors to extend their stay from days to weeks.

Kanchanaburi Province: Aside from the historic monuments of Kanchanaburi town, the chief attraction west of Bangkok is the magnificent

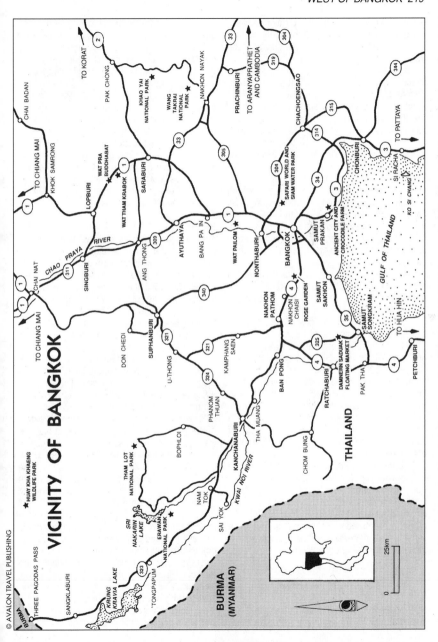

© AVALON TRAVEL PUBLISHING

VICINITY OF BANGKOK

array of rivers, lakes, and waterfalls between Kanchanaburi town and the Burmese border. Travelers can also visit the border post at Three Pagodas Pass.

Suphanburi: The modern town of Suphanburi is occasionally visited as a short stop between Kanchanaburi and Ayuthaya. A quick three-hour *samlor* tour visits the colossal seated Buddha at Wat Palelai and the ruined *prang* of Wat Mahathat. Southwest of Suphanburi is the Don Chedi Memorial, U Thong National Museum, and a weird Buddhist theme park at Wat Wai Pong Rua.

Transportation

One-day tours to the *chedi* at Nakhon Pathom and Kanchanaburi can be booked from travel agents in Bangkok. A one-day train tour is described in the following Kanchanaburi section. Quickie tours, however, are not recommended in a region so immensely rich with sightseeing attractions.

Public transportation from Bangkok is plentiful and well organized. Buses to Nakhon Pathom and Kanchanaburi depart every 15 minutes 0700-2300 from the Southern Bus Terminal in Thonburi. Discount travel agencies on Khao San Road sell minibus tickets at slightly higher cost.

All trains heading south stop in Nakhon Pathom. Departures from Hualampong station are daily at 0900, 1235, 1400, 1515, 1600, 1730, 1830, 1920, and 2155. Nakhon Pathom takes about 90 minutes to reach by train. Trains to Kanchanaburi leave the train station in Thonburi at 0800 and 1350 and take almost three hours to reach Kanchanaburi. You could, of course, take the train to Nakhon Pathom and continue to Kanchanaburi by bus.

The town of Kanchanaburi is the principal transportation hub in the region. Public buses from Kanchanaburi reach most outlying attractions. Remote sights are served by minitrucks which leave from the smaller towns. Motorcycles can be rented in Kanchanaburi and are a sensible and immensely convenient way to visit the widely scattered attractions.

NAKHON PATHOM

Nakhon Pathom, 54 km west of Bangkok, is a busy commercial center chiefly visited for its fa-

mous *chedi* in the center of town near the train station. The city is regarded as one of the oldest municipalities in Thailand and perhaps the country's first center of Buddhist studies. The surrounding countryside is renowned for its delicious pomelos, fragrant white rice, and thriving wine industry. Skip the sweetish, almost sickening white wines and try the elegant yet unpretentious reds. Thai wines and brandies have vastly improved in recent years.

Nakhon Pathom sponsors a Fruit Festival in September and an immensely popular Temple Festival each November during Loy Kratong. The town's final claim to fame is that it served as Phnom Penh in the Academy Award-winning movie, *The Killing Fields.*

History

According to tradition, the city was founded several centuries before the Christian era as a seaside port for the mythical kingdom of Suwannaphum. During this period, King Asoka the Great (272-232 B.C.) sent two senior monks from India to introduce the principles of Theravada Buddhism. Passing through Three Pagodas Pass, the main land conduit from India to Thailand, Buddhism probably made its first impact at Nakhon Pathom.

Archaeological evidence begins in the 6th century when Nakhon Pathom flourished under the patronage of the Mon people. The Mon built a Dvaravati-Buddhist empire, which thrived in central Thailand in the 6th-10th centuries. Little is known of the history or geographical extent of the Mon, though their presence at Nakhon Pathom is confirmed by local discoveries of several stone inscriptions, small *stupas,* and a coin bearing the inscription "Lord of Dvaravati." The original Pra Pathom Chedi, a pagoda of Sri Lankan style, was probably erected during the Mon Period in the late 10th century.

In the early 11th century, Nakhon Pathom and western Thailand fell to King Suryavarman, who incorporated Siam into his militaristic Khmer empire. The original Pra Pathom Chedi (a Buddhist structure) was pulled down and rebuilt in the form of a Hindu/Brahman *prang* some 40 meters high. The Khmers held the city until 1057, when it fell to King Anawratha of Bagan. Recognizing the cultural advances of the Mon, the Burmese king soon imported the artistic and religious traditions of the Mon to his powerful capital in central Myanmar.

Nakhon Pathom was abandoned in the 11th century but re-established in the 17th century by King Mahachakraphet as a defensive position against Burmese invasion. In 1860, King Mongkut ordered the restoration of the decaying *chedi,* an ancient Indian-style pagoda which he first spotted during his early years as a monk in the region.

Nakhon Pathom Chedi

The massive *chedi* at Nakhon Pathom is staggering. Soaring over 120 meters into hot blue skies, this is the most sacred Buddhist monument in Thailand and the world's largest *chedi,* surpassing even the gilded wonder in Yangon. Although the dome-shaped reliquary lacks the intricate detail of Yangon's Shwedagon, its fairyland of auxiliary *bots,* Buddha images, and curious substructures makes for a fascinating afternoon of exploration. For best impact, approach the *chedi* from the north side facing the train station.

The main *chedi* began as a simple Sri Lankan-style *stupa* constructed by the Mons in the 10th century, replaced by a Hindu-Brahman *prang* erected by the Khmers in the early 11th century. The present enormous cupola was begun in 1860 and completed in the early 20th century during the reign of King Chulalongkorn.

Before climbing into the temple complex, note the dozens of amulet booths, palmists, and foodstalls to the left of the main entrance. The stalls serve iced coffee and bamboo staffs filled with sticky rice laced with coconut milk.

Chedi: The bell-shaped *stupa,* covered with glazed orange tiles imported from China, is believed to contain a Buddha relic of great religious importance. It encases an older *stupa* of hemispherical form with a *prang* superimposed; a replica can be seen nearby. The innermost *stupa* may hold the original Dvaravati monument, though religious sanctity and inaccessibility prevent excavation. Surmounting the bulbous mound of brickwork is a triple trident (symbol of Shiva), which is in turn capped by the Royal Crown of Thailand.

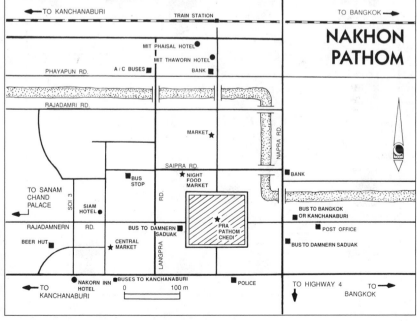

Ceremonial Halls: Flanking the Grand Staircase are two halls used for ceremonies and ordinations.

Temple Office: A large exterior mural points out the main features of the *chedi*.

North *Viharn*: This Sukothai-style standing Buddha, known as Pra Ruang Rochanarit, is an object of great veneration to the Thai peoples. The stone head, hands, and feet were discovered in Sawankalok around 1900, while the bronze body was cast later to match the stone appendages. Buried at the base are the ashes of King Vajiravudh, who completed the restoration initiated by King Mongkut and King Chulalongkorn. An adjacent Public Hall with pho-

tographs of expensive reconstruction projects is also used for ordinations of monks.

Bell Chapels: Surrounding the *chedi* are 24 bells rung by pilgrims to witness Buddha's enlightenment. You may do the same with the wooden mallets.

Buddha Poses: Set into the high-walled cloister which separates the circular walkway from the *chedi* is a remarkable series of bronze Buddhas cast in every possible position of meditation, and labeled in English with confusing translations: "The Buddha look back over one's shoulder." Note the round Chinese-style moon windows with wooden shutters.

NAKHON PATHOM CHEDI

ORIGINAL CHEDI REPLICA
NAKHON SI THAMMARAT REPLICA
NUN'S HOUSES
SEATED BUDDHA
HOLY TREES
MEDITATION CHAMBERS
MINIATURE MOUNTAIN
SOUTH VIHARN
PREACHING BUDDHA
DVARAVATI SEATED BUDDHA
CHINESE TEMPLE
SEATED BUDDHA
EAST VIHARN
RECLINING BUDDHA
WEST VIHARN
SALA
BUDDHA STATUES
CHEDI
NORTH VIHARN (PRA RUANG ROCHANARIT)
MINIATURE MOUNTAIN
BELL CHAPELS
MUSEUM
PUBLIC HALL
TEMPLE OFFICES
0   25 m
CHAOPO PRASATONG
GRAND STAIRCASES
CHEUN RUTHAI GARDEN
PRAKAN PAKKLOD
CEREMONIAL HALLS

© AVALON TRAVEL PUBLISHING

Museum: This disorganized museum on the lower platform boasts art treasures such as Dvaravati statuary and Wheels of the Law, plus a great deal of kitsch oddities such as old money and stuffed fish. The Chinese Temple and the Sala Soprong beyond the stairway are used by resting pilgrims.

Dvaravati Seated Buddha: Carved from a piece of white quartzite, this monumental stone image is widely considered one of Thailand's great artistic masterpieces. The solemn, magnificent stone figure is seated in the so-called western style, an unusual pose favored by the Mon, who apparently borrowed the arrangement from Greco-Roman models. Robe contours and Western expression might remind you of Alexander the Great, the world conqueror who led his armies to the edge of Pakistan and whose artistic styles filtered east across India to the Mons of early Thailand. Do not miss this image.

Northeast Courtyard: Down below the circular platform stands the House of Chaopo Prasatong, Prakan Pakklod, and one of many holy trees connected with the life of Buddha.

East *Viharn:* Inside sits an enlightened Buddha under a bodhi tree painted by an artist of King Rama VI, and an important mural which traces the *chedi's* architectural evolution from a white, 11th-century Mon *stupa* to a Khmer *prang* erected after Suryavarman's triumph. Both were covered by the present *chedi* erected in 1860 by King Mongkut. The side walls display portraits of 48 ancient kings and heroic warriors.

Miniature Mountain: Nakhon Pathom's great *chedi* has plenty of oddities designed to impress, edify, and confuse the visitor. Depending on whom you talk to, this artificial grotto represents either monks' meditation chambers, a low-end Disneyland, or Mt. Meru, Buddhist abode of the gods.

South *Viharn:* The central antechamber holds an earth-touching Buddha surrounded by five disciples, and a Khmer Buddha meditating beneath a hooded *naga*. In front are two decorative chimneys used by Chinese worshippers to burn incense and gold paper. The southeast courtyard is filled with decrepit nuns' quarters and sacred bodhi trees.

Southern Courtyard: At the bottom of the staircase is another Buddha seated in the European position—not as impressive as the earlier example, but better for photographs. To the left

is a replica of the original *chedi;* to the right a replica of the famous *chedi* at Nakhon Si Thammarat.

West *Viharn:* A much-venerated nine-meter Buddha cast in the reign of Rama IV reclines in the outer chamber, while a smaller image with adoring pilgrims occupies the interior chamber. Note the hilarious sign, "Please take off your shoes and keep them in this chapel before they are invisible." Impressive old wooden buildings used as monks' retreats are located inside the southwest courtyard.

Cheun Ruthai Gardens: The northeast corner of the *chedi* has yellow bodhisattvas and mechanized circulating alms bowls used as surrealistic coin tosses.

Sanam Chand Palace

Another attraction in town is the summer residence built by King Vajiravudh (Rama VI) in an eccentric melange of Thai and English Tudor architectural styles. Some of the buildings are used for private government offices and closed to the public. Most curious is the statue of Yalay, King Vajiravudh's beloved pet dog killed "by some envious people."

Thap Charoen Hall was constructed in 1911 as the residence for the king's entourage. The beautiful gardens and hall were opened to the public in 1990 after several years of restoration by the Fine Arts Department. Today, the lovely white wooden building serves as the Institute of Western Regional Culture under the supervision of Silpakorn University. The culture of western Thailand is recounted with displays of paintings by Petchburi artists, puppets from Samut Songkram, and basketry from the Thai Song tribe.

Sanam Chand Palace is two km west of Pra Pathom Chedi. Open Tues.-Sat. 0900-1700.

Accommodations

Although usually just a stopover en route to Kanchanaburi, good hotels in all price ranges are available.

Mit Thaworn: Two cheap hotels are located near the train station. The Mit Thaworn and adjacent **Mit Phaisal** have rooms acceptable for a short stay. Both are located up a short alley off the busy street market. 305 Rot Fai Rd., tel. (034) 243115, 120-250B.

Siam Hotel: Somewhat better digs a few blocks west of the chedi. Thetsaban Rd., tel. (034) 241754, 150-300B.

Nakorn Inn: Best upscale choice in town is the Nakorn Inn off the main road. This hotel has a coffee shop, convention center, and 70 a/c rooms. 55 Rajwithi Rd., tel. (034) 251152, fax (034) 254998, 500-800B.

Whale Inn: A relatively new place with cleaner rooms at reasonable prices. All rooms are a/c plus there's a restaurant, disco, snooker hall, golf driving range, and sauna facilities. 151/79 Rajwithi Rd., tel. (034) 251020, 500-800B.

Restaurants

Finding a good restaurant in Nakhon Pathom is somewhat difficult. For a quick snack, try the fruit market on the road between the railway station and Pra Pathom Chedi, or the foodstalls on the grounds of the monument. Another option is the central market on Rajavithi Road. Nakhon Pathom is known for its version of *kao lam,* sticky rice and coconut steamed in a bamboo joint.

More formal settings are located in the a/c **Beer Hut** and the **Nakorn Inn,** which features live music in the evenings.

Transportation

Ordinary buses from Bangkok's Southern Bus Terminal in Thonburi depart every 15 minutes and take an hour to reach Nakhon Pathom. Trains depart nine times daily from Bangkok's Hualampong station and twice daily from the train station in Thonburi. Trains from the south also stop in Nakhon Pathom.

To return to Bangkok or continue to Kanchanaburi, take bus 81 from the east side of the *chedi,* next to the canal. The floating market at Damnern Saduak can be reached in one hour with bus 78 from the southeast corner of the *chedi.*

KANCHANABURI

Kanchanaburi, 122 km west of Bangkok, is known for the bridge made famous by Pierre Boulle's celebrated novel of WW II, *The Bridge on the River Kwai,* and the subsequent Academy Award-winning motion picture directed by David Lean. The bridge is rather ordinary, but Kanchanaburi's relaxed atmosphere, historic sights, and nearby waterfalls, caves, and river trips make this one of the *most* enjoyable destinations in Thailand.

Allow plenty of time to explore the town and province. A minimum of three days is needed to visit the sights around town, and a one-day journey up the River Kwai is nice. Several more days are needed to visit the nearby national parks, caves, forests, and waterfalls, and to make an excursion to the Thai/Burmese border at Three Pagodas Pass. Kanchanaburi is an excellent place to discover Thai countryside without having to travel all the way to the far north or extreme south.

Topography is somewhat confusing around the region. Two River Kwais flow through the province: Kwai Yai (Big Kwai) flows from Sri Nakarin Lake, while Kwai Noi (Little Kwai) starts at Krung Kravia Lake near the Burmese border. Both rivers merge near Kanchanaburi to form the Mae Klong River, which flows into the Gulf of Thailand.

History

Located along the road to the strategic Three Pagodas Pass, Kanchanaburi and, more importantly, Kwai Yai Valley, have long been one of the pivotal trade routes and military garrison centers of Thailand. The valley was first inhabited by Neolithic tribes who fashioned pottery and crude utensils over 3,000 years ago. Archaeological evidence of early human habitation is displayed at the Ban Kao Neolithic Museum, some 40 km west of Kanchanaburi. The region was captured in the 13th century by Khmer commanders who established a military citadel and religious complex at the village of Muang Sing. The ruins of these were restored and reopened to the public in 1987. After the fall of the Khmers, Ayuthayan rulers constructed a garrison town 20 km west of Kanchanaburi. In 1548, the Burmese marched several hundred thousand warriors through Three Pagodas Pass to wage war on Ayuthaya, which fell two centuries later. To monitor Burmese aggression, King Rama I founded Kanchanaburi as a military camp. The town, valley, and jungle pass also played a pivotal role in WW II.

Kanchanaburi received worldwide attention around proposals to construct a massive dam

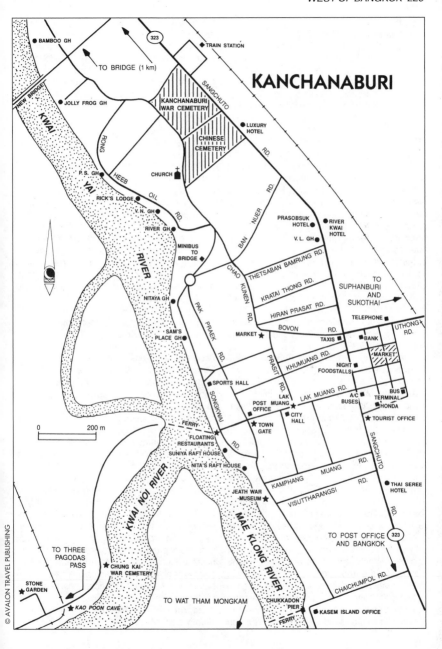

KANCHANABURI

TO BRIDGE (1 km)

323

TRAIN STATION

NEW BRIDGE

BAMBOO GH

JOLLY FROG GH

KANCHANABURI
WAR CEMETERY

SANGCHUTO

KWAI

RONG

HEEB

CHINESE
CEMETERY

LUXURY
HOTEL

P. S. GH

CHURCH

OIL

RICK'S LODGE

V. N. GH

RD.

YAI

RIVER GH

BAN NUER RD.

PRASOBSUK
HOTEL

RIVER
KWAI
HOTEL

V. L. GH

MINIBUS
TO
BRIDGE

RIVER

CHAO KUNEN

THETSABAN BAMRUNG RD.

TO
SUPHANBURI
AND
SUKOTHAI

NITAYA GH

PAK

PRAEK

KRATAI THONG RD.

HIRAN PRASAT RD.

RD.

BOVON   RD.

TELEPHONE

UTHONG
RD.

SAM'S
PLACE GH

MARKET

TAXIS

BANK

MARKET

PRASIT

KHUMUANG RD.

NIGHT
FOODSTALLS

SPORTS HALL

RD.

LAK MUANG RD.

BUS
TERMINAL

SONGKWAI

POST
OFFICE

LAK
MUANG

A/C
BUSES

HONDA

SANGCHUTO

FERRY

TOWN
GATE

CITY HALL

TOURIST OFFICE

FLOATING
RESTAURANTS

SUNIYA RAFT HOUSE

RD.

NITA'S RAFT HOUSE

KWAI NOI RIVER

JEATH WAR
MUSEUM

KAMPHANG   MUANG   RD.

THAI SEREE
HOTEL

VISUTTHARANGSI

MAE KLONG RIVER

RD.

TO THREE
PAGODAS
PASS

CHUNG KAI
WAR CEMETERY

TO POST OFFICE
AND BANGKOK

323

STONE
GARDEN

KAO POON CAVE

TO WAT THAM MONGKAM

CHUKKADON
PIER

CHAICHUMPOL RD.

KASEM ISLAND OFFICE

FERRY

0   200 m

© AVALON TRAVEL PUBLISHING

near the Burmese border. Outcries from environmentalists and Britain's Prince Charles, plus a general disenchantment over massive dam projects, led to the cancellation of the proposal. The Nam Choan Dam project was also scrapped to save several species of endangered wildlife and prevent widespread soil erosion. Environmental causes have gained widespread public support in recent times.

JEATH War Museum

First stop should be the JEATH War Museum. JEATH is an acronym for the primary nations which participated in local action: Japan, England, America/Australia, Thailand, Holland. Modeled after POW camps of the period, the simple bamboo structures contain war memorabilia, photographs of emaciated prisoners, personal recollections, and graphic descriptions of tortures committed by the Japanese. The museum is managed by a Thai monk, Maha Tomson Thongproh, who lives in the adjacent Wat Chaichumphon. More than just a museum, JEATH is a simple, immensely moving memorial to the 16,000 Allied POWs and 50,000-100,000 Asians who died from lack of medical attention, starvation, and torture during construction of the 400-km Death Railway.

The museum is open daily 0830-1630 and admission is 20B.

The Bridge over the River Kwai

Kanchanaburi's most famous sight is the simple bridge constructed in just over 16 months by some 60,000 Allied prisoners and 250,000 Asian slave-laborers. The present structure is physically uninspiring—just eight gray, riveted spans on moss-stained concrete pylons—though the historical and emotional elements are fascinating. Best times to visit are 1030, 1430, and 1630 when the Nam Tok train slowly crosses the bridge. The remainder of the day the structure serves as a footbridge across the river to cool picnic grounds on the other bank. Be careful walking across the bridge and watch out for sprinting motorcycles. A popular light-and-sound show is held at the bridge during River Kwai Week in late November or early December.

Misconceptions about the bridge are commonplace, since most visitors only know the movie *The Bridge on the River Kwai*. The iron bridge in Kanchanaburi isn't the original wooden bridge which played a pivotal role in the movie. The old wooden bridge, which once crossed the river about three km south, was abandoned by the Japanese in favor of a sturdier iron structure that was hauled up from Java in pieces. Author Boulle's character, Colonel Nicholson (portrayed by Alec Guinness), was a fictionalized commander who never existed during the construction of the bridge. Colonel Nicholson and other British engineers were portrayed in the movie as instrumental in the design of the bridge; in reality, the Japanese were solely responsible for the project. The movie also overlooked the thousands of Asians who worked on the bridge and died in appalling numbers during construction of the entire railway. Furthermore, the film portrays the escape of Commander Shear (played by William Holden) from camp to reach Allied hands in Sri Lanka and his love affair with a beautiful nurse. Shear then returns to Kanchanaburi to blow up the bridge. In fact, nobody ever escaped from Kanchanaburi and lived to tell the story.

The bridge is five km north of town—too far to walk. Hire a bike or motorcycle, or take a minibus from Chao Kunen Road.

Around the Bridge

Surrounding the bridge are several other stops worth a brief visit, plus an assortment of tourist shops and riverside restaurants. **Solos Restaurant** has good views from the patio terrace, and offers an escape from the tour buses and schoolchildren.

Train Museum: Just opposite the bridge you'll find a steam engine and an ingenious Japanese supply truck that operated on both road and rails.

Art Gallery: Some 30 meters south of the bridge is a big, garish building which features some of the finest modern murals in Thailand. Paintings on the second floor relate ancient battles between the Thais and Burmese, while third-floor murals tell Thai history and provide portraits of prime ministers and other important political figures. This private museum also features Khmer-style woodcarvings, a pair of elaborate Burmese Buddhas, and excellent paintings of Chinese deities.

Japanese War Memorial: Also located slightly south of the bridge is a simple monu-

A LIFE FOR EVERY SLEEPER

*O*ne of the most famous stories of WW II was the construction of the railway between Kanchanaburi in Thailand and Thanbyuzayat in Myanmar. Construction began on 16 September 1942 after Japanese sea routes were effectively blocked by Allied aircraft and submarine operations near Singapore and in the Straits of Malacca. To provide supplies to their bases in Myanmar, the Japanese conscripted over 50,000 Allied prisoners and 250,000 Asian laborers from Japanese-held countries in Southeast Asia. Initial estimates by engineers that completion of the 415-km railway would take five years were overruled by the Japanese High Command, who ordered the project finished in an incredibly short span of just 12 months.

As progress on the Death Railway fell behind schedule, the Japanese demanded more men who, under the most primitive conditions, worked around the clock and died in frightening numbers from malaria, dysentery, beri-beri, cholera, and starvation—described on death certificates as "Post Dysenteric Inanition." The cost was "a life for every sleeper" (railroad tie) laid over its most difficult sections.

The flimsy wooden bridge which first crossed the River Kwai was abandoned in favor of a stronger iron structure imported from Java. On 16 October 1943 the line was joined at Konkoita as Japanese film crews recorded the event for propaganda purposes. Although an estimated 50,000-100,000 lives were sacrificed, the project was not a success; the bridge was only used *once* before American B-24 bombers from Sri Lanka destroyed the fourth, fifth, and sixth spans in February 1945. The Allies controlled the bridge after the war, but sold the structure for US$2 million to the Thai government a few years later. As war reparations, the Japanese replaced the missing curved girders with two incongruously square beams ironically stamped "Made in Japan."

Kwai River Bridge

ment erected by the Japanese and dedicated to those who "died through illness during the course of the construction"—a pleasant enough euphemism.

Kanchanaburi War Cemetery

With its neatly arranged tombstones and poignant messages, this final resting place for 6,982 Allied war prisoners forms one of the most moving tableaux in Southeast Asia. A private foundation in London keeps the cemetery supplied with fresh flowers and supports the Thai gardeners who maintain the lovely grounds. The dead are eulogized on a brass plaque at the entrance, yet not a single grave marker commemorates the estimated 50,000 Asians who perished during construction of the bridge. Among the gravestone messages:

"We think of him still as the same and say: He is not dead, he is just away."

"At the going down of the sun and in the morning, we will remember them."

"Your duty nobly done, my son, sleep on. Mother."

"We shall always remember you smiling, sleep on beloved."

Chinese Cemetery

The adjacent Chinese cemetery is a study in contrasts. Pauper tombs are hidden away against the walls, while tombstones of the wealthy are elevated like Chinese pagodas. Burial sites are arranged according to the principles of *feng shui,* a Taoist belief in divine geomancy, which attempts to balance the ancient principles of yin and yang.

Other Sights

Several other modest attractions are scattered around Kanchanaburi.

Lak Muang: Kanchi's town pillar encloses a Hindu phallic symbol at the original town center, not far from an old town gate and several historic buildings now used as municipal offices. Palmists and fortune-tellers do business across the street from the pillar.

Smashed Car: A curious monument to bad driving sits on Sangchuto Road near the a/c bus terminal. Well worth a photograph.

Old Town: Unlike many of the newer towns in Thailand, Kanchanaburi retains vestiges of its past on several small streets such as Pak Praek Road and near the vegetable market on Chao Kunen Road.

River Trips

A visit to Kanchanaburi would not be complete without a boat trip. Most guesthouses can arrange short evening cruises or full-day expeditions to nearby attractions. Three-hour sunset cruises in longtail boats from Nita's Raft House cost 100B to visit the bridge and Chung Kai War Cemetery. Expensive full-day raft trips can also be arranged through better hotels and conventional travel offices such as DT Tours. River trips with "Thai Water Skiing" and "starring Master Entertainer and Dare Devil Sunya" leave on demand from Sunya Rux's Discotheque Raft.

River trips can also be made at upriver locations. Luxury raft hotels sponsor extended river trips Sept.-March, but not during the dry season when the river is low or during the dangerous rainy season. Alternatively, eight-person longtails can be chartered at Pak Sang Pier (near Nam Tok some 60 km upriver from Kanchanaburi) to visit upriver caves and waterfalls. Prices from Pak Sang Pier are posted at the train station: to Lawa Caves 300B, Sai Yok Yai Falls 500B, Daow Dung Cave 700B. For more details see **Route 323 to the Burmese Border,** below. Be prepared to bargain with the boat operator.

a life for every sleeper

Tours and Trekking

A wide variety of tours can be arranged through most guesthouses and hotels. Sample tours include: Tham Than Lot National Park, Erawan Waterfall, and sapphire mines; Erawan Falls and the bridge; and Prathat Caves, Erawan Falls, and the bridge. Mr. Pirom Angkudie, civil servant, historian, and amateur archaeologist, can be recommended for his three-hour sunset tours of nearby historical and cultural attractions. You can contact him through most guesthouses in Kanchi.

Trekking near Sangklaburi and the Burmese border is another possibility. **Travelers Trekking** in the V.N. Guesthouse leads a four-day trek that includes visits to Karen villages, an elephant ride, a bamboo river trip, a run through a bat cave, and swimming under waterfalls. Best Tours on Khao San Road in Bangkok can help with reservations.

Budget Accommodations

Local accommodations can be divided between floating guesthouses on the Kwai Yai River and conventional hotels on Sangchuto Road. River-based guesthouses in the center of town are pleasant during the week but incredibly noisy on weekends when Bangkokians flood the region. To escape the all-night parties and blasting disco boats, try the guesthouses north of the park toward the bridge.

The following guesthouses are described starting from central Kanchanaburi and moving toward the bridge.

Nita's Raft House: Several floating crash pads are located along the banks near the city park. Nita's is a popular choice, but can be very noisy at night from the floating discos. Ask for Supachai and Miss Seangthip. 27 Pakprak Rd., tel. (034) 514521, 60B communal floorspace, 100-200B private room.

Sam's Place: One of the better riverside choices in central Kanchanaburi features a beautiful foyer and cozy restaurant (with a *farang* menu), wooden reclining chairs facing a pond filled with ducks, and several detached bamboo bungalows with small porches. American-educated Sam and his staff can help with river trips, motorcycle rentals, and advice on local transportation. Songkwai Rd., tel. (034) 513971, fax (034) 512023, 100-250B fan, 200-400B a/c, 250-300B large bungalow with private bath.

Nitaya Guesthouse: At the north end of the riverside park is an old favorite with over a dozen rickety bamboo bungalows, disco boat, and river tours daily at 1300. Songkwai Rd., tel. (034) 513341, 120-180B.

River Guesthouse: Several guesthouses can be found on Soi 2 to the north of central Kanchanaburi. All are somewhat distant from the discos and fairly quiet. River Guesthouse is a simple place run by Mr. Ek, who also sponsors boat tours. 42 Rongheeboi Rd., Soi 2, tel. (034) 512491, 80-200B.

Rick's Lodge: A friendly place run by a German-speaking Thai from Bangkok, Rick's has several floating bungalows and 12 bilevel rooms senselessly crammed together back from the river. River views are blocked by trees. Try the homemade Farmhouse Bread in the Salad House across the street. 48/5 Rongheeboi Rd., Soi 2, tel. (034) 514831, 220-350B.

P.S. Guesthouse: Excellent views and a cozy restaurant make this a good choice. 54 Rongheeboi Rd., Soi 2, tel. (034) 513039, 60-100B common bath, 140-200B private bath.

Jolly Frog Guesthouse: The largest guesthouse in Kanchanaburi has over 50 rooms facing a central courtyard filled with palms and grass. Rooms inside the two-story thatched buildings are small and ordinary with mattresses placed on the floor. Services include motorcycle rentals, a spacious circular dining hall, German management, and minibuses to Bangkok daily at 1100 and 1430. 28 Maenamwae Rd., tel. (034) 514579, 120-250B.

Bamboo Guesthouse: The most idyllic guesthouse in Kanchanaburi is located at the end of a dirt road about 300 meters before the bridge. It features a big lawn with a small pond, and is often filled but otherwise a fine spot. Call first to check on vacancies. 3-5 Soi Vietnam, tel. (034) 512532, 100-250B bamboo bungalows, 250-700B upstairs rooms in a red brick building.

V.L. Guesthouse: One of the best land-based guesthouses is a modern place opposite the River Kwai Hotel. Rooms are very clean and well furnished, and include a private bath; an excellent deal for anyone who dislikes riverside accommodation. 18/11 Sangchuto Rd., tel. (034) 513546, 150-200B fan, 250-400B a/c.

Moderate Accommodations

Most midpriced rooms in the 400-800B range are located outside of town and described below under "River Kwai Raft Resorts."

Kasem Island Resort: Kanchanaburi's first upscale raft hotel features seven bamboo cottages and 20 houseboats with private baths, patios overlooking the river, and an excellent floating restaurant. Facilities are only adequate but managers are making improvements. Kasem Island head office is located at Chukadon Wharf, 27 Chaichumpol Rd., tel. (034) 513359, Bangkok reservation tel. (02) 255-3603 and fax (02) 255-3604, 750-1,000B.

Luxury Accommodations

The tourist boom finally brought the big boys to Kanchanaburi. Properties that opened over the last decade include a Sheraton, an Imperial, and a hotel operated by the Siam City chain.

River Kwai Hotel: Kanchi's oldest upscale hotel is popular with businesspeople, tour groups, and Japanese visitors. All rooms are a/c and come with private bath, TV, and video. 248 Sangchuto, tel. (034) 511184, 1,200-2,600B.

Felix River Kwai Resort: A luxurious property near the famous bridge. Facilities include two pools, tennis courts, and five restaurants. Tambon Ta Makam, tel. (034) 515061, fax (034) 515086, Bangkok tel. (02) 255-5767, fax (02) 255-5769, 3,600-6,000B.

River Kwai Raft Resorts

Kanchanaburi Province currently lists over 50 registered raft hotels on the upper reaches of the Kwai Yai (near Nam Tok and Sai Yok Falls), at Sri Nakarin Lake, and on Krung Kravia Lake near the Burmese border. The average daily per-person charge of 800B often includes three meals and boat transportation. Some are quite simple and operate without electricity; others have swimming pools and a/c rooms with hot water.

Those most popular are described below. Travel agents in Bangkok make reservations, though these are only necessary on weekends. Most of the following properties provide transportation from downtown Kanchanaburi to the raft hotel. The local tourist office and travel agents near the bus stop can also help with details and phone calls.

Home Phu Toey Resort: Probably the most popular river resort in the Kanchanaburi region. Bungalows include running water and private bath but lack electricity, phones, TVs, and other signs of "civilization." Evening meals are followed by Mon dances accompanied by Burmese gongs and cymbals. Located on the Kwai Noi River, 60 km from Kanchanaburi. Reservations can be made from travel agents in Bangkok. Upper Kwai Noi River near Pak Sang Pier, Bangkok tel. (02) 280-3488, 1,000-1,600B.

River Kwai Village Hotel: A 60-unit lodge composed of a dozen floating rafts and five long-

houses subdivided into private chalets. All rooms are a/c with full amenities. Popular with group tours from Bangkok. Upper Kwai Noi River near Pak Sang Pier (70 km from Kanchanaburi), Bangkok tel. (02) 251-7552, 800-1,000B per person including meals.

Restaurants

Kanchanaburi's best restaurants are the half dozen floating cafes tied up at the south end of the fitness park. Most are marked in Thai script only, but all specialize in seafood and highly prized river carp, favored for its fatty and succulent meat. Unfortunately, the giant *pla yi sok* (the Julien carp used for those terrific street signs) has been hunted nearly to extinction, and other species now substitute.

Krua Thien Tong: Arrive for sunset and try deep-fried freshwater catfish or frog legs fried in garlic. Songkwai Rd. Moderate.

Pae Karn: Another floating restaurant known for its *log tong* and country-style Thai dishes such as *tom yam pla* made with river carp. Songkwai Rd. Moderate.

Foodstalls: Cheap meals are found at the outdoor foodstalls on Sangchuto Road near the bus terminal.

Punee Restaurant: The first *farang* bar in Kanchi is owned by Danny and his wife, Punee. Danny does local tours, sells sapphires, rents well-maintained motorcycles, gives fishing advice ("don't bother"), operates a book exchange, and dabbles in real estate while running the bar. Ban Nuer Rd. Inexpensive.

Services

The tourist office (tel. 034-511200) on Sangchuto Road, one of the best TAT branches in Thailand, offers maps and information on river huts, plus tips on local transportation and conditions at the Burmese border. Post offices are located on Sangchuto Road and on Lak Muang Road near the city pillar. Visas can be extended at Thai Immigration, 286 Sangchuto Road. International phone service is available from the Telephone Center on Uthong Road. An excellent map of the Kanchanaburi region is published by Prannok Vidhaya Publisher, though their town details fail to list most of the newer guesthouses.

Getting There from Bangkok

Ordinary and a/c buses to Kanchanaburi leave every 15 minutes and take three hours from the Southern Bus Terminal in Thonburi. Trains for Kanchanaburi leave twice daily at 0800 and 1350 from Thonburi station.

Weekend Train Tours

Whirlwind tours sponsored by the State Railways are also possible. A special train leaves Bangkok's Hualampong station weekends at 0635, stops at the *chedi* in Nakhon Pathom for 40 minutes (0735-0815), pauses for 30 minutes at the Kanchi bridge (0930-1000), and takes a three-hour lunch break at Nam Tok (1130-1430), enough time to visit the nearby waterfall or go down to the river for a quick look. On the return trip, it stops for 45 minutes at the war cemetery (1605-1650) before arriving back in Bangkok at 1930. Whew! Advanced bookings can be made by calling the State Railways Advance Booking Office at (02) 225-6964.

The State Railways also sponsors other weekend tours of the Kanchanaburi region. The rafting program costs 340B and includes Nakhon Pathom and local sights, plus a short raft trip under the bridge. Another tour for 300B includes Nakhon Pathom, Kanchanaburi, and the Khmer ruins at Prasat Muang Sing. The final option at 280B includes Nakhon Pathom, Kanchanaburi, Sri Nakarin Dam, and Erawan Falls.

Getting Around

Bicycling is the perfect way to get around Kanchanaburi. Old bikes can be rented from most guesthouses for about 20B per day. Motorcycles cost 150-250B per day from the Honda dealer and various guesthouses. Experienced cyclists will find this an excellent way to explore the countryside and visit remote temples and caves. Motorcycle prices and conditions vary widely, so it's best to shop around. Jeep rentals cost 800-1,000B per day; shops near the bus terminal provide the cars.

Slow Train to Nowhere

A slow but romantic way to explore the historic railway is the funky third-class train which leaves Kanchanaburi daily at 0600 and 1030 and arrives in Nam Tok two hours later. The 1030 train allows you three hours to visit the river or a nearby waterfall before catching the 1530 train back to Kanchanaburi. Creaky, hair-raising, and historically poignant, many travelers consider the *Nam Tok Special* the most memorable train ride in Thailand.

Getting Away
Kanchanaburi is connected by road and rail to Bangkok and other neighboring provinces.

Bangkok: Ordinary bus 81 for Bangkok and Nakhon Pathom departs from the main bus terminal. Air-conditioned buses leave every 15 minutes from the office on Sangchuto Road. Share taxis wait at the nearby intersection.

North: Travelers heading north should go direct rather than backtrack to Bangkok. To Ayuthaya, take bus 419 from Uthong Road to Suphanburi (two to three hours), then yellow bus 703 to Ayuthaya (one hour). To Sukothai, take bus 487 to Nakhon Sawan (four hours), then bus 99 to Sukothai (three hours).

South: For Petchburi, take bus 461 to Ratchaburi, then bus 73 to Petchburi. For Hua Hin, take bus 461 to Ratchaburi, then bus 71 to Hua Hin. Bus services are also available from Ratchaburi to Surat Thani and Phuket.

Floating Market: Public transportation is also available to the floating market at Damnern Saduak. An early start is essential to reach the market during prime time, 0700-0900. From the main bus terminal in Kanchanaburi, take yellow bus 461 to Bang Pae intersection, walk down the road, then take bus 78 or the minibus to Damnern Saduak. The market is one km south. Allow two hours for the journey. Alternatively, take bus 81 to Nakhon Pathom and then bus 78 to Damnern Saduak.

SOUTH OF KANCHANABURI

South of Kanchanaburi are several temples such as Wat Tam Mongkam (five km from town), Wat Tam Sua (16 km), and Wat Pra Dong (40 km). None are major architectural triumphs, but all are unique in their sense of kitsch and unbridled commercialism.

Transportation is somewhat difficult to these southern attractions. Wat Tam Mongkam and the Tha Muang temples are easy day journeys with public transportation, but the more distant

Wat Pra Dong and the Don Chedi Memorial require private wheels. A few suggestions are given below. Motorcyclists can reach all three sites in a single day. Accommodations are unnecessary in this region since all temples can be visited on day-trips.

Wat Tam Mongkam
The Cave Temple of the Golden Dragon was chiefly known for the 75-year-old Thai nun who, meditating and whistling, floated in a pool of water. The old woman has been replaced with a younger nun who performs only for large crowds on weekends. This neat trick attracts a steady stream of devout Thais, but many *farangs* find the commercialism and zoolike atmosphere rather tawdry.

Aside from the floating meditation routine, the temple complex features nondescript modern *wats* adjacent to the parking lot, and a maze of limestone caves to the rear. The entrance is reached after a long climb up the stairs, which stop near an old Chinese hermit who sits in quiet meditation. The illuminated walkway through a cave leads to viewpoints over Kanchanaburi and the surrounding countryside.

Wat Tam Mongkam is located across the Mae Klong River, some five km south of Kanchanaburi. Visitors with rented bicycles can pedal to the ferry crossing on Chaichumpol Road, cross the river, then continue three km south to the temple. Motorcyclists can use the new bridge farther south down Sangchuto Road. Public transportation may be available; inquire at the TAT office.

Temples near Tha Muang
Two very impressive but half-completed temples are situated on a limestone hilltop near Tha Muang, 16 km south of Kanchanaburi. Wat Tam Sua, the Chinese-style pagoda to the left, is fronted by a fat, jolly Buddha surrounded by 18 superbly carved figures. To the right is Wat Tam Kao Noi which, perhaps in a show of religious competition, is separated from Wat Tam Sua by a concrete wall. This attractive Thai-style temple offers a worship hall with cool marble floors, mound-shaped tower, and gigantic Buddha complete with automated treadmill to help expedite monetary donations. From the terrace you'll enjoy excellent views over the valley of Kanchanaburi.

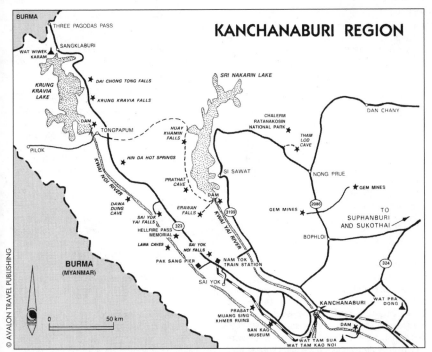

KANCHANABURI REGION

To reach the temples, take bus 461 or 81 to the dam near Tha Muang. Motorcycle taxis charge 30-40B for the roundtrip excursion to the temples, four km east.

Wat Pra Dong
This isolated temple, 40 km east of Kanchanaburi, is revered for its immense yellow-frocked stone where, according to Thai tradition, Buddha reclined before ascending to the heavens. A young monk will unlock the main *bot*. A Buddha footprint surmounts the hill to the left.

NORTH OF KANCHANABURI~ ROUTE 3199

The waterfalls, limestone mountains, caves, and other natural wonders north of Kanchanaburi comprise one of the most beautiful regions in Thailand.

Attractions are mostly natural landscapes rather than historic or religious monuments. The region boasts three immense national parks, dozens of deep caves and plunging waterfalls, and a wildlife conservation park at Khao Salakpra. Highlights include Bophloi (a gem-mining town 50 km from Kanchanaburi), Erawan Falls in Erawan National Park (65 km), Sri Nakarin Dam at the south end of Sri Nakarin Lake (70 km), Pratat Cave near Sri Nakarin Dam (75 km), Tham Lod Cave in Chalerm Ratanakosin National Park (100 km), and Huay Khamin Falls in Sri Nakarin National Park (102 km).

Erawan Falls is unquestionably the most popular sight because of its superb waterfalls and easy accessibility from Kanchanaburi.

Accommodations
Accommodations abound throughout the region. The TAT in Kanchanaburi has a complete list and can make specific recommendations. Budget hotels are located in the towns of Si Sawat, Nong

Prue, and Bophloi, but most visitors head out to stay in a lodge floating on Sri Nakarin Lake.

Kwai Yai River Huts: Fairly decent floating cottages on the lake near Si Sawat, chiefly patronized by Thais with an occasional Western visitor. Tambon Tha Kradan, tel. (02) 252-9337, 750-1,000B.

Romklao Rafts: Very small but certainly upscale place with just 10 luxury floating cottages. 51/5 Moo 2, Tambon Tha Kradan, tel. (034) 516521, 2,500-5,000B.

Erawan Resort: One of the longtime favorites with both budget and midpriced rooms in a fine setting near Khao Salak Pra Wildlife Conservation Park. 140 Moo 4 Kanchanaburi-Erawan Rd., tel. (01) 907-8210, 200-1,000B.

Pailin Rafts: Popular midpriced option with just nine bamboo structures at the edge of the lake. Tambon Tha Kradan, tel. (02) 745-2239, 900-1,000B.

Transportation
Transportation is straightforward. Popular destinations along Route 3199 such as Erawan Falls and Si Sawat can be reached with public bus 8170. Bus 325 reaches the gem mines at Bophloi and Tham Lod Cave west of Nong Prue. Inexpensive group tours to all these attractions can be arranged through most guesthouses and hotels.

Erawan Falls
The 300,000 *rai* of forested area around Erawan Falls were declared a national park in 1967. Its name was changed from Khao Salob to that of the divine elephant whose shape is found in a natural rock formation at the top of the falls. Erawan National Park consists of limestone mountains from which the Erawan Falls crash down through 10 levels before emptying into the Kwai Yai River. The lower falls and swimming pools are perpetually crowded with Thai tourists who rarely make the arduous climb to the far superior falls on the upper sections of the mountain. Keep climbing, and remember to bring along a swimsuit and sneakers for the hike. Unless you enjoy suffocating crowds, do not visit this park on weekends. As with all waterfalls in Southeast Asia, Erawan is best visited during the rainy season July-Nov. when water is most plentiful.

Accommodations are available in the park in a bamboo dormitory for 60-100B and in larger 10-person park chalets for 600B. Ten km south of the park entrance is the popular **Erawan Resort** (tel. 034-513001), where upscale bungalows cost 600-1,200B.

Erawan National Park and falls are 65 km from Kanchanaburi. A full day is necessary to enjoy the falls. Bus 8170 to Erawan departs daily at 0800 from the bus terminal and takes almost two hours to reach the park turnoff, located about one km from the park entrance. Erawan Falls is another two km west of the park entrance. The last bus back to Kanchanaburi departs around 1600.

Sri Nakarin Lake
Sri Nakarin Lake is an immense freshwater lake formed by the Sri Nakarin Dam at the southern end. Accommodations are listed above. The lake offers fishing, luxurious raft hotels, and weekend boat tours aboard the *J.R. Queen*. Prathat Cave is 10 km northwest of the dam on the west side of the lake.

Sri Nakarin National Park
The region's second most popular set of falls, Huay Khamin ("Turmeric Falls"), is located in Sri Nakarin National Park some 25 km northwest of Erawan National Park. Huay Khamin falls are actually larger and more powerful than the falls at Erawan, but the additional travel time minimizes the number of visitors.

Accommodations are available at the park headquarters and in several raft houses on the lake. The Kanchanaburi TAT can help with recommendations and reservations.

The park can be reached by taking bus 8170 to Tha Kradan Pier on the east side of the lake about 24 km north of the dam, followed by a local ferry ride across the lake to the park entrance. Visitors with private transportation can drive directly to the park via the west-side road.

Bophloi
Both blue and star sapphires are mined from open pits that pocket the farmland north and west of Bophloi. Many of the mines have been exhausted, but enough activity remains to make this a worthwhile stop for visitors interested in traditional mining activities. Gem prices are rea-

sonably low from local shops, though many of the stones are either worthless or clever synthetics. Reach Bophloi by motorcycle, jeep, or organized tour.

Chalerm Ratanakosin National Park

This 59-square-km national park, 100 km north of Kanchanaburi, is chiefly visited for its thick jungle, two immense caves of great interest to speleologists, and three waterfalls within easy walking distance of park headquarters. Tham Lod Yai, the largest of the caves with an estimated depth of over 500 meters, is filled with unusual limestone formations capped with miniature temples and images of the Buddha. The three waterfalls are Trai Trang, Than Ngun, and Than Thong.

The park has the usual choice of accommodations. Backpackers can pitch a tent near headquarters for just 20B per night. Accommodations operated by the park service include dormitories for 100B and ten-person chalets from 600B. Reservations should be made in advance through the TAT office in Kanchanaburi.

Chalerm Ratanakosin National Park can be reached with bus 325 to the small town of Nong Prue, from where minitrucks (10B) continue west to the park entrance. One-way travel consumes almost four hours, making this an overnight destination.

ROUTE 323 TO THE BURMESE BORDER

Route 323, the road northwest toward the Burmese border, is the most popular side trip from Kanchanaburi. Dozens of sights are located along the road, which parallels the Kwai Noi River. Many scenes in *The Deer Hunter* (jumping from helicopters into the river, and Russian roulette with the Viet Cong) were filmed near Sai Yok Yai Falls on the Kwai Noi River.

Attractions: Attractions in the area include the Ban Kao Museum (Neolithic remains 38 km from Kanchanaburi), Wat Muang Sing Khmer Temple (43 km), Nam Tok (the railway terminus 60 km from Kanchanaburi), Hellfire Pass Memorial (78 km), Lawa Caves (75 km), Sai Yok Yai Falls (104 km), Hin Da Hot Springs (130 km), Tongpapum (153 km), Sangklaburi (235

km), and the border crossing at Three Pagodas Pass (241 km). No wonder people spend weeks around Kanchanaburi.

Accommodations: Accommodations on Route 323 and along the Upper Kwai Noi River are among the best in the Kanchanaburi region. An excellent way to relax and enjoy the area's great natural appeal is on an upriver raft house. A few are described under **River Kwai Raft Resorts,** above. The Kanchanaburi TAT office can also make recommendations. The TAT has a complete list of over 50 guesthouses and river houses outside Kanchanaburi. River-based accommodations are also available on Krung Kravia Lake near Tongpapum. Land-based hotels and guesthouses are found in Tongpapum, Sangklaburi, and Three Pagodas Pass. More details and specific recommendations are given in the corresponding chapters.

Transportation: Transportation options include group tours, Nam Tok train, public buses, and motorcycle rentals. Inexpensive group tours are arranged by guesthouses, hotels, and travel agencies in Kanchanaburi. Prices vary sharply between low-end guesthouses and expensive travel agencies, making comparison shopping absolutely necessary. The Nam Tok train journey, described in the **Slow Train to Nowhere** section above, is an excellent way to see the countryside and enjoy one of the best train journeys in Thailand. Most visitors take the 1030 train from the central station in Kanchanaburi and return on the 1530 train from Nam Tok.

Most attractions in the Kwai Noi Valley (except for remote spots such as Prasat Muang Sing and Ban Kao Museum) can be reached with bus 8203 departing from the main bus terminal in Kanchanaburi. Bus 8203 plies the highway between Kanchanaburi and Three Pagodas Pass from sunrise until sunset. Service is frequent and buses pick up passengers every 15-30 minutes. Motorcyclists can reach most nearby sights in a single day before returning to Kanchanaburi. Alternatively, you can rent a motorcycle for several days and travel all the way up to the Burmese border at Three Pagodas Pass. Despite the danger of the horrendous driving habits of most Thais, motorcycles provide an unparalleled degree of flexibility and allow you to quickly visit even the most remote destinations.

Chung Kai War Cemetery

This war cemetery, almost identical to its counterpart in town, lies about three km away on the banks of the Kwai Noi River. Chung Kai contains some 1,750 inscribed tombstones set on the former site of the Chung Kai POW camp. The tombstones at Chung Kai and the 6,982 at the Allied War Cemetery in Kanchanaburi account for only half the estimated 16,000 Allied prisoners who died during the railway construction. The missing prisoners were cremated and left unaccounted for by the Japanese.

The cemetery is best reached with rented bicycle or motorcycle taken across the ferry near the floating restaurants on Songkwai Road. Hikers might take the ferry and then attempt to hitch a ride to the cemetery. A long wait can be expected since traffic is very light.

Kao Poon Cave

Limestone caves near Kanchanaburi often serve as Buddhist temples filled with Buddhist and Saivite images illuminated with electric lights. Kao Poon Cave, 6 km from Kanchanaburi, is behind Wat Tham Kao Poon, where friendly monks have erected English-language signs and volunteer as guides through the caves. A small donation is appropriate after the tour.

Stone Gardens

Continue over the hill from Wat Tham Kao Poon and turn right near the Thai Agricultural College, marked in Thai script only. Another left and then right leads to a curious collection of volcanic formations surrounded by poured concrete walkways.

Ban Kao Neolithic Museum

Something good did come from the construction of the Death Railway. In 1943 a Dutch prisoner of war named Van Heekeren stumbled across some Neolithic artifacts while working on the railway near Nam Tok. In 1956 an American anthropologist, Heider, confirmed the importance of Van Heekeren's discoveries. Intrigued by these reports, Thai and Danish archaeologists undertook systematic excavations in 1961 and successfully uncovered evidence that the Kwai Noi Valley had been inhabited by early humans for over 10,000 years. A new chapter in the prehistory of Southeast Asia had been opened.

A small museum housing a modest collection of pottery, ax heads, and jewelry made from animal bone has been constructed beside an open-air burial site. Major artifacts have been transferred to the National Museum in Bangkok.

Ban Kao is on a side road about 10 km off the main highway and is difficult to reach without private transportation. With the opening of Prasat Muang Sing, however, most guesthouses and hotels can now arrange day tours to Ban Kao, Muang Sing, and other nearby sights such as Sai Yok and Nam Tok. Independent travelers can take the train to Ban Kao (Tha Kilen) station, then walk or hitch the remaining two km west to Muang Sing and six km south to Ban Kao. Motorcyclists can easily visit Ban Kao and Muang Sing before continuing north to Sai Yok and Three Pagodas Pass.

Several popular raft houses are located on the Kwai Noi near the Ban Kao Museum. **River Kwai Farm** (Bangkok tel. 02-235-6433), 4 km south from Ban Kao train station, is a well-known raft lodge with rooms including meals from 600B.

Prasat Muang Sing

What were Cambodians doing so far west? This marvelous Khmer temple complex and military outpost, 45 km from Kanchanaburi, was constructed during the Lopburi Period, 1157-1207. It served as a Khmer trading post along the Kwai Noi River and protection against Burmese invasion through Three Pagodas Pass. Now completely restored, Muang Sing ("City of Lions") marks the westernmost advance of Cambodian power and provides elegant testimony to their vast territorial claims. The 460-*rai* park was declared a national historic park under the administration of the Fine Arts Department in 1987.

Muang Sing encompasses four groups of ruins composed of laterite bricks and surrounded by earthern walls arranged to suggest the cosmological symbolism so favored by Angkorian rulers. Entrance is made through reconstructed gates which flank a dusty road that leads to the central compound. A small outdoor museum to the right of the main complex contains sculptures of Mahayana Buddhist deities and stuccowork removed from the interior shrines. Prasat Muang Sing, the principal shrine, faces east toward Angkor. Hemmed in by four laterite walls oriented toward each of the cardinal directions, the interior holds a sculpture of Aval-okitesvara, which establishes the sanctuary as a Mahayana Buddhist center.

A pair of Neolithic skeletons are displayed in situ on the riverbanks to the south outside the earthern walls. Other Neolithic remains discovered near Muang Sing have been removed to the museums at Ban Kao and the National Museum in Bangkok.

Idyllic raft houses are plentiful near Prasat Muang Sing and Ban Kao to the south. Within sight of the burial site at Muang Sing are several raft houses where bamboo rooms with three meals cost from 600B per day. North of Muang Sing are the **Yang Thone River Kwai** and **River Kwai Jungle House,** two raft hotels with floating bamboo bungalows from 600B.

Prasat Muang Sing Historical Park is open daily 0800-1600, and entrance is 20B.

Nam Tok

Nam Tok, 60 km from Kanchanaburi, is a nondescript town at the end of the railway line. Most visitors arrive on the 1030 train from Kanchanaburi and leave Nam Tok on the 1530 train. Public buses back to Kanchanaburi ply the highway until nightfall. A sign posted at the train station lists suggested prices for trips up the nearby Kwai Noi River: Lawa Cave 300B, Sai Yok Yai Falls 500B, Dawa Dung Cave 700B. Be prepared to bargain with the boat operator.

The **Suvatana Hotel** in Nam Tok has basic rooms for 80-100B, while the **Sai Yok Noi Bungalows** 300 meters north along the highway has better rooms for 200-500B.

Kwai Noi River Trip

Several good explorations start from Nam Tok. Visitors short on time might hire a *samlor* or walk three km north to Sai Yok Noi (Kao Phang) Waterfall, an unremarkable and perpetually crowded place surrounded by restaurants and tacky souvenir stalls.

A better option is to take a tricycle from the train station for 10B down to Pak Sang Pier. From here, eight-person longtail boats can be hired for upriver journeys. Boat prices are listed at the train station, but most journeys are prohibitively expensive except for larger groups. A recommended six-hour trip stops at Lawa Caves (biggest cave in the region) and Sai Yok Yai

Falls, where the Russian roulette scenes from *The Deer Hunter* were filmed. This tour costs about 1,000B per boatload—not bad for five or six people.

Excellent raft hotels are located around Pak Sang. The River Kwai Village Hotel and Home Phu Toey Resort described in the Kanchanaburi chapter are two beautiful raft lodges which charge 800-1,200B for private room, boat ride from Pak Sang, and three meals. Travel agents in Bangkok and Kanchanaburi can make arrangements.

Hellfire Pass Memorial

A moving memorial to Allied prisoners and Asian conscripts who died while constructing the railway line near Hellfire Pass was erected several years ago by the Australian-Thai Chamber of Commerce. During three months of labor, over 1,000 Australian and British prisoners worked around the clock; only 300 survived the ordeal. The park consists of trails that reach Konyu Cutting, where a memorial plaque has been fastened to the rock; and Hin Tok trestle bridge, which collapsed three times during its construction. The association hopes to restore some of the track and display trains used during the construction.

The memorial is near Hellfire Pass, 80 km from Kanchanaburi and 18 km north of Nam Tok. English signs marking the turnoff are posted on Route 323. Bus travelers should alight at the Royal Thai Army Camp, then hike 500 meters to the trailhead which leads to the Konyu Cutting.

Sai Yok National Park

Tucked away inside 500-square-km Sai Yok National Park are the small but very pretty Sai Yok Yai Falls, which emerge from underground streams and tumble gracefully into the Kwai Noi River. The falls are widely celebrated in Thai poetry and song. Two large caves are located within the park boundaries but across the broad Kwai Noi River. Lawa Cave, the largest in the region, is a wonderland of dripping stalactites and stalagmites. Dawa Dung Cave is northwest of Sai Yok on the west bank of the Kwai Noi River. Other attractions inside the park include some Neolithic remains uncovered by Thai archaeologists, remains of a Japanese military camp, and a small bat cave known for its almost microscopic inhabitants.

The park entrance is about 38 km north of Nam Tok, but the falls and river are hidden three km off the main road. Bus travelers should get off at the national park sign, then flag down a passing car or face a long and dusty walk. Motorcycle taxis may be available.

Camping is permitted inside the park near the hanging bridge which vaguely resembles San Francisco's Golden Gate. The national park has several 10-person bungalows for 600-800B. Within sight of the curious bridge are several beautiful raft hotels where bamboo bungalows cost 450-600B.

Hin Da Hot Springs

Two small and very grubby swimming pools filled with warm water are located 500 meters off Route 323 about 130 km north of Kanchanaburi. Constructed by the Japanese in WW II, the two concrete tanks are now open to both male and female bathers. Not recommended

NORTH OF BANGKOK

Nestled between Bangkok and central Thailand are several small towns which have figured closely in Thai history. Bang Pa In is a riverside stop, which once served as a summer retreat for Thai kings. Lopburi, 154 km north of Bangkok, offers both 12th-century Khmer ruins and a royal residence constructed in the 17th century by King Narai. Top draw is the town of Ayuthaya, which served as the second capital of Thailand for over four centuries.

The region owes its prosperity to the rich soil and network of canals and rivers which ensure a bountiful harvest of rice. The Thai people predominate, though large numbers of Thai-Chinese merchants reside in the larger towns. Smaller numbers of Mon and Khmer live in remote villages. Climatic conditions are similar to those of Bangkok, with a rainy season July-Oct., a cool season until February, and the hot season until midsummer when the rains return.

Sightseeing Highlights

While most travelers go directly from Bangkok to Chiang Mai, a more leisurely and informative journey would include short visits to the historical sites of Ayuthaya and Lopburi just north of Bangkok, and the archaeological ruins in central Thailand.

Bang Pa In: Some 60 km north of Bangkok is a small complex of royal shrines and pavilions—once a summer getaway for the kings of Thailand. Generally visited en route to Ayuthaya, Bang Pa In is rather unexceptional, though history and architecture buffs will find it a worthwhile stopover.

Ayuthaya: The city of Ayuthaya, 85 km north of Bangkok, reigned as the political, economic, and cultural center of Thailand from 1350 until conquest by the Burmese in 1767. Set with hundreds of temples and palaces surrounded by rivers and canals, Ayuthaya was described by European traders as among the largest and most prosperous cities in the East. Though it was largely leveled by the Burmese in 1767, large-scale restoration projects have made Ayuthaya one of the most important historical and cultural destinations in Thailand. The surviving monuments are widely scattered and a full day of exploration is necessary to appreciate the magnitude of Ayuthaya. Day tours from Bangkok are not recommended.

Lopburi: One of Thailand's oldest cities, Lopburi served as a Khmer military outpost in the 13th century and as an alternative capital to Ayuthaya in the mid-17th century. Architectural attractions include a fine 12th-century Khmer temple and royal palace dating from the reign of King Narai. The town itself is small, sleepy, and rarely visited by Westerners, yet offers enough historic architecture to merit an overnight stop en route to Sukotai or the northeast.

Pra Buddhabat: Thailand's most famous Buddha footprint is located at Pra Buddhabat, a religious sanctuary near Saraburi.

Transportation

Attractions north of Bangkok can be easily visited en route to central or northern Thailand. One possible plan is to briefly visit Bang Pa In in the morning and continue up to Ayuthaya in the afternoon. A full day is necessary to properly explore Ayuthaya. Lopburi can be reached the following day on an early morning train. Allow about a half day to explore Lopburi, and perhaps make a side trip to Pra Buddhabat. Buses and trains continue north from Lopburi to Phitsanulok and Sukothai.

Ayuthaya and Lopburi—the two most important destinations north of Bangkok—are served by both bus or train. Buses to Bang Pa In and Ayuthaya depart every 15 minutes from Bangkok's Northern Bus Terminal.

Most trains go directly to Ayuthaya. Trains that stop in Bang Pa In depart Hualampong train station daily at 0827 and 0955 only. Trains to Ayuthaya depart daily at 0640, 0705, 0830, 1500, 1800, 1940, 2000, 2200. Whether ordinary, rapid, or express, all trains take about 90 minutes to reach Ayuthaya. Train travel, in general, is a relaxing and scenic way to get around Thailand.

BANG PA IN

About 60 km north of Bangkok is a strange collection of palaces and pavilions in Thai, Italian, Victorian, and Chinese architectural styles. Thai kings from the Ayuthaya Period up to the early part of the present century used the residences for summer vacations. The original palace was founded in the 17th century by King Prasat Thong (1630-1656) on an island in the middle of the Chao Praya. Successor kings vacationed here until the fall of Ayuthaya to Burmese invaders.

Early Chakri kings ignored Bang Pa In as too distant from Bangkok until King Mongkut reestablished the site in the latter half of the 19th century. King Chulalongkorn (1868-1910) erected a half dozen buildings without any great concern for architectural unity and used the retreat as a reception site for distinguished visitors. The complex was abandoned after the tragic death of the king's wife. Queen Sunandakumariratna and her children drowned in the Menam River in 1880 in full view of her royal entourage. None of the entourage attempted to rescue them because, at the time, royal law demanded death for any commoner who dared touch royalty.

Bang Pa In is more odd than amazing, but it's an easy stopover between Bangkok and Ayuthaya or a quick side trip from Ayuthaya, 20 km north. Visitors with limited time should go direct to Ayuthaya and, time permitting, backtrack to Bang Pa In for an afternoon visit.

The outer grounds of the palace, which include most of the important buildings, are open daily 0900-1800. Interior palace buildings are closed on Monday.

Attractions
Bang Pa In today no longer serves as a royal retreat but rather as a tourist site and occasional venue for state ceremonies. The original structures built by King Prasat Thong have disappeared and most of the remaining buildings are the legacy of King Chulalongkorn, who was fascinated by European architecture.

a delicate lake temple at Bang Pa In

Aisawan Thippaya Pavilion: The highlight of the small park is a delicate water pavilion erected by King Chulalongkorn to replace Prasat Thong's old palace in traditional style. Reconstructed by King Vajiravudh in reinforced concrete, the lovely building has been reproduced for several international expositions and is a favorite subject for photographers. Centerpiece is a life-sized statue of King Chulalongkorn.

Peking Palace: Pra Thinnang Warophat Piman, nicknamed the Peking Palace, was a gift from Chinese Thais who modeled the palace after a Chinese imperial court. A magnificent collection of jade, Ming Period porcelains, Chulalongkorn's intricately carved bed, and lacquer tables are displayed inside the palace. The palace itself was constructed from materials imported from China.

Royal Residence: Warophat Piman Hall, north of the landing stage at the entrance to the palace, is a Western-style palace constructed by King Chulalongkorn to replace King Mongkut's original two-story wooden residence. The building is copied from the pavilion in the Grand Palace where royalty changed regalia before mounting a palanquin. Interior chambers and anterooms are decorated with oil paintings depicting events in Thai history and scenes from Thai literature. Most rooms are closed to the public and open only for state ceremonies.

Gothic Tower: All that remains of the Uthayan Phumi Sathiana Palace (Haw Pra), an old timber structure destroyed by fire in 1938, is a curious six-sided tower in a semi-Gothic style. The hexagonal tower was reconstructed in 1990 as a gingerbread green edifice that now resembles a wedding cake.

Queen's Monument: The white marble memorial across the small bridge honors Chulalongkorn's first queen, who tragically drowned in full view of her entourage. A marble obelisk and cenotaph commemorate the event with Thai and English eulogies composed by King Chulalongkorn.

Wat Nivet Dhammapravat: A fun cable car whizzes across the river to Thailand's only European-style Buddhist temple. Erected by King Chulalongkorn for monks of the Dhammayuttika sect, the incongruous temple features an important image cast by Pradit Varakarn, court sculptor during the reigns of Mongkut and Chulalongkorn.

Transportation

Buses leave from Bangkok's Northern Bus Terminal every 30 minutes and take about one hour to reach the small town of Bang Pa In. Minitrucks from the market in Ayuthaya take 45 minutes. *Samlors* from the town to the riverside palace cost 10B. You can also take a train from Bangkok for 10B, then a *songtao* for 5B.

An interesting alternative is the Sunday morning boat trip organized by the Chao Praya Express Boat Company. The boat leaves at 0800 from Bangkok's Maharaj Pier, costs 160B, and includes stops at the Wat Pai Lom Stork Sanctuary and the Queen's Folk Arts and Handicraft Center in Bang Sai, before it returns to Bangkok around 1800.

AYUTHAYA

Ayuthaya, 85 km north of Bangkok, served as Thailand's second capital from 1350 to 1767. The city's scattered ruins, colossal Buddhas, decaying *chedis,* and multitude of soaring *wats* restored by the Fine Arts Department provide eloquent testimony to the splendor of this medieval metropolis. Recently declared a national historic park, Ayuthaya has been successfully developed into one of the country's major tourist attractions—a must-see for all visitors to Thailand.

Though Ayuthaya is often visited as a day-trip from Bangkok, it really takes a day or two of leisurely wandering to properly appreciate the sense of history evoked by the far-flung ruins. Travelers who enjoy romantic ruins and have a strong interest in Thai history should allow two full days in *both* Ayuthaya and Sukothai.

History

The first settlements near Ayuthaya were Khmer military and trading camps established in the 11th century as outposts for their distant empire. In 1350 a Thai prince named U Thong (Ramathibodi) transferred his capital from U Thong to Ayuthaya to escape a smallpox plague and provide greater military security from Burmese invaders. The site was carefully chosen at the merging of the Lopburi, Prasak, and Chao Praya Rivers where, with the creation of additional canals, the island fortress-city could be easily defended from outside attack. Ramathibodi

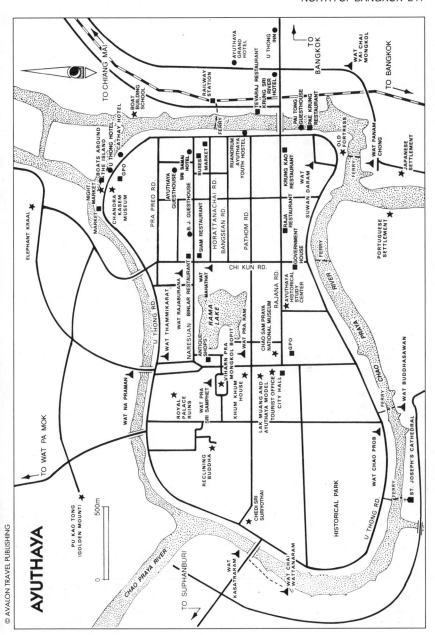

named his new city after the mythical kingdom of Ayodhya in the Hindu Ramayana epic and constructed royal palaces and temples. Sri Lankan monks soon arrived to reinforce Theravada Buddhism and maintain religious purity in the new Thai kingdom.

Ayuthaya was ruled by a succession of 33 kings of various dynasties who embellished the island capital with magnificent temples and sumptuous palaces. Ayuthayan kings, however, were not the benevolent and understanding Buddhist monarchs of Sukothai, but rather paternalistic Khmer-influenced kings who hid themselves behind walls of ritual, taboo, and sorcery. As incarnations of Shiva, they became focal points for political and religious cults which, in turn, sharply defined all levels of society.

Ayuthaya soon became the most powerful military empire in Southeast Asia. A policy of national military conscription gave Ayuthaya the strength to resist, expand, and then conquer the empires of the Burmese, Cambodians, and Muslims. In 1378, Sukothai was subjugated by King Boromaraja I, the successor of King Ramathibodi, and in 1431 Angkor fell to Ayuthaya after a siege of seven months. By the end of the 15th century, Ayuthaya controlled Southeast Asia from Vientiane in the north to Malacca in south, and from Angkor in the east to Bago in the west.

A short period of decline in the mid-16th century marked the arrival of one of Ayuthaya's greatest rulers, King Naresuan the Great (1555-1605). As a young man, Naresuan demonstrated great military capabilities against Cambodia and subsequently liberated Ayuthaya from Burmese occupation in 1586. His rare combination of dynamic leadership, personal courage, and force of personality reunited the Thai people, who had suffered from more than a decade of defeat and humiliation at the hands of the Burmese and Cambodians. Naresuan formally became king of Ayuthaya in 1590 and, in 1592, fulfilled his legendary promise to regain Ayuthaya by defeating a Burmese crown prince in a sword duel atop war elephants. For the first time in 30 years, the tables of war turned in favor of the Thais. Naresuan had successfully unified Siam into an ethnic, cultural, and political framework that included the larger international order.

Under the rule of Naresuan and subsequent kings, Ayuthaya also became an important commercial center. First on the scene were the Portuguese, who traded guns and ammunition for rice and gems. Dazzled by the city's gilded opulence and grandeur, emissaries dispatched in 1685 by Louis XIV and other astonished European visitors compared the riverine kingdom to Venice: Ayuthaya was reported to be larger and more magnificent than contemporary London or Paris. Perhaps the most famous Western trader was Constantine Phaulkon, a colorful Greek adventurer who stirred up local resentment by preaching Christianity to a Buddhist monarch named King Narai. When word spread that a dying Narai was close to conversion, xenophobic Thai nobles seized the throne and executed the Greek merchant. Westerners were expelled and Ayuthaya entered into its own Golden Age of arts—an amazing period of vibrant art, literature, and education.

After four centuries of rule, Ayuthaya went into an economic and military decline. In early 1763, an enormous Burmese army overran Chiang Mai and massed for a final assault on Ayuthaya. After two years of siege, the city capitulated and most of the citizens were either murdered or marched off to Myanmar as slave labor. Ayuthaya was burned to the ground. Tremendous art treasures, museums, countless temples, priceless libraries, and historical archives were all destroyed—a horrific act that still profoundly shocks the Thais.

Attractions

A European visitor reported in 1685 that the population of Ayuthaya exceeded one million and that the city boasted over 1,700 temples, 30,000 priests, and more than 4,000 images of Buddha, all of them gold or gilt. Contemporary Ayuthaya has three good museums with dozens of Buddhas and about 30 temples in various stages of reconstruction and renovation. Monuments are widely scattered and only the central temples near the modern town are within walking distance. A few suggestions on bicycle and *tuk tuk* rentals, as well as on boat excursions, are given below under "Getting Around."

Monuments near the city center and within walking distance of guesthouses and hotels include the Chandra Kasem Museum, Wat Rajaburana, Wat Mahathat, Rama Lake, Wat Pra Ram, Sam Praya Museum, Viharn Pra Mongkol

Bopit, Wat Pra Sri Samphet, and Wat Na Praman. A full day of walking will cover all these sights, which include the region's most important monuments.

A second set of monuments is located on the banks of the river which encircle the island of Ayuthaya. A convenient if somewhat expensive way to tour these temples and European churches is by rented boat leaving from the quay near the Chandra Kasem Museum. Alternatively, U-Thong Road can be toured by bike or minitrucks that circulate along the road and charge 10B for a ride of any distance. Temples across the river can be reached with local ferries.

Farther afield and outside the city limits is a handful of temples such as the Golden Mount and the elephant *kraal.* A chartered *songtao* is necessary to reach these monuments.

Chandra Kasem Museum

King Thammaraja constructed this 17th-century palace for his son, who subsequently claimed the throne as King Naresuan. Partially destroyed by the Burmese, the palace was reconstructed by King Mongkut and later converted into one of the three museums in Ayuthaya. The Chantura Mukh Pavilion immediately on your left features an impressive standing Buddha flanked by a pair of wooden images, and a finely detailed royal bed. Behind this pavilion stands the Piman Rajaja Pavilion, filled with rare Thai shadow puppets and dozens of Ayuthaya and Sukothai images. Outside to the rear is the startling Pisai Salak Tower, constructed by Narai to study astronomy and follow the eclipses of the moon.

Chandra Kasem is open Wed.-Sun. 0900-1600. Exit the grounds and walk past the public riverside park and Hud Ra Market.

Wat Rajaburana

King Boromaraja II constructed this temple in 1424 to commemorate his two brothers, who died on elephantback fighting for the throne after the death of their father. Boromaraja wisely skipped the battle and, in accordance with royal custom, honored his two brothers with *stupas* erected at their cremation site.

A fascinating history lies behind Wat Rajaburana. The impressive *prang* was erected several years after King Boromaraja had captured Angkor Thom, the capital of Cambodia, and while Khmer influence was still strong in central Thailand. Inside the Khmer-style *prang,* a secret crypt was constructed to guard dozens of 15th-century murals, 200 Lopburi bronzes of Khmer-Bayon style, 300 rare U-Thong Buddhas, 100,000 votive tablets, and a fabulous treasure trove of priceless gold objects.

The crypt was sealed, covered with brick and plaster, and forgotten through the ensuing centuries. Thailand's equivalent of the Tutankhamen treasure lay untouched until 1957, when scavengers broke into the crypt and stumbled on the buried treasure. Much of the booty vanished into international art markets before the government stepped in, stopped the treasure hunters, and placed the remainder in the Ayuthaya National Museum. An unknown number of items vanished and many of the ordinary votives were sold to finance construction of the Ayuthaya National Museum, but enough relics remained to constitute one of Thailand's greatest archaeological discoveries.

Wat Rajaburana has, unfortunately, been badly restored by the Fine Arts Department with shiny concrete *garudas* and other artificial embellishments that detract from its original state.

Admission to Wat Rajaburana costs 5B for Thais and 20B for Westerners.

Wat Mahathat

King Boromaraja constructed his "Temple of the Great Relic" across the street from Wat Rajaburana in 1374 to honor his dream about a relic of the Buddha. Wat Mahathat architecturally fills the link between Lopburi's 10th-century Khmer *prangs* and the 15th-century-style *prangs* that characterized most monuments in Ayuthaya. The temple once contained murals of the life of the Buddha and a large stone image in the Dvaravati style (A.D. 600-1000) seated in the European manner, perhaps imported from Nakhon Pathom. The magnificent statue was transferred in 1835 to nearby Wat Na Praman. Valuable artifacts, including a tiny gold casket said to contain Boromaraja's holy relics, were discovered during a 1956 restoration project conducted by the Fine Arts Department. Except for the casket, now displayed in the Ayuthaya National Museum, most treasures have been moved to the National Museum in Bangkok.

THE ARTS OF AYUTHAYA

*A*yuthaya from the 14th to 18th centuries was among the most powerful and wealthy kingdoms in Southeast Asia. During their four centuries of rule, a series of 33 kings constructed hundreds of glittering temples and supported the arts with lavish royal patronage. Ayuthaya rulers considered themselves heirs to the artistic and religious traditions of Sukothai, Cambodia, and Sri Lanka—a rich mixture manifested in the artistic achievements which survived the Burmese onslaught of 1767.

Some historians consider the art of Ayuthaya decadent when compared to that of earlier periods such as Sukothai and Chiang Saen. However, Ayuthaya chiefly excelled in architecture and city planning rather than sculpture and painting. And yet, a great deal of sensitive work was created before the artistic decline toward the end of the Ayuthaya era.

The Ayuthaya National Museum provides a detailed look at Ayuthaya's art, plus a superb overview of the various epochs of Thai art.

Architecture

Ayuthaya's crowning artistic achievement was its architecture. At its height, Ayuthaya boasted over 600 major monuments and temples that impressed both Asiatic and European visitors with their sheer immensity and grandeur. The majority of these monuments were initiated during the reign of King Ramathibodi, the founder of Ayuthaya, and completed during the first 150 years of the era. Another building frenzy occurred in the early 17th century during the reign of King Prasat Thong, a prolific monument builder who revived the popularity of Khmer-influenced architecture. Tradition demanded that only temples be constructed of stone and brick. Wooden structures such as royal palaces and common residences have all been destroyed by conquering Burmese arsonists.

Ayuthayan architects borrowed the forms and traditions developed by other schools, but modified them according to their own tastes. One of the most important influences was the Khmers, whose corn-cob-shaped *prang* slowly evolved in Ayuthaya from a squat and heavy form into a radically elongated and more elegant superstructure. The best examples are the magnificent *prangs* of Wat Mahathat, Wat Rajaburana, and Wat Pra Ram. Ayuthayan *prangs* were later incorporated into Bangkok religious architecture at Wat Pra Keo, Wat Arun, and Wat Po.

Ayuthayan architects were also influenced by the artistic traditions of Sri Lanka, as shown in the bell-shaped *chedis* adapted from Sri Lankan models. A new elegance emerged as local architects elongated the bulbous Sri Lankan-style *chedi* into soaring, slim spires that seem to defy gravity. Wat Sri Samphet and the memorial to Queen Suriyothai are prime examples.

Ayuthayan architecture evolved through four subperiods until the city was destroyed in 1767. The Lopburi (Khmer-Thai fusion) and U Thong styles of architecture dominated from the founding of Ayuthaya in 1350 to the end of King Boromatrailokanat's reign in 1488. Examples include Wat Pra Ram, Wat Mahathat, and Wat Rajaburana. Sukothai-influenced architecture and the Singhalese type of rounded *stupa* reached Ayuthaya in 1463 after King Boromatrailokanat left to rule the northern town of Phitsanulok. Wat Pra Sri Samphet and Wat Yai Chai Mongkol are the most famous examples. Khmer architecture regained popularity after the conquest of Cambodia by King Prasat Thong in the mid-17th century, as best demonstrated by the Khmer *prang* of Wat Chai Wattanaram.

The final phase of Ayuthayan architecture was a period of restoration of older monasteries and temples which had fallen into disrepair, and the increased popularity of the *stupa* at Wat Pu Kao Tong.

Although the temple largely lies in ruin, the monumental floor plans and wildly directed pillars are impressive for what they suggest. One classic sight (in the southeast corner) is a dismembered Buddha head firmly grasped in the clutches of the banyan trees. Take a photo and return 10 years later—it will have grown to a higher level.

Admission is 20B.

Wat Pra Ram

Wat Pra Ram was constructed in 1369 by King Ramasuan as the burial spot for his father, King Ramathibodi, the founder of Ayuthaya. The elegant Khmer-style *prang* was reconstructed in the 15th century by King Boromatrailokanat, the eighth king of Ayuthaya, and was subsequently altered by the 31st ruler, King Boromakot.

Late Ayuthayan architecture was also characterized by the use of curved foundations and roofs on *viharns,* column capitals in the form of lotus buds, and the increased use of brick and stone for domestic rather than strictly religious architecture. The surviving structures at Ayuthaya only hint at the magnificence of the former capital.

Sculpture

Ayuthaya is better known for the quality of its architecture than for its achievements in sculpture.

Ayuthayan sculpture is divided into several subperiods. Early sculpture continued the traditions of U Thong, a school of art which predates the establishment of Ayuthaya and demonstrates an indebtedness to Mon and Khmer prototypes. The second period began in 1463 when King Boromatrailokanat went to rule Phitsanulok and local sculpture came under Sukothai influence. Some pieces produced during this period exhibit the sensitive and elegant traditions of Sukothai. But, as time progressed, the spirituality of Sukothai-influenced sculpture gave way to the more ritualistic and powerful images of the third period. These late-Ayuthayan images became increasingly cold and remote as Ayuthayan kings adopted the Khmer notion of *deva raja* (god-king) and hid themselves behind palace walls. The magnificence of the royal court—as reflected by Buddhas covered with princely attire and crowned with elaborate diadems—degenerated into a passion for decoration that obliterated all detail and reduced the images to formless masses of ornamentation. The end result was stereotyped abundance without the sensitivity of earlier eras: a triumph of style over spirituality.

Ayuthayan sculptors, however, were a remarkable creative force. Among their innovations was the depiction of Buddha in a wider variety of poses than those depicted by earlier schools. Buddhas were seated with their feet on the ground in the "European fashion" once used by Dvaravati sculptors, and in the meditating mudra rather than the more common pose of touching-the-earth. Walking Buddhas were shown with alms bowls and with the weight centered on the right rather than left foot. Ayuthayan sculptors were also technical masters of large-scale bronze casting, as demonstrated by the colossal seated Buddha in Viharn Pra Mongkol Bopit. Finally, Ayuthayan sculptors increased the size and magnificence of the pedestal (a tradition carried on during the Bangkok Period) and increased exterior ornamentation to reflect the glory of Ayuthayan kings who, like the Khmer *deva raja,* identified themselves as the Buddha King.

Painting

Ayuthaya's great murals were largely destroyed during the Burmese conquest of 1767, or have disappeared due to shoddy painting techniques which left the frescoes vulnerable to the degenerative effects of rain and heat. Consequently, the best examples of Ayuthayan paintings are outside town in the *wats* of Petchburi, Uttaradit, and Nonthaburi.

The first period of Ayuthayan painting shows Khmer and Singhalese influences and the heavy use of blacks, whites, and reds with dashes of vermilion and gold leaf to ornament the costumes of deities. Crypt murals inside the main *prang* of Wat Rajaburana form the finest surviving example of early Ayuthayan painting. Illustrations from manuscripts and religious documents show the gradual development of Sukothai influence and the increased use of bright colors during the second period. Late Ayuthayan painting is typically Thai, with bright colors, representations of trees and wildlife, and the innovative use of zigzag lines to compartmentalize scenes. Ayuthaya's sole surviving example of late-period painting is in the pavilion at Wat Buddhaisawan, where interior frescoes relate important religious and secular works. Outstanding examples of late-Ayuthayan painting are found in Petchburi at Wat Yai Suwannaram and Wat Ko Keo Suttaram, in Uttaradit at Wat Pra Boromathat, and in Nonthaburi at Wat Po Bang Oh and Wat Prasat.

The temple consists of symmetrical sanctuaries which flank a *prang* decorated with miniature *chedis* and stuccowork interspersed with *garudas, nagas,* and walking Buddhas. Although less monumental than Wat Mahathat or Wat Rajaburana, Wat Pra Ram boasts a stunning location. The temple casts a beautiful reflection in the placid lily ponds.

Ayuthaya National Museum

Chao Sam Praya, Thailand's second-largest museum, was constructed in 1959 from sale proceeds of votive tablets recovered from Wat Rajaburana, and was named after Prince Sam Praya (King Boromaraja II), the founder of Wat Rajaburana. The museum consists of a central hall with two floors, and a second building opened in 1970. All major art styles are represented—Dvaravati, Lopburi, U-Thong, Sukothai, and, of course, Ayuthaya. Ayuthayan kings were apparently avid collectors of early Thai art, though the best-represented styles are those of the Lopburi, U-Thong, and Ayuthaya Periods.

The main floor of the central hall holds dozens of statues, votives, lacquer cabinets, decorated palm-leaf manuscripts, and priceless objects discovered inside the left shoulder of the Pra Mongkol Bopit Buddha. Displays are arranged in chronological order and a careful inspection will provide a good overview of the artistic legacy of Thailand. Highlights on the main floor include a colossal bronze Buddha head with square face and broad features typical of the U-Thong Period, and a Dvaravati-style seated Buddha carved from white crystalline stone.

The second floor features a main room filled with lead and terra-cotta votive tablets, palm-leaf manuscript cabinets, and crystal objects found during the restoration of Wat Yai Chai Mongkol in 1980. Highlights of the upper floor are displayed in antechambers to the east and west. The small room on the east side contains dazzling gold objects unearthed in 1956 from the central *prang* of Wat Rajaburana. The western room holds the previously described Buddha relic from Wat Mahathat. Look carefully: it's one-third the size of a rice grain and protected by five bronze stupas inserted one inside the other.

The modern addition to the rear offers a dusty and rather neglected collection of artifacts not native to Ayuthaya.

Chao Sam Praya Museum is open Wed.-Sun. 0900-1600; admission is 20B.

Ayuthaya Historical Study Center

Located on Rajana Road near the Provincial Teachers College is a modern museum designed to relate the history of Ayuthaya. Opened in August 1990, the complex was constructed with a grant from the Japanese government on the site of an old Japanese settlement. Five exhibitions are included: Ayuthaya as the capital, port, seat of government, center of the Thai community, and center of international relations with the Western world. Top sights are a Chinese commercial ship, scale models of old Ayuthaya and the elephant *kraal,* and murals depicting merit-making ceremonies at Pra Buddhabat in Saraburi, an annual event attended by the citizens of Ayuthaya. Other murals illustrate ordination ceremonies, the rice-planting season, an ancient theater, a marriage ceremony, and a Thai funeral.

The Ayuthaya Historical Center is open Wed.-Sun. 0900-1700. Admission is a reasonable 20B for Thais and a stiff 100B for Western tourists.

Lak Muang

Across the street from the National Museum lies Ayuthaya's modern city pillar. It features a scale model of the city which helps with local orientation.

Khum Khum House

Constructed in 1894 as the city jail and now used by the Fine Arts Department, Khum Khum House is an outstanding example of traditional domestic Thai architecture. The compound is surrounded by moats and elevated on teak piles that support a central *sala* roofed with dried palm leaves.

Viharn Pra Mongkol Bopit

One of the largest bronze Buddha images in Thailand is located inside a modern and very claustrophobic *viharn* immediately south of Wat Pra Sri Samphet. Originally erected during the Ayuthaya Period, the old *viharn* and brooding image were badly damaged in 1767 when the roof collapsed and broke off the statue's top-knot and right arm. The image was repaired but allowed to remain outdoors until 1951, when the present shelter was erected to protect the enormous statue. Perhaps the Buddha, with its black coating and mysterious mother-of-pearl eyes, should have been left alone—an image of this size and power needs a great deal of room.

Today the statue is an object of great veneration to the Thais. The date of the image is uncertain, though it displays both U-Thong and Sukothai influences and may have been cast in the 15th century.

Adjacent to the *viharn* is a large parking lot and a shopping complex that formerly served as royal cremation grounds. Several of the open-air shops and restaurants sell basketry, locally produced knives, imitation antiques, cold drinks, and spicy soups such as *tam yam kung.*

Wat Pra Sri Samphet

This famous trio of 15th-century Sri Lankan-style *chedis* is the most important temple complex within the former royal palace compound, similar in function to Wat Pra Keo in Bangkok. The temple was founded in the 15th century by King Boromatrailokanat and expanded by his successors. As with Wat Pra Keo, Wat Pra Sri Samphet served as the private chapel and ceremonial courtyard for the kings of Ayuthaya.

The temple is composed of three famous *chedis* which stand on a long terrace linked by stone *mondops*. In the manner of Khmer monuments at Angkor Wat, all served as royal tombs for Thai monarchs rather than as simple memorials to the Buddha. All once contained secret chambers adorned with frescoes and votive offerings for the dead, and in conformity with classical rules all were constructed on a circular ground plan with elongated cupolas flattened to accommodate a double-layered reliquary plinth. The east *chedi* was erected by King Ramathibodi in 1492 to enshrine the ashes of his father, while the central shrine holds the remains of his elder brother, King Boromaraja III. The westernmost *chedi* was built in 1540 to contain the ashes of King Ramathibodi II.

Their perfect symmetry has made the *chedis* one of the most photographed scenes in Ayuthaya and the very essence of Middle Kingdom architecture. Unfortunately, insensitive restoration projects by the Fine Arts Department

and repeated whitewashings have tragically obliterated all architectural detail.

Several famous Buddhas were discovered in the ruins after the destruction of Ayuthaya in 1767. The most famous image, Pra Sri Samphet, is a 16-meter bronze Buddha once covered with gold leaf from which the temple received its name. The image was stripped by the Burmese and subsequently regained by King Rama I, who took it to Wat Po in Bangkok. Pra Buddha Singh, another national treasure, also now resides in Bangkok at the National Museum, while Pra Buddha Lokanat has been transferred to the west *viharn* of Wat Po.

Admission is 20B, but the *prangs* can be easily seen and photographed from the road. A cluster of small antique shops and restaurants is located just opposite Sri Samphet. Stonecarving is the local specialty. Excellent-quality Cambodian images, Ganeshas, and standing Ayuthayan Buddhas are sold at reasonable prices.

Royal Palace

North of Wat Pra Sri Samphet are some scattered foundations and modest ruins of the old royal palace. The site was chosen by King Boromatrailokanat, who began construction of the palace and Wat Pra Sri Samphet in 1448. The complex was later expanded by several kings,

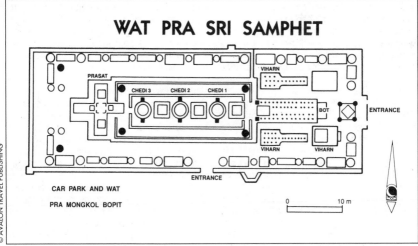

WAT PRA SRI SAMPHET

PRASAT

CHEDI 3   CHEDI 2   CHEDI 1

VIHARN

BOT

ENTRANCE

VIHARN   VIHARN

ENTRANCE

CAR PARK AND WAT

PRA MONGKOL BOPIT

0   10 m

such as Narai, Prasat Thong, and Pra Petracha, who erected reception halls, audience chambers, military review stands, and a royal palace covered with golden tiles.

The palace was burned and completely destroyed by the Burmese in 1767. The remaining brickwork, stucco molding, and Buddhas were removed to Bangkok by early Chakri kings to help rebuild the capital. All that remains today of the royal palace are narrow footpaths and brick foundations which distinguish the ground plans; a great deal of imagination is needed to recreate the palace's former magnificence and lost grandeur.

Wat Na Praman

This tremendous *bot,* across the river from the old royal palace, is one of the most impressive temples in Ayuthaya. The foundation date is unknown, but documents record restoration projects during the reign of King Boromakot (1753-59) and by the governor of Ayuthaya (1824-51) in the Bangkok Period. Wat Na Praman (Wat Pra Meru) was one of the few temples which survived the Burmese destruction of 1767.

Wat Na Praman consists of a large, recently rebuilt *bot* on the left, and a small but very important *viharn* on the right. A long and rather convoluted history of the primary temple is given on the exterior notice board. The main *bot* is an elegant structure elevated on a stepped terrace and covered with varnished tiles over a four-tiered roof. Magnificent examples of classic Ayuthayan architecture are displayed in the monumental entrances, twin facades flanked by smaller porticoes, windows barred with stone colonnades, and beautifully carved pediments over the southern entrance.

The interior is equally remarkable. The centerpiece altar displays a rare gold-leaf, six-meter Ayuthaya-style Buddha surrounded by 16 octagonal painted pillars, highly polished floors, and roofs carved with concentric lotus buds. Wat Na Praman is an excellent place to relax and meditate away from the more touristy temples in Ayuthaya.

To the right of the *bot* is a small chapel which guards a green stone Dvaravati Buddha (Pra Kantharat) seated in European fashion with splayed feet resting on a lotus flower and hands curiously placed on the knees. The broad Mon face and firm facial expression exude a meditative serenity rarely experienced in Thai sculpture. Although located in a modest and often neglected setting, this powerful image richly deserves its reputation as one of the masterpieces of Mon Buddhist art.

The combination of striking architecture, stunning sculpture, and pleasant surroundings makes Wat Na Praman one of the finest experiences in Ayuthaya: a refreshing change from the over-restored and dead monuments controlled by the Fine Arts Department.

Admission is 20B.

Reclining Buddha

Wat Logya Suthat is known for its picturesque 20-meter statue of a reclining Buddha. The image features a very long face and a vertical arm supporting the head which rests on a lotus pillow, a pose characteristic of 16th-century Ayuthaya. The large wooden *viharn* which once covered the image has disappeared, leaving the Buddha exposed to the elements with the contented cows that occasionally graze in nearby grasses. Cokes at the refreshment stand are expensive!

Chedi Sri Suriyothai

The only remaining part of Wat Suan Luang Sopsawan is a rather inelegant and heavily restored *chedi* dedicated to Queen Suriyothai, the wife of King Maha Chakraphet. According to Thai chronicles, the queen sacrificed her life in 1563 by intervening during an elephant duel between King Chakraphet and a Burmese general. Wat Suan Luang Sopsawan was erected at the cremation site of the queen.

Wat Chai Wattanaram

One of the most intriguing monuments in Ayuthaya is located at the southwestern edge of town and across the Chao Praya River. Wat Chai Wattanaram was constructed in 1630 by King Prasat Thong on the site of his mother's palace, and modeled after the Khmer monument at Angkor Wat.

The temple can be approached by crossing the nearby bridge and following the trail to the restored monument. The ruins include a Khmer *prang* surrounded by a square cloister interspersed with well-preserved *chedis* capped with wooden, coffered roofs. Stucco details include

COSMIC SYMBOLOGY
AND THE ARCHITECTURE OF AYUTHAYA

*T*hailand's architecture and the temples of Ayuthaya were designed to symbolize aspects of Theravada Buddhism and the powerful belief in Hindu cosmology. Most elements displayed today began as Hindu concepts which filtered through the Khmer Empire and were finally reinterpreted with some degree of originality by Thai architects. A short summary may help you understand the motivations and design considerations of local architects.

As with Angkor Wat in Cambodia, Thai architecture embodies in stone the Hindu concept of cosmology. Hinduism teaches that the world is composed of countless universes which, like their human counterparts, also experience endless cycles of destruction and rebirth. Each universe is dominated by a magical mountain, Mt. Meru, the mythical home of the gods. This colossal mountain is surrounded by seven subordinate mountain ranges and seven seas, beyond which lie the four major continents, one in each cardinal direction. Below Mt. Meru are the four levels of hell inhabited by guardian demons with supernatural powers. The upper levels of Mt. Meru contain the world of angels, guardians of the four cardinal directions, and, at the summit, the city of gods where Indra reigns as king. Above Mt. Meru tower more levels of heaven, inhabited by abstract beings nearing nirvana.

Kings throughout most of Southeast Asia strived to re-create this cosmological order by modeling their royal palaces, temples, and general city plan after the Hindu universe. Ayuthaya, for example, was laid out as the cosmic center of the universe with four important cities in each cardinal direction:

Sukothai to the north (the direction of death), Prapadang to the south (life), Nakhon Nayon to the east (birth), and Suphanburi to the west (dying). The city was constructed as a giant mandala with the royal palace at the center, surrounded by three circles of earthen ramparts and a series of circular moats to represent the great seas.

Hindu cosmology also dictates the shape and arrangement of individual temples. Centerpiece was a massive tower which represented Mt. Meru. The tower was divided into 33 lesser tiers to symbolize the 33 levels of heaven. A row of demon guardian figures was often added just below the seventh tier. *Prangs* were surmounted by a *vajra* or thunderbolt, the heavenly symbol of Indra, while *chedis* were topped by a circular orb which represented the core of nirvana. To the west and east—the axis of purity—were the *bot* (ordination hall) and *viharn* (meeting hall). Moats surrounding the temple complex represent the primordial oceans which separate the world of humans from the abode of gods.

Thai architects reinterpreted Hindu forms in several ways. *Prangs* and *chedis* were subdivided into the familiar 33 tiers, but Thai love of curvature brought along redented corners which added vertical lines, and a bulbous parabolic shape which gave the monument a sense of soaring grace. Thai propensity for asymmetry inspired the use of trapezoidal doors and window frames, tapered columns capped with lotus bud finials, and overlapping roofs which added an effect of soft sensuality. The end result was Hindu cosmology mixed with Thai sensibility: one of the great triumphs of Southeast Asian architecture.

additional embellishments of Lanna Thai and Ayuthaya origins.

The overall effect—especially at sunset—is overwhelming: a magnificent temple with headless Buddha torsos being swallowed by creeping vines, cows grazing next to the leaning *prangs*. . . everything you ever imagined about mysterious temples of the East.

St. Joseph's Cathedral
Western architecture in Ayuthaya is the legacy of a period of trade with European powers during

the 17th and 18th centuries. European architectural themes introduced to Ayuthaya during the reign of King Narai (1656-1688) include radiating arches, large windows constructed without claustras, and the use of masonry on residential buildings. Windows constructed without claustras remained popular after the death of King Narai, though the other two innovations faded away.

Western capitalists were required to live outside the city limits and could only enter Ayuthaya on official business. The Catholic community

pre-restoration Wattanaram

was thus served by this 17th-century church built by Monsignor de Beryte during the reign of King Narai. The modest church has been restored several times and still functions as an active house of worship.

A small ferry leaves from the dock at the end of a narrow dirt path off U-Thong Road.

Wat Buddhasawan

Wat Buddhasawan, consecrated in 1353 by the prince of U Thong (King Ramathibodi), who lived on the site during construction of his new capital, features the most perfect reproduction of a Cambodian *prang* in Ayuthaya. The general layout is derived from Angkor Wat, with a large central *prang,* representing the Buddhist heaven of Mt. Meru, surrounded by six smaller *prangs* which signify the outer heavens. A long series of seated Buddhas fills the open gallery that surrounds the central *prang.* The niche in the northern wall contains a standing Buddha image cast during the reign of King Rama I to replace a statue removed to the Royal Pantheon at Wat Pra Keo in Bangkok.

Adjacent to the *prang* is a large, modern *wat* and a public park which contains a statue of King Ramathibodi flanked by two soldiers.

A small ferry shuttles across the river; the one-way journey costs 5-10B.

Portuguese Settlement

During the reign of King Narai, foreign traders were encouraged to settle and set up residential centers south of Ayuthaya. The Portuguese arrived in 1511 after Viceroy Albuquerque sent a trading mission headed by Duarte Fernandez. Portuguese influence was tempered by the Dutch, who enjoyed a monopoly on the hide trade with Japan, and by the French, who sent Jesuit missionaries to Ayuthaya in 1673. Western influence peaked in the reign of King Narai and then sharply declined under subsequent, more xenophobic rulers.

All of the Western residential enclaves constructed during the 17th and 18th centuries were destroyed in 1767 by the Burmese conquest of Ayuthaya. The former Portuguese community is marked with a memorial plaque.

Japanese Settlement

Soon after the Portuguese established trade agreements with Ayuthaya in 1516, Japanese entrepreneurs arrived to serve as merchants, soldiers, and diplomats. The most famous arrival was a Japanese chief named Nagamasa Yamada, who was later named viceroy of Nakhon Si Thammarat in southern Thailand.

The site of the former Japanese community is marked with a stone inscription, memorial hall, and Japanese-style gate erected by the Thai-Japanese Society.

Wat Panam Chong

One of the oldest and largest temples in Ayuthaya lies on the Chao Praya River southeast of town. According to Thai chronicles, Wat Panam Chong was founded by the prince of U-Thong in 1324, 26 years before the formal establishment of Ayuthaya.

The temple was constructed to house a gigantic Buddha image donated by a Chinese emperor whose daughter had married a local Thai prince. Constructed of brick and stucco covered with gold leaf, Pra Chao Panam measures 19 meters in height and almost 14 meters in breadth—the largest single-cast bronze Buddha in Thailand. The image has been restored several times, but remains a source of great power and inspiration to Thai and Chinese pilgrims who divine their fortunes under the watchful gaze of the great Buddha.

The internal walls feature prayer flags, paper lanterns, and hundreds of small niches filled with votive statues of the Buddha—a rare element in Thai architecture.

Special note should be made of the Sukothai statues inside the small *viharn* to the left of the main *bot.* The 14th-century image on the left was discovered in 1956 when its heavy plaster covering cracked to reveal a statue estimated to be 60% pure gold.

Surrounding the exterior courtyard are dozens of stucco-covered Buddhas and grassy grounds kept neatly trimmed by a small army of devotees.

Wat Yai Chai Mongkol

Dominating the landscape southeast of town is the temple and *chedi* of Wat Yai Chai Mongkol. The monastery was established in 1360 by King Ramathibodi as Wat Chao Praya Thai ("Temple of the Supreme Patriach") for Thai monks who had returned from religious studies in Sri Lanka. The sect, known as Pa Kao, devoted itself to strict meditation, in contrast to other sects which emphasized the study of Buddhist scriptures. The temple now hosts a large community of *mae chi,* Buddhist nuns, who maintain the buildings and keep the lawns in good condition.

The present *wat* derives its name from the towering Chedi Chai Mongkol, located within the fortified temple compound and elevated on a rectangular base bisected by smaller *chedis.* The whitewashed tower was constructed by King Naresuan to commemorate his single-handed slaying of a Burmese crown prince in 1592. The infamous battle was fought on elephantback near Suphanburi and reestablished Thai control of the central Chao Praya plains.

Encircling the massive *chedi* are some 135 Buddhas which once sat in a rectangular cloister marked only by surviving columns. Also within the perimeter wall is a huge reclining Buddha image of the Ayuthaya Period, still highly regarded by local Thais. To the rear is the spirit house of King Naresuan, patronized by Thais who seek counsel from the king's spirit through female mediums.

Wat Suwan Daram

This rarely visited temple is one of the most attractive and fascinating in Ayuthaya. Wat Suwan Daram was constructed by the grandfather of the first king of the Chakri dynasty at the end of the Ayuthaya Period, and was subsequently restored by King Rama II after his accession to the throne.

The curving, concave foundation of the boat-shaped *bot* illustrates mankind's voyage toward nirvana. Elaborate doors and pediments decorated with carved wood complete the exterior detail.

The highlights of the temple are the interior murals in the *bot,* which date from the period of Rama II and rank among the best in Thailand. Painted with great talent, these frescoes depict scenes from the Vessantara and Suvanasama Jatakas with an assembly of divinities in the upper registers. The wall opposite the altar relates the victory of the Buddha over Mara and the spirits of evil. Ayuthaya-style Buddhas fill the central altar.

Also on the temple grounds are a *kambarian, chedi,* and *viharn* completed during the reign of King Chulalongkorn, with modern murals depicting the life of King Naresuan the Great.

Unlike most temples in Ayuthaya, Wat Suwan Daram still serves as an active monastery where religious life continues in traditional fashion. The *bot* is kept locked, but young monks anxious to practice their English can open the building.

Pu Kao Tong ("Golden Mount")

Situated in the open countryside almost five km from town is the gigantic silhouette of Pu Kao Tong, the Golden Mountain of Ayuthaya. The monastery was founded in 1387 by King Ramasuan, but the *chedi* was built by the Burmese to commemorate their conquest of Ayuthaya in 1569 and subsequently remodeled in Thai style by King Boromakot. The Ayuthaya-style *chedi* features four niches which rest on square-stepped platforms reached by monumental staircases.

To commemorate the 2,500th anniversary of Buddha's birthday, the towering *chedi* was capped in 1956 with a 2.5-kg solid-gold orb. Somebody immediately stole it, but views from the top of the 80-meter *chedi* remain outstanding, especially during the rainy season when the surrounding ricefields are flooded. Hire a *tuk tuk* or *samlor* to reach Pu Kao Tong.

Elephant *Kraal*

One of the few surviving elephant *kraals* in Thailand is located on Pu Kao Road, some three km northwest of town. Inside the teak stockade, wild elephants were once herded and battle-trained under the watchful gaze of royalty and spectators. Hunters would gather up to 150 beasts before slowly leading them through the bottleneck opening into the *kraal*. The elephants were then lassoed with rattan cables and selected according to their size and color; white and reddish elephants were favored over gray or mixed-colored animals.

The present structure includes a royal pavilion, elephant gateway, stockade of teak posts, holy *sala* where hunters performed purification ceremonies before the chase, central altar which once held an image of Ganesha, and elephant statue near the spectators' arena. Old-fashioned elephant roundups were re-created here in 1891 for Czar Nicholas II and in 1962 for Danish royalty.

Accommodations—Guesthouses

Several new guesthouses have opened in recent years to provide cheap accommodations for backpackers.

Ayuthaya Guesthouse: Formerly known as B.J. Guesthouse, Ayuthaya's original homestay is 50 meters up a small alley (Chao Phrom Road) running north from Naresuan Road. Mr. Hong Singha Paisal has eight rooms in an old teak house with great atmosphere. Bicycles can be rented from the outdoor patio. 16/2 Naresuan Rd., tel. (035) 251468, 100-150B.

B.J. Guesthouse: The most popular guesthouse in Ayuthaya has 20 rooms in a cinderblock building about 10 minutes west of the market. Banjong, the lady owner, is a good cook and can help with travel tips. They also operate another property a few doors down the street. 19/29 Naresuan Rd., tel. (035) 246046, 60B dorm, 100-120B rooms.

Ruandrum Ayuthaya Youth Hostel: Perhaps the most beautiful lodging in Ayuthaya are these teak houses overlooking the river. The central wing was built by an Ayuthayan aristocrat

in the traditional *panya* style found in central Thailand. The owner, Praphan Sukarechit (Kimjeng), has renovated the adjacent homes and refurbished all the rooms with antiques. Curiosities on the grounds include old rowing boats, a kitchen constructed on a floating barge, wooden door frames from the old elephant *kraal,* and other antiques from Kimjeng's antique shop. Rooms are somewhat expensive for a youth hostel, but Kimjeng also intends to open a budget dormitory for backpackers. 48 U-Thong Rd., tel. (035) 241978, 150-200B. The dormitory costs around 100B per person.

Pai Tong Guesthouse: A floating hotel on a reconstructed barge. Rooms are small and the atmosphere dark and dank, but two good restaurants are located nearby. U-Thong Rd., 80-100B.

Accommodations—Hotels

Ayuthaya has a very limited selection of hotels since most tourists visit the town on day-trips from Bangkok.

Sri Samai Hotel: Ayuthaya's central hotel was once a clean and comfortable place with a fairly decent restaurant. Standards, unfortunately, have dropped and the hotel can no longer be recommended aside from its convenient location near the marketplace. 12 Chao Prom Rd., tel. (035) 251104, 300-400B fan, 400-500B a/c.

U-Thong Hotel: A rudimentary hotel for those who want traditional facilities at moderate cost. The U-Thong has rather dirty rooms with fan and common bath, and a few a/c rooms with private bath. Avoid rooms facing the street. The nearby Cathay Hotel is similar in quality and price. 86 U-Thong Rd., tel. (035) 251136, 150-300B.

U Thong Inn: Two km east of Ayuthaya and rather isolated from central Ayuthaya is the first semiluxurious hotel in town. 210 Rajana Rd., tel. (035) 242236, fax (035) 242235, 800-1,200B a/c.

Krung Sri River Hotel: A new hotel near the train station with an outdoor swimming pool, health club, bowling alley, Pasak coffee shop, and 202 tastefully decorated rooms. 27/2 Rajana Rd., tel. (035) 244333, fax (035) 243777, 1,600-2,200B.

Ayuthaya Grand Hotel: Another recent addition to the luxury hotel market in Ayuthaya. All the standard facilities such as a pool, a snooker hall, and travel services. 55/5 Rajana Rd., tel. (035) 335483, fax (035) 335492, Bangkok tel. (02) 511-1029, 1,200-1,800B.

Restaurants

Most travelers dine in their guesthouses or at the market, though several good restaurants are located along the river and near the monuments on Chi Kun Road.

Night Market: The old night market has been relocated from downtown to a new location on the river across from the Chandra Kasem Museum. A small selection of foodstalls complement the hawkers' emporiums. A comfortable place to spend an evening.

Pae Krung Kao Floating Restaurant: The better of Ayuthaya's two floating restaurants is hardly spectacular, but the atmosphere is relaxed and the food tasty. U Thong Rd. Moderate.

Krung Kao Restaurant: A small, modern, air-conditioned spot with Thai specialties and an English-language menu. Try the pepper steak or chicken sautéed with garlic. Located on Rajana Rd. near the bridge. Budget.

Youth Hostel: Kimjeng's wife operates a well-appointed restaurant furnished with antiques and knickknacks. The menu includes both Thai and Western dishes. 48 U-Thong Rd. Moderate.

Tevaraj Restaurant: Riverside dining in a large bamboo hall with a small attached floating pavilion. Pictures of cabaret singers are displayed at the front. A big place popular with Thais and tour groups. Railway Station Rd., just over the bridge. Moderate to expensive.

Binlar Restaurant: A large, open-air nightclub with rock music and Thai cabaret singers. Good food at reasonable prices, a popular hangout in the evenings. Naresuan Rd. Budget to moderate.

Siam Restaurant: Just opposite Wat Mahathat is a small a/c restaurant that offers a welcome escape from the heat. Chi Kun Rd. Moderate.

Raja Restaurant: Dine outdoors surrounded by ponds filled with water lilies. Great atmosphere in a very quiet location. Rajana Rd. Moderate.

Getting There

Ayuthaya is 86 km north of Bangkok and can be reached by bus or train.

Bus: Buses leave every half hour from Bangkok's Northern Bus Terminal and take about two hours to reach Ayuthaya. Most buses terminate at the marketplace in the center of town. Stay on the bus until it arrives downtown; get off at the bridge and you are fed to mercenary taxi drivers. Some buses will drop you on the highway about five km east of town. *Tuk tuk* drivers will then yell, "No bus, no bus," but a public bus into town rolls by every 15 minutes. Walk to the intersection and wait at the corner.

Train: Trains leave Bangkok hourly and take about two hours to reach Ayuthaya. From the station, stroll across the road and walk down to the river, where ferries continue across to town. Bicycles can be rented south of the train station past the Tevaraj Restaurant.

Boat: Public boats no longer operate between Ayuthaya and Bangkok or Bang Pa In. However, one-day luxury excursions to Ayuthaya and Bang Pa In are organized by the Oriental Hotel and Shangri La Hotel. These quickie trips leave daily at 0800 and cost 1,200B with lunch.

Getting Around

Most visitors attempt to see Ayuthaya on a single day-trip from Bangkok—a serious mistake. Ayuthaya is a sprawling place with dozens of great temples that deserve a day or two of exploration. Only the central temples can be reached on foot. Rent either a bicycle, longtail boat, or minitruck for a day tour of all of Ayuthaya. Bicycles can be rented south of the train station past the Tevaraj Restaurant near the temple, and from Bai Thong Guesthouse. Motorcycles are no longer available in Ayuthaya.

Six-person longtail boats chartered from the landing stage opposite Chandra Kasem Museum cost 300-500B for the standard three-hour tour. During the dry season only the lower half of Ayuthaya can be reached due to low waters. Boats can also be hired to Bang Pa In: look for the "Boat Trid Bang Pa In" sign.

Minitrucks cost 250-400B for an afternoon tour which should include the Golden Mount, Wat Chai Wattanaram, St. Joseph's Cathedral, and Wat Panam Chong. Temples on the southern riverbanks are served by small ferries for 5B.

Local *tuk tuks* and minitrucks cost 20-30B for any distance. Ayuthaya, with over 1,100 registered three-wheelers, claims the title of *tuk tuk* capital of Thailand.

Leaving Ayuthaya

Minibuses to Bang Pa In leave from the market on Naresuan Road. To Kanchanaburi, take a yellow bus from the market to Suphanburi, from where buses continue to Kanchanaburi. Buses to Sukothai and Bangkok leave hourly from the market. Trains north to Phitsanulok and Chiang Mai depart eight times daily.

LOPBURI

Lying 150 km north of Bangkok is the pleasant and friendly little town of Lopburi, one of the oldest and most historic sites in Thailand. Lopburi is rarely visited by Westerners and initial impressions are hardly spectacular, though the town offers enough good architecture and historical background to merit an overnight stop.

Local people are friendly, hospitable, and often happy to show visitors around the major sites and point out the better restaurants and nightclubs. The study of English seems to be a major preoccupation with the population, who will gladly exchange guide services for a few hours of English conversation.

Lopburi is divided between the historic old town near the train station and the new town three km east. The old town has all the temples plus several good budget hotels near the train station. The only reasons to visit the new town are the main bus terminal at the first oversized traffic circle (Sakao Circle) and the nightclubs and swimming pool along the main road towards the second circle. Minibuses shuttle between the old and new town until about 2000.

All major attractions are in the old town near the train station. Hurried visitors can visit the most important sites in about three hours of walking, then continue north by train or bus. Note: the Fine Arts Department now collects a 20B admission fee for most monuments. Although the Royal Palace and Wat Mahathat are worth the cost, other monuments can be easily viewed and photographed from the street.

Lopburi's friendly population, pleasant pace of life, and small selection of historical attractions make it a fine place to break the northward journey.

History

Lopburi has been home to Neolithic settlers, an independent Dvaravati kingdom called Lavo (6th-10th centuries), a Khmer military outpost (10th-13th centuries), and a subcapital during the Ayuthaya Period (1350-1767). It was during the third period that Cambodian architectural and artistic patterns fused with traditional Mon styles to produce the famous Lopburi style— one of Thailand's most important and distinctive regional art movements.

The city has ridden the roller coaster of Thai history. Scholars believe the city (then called Lavo) was established some 1,400 years ago as the capital of a Mon kingdom which extended northward to the Mekong River. According to tradition, Lopburi helped establish the northern Mon kingdom of Haripunchai (Lamphun) by sending up a number of holy men and providing national leadership under Cham Devi, the daughter of a Buddhist ruler. The dynasty lasted until the middle of the 11th century. All traces of Lavo have disappeared aside from some Dvaravati artifacts displayed in the Lopburi National Museum.

Lavo declined near the end of the 9th century as Angkor succeeded in replacing Dvaravati's hegemony over central Southeast Asia. In fact, sometime during the early 11th century, Lopburi was aided by the Khmers during a skirmish against an army from Haripunchai. Lopburi was incorporated into the Angkor empire during the reign of Suryavarman I (1007-1050). As a province of Angkor, Lopburi was ruled by Cambodian governors yet maintained a cultural and religious tradition as heir to the Dvaravati Kingdom. Lopburi remained a Khmer outpost until the rise of Sukothai in the late 13th century. Khmer influence is still evident in the Cambodian architecture of Prang Khaek, San Pra Kan, Wat Mahathat, and Prang Sam Yot, a Hindu shrine which appears on the back of the 500B note.

The city was largely abandoned after the demise of the Khmers until the ascension of King Narai, who ruled Ayuthaya from 1657 to 1688. Lopburi then entered its most brilliant phase, serving as the alternative capital to Ayuthaya after the Gulf of Siam was blockaded by Dutch ships. Even after the gulf reopened to international trade, King Narai continued to spend up to nine months of each year at his palace in Lopburi, nicknamed the "Versailles of Siam." European influences were introduced on an unprecedented scale. Narai called in French Jesuit missionaries to discuss religion and invited French architects to help design and construct his new residence. European architects also helped design his military forts in Ayuthaya, Bangkok, and Nonthaburi, while exquisite gifts were exchanged between Narai and the "Sun King," Louis XIV. The city was filled with diplomats and merchants from all parts of Europe, Persia, India, China, and Japan. The high-powered phase ended in March 1688 after the death of Narai and the execution of his controversial advisor, Constantine Phaulkon.

Lopburi was abandoned in favor of Ayuthaya during the reign of King Petraja (1688-1703) and fell into a state of neglect and dilapidation over the next 150 years. A modest revival occurred in the mid-19th century when King Rama III reestablished Lopburi as an alternative capital to Bangkok and restored the Chantara Phisan Pavilion inside the royal complex. A residence was subsequently built by King Mongkut, who used Lopburi as a vacation resort.

Royal Palace

The enormous complex constructed by King Narai between 1665 and 1677 displays a combination of European and Khmer styles. The palace was restored by King Rama III 150 years

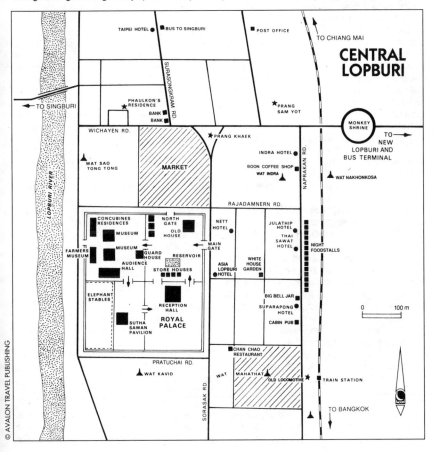

CENTRAL LOPBURI

later, and further improvements were conducted in the 1860s by King Mongkut. The main entrance is on Sorasak Road near the Asia Lopburi Hotel. The palace and museums are open Wed.-Sun. 0900-1700. Admission is 20B.

A beautiful old house stands immediately to the right of the main eastern gateway. To the left are remnants of a water reservoir and storage houses while straight ahead, through the crenellated walls, are the inner courtyard and central buildings. The middle wall is pocketed with hundreds of small niches which once held glowing oil lamps, doubtless an impressive sight on royal celebrations.

Chantara Phisan Pavilion: The museum on the right was constructed in 1665 as the royal residence of King Narai. French architects designed the palace, which shows European influence in its pointed doorway arches. Restored by King Rama III, today it serves as the Lopburi National Museum with a small but worthwhile collection of Lopburi and Dvaravati images. Impressive statuary is placed on the palace grounds.

Sutha Vinchai Pavilion: Phiman Mongkut Pavilion, on the left, was constructed by King Mongkut and now serves as an extension of the National Museum in Bangkok. The top level of the three-story building holds the private apartment and study of King Mongkut. To the rear is a Farmer's Museum, which exhibits rare tools and farming artifacts, and eight bijou houses which once guarded the king's concubines.

Audience Hall: The Dusit Sawan Thanya Mahaprasat, an eerie hollow shell to the left of the museums, originally served as an audience hall for ambassadors and high-ranking foreign visitors. King Narai hosted guests from the court of King Louis XIV inside the hall once fitted with huge mirrors designed to imitate the Hall of Mirrors in Versailles.

Sutha Sawan Pavilion: Below the central courtyard is another audience hall which served as the final residence of King Narai until his death in 1688. Elephant *kraals* are found beyond the wide gates.

To truly understand the grandeur of the royal court, imagine it laid out with gardens, fountains, and statues surrounded by sumptuously dressed royalty, military leaders, and lovely concubines.

Wat Mahathat

Lopburi's finest architectural treasure and one of Thailand's best examples of Khmer provincial art is located just opposite the train station. The temple was constructed by the Khmers in the 12th century on the ruins of an earlier temple, but was heavily renovated by Siamese kings during the Ayuthaya and Sukothai Periods. Centerpiece is the Khmer *prang* richly embellished with outstanding stucco lintels lacking the foliage ornamentation popular during the late 12th century. A beautiful and imposing sight, the *prang* architecturally marks the transition from pure Khmer to the Siamese style favored in Ayuthaya.

Also on the grounds is a large brick *viharn* which dates from the reign of King Narai and shows European and Persian influences in its pointed arch window. *Chedis* nearby are later constructions dating from the Sukothai and Ayuthaya Periods. Only traces of the square cloister which once surrounded the central *prang* remain visible.

Admission at the northern entrance is 20B. While some visitors are content to snap a few photos over the wall, this monument is worth the admission fee.

Near the station is a locomotive manufactured in 1919 by North British Locomotive, and a decrepit Khmer temple with odd European statues and racist posters illustrating human evolution.

Wat Nakhonkosa

Bangkok's Fine Arts Department has recently completed restoration on the ruins of this 12th-century Khmer *chedi, viharn,* and small *prang* originally dedicated to Hindu gods. Lopburi and U-Thong images uncovered from the lower *chedi* are now displayed in the Lopburi Museum.

Monkey Shrine

San Pra Khan—the so-called Kala Temple—consists of the ruins of a large 10th-century Khmer *prang,* the dimensions of which indicate its once considerable size, as well as a small later temple noted for its sandstone doorway graced with images of Vishnu and *nagas*. To the rear stands a modern and rather nondescript temple erected in 1953 with statues of Hindu divinities highly revered by the Thai people. The temple is dedicated to, and dominated by, a gold-covered, four-armed image of Kala, the

Hindu god of time and death, incongruously capped with the head of Buddha. Behind is an elevated courtyard and giant banyan tree inhabited by aggressive monkeys that snatch purses and cameras from unsuspecting tourists. Hold onto your bags!

Prang Sam Yot

Prang Sam Yot—"Temple of the Three Towers"—is a fairly well-preserved example of Bayon-style Khmer architecture which, together with Wat Mahathat, once served as one of Lopburi's two principal Hindu temples. Archaeologists believe the structure was originally dedicated to Hindu gods and later converted into a Buddhist sanctuary as suggested by the modest interior collection of *nagas,* Hindu images, and life-sized Buddhas in the Lopburi style.

Regarded as the primary landmark in Lopburi, the complex consists of a central corridor which links three laterite towers dedicated to Brahma, Shiva, and Vishnu. This finely balanced trio currently graces the back of Thailand's 500B currency note, though perfect symmetry has been marred by an east *viharn* erected during the reign of King Narai. The floor plan resembles a Greek cross with corbelled-roof porticoes on four sides.

Prang Khaek

The busiest intersection in Lopburi encircles a Hindu shrine erected in the 11th century by the Khmers, and restored in the 17th century by King Narai. The strange location intrigues more than the monument itself.

Wat Sao Tong Tong

Northwest of the Royal Palace stands another temple complex filled with an odd assortment of monuments. The *viharn* (Pra Viharn) to the right of the gaudily painted modern *wat* was originally constructed by King Narai to serve as a Christian chapel for Western diplomats. Though heavily restored in a pseudo-Western style, Pra Viharn shows typical Ayuthayan details such as tall and slightly concave foundations, superimposed roofs, and pilasters decorated with foliage capitals. The elegant structure—now a Buddhist sanctuary—features an immense seated Buddha and recessed wall niches filled with a collection of small but remarkable Lopburi images.

Outside the temple is a modern *sala* which displays a carved wooden pulpit dating from the Ayuthaya Period, monastic buildings constructed by King Narai, and distinctive residences erected for visiting ambassadors and Christian missionaries.

Phaulkon's Residence

This complex displays a broad patchwork of architectural styles in which European predominates, but not to the exclusion of Thai influences. Chao Praya Wichayen was originally constructed by King Narai as a residence for a French ambassador sent from the court of King Louis XIV, but later became the final home to an infamous Greek adventurer named Constantine Phaulkon. Phaulkon's attempts to convert Narai to Christianity resulted in his beheading, the ouster of all Westerners from the royal courts in Lopburi and Ayuthaya, and the near-complete destruction of his residence and all ancillary buildings!

The narrow courtyard to the rear holds a Roman Catholic church, Jesuit residence, and remains of a bell-shaped tower. To the east are residences constructed for members of the 1685 French mission.

The complex has been completely restored, though there's less of interest here than at the Royal Palace and Wat Mahathat.

Accommodations

Hotels in Lopburi are basic but reasonably clean, proprietors friendly, and prices low—a great change from towns dominated by mass tourism.

Asia Lopburi Hotel: Best bet for comfortable lodgings in the center of town is the basic hotel just opposite the Royal Palace. 1 Sorasak, tel. (036) 411892, 140-180B fan, 280-350B a/c.

Naprakan Road Hotels: Several inexpensive hotels are strung along Naprakan Road just opposite the train station. Rooms at the **Suparapong, Thai Sawat, Julathip,** and **Indra** start from 120B fan and 250B a/c. Ask for the cheapest room rather than accept the more expensive options offered by the manager.

Nett Hotel: Tucked away in a quiet alley, this convenient hotel has large, clean rooms and homey decorations. Check this one if the Asia Lopburi is filled. 17/1 Rajadamnern Rd., tel. (036) 411738, 150-300B fan, 300-400B a/c.

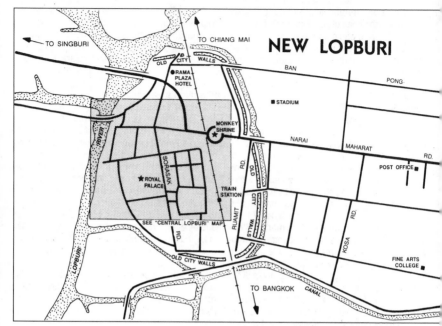

Taipei Hotel: Another decent budget hotel just past the Honda dealership. 29/6 Surasongkram Rd., tel. (036) 411524, 120-180B fan, 200-260B a/c.

Rama Plaza Hotel: A new business traveler's hotel with better rooms than those in the older places in town. 4 Banpong Rd., tel. (036) 411663, 220-320B fan, 320-450B a/c.

Lopburi Inn: Located in New Lopburi on the main road between the two traffic circles, this is the only hotel in town with a/c rooms and modern facilities. 28/9 Narai Maharat Rd., tel. (036) 412300, fax (036) 411917, 600-800B.

Lopburi Inn Resort: Best in town, also located way out in New Lopburi. 144 Tambon Tha Sala, tel. (036) 420777, fax (036) 412010, 2,200-2,800B.

Restaurants

Lopburi offers a limited number of simple restaurants. Snacks are available from the **night market** on Naprakan Road opposite the Julathip and Thai Sawat Hotels. The Chinese restaurant in the **Asia Lopburi Hotel** serves both Chinese and Thai dishes in fairly comfortable surroundings. An es-

cape from the heat is provided by the two branches of a/c **Foremost Restaurant** on Napraka Road and just north of the **Traveler's Drop In.** Other popular restaurants include the **White House Garden** in the center of town, upscale **Chan Chao Restaurant** near Wat Mahathat, and **Boon Coffee Shop** near the Indra Hotel.

Entertainment

Nightclubs and discos are located in New Lopburi near the first traffic circle. The most popular spot is **Chao Praya Nightclub,** where live music is offered during the week and disco on weekends. Back in the old town, **Big Bell Bar** adjacent to the Suparapong Hotel is a popular spot to spend an evening.

Thai classical dance and music can be found at the Nartasin School of Art, where young students from nearby provinces train for professional careers in the performing arts. Mornings around 1000 are the best time to observe the students and take a tour of the facilities. Nartasin (Vithayalia Kalasilpa University) is in New Lopburi, about three km from old town. Take a

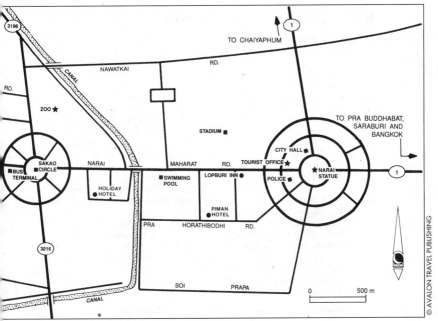

blue *songtao* from Three Pagodas bus stop to the first traffic circle, walk 10 minutes south, then west along the canal to the Fine Arts College.

Lopburi's municipal **swimming pool** is on the right side of the road in New Lopburi, about one km beyond Sakao Circle. It's open daily 1000-2000 and charges a 25B admission fee.

Transportation
Lopburi, 150 km north of Bangkok and 75 km from Ayuthaya, can be visited as an overnight excursion or as an afternoon trip from Ayuthaya. Rushed travelers can leave their bags at the train station, conduct a three-hour walking tour, and continue by night train to either Phitsanulok or Chiang Mai.

Bus: Buses leave Bangkok's Northern Terminal every 30 minutes 0600-1900 and take about three hours to reach Lopburi. Buses from the central market in Ayuthaya leave every 30 minutes.

Lopburi can also be reached direct from Kanchanaburi, avoiding the nightmare of travel connections in Bangkok. From Kanchanaburi, take a bus to Suphanburi (two hours) where buses continue up to Singburi (three hours) and on to Lopburi (30 minutes). Travelers coming from Korat and the northeast should transfer to a connecting bus in Saraburi. The Lopburi bus station is in the new town about two km east of old town. To reach the station from old town, take any *songtao* going west.

Train: Trains from Bangkok's Hualampong station depart every two hours 0600-2000 and take about three hours to reach Lopburi. The train from Ayuthaya takes an hour and passes through lovely scenery of ricefields and idyllic villages. The express sleeper train from Bangkok to Chiang Mai passes through Lopburi at 2020. Reservations should be made on arrival in Lopburi. The Lopburi station is conveniently located within walking distance of all attractions and the budget hotels in the old town.

SARABURI AND PRA BUDDHABAT

Saraburi is a small provincial town 113 km from Bangkok on the highway to the northeastern

JUST SAY NO AT OPIUM PIPE MONASTERY

*C*an a radical therapy concocted of strange herbs and rigorous spiritual practice cure hard-core drug addiction? For over 30 years, a Thai monk named Pra Chamroon Parnchand has been saving addicts with an extraordinary 70% success rate. His unorthodox yet highly efficacious treatments won him the prestigious Ramon Magsaysay Award for Public Service in 1975, and his worldwide reputation ensures a steady stream of opium, heroin, cocaine, and crack cocaine addicts.

Although all patients are ensured absolute privacy, visitors over the past two decades have included American lawyers, stockbrokers, corporate presidents, Asian politicians, Italian fashion designers, rock stars, senior Islamic religious authorities, disciples of the Dalai Lama, sons and daughters of the rich and famous, and an African-American Vietnam veteran (Gordon Baltimore from Harlem) who now welcomes nervous arrivals. All share the same quarters and conduct therapy together.

The 15-day rehabilitation course begins with a sacred vow never to use drugs again; the oath is written on rice paper and swallowed. The first five days include detoxifying vomit sessions in which patients drink a potion made from 100 wild plants which grow on the monastery grounds; it "tastes like stale tobacco that burns like fire." Long gulps of holy water are followed by convulsions and violent spasms of vomiting which remove the toxic waste of years of addiction. Afternoons are spent in herbal saunas spiced with lemongrass to purify the blood and morning glory to restore the eyesight. The final 10 days involve working in the fields and helping the resident monks with construction projects. The treatment has been broadened with religious and psychological elements. To date, more than 100,000 drug addicts have taken the treatment, which is completely free aside from voluntary contributions.

Wat Tham Krabok ("Opium Pipe Monastery") is located in a hillside monastery some 125 km north of Bangkok and 25 km from Saraburi, midway between Lopburi and Saraburi. Anyone with a serious drug problem may want to seek out the extraordinary treatments offered by Pra Chamroon Parnchand. Casual visitors are also welcome.

town of Korat. Saraburi has little of interest aside from the shrine at Pra Buddhabat and the drug rehabilitation center at Wat Tham Krabok. Most travelers visit the two sites on side trips from Lopburi.

Pra Buddhabat

Pra Buddhabat, 29 km from Saraburi toward Lopburi, is regarded as one of the finest examples of classic architecture in Thailand and is the site of the country's most sacred festival. Along with temples in Doi Suthep, Nakhon Phanom, and Nakhon Si Thammarat, Pra Buddhabat constitutes one of the four most sacred destinations in Thailand. The temple was originally constructed by the kings of Ayuthaya but destroyed by the Burmese in 1765. The present structure was erected by the early kings of Bangkok and improved upon by subsequent rulers.

Entrance is made up a long staircase flanked by a pair of impressive, undulating *nagas* which symbolically transport the visitor from the earthly realm to the heavenly home of the Buddha. The most significant building is an elegant *mondop* that enshrines a two-meter footprint. According to Thai tradition, the footprint was discovered in 1606 by a hunter chasing a deer. Standing on a broad marble platform, the *mondop* features a highly ornate pyramidal roof decorated with a profusion of glass and gold mosaics. Inside the structure is the gold-leaf footprint filled with coins tossed by pilgrims. Also note the elaborate doors inlaid with mother-of-pearl, constructed during the reign of King Rama I.

Pra Buddhabat is considered a powerful place filled with divine magic. Thais believe they can improve their karma by tossing coins into the footprint, ringing the bells with bamboo sticks, and throwing fortune-telling sticks *(siem si)* which now compete with electronic counterparts. Other legends claim you will live a full 93 years if you ring all 93 bells and count them correctly, and that three visits to Pra Buddhabat ensures admittance into heaven.

The temple complex includes several other beautiful and significant buildings. Viharn Luang features a museum filled with religious paraphernalia and donations from pious visitors.

Several small *chedis* and *bots* and a temple dedicated to Kala are also located on the temple grounds.

The best time to visit Pra Buddhabat is during the religious festivals held twice yearly in the early spring and late fall. An estimated 800,000 pilgrims arrive to improve their karma and enjoy entertainment provided by Ferris wheels, magicians, beggars, swindlers, and folk shows of *likay* and *khon.* The first festival, held in the third lunar month, is popular with Chinese since it corresponds with the Chinese New Year. The second festival in the fourth lunar month is mainly attended by Thai pilgrims.

While the festivals are still popular events that celebrate the primordial concept of agricultural society, some of the significance has been lost to modernization, which downplays the importance of cyclical festivals.

Accommodations

Pra Buddhabat Hotels: The **Suk Sant** and the larger **Thanin Hotel** on the main road in Pra Buddhabat have fan-cooled rooms for 120-180B.

Saraburi Hotels: Saraburi has six hotels with both fan and a/c rooms. **Kiaw An Hotel** (tel. 036-211656) at 273 Phahonyothin Rd. has fan rooms for 120B and a/c from 260B. Other hotels in the same price range include the **Saen Suk** (tel. 036-211104) at 194 Phahonyothin Rd. and the **Sap Sin** (tel. 036-211047) at 471 Phahonyothin Rd.

Transportation

Buses and *songtaos* to Pra Buddhabat leave from the bus terminal in New Lopburi. Keep your eyes open for the hillside monastery on the right side of the road. Pra Buddhabat and Wat Tham Krabok are also served by buses and *songtaos* leaving from the Saraburi bus terminal on Banthat Road and from the bus stop near the Bank of Asia.

APPENDIX
SUGGESTED RESOURCES

The following books will help orient you to Southeast Asia and Thailand, discuss the impact of mass tourism on third-world destinations, and fire up your imagination. All books are best read before departure, though *Mai Pen Rai, Culture Shock,* and *Thai Ways*—three highly recommended paperbacks—are available in Bangkok bookstores.

GENERAL TRAVEL LITERATURE

Bloodworth, Dennis. *An Eye For The Dragon.* New York: Farrar, Straus and Giroux, 1970. The former Far East correspondent of *The Observer* incisively examines the comedies and tragedies of Asia, from the fanatic wranglings of Sukarno to racial tensions in Malaysia. Bloodworth makes history and politics—often dry and dull subjects—fascinating and memorable.

Buruma, Ian. *God's Dust.* New York: Farrar, Straus and Giroux, 1989. The former arts editor for the *Far Eastern Economic Review* provides sharp and unsentimental observations of various Asian countries, including 40 pages on Thailand. Buruma questions the survival of Asian cultures against the impact of Westernization.

Fenton, James. *All the Wrong Places.* New York: Atlantic Monthly Press, 1988. In this work, James Fenton—journalist, poet, and critic—is jaundiced, self-indulgent, hard-hitting, and more concerned with personal impressions than scholarly dissertation. The result is a mesmerizing book full of great perceptions.

Iyer, Pico. *Video Night in Kathmandu.* New York: Vintage, 1988. Iyer's incongruous collection of essays uncovers the Coca-colonization of the Far East in a refreshingly humorous and perceptive style. His heartbreaking accounts of decay in the Philippines, brothels in Bangkok, and cultural collisions in Bali form the finest travel writing in the last decade. Do not miss this book.

Nelson, Theodora, and Andrea Gross. *Good Books for the Curious Traveler—Asia and the South Pacific.* Boulder, CO: Johnson Publishing, 1989. Outstanding in-depth reviews of over 350 books, including almost 50 titles to Southeast Asia. Written with sensitivity and great insight. The authors also run a service that matches books with a traveler's itinerary. Write to Travel Source, 20103 La Roda Court, Cupertino, CA 95014, tel. (408) 446-0600.

Richter, Linda. *The Politics of Tourism in Asia.* Honolulu: University of Hawaii Press, 1989. A scholarly study of the complex political problems which confront the tourist industries in Thailand, the Philippines, and other Asian destinations. Filled with surprising conclusions about the impact of multinational firms and the importance of targeting grass-roots travelers rather than upscale tourists.

Schwartz, Brian. *A World of Villages.* New York: Crown Publishers, 1986. A superbly written journal of a six-year journey to the most remote villages in the world. Rich tales of unforgettable people and lands of infinite variety and beauty.

Shales, Melissa, ed. *The Traveler's Handbook.* Chester, CT: Globe Pequot Press, 1988. Fifth edition of the award-winning guide that puts together the contributions of over 80 experienced travelers, all authorities in their particular fields. Practical suggestions on climate, maps, airfares, internal transportation, backpacking, visas, money, health, and theft.

Simon, Ted. *Jupiter's Travels.* New York: Doubleday, 1980. Fascinating account of a 63,000-km motorcycle journey (500cc Triumph Tiger) from Europe, down the continent of Africa, and across South America, Australia, and India. And what does Ted do now? Raises organic produce in Northern California.

Theroux, Paul. *The Great Railway Bazaar.* New York: Houghton Mifflin, 1975. One of the world's finest travel writers journeys from London to Tokyo and back by rail. Rather than a dry discourse on history or sights, Theroux's masterpiece of observation keeps you riveted with personal encounters of the first order. Highly recommended.

Viviano, Frank. *Dispatches from the Pacific Century.* New York: Addison Wesley, 1993. Frank Viviano, foreign correspondent for the *San Francisco Chronicle,* has reported extensively on Asia. His 18-part narrative focuses on his encounters with ordinary individuals, rather than dry interviews with politicians or businesspeople. Viviano's consistently elegant prose and keen interest in the human element make *Dispatches* the best overview since *An Eye for the Dragon.*

DESCRIPTION AND TRAVEL

APA Insight Guides. *Thailand.* Singapore: APA Publications, 1995. Superb photography and lush text make this a useful introduction to the country. Read before traveling.

Clarac, Achille. *Guide to Thailand.* Malaysia: Oxford University Press, 1981. Published over a decade ago, but still the most comprehensive guide to the architecture of Thailand. Dated travel information but highly recommended for historical background and temple descriptions.

Jones, Tristan. *To Venture Further.* Grafton: Hearst Marine Books, 1988. Amazing true tale of how the author and his crew completed the first crossing of the Isthmus of Kra in a longtail boat; both Jones and his assistants were disabled or amputees. A memorial to the crossing is found on the southern coast of Phuket.

O'Reilly, James, and Larry Habegger. *Travelers' Tales Thailand.* Sebastopol, CA: O'Reilly & Associates, 1993. The first of a new series of travel books designed to deepen and enrich your experience in Thailand. Rather than do another guidebook, O'Reilly & Associates collected the finest descriptive writings of 46 talented writers, such as Pico Iyer, Simon Winchester, Norman Lewis, and John Hoskins. Excellent background reading.

Smithies, Michael. *Old Bangkok.* Singapore: Oxford University Press, 1988. Professor Smithies leads you around modern Bangkok but describes the modern attractions in erudite terms.

Valli, Eric, and Diane Summers. *Nest Gatherers of Tiger Cave.* London: Thames and Hudson, 1992. Large-format photography of birds' nests in Southern Thailand. The authors spent over a year living and working with nest collectors on Ko Phi Phi.

Veran, Geo. *50 Trips through Siam's Canals.* Bangkok: Duang Kamol, 1979. A fascinating but outdated guide to the confusing labyrinth of rivers and canals that stretch across southern Thailand. Included are over 30 maps, Thai prices, and brief descriptions of the temples. Later attempts to describe these canals have been less than successful.

HISTORY

Bock, Carl. *Temples and Elephants.* Singapore: Oxford University Press, 1986. Late 19th-century account of the remarkable expedition of Bock from Bangkok to the Golden Triangle. A valuable record of life in Old Siam as seen through the eyes of a percipient traveler.

Davis, Bonnie. *Postcards of Old Siam.* Singapore: Times Editions, 1987. A fascinating pictorial record of the Siamese kingdom from 1883 to WW II told with reproductions of hand-tinted black-and-white postcards.

Gray, Anthony. *The Bangkok Secret.* London: Pan, 1990. A melodramatic novel based on the mysterious death of King Ananda in 1946. The story draws heavily on Thai exotica—drug smugglers, student activists, hilltribe shamans. Gray's semi-pornographic prose and heavy cribbing from *The Devil's Discus* make the novel just as murky as whatever happened in 1946. For obvious reasons, the book is banned in Thailand.

Kruger, Rayne. *The Devil's Discus.* London: Cassell, 1964. The best historical narrative on the death of King Ananda. Sets the stage for events following the national calamity—the purge of the ruling liberals and rise of right-wing generals who oversaw three decades of repressive government until the democratic revolution of 1976. The book is banned in Thailand.

Leonowens, Anna. *The English Governess at the Siamese Court.* Singapore, Oxford University Press, 1988. The overimaginative yet entertaining memoirs of the 19th-century English governess that inspired *The King and I.* Originally written in 1870 but reprinted by Oxford in Asia.

Vincent, Frank. *The Land of the White Elephant.* New York: Harper & Brothers, 1881. One of the best travelogues of the era recounts the adventures of an observant man with cultivated tastes and catholic interests. Vincent describes his encounter with the king of Siam before tramping across the country to visit Angkor, rediscovered only 13 years prior to the publication of the book. Several of the wonderful illustrations are reproduced in this book.

Warren, William. *The Legendary American.* Boston: Houghton Mifflin, 1970. The remarkable career and strange disappearance of Jim Thompson is retold by one of Thailand's most prolific writers. Thompson almost single-handedly revived the mordant silk weaving industry in Thailand; his mysterious disappearance in the hill resort of Cameron Highlands, Malaysia, remains one of Southeast Asia's great puzzles.

Wyatt, David. *Thailand: A Short History.* New Haven: Yale University Press, 1984. The best available synopsis on Thailand is a scholarly yet catchy read for both serious students and interested laypeople seeking insight into the convolutions of Siamese history.

CURRENT EVENTS

Kulick, Elliott, and Dick Wilson. *Thailand's Turn:* *Profile of a New Dragon.* New York, Martins Press, 1993. Kulick, an international lawyer, and Wilson, a former editor at the *Far Eastern Economic Review,* combined their talents to produce an excellent 200-page introduction to the state of modern Thailand. It covers the problems of deforestation, landless peasants, industrial pollution, AIDS, soaring crime rates, and loss of Buddhist values. Kulick and Wilson then put forth the reasons why Thailand will meet the challenges of the next century with more success than their authoritarian neighbors. Let's hope these two are prophets in their own time.

Laothamatas, Anek. *Business Associations and the New Political Economy of Thailand.* Boulder, CO: Westview Press, 1993. Is the present government just another periodic break from military rule, or has the military elite really given up the reins of power? Major changes are suggested by the rise of nonbureaucratic institutions within the government and the ability of business interests to affect government policy. This new political model is explained in the work of Anek Laothamatas as well as in *Demi Democracy* by Likhit Dhiravegin.

Wright, Joseph. *The Balancing Act: A History of Modern Thailand.* Bangkok: Asia Books, 1991. Solid analytical framework and careful attention to detail make this a useful guide to modern Thai politics. Wright's assertion that Thailand's political culture will forever be controlled by elites helps us understand the failure of democracy but also undermines recent changes that indicate otherwise.

THE ENVIRONMENT

Boyd, Ashley, and Collin Piprell. *Thailand: The Kingdom Beneath the Sea.* Bangkok: Artasia Press, 1990. Superb photography, detailed descriptions of marinelife, and tips for scuba divers. Reprinted in 1994 by Hippocrene Books as *Diving in Thailand.*

Caufield, Catherine. *In The Rainforest.* Chicago: University of Chicago Press, 1984. Marvelous descriptive writings on tropical forests and their ongoing destruction—a story of corruption, greed, disaster, and murder told in a sympathetic yet impassioned voice.

Gray, Denis, and Collin Piprell. *The National Parks of Thailand*. Bangkok: Communications Resources, 1991. An excellent survey of 30 national parks and wildlife sanctuaries, plus background on problems faced by park rangers working to save the remaining wildlife in the parks.

Lekagul, Boonsong, and Jeffrey McNeely. *Mammals of Thailand*. Bangkok: Association for the Conservation of Wildlife, 1988. The finest overview of wildlife in Thailand is enriched with maps, photos, and sketches by two of the leading environmentalists in the country.

Lekagul, Boonsong, and Philip Round. *The Birds of Thailand*. Bangkok: Sahakarn Bhaet, 1991. A newer publication that updates the original 1974 guide written by Lekagul and Edward Cronin.

McNeely, Jeffrey, and Paul Spencer Wachtel. *Soul of the Tiger: Searching for Nature's Answers in Exotic Southeast Asia*. New York: Doubleday, 1991. This timely and ambitious book argues that the ancient relationships between humanity and nature provide the best hopes for saving the environment.

Rush, James. *The Last Tree: Reclaiming the Environment in Tropical Asia*. New York: The Asia Society, 1992. Rush uses his expertise as an historian to recount how the Asian environment has been plundered, polluted, and wrecked to the point of exhaustion in less than five decades. Rush blames both the Western world and its insatiable need for natural resources, and the Asian power elite who allow the rape to continue. Money, of course, is the motive.

ART AND ARCHITECTURE

Boisselier, Jean. *The Heritage of Thai Sculpture*. Bangkok: Asia Books, 1987. Written by one of the world's leading authorities on the art of Southeast Asia, the original 1974 edition has been reprinted and is now available from Asia Books in Bangkok.

Conway, Susan. *Thai Textiles*. Seattle: University of Washington Press, 1992. A richly illustrated work that traces the evolution of Thai weaving and costumes from early kingdoms to the 20th century.

Gosling, Betty. *Sukothai: Its History, Culture, and Art*. Singapore: Oxford University Press, 1990. Authoritative survey of the ruins of Sukothai and the lives of the kings who commissioned their construction.

Poshyananda, Apinan. *Modern Art in Thailand*. Singapore: Oxford University Press, 1993. The most important and brutally honest survey of modern Thai art is based on the author's doctoral research at Cornell. Apinan shows how Thai modernism traces its genealogy from Western sources, then continues to evolve through court patronage, nationalistic movements, the turbulent 1970s, and the unending military coups. Apinan's insight and brutal honesty about the current state of Thai art make this a rare and remarkable book.

Siribhadra, Smitthi, and Elizabeth Moore. *Palaces of the Gods: Khmer Art and Architecture in Thailand*. Bangkok: River Books, 1991. An expensive large-format book loaded with excellent photos of Cambodian monuments, all graciously described by the art historian from London's School of Oriental and African Studies.

Van Beek, Steve, and Luca Invernizzi Tettoni. *Arts of Thailand*. New York: Thames and Hudson, 1991. The best introductory guidebook to Thai arts in print. Rich text and great photos.

Warren, William, and Luca Invernizzi Tettoni. *Legendary Thailand*. Hong Kong: Travel Publishing Asia Limited, 1986. Outstanding photographs and clean text; a good introduction to the land and people.

Warren, William, and Luca Invernizzi Tettoni. *Thai Style*. Bangkok: Asia Books, 1988. Thai interior design ranks with Japanese as among the most elegant and highly refined in the world. Bill and Luca will convince you of the sensitive creativity of the Thai people.

FOOD AND SHOPPING

Brennan, Jennifer. *Thai Cooking*. London: Futura Publications, 1984. The California author lived in Thailand for almost a decade during the 1960s and returned home to teach her culinary secrets. Her book offers both dependable recipes and superb insight into the authentic styles of regional cooking.

Hoskin, John. *A Buyer's Guide to Thai Gems and Jewellery*. Bangkok: Asia Books, 1988. Essential reading for anyone contemplating a sizable purchase of gems in Thailand. Excellent photography by Michael Freeman.

Kahrs, Kurt. **Thai Cooking.** Bangkok: Asia Books, 1990. The executive chef at the Menan Hotel in Bangkok serves up delicious recipes from the various regions of Thailand. Color photographs help you visualize the final masterpiece.

Piper, Jacqueline. *Fruits of Southeast Asia*. Singapore: Oxford University Press, 1988. Practical background on the use of tropical fruits in cooking, medicine, and rituals accompanied with helpful photos and early botanical illustrations.

Reimer, Joe, and Ronald Krannich. *Shopping in Exotic Thailand*. Manassas, VA: Impact Publications, 1990. Step-by-step guide to the secrets of shopping in Thailand with detailed descriptions of shopping centers, arcades, factory outlets, and exclusive boutiques.

HEALTH

Dawood, Richard, M.D. *Traveller's Health, How to Stay Healthy Abroad*. Oxford University Press, 1994. This guide to healthy travel is very comprehensive and medically authoritative, though highly technical.

Hatt, John. *The Tropical Traveller*. Hippocrene, 1984. A readable book which served as the bible of healthy travel for many years. Remains useful for its clear descriptions of health and related travel issues such as theft, communication, and culture shock.

IAMAT Directory. The International Association for Medical Assistance to Travelers (IAMAT) in Lewiston, New York, publishes a worldwide directory of English-speaking physicians whose qualifications meet IAMAT standards and who have agreed to treat members for a set fee. Membership in IAMAT is free.

Schroeder, Dirk G., ScD, MPH. *Staying Healthy in Asia, Africa, and Latin America*. Moon Publications, 1999. A handy and compact guide that updates the original publication from Volunteers in Asia. The book includes three chapters on the prevention of illness and general health maintenance on the road, while the remainder describes the diagnosis and treatment of illnesses common to foreign countries. Written for the average traveler in a lively and direct tone.

The Travel Clinic Directory. A free list of physicians specializing in travel medicine in the United States is available from Connaught Laboratories (tel. 717-839-7187) in Swiftwater, Pennsylvania.

Werner, David. *Where There Is No Doctor*. Hesperian Foundation, 1992. A health-care handbook written in nontechnical language with information on children's diseases, pregnancy, use of drugs with recommended dosage, and first aid in third-world countries. Designed for both certified professionals and Peace Corp volunteers intending to work abroad in remote villages.

HUMOR AND PERSONAL TALES

Eckardt, James. *Waylaid by the Bimbos*. Bangkok: Post Publishing, 1991. James Eckardt—writer-in-residence and former dominant guru in Songkhla—finally received worldwide acclaim with his deranged ramblings that resemble a Thai-style Fear and Loathing in the Land of Smiles. A weird and funny work recommended for twisted readers.

Eckardt, James. *Running With the Sharks*. Bangkok: Post Publishing, 1993. An adventure story set in South Thailand filled with assorted characters such as escapist spearfishermen, a heroin smuggler, ex-pirates, and Burmese crewmen armed with M-16s.

Hollinger, Carol. *Mai Pen Rai*. Boston: Houghton Mifflin, 1965. The story of an American housewife's humorous introduction to life in Bangkok. One of the warmest books you will ever read. Highly recommended.

Stephens, Harold. *Asian Portraits*. Hong Kong: Travel Publishing Asia, 1983. Adventurer and free spirit Stephens ran away from his English teaching position in the United States to live out his fantasies in Southeast Asia. The prolific author describes many of the fascinating expatriates he has met over the years.

CULTURE

Cooper, Robert, and Nanthapa. *Culture Shock Thailand*. Singapore: Times Editions, 1993. A humorous paperback that succinctly explains the Thai people, their customs, and hidden rules of social etiquette. Filled with great insight and charm but minimal clichés about the "Land of Smiles." Widely available in Bangkok bookstores; highly recommended.

Cooper, Robert. *Thais Mean Business: The Foreign Businessman's Guide to Doing Business in Thailand*. Singapore: Times Editions, 1993. Cooper, an anthropologist, and his wife Nanthapa forgo ludicrous cultural fantasies to explain cultural idiosyncrasies and prove that cultural awareness is profitable. A serious subject treated with great humor.

Fieg, John Paul. *A Common Core: Thais and Americans*. New York: Intercultural Press, 1989. A fine book explaining with great insight the key similarities and differences between Western and Thai cultures. Highly recommended for any visitor who intends to live or work in Thailand.

Segaller, Denis. *Thai Ways*. Bangkok: Allied Newspapers, 1984. A collection of short essays on Thai ceremonies, festivals, customs, and beliefs. This and the sequel *More Thai Ways* are great books to read while traveling in the country.

Smithies, Michael. *Bight of Bangkok*. Singapore, Heinemann Asia, 1994. The widely published scholar of Asia addresses the forces of modernization in this hard-hitting but realistic look into the underside of a threatened Thai society. His dozen fictional profiles of local residents are based on real stories collected from local newspapers: the mother who trades her two teenage daughters for a red motorcycle; the transvestite hooker with a heart of gold; a three-year-old Buddhist faith healer in the northeast.

HILLTRIBES

Anderson, Edward. *Plants and People of the Golden Triangle: Ethnobotany of the Hill Tribes of Northern Thailand*. Portland, OR: Dioscorides Press, 1994. A botanist at the Desert Botanical Garden in Phoenix, Anderson explores the ethnobotany of the hilltribes and problems associated with the loss of plants used for medicinal purposes, construction, and pleasure.

Campbell, Margaret. *From the Hands of the Hills*. Hong Kong: Media TransAsia, 1978. Lavishly illustrated guide to the handicrafts of the hilltribes.

Grunfeld, Frederic. *Wayfarers of the Thai Forest: The Akha*. New York: Time-Life Books, 1982. Photographic essay on the poorest and most ill-treated of the northern tribes.

Lewis, Paul, and Elaine Lewis. *Peoples of the Golden Triangle*. London: Thames and Hudson, 1984. Paul and Elaine have worked as missionaries in northern Thailand since 1947. This lavishly illustrated book is the best guide available to these intriguing peoples.

Wijeyewardene, Gehen, ed. *Ethnic Groups Across National Boundaries in Southeast Asia*. Singapore: Institute of Southeast Asian Studies, 1990. This collection of essays argues ethnicity is a modern invention, despite the claims of anthropologists who believe ethnicity can be defined by language and historical migrations. The minorities of Thailand threaten government assertions of racial purity and cultural superiority; this sets them on a collision course with the ruling state.

RELIGION

Ross, Nancy. *Three Ways of Asian Wisdom.* New York: Simon and Schuster, 1966. A great and powerful book—beautifully written, well organized, and full of love and understanding. Now considered among the finest books on Asian religions; a superb introduction for the reasonably intelligent reader without prior exposure to Hinduism, Buddhism, and Zen. Highly recommended.

Ward, Timothy. *What the Buddha Never Taught.* Berkeley, CA: Celestial Arts, 1993. Timothy Ward recounts his experiences at a Buddhist monastery in northeastern Thailand (Wat Pa Nanachat) and describes the conflict and disillusion encountered by many Westerners during their initial encounters with Buddhist monastic practices. An amusing but superficial tale told by a young man who stayed only six weeks before reaching his sad and misguided conclusions.

Weir, Bill. *A Guide to Buddhist Monasteries and Meditation Centers in Thailand.* Bangkok: World Fellowship of Buddhists, 1995. The best currently available survey of the meditation retreats of Thailand was meticulously researched and compiled by the author of Moon Publications' guides to Arizona and Utah. Bill's superb tome includes a brief description of Buddhism, advice on living for extended periods in a retreat, and an exhaustive list of all temples that accept Western novices.

Wray, Elizabeth. *Ten Lives of the Buddha.* This beautifully illustrated book describes the final 10 lives of the Buddha from the ancient Jataka tales of the Mahabharta. Filled with rare photos of murals from Wat Suwannaram in Thonburi, Wat Yai Intharam in Chonburi, and Wat Buddhasawan in Ayuthaya.

DRUGS AND PROSTITUTION

Belanger, Francis. *Drugs, the U.S., and Khun Sa.* Bangkok: DK Books, 1989. A brief survey of opium production and profile of drug kingpin Khun Sa. Now badly dated but useful for its hard-hitting accusations against almost everyone connected with the drug industry.

Marshall, Jonathan. *Drug Wars—Corruption, Counterinsurgency and Covert Operations in the Third World.* San Francisco: Cohan & Cohen, 1991. A former economics editor at the *San Francisco Chronicle,* Marshall provides further support to the views of Alfred McCoy that America's costly war to stop drugs at their source has been both hypocritical and ineffective.

McCoy, Alfred. *The Politics of Heroin: CIA Complicity in the Global Drug Trade.* New York: Lawrence Hill, 1991. The Wisconsin University history professor updates his 1972 classic with new information on CIA collaboration with Thai heroin smugglers, Panama's Noriega, Afghan *mujahedeen,* the Sandinistas, and the Pakistani military.

Moore, Christopher. *A Killing Smile.* Bangkok: White Lotus, 1991. Moore peers into the rotten world of bars and prostitution. This fictional account of life in Bangkok's Thermae Cafe then becomes a pedantic lecture on morality with an unbalanced mix of honest *farang* and corrupt bargirls. His "Land of Smiles" trilogy continues with *A Bewitching Smile* and *A Haunting Smile.*

Truong, Thanh Dam. *Sex, Money and Morality: Prostitution and Tourism in Southeast Asia.* London: Zed Press, 1994. A critical and highly charged account of the sex industry in Thailand. Zed Press also publishes *Access to Justice: The Struggle for Human Rights in Southeast Asia.*

THAI AUTHORS

Ekachai, Samitsuda. *Behind the Smile: Voices of Thailand.* Bangkok: Post Publishing, 1990. Revealing interviews by a *Bangkok Post* journalist with impoverished Thai peasants in the Northeast. Valuable insight into the effect of unparalleled economic growth on the rural poor of Thailand.

Majupuria, Trilok Chandra. *Erawan Shrine and Brahma Worship in Thailand.* Bangkok: Tepress

Press, 1990. Concise introduction to the complexities of Thai religion and animistic practices that overlay contemporary Buddhism.

Pramoj, Kukrit. *Four Reigns.* Bangkok: DK Books, 1953. Historical romance spanning the reigns of Rama V to Rama VIII written by a former prime minister and movie star *(The Ugly American).* Pramoj's novel about a noble family has been remade into films, plays, and TV dramas that feature the central character as the archetypical femme fatale.

Rajadhon, Phya Anuman. *Some Traditions of the Thai.* Bangkok: DK Books, 1993. Detailed essays on traditional society written by one of Thailand's leading scholars.

Sivaraksa, Sulak. *Siam in Crisis.* Bangkok: DK Books, 1986. An unusual analysis of Thai politics from one of Thailand's leading intellectuals and political dissidents. Sivaraksa melds Thai Buddhism with his admiration for individualism into themes of disenfranchisement in a burgeoning economy. Although he was forced to flee the country several years ago after accusations of lese majesty, Sivaraksa has returned to continue his biting criticisms of Thai society.

Sudham, Pira. *People of Esarn.* Bangkok: Siam Media International, 1988. Thailand's most well-known author who writes in the English language brings great insight into the realities of poverty in northeastern Thailand. Sudham also wrote *Siamese Drama* (1983) and *Monsoon Country* (1988), and today enjoys a lifestyle in striking contrast to his impoverished background—successful businessman and former president of the Siam Wine Society.

GOOD READING

Conrad, Joseph. *Lord Jim.* London: Penguin, 1900. Conrad's place as one of the greatest writers in the English language was established several years after his visit to Bangkok in 1887 to assume control of a vessel carrying teak to Australia. His three-week visit to Bangkok was spent in the billiards room at the Oriental Hotel (he never stayed there) and on a leisurely excursion to Ayuthaya by two-wheeled gig.

Eames, Andrew. *Crossing the Shadow Line.* London, Hodder and Stoughton, 1986. Eames's account of a two-year odyssey through Southeast Asia speaks of crossing Joseph Conrad's "shadow line" between sanity and madness, youth and maturity. His vivid reporting and personal candor cover the philosophical matters faced by many modern travelers.

Gray, Spaulding. *Swimming to Cambodia.* New York: Theater Group, 1985. Monologist Gray describes his experiences in Thailand during the production of *The Killing Fields* with great insight into the emotional impact of Thailand on a Western visitor. The book later became the movie of the same name.

Maugham, Somerset. *The Gentleman in the Parlour.* London: Heinemann, 1930. A record of the author's journey from Yangon to Haiphong in the early 1920s. Perhaps inspired by a meeting with Joseph Conrad in the spring of 1918, Maugham's subsequent 60 years of creative output eventually shaped many popular conceptions of life in Southeast Asia.

Thompson, Thomas. *Serpentine.* New York: Doubleday, 1979. The true story of Charles Sobhraj, the so-called "bikini killer," who terrorized the continent from India to Thailand until his capture by the Indian police. A compelling, exotic, glamorous, and completely frightening story about psychopaths who wander the backstreets of Southeast Asia.

Young, Gavin. *In Search of Conrad.* London: Hutchinson, 1991. A well-known British writer attempts to retrace the steps of Conrad while interlacing his impressions of the region with quirky opinions about contemporary social issues.

ELECTRONIC SOURCES OF TRAVEL INFORMATION

Surfing the information superhighway is the hottest way to find travel information about every nook and cranny of the planet. With enough hardware and computer expertise you could:
• Retrieve a 40-page country report on Thailand, courtesy of a World Wide Web site

- Add a chapter or two of visitor comments from the Rec.Travel Library at the University of Manitoba in Winnipeg
- Read the CIA's assessment of the country, including concise and detailed advice helpful to the traveler
- Attach a satellite photo of current weather patterns over a map of the country
- Pick up the latest news on political and economic developments from various news services
- Find current travel advisories issued by the U.S. State Department
- Determine the currency exchange rate from Global Network Navigator
- Chat online with a famous travel writer
- Ask for travel advice from an expatriate in Bangkok
- Uncover the newest nightclubs recommended by Worldview Systems
- Check out upcoming adventure tours offered by Mountain Travel Sobek
- Print the whole thing out
- Return your copy of *Bangkok Handbook* for a refund

Internet Resources

The easiest way to get started is with a major on-line service such as America Online (tel. 800-827-6364), CompuServe (tel. 800-848-8199), Prodigy (tel. 800-776-3449), or Delphi (tel. 800-695-4005). All offer special travel forums, e-mail addresses, chat lines, and limited access to the Internet.

You can also get connected directly to the Net through an Internet provider such as Netcom (tel. 800-353-6600). Once hooked up—and familiar with terms like Mosaic, World Wide Web, Gopher, Archie, and Usenet—you're part of an electronic community consisting of over 20 million individuals and 10,000 databases covering every possible field of human endeavor.

The biggest problem is navigating the murky waters of cyberspace. A good place to start is the Traveler's Center from the Global Network Navigator (GNN) Travel Center, a project of O'Reilly & Associates (tel. 800-998-9938) in Northern California. GNN combs the Internet gathering the best travel tips for their readers and dividing it into five sections: Editor's Notes (new communications and editorial advice), Notes from the Road (columns from regional correspondents), Internet Resources (information gathered from websites), Traveler's Marketplace (commercial listings), and Regions in Focus (such as Thailand).

Perhaps the largest travel database is Rec.Travel Library, a nonprofit information service established by the University of Manitoba in Winnipeg with mirror server sites around the world. Rec.Travel is the repository for thousands of travel resources covering every possible topic and worldwide destination. Rec.Travel Library may be reached via tel. (204) 992-2312, fax (204) 831-5583, e-mail: lucas@mbnet.mb.ca, or website www.mbnet.mb.ca/lucas

Two net groups worth checking for online chat are rec.travel.asia (general travel talk) and soc.culture.thailand (political, social issues, etc.).

Travel Publishers and Services

Contact Moon Publications for the current issue of *Travel Matters,* search for health tips, download the Moon booklist, and contact Moon authors.

Moon Sites:
- Moon: www.moon.com
- Carl Parkes e-mail: cparkes@moon.com

General Travel:
- Adventure Travel Books: www.gorp.com/atbook.htm
- American Institute of Foreign Studies: www.aifs.org
- Asiaville: www.asiaville.com
- Council on International Educational Exchange: www.ciee.org
- City Net: www.city.net
- Fodor WorldView: gnn.com/gnn/bus/wview/index.html
- Global Travel Village: www.neptune.com
- Homestay Exchange: hospex.icm.edu.pl
- International Honors Program: world.std.com/~ihp/ihp.html
- Microsoft Expedia: expedia.msn.com

- Pacific Area Travel Association: www.singapore .com/pata/
- TEN-IO Travel: www.ten-io.com
- Travel Library: ftp.cc.umanitoba.ca
- U.S. State Department Travel Warnings: travel.state.gov
- Youth Hostels: www.hostels.com/

Academic Organizations (Southeast Asia):
- Australia National University: coombs.anu.edu.au/WWWVL-AsianStudies.html
- Cornell: www.arts.cornell.edu/seasia
- Northern Illinois University: www.niu.edu/acad/cseas
- UC Berkeley: violet.berkeley.edu/~csasweb
- UC Berkeley: garnet.berkeley.edu:4252/seascalinfo
- University of Michigan: www.umich.edu:80/~iinet/csseas

Adventure Travel:
- Adventure Travel Society: www.adventure-travel.com
- *Asian Dive Magazine:* www.asian-diver.com
- Asian-Transpacific Journeys: www.southeastasia.com
- Earthwatch: www.earthwatch.org
- Journeys International: www.journeys-intl.com
- Mountain Travel Sobek: www.mtsobek.com
- Sea Canoes: www.seacanoe.com
- See & Sea Dive: www.batnet.com/see&sea
- Siam Divers: www.siamdivers.com

Asian Magazines and Newspapers:
- *Asia Inc:* www.asia-inc.com/index.html
- *Asiaweek:* pathfinder.com/@ @G4FHi2Eq9gIAQGB4/Asiaweek
- *Bangkok Post:* www.bangkokpost.net
- *Business Traveler:* www.biztravel.com
- *Far Eastern Economic Review:* www.feer.com

Environmental and Human Rights Groups:
- Amnesty International: www.amnesty.org
- Rainforest Action Network: www.ran.org/ran
- U.S. State Department Human Rights Reports: www.gdn.org/ftp/US_State_Department/Human_Rights_Report_1998

Health:
- Center for Disease Control: www.cdc.gov/cdc.htm
- Stanford Medical Center: www-leland.stanford.edu/~naked/stms
- WHO Tropical Disease Center: www.who.int
- Wisconsin Health Clinic: www.intmed.mcw.edu/travel.html

Maps:
- U.S. Government: www.usgs.gov/
- Map Archive: www.lib.utexas.edu

Thailand Sites:
- Asia Online: www.asia-online.com
- Bangkok Airways: www.bkkair.co.th
- *Bangkok Metro Magazine:* www.bkkmetro.com
- *Chiang Mai News:* www.chiangmainews.com
- *Chiang Mai & Chiang Rai Magazine:* www.infothai.com/wtcmcr
- Coalition Against Prostitution: www.capcat.ksc.net
- Diethelm Tours: www.asiatour.com
- Issan Guide: www.thaiguide.com
- Ko Phangan: www.kohphangan.com
- Ko Samui: www.sawadee.com
- Loxley ISP: www.loxinfo.co.th
- Ministry of Foreign Affairs: www.mfa.go.th
- Pattaya: www.pattaya.com
- Phuket Info: www.phuket.com
- *Phuket Gazette:* www.phuketgazette.net
- Siam Net: www.siam.net
- TAT: www.tat.or.th
- TAT: www.tourismthailand.org
- Thai Airways: www.thaiair.com

- Thai Embassy Bangkok:
  www.inet.co.th/org/usis/embindex.htm
- Thai Embassy U.S.A.: www.thaiembdc.org
- Thai Focus: www.thaifocus.com
- Thai Index: www.thaiindex.com
- Thailand Big Picture: www.nectec.or.th/

Travel Media:
- Amazon Books: www.amazon.com
- Book Passage: www.bookpassage.com
- Condé Nast *Traveler:* travel.epicurious.com
- Lonely Planet: www.lonelyplanet.com
- Outside: www.starwave.com/outside
- Speciality Travel Index: www.spectrav.com
- Travel Channel: www.travelchannel.com
- Travelocity: www.travelocity.com

THE THAI LANGUAGE

Far too many travel books have called Thai an impossible language. The truth is that the vocabulary and syntax are not difficult to grasp and dedicated students can learn to speak some Thai within a few weeks. Even a few rudimentary phrases will help you make friends and save money.

Thai is a monosyllabic, tonal language with 44 consonants, 24 vowels, and five tones. Script is written from left to right without separation between words. There are no prefixes or suffixes, genders, articles, plurals, or verb conjugations. If this makes Thai seem a simple language, think again.

Thai is a tonal language in which each syllable cluster can be pronounced with five different tones: low, middle, high, rising, or falling. Each tone completely changes the meaning of the word. *Suay* with a rising tone means "beautiful" but with a falling tone means "bad fortune." Therefore, Thai pronunciation should be checked with a native speaker for the correct inflection.

Thai Script

The principal "letters" you see in Thai script are the consonants; vowels are represented by a series of squiggles written above, below, behind, or in front of the consonants. This complication means that most visitors should first learn to speak a modest vocabulary before attempting to learn any Thai script. Additionally, most signs at tourist destinations and along highways now show both Thai and Western script, so Westerners on shorter vacations will have few problems making sense of the more important signs in the country.

From English to Thai

Translating English into Thai also poses problems. A few years ago, Pepsi-Cola entered the local soft drink market with their familiar slogan, "Come Alive, Join the Pepsi Generation." But the translation came out as "Drink Pepsi and Bring Your Ancestors Back from the Dead." The wording was quickly changed, but humor columnist Joe Bob noted that the mistranslated promotion was "the only thing that could make Texans swear off all forms of drinking permanently."

Thai Challenges

Westerners who speak non-tonal languages such as English will find that tones are initially a big challenge since we are not accustomed to listening to or associating tones with words in this way. But this must be done. To speak Thai without including the proper tone will result in confusion and, in many cases, peals of laughter from highly amused Thais who appreciate your efforts but find your tonal mishaps a source of constant fun.

Tonal ignorance is the biggest challenge, but another problem for Western visitors is our tendency to use Western-style inflection in our sentences, such as a rising inflection at the end of any sentence that is a question. "Where did you go today?" is pronounced with a rising "today" to indicate that this is a question and not a statement. We also indicate anger, joy, threats, sexiness and other emotions with our Western tonal inflections. You'll have to break these tendencies—and the urge to express emotions with your tone—to speak Thai properly.

An additional obstacle to speaking and learning Thai is that many consonants, vowels, and diphthongs are completely unique sounds with no equivalents in English or other Western languages and no accepted standardization of spelling. Thus, Thai words can be spelled several different ways—such as the avenue in Bangkok variously rendered as Rajadamnern, Ratchadamnoen, and Rajdamnoen. A town south of Bangkok can be spelled either Petchburi, Petchaburi, or Phetchaburi. In general the transliteration from Thai sounds to Western script is a very imprecise science and what you read may not exactly correlate with the proper Thai pronunciation. Several unique Thai sounds cannot properly be expressed with Roman letters. For example, there are sounds midway between "d" and "t" and others midway between "b" and "p". Fortunately, Thai pronunciation is much more logical and consistent than English. Pity the poor Thai student studying English when confronted with cough, rough, though, thought, and through!

The best way for Westerners to get around this stumbling block is to listen carefully to Thai speakers and ask for their help with your pronunciation at every possible opportunity. The simplest possible spelling has been used in this book, but it's no more correct than the system used in other travel guidebooks.

Pronunciation

Thai uses five different tones—low, middle, high, falling, and rising—to alter the meaning of each word in five different ways. The individual tones are represented as low tone (`` ` ``), high tone (´), falling tone (^), and rising tone ( ). No mark is used to indicate middle tones.

The pitch of each tone is determined by average vocal range. Low, middle, and high tones are variations of one's average tonal range, and each tone is pronounced evenly with no vocal inflection. They don't rise or fall but are flat tones spoken at slightly different vocal ranges.

The falling tone is spoken with an obvious drop in pitch, with the loudest part at the beginning of the tone with a quick drop-off into vocal oblivion. The rising tone is quite similar to the Western tone use when asking a question. "Yes?" has the same tonal pattern as the rising tone *"măi."*

The Thai word *mai* is a classic example of the effect of tonal variation which has different meanings depending on the tone. The low-tone *mài* (say it low and soft) means "new," the no-tone (or middle-tone) *mai* means "burn," and the high-tone (say it a little louder and at a higher pitch) *mái* means "question?" The falling-tone *mâi* is a negative indicator, and the rising-tone *măi* means "wood." Therefore, if you say "Mai, mai, mai, mai, mai" with five different inflections, you have said "New wood doesn't burn, does it?" This same principal applies to all other Thai words, which means that you must memorize not only the word but also the proper tone for each particular meaning.

Pronunciation Tips

The various ways to pronounce consonants and vowels are described below, though Thai has a few other common quirks to keep in mind.

B: The Thai "b" is pronounced like the English "p." For example, King Bhumibol is actually pronounced King Pumiphon. The "l" changes to the sound of an "n" (see below).

V: The "v" sound doesn't exist in the Thai language. Any Thai word with a "v" should be pronounced as if written with a "w." Sukumvit Road is actually pronounced "Sukumwit Road."

L and R: These two letters are often used interchangeably in written English and their pronunciation changes to "n" when used at the end of a word. Satul (a fairly rare spelling of a town in southern Thailand) is therefore pronounced "Satun," while *banhar* is pronounced as "banharn."

A and U: These two letters are also used interchangeably in the English transliteration of the Thai language. Therefore, you will find "tam" and "tum" to have the same meaning.

Consonants and Vowels

When you read a Thai word written in English script, you may need to pronounce the word with an original Thai tone. Most of these English transliterations are pronounced the same as in English, though the following letters and combinations of letters have slightly different pronunciations that you might expect.

Once again, the best way to figure out correct pronunciation is to listen to a native Thai speaker or purchase a Thai language cassette or CD-ROM as a learning tool.

Consonants

Most of the 44 Thai consonants are pronounced exactly like English, though the following English-script equivalent of Thai consonants have unique sounds which should be mastered.

th / as a "d" or the "t" in "tea" rather than the "th" in "the"

ph / as the "p" in "put" and never as the "ph" in phone

kh / as the "k" in "keep

k / flat and closer or a "g" than a "k" sound

t / flat and closer to a "d" than a "t" sound

p / flat and closer to a "b" than a "p" sound

ng / as the "ng" at the end of "sing"

r / flat and closer to a "l" than a "r" sound

Vowels

Many Thai vowels carry unique types of sounds somewhat different than in English.

a / short "a" as in "dad"

aa / long "a" as in "father"
ai / long "i" as the "i" in "pipe"
ae / nasal "a" as in "bat"
ao / nasal inflection as in "now"
aw / as in "awe"
ay / long "I" as in "buy"
e / as the "e" in "pen"
ee / as the "ee" in "feet"
eh / as the "a" in "gate"
eu / as the "deux" sound in French
i / as the "i" in "tip"
ia / say "eee" then "yah"
o / as the "o" in "bone"
oe / short "u" sound as in "hut"
oh / as the "o" in "toe"
u / as the "u" in "loot"
uu / as the "oo" in "food"

More Language Tips

Several other important points should be made before launching into a list of words and useful phrases.

Polite Particles: Expressions of politeness are tacked to the end of most sentences, depending on whether the speaker is male or female. Male speakers should add *"kráp"* (with a high and strong tone!) at the end of most statements or questions, while females should add *"kà"* (with a soft and falling tone). Thus, men use the phrase *"sawàsdee kráp"* (a general greeting) while females say *"sawàsdee kà."*

Negatives with Falling Tone *"Mai":* Negatives are indicated by putting a falling tone *"mâi"* before a verb or adjective. For example, *"sabai"* means "well" and *"mâi sabai"* means "not well."

Questions with Rising Tone *"Mǎi":* Questions are created by adding a rising tone *"mǎi"* at the end of a phrase, somewhat similar to tacking on "isn't it?" to an English language statement. Therefore, *"kow dai mǎi"* means "may I come in?" Remember, when asking a question to a Thai, add a *"mǎi"* to the end of the sentence rather than raising the inflection of the final word (as you normally do in English).

Common Expressions

Here are a few phrases for the first-time visitor.

Mâi pen rai: Roughly translates to "Never mind" or "It doesn't matter." It suggests a state of mind similar to the Buddhist disregard of the unimportant events of life since what happens is inevitable and it doesn't help to get uptight. This rather happy-go-lucky attitude is an essential element of the Thai spirit, although it can irritate the rigid Westerner. Learning to say *mâi pen rai* in the event of a delayed train or lost luggage will help you keep your sanity while on the road.

Sanùk: "Pleasure" or "fun." Thais believe life is meaningless without fun! High value is placed on whether something is pleasurable or not. Food, drink, sex, sports, festivals, and fairs are all great fun. Even a poorly paid job is acceptable if pleasurable. *Tuk tuk* drivers roar around corners on two wheels for the sake of *sanùk.*

Pai tio: To wander aimlessly, hang out, or just waste time. Going *pai tio* is definitely *sanuk.* Strolling aimlessly on a warm evening is the ultimate in *pai tio.* When a Thai asks you where you are going, just respond with a friendly *"pai tio."*

USEFUL TRAVELER'S PHRASES AND VOCABULARY

Greetings

hello / *sawàsdee*
How are you? / *pen yangai?*
I'm fine. / *sabày dit*
Thank you. / *kàwp khun*
Excuse me. / *khǎw thâwt*
Good luck. / *chôck dee*
please / *kor*

Language Difficulties

Do you understand? / *khâw jai mǎi?*
I don't understand. / *mâi khâw jai*
I speak little Thai. / *puût pasǎ Thai nitnòy*
It doesn't matter. / *mâi pen rai*

Questions, Requests, and Answers

Can I take a photo? / *tai ruûp dâi mâi?*

How far? / *kiai taôrai?*

How long? / *nan taôrai?*

How much? / *taô rai?*

How? / *yang rai?*

I don't know. / *mâi róo*

I want . . . /
   dichán tonggam . . . (spoken by female)

I want . . . /
   pǒm tonggam . . . (spoken by male)

What does that mean? /
   maǎi kwarm wâa arai?

What is the problem? / *mee punhǎa arai?*

What's this called in Thai? /
   née pasǎ Thai riâk waâ arrai?

When? / *meûa rai?*

Where is . . . ? / *. . . yutînǎi?*

Where? / *tinǎi?*

Who? / *krai?*

Why? / *tammǎi?*

don't have / *mâi mee*

don't want / *mâi aò*

no / *mâi*

no good / *mâi dee*

okay / *oh-kay*

sorry / *kǒr tôwt*

yes / *châi*

Transportation

Where is the bus station? /
   sattǎni rót may yutînǎi?

How many buses per day? /
   rót may òrk wan la geè tiâo?

When is the first bus? /
   rót may tiâo râck òrk geè mong?

When is the last bus? /
   rót may tiâo sutái òrk geè mong?

When is the next bus? /
   rót may tiâo nâa òrk geè mong

When does the bus arrive? /
   rót may maa tỷ ng geè mong?

Where can I leave my luggage? /
   gapao ao wai têe nǎi dee?

Can you buy a ticket for me? /
   chuây sỷ y tǔa hâi dichán (spoken by female)

Can you buy a ticket for me? /
   chuây sỷ y tǔa hâi pǒm (spoken by male)

Please write down the timetable. /
   chuây kiǎn

boat / *rya*

boat dock / *tah rya*

boat, longtail / *rya hang yao*

bus, air-conditioned / *rót tooa*

bus, mini / *rót sǒng tǎyo*

bus, ordinary / *rót tammada*

bus station / *sattǎni rót may*

express / *duan*

ferry / *rya doy sam*

ferry pier / *thaa rya doy sam*

plane / *kryang bin*

seat / *têe nâng*

sleeper / *tôa non*

ticket / *tǔa*

timetable / *tarang welaa*

train / *rót fai*

train station / *sattǎni rót fai*

Vehicle Rentals

Where can I rent a bicycle? /
   châo rót jakayarn têe nǎi?

Where can I rent a car and driver? /
   châo rót próm kon úp daî têe nǎi?

Where can I rent a motorcycle? /
   châo rót motorsay têe nǎi?

Where can I hire a boat? /
   châo rya têe nǎi?

How much per hour? /
   káh châo chuamong la tâorai?

How much for a half-day? / *kryng wan tâorai?*

How much for one day? / *wan nỳing tâorai?*

bicycle / *rót jàkrayan*

driver/guide / *kon kúp rót*

motorcycle / *rót motorsai*

motorcycle taxi / *rót motorsai láp jârng*

taxi / *teksî*

Destinations

airline office / *têe tam ngam saăi kam bin*
airport / *sanăm bin*
bank / *tanakan*
beach / *hàt*
bookshop / *rám kăi nangsyý*
drugstore / *ráhn kaiyăa*
embassy / *sathăn tôot*
gas station / *pam namman*
hospital / *rong payabaan*
market / *talaàt*
museum / *pipitaphan*
police station / *sattăni tamrùat*
post office / *praisinee*
restaurant / *ráan ahăan*
temple / *wàt*
tourist office / *samnakngan karn tong tiâo*

Accommodations

May I see the room? / *doo hôrg dâi măi?*
Can you give me a discount? /
   lòt raakah dâi măi?
bathroom / *hông naám*
bathroom, men's / *hông naám chai*
bathroom, women's / *hong naám ying*
dormitory / *hŏr púck*
guesthouse / *guest how*
hotel / *rong raem*
hotel, budget / *rong raem tùke*
hotel, good / *rong raem dee*
mosquito net / *mûng*
room with air-conditioning / *hông air*
room with bath / *hông têe mee hông naam*
room, double / *hông kôo*
room, single / *hông dêeo*
room, triple / *hông non sărm kon*
sheets / *pâr poo têe non*
shower / *aàp naám duay fárk bua*
shower with hot water / *naám ron*
telephone (noun) / *tora sap*
towel / *pâr chét tua*

Medical

I need a doctor. / *tong hăa mŏr*
I need a dentist. / *tong hăa mŏr fun*
Please help. / *chuây duây*
cold (adj.) / *pen wàt*
diarrhea / *tóng dern*
drugstore / *rárn kai yaa*
emergency / *chúg chĕrn*
fever / *kaî*
headache / *puàt hua*
hospital / *rong payabuarn*
sick / *mâi sabai*
sore throat / *jèp kor*

Shopping

How much is this? / *nee taôrai?*
Do you have? / *mee măi?*
Do you have anything cheaper? /
   toòk gwa née mee măi?
Can you give me a better price? /
   loàt raakah dâi măi?
I will come back. /
   dichán ja giàp maa (spoken by female)
I will come back. /
   pŏm ja giàp maa (spoken by male)
new / *mai*
old / *gaò*
too big / *yài kern pai*
too expensive / *paeng pai*
too small / *lék kern pai*

Personal Questions

What is your name? / *khun chêu arrai?*
My name is . . . /
   dichán chêu . . . (spoken by female)
My name is . . .
   pŏm chêu . . . (spoken by male)
Where are you from? / *khun maa jàk năi?*
I come from . . . /
   dichăn maa jàak . . . (spoken by female)
I come from . . . /
   phŏm maa jàak . . . (spoken by male)

America/Canada/Australia /
    Ameriga/Kanada/Australia
British/French/Italian / *Angrit/Farangset/Italee*
Where are you going? / *pai nǎi?*
I'm just having fun. / *pai thîaw*
How old are you? / *kun aayú taôrai?*

Family Status

married / *tangngam layo*
single / *pen soàt*
husband / *sǎr mee*
wife / *phanlaya*
mother / *mâre*
father / *pôr*
children / *lûke*
son / *lûke chai*
daughter / *sǎo*
brother / *pêe (older), nóng (younger)*
sister / *chai (older), sǎo (younger)*

Flattery

The food is delicious. / *ahǎan arròi*
The food is excellent. / *arròi maâk*
Cheers! / *chai yo*
I had a great time. /
    dâi ráb kwam sanùk sabai
I love this town. / *myang nêe pǒm chôp mârk*
    (spoken by female)
I love this town. /
    myang nêe dichán chôp mârk
    (spoken by male)
beautiful / *suǎy maâk*
excellent / *dee maâk*
good / *dee*
interesting / *nâr son jai maâk*

Directions

How far is it to . . . ? / *pai . . . taôrai?*
How many kilometers? / *gi kilo pai?*
I want to see . . . /
    dichán yùck doo . . . (spoken by female)
I want to see . . . /
    pǒm yùck doo . . . (spoken by male)

I'm going to . . . / *pai . . .*
Let's go. / *pai ler ee*
Stop here. / *yùd tî nêe*
Wait here. / *ror têe nêe*
Where can I get a map? /
    sýy pǎntêe têe nǎi dâi?
fast / *rayo*
slow / *cháa*
slow down / *cha cha noi*
straight ahead / *trong pai*
turn left / *leó sai*
turn right / *leó kwǎ*
east / *tawanòrk*
north / *neua*
south / *tâi*
west / *tawantòk*

Geographical Terminology

bay / *ào*
beach / *hàt*
bridge / *saphan*
canal / *klong*
cape / *laem*
city / *nakhon*
district / *amphoe*
hill / *khâo*
island / *kò*
lane / *soi*
mountain / *doi*
pier / *tha*
province / *changwàt*
river / *mae nám*
street / *thanôn*
town / *muang*
village / *ban*
waterfall / *nám tòk*

Time

What is the time? / *kee mohng láew?*
afternoon / *bai*
day / *wan*
evening / *yen*

month / *deuan*

morning / *ton chaó*

now / *deeo née*

this evening / *ye née*

today / *wan née*

tomorrow / *prung née*

tonight / *kern née*

year / *pee*

yesterday / *mya wan née*

Days of the Week

Sunday / *wan aathit*

Monday / *wan jan*

Tuesday / *wan ang kan*

Wednesday / *wan poót*

Thursday / *wan prýhàrt*

Friday / *wan sòok*

Saturday / *wan sǎo*

Numbers

0	*suun*
1	*neùng*
2	*sǒng*
3	*sǎm*
4	*si*
5	*hâ*
6	*hòk*
7	*jèt*
8	*baàt*
9	*gôw*
10	*sìp*
11	*sìp-èt*
12	*sìp-sǒng*
13	*sìp-sǎm*
14	*sìp-si*
15	*sìp-hâ*
16	*sìp-hòk*
17	*sìp-jèt*
18	*sìp-baàt*
19	*sìp-gôw*
20	*yî-sìp*
30	*sǎm-sìp*
40	*si-sìp*
50	*hâ-sìp*
60	*hòk-sìp*
70	*jèt-sìp*
80	*baàt-sìp*
90	*gôw-sìp*
100	*neùng rói*
500	*hâ rói*
1,000	*neùng pan*
10,000	*mern*
20,000	*sǒng mern*
100,000	*sǎn*
1,000,000	*lárn*

FOOD PHRASES AND VOCABULARY

General Terms

to eat / *kin*

to drink / *duem*

breakfast / *ahâan cháo*

lunch / *ahâan glang wan*

dinner / *ahâan kam*

snack / *klaem*

classic meal of the north / *khan toke*

Ordering

Please bring me the menu. / *kǒr doo menu*

May I have . . . ? / *kǒr . . . ?*

Let's eat! / *cher tarn ná kâ (spoken by female)*

Let's eat! / *chern tam ná kráp (spoken by male)*

The bill please. / *kǒr check bin*

Have you eaten? / *Kin khâo?*

Do you have . . . ? / *. . . mi mâi?*

I'm a vegetarian. / *kin jeh*

I can't eat beef. / *kin néua mâi dâi*

I can't eat pork. / *kin mu mâi dâi*

I don't like hot or spicy. / *mâi châwp phèt*

I like it hot and spicy. / *châwp phèt*

I can eat Thai food. / *kin ahâan Thai pen*

Places to Eat

cafe / *raan*
cafe, Chinese thick-rice / *ráan khâo tôm*
cafe, curry-and-rice / *ráan khâo kaeng*
garden restaurant / *ráan suan*
market / *talaat*
night market / *talaat toh rung*
noodle shop / *ráan kuay teow*
restaurant / *ráan ahâan*
vegetarian restaurant /
   ráan ahâan mangsâwirát

Adjectives

bitter / *khôm*
cold / *yen*
dry (without soup) / *haeng*
hot (temperature) / *ráwn*
hot and spicy / *châwp phèt*
hot, a little / *phèt nít nòy*
hot, not at all / *mâi phèt*
large, big / *yai*
liquid (as in curry or soup) / *gaeng*
raw, half-cooked / *dip*
salty / *khem*
sour / *brio*
spicy / *phèt*

Basic Ingredients

bread / *khanôm pan*
cake, biscuit / *khanôm*
egg / *khài*
salt / *kleua*
salted egg / *khài khem*
sugar / *nám tan*

Beverages

coffee, iced, black with sugar / *o liang*
ice / *nám khǎeng*
lemon juice / *nám manao*
milk / *nom*
orange juice / *nám sǒm*
rice liquor / *lâo kǎo*
rum, made from sugar cane / *sàng sǒm*

tea / *nám cha*
water, boiled / *nám tôm*
water, drinking / *nám dèum*
water, plain / *nám plào*
water, purified bottled / *nám dèum khùat*
whiskey, Thai (national brand) / *Mêkǒng*

Cooking Methods

baked, toasted / *ping*
barbecued, roasted / *yang*
boiled / *dom*
boiled until jelled / *long*
fried / *pat*
ground, grated / *see*
roasted / *phao*
steamed / *neung*
stir-fried / *taud*
stuffed / *sawd sai*

Fruits

banana / *klûay*
coconut / *máphráo*
custard apple / *náwy naa*
durian / *thúrian*
guava / *faràng*
jackfruit / *khanun*
lime / *mánao*
longan / *lam yài*
mandarin orange / *sôm*
mango / *mámûang*
mangosteen / *mangkút*
papaya / *málákaw*
pineapple / *sàppàrót*
pomelo / *sôm oh*
rambeh / *máfai*
rambutan / *ngáw*
rose apple / *chom phû*
sapodilla / *lamut*
tamarind / *mákhǎm*
watermelon / *taeng moh*

Meats

beef / *núa*
bird / *nok*
chicken / *gài*
duck / *pèt*
frog / *kob*
meatball / *luchin nua*
pork / *mú*
poultry / *gài lae pèt*
quail / *nok krataa*
rabbit / *kratai*
spiced minced ground beef / *laab*
spicy sausages / *nem*
tongue / *lin*

Seafood

crab / *pu*
dried fish / *kûng haeng*
fish / *pla*
lobster / *kûng talai*
mussel / *hôi malaeng po*
oyster / *hoi naang rom*
prawn / *kûng foi*
scallop / *hôi shell*
shellfish / *hôi*

Vegetables

bean / *thua phuu*
bean sprouts / *thua ngok*
bitter melon / *márá jeen*
brinjal / *màkhěua prà*
cabbage / *phàk kà làm*
cauliflower / *dàwk kà làm*
corn / *khâo phôht*
cucumber / *taeng kwa*
eggplant / *màkhěua mûang*
garlic / *kràtiam*
lettuce / *phàk kàat*
long bean / *thùa fák yao*
mushroom / *hèt*
onion bulb / *hua hǎwm*
onion scallions / *tôn hǎwm*
peanuts / *tùa lisǒng*
potato / *man faràng*
pumpkin / *fák thawng*
spinach / *pàk kôhm*
taro / *pheùak*
tomato / *màkhěua thêt*

GLOSSARY

aahan—food

achaan—religious leader; teacher

amphoe—district

amphoe muang—provincial capital

ao—bay

apsara—female celestial being

Avalokitesvara—a principal bodhisattva

baht—a Thai unit of currency; also, a unit of weight used to measure gold that equals approximately 15.2 grams

bai semas—eight boundary stones defining consecrated ground and helping to ward off evil spirits; often protected by small, richly decorated tabernacles with spires and runic symbols

ban—village

ba nam ran—hot springs

bang—village along a waterway

bhikku—Buddhist monk

bo—tree under which the Buddha became enlightened

bodhisattva—saint in Mahayana Buddhism; the future Buddha in previous incarnations in Theravada Buddhism; an enlightened being who has returned to help humans

bot—temple building for sermons and services; surrounded by foundation stones

Brahma—four-faced creator in Hindu mythology

bung—lake or swamp

buri—town

chang—elephant

changwat—province

chao nam—sea gypsies

chedi—decorative spire containing amulets or religious icons

chiang—town or city

chofa—slender, curved temple decoration adorning the ends of roofline ridges; symbolizes the *garuda*

deva—angel or divine being

devaraja—divine king

dhammachakha—Buddhist Wheel of Law; circular motif used in Dvaravati sculpture

dharma—law and teachings of the Buddha

doi—mountain

Erawan—mythical three-headed white elephant; mount of Indra

farang—foreigner of European descent

Ganesha—elephant-headed Hindu god of literature and success

garuda—mythical animal with bird head and human torso; the mount of Vishnu; half-brother and enemy of the *naga*

gatoei—transvestite

gopura—Khmer ornamental covered gateway

hang yao—longtail boat

Hanuman—mythical monkey warrior who leads the monkey army in the Ramakien epic

harmika—the small pavilion near the summit of a *chedi* that symbolizes the Buddha's seat of meditation

hat—beach

hin—stone

ho trai—temple library

ikat—a woven fabric in which the yarn is tie-dyed before the weaving process begins

Indra—chief Hindu god of heaven; resides at the top of Mt. Meru

Issan—Northeastern Thailand

Jatakas—previous life stories of the Buddha

Jiin—Chinese

kaeng—rapids

kambarian—sermon hall

kamphang—wall

kan tuei—carved wood supporting roof eaves

kaw lae—traditional fishing boats of southern Thailand

keo—gem, precious stone, honorific title

khaen—reed instrument common to northeastern Thailand

khao—hill or mountain

khon—masked dance-drama based on Ramakien stories

kinnari—mythical animal with bird and female elements

klawng—Thai drums

klong—canal
ko—island; also koh
kuay haeng—Chinese-style work shirt
kuti—small huts used as monk residences

laem—cape or point
lakhon—Thai classical dance-drama
lak muang—city pillar; home to animist spirits
lao khao—white liquor popular in the northeast
likay—Thai folk dance
longyi—a sarong
luang—royal

mae chi—Buddhist nuns
mae nam—river
mahathat—honorific term for very sacred temples which contain Buddha relics
Mahayana—One of the two principal Buddhist sects; Zen and Nichiren traditions
mai ku—pan pipe played at Thai kickboxing events
mai pen rai—"What will be, will be" or "Never mind"
Mara—evil goddess who tempted the Buddha during his meditations
maw hawn—Thai work shirt
maw kwan—triangular-shaped pillow
metta—loving kindness
mondop—temple building erected over a sacred relic, often a footprint of the Buddha
Mt. Meru—mythical mountain abode of the gods; symbolized by the prang and chedi in Thai and Khmer architecture
muang—small town or city
muay Thai—Thai kickboxing
muban—village
mudra—symbolic hand gesture of the Buddha
mut mee—tie-dyed silk

naga—mythical animal; the snake which protected the Buddha against rain
nakhon—large town or city; also nakorn
nam tok—waterfall
nang—Thai shadow play
ngop—traditional Khmer rice farmer's hat
nirvana—a state of enlightenment
nong—lake or swamp

pa tai—batik
Pak Thai—people of southern Thailand
paknam—estuary

Pali—scriptural language derived from Sanskrit; language of Thai Theravada texts
phanom—hill or mountain
phi—spirit or apparition
phi pat—Thai classical orchestra
phu—hill or mountain
pla buk—giant catfish, now found mostly in the Mekong River
pong lang—musical instrument made of resonant logs
pra phum earth spirits
pra—honorific title given to important Buddhas and temples; also spelled phra
prang—solid spire-shaped temple building containing religious icons
prasat—royal religious edifice with distinctive rooflines
pratu—decorated door

rai—1,600 square meters
ram muay—Thai boxing dance
ram wong—traditional Thai dance
Ramakien—Thai version of the Ramayana epic; recounts the adventures of Rama and Sita and their battles with Totsakan, king of the demons
reua duan—river express boat
reua kam fak—cross-river boat
rot thammada—ordinary bus
rot thua—tour bus

sala—open-air building used for resting
sala klang—provincial offices
samlor—three-wheeled pedicab
sanam—open grounds
sangha—monastic community
sanjao—shrine
sanuk—"Life is a pleasure"
saphan—bridge
sema—sacred boundary stones placed at corners and axis of the bot
Shiva—Hindu god of death, destruction, and regeneration
soi—lane
songkran—Thai new year
songtao—small pickup truck used for public transportation
sra—pond
stang—a basic unit of currency; 100 stang equal one baht

stupa—synonymous with *chedi*

suan—garden

susaan—cemetery

taam sabai—comfortable with one's environment

takraw—a popular Thai ball game

talaat nam—floating market

talat—market

tambon—precinct

tha—pier

thale—sea

tham—cave

thanon—road

that—northeastern religious shrine; reliquary for religious objects

thep—angel or divine being

Theravada—one of the two principal Buddhist sects; the main form of Buddhism in Thailand; also called Hinayana or the Lesser Vehicle

thung—savannah

thu thong—monks who have to take ascetic vows

tom kha kai—a rich chicken and coconut-milk soup flavored with lemongrass, lime leaves, galangal, and shallots; an essential element of Thai cuisine served throughout the country

tongteung—rattan

Tripitaka—Theravada Buddhist scriptures

trok—the smallest of all roads; refers to a very small alley generally running off a slightly larger *soi.*

tuk tuk—three-wheeled motorized transportation

ubosot—another term for *bot*

vajra—thunderbolt of Vishnu

viharn—major temple building similar to but less important than the *bot*

vipassana—Buddhist insight meditation

Vishnu—a Hindu god

wai—Thai greeting with palms pressed together

wai kin—a Thai dance

wang—royal palace

wan pra—Buddhist holy days

wat—temple complex, not a single building

ACCOMMODATIONS INDEX

AA Pattaya Hotel: 206
Amari Airport Hotel: 160
Amari Orchid Resort: 207-208
Ambassador Hotel: 160
Ambassador Jomtien: 208
Anna Guesthouse: 149
A-One Inn: 154-156
Apex Hotel: 207
Apple 2 Guesthouse: 146-147
Asia Guesthouse: 151
Asia Lopburi Hotel: 257
Atlanta Hotel: 157
Ayuthaya Grand Hotel: 252-253
Ayuthaya Guesthouse: 252
Bamboo Guesthouse: 229
Bang Saen Beach Resort: 193
Ban Sukchoke Resort: 139
Bed and Breakfast Guesthouse:
    154
Benz Bungalow: 195
B.J. Guesthouse: 252
Bossotel Inn: 151
Boston Inn: 150
Buddy Guesthouse: 146
Caesar Palace Hotel: 207
Central Guesthouse: 146
Central Plaza Hotel: 160
Champ Guesthouse: 151
Chao Phaya Guesthouse: 150
Chart Guesthouse: 146
C.H. Guesthouse: 146
Chinatown Hotel: 150
Chris Guesthouse: 206
Comfort Inn Airport: 160
Crown Hotel: 157
Diana Inn (Bangkok): 149
Diana Inn (Pattaya): 207
Dusit Resort Hotel: 208
Dusit Thani Hotel: 154
Dynasty Inn: 157
Eastiny Inn & Minimart: 207
Eiger Bar: 206
Elephant & Castle Pub: 206
Erawan Resort: 234
Europa Inn: 206
Felix River Kwai Resort: 230
Flipper Lodge Hotel: 207
Freddy's #2 Guesthouse: 149
Golden Bangkok Guesthouse: 151

Grace Hotel: 157-160
Grand Bungalows: 193
Grand Hyatt Erawan: 156
Green House: 195
Happy Inn: 157
Hello Guesthouse: 146
Highfive Hotel: 206
Hilton International Hotel: 156
Holiday Inn Crowne Plaza: 154
Home Phu Toey Resort: 230
Honey Guesthouse: 149
Honey Lodge: 207
Hotel Norge: 206
Icon, The: 208
Indra Hotel: 257
Inn of the Golden Crab: 206
Joiles Momei Hotel: 206
Jolly Frog Guesthouse: 229
Julathip Hotel: 257
Kabana Inn: 151
Kasem Island Resort: 230
Kenny Guesthouse: 149
Khao San Palace Hotel: 147
Kiaw An Hotel: 261
King's Mansion: 151
Krit Thai Mansion: 156
Krung Sri River Hotel: 252
Kwai Yai River Rafts: 234
L.A. Guesthouse: 149
Landmark Hotel: 160
Lee #3 Guesthouse: 149
Lek Guesthouse: 146
Lek Hotel: 207
Lopburi Inn: 258
Lopburi Inn Resort: 258
Madam Guesthouse: 149
Madras Lodge: 151
Magic Guesthouse: 207
Majestic Hotel: 148
Malaysia Hotel: 150
Ma Maison Hotel and Restaurant:
    206
Marriott Royal Garden Riverside
    Hotel: 154
Maxim's Inn: 160
Mermaid's Beach Resort: 208
Merry V Guesthouse: 147
Miami Hotel: 157
Mit Phaisal: 223

Mit Thaworn: 223
Monarch Lee Gardens: 154
Mongkol Guesthouse: 206
Montien Hotel: 154
Montien Pattaya: 208
Muangphol Lodging Department:
    156
Naaz Guesthouse: 151
Nakorn Inn: 224
Nana City Inn: 157
Nana Hotel: 157
Nett Hotel: 257
New Empire Hotel: 150
New Merry V Guesthouse: 147
New Rotel: 151-152
New Siam Guesthouse: 147
New World House: 147-148
Niagra Hotel: 152
Nipa Guesthouse: 206
Nita's Raft House: 229
Nitaya Guesthouse: 229
Nith Charoen Hotel: 147
Noknoi Hotel: 139
Oriental Hotel: 154
Pailin Rafts: 234
Pai Tong Guesthouse: 252
Palm Villa: 207
Pattaya Park Beach Resort: 204
Peachy Guesthouse: 147
Ploy Guesthouse: 146
Porn Hotel: 206
Pranee Building: 156
President Inn: 160
Prince of Pattaya Beach Hotel:
    207
Privacy Guesthouse: 146
Privacy Hotel: 150
PS Guesthouse (Ayuthaya): 206
P.S. Guesthouse (Kanchanaburi):
    229
Rama Gardens Hotel: 160
Rama Plaza Hotel: 258
Regent Hotel: 156
Rick's Lodge: 229
Rising Sun Hotel: 206
River Guesthouse: 229
River Kwai Farm: 236
River Kwai Hotel: 230
River Kwai Jungle House: 237

River Kwai Village Hotel: 230-231
Riverview Guesthouse: 150
Riviera Beach Hotel: 206
Romklao Rafts: 234
Roof Garden Guesthouse: 147
Rose Hotel: 152
Rovers Return Hotel: 206
Royal Cliff Hotel: 208
Royal Garden Resort: 207
Royal Hotel: 148
Royal Orchid Sheraton Hotel: 154
Ruandrum Ayuthaya Youth
   Hostel: 252
Saen Suk: 261
Sailor Inn: 206
Sai Yok Noi Bungalows: 237
Samchai Hotel: 193
Samsen 6 Guesthouses: 147
Sam's Place: 229
Sap Sin: 261
Sawasdee Guesthouse: 147
Sawasdee Krungthep Inn: 147
Shangri La Hotel: 154
Siam Guesthouse: 206

Siam Hotel: 224
Siam Intercontinental Hotel: 156
Siam Oriental Guesthouse: 146
Sichang Palace: 195
Sichang View Resort: 195
Siri Wattana Hotel: 193
Sri Pitsanuk Bungalow: 195
Sri Samai Hotel: 252
Sukothai, The: 154
Suk Sant: 261
Sunbeam Hotel: 206-207
Sunny Guesthouse: 151
Sunshine Hotel: 207
Suparapong: 257
Sureena Bed and Breakfast: 206
Suriwong Hotel: 152
Suvatana Hotel: 237
Swan Hotel: 151
Swiss Park Hotel: 160
Swissotel: 152
Taipei Hotel: 258
Tara Hotel: 160
Tavee Guest House: 147
Texxan Inn: 206

Thai: 149
Thai Sawat: 257
Thanin Hotel: 261
Tiew Pai Guesthouse: 195
Top Bungalows: 195
Top House: 206
Truly Yours Guesthouse: 147
TT 1 Guesthouse: 150
TT 2 Guesthouse: 150
Turk Guesthouse and Cafe: 149
Uncle Rey's Guesthouse: 157
U Thong Hotel: 252
U Thong Inn: 252
U Thumphorn: 207
Viengtai Hotel: 148
V.L. Guesthouse: 229
Whale Inn: 224
White House, The: 206
White Inn: 157
Wong Amat: 208
Yang Thone Rive Kwai: 237
YMCA Collins House: 153
Youth Hostel: 147
YWCA: 153

RESTAURANT INDEX

Ad Makers: 183
Airplane: 168
Akamon: 209
Akbar's: 169
Alfredo: 170
Ali Baba: 209-210
All Gaengs: 165
Amarin Plaza: 167
Ambassador Food Center: 169
Anna's Café: 164
Anzac: 210
Apostrophe's Restaurant: 162
Art House: 171
Asia Lopburi Hotel: 258
Atlanta Hotel: 169
Au Bon Coin: 211
Australian Club: 165
Baan Kanitha: 171
Baan Khun Phor: 167
Bahay Philipino: 210
Balcony, The: 211
Bali Restaurant: 168
Ban Chiang: 165
Bankeo Restaurant: 169
Barbican: 181
Barley House: 171
Beer Garden: 166
Beer Hut: 224
Benihana: 209
B.H. International Restaurant & Beer House: 178
BH Vietnamese Restaurant: 169
Binlar Restaurant: 253
Bismi Restaurant: 164
Bistango: 171
Black Scene: 171
Blue Fox: 163
Blue River: 212
Blues Jazz: 184
Bobby Arms: 164
Boon Coffee Shop: 258
Borsolino: 211
Bourbon Street: 170, 178, 184
Bruno's Restaurant and Wine Bar: 210-211
Bua Garden: 165
Buddy Café: 162
Bull's Head, The: 183
Bussaracum: 165-166

Bussaracum 2: 166
Cabbages and Condoms: 169
Café, The: 170
Café Deco: 170
Cairns Stonegrill Restaurant: 165
Captain's Corner Steak House: 211
Central Department Store: 163
Chabad House: 162
Chalet Swiss: 210
Chan Chao Restaurant: 258
Chandrapen: 163
Charuvan Duck Shop: 163
Cheap Charlie's: 169
Chochana: 162
Club Tacoco: 171
Coca Noodles (Siam Square): 167
Coca Noodles (Silom Road): 164
Cue: 171
Dachanee: 162
Deen Muslim Restaurant: 164
Delaney's (Bangkok): 181
Delaney's Irish Pub (Pattaya): 210
Denny's Corner: 184
Deutsches Haus: 210
Dhaba Indian Café: 169
Djit Pochana: 170
Dolf Riks: 210
Duke's: 171
Dux Bar and Grill: 168
Eat Me!: 164
Elephant & Castle Pub: 206
El Gordo's Cantina: 165
El Toro Steak House: 211
Fawlty Towers: 210
FM 228: 181
Foremost Restaurant: 258
Gianni's: 167
Gourmet Gallery: 171
Green Bottle: 211
Green Tree: 211
Greg's Kitchen: 210
Gulliver's Traveller's Tavern: 180
Hard Rock Café: 183
Harmonics: 184
Hartmannsdorfer Bauhaus: 183
Hemlock: 162, 180
Henry J. Bean's Bar & Grill: 211
Himali Cha Cha: 164

Home & Garden Restaurant: 194
Hopf Brew House: 211
Huntsman Pub: 183
Imageries by the Glass: 183
Indian Hut: 164
Inter Restaurant: 167
Isn't Classic: 165
JJ Park: 181
Joe's Place: 170
Jool's: 183
Joy Luck Club: 180
Kanit's: 163
Khing Klao: 170
Kiaow Tra Wang Chun: 163
Koreana (Bangkok): 167
Koreana (Pattaya): 210
Krai Si: 162
Krit Thai Mansion: 156
Krua Thien Tong: 231
Krung Kao Restaurant: 253
Krung Seoul: 210
La Fontana: 167
La Gritta: 211
Laicram: 171
La Rotonde Grill: 166
Larry's Dive Shop (and Bar and Grill): 170
Le Café Royale: 211
Le Dalat: 171
Lemongrass Restaurant: 170
Le Moulin De Sommai: 168
L'Hexagone: 171
Library, The: 171
Lobster Pot: 212
Lum Gai Yia: 169
Mai Kai Supper Club: 210
Major Bowl Pub & Restaurant: 184
Ma Maison Hotel and Restaurant: 206, 211
Mang Gorn Luang: 171-172
Mango Tree, The: 164
Maria Bakery: 163
Maria Restaurant: 162
Maxwell's American Diner: 211
May Kaidee: 162
MBK Shopping Center: 166
Moghul Room: 169
Mon Ami Pierrot: 210
Moon River Pub: 211

Moonshine: 212
Motta Mahal: 210
Mr. Chew's Shark Fin Restaurant:
   126
Nakorn Inn: 224
Nang Nual: 212
Napoleon Lounge: 177
Nasir Al-Masri: 169
New Light Coffee House: 167
New World Shopping Center: 162
Nguan Lee Lang Suan: 168
19th Hole: 211
Normandie Grill: 165
Old Dutch Café: 178, 210
Oldies Goldies: 166
Old Siam: 178
Once Upon a Time: 165
O'Reillys Irish Pub: 181
Pae Krung Kao Floating
   Restaurant: 253
Pae Yarn: 231
Pan Pan: 167-168
PIC Kitchen: 208
Piman: 171
Pinnacle Hotel: 163
Pinnacle Revolving Restaurant,
   The: 212
Planet Hollywood: 183
Prince of Wales, The: 184
Pueng Kaew: 171
Punee Restaurant: 231
Raja Restaurant: 253
Rancho Tejas: 212
Ratsstube: 163
Restaurant Heidelberg: 169
Riley's Pub Café: 169
River City Barbecue: 165
Robinson's Department Store
   (Silom Road): 163
Robinson's Department Store
   (Sukumvit Road): 169

Royal Hotel Coffee Shop: 162
Ruam Rudi Kitchen: 168
Ruandrum Ayuthaya Youth Hos-
   tel: 253
Rueng Pueng: 166
Ruen Pak: 171
Ruen Thai: 208
Sala Maekong: 209
Sala Rim Nam: 165
Salathip: 165
Sallim Restaurant: 132
Sally's Kitchenette: 170
Sanuk Nuek: 171
Sarah Jane's: 167
Savoey Seafood: 212
Seafood Market Restaurant: 170
See Fah Restaurant: 166-167
September: 171
Ship Inn: 178
Siam Center: 166
Siam Intercontinental: 167
Siam Restaurant: 253
Silom Plaza Hotel: 163-164
Silom Village Trade Center: 163
Silver Dollar: 184
Simla Café: 164
Singapore Chicken Rice: 171
Singha Bier Haus: 170
Sizzler: 211
Solos Restaurant: 226
Somsak: 209
Song Muai: 180
Sorn Daeng Restaurant: 162
Sphinx: 181
Sportsman Grill: 206
Sportsman's Inn: 210
Sugar Hut: 209
Sun Far Myanmar Food Centre:
   165
Swiss Food: 210

Tamil Nadu: 164
Tangerine's: 170
Telephone: 181
Tevaraj Restaurant: 253
Texas Lone Star Saloon: 178
Thai House: 209
Thai Room: 165
Thang Long: 209
Thanying Princess: 167
Thong Lee Restaurant: 170
Thong U Rai: 171
Thong U-Rai Chicken: 171
Tiara Restaurant: 166
Tom's Quik Pizza: 164
Trattoria d'Roberto: 164
Traveler's Drop In: 258
Tum Nak Thai: 171
Turk Guesthouse and Café: 149
Vegeta: 167
Via Convent: 165
Victoria Bar & Pub: 183
Vientiane: 209
Vijit's: 162
Vito's Restaurant: 168
Wanakarm: 171
White House Garden: 258
Whole Earth Restaurant (Soi Lang
   Suan): 168
Whole Earth Restaurant
   (Sukumvit Road): 170
Wild Chicken: 212
Wild Mango: 209
Witch's Tavern: 171, 184
Wit's Oyster Bar: 168
Woodland's Inn: 164
World Trade Centre: 167
Yamato: 209
Yok Yor: 162
Yong Lee Restaurant: 169
Zeppelin: 210

INDEX

A

accommodations: 37-38, 44-46;
Ayuthaya 252-253; Bangkok
142-160; Bang Saen 193; Kanchanaburi 229-231; Lopburi
257-258; Nakhon Pathom 223-
224; Pattaya 205-208; Route
3199 Area 233-234; Si Racha
193; *see also* hotel index
addresses: 101-102
admission fees: 103
agrarian values: 23-24
AIDS: 57-58
air travel: 78-86
Aisawan Thippaya Pavilion: 240
Alaungpaya, King: 10-11
Amporn Pimok Pavilion: 109
amulets: 118-119
amusement parks: Ocean World
192; *see also* water parks
Ananda Mahidol, King: 17-18
Ancient City: 139-140
Angkor Wat model: 104
antiques: 53; shopping 185
aquariums: 192
architecture: Ayuthaya 244-245,
249; Bangkok 131, 139-140
architecture, temple: 28-31
art collections: gallery in Kanchanaburi 226; Jim Thompson
House 130; Khun Prasart
Vongsakul Museum 137; Na-
tional Art Gallery 114; National
Museum 109-113; Suan
Pakkard Palace 131
arts: Ayuthaya 244-245
Asalha Puja: 43
attire: 27
auto racing: 205
Automated Teller Machines
(ATMs): 69
Ayuthaya: 240-254
Ayuthaya Historical Study Center:
246
Ayuthaya Kingdom: 9-11
Ayuthaya National Museum: 245-
246
Ayuthaya Swan Boat Races: 44

B

Baan Baht: 118
Banglampoo: accommodations
144-149; bus routes 146; food
161-163
Bang Pa In: 239-240
Bang Saen: 192-193
Bang Saray: 199
Ban Kao Neolithic Museum: 236
banks: 67
bargaining: 52
bars: 175-185
beaches: Bang Saen 192; Jomtien
208; Ko Larn 199; Pattaya 202
beer: 50
bell towers: Wat Pra Keo 108
Bhumibol Adulyadej, King: 18-20
bicycling: Kanchanaburi 231;
Pattaya 205
Big Buddha Hill: 197
Bira Circuit: 205
bird sanctuaries: Wat Pailom 138
boat rentals: 203
boat trips: Ayuthaya 253; Bangkok
133-137; Bang Pa In 240; River
Kwai 228, 237; Sri Nakarin Lake
234
bookstores: Bangkok 77; Pattaya
215
Boonsamakan Vegetarian Hall:
122-123
Bophloi: 234-235
bot: 28-30
boxing instruction: 204-205
boxing, Thai: 178
breweries: Hopf Brew House 211

BUDDHA STATUES

Buddha at Nakhon Pathom
Chedi: 222, 223
Golden Buddha at Wat
Traimit: 126
Reclining Buddha at
Ayuthaya: 248
Reclining Buddha at Wat
Po: 116

Bridge over the River Kwai: 226,
227
bronzeware: 54
Buddha images: export of 53-54,
64; proper conduct around: 26-27
Buddhism: 23, 29; Buddhist festivals 41
budget activities: 100
Burma: 1, 4
bus travel: Ayuthaya 253, 254;
Bangkok 90-92, 93-94; Bang Pa
In 240; Kanchanaburi 231, 232;
Lopburi 259, 261; Pattaya 215-
217; west of Bangkok 220, 224
business hours: 73-74

C

camping: Ko Si Chang 195; Sai
Yok National Park 237-238
canals: 135-137
car rental: Kanchanaburi 231;
Pattaya 216
caves: Kao Poon 236
Celadon pottery: 54
cemeteries: 227-228, 236
Center for Responsible Tourism: 22
Centers for Disease Control
(CDC): 54
Chakrabongse House: 135
Chakri Day: 42
Chakri Maha Prasat: 109
Chalerm Ratanakosin National
Park: 235
Chandra Kasem Museum: 243
Chantara Phisan Pavilion (Lopburi
National Museum): 256
Chao Phaya Express Boat: 95
Chapel of the Emerald Buddha:
105-108
Chatuchak Weekend Market: 187-
188
chedi: 30; in Nakhon Pathom 221-
223
Chedi Sri Suriyothai: 248
Cheun Ruthai Gardens: 223
children, traveling with: 38
chili peppers: 48
Chinese Cemetery: 228
Chinese lanterns: 124

Chinese New Year: 42
Chinese opera: 123, 126
Chinese people: 25-26
Chinese temples: 118, 127
Chonburi Fair: 42
Chulalongkorn Day: 43
Chulalongkorn, King: 15-16, 98, 239-240
Chulalongkorn's Summer Palace: 194
Chung Kai War Cemetery: 236
churches: Holy Rosary 133; St. Joseph's 249-250; Santa Cruz 135; *see also* temples
climate: 6-8, 74
cloth market: 128
coffee: 50
Coin Museum: 104
College of Traditional Medicine: 116
conduct: 26-28
Coronation Day: 43
cosmology: 249
counterfeit merchandise: 53
crafts: 54, 186
credit cards: 67-69
crime: 24-25, 58-60, 92, 103, 215
crocodile farms: 140, 199
cruises: *see* boat trips
cuisine: 46-52
cultural performances: 173-175
currency: 65-69
curry: 47
customs (import/export): 62-64
customs, social: 26-28

D
Damnern Saduak Floating Market: 138-139
dance: 31-32; Bangkok 173-175; Lopburi 258-259
demographics: 21-26
dental care: 58
diarrhea: 55
dining etiquette: 51-52
diplomatic offices: 61-63
discos: Bangkok 175-185; Lopburi 258; Pattaya 212-214
diving: 202-203
Don Chedi Memorial Fair: 42
drama: 31-32
dress regulations: 103
drugs: 59-60; rehabilitation facilities 260

Dusit Zoo: 122
Dvaravati Seated Buddha: 223

EF
Earth Goddess Statue: 114
electricity: 74
electronic information resources: 269-272
elephant *kraals*: 252, 256
embassies: 61-63
entry permits: 61-62
Erawan Falls: 233, 234
Erawan Shrine: 132-133
exchange rates: 65-66
expenses: 36-38
Farmer's Museum: 256
fax services: 73
festivals: 40-44
fishing: Pattaya 203-204
floating market: Bangkok 129-130; Damnern Saduak 138-139
food: 46-52; Bangkok 161-172; Kanchanaburi 231; Lopburi 258; Nakhon Pathom 224; Pattaya 208-212; vocabulary 279-281; *see also* Restaurant Index
fraud: 58-59, 68-69, 103
fruit juice: 49-50

GH
Gallery of Pre-Thai History: 111
garbage: 98
gardens: Cheun Ruthai 223; Nong Nooch Tropical Gardens 199; Rose Garden 140
gay bars: Bangkok 181-182; Pattaya 213-214
gems: 53
geography: 5-6
getting there: 78-85
Giant Swing: 118
glass-bottom boat trips: 202
glossary: 282-284
go-carts: 205
Golden Buddha: 126
Golden Mountain: 119
Golden Mountain of Ayuthaya: 251-252
gold shops: 123, 126
golf: Bang Pra Golf Course 192-193; Pattaya 204
government agencies: 75-76
Guan U Shrine: 124
guesthouses: 44-45

health: 54-58
Hellfire Pass Memorial: 237
Hepatitis (A and B): 55
hierarchy: 24
Hin Da Hot Springs: 238
Hinduism: 41
Hindu Shrine: 118
history: general 8-20; Ayuthaya 240-242; Bangkok 97-98; Lopburi 254-255
holidays: 40-41
Holy Rosary Church: 133
horseback riding: 204
hospitals: 58
hot springs: 238
hotels: 45-46; *see also* accommodations and separate Accommodations Index

IJ
illegal drugs: 59-60
immunizations: 54
information sources: 74-78
international clock: 73
International Drivers License: 64
International Student Identity Cards (ISIC): 64
International Youth Hostel Cards: 64
Internet information: 76
Japanese settlement: 250
Japanese War Memorial: 226-227
JEATH War Museum: 226
jewels: 53
Jomtien Beach: 208

K
Kala Temple: 256-257
Kamthieng House: 131
Kanchanaburi: 224-232
Kanchanaburi War Cemetery: 227-228
Kao Poon Cave: 236
karaoke bars: 177, 181, 182
Khao Khiew Open Zoo: 192
Khao Phansa: 43
Khao Pra Yai: 197
khon: 31, 112
Khum Khum House: 246
kickboxing: 178
King and I, The: 14
King's Birthday Festival: 44
Ko Krok: 202
Ko Larn: 199-202

Ko Loi: 193
Ko Loi Temple: 193
Ko Pai: 202
Ko Sak: 202
Ko Si Chang: 194-195
kraals: 252, 256
Kwai, River: 44

L
lacquerware: 54
lakhon: 31-32
Lak Muang (Ayuthaya): 246
Lak Muang (Bangkok): 109
Lak Muang (Kanchanaburi): 228
land: 5-6
land measurements: 74
Lang Boya: 127
language: 27-28, 273-284
Leonowens, Anna: 14
libraries: 77-78
likay: 31
Little India: 128
live music: 180-185
Lohaprasat: 118
Lopburi: 254-259
Lopburi National Museum: 256
Loy Kratong: 43-44
Luang Kocha Mosque: 124
luggage: 38-39
Lumpini Park: 133
lunar calendar: 40

M
mail: 70-71, 215
Makha Puja: 42
malaria: 55-56
Manangasila stone: 104
maps: 76, 215; *see also specific place*
Marble Temple: 121
massage parlors: 179
massage: Wat Po 116
mausoleum: 105
medical care facilities: 58
meditation retreats: 29
Mekong whiskey: 51
Memorial Bridge: 135
metric system: 74
Miniature Mountain: 223
Mini Siam: 197, 205
monasteries: Wat Suwan Daram 251; Wat Tham Krabok 260
mondop: 30
money: 65-69

Mongkut, King: 13-14, 98
Monkey Cliff: 192
Monkey Shrine: 256-257
monks: 27
monsoons: 6-8
mosques: Luang Kocha 124
motorbikes: 195, 216
mountain biking: 205
movies filmed in Thailand: 33-35
Muang Boran: 139-140
murals: Ayuthaya Historical Study Center 246; Wat Bowonivet 120; Wat Pra Keo 104-108; Wat Suthat 117-118
murder: 24-25
museums: Ancient City 139-140; Ayuthaya Historical Study Center 246; Ayuthaya National Museum 245-246; Ban Kao Neolithic Museum 236; Chandra Kasem Museum 243; Coin Museum 104; Farmer's Museum (at Lopburi Royal Palace) 256; JEATH War Museum 226; Lopburi National Museum 256; Nakhon Pathom *Chedi* Museum 223; National Museum 109-113; Royal Barges Museum 129; Train Museum 226; Viharn Luang at Pra Buddhabat 260-261; Wat Pra Keo Museum 109
music, live: 180-185
Myanmar: 1, 4

NO
Nakhon Pathom: 220-224
Nakhon Pathom *Chedi*: 221-223
Nakhon Pathom *Chedi* Museum: 223
Naklua: 208
Nam Choan Dam project: 224-226
Nam Tok: 237
Nana Entertainment Plaza: 176, 177
Nangklao, King Phra: 13
Narai, King: 254-255
Naresuan the Great: 242, 251
Nartasin School of Art: 258-259
NASA Spacedrome Disco: 184
National Art Gallery: 114
National Museum: 109-113
national parks: Chalerm Ratanakosin 235; Erawan 234; Sai Yok 237-238; Sri Nakarin 234

New Year: 42-43
nielloware: 54
nightlife: Bangkok 175-185; Lopburi 258; Pattaya 212-214
Nong Nooch Tropical Gardens: 199
Nonthaburi: 138
noodle dishes: 47
Ocean World: 192
opera: 123, 126
Opium Pipe Monastery: 260
orientataion: 99-102

PQ
packages (shipping): 70-71
packing: 38-39
Pah Fah Pavilion: 118
painting: 245
palanquins: 112
parcel post: 70-71
passports: 61
Pasteur Institute: 131-132
Pattaya: 196-217
Pattaya Elephant Village: 199
Pattaya Festival: 42
Pattaya Tower and Water Park: 204
Pei Ying School: 124
Peking Palace: 240
phallic shrine: 130
Phaulkon, Constantine: 257
Phibul Songkram: 16-17
Phimai Historical Fair: 44
Phimuk Monthain Gallery: 112
Phutthalaetia, King Phra: 13
planning the trip: 36-39
Po Kao Tong (Golden Mount): 251-252
Portuguese settlement: 250
postal service: 70-71, 215

PALACES

Chulalongkorn's Summer Palace: 194
Peking Palace: 240
Royal Palace (Bangkok): 108
Royal Palace (Lopburi): 255-256
Sanam Chand: 223
Suan Pakkard: 131
Vimanmek: 121-122
Warophat Piman Hall: 240

Pra Arthit Fort: 119
Pra Buddhabat: 259-261
Pra Chamroon Parnchand: 260
Prajadhipok, King: 16-17
prang: 30, 31
Prang Khaek: 257
Prang Sam Yot: 257
Pra Pathom Chedi Fair: 44
Pra Pradang Songkran Festival: 43
Pra Ruang Rochanarit standing
  Buddha: 222
Prasart Museum: 137
prasat: 30-31
Prasat Muang Sing: 236-237
Pra Sumane: 119
Pra Viharn Yot: 104
precious stones: 53
precipitation: 6-8
Pridi Panomyong: 16-18
produce markets: 188
pronunciation of Thai language:
  274-275
prostitution: 175-179; Pattaya 212-
  214
publications: 215
Queen's Birthday Festival: 43
Queen's Monument: 240

R

Rachini School: 135
rainfall: 6-8
Rajawong Pier: 122
Rama I: 10, 12-13, 240-242
Rama II: 13
Rama III: 13
Rama IV: 13-14
Rama V: 15-16
Rama VI: 16
Rama VII: 16-17
Rama VIII: 17-18
Ramakien Murals: 104
Ramathibodi I, King: 10, 12-13,
  240-242
Ramkamheng, King: 8-9
reading list: 262-269
Reclining Buddha, Ayuthaya: 248
Reclining Buddha, Wat Po: 116
reptile farms: Crocodile Farm 140;
  Crocodile Farm and Million Year
  Stone Park 199; Saowapha In-
  stitute (Snake Farm) 131-132
reservations, accommodations:
  143-144

resources: 262-272
responsible tourism: 22
rice: 47
riverboat travel: 95
River Kwai Historical Week: 44
river tours: 133-137
rock 'n' roll: 180-185
Rose Garden: 140
Royal Barges Museum: 129
royal family: 18-20, 26
Royal Palace (Bangkok): 108-109
Royal Palace (Lopburi): 255-256
Royal Palace ruins (Ayuthaya):
  247-248
Royal Pantheon: 104
Royal Ploughing Ceremony: 43

S

Safari World: 137
safety: 58-60, 92
St. Joseph's Cathedral: 249-250
Sai Yok National Park: 237-238
salads: 47-48
samlors: 195
Sampeng Lane: 123-124
Samphran Elephant Park: 141
Sanam Chand Palace: 223
San Chao Por Khao Yai (Chinese
  Temple): 194
San Pra Khan: 256-257
Santa Cruz Church: 135
Saowapha Institute: 131-132
sapphire mining: 234-235
Saraburi: 259-261
scams: 58-59, 68-69, 103
scuba diving: 202-203
sculpture: 245
seasons: 6-8, 74
Seni Pramoj: 17
sex shows: 175-179
shadow puppets: 31, 112
shopping: 52-54, 185-188
Siam Society: 96, 130-131
Siam Water Park: 137
sightseeing highlights: 3; East
  Coast 189-191; Kanchanaburi
  218-220; Nakhon Pathom 218;
  north of Bangkok 238; Ratchaburi 218; Suphanburi 220
silk: 53, 185
Si Racha: 193-194
Sirindhorn, Princess Mahachakri:
  20

Skytrain: 95
Smashed Car at Kanchanaburi:
  228
snacks: 49
snake farm: 131-132
social customs: 26-28
societal values: 22-25
Songkran: 42-43
songtaos: 216
soup: 46
spirit house of King Naresuan: 251
Sri Nakarin Lake: 234
Sri Nakarin National Park: 234
statues: Wat Benjamabopit 121;
  Wat Po 114, 116; Wat Pra Keo
  105, 108-109; Wat Suthat 117;
  see also Buddha statues
Stone Gardens: 236
street names: 101-102
Suan Pakkard Palace: 131
Sukothai Kingdom: 8-9
Sunandakumariratna, Queen:
  239-240
Suthorn Phu Day: 43

T

Taksin, General: 11-12
Tamnak Daeng (Red House): 111
tampons: 38, 56-57
Tang Toh Gang: 123
taxis: 93
telephone service: 71-73, 215
temperatures: 6-8, 74
temple architecture: 28-31
temples: Chinese 118, 127; Kala
  Temple 256-257; Ko Loi 193;
  Pra Buddhabat 260-261; Prasat
  Muang Sing 236-237; San Chao
  Por Khao Yai 194; Wat Arun
  128-129; Wat Benjamabopit
  (Marble Temple) 121; Wat
  Bowonivet 120-121; Wat Bud-
  dhaisawan 111; Wat Buddha-
  sawan 250; Wat Chaichana
  Songkram 127; Wat Chai Wat-
  tanaram 248-249; Wat
  Chakrawat Rachawas 127-128;
  Wat Dusitaram 129; Wat In-
  draram 121; Wat Kalayamit
  129, 135; Wat Kanikaphon 127;
  Wat Kanmatuyaram 127; Wat
  Koh 124-125; Wat Kusan
  Samakorn 127; Wat Leng Nee

Yee 127; Wat Mahathat (Ayuthaya) 243-244; Wat Mahathat (Bangkok) 113-114; Wat Mahathat (Lopburi) 256; Wat Nakhonkosa 256; Wat Na Praman 248; Wat Nivet Dhammapravat 240; Wat Panam Chong 250-251; Wat Pathom Kongka 125; Wat Po 114-116; Wat Pra Dong 233; Wat Pra Keo 104-109; Wat Pra Ram 244-245; Wat Pra Sri Samphet 246-247; Wat Prayoon 129, 135; Wat Rajabopit 116-117; Wat Rajaburana 243; Wat Rajanada 118; Wat Rajapradit 116; Wat Rakang Kositharam 135; Wat Sampha Tawong 124-125; Wat Sao Tong Tong 257; Wat Sri Maha Racha 193; Wat Suthat 117-118; Wat Suwan Daram 251; Wat Suwannaram 129; Wat Tam Kao Noi 232-233; Wat Tam Mongkam 232; Wat Tam Sua 232-233; Wat Thamakai 137; Wat Tham Krabok 260; Wat Thammachat 133-135; Wat Thamma Mongkol 133; Wat Thong Noppakhun 133-135; Wat Traimit (Temple of the Golden Buddha) 126; Wat Yai Chai Mongkol 251; Wat Yansangwararam 199
Thai Human Imagery Museum: 141
Thai people: 21-25
Thammasart University: 135
Tha Muang: 232-233
theater: 31-32, 174-175
theft: 58-59, 92
Thompson, Jim: 130
Thonburi: 11, 128-130
time: 73, 75
tipping: 52
Tod Kathin: 43
tourism: 22
Tourism Authority of Thailand (TAT): 59, 76
tourist offices: Kanchanaburi 231; Pattaya 214-215
tours: Kanchanaburi 229, 231; river 133-137; to Bangkok 95-96; walking tours 102-104
touts: 53, 103
traffic problems: 98
Train Museum: 226
train travel: Ayuthaya 253, 254; Bangkok 86-90; Kanchanaburi 231-232; Lopburi 259; Pattaya 215, 217; west of Bangkok 220, 224
transvestite revues: Bangkok 177, 179-180; Pattaya 206, 214
travel agencies: 95-96, 215
traveler's checks: 66-67
tuk tuks: 93

UV
University Aquarium: 192
U.S. State Department: 60
Uthayan Phumi Sathiana Palace remains: 240
U Thong, King: 10, 12-13, 240-242
vaccinations: 54
Vajiravudh, King: 16
value-added tax: 66
Vegetarian Festival: 123
viharn: 30
Viharn Pra Mongkol Bopit: 246
Vimanmek Palace: 121-122
Visaka Puja: 43
visas: 61-62, 216
Vithayalia Kalasilpa University: 258-259
vocabulary: 273-284
Volunteer Guide Group Tours: 96

WXYZ
wai: 27
walking tours: 102-104, 132
Warophat Piman Hall: 240
wat: 28
Wat Arun: 128-129
Wat Benjamabopit (Marble Temple): 121
Wat Bowonivet: 120-121
Wat Buddhaisawan: 111
Wat Buddhasawan: 250
Wat Chaichana Songkram: 127
Wat Chai Wattanaram: 248-249
Wat Chakrawat Rachawas: 127-128
Wat Dusitaram: 129
Wat Indraram: 121
Wat Kalayamit: 129, 135
Wat Kanikaphon: 127
Wat Kanmatuyaram: 127
Wat Koh: 124-125
Wat Kusan Samakorn: 127
Wat Leng Nee Yee: 127
Wat Mahathat (Ayuthaya): 243-244
Wat Mahathat (Bangkok): 113-114
Wat Mahathat (Lopburi): 256
Wat Nakhonkosa: 256
Wat Na Praman: 248
Wat Nivet Dhammapravat: 240
Wat Pailom Bird Sanctuary: 138
Wat Panam Chong: 250-251
Wat Pathom Kongka: 125
Wat Po: 114-116
Wat Pra Buddhapat Fair: 42
Wat Pra Dong: 233
Wat Pra Keo: 104-109
Wat Pra Keo Museum: 109
Wat Pra Ram: 244-245
Wat Pra Sri Samphet: 246-247
Wat Prayoon: 129, 135
Wat Rajabopit: 116-117
Wat Rajaburana: 243
Wat Rajanada: 118
Wat Rajapradit: 116
Wat Rakang Kositharam: 135
Wat Saket Fair: 44
Wat Sampha Tawong: 124-125
Wat Sao Tong Tong: 257
Wat Sri Maha Racha: 193
Wat Suthat: 117-118
Wat Suwan Daram: 251
Wat Suwannaram: 129
Wat Tam Kao Noi: 232-233
Wat Tam Mongkam: 232
Wat Tam Sua: 232-233
Wat Thamakai: 137
Wat Tham Krabok: 260

WILDLIFE PARKS

Monkey Cliff: 192
Pattaya Elephant Village: 199
Safari World: 137
Wat Pailom Bird Sanctuary: 138
see also reptile farms

Wat Thammachat: 133-135
Wat Thamma Mongkol: 133
Wat Thong Noppakhun: 133-135
Wat Traimit (Temple of the Golden Buddha): 126
Wat Yai Chai Mongkol: 251
Wat Yansangwararam: 199
water: 48-49

water parks: Ocean World 192; Pattaya Tower and Water Park 204; Siam Water Park 137
waterfalls: 233, 234
weather: 6-8, 74
Websites: 269-272
wedding shops: 126
whiskey: 51

windsurfing: 203
women's issues: 56-57, 60
yacht rentals: 203
yeast infections: 38, 56
zoos: Crocodile Farm and Million Year Stone Park 199; Dusit 122; Khao Khiew Open Zoo 192

ABOUT THE AUTHOR

Carl Parkes, author of *Thailand Handbook, Southeast Asia Handbook,* and *Bangkok Handbook,* was born into an American Air Force family and spent his childhood in California, Nebraska, Alabama, and Japan, where his love of Asia first began. After graduating from the University of California at Santa Barbara, Carl traveled throughout Europe and later returned to work in Hawaii, Lake Tahoe, Aspen, Salt Lake City, and, finally, San Francisco.

But childhood memories of Asia continued to pull him eastward. After a 12-month journey across Asia, Carl returned to San Francisco to work as a stockbroker and plan his escape from the nine-to-five world. A chance encounter in Singapore with publisher Bill Dalton offered a more intriguing option: research and write a travel guidebook to Southeast Asia—one that addressed more than travel practicalities by exploring the region's rich culture and history.

Carl fervently believes that travel is an immensely rewarding undertaking that affirms the basic truths of life. "Travel is much more than just monuments and ruins. It's an opportunity to reach out and discover what's best about the world. Travel enriches our lives, spreads prosperity, dissolves political barriers, promotes international peace, and brings excitement and change to our lives."

Carl also believes in the importance of political, economic, and environmental issues. "Historical sites and beaches make for wonderful memories, but national agendas such as human rights and rainforest preservation are just as fascinating in their own right. Understanding the contemporary scene enriches travel experiences and opens avenues rarely explored by the visitor."

In addition to his guidebooks for Moon Publications, Carl also writes for Fodor's *Worldview*

Systems, PATA Travel News America, and *Pacific Rim News Service.* Carl also has updated portions of *Indonesia Handbook* for Moon Publications, lectured onboard *Pearl Cruises,* and appeared on CNN and the Travel Channel with Arthur Frommer. In 1995, Carl won the Lowell Thomas Award from the Society of American Travel Writers in the travel guidebook category for his *Southeast Asia Handbook.*

Besides travel writing, Carl enjoys straight-ahead jazz, photography, Anchor Steam beer, opera, art openings, poetry readings, and samba nightclubs in his favorite city of San Francisco. Future plans include more books on his favorite destinations in Southeast Asia.

READER SURVEY

Knowing a bit about you and your travel experiences will help me improve this book for the next edition. Please take a few minutes to complete this form and share your tips with the next traveler. Remember to send along corrected copies of photocopied maps from this book and business cards collected from your favorite hotels and restaurants. All contributors will be acknowledged in the next edition.

The author also appreciates correspondence from expatriates living in Thailand and other local residents with special insight into travel conditions. Research correspondents are also needed to help update several Moon Handbooks to destinations in Southeast Asia. You may write to Moon Publications at the address below or contact the author directly via e-mail: cparkes@moon.com.

Send the following survey to:
Carl Parkes/Reader Survey
Bangkok Handbook
Moon Travel Handbooks
5855 Beaudry St.
Emeryville, CA 94608
USA

Date of Letter: _____

1. Gender: ☐ male   ☐ female

2. Age: ☐ under 25   ☐ 25-30   ☐ 31-35   ☐ 36-40
☐ 41-50   ☐ 51+

3. Status: ☐ single   ☐ married

4. Income: ☐ $20K   ☐ $20-30K   ☐ $30-40K   ☐ $40-50K
☐ $50K+

5. Occupation: _____

6. Education: ☐ high school   ☐ some college   ☐ college grad   ☐ post grad

7. Travel style: ☐ budget   ☐ moderate   ☐ luxury

8. Vacations: ☐ once yearly   ☐ twice yearly   ☐ 3+ yearly

9. Why do you travel? _____

_____

10. What's best about travel? _____

_____

11. What's worst about travel? _____

_____

12. This Journey:

Length of time: _____

    Enough time? _____

Countries visited: _____

Countries planned for next visit: _____

Season: _____

How was the weather? _____

Travel companions? _____

Do you prefer solo travel or with companions? _____

Purpose of Trip?

  a. ☐ Pleasure b. ☐ Study   c. ☐ Work   d. ☐ Volunteer e. ☐ Hanging out

Main Activities?

  a. ☐ Sights   b. ☐ Culture   c. ☐ Beaches and outdoor activities
  d. ☐ Meeting people   e. ☐ Nightlife and entertainment
  f. ☐ Food and shopping

Main regions? Please give specific locations:

  a. ☐ Cities _____

  b. ☐ Smaller towns _____

  c. ☐ Beaches and islands _____

  d. ☐ Mountains _____

Primary modes of transportation? _____

Expenses:

  a. Total: _____

  b. Average daily expenses: _____

c. Average hotel price: _____

d. Average meal price: _____

e. Total airfare: _____

f. Shopping expenses: _____

Unexpected encounters: _____

13. Favorites:

a. Countries: _____

_____

b. Hotels and guesthouses (include address, price, description): _____

_____

c. Restaurants (address, price range, favorite dishes): _____

_____

d. Airline: _____

_____

e. Cuisine: _____

_____

f. Nightspots: _____

_____

g. Cultural events: _____

_____

h. Outdoor adventures: _____

_____

i. Temples or historical sites: _____

_____

j. Beaches: _____

_____

k. People: _____

_____

_____

14. This Book:

Where did you buy this book? _____

Why did you select Moon Publications? _____

What other Moon Handbooks have you used? _____

What other guidebooks have you used? _____

What is your favorite series of guides? _____

How does this book compare with other guides? _____

Your opinion about the following:

    a. Hotel listings (how accurate?) _____

    b. Restaurants _____

    c. Background information _____

    d. Maps _____

    e. Charts _____

    f. Photography _____

    g. Writer's attitude _____

    h. Price of this book _____

    i. Distribution _____

    j. Design and layout _____

How accurate did you find the following information?

a. Hotel prices _____

b. Restaurant recommendations _____

c. Maps _____

d. Charts _____

e. Writer's opinions _____

Favorite introduction section (history, government, etc., none) _____

Did you use the hotel charts? _____

Weakest points of this book: _____

Suggestions for improvements: _____

How does this book compare with the competition? _____

15. Name and Address

_____

_____

_____

_____

Thanks for your help!

MOON TRAVEL HANDBOOKS
LOSE YOURSELF IN THE EXPERIENCE, NOT THE CROWD

For more than 25 years, Moon Travel Handbooks have been the guidebooks of choice for adventurous travelers. Our award-winning Handbook series provides focused, comprehensive coverage of distinct destinations all over the world. Each Handbook is like an entire bookcase of cultural insight and introductory information in one portable volume. Our goal at Moon is to give travelers all the background and practical information they'll need for an extraordinary travel experience.

The following pages include a complete list of Handbooks, covering North America and Hawaii, Mexico, Latin America and the Caribbean, and Asia and the Pacific. Please check our Web site at **www.moon.com** for current prices and editions, or see your local bookseller.

"An in-depth dunk into the land, the people and their history, arts, and politics."
—*Student Travels*

"I consider these books to be superior to Lonely Planet. When Moon produces a book it is more humorous, incisive, and off-beat."
—*Toronto Sun*

"Outdoor enthusiasts gravitate to the well-written Moon Travel Handbooks. In addition to politically correct historic and cultural features, the series focuses on flora, fauna and outdoor recreation. Maps and meticulous directions also are a trademark of Moon guides."
—*Houston Chronicle*

"Moon [Travel Handbooks] . . . bring a healthy respect to the places they investigate. Best of all, they provide a host of odd nuggets that give a place texture and prod the wary traveler from the beaten path. The finest are written with such care and insight they deserve listing as literature."
—*American Geographical Society*

"Moon Travel Handbooks offer in-depth historical essays and useful maps, enhanced by a sense of humor and a neat, compact format."
—*Swing*

"Perfect for the more adventurous, these are long on history, sightseeing and nitty-gritty information and very price-specific."
—*Columbus Dispatch*

"Moon guides manage to be comprehensive and countercultural at the same time . . . Handbooks are packed with maps, photographs, drawings, and sidebars that constitute a college-level introduction to each country's history, culture, people, and crafts."
—*National Geographic Traveler*

"Few travel guides do a better job helping travelers create their own itineraries than the Moon Travel Handbook series. The authors have a knack for homing in on the essentials."
—**Colorado Springs** *Gazette Telegraph*

MEXICO

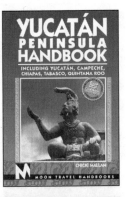

"These books will delight the armchair traveler, aid the undecided person in selecting a destination, and guide the seasoned road warrior looking for lesser-known hideaways."
—*Mexican Meanderings* Newsletter

"From tourist traps to off-the-beaten track hideaways, these guides offer consistent, accurate details without pretension."
—*Foreign Service Journal*

Archaeological Mexico	**$19.95**
Andrew Coe	420 pages, 27 maps
Baja Handbook	**$16.95**
Joe Cummings	540 pages, 46 maps
Cabo Handbook	**$14.95**
Joe Cummings	270 pages, 17 maps
Cancún Handbook	**$14.95**
Chicki Mallan	240 pages, 25 maps
Colonial Mexico	**$18.95**
Chicki Mallan	400 pages, 38 maps
Mexico Handbook	**$21.95**
Joe Cummings and Chicki Mallan	1,200 pages, 201 maps
Northern Mexico Handbook	**$17.95**
Joe Cummings	610 pages, 69 maps
Pacific Mexico Handbook	**$17.95**
Bruce Whipperman	580 pages, 68 maps
Puerto Vallarta Handbook	**$14.95**
Bruce Whipperman	330 pages, 36 maps
Yucatán Handbook	**$16.95**
Chicki Mallan	400 pages, 52 maps

"Beyond question, the most comprehensive Mexican resources available for those who prefer deep travel to shallow tourism. But don't worry, the fiesta-fun stuff's all here too."
—*New York Daily News*

LATIN AMERICA AND THE CARIBBEAN

"Solidly packed with practical information and full of significant cultural asides that will enlighten you on the whys and wherefores of things you might easily see but not easily grasp."

—Boston Globe

Belize Handbook	**$15.95**
Chicki Mallan and Patti Lange	390 pages, 45 maps
Caribbean Vacations	**$18.95**
Karl Luntta	910 pages, 64 maps
Costa Rica Handbook	**$19.95**
Christopher P. Baker	780 pages, 73 maps
Cuba Handbook	**$19.95**
Christopher P. Baker	740 pages, 70 maps
Dominican Republic Handbook	**$15.95**
Gaylord Dold	420 pages, 24 maps
Ecuador Handbook	**$16.95**
Julian Smith	450 pages, 43 maps
Honduras Handbook	**$15.95**
Chris Humphrey	330 pages, 40 maps
Jamaica Handbook	**$15.95**
Karl Luntta	330 pages, 17 maps
Virgin Islands Handbook	**$13.95**
Karl Luntta	220 pages, 19 maps

NORTH AMERICA AND HAWAII

"These domestic guides convey the same sense of exoticism that their foreign counterparts do, making home-country travel seem like far-flung adventure."

—Sierra Magazine

Alaska-Yukon Handbook	**$17.95**
Deke Castleman and Don Pitcher	530 pages, 92 maps
Alberta and the Northwest Territories Handbook	**$18.95**
Andrew Hempstead	520 pages, 79 maps
Arizona Handbook	**$18.95**
Bill Weir	600 pages, 36 maps
Atlantic Canada Handbook	**$18.95**
Mark Morris	490 pages, 60 maps
Big Island of Hawaii Handbook	**$15.95**
J.D. Bisignani	390 pages, 25 maps
Boston Handbook	**$13.95**
Jeff Perk	200 pages, 20 maps
British Columbia Handbook	**$16.95**
Jane King and Andrew Hempstead	430 pages, 69 maps

Canadian Rockies Handbook	**$14.95**
Andrew Hempstead	220 pages, 22 maps
Colorado Handbook	**$17.95**
Stephen Metzger	480 pages, 46 maps
Georgia Handbook	**$17.95**
Kap Stann	380 pages, 44 maps
Grand Canyon Handbook	**$14.95**
Bill Weir	220 pages, 10 maps
Hawaii Handbook	**$19.95**
J.D. Bisignani	1,030 pages, 88 maps
Honolulu-Waikiki Handbook	**$14.95**
J.D. Bisignani	360 pages, 20 maps
Idaho Handbook	**$18.95**
Don Root	610 pages, 42 maps
Kauai Handbook	**$15.95**
J.D. Bisignani	320 pages, 23 maps
Los Angeles Handbook	**$16.95**
Kim Weir	370 pages, 15 maps
Maine Handbook	**$18.95**
Kathleen M. Brandes	660 pages, 27 maps
Massachusetts Handbook	**$18.95**
Jeff Perk	600 pages, 23 maps
Maui Handbook	**$15.95**
J.D. Bisignani	450 pages, 37 maps
Michigan Handbook	**$15.95**
Tina Lassen	360 pages, 32 maps
Montana Handbook	**$17.95**
Judy Jewell and W.C. McRae	490 pages, 52 maps
Nevada Handbook	**$18.95**
Deke Castleman	530 pages, 40 maps
New Hampshire Handbook	**$18.95**
Steve Lantos	500 pages, 18 maps
New Mexico Handbook	**$15.95**
Stephen Metzger	360 pages, 47 maps
New York Handbook	**$19.95**
Christiane Bird	780 pages, 95 maps
New York City Handbook	**$13.95**
Christiane Bird	300 pages, 20 maps
North Carolina Handbook	**$14.95**
Rob Hirtz and Jenny Daughtry Hirtz	320 pages, 27 maps
Northern California Handbook	**$19.95**
Kim Weir	800 pages, 50 maps
Ohio Handbook	**$15.95**
David K. Wright	340 pages, 18 maps
Oregon Handbook	**$17.95**
Stuart Warren and Ted Long Ishikawa	590 pages, 34 maps

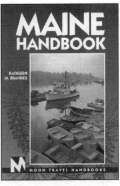

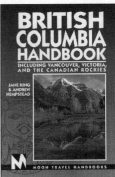

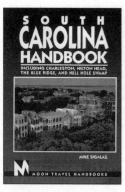

Pennsylvania Handbook	**$18.95**
Joanne Miller	448 pages, 40 maps
Road Trip USA	**$24.00**
Jamie Jensen	940 pages, 175 maps
Road Trip USA Getaways: Chicago	**$9.95**
	60 pages, 1 map
Road Trip USA Getaways: Seattle	**$9.95**
	60 pages, 1 map
Santa Fe-Taos Handbook	**$13.95**
Stephen Metzger	160 pages, 13 maps
South Carolina Handbook	**$16.95**
Mike Sigalas	400 pages, 20 maps
Southern California Handbook	**$19.95**
Kim Weir	720 pages, 26 maps
Tennessee Handbook	**$17.95**
Jeff Bradley	530 pages, 42 maps
Texas Handbook	**$18.95**
Joe Cummings	690 pages, 70 maps
Utah Handbook	**$17.95**
Bill Weir and W.C. McRae	490 pages, 40 maps
Virginia Handbook	**$15.95**
Julian Smith	410 pages, 37 maps
Washington Handbook	**$19.95**
Don Pitcher	840 pages, 111 maps
Wisconsin Handbook	**$18.95**
Thomas Huhti	590 pages, 69 maps
Wyoming Handbook	**$17.95**
Don Pitcher	610 pages, 80 maps

ASIA AND THE PACIFIC

"Scores of maps, detailed practical info down to business hours of small-town libraries. You can't beat the Asian titles for sheer heft. (The) series is sort of an American Lonely Planet, with better writing but fewer titles. (The) individual voice of researchers comes through."

—Travel & Leisure

Australia Handbook	**$21.95**
Marael Johnson, Andrew Hempstead,	
and Nadina Purdon	940 pages, 141 maps
Bali Handbook	**$19.95**
Bill Dalton	750 pages, 54 maps
Fiji Islands Handbook	**$14.95**
David Stanley	350 pages, 42 maps
Hong Kong Handbook	**$16.95**
Kerry Moran	378 pages, 49 maps

Indonesia Handbook	**$25.00**
Bill Dalton	1,380 pages, 249 maps
Micronesia Handbook	**$16.95**
Neil M. Levy	340 pages, 70 maps
Nepal Handbook	**$18.95**
Kerry Moran	490 pages, 51 maps
New Zealand Handbook	**$19.95**
Jane King	620 pages, 81 maps
Outback Australia Handbook	**$18.95**
Marael Johnson	450 pages, 57 maps
Philippines Handbook	**$17.95**
Peter Harper and Laurie Fullerton	670 pages, 116 maps
Singapore Handbook	**$15.95**
Carl Parkes	350 pages, 29 maps
South Korea Handbook	**$19.95**
Robert Nilsen	820 pages, 141 maps
South Pacific Handbook	**$24.00**
David Stanley	920 pages, 147 maps
Southeast Asia Handbook	**$21.95**
Carl Parkes	1,080 pages, 204 maps
Tahiti Handbook	**$15.95**
David Stanley	450 pages, 51 maps
Thailand Handbook	**$19.95**
Carl Parkes	860 pages, 142 maps
Vietnam, Cambodia & Laos Handbook	**$18.95**
Michael Buckley	760 pages, 116 maps

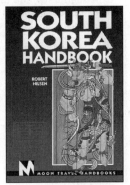

OTHER GREAT TITLES FROM MOON

"For hardy wanderers, few guides come more highly
recommended than the Handbooks. They include good
maps, steer clear of fluff and flackery, and offer plenty of
money-saving tips. They also give you the kind of
information that visitors to strange lands—on any budget—
need to survive."

—US News & World Report

Moon Handbook	**$10.00**
Carl Koppeschaar	150 pages, 8 maps
The Practical Nomad: How to Travel Around the World	**$17.95**
Edward Hasbrouck	580 pages
Staying Healthy in Asia, Africa, and Latin America	**$11.95**
Dirk Schroeder	230 pages, 4 maps

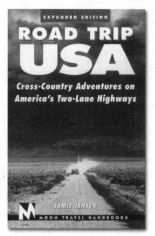

THE PRACTICAL NOMAD

✈ TAKE THE PLUNGE

"The greatest barriers to long-term travel by Americans are the disempowered feelings that leave them afraid to ask for the time off. Just do it."

✈ TAKE NOTHING FOR GRANTED

"Even 'What time is it?' is a highly politicized question in some areas, and the answer may depend on your informant's ethnicity and political allegiance as well as the proximity of the secret police."

✈ TAKE THIS BOOK

$17.95   580 pages

With experience helping thousands of his globetrotting clients plan their trips around the world, travel industry insider Edward Hasbrouck provides the secrets that can save readers money and valuable travel time.
An indispensable complement to destination-specific travel guides, *The Practical Nomad* includes:

    airfare strategies

    ticket discounts

    long-term travel considerations

    travel documents

    border crossings

    entry requirements

    government offices

    travel publications

    Internet information resources

"One of the best travel advice books ever published. . . .
A fantastic resource."
—Big World

U.S.~METRIC CONVERSION

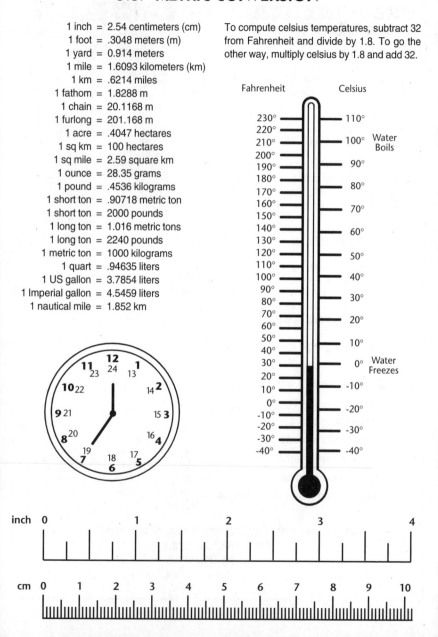

1 inch = 2.54 centimeters (cm)
1 foot = .3048 meters (m)
1 yard = 0.914 meters
1 mile = 1.6093 kilometers (km)
1 km = .6214 miles
1 fathom = 1.8288 m
1 chain = 20.1168 m
1 furlong = 201.168 m
1 acre = .4047 hectares
1 sq km = 100 hectares
1 sq mile = 2.59 square km
1 ounce = 28.35 grams
1 pound = .4536 kilograms
1 short ton = .90718 metric ton
1 short ton = 2000 pounds
1 long ton = 1.016 metric tons
1 long ton = 2240 pounds
1 metric ton = 1000 kilograms
1 quart = .94635 liters
1 US gallon = 3.7854 liters
1 Imperial gallon = 4.5459 liters
1 nautical mile = 1.852 km

To compute celsius temperatures, subtract 32 from Fahrenheit and divide by 1.8. To go the other way, multiply celsius by 1.8 and add 32.